Perl: The Complete Reference

Martin C. Brown

Osborne/**McGraw-Hill**

Berkeley New York St. Louis San Francisco
Auckland Bogotá Hamburg London Madrid
Mexico City Milan Montreal New Delhi Panama City
Paris São Paulo Singapore Sydney
Tokyo Toronto

Osborne/**McGraw-Hill**
2600 Tenth Street
Berkeley, California 94710
U.S.A.

For information on translations or book distributors outside the U.S.A., or to arrange bulk purchase discounts for sales promotions, premiums, or fund-raisers, please contact Osborne/**McGraw-Hill** at the above address.

Perl: The Complete Reference

1234567890 DOC DOC 90198765432109

ISBN 0-07-212000-2

Publisher
Brandon A. Nordin

Associate Publisher and Editor-in-Chief
Scott Rogers

Acquisitions Editor
Wendy Rinaldi

Project Editor
Madhu Prasher

Editorial Assistant
Monika Faltiss

Technical Editors
Mark Strivens and Rima Regas

Copy Editor
Judith Brown

Proofreaders
Carol Burbo and Barbara Brodnitz

Indexer
Valerie Robbins

Computer Designers
Ann Sellers and Roberta Steele

Illustrators
Brian Wells and Beth Young

To my wife,
who lets me keep the house running
and sit at the keyboard.

About the Author...

Martin C. Brown is an IT Manager and freelance consultant with 15 years of multi-platform administration and programming experience in Perl, Shellscript, Basic, Pascal, C/C++, Java, JavaScript, VBScript, and Awk. Martin is also the author of two computer books.

Contents at a Glance

Part IV Enhancing the User Interface

Part V Perl for the Web

Part VI Getting "Inside" Perl

Part VII Cross-Platform Perl

Part VIII Fun

Part IX Appendixes

Contents

Part II

Advanced Perl Programming

Part V

Perl for the Web

Part VI

Getting "Inside" Perl

Part VII

Cross-Platform Perl

Acknowledgments

First of all, I'd like to thank my wife, who stood by me when I decided to make the leap from part-time to full-time writing. Without her support this book would never have been written (by me at least), and I'd be doing a 9-to-5 job somewhere without ever realizing how much of a pleasure writing full time is.

Next, I'd like to thank Wendy Rinaldi, my acquisitions editor, for asking me to write the book, and for the constant support and encouragement required to keep me writing. Monika Faltiss helped keep me on track timewise, and reminded me when I forgot to send screenshots or edits. I'd also like to thank the rest of the team: Madhu Prasher (project editor), Judith Brown (copy editor), and Ron Hull, among many others.

For technical input, thanks go to Rima S. Regas and Mark Strivens, who managed to spot errors in the technical and discussion content, as well as provide some input on content and layout in the earlier stages. I should also thank Hugo van der Sanden and Ann-Marie Mallon for offering to step in when they did.

It's not possible to write a Perl book without thanking Perl's original author and the current maintainers. That includes Larry Wall, Tom Christiansen, Randal L. Schwartz, Sriram Srinivasan, Gurusamy Sarathay, and many many others.

Finally, I'd like to thank Spip, the channel bot on the #beos channel of IRCNet. He features, in some small part, in Chapter 25, and is a good companion, electronic or otherwise. I guess I should thank the other members of the channel, including Woonjas, RedHeat, drag, Tao, Naguel, wossname, and the rest of the #beos gang.

If there's anybody I've forgotten to acknowledge, I apologize unreservedly in advance now. I have done my best to check and verify all sources and contact all parties involved but it's perfectly possible for me to make a mistake.

Introduction

As the title suggests, this book is a complete reference to the Perl programming language. As such, it includes details of everything you want to know about statements, expressions, functions, and regular expressions within Perl. Some highlights of the book include the creation of useful packages and modules, using Perl on the command line and Tk as a cross-platform user interface solution. There are also several chapters dedicated to the design and use of the supported data structures within Perl, and to the processes available for accessing external data structures and databases.

Interprocess communication, either between processes on the same machine or between processes on different machines, is also a topic for discussion. The former is handled by a number of tricks and some system-dependent features. For the latter machine communication, you can use network sockets. An alternative solution to the problems of processing between multiple processes is to use threads, which are small, "lightweight" execution sequences that are still owned in their entirety by their parent process, and we also look at how threads can be used to solve these problems.

A large portion of the book is given over to the process of getting inside Perl. We examine how Perl works as it parses a Perl script and how that process can be modified with compiler pragmas. Then we move on to the process of extending Perl by writing an interface between Perl and a C function. This allows Perl to use and access an unlimited number of extensions and enhancements to the core Perl language. You can also do the reverse. You can embed the Perl interpreter into a C program, allowing you to use the advanced features of Perl within a C program. You could even build the interpreter into an application to provide a built-in scripting language.

A recent development in the Perl interpreter has allowed the creation of a Perl compiler (which is in itself a bit of a misnomer; see Chapter 1 for details). With the compiler you can do many things, including produce some detailed output on the real structure and execution path that your script takes. One of the most significant and useful features, though, is that you can take a Perl script and produce a stand-alone executable program.

Perl is also a good cross-platform development tool. See Chapter 1 for a list of some of the platforms that Perl has been ported to. We take a close look at the three main platforms—Unix, Windows, and MacOS—and how they differ, before taking a more generalized view of how to program with Perl in a cross-platform world and ensure the cross-platform compatibility.

Finally, the appendixes provide a quick and detailed reference to the Perl functions, error messages, and the standard Perl library that comes with every distribution.

Of course, even with the best intentions, it's possible to have forgotten some element, or not to have gone through a particular element to a deep enough degree, although I hope this won't be the case for most readers.

Who Is the Book For?

I haven't targeted the book at any specific group of Perl users. To put it simply, if you program in Perl, you will find this book useful. As a reference, most people should find it useful to keep on the desk or the shelf just as a quick means of looking up a particular function or feature. For learners and expert users alike, the information in this book will be invaluable.

You should also find the book useful if you want to know how to do a particular task in Perl, since you'll also find working, real-world examples of the different features of Perl within the book. If you are looking for more examples, you might want to look at *Perl Annotated Archives*, which contains over 100 scripts to solve a myriad of different problems.

How to Use This Book

Pick it up, look up the feature you want to get more information on from the contents or the index, and read! The scripts and script fragments included in the book should all work without modification on your machine. Be aware though that not all platforms support all Perl features. Use Chapters 21 through 24 if you are unsure of a feature.

If you want purely reference information—that is, you want to look up the arguments and return values to a function—then use the appendixes at the back. For discussion, examples, and detailed information on a particular feature, use one of the earlier chapters. You should find references between the chapters and appendixes in both directions to help you get more information.

The bulk of the book covers the core version of Perl as it is supported and developed under Unix. See Chapter 21 for details on using Perl on the Unix platform. If you are programming under Windows or MacOS, then please read Chapter 22 or 23, respectively, for details on how to obtain, compile, and program Perl on those two platforms.

Chapter Breakdown

Each chapter in the book attempts to cover a different aspect of the solutions that Perl is able to provide.

Chapter 1 looks at the background of Perl and the fundamental abilities that you will need to use and understand in order to make the best use of Perl.

Chapter 2 examines the basic processes behind programming in Perl, including the basics of expressions and statements, and the creation and use of the base data types.

Chapter 3 discusses the base user interface available—the screen and the keyboard—and also deals with reading from and writing to files, which are essentially all the screen and keyboard are to a program anyway.

Chapter 4 looks at the basics of data manipulation with scalars, and also at the use of regular expressions for searching, matching, and extracting strings from variables and files.

Chapter 5 starts off the discussion of the more complex developmental processes by looking at how you can use packages and modules within Perl to promote code reuse.

Chapter 6 covers the management of external data, that is, files, users, groups, and time.

Chapter 7 looks at the more complex data structures available in Perl—arrays and hashes. We go beyond the normal uses of these structures and look at other ways they can be employed to aid in the programming process. We also take the opportunity to examine references, which provide a different way of accessing and using information stored in variables, and this leads us on to nested data structures and object-oriented programming. This final section also leads to tied data structures—a system whereby information from an external source can be attached to an internal data structure.

Chapter 8 expands on many of the principles in Chapter 7 and covers data persistence—the storage of information in external databases, both homegrown and using systems such as DBM, Oracle, and ODBC sources.

Chapter 9 describes the processing required within Perl to support communication over standard network sockets, such as those used for communication over the Internet.

Chapter 10 discusses the processes involved in interprocess communication, using both standard filehandles and System V IPC functions. The chapter also describes the methods available for creating, controlling, and communicating with external processes.

Chapter 11 looks at ways to improve on the models so far discussed for running Perl scripts and executing Perl programs. This covers the use of Perl on the command line, executing scripts dynamically within a Perl interpreter, and how to use threads as a better alternative for running multiple processes.

Chapter 12 examines ways to make Perl more user friendly by discussing the use of the command line as a quick interface for the user. POD, or Plain Old Documentation, is a system that is cross-platform compatible and provides a very simple documentation environment that includes support for creating text, man page, and HTML documentation for your Perl scripts.

Chapter 13 takes a detailed look at Perl/Tk—the Perl interface to the Tk user interface development system.

Chapter 14 describes the environment available to you when you are writing web scripts. This covers the physical environment of a script and also the ways of communicating between the web server, the user's browser, and a Perl script, otherwise known as CGI.

Chapter 15 goes into more detail about the web development process and covers the specifics of web programming with Perl, including a useful checklist of the security issues surrounding the web programming process.

Chapter 16 starts our look into the insides of the Perl interpreter by describing how a Perl script is dissected and then compiled and parsed into a working program. A Perl pragma can be used to control the operation of the interpreter, and we take a look at the available pragmas that come as part of the standard distribution.

Chapter 17 builds on the information in Chapter 16 and describes the processes involved in extending Perl with external C functions and embedding Perl into C programs.

Chapter 18 covers the essential process of debugging Perl scripts, both at a simple level and at deeper levels within the Perl interpreter. We also look at how to debug regular expressions and how to use the Perl profiler to determine which parts of your Perl script need optimization.

Chapter 19 looks in detail at the Perl compiler. This supports several different systems that take a Perl script and produce a number of different reports and output formats. At a simple level this includes a parsing tree that describes the real execution profile of your script, and at the other end of the scale, the compiler supports the creation of stand-alone Perl binaries.

Chapter 20 discusses the processes involved in releasing a Perl module to the Perl community. In particular it describes the **MakeMaker** utility for creating Perl Makefiles that can compile and automatically install Perl extensions.

Chapter 21 starts the section on using Perl under different platforms. This first chapter looks at using Perl under Unix, its original development platform.

Chapter 22 looks at the specifics of using Perl under Windows and includes detailed information on the additional modules available for Windows Perl programming.

Chapter 23 looks at the specifics of Perl under MacOS, including details of how you can get around the lack of a command line interface using extensions to the Perl interpreter that come with the MacPerl application.

Chapter 24 takes a step back from the previous chapters and instead concentrates on ways in which you can write Perl programs that are cross-platform compatible, even if you don't know what the destination platform is.

Chapter 25 shows that Perl can be used for more than managing machines and providing a language for writing web scripts. Perl is a general-purpose language and, with some thought, can be used for a great many more things than you first realize.

The appendixes provide a quick reference resource for further information (Appendix A), Perl functions (Appendix B), and Perl operators and variables (Appendix C). Appendix D contains a list of the error messages that might be generated when compiling a Perl script.

Appendix E is a complete reference to the standard Perl library—the modules and packages that are supplied as standard with all Perl distributions—while Appendix F is a quick overview of the modules and extensions available for Perl from CPAN, the Comprehensive Perl Archive Network.

Conventions Used in This Book

All Perl keywords are highlighted in **bold**, but functions are listed without parentheses. This is because the C functions on which the Perl versions may be based are shown like **this()**.

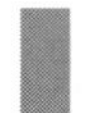

```
Examples and code are displayed using a fixed-width font.
```

Function descriptions are formatted using the same fixed-width font.

Notes are formatted like this and include additional information about a particular topic. You'll also find similarly formatted "Warnings," which highlight possible dangerous tools or tricks to watch out for when programming.

Contacting the Author

I always welcome comments and suggestions on my work. I particularly appreciate guides and recommendations on better ways of achieving different goals, especially with a language as varied and capable as Perl. The best way to contact me is via email. You can use either books@mcwords.com (preferred) or mc@whoever.com. Alternatively, visit my website, http://www.mcwords.com, which contains resources and updated information about the scripts and contents of this book.

The Complete Reference

Part I

Basic Perl Programming

The Complete Reference

Chapter 1

Perl Backgrounder

Perl is many different things to many different people. The most fundamental aspect of Perl is that it's a high-level programming language written originally by Larry Wall and now supported and developed by a cast of thousands. The Perl language semantics are largely based on the C programming language, inheriting many of the best features of **sed**, **awk**, the Unix **shell**, and at least a dozen other tools and languages.

Although it is a bad idea to pigeonhole any language and attribute it to a specific list of tasks, Perl is particularly strong at process, file, and text manipulation. This makes it especially useful for system utilities, software tools, systems management tasks, database access, graphical programming, networking, and world web programming. These strengths make it particularly attractive to CGI script authors, systems administrators, mathematicians, journalists, and just about anybody who needs to write applications and utilities very quickly.

Perl has its roots firmly planted in the Unix environment, but it has since become a cross-platform development tool. Perl runs on IBM mainframes; AS/400s; Windows NT, 95, and 98; OS/2; Novell Netware; Cray supercomputers; Digital's VMS; Tandem Guardian; HP MPE/ix; MacOS; and all flavors of Unix, including Linux. In addition, Perl has been ported to dozens of smaller operating systems, including BeOS, Acorn's RISCOS, and machines such as the Amiga.

Larry Wall is a strong proponent of free software, and Perl is no exception. Perl, including the source code, the standard Perl library, the optional modules, and all of the documentation, is provided free and is supported entirely by its user community.

Before we get into the details of how to program in Perl, it's worth taking the time to familiarize yourself with where Perl has come from, what it can be used for, and how it stacks up against other languages. We'll also look at some popular "mythconceptions" about what Perl is and at some success stories of how Perl has helped a variety of organizations solve an equally varied range of problems.

What Does PERL Stand For?

There is a lot of controversy and rumor about exactly what PERL stands for and if, in fact, it stands for anything. According to Larry Wall, the original acronym stood for Practical Extraction and Reporting Language, and this relates to the original development purpose, which was a tool for processing a large amount of textual report information.

Over the years, other solutions have been proposed for the PERL acronym. The most popular recent version is Pathologically Eclectic Rubbish Lister. Luckily, a rough translation of that expansion equates to the original version!

Versions and Naming Conventions

The current version of Perl that you should use is version 5. Although version 4 is available, it has fewer features, is relatively limited, and is no longer maintained. The last patch version of version 4 was 4.036, released in 1992. Version 5 is essentially still in development, with the latest stable release being 5.005_02. A number of experimental versions of the language are also available, but it is probably best to avoid these in production-based systems.

It has been a common practice in recent years to refer to Perl with the informal names of perl4 and perl5, which correspond to the 4.036 and 5.x versions of the language. It is quicker to say perl5 than "the 5.005 release of Perl." However, this also led to some confusion that there is a separate language called perl5, which is not true. Perl5 is just the popular name for the most recent major release (October 1994). Perl4 was the last major release (March 1991). There was also a perl1 (January 1988), a perl2 (June 1988), and a perl3 (October 1989).

There is also a certain amount of confusion regarding the capitalization of Perl. Should it be written Perl or perl? Larry Wall now uses Perl to signify the language proper and perl to signify the implementation of the language. Therefore, perl can parse Perl. In essence, however, it really doesn't make a huge amount of difference. That said, you will find that the executable version of perl is installed with a name in lowercase.

Perl History

Perl is a relatively old language, with the first version having been released in 1988. Larry Wall describes the history thus:

Perl 0—Introduced to Larry Wall's office associates

Perl 1—Introduced Perl to the world

Perl 2—Introduced Harry Spencer's regular expression package

Perl 3—Introduced the ability to handle binary data

Perl 4—Introduced the first "Camel" book (Programming Perl, by Larry Wall, Tom Christiansen and Randal L Schwartz, O'Reilly & Associates). We mostly just switched version numbers, so the book could refer to 4.000.

Perl 5—Introduced everything else, including the ability to introduce everything else.

Main Perl Features

Perl contains many features that most Perl programmers are not even aware of, let alone use. Some of the most basic features are described here.

Perl Is Free

It may not seem like a major feature, but in fact being free is very important. Some languages, such as C (which is free with compilers such as GNU's **gcc**), have been commercialized by MetroWerks, Microsoft, and other companies. Other languages, such as Visual Basic, are entirely commercial. Perl's source code is open and free—anybody can download the C source that constitutes a Perl interpreter. Furthermore, you can easily extend the core functionality of Perl both within the realms of the interpreted language and by modifying the Perl source code.

Perl Is Simple to Learn, Concise, and Easy to Read

Because of its history and roots, most people with any programming experience will be able to program with Perl. It has a syntax similar to C and shell script, among others, but with a less restrictive format. Many things are quicker written in Perl because of the number of built-in functions and logical assumptions that the Perl interpreter makes during execution. It's also easy to read, because the code can be written in a clear and concise format that almost reads like an English sentence.

Perl Is Fast

As we will see shortly, Perl is not an interpreter in the strictest sense—the code is compiled before it is executed. Compared to most scripting languages, this makes execution almost as fast as compiled C code. But, because the code is still interpreted, there is no compilation process, and applications can be written much faster than with other languages without any of the performance problems normally associated with an interpreted language.

Perl Is Extensible

You can write Perl-based packages and modules that extend the functionality of the language. You can also use external C code that can be called directly by Perl to extend the functionality further. The reverse is also true: the Perl interpreter can be incorporated directly into many languages, including C. This allows your C programs to use the functionality of the Perl interpreter without calling an external program.

Perl Has Flexible Data Types

You can create simple variables that contain text or numbers, and Perl will treat the variable data accordingly at the time it is used. You can increment text values (such as hexadecimal) directly, without any conversion, and strings can be interpolated with each other without requiring external functions to concatenate or combine the results.

You can also handle arrays of values as simple lists, as typical indexed arrays, and even as stacks of information. Lastly, you can model complex data using hashes—a form of associative array where the list of the information is indexed via strings instead of numbers.

Perl Is Object Oriented

Perl supports all of the object-oriented features—inheritance, polymorphism, and encapsulation. There are no restrictions on when or where you make use of object-oriented features. There is no boundary as there is with C and C++.

Perl Is Collaborative

There is a huge network of Perl programmers worldwide. Most programmers supply, and use, the modules and scripts supplied via CPAN, the Comprehensive Perl Archive Network. This is a repository of the best modules and scripts available. Using an existing prewritten module can save you hundreds, perhaps even thousands of hours of development time.

Compiler or Interpreter

Different languages work in different ways. They are either compiled or interpreted. A compiled language is translated from the original source into a platform-specific machine code. This machine code is referred to as an *executable*. There is no direct relation between the machine code and the original source: it is not possible to reverse the compilation process and produce the source code. This means that the compiled executable is safe from intellectual property piracy.

An interpreted language, on the other hand, reads the original source code and interprets each of the statements in order to perform the different operations. The source code is therefore executed at run time. This has some advantages: Because there is no compilation process, the development of interpreted code should be significantly quicker. Interpreted code also tends to be smaller and easier to distribute. The disadvantages are that the original source must be supplied in order to execute the program, and an interpreted program is generally slower than a compiled executable because of the way the code is executed.

Perl fits neither of these descriptions in the real sense. The internals of Perl are such that the individual elements of a script are compiled into a tree of *opcodes*. Opcodes are similar in concept to machine code. However, whereas machine code is executed directly by hardware, opcodes are executed by a virtual machine. The opcodes are highly optimized objects designed to perform a specific function. This is similar, but not identical, to the way Java works.

In essence, at the time of executing a Perl script, it is compiled into opcodes, which in turn are executed via a virtual machine. This enables Perl to provide all the advantages of a scripting language in combination with the fast execution of a compiled program.

Keeping all of that mind, however, with the most recent versions, there have been some advances in a Perl compiler that takes native Perl scripts and converts them into directly executable machine code. We'll cover the compiler and Perl internals later in this book.

Similar Programming Languages

We already know that Perl has its history in a number of different languages. It shares several features and abilities with many of the standard tools supplied with any Unix workstation. It also shares some common features and abilities with many related languages, even if it doesn't necessarily share the same heritage.

With regard to specific features, abilities, and performance, Perl compares favorably against some languages, and less favorably against others. A lot of the advantages and disadvantages are a matter of personal choice. For example, for text handling, there is very little to choose between **awk** and Perl. However, personally I prefer Perl for those tasks that involve file handling directly within the code, and **awk** when using it as a filter as part of a shell script.

Unix Shells

Any of the Unix shells—**sh**, **csh**, **ksh**, or even **bash**—share the same basic set of facilities. They are particularly good at running external programs and at most forms of file management where the shell's ability to work directly with many of the standard Unix utilities enables rapid development of systems management tools.

However, where most shells fail is in their variable- and data-handling routines. In nearly all cases you need to use the facilities provided by shell tools such as **cut**, **paste**, and **sort** to achieve the same level of functionality as that provided natively by Perl.

Tcl

Tcl (Tool Command Language) was developed as an embeddable scripting language. A lot of the original design centered around a macrolike language for helping with shell-based applications. Tcl was never really developed as a general-purpose scripting language, although many people use it as such. In fact, Tcl was designed with the philosophy that you should actually use two or more languages when developing large software systems.

Tcl's variables are very different from those in Perl. Because it was designed with the typical shell-based string handling in mind, strings are null terminated (as they are in C). This means that Tcl cannot be used for handling binary data. Compared to Perl,

Tcl is also generally slower on iterative operations over strings. You cannot pass arrays by value or by reference; they can only be passed by name. This makes programming more complex, although not impossible.

Lists in Tcl are actually stored as a single string, and arrays are stored within what Perl would treat as a hash. Accessing a true Tcl array is therefore slightly slower, as it has to look up associative entries in order to decipher the true values. The data-handling problems also extend to numbers, which Tcl stores as strings and converts to numbers only when a calculation is required. This slows mathematical operations significantly.

Unlike Perl, which parses the script first before optimizing and then executing, Tcl is a true interpreter, and each line is interpreted and optimized individually at execution time. This reduces the optimization options available to Tcl. Perl, on the other hand, can optimize source lines, code blocks, and even entire functions if the compilation process allows. The same Tcl interpretation technique also means that the only way to debug Tcl code and search for syntactic errors is to actually execute the code. Because Perl goes through the precompilation stage, it can check for syntactic and other possible/probable errors without actually executing the code.

Finally, the code base of the standard Tcl package does not include many of the functions and abilities of the Perl language. This is especially important if you are trying to write a cross-platform POSIX-compliant application. Perl supports the entire POSIX function set, but Tcl supports a much smaller subset of the POSIX function set, even using external packages.

It should be clear from this description that Perl is a better alternative to Tcl in situations where you want easy access to the rest of the OS. Most significantly, Tcl will never be a general-purpose scripting language. Tcl will on the other hand be a good solution if you want to embed a scripting language inside another language.

Python

Python was developed as an object-oriented language and is well thought out, interpreted, byte compiled, extensible, and a largely procedural programming language. Like Perl, it's good at text processing and even general-purpose programming. Python also has a good history in the realm of GUI-based application development. Compared to Perl, Python has fewer users, but it is gaining acceptance as a practical rapid application development tool.

Unlike Perl, Python does not resemble C, and it doesn't resemble Unix-style tools like **awk** either. Python was designed from scratch to be object oriented and has clear module semantics. This can make it confusing to use, as the name spaces get complex to resolve. On the other hand, this makes it much more structured, which can ease development for those with structured minds.

I'm not aware of anything that is better in Python than in Perl. They both share object features, and the two are almost identical in execution speed. However, the reverse is not true: Perl has better regular expression features, and the level of integration between Perl and the Unix environment is hard to beat (although it can probably be solved within Python using a suitably written external module).

In general, there is not a lot to tip the scales in favor of one of the two languages. Perl will appeal to those people who already know C or Unix shell utilities. Perl is also older and more widespread, and there is a much larger library of contributed modules and scripts. Python, on the other hand, may appeal to those people who have experience with more object-oriented languages such as Java or Modula-2.

Both languages provide easy control and access when it comes to the external environment in which they work. Perl arguably fills the role better though, because many of the standard system functions you are used to are supported natively by the language, without requiring external modules. The technical support for the two languages is also very similar, with both using websites and newsgroups to help users program in the new language.

Finally, it's worth mentioning that of all the scripting languages available, Perl and Python are two of the most stable platforms for development. There are, however, some minor differences. First, Perl provides quite advanced functions and mechanisms for tracking errors and faults in the scripts. However, making extensive use of these facilities can still cause problems. For example, calling the system **truncate()** function within Perl will cause the whole interpreter to crash. Python, on the other hand, uses a system of error trapping that will immediately identify a problem like this before it occurs, allowing you to account for it in your applications. This is largely due to the application development nature of the language.

Java

At first viewing, Java seems to be a friendlier, interpreted version of C++. Depending on your point of view, this can either be an advantage or a disadvantage. Java probably inherits less than a third of the complexity of C++, but it retains much of the complexity of its brethren.

Java was designed primarily as an implementation-independent language, originally with web-based intentions, but now as a more general-purpose solution to a variety of problems. Like Perl, Java is byte compiled, but unlike Perl, programs are supplied in byte-compiled format and then executed via a Java virtual machine at execution time.

Because of its roots and its complexity, Java cannot really be considered as a direct competitor to Perl. It is difficult to use Java as a rapid development tool and virtually impossible to use it for most of the simple text processing and system administration tasks that Perl is best known for.

C/C++

Perl itself is written in C. You can download and view the Perl source code if you so wish, but it's not for the fainthearted! Many of the structures and semantics of the two languages are very similar. For example, both C and Perl use semicolons as end-of-line terminators. They also share the same code block and indentation features. However, Perl tends to be stricter when it comes to code block definitions—you always require curly brackets, for example—but most C programmers will be comfortable with the Perl environment.

Perl is object oriented like C++. Both share the same abilities of inheritance, polymorphism, and encapsulation. However, object orientation in Perl is easier to use compared to the complexities of constructors and inheritance found in C++. In addition to all this, there is no distinction between the standard and object-oriented implementations of Perl as there is with C and C++. This means you can mix and match different variables, objects, and other data types within a single Perl application—something that would be difficult to achieve easily with C and C++.

Because Perl is basically an interpreted language (as mentioned earlier), development is generally quicker than writing in native C. Perl also has many more built-in facilities and abilities that would otherwise need to be handwritten in C/C++. For example, regular expressions and many of the data-handling features would require a significant amount of programming to reproduce in C with the same ease of use available in Perl.

Because of Perl's roots in C, it is also possible to extend Perl with C source code and vice versa: you can embed Perl programs in C source code.

awk/gawk

Although a lot of syntax is different, **awk**, and **gawk** (the GNU projects version) are functionally subsets of Perl. It's also clear from the history of Perl that many of the features have been inherited directly from those of **awk**. Indeed, **awk** was designed as a reporting language with the emphasis on making the process of reporting via the shell significantly easier. Without **awk** you would have to employ a number of external utilities such as **cut**, **expr**, and **sort**, and the solution would be neither quick nor elegant.

There are some things that Perl has built-in support for that **awk** does not. For example, there is no network socket class, and **awk** is largely ignorant of external files compared to the file manipulation and management functions found in Perl. However, some advantages **awk** has over Perl are summarized here:

- **awk** is simpler, and the syntax is more structured and regular.
- Although gaining acceptance, Perl has yet to be included as standard with many operating systems. **awk** has been supplied with Unix almost since it was first released.
- **awk** can be smaller and therefore much quicker to execute for small programs.
- **awk** supports more advanced regular expressions. You can use a regular expression for replacement, and you can search text in substitutions.

Popular "Mythconceptions"

Despite its history and wide use in many different areas, there are still a number of myths about what Perl is, where it should be used, and even why it was invented. Here's a quick list of the popular mythconceptions of the Perl language.

Only for the Web

Probably the most famous of the myths is that Perl is a language used, designed, and developed exclusively for developing web-based applications. In fact, this could not be more wrong. Version 1.0 of Perl, the first released to the world, shipped in 1988—several years before the web and HTML as we know it today were in general use. In fact, Perl was inherited as a good design tool for web server applications based on its ease of use and flexibility. The text-handling features are especially useful when working within the web environment. There are libraries of database interfaces, client-server modules, networking features, and even GUI toolkits to enable you to write entire applications directly within Perl.

Not Maintenance Friendly

Any good (or bad) programmer will tell you that anybody can write unmaintainable code in any language. Many companies and individuals write maintainable programs using Perl. A lot of people would argue that Perl's structured style, easily readable source code, and modular format make it more maintainable than languages such as C, C++, and Java.

Hacker Culture

Perl is used by a variety of companies, organizations, and individuals. Everybody from programming beginners through "hackers" up to multinational corporations use Perl to solve their problems. It can hardly be classed as a hackers-only language. Moreover, it is maintained by the same range of people, which means you get the best of both worlds—real-world features, with top-class behind-the-scenes algorithms.

It's a Scripting Language

In Perl, there is no difference between a script and program. Many large programs and projects have been written entirely in Perl. A good example is majordomo, the main mailing list manager used on the Internet. It's written entirely in Perl. See the upcoming section "Perl Success Stories" for more examples of where Perl has made a difference, despite its scripting label.

No Support

The Perl community is one of the largest on the Internet, and you should be able to find someone, somewhere, who can answer your questions or help you with your problems. The Perl Clinic (see Appendix A) offers free advice and support to Perl programmers.

All Perl Programs Are Free

Although you generally write and use Perl programs in their native source form, this does not mean that everything you write is free. Perl programs are your own intellectual property and can be bought, sold, and licensed just like any other program. If you are worried about somebody stealing your code, source filters and bytecode compilers will render your code only useful for execution and unreadable by the casual software pirate.

No Development Environment

Development environments are only really required when you need to compile source code into object files. Because Perl scripts are written in normal text, you can use any editor to write and use Perl programs. Under Unix, the favorites are **emacs** and **vi**, and both have Perl modes to make syntax checking and formatting easier. Under Windows NT, you can also use **emacs**, or you can use SolutionSoft's PerlBuilder, which is an interactive environment for Perl programs. Alternatively, you can use the ActiveState debugger, which will provide you with a direct environment for executing and editing Perl statements. On the Mac, BBEdit has a Perl mode that colors the syntax of the Perl source to make it easier to read.

Additionally, because Perl programs are text based, you can use any source code revision control system. The most popular under Unix are RCS and CVS.

Perl Is a GNU Project

While the GNU project includes Perl in its distributions, there is no such thing as "GNU Perl." Perl is not produced or maintained by GNU and the Free Software Foundation. Perl is also made available on a much more open license than the GNU Public License.

Note *GNU stands for the recursive GNU's Not Unix, and is part of the Free Software Foundation, an organization devoted to providing a suite of useful user software for free.*

Perl Is Difficult to Learn

Because Perl is similar to a number of different languages it is not only easy to learn but also easy to continue learning. Its structure and format is very similar to C, **awk**, shell script, and, to a greater or lesser extent, even BASIC. If you have ever done any form of programming, you're half way toward learning programming in Perl.

In many cases you will only use a very small subset of Perl to complete most tasks. The guiding motto for Perl development is "there's more than one way to do it." This makes Perl's learning curve very shallow and very long. Perl is a large language with a great many features, and there is a lot you can learn if you want to.

Perl Success Stories

Perl has been used by thousands of different corporations to tackle and solve different problems. For most people it has reduced the development time for their desired application by days, weeks, or even months. Below is a sample of the bigger companies that have used Perl. I've tried to include testimonials and deeper examples of how Perl was the better solution where the information has been available.

- Amazon.com, one of the Internet's best known and most successful e-commerce sites, used Perl to develop an entire editorial production and control system. This integrates the authoring, maintenance (including version control and searching), and output of the editorial content of the entire Amazon.com website.
- Netscape engineers wrote a content management and delivery system with logging, analysis, and feedback on use in three months using Perl.
- In order to get around many cross-platform development problems, SPEC (the Standard Performance Evaluation Corporation) used Perl as a wrapper around the C code that is used to test performance. With Perl's ability to import and dynamically use external C code in combination with its object-oriented abilities, SPEC generated a test system that was easily portable from Unix to the Windows NT platform.
- Using an old 60MHz Pentium and Perl, a New England hospital implemented a distributed printing system that connected 20,000 PC workstations to 3,000 printers spread over an entire city.

Chapter 2

Perl Basics

It's difficult to describe the basics of Perl in a few simple statements. Perl is a very straightforward language; there are few complications or complexities for a simple program. That said, it is possible for Perl programs to be overtly cryptic and almost impossible to read.

Let's start by having a look at the most fundamental part of a Perl program—a simple statement used to demonstrate every programming language:

```
print "Hello World!";
```

This is an incredibly simple example, but it demonstrates a few of the basic principles. This example uses a function, which is one of the basic elements of a Perl script. The function is followed by a quoted string, and the line is terminated by a semicolon. This last point is one of the most important. A Perl statement can span multiple lines within the source code, but the statement is only completed once the semicolon is reached. To demonstrate this, you could rewrite the above example as

```
print
"Hello World!";
```

The result would be the same.

Note well that we have not had to insert any form of "preamble" as we would with languages like C or Pascal, nor do we have to formally close the program with an exit statement. The script starts with the first statement, and it's perfectly natural for a program to simply end. Perl treats this as normal operation. For most people this makes development time quicker and programs simpler and easier to understand.

A Perl script is made up of a combination of declarations and statements:

- A *declaration* is a statement of fact. It defines the existence of something and probably its value or format. There is no commitment in a declaration of how the entity will be used or indeed if it will be used. For example, when you create a variable and assign it a value, it is a declaration.
- A *statement* is the opposite. It is a command or instruction to perform a particular operation. The act of adding two numbers together is a good example of a statement.

In addition, statements are made up of a combination of operators and functions.

- An *operator* performs an operation on a value and should be thought of as a verb. For example, when you add two numbers together, you use an operator—the plus (+) sign.
- A *function* should be thought of as a list of statements and operators combined into a single verb. Perhaps the easiest analogy is a sentence or paragraph.

If you put all of these elements together, you can produce a simple Perl script that adds two numbers together (with the plus operator). The result is assigned to a variable (using the equal sign operator), making a declaration. The result is then printed out (using a function), which forms the statement. You can see the Perl version below:

```
$result = 45 + 25;
print "$result\n";
```

Note *The terms operator, function, and subroutine tend to be used interchangeably. It is best not to get bogged down in the detail of which element is which.*

Before we dig further into the specifics, it is worth remembering the following when looking at the example code fragment and, indeed, when programming Perl:

- There is no "right" way to do things in Perl. There may be more efficient, more elegant, or simply more straightforward methods, but it is possible to achieve the same result in a number of different ways. This is called the TMTOWTDI syndrome (pronounced "tim-today"), or "There's More Than One Way To Do It."

In this chapter, we will look at the basic components of Perl that go to make a Perl program: variables, operators, and statements. There are other elements to consider, but for the basics, these are the three main components of which you need to be aware.

Variables

You use variables to store information in a named location. There are many different types of variable, and each can be used for a different type of information. Perl supports three main variable types: scalars, arrays, and hashes. Scalars store simple information such as numbers and text strings. Arrays store lists of numbers and strings where each entry in the list is identified by a number. Hashes also store lists of numbers and strings, but the individual elements are referenced strings instead of numbers.

Unlike many other languages, the different types of variables in Perl are identified by a leading special character. Therefore **$var** is a scalar, **@var** is an array, and **%var** is a hash. Each variable type has its own name space. This means that in the list of example variables, each would be a separate variable containing a different selection of information:

```
$var = "Hello World!";
@var = qw/Martin Brown/;
print $var,"\n";
```

This would result in

```
Hello World!
```

But

```
print @var,"\n";
```

results in

```
Martin Brown
```

A variable name must start with a letter and can then contain any mixture of letters, numbers, and underscores. The use of any other character will be treated as an operator by Perl.

Scalars

A scalar is the most basic form of data container available within Perl. All other data types within Perl use a scalar as the base data type. For example, an array is an array of scalars, and a hash is a hash of scalars. Scalars can only hold singular pieces of information; that is, a scalar can store numbers, strings, or references. A scalar cannot contain multiple values, but it can contain a reference that points to an array or hash that contains multiple values. We will look at references later in this chapter.

Perl treats strings and numbers almost equally. There is no way to define a scalar as containing a number or a string; a scalar just contains a value. Perl will decide at the time the variable is used whether the value should be interpreted as a number or string. This also extends to references: a reference can be a reference to another scalar, to an array or hash, or even to an object.

To define or assign a value to a scalar variable, you must specify the value and the variable name with an equal sign (the operator). For example:

```
$age = 26;
```

This would store the value of 26 in the variable **$age**. The value assigned to the variable is called a *literal* because it is a static (noncomputed) value. However, the statement

```
$pi = 3.1415126;
```

signifies that **$pi** should be a floating point value. Perl will treat both **$age** and **$pi** with the same regard.

There is also no way of specifying the precision of a number. Theoretically, all numbers are stored as floating point values (the equivalent of doubles in C). However, Perl will also make educated and intelligent guesses based on the variable value as to the result of a particular expression. Arithmetic with integers results in integer values, whereas floating point values produce floating point results when printed. Furthermore, you can also specify a floating point number using scientific notation:

```
$speed_of_light = 2.997e08;
```

For strings, Perl uses different quotes to define the format of the string. For example, single quotes and double quotes define a string:

```
$name = 'Martin';
$fullname = 'Martin C Brown';
$book = "Perl Complete Reference";
```

The difference is that double quotes define a string with interpolation; that is, the contents of the string can be evaluated. So the following statements evaluate separately:

```
$name = 'Martin C Brown';
$msg = 'Hello $name\n';
$realmsg = "Hello $name\n";
```

The value of **$msg** would be printed as

```
Hello $name\n
```

without any trailing newline (the \n character), but the value of **$realmsg** would be printed as

```
Hello Martin C Brown
```

including a trailing newline character.

This is a very important distinction to understand, as it will affect many of the operations and statements you execute in Perl, not to mention the legibility of the strings you print out!

It's also worth noting, as mentioned before, that scalars are automatically converted between the necessary formats in order to achieve the desired results. For example,

```
$value = '123';
print $value + 1, "\n";
```

would print out a value of 124. Perl automatically converts the string value into a number before applying the operator and adding one to the value. The newline, represented by the leading backslash character, is already specified as a string, and so needs no conversion, but it is interpreted. There are a number of backslash interpreted characters available, and you will probably be familiar with many of them already.

Incidentally, you can assign single words to scalars without quotes:

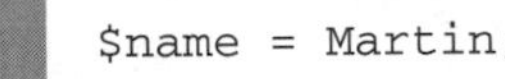

```
$name = Martin;
```

However, this is an ambiguous statement and is not recommended. If Martin was defined as a function, then the value of $name would be the result returned from a call to the Martin function.

You do not have to predefine variables; they will automatically be created when first used. Their initial value will be null, either "" for a string or 0 (zero) for a number. Depending on where you use them, a scalar (and other types of variables) will be interpreted automatically as strings, numbers, or as a Boolean (true or false) value. Different operators and functions expect and return different scalar values.

Perl also supports one final special value for a scalar. The undefined value, **undef**, can be used to identify certain error conditions and the existence, or otherwise, of information in arrays and hashes. The **undef** is most widely used as a return value from a function that would otherwise supply a value of zero that could be genuine. For example, the location of the file pointer within a filehandle could genuinely be at zero, so the **tell** function returns the **undef** value if the location cannot be determined.

Arrays

An array is a list of scalars. You can use an array to store a list of information, to act as a stack (we'll look at stacks in a later chapter), or to act as a container for more complex data structures. The scalar values can be a type of data that can be stored in a scalar: a number, string, or reference.

You can define an array in several different ways, and like scalars, arrays can be generated and returned by functions and statements. The most basic method is to define an empty array:

```
@array = ();
```

Perl does not require you to define variables before you use them; they can be defined at the point you first want to use them. The above example is therefore just an example of how an array can be defined.

The individual scalars of an array are referred to as elements, and each element is referenced by a number. You can use an array to store an indexed list of scalar information. For example, you can use an array to store a list of days of the week, starting with Sunday:

```
@days = ("Sun", "Mon", "Tue", "Wed", "Thu", "Fri", "Sat");
```

This is the long format for predefining the contents of an array. The following examples fill the arrays with the same information:

```
@days = qw/Sun Mon Tue Wed Thu Fri Sat/;
$days[0] = "Sun";
$days[1] = "Mon";
...$days[6] = "Sat";
```

The first example uses the qw operator to automatically quote the bare words, and the spaces separate the individual words into the separate elements of the array. Note that the **qw** operator returns an array, which Perl then automatically assigns to the array you are creating. We'll see later that the same operator can be used to supply lists to other functions without requiring you to create a named array.

If you are unable to automatically fill an array with a list of values, you can set the value of each element individually. You refer to an element of an array by specifying the array name with a dollar sign, because you are referring to a single scalar value within the array. The index notation for an array is square brackets, as in **$days[0]**, which returns the scalar value of element zero from the array.

The first element of an array is element zero, the second element has an index of one, the third, two, and so on. This may not be a problem if you are using the array to hold a list of values. However, if you are using the array as an indexed list of values, then it's unlikely you want to refer to an entry with a value of zero. The example below populates an array with a list of months:

```
@months = qw/Jan Feb Mar Apr May Jun Jul Aug Sep Oct Nov Dec/;
```

The problem should be obvious: month three, which should be March, will be stored in the array as April. You can solve this either by using the direct notation above, never specifying a value for index zero (not recommended), or by using the special **JUNK** placeholder with the qw operator:

```
@months = qw/JUNK Jan Feb Mar Apr May Jun Jul Aug Sep Oct Nov Dec/;
```

This will correctly reference month three as March.

If you want to find out the number of elements in an array, you have two possible methods. The **$#months** notation returns the index of the largest element in the array.

However, using the **@months** notation when the operator or function is expecting a scalar value, rather than an array value, will return the number of elements in the array. You can also force the value to be returned as a scalar by using the **scalar** keyword.

Sometimes it's also necessary to refer to elements of an array referenced from the last, rather than the first, element. For example, to access the last argument of the **@months** array, you would specify an index of –1.

It's also possible to use a statement to select an element from the array; for example,

```
$month = 3;
@months = qw/JUNK Jan Feb Mar Apr May Jun Jul Aug Sep Oct Nov Dec/;
print $months[$month-1];
```

would print out Feb. The statement in the square brackets is evaluated before evaluating the value of the array index.

Finally, you can also use a list of index entries in order to create a new array from an existing list or array. When referring to the entire array, or an array slice, you must use the @ notation, hence,

```
print @months[3,6,9,12],"\n";
```

would output MarJunSepDec, and

```
print @months[3..6,9,12],"\n";
```

would output MarAprMayJunSepDec.

We'll look at further ways of managing and handling arrays when we examine complex data structures in Chapter 7.

Hashes

One problem with arrays is that the information is stored sequentially, using a numeric index reference. This causes problems when you have to delete, insert, and update information in an array, because you must reorganize the sequence each time you make a change. Furthermore, you need to know what information is stored in each index location in order to update the information. This makes using arrays for anything other than simple lists very complex.

A better alternative for managing complex list data is a hash. A hash uses strings as the index values instead of the arbitrary integer value. This means that a hash has no sense of order (there is no natural progression of the index values), and there is no first or last addressable element. Conversely, it also means that additional values can be added to the hash without requiring you to reorganize the list contents.

The real advantage though is that you can refer to an element of a hash by name, instead of by number. Let's look at an example. Imagine you want the reverse of the earlier months array—that is, you want to return a number based on a month name. You can use a hash, with the month names as the index (or key) of the hash and the month number as the corresponding value.

Note *Hashes are often called associative arrays, because a string index is associated with a scalar value. However, this is too long for general use, the name hash is quicker and easier to use.*

First, use long notation to populate the hash:

```
$monthtonum{'Jan'} = 1;
$monthtonum{'Feb'} = 2;
...$monthtonum{'Dec'} = 12;
```

Note that curly brackets, not square brackets, are used to specify the key value. This signifies to Perl that you are referencing the index of a hash, not an array (remember that Perl has different name spaces for the different variable types). The entire hash can be identified by a prefix of a percentage sign, as in **%monthtonum**.

Because the keys to a hash are not automatically implied, you must supply the key as well as the value when you are populating a hash. It is still possible to assign a list to a hash, but Perl interprets alternate elements of the list as keys and values. For example, to populate a hash with short day names as the keys and corresponding long names as the values, you could use

```
%longday = ("Sun", "Sunday", "Mon", "Monday", "Tue", "Tuesday",
            "Wed", "Wednesday", "Thu", "Thursday", "Fri", "Friday",
            "Sat", "Saturday");
```

However, this is not only very difficult to understand but also unclear as to exactly what is being achieved. Perl provides an alternative operator for defining the key and value pairs—the => operator. This syntax is much clearer, enabling you to identify both the key and corresponding value. You can therefore rewrite the previous hash population statement as

```
%longday = ("Sun" => "Sunday",
            "Mon" => "Monday",
            "Tue" => "Tuesday",
            "Wed" => "Wednesday",
            "Thu" => "Thursday",
            "Fri" => "Friday",
            "Sat" => "Saturday"
           );
```

If you refer to the entire hash using **%longday**, then it will be converted back to a list of key and value pairs as in the first example. The alternative is to use the **keys** and **values** functions, which return the appropriate keys or values of an entire hash as a list. In both cases the list is in arbitrary order, and there is no guarantee that two sequential calls to list the hash contents will produce the list in the same order. In these cases you can use the sort or reverse functions to place a suitable order on the lists.

Further examples of how to use hashes will be given when we examine the operators, functions, and complex data structures that can be used with arrays and hashes in Chapter 7.

Localization

By default, all variables are defined globally. This means you can access a defined variable from any location within a single script. However, it is often useful, if not sometimes essential, to localize a particular variable within a code block.

We will consider two keywords at this point that specify the locality of a variable: **my** and **local**. The **local** keyword localizes a variable only within the current code block. The **my** keyword hides a variable entirely from the outside world. The use of **my** is encouraged over **local** since it achieves what most people (particularly those who have previously programmed in C) consider to be variable localization.

To see how this works, let's look at a simple script using a subroutine to demonstrate the localization:

```
sub simplefunction
{
   my $variable = "Martin Brown";
   print "In function variable = $variable\n";
}
my $variable = "Hello World!";
print "Outside function variable = $variable\n";
simplefunction();
print "Outside function variable = $variable\n";
```

Executing this script produces the following:

```
Outside function variable = Hello World!
In function variable = Martin Brown
```

You can see from this that although we have a variable, **$variable**, because it has been defined and localized within the main body of the Perl script and separately defined and localized within the function, the values printed are different.

We'll see more examples of localization and how it can be employed throughout the rest of the book.

Special Variables

Perl keeps an internal list of special variables that supply information and data about the current scripts environment. We will look at each of the available variables in alphabetical order, divided into the three main data types: scalars, arrays, and hashes.

Note that Perl uses a combination of special characters and names to refer to the individual variables. To use the long (named) variables, you must include the **English** module by placing

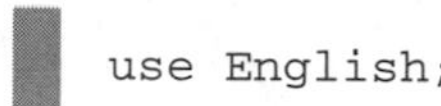

```
use English;
```

at the top of your program. By including this module, the longer names will be aliased to the shortened versions. Although there is no standard for using either format, because the shortened versions are the default, you will see them used more widely. The long version of the name is specified last in the lists that follow.

In the lists of variables, the minimum amount of information has been supplied to enable you to identify the individual variables. More extensive examples of the usage of each variable will be available throughout the rest of this book.

If you import the FileHandle module, the variables that affect the currently selected filehandle can be set to affect only specific filehandles. To use the variables in this way, you can either use

```
method FILEHANDLE EXPR
```

or

```
FILEHANDLE->method(EXPR)
```

Scalar Variables

In this section, you learn what the scalar variables does.

$_
$ARG The default input and pattern searching space. For many functions and operations, if no specific variable is specified, the default input space will be used. For example,

```
$_ = "Hello World\n";
print;
```

would print the "Hello World" message. The same variable is also used in regular expression substitution and pattern matches. We'll look at this more closely in Chapter 4.

Perl will automatically use the default space in the following situations even if you do not specify it:

- Unary functions, such as **ord** and **int**.
- All file tests except **-t**, which defaults to STDIN.
- Most of the functions that support lists as arguments (see Appendix B).
- The pattern matching operations, **m//**, **s///**, and **tr///** when used without an =~ operator.
- The default iterator variable in a **for** or **foreach** loop, if no other variable is supplied.
- The implicit operator in **map** and **grep** functions.
- The default place to store an input record when reading from a filehandle.

$<DIGITS> Contains the regular expression specified within the corresponding parentheses from the last regular expression match.

$&
$MATCH The string matched by the last successful pattern match.

$’
$PREMATCH The string preceding the information matched by the last pattern match.

$’
$POSTMATCH The string following the information matched by the last pattern match.

$+
$LAST_PAREN_MATCH The last bracket match by the last regular expression search pattern.

$*
$MULTILINE_MATCHING Set to 1 to do multiline pattern matching within a string. The default value is zero. The use of this variable has been superseded by the **/s** and **/m** modifiers to regular expressions.

$.
$NR
$INPUT_LINE_NUMBER
input_line_number HANDLE EXPR The current input line number of the last file from which you read. This can be either the keyboard or an external file or other filehandle (such as a network socket).

$/
$RS
$INPUT_RECORD_SEPARATOR
input_record_separator HANDLE EXPR The current input record separator. This is newline by default, but can be set to any string to enable you to read in delimited text files that use one or more special characters to separate the records. You can also undefine the variable, which will allow you to read in an entire file.

$|
$OUTPUT_AUTOFLUSH
autoflush HANDLE EXPR By default all output is buffered (providing the OS supports it). This means all information to be written is stored temporarily in memory and periodically flushed, and the value of **$|** is set to zero. If it is set to non-zero, the filehandle (current, or specified) will be automatically flushed after each write operation.

$,
$OFS
$OUTPUT_FIELD_SEPARATOR
output_field_separator HANDLE EXPR The default output separator for the print series of functions. By default, print outputs the comma-separated fields you specify without any delimiter. You can set this variable to commas, tabs, or any other value to insert a different delimiter.

$
$ORS
$OUTPUT_RECORD_SEPARATOR
output_record_separator HANDLE EXPR The default output record separator. Ordinarily, print outputs individual records without a standard separator, and no trailing newline or other record separator is output.

$"
$LIST_SEPARATOR This defines the separator inserted between elements of an array output within a double-quoted string. The default is a single space.

$;
$SUBSEP
$SUBSCRIPT_SEPARATOR The separator used when emulating multidimensional arrays. If you refer to a hash element as

```
$foo{$a,$b,$c}
```

it really means

```
$foo{join($;,$a,$b,$c)}
```

The default value is "\034."

$#
$OFMT The default number format to use when printing numbers. The value format matches the format of numbers printed via printf and is initially set to **%.ng**, where n is the number of digits to display for a floating point number as defined by your operating system (this is the value of **DBL_DIG** from float.h under Unix).

$%
$FORMAT_PAGE_NUMBER The page number of the current output channel.

$=
$FORMAT_LINES_PER_PAGE The number of printable lines of the current page.

$-
$FORMAT_LINES_LEFT The number of lines available to print to on the current page.

$~
$FORMAT_NAME The name of the current report format in use by the current output channel. This is set by default to the name of the filehandle.

$^
$FORMAT_TOP_NAME The name of the current top-of-page output format for the current output channel. The default name is the filehandle with **_TOP** appended.

$:
$FORMAT_LINE_BREAK_CHARACTERS The set of characters after which a string may be broken to fill continuation fields. The default is "\n-," to allow strings to be broken on newlines or hyphens.

$^L
$FORMAT_FORMFEED The character to be used to send a form feed to the output channel. This is set to "\b" by default.

$ARGV The name of the current file when reading from the default filehandle <>.

$^A
$ACCUMULATOR When outputting formatted information via the reporting system, the **formline** functions put the formatted results into **$^A**, and the **write** function then outputs and empties the accumulator variable. This the current value of the **write** accumulator for **format** lines.

$?
$CHILD_ERROR The status returned by the last external command (via backticks or **system**) or the last pipe close. This is the value returned by **wait**, so the true return value is **$? >> 8**, and **$? & 127** is the number of the signal received by the process, if appropriate.

$!
$ERRNO
$OS_ERROR Returns the error number or error string, according to the context in which it is used. This is equivalent to the errno value and can be used to print the error number or error string when a particular system or function call has failed.

$^E
$EXTENDED_OS_ERROR Contains extended error information for operating systems other than Unix. Under Unix the value equals the value of **$!**. We'll look more closely at the use of this variable when we study the use of Perl as a cross-platform development solution.

$@
$EVAL_ERROR The error message returned by the Perl interpreter when Perl has been executed via the **eval** function. If null, then the last **eval** call executed successfully.

$$
$PID
$PROCESS_ID The process number of the Perl interpreter executing the current script.

$<
$UID
$REAL_USER_ID The real ID of the user currently executing the interpreter that is executing the script.

$>
$EUID
$EFFECTIVE_USER_ID The effective user ID of the current process.

$(
$GID
$REAL_GROUP_ID The real group ID of the current process. If the OS supports multiple simultaneous group membership, this returns a space-separated list of group IDs.

$)
$EGID
$EFFECTIVE_GROUP_ID The effective group ID of the process. If the OS supports multiple simultaneous group membership, this returns a space-separated list of group IDs.

$0
$PROGRAM_NAME The name of the file containing the script currently being executed.

$[The index of the first element in an array, or of the first character in a substring. The default is zero, but can be set to any value. In general, this is useful only when emulating **awk**, since functions and other constructs can emulate the same functionality.

$]
$PERL_VERSION The version + patchlevel/1000 of the Perl interpreter. This can be used to determine the version number of Perl being used, and therefore what functions and abilities the current interpreter supports.

$^D
$DEBUGGING The value of the current debugging flags.

$^F
$SYSTEM_FD_MAX The maximum system file descriptor number—usually two. System file descriptors are duplicated across **exec**'d processes, although higher descriptors are not.

$^H The status of syntax checks enabled by compiler hints, such as **use strict**.

$^I
$INPLACE_EDIT The value of the inplace-edit extension (enabled via the –i switch on the command line).

$^M The size of the emergency pool reserved for use by Perl and the **die** function when Perl runs out of memory. This is the only standard method available for trapping Perl memory overuse during execution.

$^O
$OSNAME The operating system name, as determined via the configuration system during compilation.

$^P
$PERLDB The internal variable that enables you to specify the debugging value. We'll look at this in more detail when we examine the Perl debugger.

$^R The value of the last evaluation in a **(?{ code })** block within a regular expression.

$^S The current interpreter state. The value is undefined if the parsing of the current module is not finished. It is true if inside an evaluation block, otherwise, false.

$^T
$BASETIME The time at which the script started running, defined as the number of seconds since the epoch.

$^W
$WARNING The current value of the warning switch (specified via the **-w** command line option).

$^X
$EXECUTABLE_NAME The name of the Perl binary being executed, as determined via the value of C's **argv[0]**.

Array Variables

This section explains the different array variables.

@ARGV The @ARGV array contains the list of the command line arguments supplied to the script. Note that the first value, at index zero, is the first argument, not the name of the script.

@INC The list of directories that Perl should examine when importing modules via the do, require, or use constructs (see the sections on **use** and **require** in Chapter 5).

@_ Within a subroutine (or function), the @_ array contains the list of parameters supplied to the function.

Hash Variables

The hash variables are as follows.

%INC Contains a list of the files that have been included via do or require. The key is the file you specified, and the value is the actual location of the imported file.

%ENV The list of variables as supplied by the current environment. The key is the name of the environment variable, and the corresponding value is the variable's value. Setting a value in the hash changes the environment variable for child processes.

%SIG The keys of the **%SIG** hash correspond to the signals available on the current machine. The value corresponds to how the signal will be handled. You use this mechanism to support signal handlers within Perl. We'll look at this in more detail when we examine in Chapter 10.

Operators

An operator is a string or sequence of special characters that perform an operation on a statement. For example, the plus sign adds two numbers together. Operators can be further subdivided into numeric and string operators, depending on the type of scalar value they expect to work on. Furthermore, there are a number of operators for testing and comparing, and for logical operations on scalars and statements.

All operators have precedence—the priority with which they are executed when multiple operators are present in a statement. In most cases the operator precedence is identical to the precedence prevalent in C, although this is not always the case. In Table 2-1 you can see the precedence of the different operators available in Perl. The precedence shown determines which side of the operator statement is evaluated first. The "Nonassoc" entries are special cases. Please refer to the operator descriptions that follow for more information.

The table is shown in precedence order, so for example, in the statement

```
$variable = 123 + 45 * 56;
```

Precedence	Operator(s)
Left	Terms and list operators
Left	->
Nonassoc	++ —
Right	**
Right	! ~ \ and unary + and –
Left	=~ !~
Left	* / % x
Left	+ - .
Left	<< >>
Nonassoc	Named unary operators
Nonassoc	< > <= >= lt gt le ge
Nonassoc	== != <=> eq ne cmp
Left	&
Left	| ^
Left	&&
Left	||
Nonassoc	.. ...
Right	?:
Right	= += -= *= etc.
Left	, =>
Nonassoc	List operators
Right	not
Left	and
Left	or xor

Table 2-1. *Operator Precedence*

the multiplication has a higher precedence than the addition, so the result will be 2643. You can also force the precedence of different statements by using parentheses. To make the above example clearer, it could be rewritten as

```
$variable = 123 + (45 * 56);
```

Of course, the reverse is true. If you want the first two values added together before being multiplied by 56, then you could write the statement as

```
$variable = (123 + 45) * 56;
```

In the details below I have collated the different operators by the operation they perform. You can refer to Table 2-1 to decipher the operators' precedence. I have also included only the basic operators at this point. Other operators, such as quotes, regular expressions, transformations, and other complex operators, will be dealt with separately in the forthcoming chapters.

Numeric Operators

The first numeric operators are the increment, **++**, and decrement, **--**, operators, which work exactly as they do in C. When used in front of a statement, the statement is incremented or decremented before being used. When used after a statement, the value is incremented or decremented after the entire statement has been evaluated. For example,

```
$var = 23;
print ++$var,"\n";
```

prints a value of 24, but the script

```
$var = 23;
print $var++,"\n";
```

prints a value of 23. If you print the value of **$var** now, you should get 24:

```
print $var,"\n";
```

The increment operator has one other trick up its sleeve. When used with an alphabetical or alphanumeric value, the increment is executed as a string, incrementing each character within its range:

```
print ++('Az');              #prints 'Ba'
print ++('a0');              #prints 'a1'
```

The decrement operator does not work in the same way.
The available numeric operators are summarized in Table 2-2.

String Operators

The equivalent of + for strings is the period. Using a period concatenates two strings, for example,

```
$string = 'Hello' . ' ' . 'World!';
print $string,"\n";
```

would print out the familiar "Hello World!" message.

There is also a multiplication operator for strings, **x**, which allows you to repeat a string for the specified number of times. The string is taken from the left of the operator, and the multiplication value is taken from the right. So,

```
print '=' x 80;
```

would print a row of equal signs 80 characters wide.

Operator	Action
+	Adds the two statements.
-	Subtracts the statement on the right from the statement on the left.
*	Multiplies the statement on the right by the statement on the left.
/	Divides the statement on the left by the statement on the right.
**	Exponential—that is, the statement on the left is raised to the power of the statement on the right.
%	Returns the modulus of two numbers. The *modulus* is the integer remainder when the left statement is divided by the right statement. For example, 8 % 3 is 2.

Table 2-2. *Numeric Operators*

Equality and Relational Operators

It is important to be able to test the equality of two statements. This ability enables you to produce test statements and make decisions based on the results of the test. It is also useful to be able to compare the relation between two statements (particularly strings). Table 2-3 lists equality and relational operators.

Operator	Action
<	Returns true if the left statement is numerically less than the right statement.
>	Returns true if the left statement is numerically greater than the right statement.
<=	Returns true if the left statement is numerically less than or equal to the right statement.
>=	Returns true if the left statement is numerically greater than or equal to the right statement.
==	Returns true if the left statement is numerically equal to the right statement.
!=	Returns true if the left statement is numerically not equal to the right statement.
<=>	Returns –1, 0, or 1 depending on whether the left statement is numerically less than, equal to, or greater than the right statement.
lt	Returns true if the left statement is stringwise less than the right statement.
gt	Returns true if the left statement is stringwise greater than the right statement.
le	Returns true if the left statement is stringwise less than or equal to the right statement.
ge	Returns true if the left statement is stringwise greater than or equal to the right statement.

Table 2-3. *Equality and Relational Operators*

Operator	Action
eq	Returns true if the left statement is stringwise equal to the right statement.
ne	Returns true if the left statement is stringwise not equal to the right statement.
cmp	Returns –1, 0, or 1 depending on whether the left statement is stringwise less than, equal to, or greater than the right statement.

Table 2-3. *Equality and Relational Operators* (continued)

It is important to appreciate the difference between comparing numbers and strings. The tests

```
$var = 1;
print "Right!" if ($var == 1);
```

and

```
$var = 1;
print "Wrong!" if ($var eq 1);
```

are not testing the same thing, although both will work.

The easiest way to remember which operator to use is that numeric comparisons use special characters; string comparisons use words.

Logical Operators

Logical operators allow you to compare and evaluate logical (Boolean) expressions. See Table 2-4 for the list of logical operators supported. In a list context, the logical operators are evaluated right statement first. Care must be taken, therefore, if using logical operators in function calls.

It is worth noting that logical operators in Perl return the last value evaluated. This is different from C, in which individual statements must be encapsulated within parentheses to evaluate multiple statements simultaneously. For example, the statement below is a practical way of discovering a user's login:

```
$login = $ENV{'USER'} || $ENV{'LOGNAME'} || getlogin();
```

Operator	Action
&&	Logical AND. The evaluation returns true only if both the left and right statements are logically true.
||	Logical OR. The evaluation returns true if one or the other of the statements is true.
!	Logical NOT. The evaluation returns the opposite of the statement on the right.

Table 2-4. *Logical Operators*

Each statement is evaluated, and the one that returns a value will be assigned to the $login variable. This is far more practical and certainly easier to read.

If you prefer, you can use **and** and **or** in place of **&&** and ||. The advantage is that they have a much lower precedence, which means they can safely be used in list contexts. For example,

```
unlink 'rod', 'jane', 'freddy' || die "Error deleting files";
```

would actually evaluate the result of the **die** statement against the value of 'freddy', which is not the desired result. You would instead have to write that statement as

```
unlink('rod', 'jane', 'freddy') || die "Error deleting files";
```

Using **or**, you can return to the previous format:

```
unlink 'rod', 'jane', 'freddy' or die "Error deleting files";
```

As a rule you should use || and && in preference to **or** and **and**.

Bitwise Operators

You can perform bitwise operations on scalars to operate on individual bits within the value. There are three main bitwise operators, and **&**, or |, and exclusive or ^. For example, the **&** operator returns the two statements anded together bit by bit.

You can also shift numbers by a number of bits left and right using the shift operators << and >>, respectively. You will need to know binary mathematics to understand it fully, but it's demonstrated with an example:

```
print 1 << 4,"\n";
```

If you look at Table 2-5, you can see the standard binary table. If you shift the value of 1 four places to the left, as in the example, the 1 will be in the 16 column, and the result will therefore be 16. This also works with other numbers; so 7 shifted to the left twice equals 28. Right-shift performs the opposite; **–16 >> 4** equals 1.

The last bitwise operator is ~, which returns the bitwise negation, or ones complement of a number. See Table 2-6 for a simple demonstration.

Remember though that Perl uses 32 bit integers for calculations, and not the 8 bit integers I've used in this example.

Range Operator

The range operator **..** allows you to define a range between the left and right statements. The result of using the operator depends on the context. In a list context, it returns an array of values from the right operator to the left in steps of one element. For example, to extract elements 4 to 5 from an array, you might use

```
print $months[3..5];
```

You can also use it within for and foreach loops:

```
for(1..1000) {
...
}
```

If the operands are strings, Perl makes use of the auto-increment feature; so you can refer to the entire uppercase alphabet with

```
@alphabet = ('A' .. 'Z');
```

Or to get a list of days of the month with leading zeros:

```
@days = ('01' .. '31');
```

128	64	32	16	8	4	2	1
0	0	0	0	0	0	0	1

Table 2-5. *Binary Table with a Value of One*

	128	64	32	16	8	4	2	1
28	0	0	0	1	1	1	0	0
~28	1	1	1	0	0	0	1	1

Table 2-6. *Bitwise Negation, or Ones Complement*

In a scalar context, the .. operator acts as a toggle. The range operator is false as long as the left statement is false. Once the left statement is true, the range operator also becomes true. The operator then stays true until the right statement becomes true, at which point the range operator becomes false, and so the process continues. This can be used to toggle between two states where the range between the scalars is relevant. The example given in the documentation is that of a mail message, which is logically divided into a message header and a message body. You could therefore use the following fragment to parse an email message:

```
while(<>)
{
    $in_header = 1 ../^$/;
    $in_body = /^$/ .. eof();
}
```

If you do not want to test the right statement until the next evaluation, you can use the ... operator in place of the .. operator.

Assignment Operators

The standard assignment operator is the equal sign =. It assigns the result of the evaluation of the statement on the right side to the statement on the left. In addition to the standard operator, you can combine operators with the assignment operator to shorten operations. For example, to add a number to an existing variable, you would logically use

```
$var = $var +15;
```

However, Perl allows you to shorten this to

```
$var += 15;
```

The same combination can be made with the following operators:

```
**=, +=, -=, .=, *=, /=, %=, x=, &=, |=, ^=, <<=, >>=, &&=, ||=
```

This is similar to C, although Perl provides a larger range of assignment operators. Also, unlike C, Perl supports an assignment expression as an lvalue, which allows you to combine two separate statements such as

```
$var += 3;
$var *= 4;
```

into a single line:

```
($var += 3) *= 4;
```

Terms and List Operators

A term has the highest precedence in Perl. A term includes variables, quotes, and functions with arguments or entire statements that are in parentheses. List operators (commas or returns from arrays or hashes) are evaluated in order before being passed to the next highest function or operator. For example:

```
print $foo, exit();
print($foo,exit());
```

Both evaluate the function exit before passing the information back to **print** to be output. This means both lines will exit the script before the result is printed, which is probably not what you want. You need to raise the print statement to a higher precedence using parentheses:

```
(print $foo), exit();
print($foo), exit();
```

Comma Operator

Binary , is the list operator. In a scalar context it evaluates the statement on the left, disposes of the value, and then evaluates and returns the result of the right statement. This allows you to write fragments like this:

```
$string = ("Hello", "World");
```

The "Hello" in this instance will be discarded and the $string variable will now contain the string "World".

The => operator is just a synonym for the comma operator but is most useful when using arguments that come in pairs, for example, hash index and value arguments.

Arrow Operator

The **->** is the infix dereference operator, the same as in C. If the right statement is a subscript, then the left side must be a hard or symbolic reference to an array or hash. Otherwise, if the right side is a method name or scalar variable containing a reference to a method name, then the left side must be either an object or a class name.

Regular Expression

The =~ operator binds a scalar expression to a pattern match (regular expression). We'll look at this more closely when we examine regular expressions later in Chapter 4. The !~ operator is identical except that the return value is logically negated.

Statements

Any Perl program is a combination of expressions, declarations, and statements. An expression (**EXPR**) is any sequence that can be evaluated (for example, a calculation), typically made up of literals, variables, operators, functions, and subroutines. A declaration is an assertion that something exists, for example, the definition of a variable. A statement is a command to the computer that describes what to do next.

We have already considered the bulk of expressions and declarations; we now need to consider how to control the flow of these expressions and declarations in order to develop a sequence that will control what our Perl program actually achieves.

To do this, you use statements. A statement is an evaluated expression. Every statement must end in a semicolon. The only exception to this rule is when a simple statement is the last statement in a block. In this case the semicolon is optional. However, in order to make the code easy to extend, a semicolon is advised in all situations.

Code Blocks

When you define a series of statements within a specific scope, either the entire program, an evaluated block (via the eval function), or within a brace-delimited ({})section, it is called a *block*. Blocks are used in combination with expressions in order to form compound statements.

You can define a block within a script by enclosing the statements and expressions in a pair of braces. This is a simple code block:

```
{
   print "Hello World!\n";
}
```

Blocks may be nested. Because a block is a sequence of expressions and declarations (and even other statements and blocks), the use of a block is the only way to define functions and subroutines. It is therefore implicit that a single file (either the main script or one included in the main script) is also a code block.

We will refer to code blocks using the standard BLOCK.

Labels

All blocks and loop statements can have an optional label. This way you can label a code block and then jump to that code block at any point within the program. Note that this is different from a function: a labeled block does not return to the caller once the block has been executed and evaluated. We'll see examples of how to use labels and labeled blocks later in this chapter.

Conditional Statements

Now that you understand what a statement is and what a code block is, you can begin to form conditional statements. A conditional statement is one that relies on the result of an evaluated expression to decide whether a statement or code block should be executed.

There are two simple conditional statements. The **if** statement is identical to the English equivalent. It is designed to ask a question (based on an expression) and execute the statement or code block if the result of the evaluated expression returns true. There are five different formats for the **if** statement:

```
if (EXPR)
if (EXPR) {BLOCK}
if (EXPR) {BLOCK} else {BLOCK}
if (EXPR) {BLOCK} elsif (EXPR) {BLOCK} ...
if (EXPR) {BLOCK} elsif (EXPR) {BLOCK} ...else {BLOCK}
```

Note that in each case the condition is defined in terms of code blocks, not statements. Unlike C, braces are required.

The first format is used at the end of a statement, as in:

```
print "Happy Birthday!\n" if ($date == $today);
```

In this instance the message will only be printed if the expression evaluates to a true value.

The second format is the more familiar conditional statement:

```
if ($date == $today)
{
   print "Happy Birthday!\n";
}
```

This produces the same result as the previous example, but because the condition can be followed by a code block, you can insert additional statements and expressions.

The third format allows for exceptions. If the expression evaluates to true, then the first block is executed; otherwise (**else**), the second block is executed:

```
if ($date == $today)
{
   print "Happy Birthday!\n";
}
else
{
   print "Happy Unbirthday!\n";
}
```

The fourth form allows for additional tests if the first expression does not return true. The **elsif** can be repeated an infinite number of times to test as many different alternatives as are required:

```
if ($date == $today)
{
   print "Happy Birthday!\n";
}
elsif ($date == $christmas)
{
   print "Happy Christmas!\n";
}
```

Finally, the fifth form allows for both additional tests and a final exception if all the other tests fail:

```
if ($date == $today)
{
   print "Happy Birthday!\n";
}
```

```
elsif ($date == $christmas)
{
   print "Happy Christmas!\n";
}
else
{
   print "Happy Unbirthday!\n";
}
```

If you use **unless** in place of **if**, then the test is reversed; so,

```
print "Happy Unbirthday!\n" unless ($date == $today);
```

is equivalent to

```
print "Happy Unbirthday!\n" if ($date != $today);
```

However, if you want to make multiple tests, there is no **elsunless**, only **elsif**. It is more sensible to use **unless** only in situations where there is a single statement or code block; using **unless** and **else** or **elsif** only confuses the process. For example, the following is a less elegant solution to the above **if...else** example

```
unless ($date != $today)
{
   print "Happy Unbirthday!\n";
}
else
{
   print "Happy Birthday!\n";
}
```

although it achieves the same result—TMTOWTDI syndrome!

The final conditional statement is actually an operator—the conditional operator. It is synonymous with the **if...else** conditional statement but is shorter and more compact. The format for the operator is

```
(expression) ? (statement if true) : (statement if false)
```

For example, we can emulate the above example:

```
($date == $today) ? print "Happy Birthday!\n" : print "Happy Unbirthday!\n";
```

Furthermore, because it is an operator, it can be incorporated directly into expressions where you would otherwise require statements. This means you can compound the above example to the following:

```
print "Happy ", ($date == $today) ? "Birthday!\n" : "Unbirthday!\n";
```

Loops

Perl supports a number of different loops, and all of them should be familiar to programmers. Perl supports four main loop types: while, until, for, and foreach.

The while loop has three forms:

```
while EXPRLABEL
while (EXPR) BLOCKLABEL
while (EXPR) BLOCK continue BLOCK
```

The first format allows simple statements to be executed. The expression is evaluated first, and then the statement is evaluated. For example:

```
$linecount while !eof();
```

The exception to this rule is when it is combined with a preceding do {} block, as in

```
do
{
   $calc += ($fact*$ivalue);
} while $calc <100;
```

In this case the code block is executed first, and the conditional expression is only evaluated at the end of each loop iteration.

The second two forms of the while loop repeatedly execute the code block as long as the result from the conditional expression is true. If the optional continue block is included, then it is executed after the main code block, and when the execution skips to the next iteration as part of a loop control statement (see the Loop Control section below). In general practice, continue blocks are not used, but they are included to allow us to reproduce a **for** loop using a **while** loop.

The inverse of the **while** loop is the **until** loop, which evaluates the conditional expression and reiterates over the loop only when the expression returns false. Once the expression returns true, the loop ends. In the case of a **do...until** loop, the conditional expression is only evaluated at the end of the code block. In an **until (EXPR) BLOCK** loop, the expression is evaluated before the block executes. Using an **until** loop, you could rewrite the above example as

```
do
{
   $calc += ($fact*$ivalue);
} until $calc >= 100;
```

A **for** loop is basically a **while** loop with an additional expression used to reevaluate the original conditional expression. This is written as three separate expressions, which together form the initialization. The format of the **for** loop is

```
LABEL for (EXPR; EXPR; EXPR) BLOCK
```

Thus you can write a loop to iterate 100 times like this:

```
for ($i=0;$i<100;$i++)
{
...
}
```

You can place multiple variables into the expressions using the standard list operator (the comma):

```
for ($i=0, $j=0;$i<100;$i++,$j++)
```

This is more practical than C, where you would require two nested loops to achieve the same result. Furthermore, the expressions are optional, so you can create an infinite loop like this:

```
for(;;)
{
...
}
```

Loop control statements can then be employed to exit the loop at the appropriate point.

The last loop type is the **foreach** loop, which has a format like this:

```
LABEL foreach VAR (LIST) BLOCK
LABEL foreach VAR (LIST) BLOCK continue BLOCK
```

This is identical to the **for** loop available within the shell. For those not familiar with the operator of the shell's **for** loop, let's look at a more practical example. Imagine that you want to iterate through a list of values stored in an array printing each value (we'll use the month list from our earlier variables example). Using a **for** loop, you can achieve this using

```
for ($index=0;$index<=@months;$index++)
{
   print "$months[$index]\n";
}
```

This is messy because you're manually selecting the individual elements from the array and using an additional variable, **$index**, to extract the information. Using a **foreach** loop, you can simplify the process:

```
for (@months)
{
   print "$_\n";
}
```

Perl has automatically separated the elements, placing each element of the array into the default input space. Each iteration of the loop will take the next element of the array. The list can be any expression, and you can supply an optional variable for the loop to place each value of the list into. To print out each word on an individual line from a file, you could use the example below:

```
while (<FILE>)
{
   chomp;
   foreach $word (split)
   {
      print "$word\n";
   }
}
```

The **foreach** loop can even be used to iterate through a hash, providing you return the list of values or keys from the hash as the list:

```
foreach $key (keys %monthstonum)
{
   print "Month $monthstonum{$key} is $key\n";
}
```

Note *The **for** and **foreach** keywords are synonymous. You can use either keyword to use either type of loop. However, as with other parts of the Perl language, you should use them as listed here so that it is obvious to readers of your source code what you are trying to achieve.*

Loop Control

There are three loop control keywords: **next**, **last**, and **redo**. The **next** keyword skips the remainder of the code block, forcing the loop to proceed to the next value in the loop. For example,

```
while (<DATA>)
{
   next if /^#/;
}
```

would skip lines from the file if they started with a hash symbol, which is the standard comment style under Unix. If there is a continue block, it is executed before execution proceeds to the next iteration of the loop.

The **last** keyword ends the loop entirely, skipping the remaining statements in the code block, as well as dropping out of the loop. This is best used to escape a loop when an alternative condition has been reached within a loop that cannot otherwise be trapped. The **last** keyword is therefore identical to the **break** keyword in C and Shellscript. For example,

```
while (<DATA>)
{
   last if ($found);
}
```

would exit the loop if the value of **$found** was true, regardless of whether the end of the file had actually been reached. The **continue** block is not executed.

The **redo** keyword reexecutes the code block without reevaluating the conditional statement for the loop. This skips the remainder of the code block and also the **continue** block before the main code block is reexecuted. This is especially useful if you want to reiterate over a code block based on a condition that is unrelated to the loop condition. For example, the code below would read the next line from a file if the current line terminates with a backslash.

```
while(<DATA>)
{
    if (s#\\$#)
    {
        $_ .= <DATA>;
        redo;
    }
}
```

In all cases the loop control keyword affects the current (innermost) loop. You can supply an optional label, at which point the keyword will affect the corresponding named block. This allows you to nest and control loops:

```
OUTER:
while(<DATA>)
{
    chomp;
    @linearray=split;
    foreach $word (@linearray)
    {
        next OUTER if ($word =~ /next/i)
    }
}
```

This would skip the current input line from the file if there was a word "next" in the input line while allowing the remainder of the words from the file to be processed.

Perl considers all the keywords here to be operators, rather than functions or statements. This allows you to use them in an expression as you would any other operator, rather than using them in more simple statements.

Emulating case or switch

If you are used to working in C or Shellscript, you will probably be used to using a case or switch conditional statement to make selections from multiple expressions. There is no equivalent in Perl, although you can use a number of different methods to emulate the same functionality. The most obvious is to use an **if...elsif...else** combination. However, this can be difficult to follow and complex to debug.

A more elegant solution is to use a labeled code block with loop control operators. For example:

```
SWITCH:
{
   if ($date == $today) { print "Happy Birthday!\n";   last SWITCH; }
   if ($date != $today) { print "Happy Unbirthday!\n"; last SWITCH; }
   if ($date == $xmas)  { print "Happy Christmas!\n";  last SWITCH; }
}
```

This is not as strange as it appears once you realize that you can use the loop control operators **last**, **next**, and **redo** within any block. This also means you could write to the same script as

```
SWITCH:
{
   print "Happy Birthday!\n",   last SWITCH if ($date == $today);
   print "Happy Unbirthday!\n", last SWITCH if ($date != $today);
   print "Happy Christmas!\n",  last SWITCH if ($date == $xmas);
}
```

Or for a more formatted solution that will appeal to C and Shellscript programmers:

```
SWITCH:
{
   ($date == $today)    && do {
                                 print "Happy Birthday!\n";
                                 last SWITCH;
                           }
   ($date != $today)    && do {
                                 print "Happy Unbirthday!\n";
                                 last SWITCH;
                           }
   ($date == $xmas)     && do {
                                 print "Happy Christmas!\n";
                                 last SWITCH;
                           }
}
```

Note that in this last example you could exclude the label. The **do {}** blocks are not loops, and so the last command would ignore them and instead drop out of the parent **SWITCH** block.

goto

BASIC programmers will be immediately happy when they realize that Perl has a goto statement. For purists, goto is a bad idea, and in many cases it is actually a dangerous option when subroutines and functions are available. There are three basic forms: **goto LABEL, goto EXPR**, and **goto &NAME**.

In each case, execution is moved from the current location to the destination. In the case of **goto LABEL**, execution stops at the current point and resumes at the point of the label specified. It cannot be used to jump to a point inside a block that needs initialization, such as a subroutine for loop. However, it can be used to jump to any other point within the current or parent block, including jumping out of subroutines. As has already been stated, the use of **goto** is deprecated. It is always possible to use a control flow statement (**next**, **redo**, etc.), function, or subroutine to achieve the same result without any of the dangers.

The second form is essentially just an extended form of **goto LABEL**. Perl expects the expression to evaluate dynamically at execution time to a label by name. This allows for computed gotos similar to those available in FORTRAN, but like **goto LABEL**, its use is deprecated.

The **goto &NAME** statement is more complex. It allows you to replace the currently executing subroutine with a call to the specified subroutine instead. This allows you to automatically call a different subroutine based on the current environment and is used by the autoload mechanism (see the **Autoload** module in Appendix E) to dynamically select alternative routines. The statement works such that even the caller will be unable to tell whether the requested subroutine or the one specified by **goto** was executed first.

Literal Tokens

There are four special tokens which have additional meaning in a Perl script. The **__LINE__** and **__FILE__** tokens represent the current script's line number, and current script name. They cannot be used in interpolated string, only separately. See Chapter 3 for an example of using these two functions.

The **__END__** token signifies to the Perl interpreter that this is the logical end of the script, even though there may be more text following this token. This is often used to incorporate release notes or documentation within the script without it affecting the script's execution. The data contained after the **__END__** token can be read using the DATA filehandle.

The **__DATA_** token is similar to the **__END__** token, except that it opens the DATA filehandle within the current package namespace. This enables you to have multiple **__DATA__** date blocks for each package. Both the **__DATA__** and **__END__** tokens are used with the **AutoLoader** and **SelfLoader** modules. See Appendix E for more information.

The Complete Reference

Chapter 3

The User Interface

It is inevitable that at some point you will need to communicate with the outside world. We will consider three basic outside influences in this chapter: screen, keyboard, and files. In fact, Perl works much like many other languages. The default input and output devices are the screen and the keyboard, but these devices can also be referenced via files.

Unlike C, Perl uses, within reason, the same set of functions for communicating with the terminal, keyboard, pipes (external commands or command input), network sockets, and files. This creates less confusion while you are working and helps optimize the language. This means that many of the functions we will look at can be used not only for accessing files but also for accessing any kind of external data stream outside of the main Perl script.

The basics of handling files are simple: you associate a *filehandle* with an external entity (usually a file) and then use a variety of operators and functions within Perl to read and update the data stored within the data stream associated with the filehandle. This is similar to other languages that use the same structure. In C, for example, a **FILE** structure contains all the information on a data stream and acts as the reference point for using the data stored within that stream.

The basic way of communicating information to a user is via the two functions **print** and **printf**. Both of these print information to the terminal or to a specified filehandle (see **print** below). The only difference between the two functions is that **print** simply outputs the values of the list of expressions supplied. Thus it ignores any specific formatting or interpretation of the information (interpolation still works, since that is a function of the quote operators, not the function).

The **printf** function is essentially identical to the C **printf()** function. Using a special format string, the resulting expression list can be formatted and interpreted according to the specified format. This gives greater control over the justification of values and the number of decimal points printed for floating point numbers.

In general use, **print** is used significantly more than **printf**. You generally only use **printf** when you need to format the output of a number of strings or numbers in a single instance. The use of **print** is preferred since it is both quicker (to write and use) and less prone to errors (because there is no format string).

For list information, a more practical solution is the Perl reporting system. Using a special format string (similar to the one used by **printf**) and a collection of functions, you can create simple lists and complex reports with relative ease. We'll look at the Perl reporting mechanism in Chapter 12.

Specifying Data

Although we have already seen the different methods available for placing information in variables, there are simpler ways of introducing static information into a Perl script. For the purposes of the user interface, as well as other parts of Perl, we need to know what these methods are and where they can be used.

Quotes

Quotes are used to separate static information from the operators, functions, and expressions that make up a typical Perl statement. In Perl, quotes also act like operators, providing various methods for interpolating other pieces of information into the quoted values. The supported quote types are summarized in Table 3-1.

Perl takes the quotes literally, with the value starting with the first quote character and only ending with the final quote character. You can, for example, include a newline in a string, not only by using the normal control character notation, but also by inserting a newline character into the Perl source code. For example:

```
print "Hello Martin
This is a new line...\n";
```

This results in

```
Hello Martin
This is a new line...
```

However, be warned that this system has its disadvantages. Unless you are careful, the Perl parser will bail out if it never sees the closing quote. Worse still, you may accidentally be including Perl statements in your quoted strings. If you want to print large volumes of text included directly within a Perl script, see "Here Documents" a bit later in this chapter.

Customary	Generic	Meaning	Interpolates
''	q//	Literal text	No
""	qq//	Literal text	Yes
"	qx//	Command	Yes
()	qw//	Word list	No
//	m//	Pattern match	Yes
s///	s///	Substitution	Yes
y///	tr///	Translation	No

Table 3-1. *Perl Quotes*

Variable Interpolation

As we have already seen, you can insert variables directly into double-quoted strings. This is called *variable interpolation*, and Perl supports the interpolation of both scalar and list values directly into double-quoted strings. It simplifies the process of string concatenation. You can avoid using the concatenation operator, or using a special function as you have to in C where **strcat** and **strcpy** are required to combine and copy strings.

Interpolation only works with scalar values. That means you can only incorporate scalars—the individual scalar elements or slices of an array or hash—or entire arrays, but you cannot interpolate entire hashes. This is logical, since there is no logical order or format to an entire hash, only to the keys or values of the hash. In fact, the Perl parser only looks for expressions that start with **$** or **@** (and the backslash, for the special characters listed in Tables 3-1 and 3-2). This restriction does not stop you from printing the values of a hash, since you can refer to the elements and slices of a hash directly (because they start with **$** and **@**, respectively).

For example, in the code

```
$name = 'Martin Brown';
print "Your name is $name\n";
```

the assignation to the **$name** variable is not interpolated, since single quotes are used. The **print** statement on the other hand is interpolated, because double quotes are specified, and the result is that the message printed is

```
Your name is Martin Brown
```

Incidentally, interpolation is recursive. This enables you to specify control characters and variables within scalars that are then printed. You could rewrite the above example as follows:

```
$name = "Martin Brown\n";
print "Your name is $name";
```

Note, however, that you have to specify double quotes for the variable assignation, since it is the resultant value of the **$name** scalar that contains the value of the interpolated string. This is what I would class as indirect recursion, since the actual interpolation occurs each time a value is returned from an expression, depending on the quotes used around the expression.

Here Documents

When incorporating large volumes of text, using quoted strings becomes cumbersome. A better solution is to use what Perl calls a *here document*. This allows you to specify that all of the characters and lines up to a specified delimiter be treated as a quotable string that can be passed directly to a specific function. The specification allows for control characters and interpolation and can act as a direct replacement for multiple **print** statements or from messy multiline quoted strings. The format for a here document is as follows:

```
function <<MARKER;
text
MARKER
```

Note the format of **MARKER**, which immediately follows the **<<** operator. Perl treats any text following the **<<** operator as the termination string for the included text. For example:

```
print <<EOF;
Hello $name
EOF
```

The type of quote and format of the marker are entirely at your discretion. A marker without quotes is treated like one with double quotes, but you can also use here documents to run commands by using backtick quotes:

```
print <<'EOF';
ls -l /etc
du -sk /usr/local
EOF
```

Or you can specify the same string a multiple number of times:

```
print <<"" x 5;
-----
```

This would print the next line five times. The initial empty string tells Perl to treat the next blank line as the terminator.

The only rule to remember when using here documents is to be sure you place a semicolon after the terminating string in the original statement; otherwise Perl treats both the original statement and the here document as one entire statement, as can be seen in this example,

```
print <<EOF
123
EOF
+456;
```

which actually prints 579.

Essentially, a here document is a special type of quote operator that allows you to specify multiline information in a simple and straightforward way.

Special Characters

When using a double-quoted string, you can insert various control characters using the same basic notation as C and Unix. This allows you to insert special characters into strings—both those used as the values for scalar variables and those used directly within statements. In addition to the "named" variables, you can insert special characters using their octal or hexadecimal values, or as control characters. Table 3-2 lists the characters supported within Perl.

Code	Result
\t	Tab
\n	Newline
\r	Carriage return
\f	Form feed
\b	Backspace
\a	Alarm (bell)
\e	Escape
\007	Bell character in octal
\x07	Bell character in hexadecimal
\cC	Control-C

Table 3-2. *Backslash Characters*

It is also possible to insert special characters into double-quoted strings that affect the subsequent characters and words. These are not quite so useful for static string information, but they can help the formatting of variable information. Table 3-3 lists the various options.

For example, if you wanted to enforce sentence case, in which the first character of a string is converted to uppercase, you might use

```
print "The message is \u$message, from $who\n";
```

Or if you wanted to convert the message entirely into uppercase:

```
print "The message is \U$message\E, from $who\n";
```

These characters can be used in any set of quotes that interpolate variables.

Filehandles

A filehandle is a named internal Perl structure that associates a physical file with a name. A filehandle can be reused. It is not permanently attached to a single file, nor is it permanently related to a particular file name. The name of the filehandle and the name of the file are not related.

As far as Perl is concerned, all operating systems support three basic filehandles—**STDIN**, **STDOUT**, and **STDERR**. The exact interpretation of the filehandle and the device or file it is associated with depend on the OS and the Perl implementation. Table 3-4 shows the relationship between Perl filehandles and the underlying C file descriptors.

Code	Result
\u	Force next character to uppercase.
\l	Force next character to lowercase.
\U	Force all following characters to uppercase.
\L	Force all following characters to lowercase.
\Q	Backslash all following nonalphanumeric characters.
\E	End \U, \L, or \Q.

Table 3-3. *Formatting Strings Inline*

Perl Filehandle	C File Descriptor	Associated Device	Access Mode
STDIN	0	Keyboard/terminal	Write-only
STDOUT	1	Monitor/terminal	Read-only
STDERR	2	Monitor/terminal	Write-only

Table 3-4. *Standard Perl Filehandles*

Note *Perl also supports two further filehandles, **ARGV** and **DATA**, we'll examine these more closely in Chapter 11.*

All filehandles are capable of read/write access, so you can read from and update any file or device associated with a filehandle. However, when you associate a filehandle, you can specify the mode in which the filehandle is opened. This option prevents you from accidentally updating or overwriting information in a file that you only wanted to read. You can see from Table 3-4 the access modes for the standard filehandles.

All filehandles are by default buffered on both input and output. In most cases, this helps to improve performance by reading more than is needed from the physical device, or by block writing to a physical device. Information is buffered on a block-by-block basis (the underlying OS defines the block size). The only exception to this rule is **STDOUT**, which is buffered on a line basis: appending the newline character to a printed string will automatically flush the buffer. You can switch the buffering for the currently selected filehandle by setting the value of the **$|** variable to any value other than zero. It's also possible to set the buffering on other files if you use the **IO::Handle** module with the **autoflush** method. For example, the following code turns buffering off for the **DOOR** filehandle.

```
use IO::Handle;
open(DOOR,"<file.in") or die "Couldn't open file";
autoflush DOOR 1;
```

To switch it back on again:

```
autoflush DOOR 0;
```

Note *In the above example, the arguments to **open** are placed in parentheses to ensure that the **or** operator checks the entire statement, not the value of the file name.*

A filehandle can be referred to either by static token or an expression. If an expression is specified, then the value of the expression is used as the filehandle name. Note that a filehandle token does not have a special preceding character, as with a variable, and the name is written in uppercase. This is to help separate a filehandle from a normal variable. If the filehandle is referred to by an expression, then the result of the expression is used as the filehandle name.

The only limitation with a filehandle is that it cannot be supplied directly to a user-defined function. In this instance you must use a *typeglob*. This is a special type of identifier that enables you to refer to different types of variables by prefixing the name with an asterisk. This allows a typeglob to refer to all, or any, of **$name**, **@name**, **%name**, or **name** with ***name**. How the typeglob is used, and therefore which interpretation is employed, is at the discretion of the expression or statement using the typeglob. See Chapter 5 for more information on the symbol table and the use of typeglobs in functions.

Opening and Closing Files

A fundamental part of the Perl language is its ability to read and process file data very quickly. In Chapter 1 we saw how the historical development of Perl was geared toward text processing long before it gained the general-purpose status it holds now.

All file data is exchanged through the use of a filehandle, which associates an external data source (a file, network socket, external program, pipe) with an internal data structure (the filehandle). The method with which you associate the filehandle differs depending on the type of external data source, although many of the functions used to access the data available with the filehandle are the same. For files, you use the **open** function to open ordinary files and the **sysopen** function to handle more complex opening procedures. The **close** function is used to close any open filehandle, regardless of how it was opened.

open

The **open** function is almost certainly one of the most complicated to understand when you first approach the Perl language. Once grasped, however, it becomes easy and almost second nature in use, often making the methods employed in other languages seem clumsy and constricting.

```
open FILEHANDLE, EXPR
open FILEHANDLE
```

The first form is the one used most often. The **FILEHANDLE** is a token name that allows you to refer to a file with a specific name. A **FILEHANDLE** in any function can alternatively be an expression, which is evaluated; the value being used as the filehandle name. If the expression supplied does not evaluate to a suitable value, Perl does not make one up for you. You must ensure, therefore, that the expression you supply in place of **FILEHANDLE** evaluates to something identifiable.

The **EXPR** is more complex. Perl takes the value supplied, interpolates the string where necessary, and then strips any leading or trailing white space. The string is then examined for special characters at the start and end of the string that defines the mode and type of file to be opened.

The basic operators are the greater-than/less-than signs. The syntax is taken from the shell, which uses a less-than sign to pass file contents to the standard input of a command. Within Perl, this translates to this:

```
open(DATA, "<file.txt");
```

The **EXPR** for the function shows that the file is being opened read-only. If you want to write to a file, you use the greater-than sign:

```
open(DATA, ">file.txt");
```

This example actually truncates (empties) the file before opening it for writing, which may not be the desired effect. If you want to open a file for reading and writing, you can put a plus sign before the **>** or **<** characters.

For example, to open a file for updating without truncating it:

```
open(DATA, "+<file.txt");
```

To truncate the file first:

```
open DATA, "+>file.txt" or die "Couldn't open file file.txt, $!";
```

Note that in the example above I've combined the **open** function with the **die** function to report an error if the **open** failed. This shows a basic principle of nearly all Perl functions. They all return **truetrue** (a value greater than zero) if the function was a success, so you can easily combine it with a **warn** or **die** function to report errors. (See the end of this chapter for more information on these two functions.) So, in this example, if the **open** function returns true, then the **die** function will not be executed. However, if it returns **false** (zero), indicating a failure, then the **die** function will be executed. This is quicker and significantly more efficient than using **if** statements to test the success of functions.

This also demonstrates a basic principle of any programming: you must be able to track and trace errors. Perl has a simple but effective method of error checking that we'll see in various examples throughout the rest of the book. In this case, not being able to open a file is a serious problem, so there is little point in continuing.

One final item to mention for this example is that I've left out the parentheses (which is valid in Perl; they are optional for all function arguments, but essential for other lists) and used **or** as the operator, which checks the function's success. Using **or** is safe in a list context because it has a lower precedence than the list supplied to the **open** function. If you wanted to use the || operator, you would have to enclose the arguments in parentheses; otherwise the operator would act on the **EXPR** and **die** function:

```
open(DATA,"+>file.txt") || die "Couldn't open file file.txt, $!";
```

In both of the previous cases, the file has been opened for updating, but the file pointer that describes the current position within the file is at the start of the file. If you want to append, you can also use shell-style operators:

```
open(DATA, ">>file.txt");
```

A double **>>** opens the file for appending, placing the file pointer at the end, so that you can immediately start appending information. However, you can't read from it unless you also place a plus sign in front of it:

```
open(DATA, "+>>file.txt");
```

The list of tricks for opening files does not end there. Let's imagine a situation in which you need to read the contents of a compressed file within a script. The normal method would be to use a function to call an external program that uncompresses the file so you can read it, before recompressing the file once you finish. But this is very time consuming, and on systems that have limited resources (CPU and disk space), it is extremely wasteful.

With Perl, you can open a filehandle that is associated with the output of an external command. The **gzcat** function decompresses Gzipped files on the fly, sending the output to the commands stdout without actually decompressing the file to its full size. You can use Perl to read in this information directly by using a pipe at the end of the **EXPR**:

```
open(GZDATA, "gzcat file.gz|");
```

You can now use one of the many functions that read from a filehandle to process the data being decompressed on the fly. You haven't created a temporary file, nor will you have to recompress the data once you've finished reading it. The opposite is also true. So you could, for example, send an email message by using the **mail** program and opening a filehandle to which you can write the email message:

```
open(EMAIL, "|mail mc@mcwords.com");
```

The only limitation to this is that you cannot open an external program for both reading and writing; the pipes work only one way—read when at the end, write when at the start.

You can also open **STDIN** and **STDOUT** directly by specifying "-" and ">-," respectively.

The next forms allow you to duplicate a filehandle. This is again similar to the shell tradition of being able to redirect information not to just one file, but to multiple files. The duplication can be specified by the existing filehandle name:

```
open(SECOUT,">&STDOUT");
```

This is especially useful if you want to save the information that would normally be printed to **STDOUT** and **STDERR**. You duplicate the two standard filehandles to new filehandles. You can then respecify the destination for **STDOUT** and **STDERR**, perhaps to an external log file. This will force all output and errors to the new location, without losing the ability to report information to the real standard output and error using the duplicated filehandles. For example:

```
open(SECOUT,">&STDOUT");
open(SECERR,">&STDERR");
open(STDOUT,">stdlog.txt");
open(STDERR,">stderr.txt");
```

In the above example, all standard prints will go to the stdlog.txt file, while errors will go to stderr.txt. If you needed to, however, you could still report to the real standard output and error by using the **SECOUT** and **SECERR** filehandles.

The penultimate form of the **open** function emulates the functionality of the **fdopen** system function. It associates a filehandle with a specific file descriptor number. For example, the following line opens **STDIN** by file descriptor:

```
open(SECIN,"<&=1");
```

The final two formats are really extensions of the earlier pipe expressions. Instead of starting a new program from the current script, an explicit **fork** is done, creating a new child process. The return value of **open** is the process ID of the child. The filehandle is normal as far as the parent is concerned. However, the input and output to the parent filehandle is piped to the **STDOUT** or **STDIN**, respectively, of the child.

There is little advantage in this method of using a piped command, except that it can be useful in secure situations where you want to control the method used to execute the external command. For example, the earlier **gzcat** example could be rewritten as

```
open(GZDATA,"-|") or exec 'gzcat', 'file.gz';
```

and the email example could be written as

```
open(EMAIL, "|-") or exec 'mail' 'mc@mcwords.com';
```

Note that in both cases communication is still one way: you can still only read from a "-|"-based **open**. See Chapter 10 for examples of two-way pipes.

The full list of available expressions for opening files is shown in Table 3-5.

sysopen

The **sysopen** function is similar to the main **open** function, except that it uses the system **open()** function, using the parameters supplied to it as the parameters for the system function:

```
sysopen FILEHANDLE, FILENAME, MODE, PERMS
sysopen FILEHANDLE, FILENAME, MODE
```

There are some differences between the **sysopen** and **open** functions. The **FILENAME** argument is not interpreted by **sysopen**. The special codes used with **open** are interpreted as elements of the file name. In essence, the **FILENAME** argument is taken literally. This allows you to take information from a user that specifies the full pathname to a file and use it directly without requiring variable interpolation.

Because of this difference, the format in which a file is opened is taken from **MODE**. The value of **MODE** is a bitset using the constants defined in the system's fcntl.h header file. Perl can either use the numbers directly or use word equivalents if the standard **Fcntl** module has been imported. Because it's a bitset, you'll need to **OR** the values together to produce the final mode. There are some standard values if you want to remain completely portable. A **MODE** of zero opens the file read-only; one, write-only; and two, read/write. These correspond to the constants **O_RDONLY**, **O_WRONLY**, and **O_RDWR** which are defined in the **Fcntl** module.

Two other standard constants are **O_CREAT**, which creates a file if it does not already exist, and **O_TRUNC**, which truncates a file before it is read or written.

Expression	Result
"filename"	Opens the file for reading only.
"<filename"	Opens the file for reading only.
">filename"	Truncates and opens the file for writing.
"+<filename"	Opens the file for reading and writing.
"+>filename"	Truncates and opens the file for reading and writing.
"|command"	Runs the command and pipes the output to the filehandle.
"command|"	Pipes the output from the filehandle to the input of command.
"-"	Opens **STDIN**.
">-"	Opens **STDOUT**.
"<&FILEHANDLE"	Duplicates specified **FILEHANDLE** or file descriptor if numeric, for reading.
">&FILEHANDLE"	Duplicates specified **FILEHANDLE** or file descriptor if numeric, for writing.
"<&=N"	Opens the file descriptor matching **N**, essentially identical to C's **fdopen()**.
"|-" and "-|"	Opens a pipe to a forked command.

Table 3-5. *Options for Opening Files*

For example, to open a file for updating, emulating the **"+<filename"** format from **open**:

```
sysopen(DATA, "file.txt",O_RDWR);
```

Or to truncate the file before updating:

```
sysopen(DATA, "file.txt",O_RDWR|O_TRUNC);
```

The **PERMS** argument specifies the file permissions for the file specified if it has to be created (provided **O_CREAT** has been specified in **MODE**). This should be specified in standard octal notation, and Perl uses a default of **0x666** if **PERMS** are not defined. The values are modified according to your current **umask** if applicable (see Chapter 7).

close

To close a filehandle, and therefore disassociate the filehandle from the corresponding file, you use the **close** function. This flushes the filehandle's buffers and closes the system's file descriptor.

```
close FILEHANDLE
close
```

If no **FILEHANDLE** is specified, then it closes the currently selected filehandle. It returns **true** only if it could successfully flush the buffers and close the file. If you have been writing to a file, then **close** can be used as an effective method of checking that information has been successfully written. For example:

```
open(DATA,"+<data.txt") || die "Can't open data.txt";
   #do some work
close(DATA) || die "Couldn't close file properly";
```

However, if you are not worried about the file condition (for example, you are reading from a file), you do not need to close a filehandle before reassigning the filehandle to a new file. The **open** function implicitly closes the previous file before opening the new one, but be warned that there is no way of guaranteeing the file status in this way.

When you open a pipe, either via the **pipe** function or via **open,** the function will return **false** if one of the related system calls fails. Alternatively, if the program called via the pipe returns an exit status other than zero, the return value from the called program is placed in **$?**. In either case, closing a pipe waits for the child process to exit before returning.

Reading and Writing Filehandles

Once you have an open filehandle, you need to be able to read and write information. There are a number of different ways of reading and writing data, although it's likely you'll stick to one or two methods that you find you prefer.

The <FILEHANDLE> operator

The main method of reading the information from an open filehandle is the **<FILEHANDLE>** operator. In a scalar context it returns a single line from the filehandle. For example:

```
print "What is your name?\n";
$name = <STDIN>;
print "Hello $name\n";
```

I've used **STDIN** to demonstrate how to read information from the keyboard or terminal. Since it is already open, I don't have to worry about opening it beforehand.

When you use the **<FILEHANDLE>** operator in a list context, it returns a list of lines from the specified filehandle. For example, to import all the lines from a file into an array:

```
open(DATA,"<import.txt") or die "Can't open data";
@lines = <DATA>;
close(DATA);
```

Note *Although this operation looks dangerous, Perl lets you go ahead and read the entire contents of a file into a single variable. Perl dynamically allocates all of the memory it needs. The only limitation is the amount of physical and virtual memory your machine has.*

Although it appears that **<FILEHANDLE>** only reads in lines from the file, you can specify a different record separator using the **$/** or **$INPUT_RECORD_SEPARATOR** variable. This enables you to read in character-separated data files. On the Mac, for example, a program called TouchBase Pro supports the export of name and address information using a record separator with an ASCII value of 252; hence you could use Perl to import this information using a script like this:

```
open(DATA,"+<tbpro.dat") or die "Can't open tbpro.dat, $!\n";
$/ = "\374";
while(<DATA>)
{
    # Process and update a record
}
```

I've introduced two new things here. One is the use of the special **$!** variable to report the error returned by the **open** function if it fails. The other is that I've enclosed the **<FILEHANDLE>** operator within a **while** loop. Because the **<FILEHANDLE>** operator returns a single record in a scalar context, you can use it within a **while** loop to work through a file until the end. Each iteration of the loop will return a new record, and the data is placed into the **$_** default input space.

readline

The **readline** function is actually the internal function used by Perl to handle the **<FILEHANDLE>** operator function.

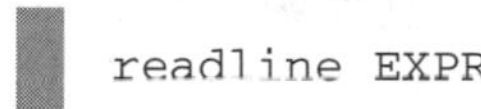

```
readline EXPR
```

The only difference is that **readline** accepts an expression directly, instead of the usual filehandle. This means you need to pass a typeglob to the **readline** function, instead of the normal filehandle. However, the same rules apply. The function reads in records from the filehandle using the value of **$/** as a record separator. So to duplicate the **while** statement above, you would use

```
while(readline *DATA)
```

getc

The **getc** function returns a single character from the specified **FILEHANDLE**, or **STDIN** if none is specified:

```
getc FILEHANDLE
getc
```

If there was an error, or the filehandle is at end of file, then **undef** is returned instead. Unfortunately, because of the buffering on filehandles, you can't use it effectively to get nonbuffered single characters. There is a trick for this, and we'll examine some techniques for this in Chapter 13.

read

Whereas the **<FILEHANDLE>** operator or **readline** function reads data from a filehandle using the input record separator, the **read** function reads a block of information from the buffered filehandle:

```
read FILEHANDLE, SCALAR, LENGTH, OFFSET
read FILEHANDLE, SCALAR, LENGTH
```

The length of the data read is defined by **LENGTH**, and the data is placed at the start of **SCALAR** if no **OFFSET** is specified. Otherwise data is placed after **OFFSET** bytes in

SCALAR, allowing you to append information from the filehandle to the existing scalar string. The function returns the number of bytes read on success, zero at end of file, or **undef** if there was an error.

This function can be used to read fixed-length records from files, just like the system **fread()** function on which it is based. However, it must be used in combination with **print** and **seek** to ensure that the buffering system works correctly without overwriting existing data. For a more reliable method of reading and writing fixed-length data, and for the equivalent of the system **read()** function, see the section "**sysread**" later in the chapter.

print

For all the different methods used for reading information from filehandles, the main function for writing information back is the **print** function. Unlike C, in Perl **print** is not just used for outputting information to the screen; it can be used to print information to any open filehandle. This is largely due to the way Perl structures its internal data. Because scalars are stored precisely, without using the traditional null termination seen in other languages, it's safe to use the **print** function to output both variable and fixed-length information.

```
print FILEHANDLE LIST
print LIST
print
```

The most common error a new Perl programmer makes is to place a comma between the ***FILEHANDLE*** *and* ***LIST****. This often causes undesired results, because to the* ***print*** *function, the comma makes* ***FILEHANDLE*** *the first element of the* ***LIST*** *to be evaluated and printed.*

The **print** function prints the evaluated value of **LIST** to **FILEHANDLE**, or to the current output filehandle (**STDOUT** by default). For example:

```
print "Hello World!\n";
```

Or

```
print "Hello", $name, "\nHow are you today?\n";
```

which prints

```
Hello Martin
How are you today?
```

Note that a **LIST** rather than string interpolation is used in the last example. You can achieve the same result using a here document with the **print** function:

```
print <<EOT;
Hello $name
How are you today?
EOT
```

Because the argument to the **print** function is a **LIST**, the individual elements of the list are evaluated before the results are passed to **print**, which then outputs the values. You need to be careful when incorporating a **print** statement within a larger statement, especially one that itself uses a **LIST** context. For example, the line

```
print "Hello ", print "How are you today?";
```

actually prints

```
How are you today?Hello 1
```

The second element to the **print** function is evaluated first, resulting in the message, and then the resulting list values are output by **print**, which explains the 1—the return value from the nested **print** function.

To get around this problem, you can use parentheses to enclose the list of values for **print**,

```
print("Hello "),print "How are you today?";
```

which correctly outputs the message "Hello How are you today?" However, care should be taken with the parentheses, since you can also get unexpected results:

```
print (1+2)*3, "\n";
```

Only the first calculation is printed, since the parser assumes the parentheses specify the **LIST** to the **print** function. The remaining values are ignored, since they no longer form part of a valid expression. Perl doesn't produce an error because you are still defining valid Perl code—even though the values of the list are never used.

The correct way to write the equation above is

```
print(((1+2)*3),"\n");
```

If no **LIST** is specified, the value of **$_** is printed instead. The **print** function returns true (1) on success and zero on failure.

printf

Although **print** is incredibly useful, it suffers from a lack of format. The Perl parser decides how a particular value is printed. This means that floating-point numbers are printed as such, when you may wish to restrict the number of places past the decimal point that the number is printed. Alternatively, you may wish to left- rather than right-justify strings when you print them.

```
printf FILEHANDLE FORMAT, LIST
printf FORMAT, LIST
```

Within C, the only function available is **printf**, which uses a formatting string as the first element and formats the remaining values in the list according to the format specified in the format string. Each format is called a *format conversion* and is made up of an initial percent sign, followed by some optional flags, and finally a single character that defines how the value in the list is printed. Each format conversion string relates to the corresponding value in the remainder of the argument list.

For example, the statement

```
printf "%d\n", 3.1415126;
```

only prints the number 3. The "%d" conversion format determines that an integer should be printed. Alternatively, you can define a "currency" format like this,

```
printf "The cost is $%6.2f\n",499;
```

which would print

```
The cost is $499.00
```

The **printf** function accepts the format conversions in Table 3-6.

Perl also supports flags that optionally adjust the output format. These are specified between the % and conversion letter, as shown in Table 3-7.

Format	Result
%%	A percent sign.
%c	A character with the given ASCII code.
%s	A string.
%d	A signed integer (decimal).
%u	An unsigned integer (decimal).
%o	An unsigned integer (octal).
%x	An unsigned integer (hexadecimal).
%X	An unsigned integer (hexadecimal using uppercase characters).
%e	A floating-point number (scientific notation).
%E	A floating-point number (scientific notation using "G" in place of "e").
%f	A floating-point number (fixed decimal notation).
%g	A floating-point number ($e or %f notation according to value size).
%G	A floating-point number (as %g, but using "G " in place of "g" when appropriate).
%p	A pointer (prints the memory address of the value in hexadecimal).
%n	Stores the number of characters output so far into the next variable in the parameter list.
%i	A synonym for %d.
%D	A synonym for C %ld.
%U	A synonym for C %lu.
%O	A synonym for C %lo.

Table 3-6. *Conversion Formats for printf*

Flag	Result
space	Prefix positive number with a space.
+	Prefix positive number with a plus sign.
-	Left-justify within field.
0	Use zeros, not spaces, to right-justify.
#	Prefix non-zero octal with "0" and hexadecimal with "0x."
number	Minimum field width.
.number	Specify precision (number of digits after decimal point) for floating-point numbers.
l	Interpret integer as C type "long" or "unsigned long."
h	Interpret integer as C type "short" or "unsigned short."
V	Interpret integer as Perl's standard integer type.

Table 3-7. *Formatting Flags for printf Conversion Formats*

If you do not require a specific output format, you should use **print** in preference to **printf**, as it's faster and less prone to errors induced by the format string.

Nonbuffered I/O

Using the standard **read** and **print** functions can cause problems if you want to access fixed blocks of data that are not separated by a recognizable record or if you want to avoid the problems associated with buffered input. In particular, this can cause delayed reads and writes, and, overall, make the system seem inefficient compared to a direct access system.

To get around this, you can use the **sysread** and **syswrite** functions, which emulate the underlying **fread** and **fwrite** functions. They read and write a block of data of a specified size, ignoring the usual field and record boundaries of the **<FILEHANDLE>** operator and the **read** and **print** functions.

sysread

The **sysread** function reads a fixed number of bytes from a specified filehandle into a scalar variable:

```
sysread FILEHANDLE, SCALAR, LENGTH, OFFSET
sysread FILEHANDLE, SCALAR, LENGTH
```

If **OFFSET** is specified, then data is written to **SCALAR** from **OFFSET** bytes, effectively appending the information from a specific point. If **OFFSET** is negative, data is written from the number of bytes specified counted backwards from the end of the string.

The function is based on the system **read()** function, and therefore it avoids the normal buffering supported by standard streams-based **stdio** functions.

syswrite

The **syswrite** function is the exact opposite of **sysread**. It writes a fixed-sized block of information from a scalar to a filehandle:

```
syswrite FILEHANDLE, SCALAR, LENGTH, OFFSET
syswrite FILEHANDLE, SCALAR, LENGTH
```

If **OFFSET** has been specified, then **LENGTH** bytes are read from the **SCALAR** and written to **FILEHANDLE**. If the length of the scalar is less than **LENGTH**, the data is padded with nulls.

In both cases, you should avoid using the **sysread** and **syswrite** functions with the functions that do use buffered I/O, including **print**, **seek**, **tell**, **write**, and especially **read**.

If you use these two functions in combination with the **sysseek** function (discussed later in the chapter), you can update a database with a fixed record size:

```
open(DATABASE,"+<datafile") or die "Can't open datafile";
$recloc = 0;
while(sysread(DATABASE,$record,80))
{
```

```
        # Find the record we're looking for
        if ($found)
        {
                last; # quit out of the read loop
        }
        $recloc += 80; #Otherwise, record the next record start
}
# Update the information
sysseek(DATABASE,$recloc,SEEK_SET); #Go back to the start of the
record
syswrite(DATABASE,$record,80); #Write the record back, replacing
the old version
```

You can't use the **tell** function, since that takes into account the usual buffering; so you have to calculate the file position manually by totaling up the bytes read from the database. If you had used **read**, **seek**, and **print**, then the standard buffering used may have affected the results, probably overwriting information. Using **sysread** guarantees that the information read and written from the filehandle is what you received and supplied.

Locating Your Position Within a File

When reading and writing files using the standard line-based or record-based methods, you are normally processing individual records in sequence—outputting or formatting the results as you read in the entire file in sequence. However, if you are accessing fixed-length information—for example, a database—you are likely to require access to the information in a more random fashion. In order to work correctly, you need to be able to discover your current location and set a new location within the file.

tell

The first requirement is to find your position within a file, which you do using the **tell** function:

```
tell FILEHANDLE
tell
```

This returns the position of the file pointer, in bytes, within **FILEHANDLE** if specified, or the current default selected filehandle if none is specified. The function returns **undef** if there is a problem getting the file position information, since a value of zero could just indicate that you're at the start of the file.

seek

The **seek** function positions the file pointer to the specified number of bytes within a file:

```
seek FILEHANDLE, POSITION, WHENCE
```

The function uses the **fseek** system function, and you have the same ability to position relative to three different points: the start, end, and current position. You do this by specifying a value for **WHENCE**. The possible values are zero, one, and two for positions relative to the start, current, and end of the file. If you import the **IO::Seekable** module, you can use the constants **SEEK_SET**, **SEEK_CUR**, and **SEEK_END**, respectively.

Zero sets the positioning relative to the start of the file. For example, the line

```
seek DATA, 256, 0;
```

sets the file pointer to the 256th byte in the file. Using a value of one sets the position relative to the current position; so the line

```
seek DATA, 128, 1;
```

moves the file point onto byte 384, while the line

```
seek DATA, -128, SEEK_CUR;
```

moves back to byte 256.

A **WHENCE** value of two moves the file relative to the end of the file, and the value of **POSITION** is generally specified as a negative number. You can move to a point 80 bytes from the end of the file using a line like this:

```
seek DATA, -80, SEEK_END;
```

It's worth noting that the **seek** function resets the end-of-file condition. You can use the **SEEK_CUR** constant with a **WHENCE** value of zero to achieve this, since the overall effect is to move nowhere. If you were to use the **SEEK_SET** or **SEEK_END** function, you'd have to use the **tell** function to discover the current location.

sysseek

As you already know, the bulk of the functions that use filehandles rely on the buffering provided by the system's **stdio** functions. The **sysseek** function is essentially identical to the **seek** function, except that it ignores the buffering on filehandles:

```
sysseek FILEHANDLE, WHENCE, POSITION
```

In the earlier database example, you might want to move to the last record in a database, which you could do with

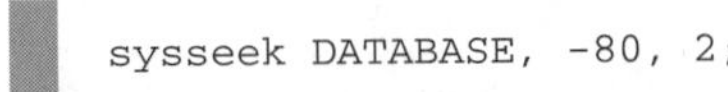

```
sysseek DATABASE, -80, 2;
```

Miscellaneous Control Functions

There are a few functions which do not conveniently fall into one of the sections we have already discussed. They are functions that primarily control the operation or control of a filehandle, or they may return some additional information for a specific filehandle.

binmode

On older operating systems, there is a distinction between textual and binary files. The difference occurs because Perl converts automatically between external file formats that contain two characters for line separation. MS-DOS, for example, uses **CR LF** to terminate lines, which Perl translates internally to **LF**, converting them back when information is written.

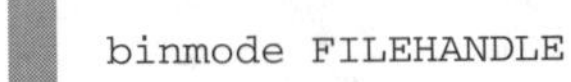

```
binmode FILEHANDLE
```

This obviously causes a problem when opening files for binary access, since you will lose information in the internal representation and can corrupt the files due to the conversion process. To get around this problem, you can use the **binmode** function, which forces Perl to ignore line termination, thus preventing it from doing any form of conversion. To use it, open a filehandle, and then call the **binmode** function with the new filehandle. For example:

```
open(DATA,"+<input.bin") or die "Couldn't open the file input.bin\n";
binmode(DATA) or die "Couldn't set binary mode on input.bin\n";
...
```

The **binmode** function returns the usual **true/false** on success/failure. Once set, there is no way to unset binary mode short of closing the filehandle and reopening it, although you're unlikely to want to change the interpretation of an open file anyway.

The function has no effect on systems that make no distinction between formats, such as Unix and MacOS.

eof

Although all functions and operators that read information automatically detect the end-of-file condition and return a suitable error code to the user, it is sometimes necessary to check the status outside of such a test. The **eof** function supports this action:

```
eof FILEHANDLE
eof()
eof
```

If **eof** is specified with a **FILEHANDLE**, then it checks whether the next read from the specified filehandle will return an end-of-file condition. The function returns **true** if the end-of-file condition exists, or **undef** otherwise.

When called with parentheses, it returns **true** when the end of file has been reached for the last file within a **while(<>)** loop (see Chapter 9). For example, the following code prints an error message when it realizes it's running out of source text:

```
while(<>)
{
    if(eof())
    {
        print "Running out of data!!\n";
    }
...
}
```

When used without a filehandle or parentheses, the function detects the end-of-file condition for the end of file within the current file of a **while(<>)** loop. So the example below prints a separator between each file that is printed:

```
while(<>)
{
    print;
    if (eof)
    {
        print "\n",'=' x 50,"\n\n";
    }
}
```

The actual method used by Perl for discovering the end-of-file condition is to get a byte of information from the required filehandle and then push the character back onto the input stream of the filehandle with the C **ungetc()** function. This makes it useless in an interactive context, so it may catch keystrokes that you are trying to read.

fileno

The **fileno** function returns the underlying operating system file descriptor for the specified filehandle:

```
fileno FILEHANDLE
```

Essentially this function is only used when you require the file descriptor number instead of the filehandle. The **select** function is a classic example that requires the number in order to create the necessary bitsets used to monitor the filehandles. The function can also be used when duplicating filehandles (although you can do that easier by name) and detecting whether two filehandles are duplicated:

```
print "Dupes\n" if (fileno(DATA) == fileno(SRC));
```

select

There are two forms of **select**. One sets the default filehandle, and the other is used for the more complex act of handling multiple I/O effectively. We will deal only with the first in this section. See Chapter 6 for the second format.

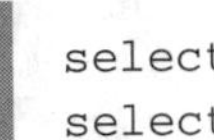

```
select FILEHANDLE
select
```

The **select** function returns the default filehandle name and sets the default filehandle to **FILEHANDLE**. This is the default filehandle used by functions such as **print** and **read** when the user does not specify a **FILEHANDLE**. If no **FILEHANDLE** is specified, the name of the current filehandle is returned.

For example, to switch buffering off for another filehandle, you could use this code:

```
$stdfh = select DATA;
$| = 1;
select $stdfh;
```

This works because **select** returns the current filehandle before setting it to the new supplied value.

This trick is also sometimes useful when you are formatting and producing reports using the Perl reporting mechanism. However, in both cases, there are now convenient ways of modifying report formats and setting the buffering of filehandles.

If you import the **FileHandle** module, then you can switch buffering off with

```
use FileHandle;
autoflush(DATA);
```

Alternatively, using the method syntax, you can set the format options for two separate reports:

```
use FileHandle;
DETAILS->format_top_name("Detailed Phone Statistics");
SUMMARY->format_top_name("Summary Phone Statistics");
```

This virtually eliminates the need for **select** altogether, but it remains for historical compatibility.

truncate

You can truncate (empty) a specific filehandle to trim it down to a specific size:

```
truncate FILEHANDLE, LENGTH
```

For example, to reset the size of an error log, perhaps after the full contents have been printed, you can use this line:

```
truncate LOGFILE, 1024;
```

The function causes a fatal error if your system does not support the underlying **truncate** function, or returns **true** if the operation is successful.

Error Messages

We saw earlier that the **STDERR** filehandle is classed as a separate output device under many operating systems, most notably Unix. This can be used to report errors that can be separately trapped by the host operating system and environment. However, when using a statement such as

```
open(DATA, "file") or print STDERR "Couldn't open the file\n";
```

the actual aim of the statement is not immediately obvious. Worse, without converting the single-line statement into a more complex **unless** condition, you have no way of raising an exception for the error you have trapped. All you can do is print out an error message.

A better method is to use one of the two error functions, **warn** or **die**:

```
warn LIST
die LIST
```

In both cases, the functions print out the value of the **LIST** you supply and raise an exception to the Perl interpreter. This has no direct effect in normal use, but within an **eval** block, it has special significance.

The only difference between the two functions is that **warn** only raises an exception and prints the error; **die** also calls **exit**, which causes a script to exit prematurely and an **eval** block to terminate.

```
chdir('/etc') or die "Can't change directory";
chdir('/etc') or warn "Can't change directory";
```

In the case of **warn**, if the variable **$@** contains a value (from a previous **eval** call) and **LIST** is empty, then the value of **$@** is printed with "\t...caught" appended to the end. If both the **$@** variable and the supplied **LIST** are empty, then the message "Warning: Something's wrong" is printed.

For **die**, if the value of **LIST** does not end in a newline, Perl adds the current script and line number to the message that is printed. It's a good idea in these situations to ensure you append ", stopped" or a similar message to the value of **LIST**. This will print a more sensible message when the script and line number information is appended.

If **LIST** is empty and **$@** already contains a value, then the string "\t...propagated" is printed; and if **LIST** is empty, then the string "Died" is printed instead. When called within an **eval** block, the value of **LIST** is inserted into the **$@** variable, and the **eval** block exits with an undefined value. We'll cover this in more detail when we examine the use of the **eval** function.

The return code given by the script when **die** is called depends on the context. If the **$!** error variable contains a value, then that is used as the error code. If **$!** is zero, then the value of **$!** shifted to the right eight times (**$! >> 8**) is used. This correctly prints the error number retrieved from an external program execution via backticks. If the value is still zero, a value of 255 is passed to the **exit** function and returned instead.

If you want to use the script name and line numbers within your error messages, you can use the special tokens **__FILE__** and **__LINE__**, respectively. For example:

```
chdir('/etc') or die "Can't change dir in ",__FILE__," line ",
__LINE__, "\n";
```

If you failed to change the directory, this would print

```
Can't change dir in adduser.pl line 35
```

Chapter 4

Data Manipulation

It is difficult to write a program of reasonable length (i.e., something more than "Hello World") that does not involve some form of data manipulation, even if it's a simple calculation. In this chapter we'll be examining all of the different ways you can manipulate scalar data. Many of the common operations on scalars (strings or numbers) are handled by the standard Perl operators outlined in Chapter 2.

Perl also supplies a number of built-in functions for managing variables, performing complex numerical calculations, and finding your way around strings. However, simple string concatenation and extraction is not always enough. A more pragmatic solution is required that can identify individual elements based on an expression.

Perl uses the now standard regular expression engine seen in everything from **sed** to Microsoft Word, albeit with some additional extensions that provide more flexibility and, ultimately, more control over the regular expression matching and replacement process.

Variable Management

Creating variables is easy in Perl. Unlike other languages, you can create a new variable without having to predeclare it first. You can also assign values to variables directly during calls to functions and operators, and even work on variables directly within external functions that you call. Perl also supports two functions for controlling variables. One, **defined**, tests whether a variable has been defined with a real value in the name space (see Chapter 5), while the other, **undef**, allows you to undefine a variable within the current name space.

```
defined EXPR
```

The **defined** function returns true only if the value of **EXPR** has a real value. A scalar that contains no valid string, numeric value, or reference is known as the undefined value, or **undef** for short. On array and hash elements it returns true only if the specified element has a valid value. On whole arrays or hashes it returns true only when memory has been allocated for the elements. That is, a new, empty array is undefined, but "used" empty arrays would return true.

The use of the **undef** value means you can distinguish between a real empty string and one that contains a value that would be interpreted as empty, for example, one with a single null value. Its most common use though is to return an error from a function that could genuinely return a zero value. For example, in Chapter 3, the **tell** function returns the **undef** value when the position of the file cannot be determined.

The **undef** function undefines the scalar, entire array or hash, or subroutine name (with **&** prefix) specified in **EXPR**. Whether **EXPR** is specified or not, the function returns the undefined value:

```
undef EXPR
undef
```

This frees the memory used by EXPR, e.g.:

```
[existing code block starting $var =...]
```

This will only print the message once, since the variable was freed in the third line. The variable will not have been redefined in the fourth line because no value, assumed or other, has been implied. The **undef** function also returns the undefined value, which can be assigned to a scalar or scalar element as we saw in Chapter 2.

During the execution of a loop or **continue** block, it is sometimes necessary to reset the variables that have been used to store temporary information. Although you could arguably do this with multiple **undef** statements (which is fine for a small number of variables), this is not always practical, and it doesn't reset the global variables or **??** searches (you'll see an example of this shortly). You can use the **reset** function to clear all of the variables starting with a particular letter or letter range:

```
reset EXPR
reset
```

For example, to clear all of the variables starting with "a":

```
reset 'a';
```

Or to clear all the variables beginning with uppercase characters from "A" to "Z":

```
reset 'A-Z';
```

This is not recommended however, since you will clear out the global **ARGV**, **INC** arrays, and the **ENV** and **SIG** hashes.

If you want to reset a **?PATTERN?** match so that it matches again on the next iteration of the loop, use the **reset** function without any arguments:

```
reset;
```

Working with Numbers

Most of the numerical abilities of Perl are handled by the operators we covered in Chapter 2. Perl also sports a range of supporting functions for other less used mathematical operations.

Mathematical Functions and Operators

When you are concerned only with magnitude—for example, when comparing the size of two objects—the designation of negative or positive is not required. You can use the **abs** function to return the absolute value of a number:

```
abs EXPR
abs
```

For example, the code

```
print abs(-1.295476);
```

should print a value of 1.295476. Obviously, using a positive value with **abs** will return the same positive value or, more correctly, nondesignated value: all positive values imply a + sign in front of them. The **abs** function takes its value from **$_** if no argument is specified.

Using the same number you can also return its integer component using the **int** function:

```
int EXPR
int
```

Extending the above example,

```
print int abs(-1.295476);
```

should print a value of 1. The only problem with the **int** function is that it does strictly remove the fractional component of a number; no rounding of any sort is done. If you want to return a number that has been rounded to a number of decimal places, use the **printf** or **sprintf** function:

```
printf("%.2f",abs(-1.295476));
```

This will round the number to two decimal places—a value of 1.3 in this example.

Unlike C, which uses the **pow()** function, Perl uses the ** operator to raise a number to the power; for example,

```
$square = 4**2;
```

returns 16, or 4 raised to the power of 2. To raise the natural base number *e* to the power, you need to use the **exp** function:

```
exp EXPR
exp
```

If you do not supply an argument, it calculates the exponential of the **$_** variable. For example, to find the square of *e*:

```
$square = exp(2);
```

The inverse of the exponential operator for squared numbers is the **sqrt** function:

```
sqrt EXPR
sqrt
```

So to find the original value of the exponential, you might use

```
$var = sqrt(exp(2));
```

which should assign the value of the natural base number to the **$var** variable.

To calculate the nth root of a number, use the ** operator with a fractional number in the form,

```
$var = $num**(1/$n);
```

where **$n** is the nth root. To find the cube root of 16,777,216, you might use

```
$var = 16777216**(1/3);
```

which should return a value of 256.

To find the logarithm (base *e*) of a number, you need to use the **log** function:

```
log EXPR
log
```

As with other mathematical (and in fact most) functions, if you neglect to specify an expression, it uses the value of **$_**.

Trigonometric Functions

There are three built-in trigonometric functions for calculating **atan2**, **cos**, and **sin**:

```
atan2 X,Y
cos EXPR
sin EXPR
```

For the equivalent functions of **acos**, **asin**, and **tan**, you should use the **POSIX** module, which defines the missing functions. Unless you are doing trigonometric calculations, there is little use for these functions in everyday life. However, you can use the **sin** function to calculate your biorhythms using the simple script shown below, assuming you know the number of days you have been alive:

```
use Math::Complex;
my ($phys_step, $emot_step, $inte_step) = (23, 28, 33);
my ($phys, $emot, $inte);

print "Enter the number of days you been alive:\n";
my $alive = <STDIN> ;

$phys = int(sin(((pi*($alive%$phys_step))/($phys_step/2)))*100);
$emot = int(sin(((pi*($alive%$emot_step))/($emot_step/2)))*100);
$inte = int(sin(((pi*($alive%$inte_step))/($inte_step/2)))*100);

print "Your Physical is $phys%, Emotional $emot%, Intellectual $inte%\n";
```

Conversion Between Bases

Perl provides automatic conversion to decimal for octal and hexadecimal numbers specified in the 0777 and 0x formats, respectively. However, Perl automatically interprets these into decimal numbers, and the conversion only takes place on literals inserted directly into the Perl code. To interpret hexadecimal and octal numbers imported from an external source, you need to use the **hex** and **oct** functions:

```
hex EXPR
hex
oct EXPR
oct
```

The **hex** function recognizes numbers both in "ff47ace3" and "oxff47ace3" formats, the value of which can be displayed with:

```
print hex("ff47ace3");
```

The octal function performs the same function on octal numbers:

```
print oct("755");
```

Like **hex**, the **oct** function accepts numbers in the literal format, so you can interpret numbers as they would be written within Perl:

```
print oct("0755")," and ", oct("0x7f"),"\n";
```

In either case, the functions will attempt to convert **$_** if you do not specify an argument. If you try to convert a number or string that is not a valid number in the specified base, then the functions return zero.

To print a hexadecimal or octal number, use **printf** or use **sprintf** to translate a base value to a formatted string. Note the leading characters in the printed string:

```
printf("0%o 0x%x\n", oct("755"), hex("7f"));
```

Conversion Between Characters and Numbers

You know from the earlier discussions on interpolation that you can refer to some characters with a special backslashed sequence. This is useful for introducing tabs, newlines, and other terminal-related formatting characters. It is also possible to specify characters using octal and hexadecimal characters into an interpolated string. For example, the two lines

```
print "\007";
print "\x07";
```

print the octal and hexadecimal values; in this case the "bell" character. Often though it is useful to be able to specify a character by its decimal number and to convert the character back to its decimal equivalent in the ASCII table. The two functions **chr** and **ord** perform each of those conversions, respectively:

```
chr EXPR
chr
```

The **chr** function returns the character matching the value of **EXPR** or **$_** if **EXPR** is not specified. The value is matched against the current ASCII table for the operating system, so it could reveal different values on different platforms' characters with an ASCII value of 128 or higher. This may or may not be useful.

```
ord EXPR
ord
```

The **ord** function returns the numeric value of the first character of **EXPR** or **$_** if **EXPR** is not specified. The return value is returned according to the current ASCII table and is always unsigned.

Although it is possible to use this function to get a list of numbers for an entire string (using a loop and the **substr** function), an easier solution is to use the **pack** function. You'll see descriptions and examples of each function later in this chapter.

Random Numbers

Perl provides a built-in random number generator. All random numbers need a "seed" value. The value is used in an algorithm, usually based on the precision, or lack thereof, for a specific calculation. The format for the **rand** function is

```
rand EXPR
rand
```

The function returns a floating point random number between zero and **EXPR** or between zero and one (including zero, but not including one) if **EXPR** is not specified. If you want an integer random number, just use the **int** function to return a reasonable value, as in this example:

```
print int(rand(16)),"\n";
```

You can use the **srand** function to see the random number generator with a specific value:

```
srand EXPR
```

The **rand** function automatically calls the **srand** function the first time **rand** is called if you don't specifically seed the random number generator. The default seed value is the value returned by the **time** function, which returns the number of seconds from the epoch (usually January 1, 1970 UTC—although it's dependent on your platform). The problem is that this is not a good seed number, since its value is predictable. Instead, you might want to try a calculation based on a combination of the current time, the current process ID, and perhaps the user ID to seed the generator with an unpredictable value.

I've used the following calculation as a good seed, although it's far from perfect:

```
srand((time() ^ (time() % $])) ^ exp(length($0))**$$);
```

By mixing the unpredictable values of the current time and process ID with predictable values such as the length of the current script and the Perl version number, you should get a reasonable seed value.

The program below calculates the number of random numbers generated before a duplicate value is returned:

```
my %randres;
my $counter = 1;

srand((time() ^ (time() % $])) ^ exp(length($0))**$$);

while (my $val = rand())
{
    last if (defined($randres{$val}));
    print "Current count is $counter\n" if (($counter %10000) == 0);
    $randres{$val} = 1;
    $counter++;
}

print "Out of $counter tries I encountered a duplicate random number\n";
```

Whatever seed value you choose, the internal random number generator is unlikely to give you more than 500 numbers before a duplicate appears. This makes it unsuitable for secure purposes, since you need a random number that cannot otherwise be predicted. The **Math::TrulyRandom** module provides a more robust system for providing random numbers. If you insert the **truly_random_value** function in place of the **rand** function in the program above, you can see how long it takes before a random number reappears. I've attained 20,574 unique random numbers with this function using the test script above; this should be more than enough for most uses.

Working with Very Small Integers

Perl uses 32-bit integers for storing integers and for all of its integer-based math. Occasionally, however, it is necessary to store and handle integers that are smaller than the standard 32-bit integers. This is especially true in databases where you may wish to store a block of Boolean values: even using a single character for each Boolean value will take up 8 bits. A better solution is to use the **vec** function, which supports the storage of multiple integers as strings:

```
vec EXPR, OFFSET, BITS
```

The **EXPR** is the scalar that will be used to store the information; the **OFFSET** and **BITS** arguments define the element of the integer string and the size of each element, respectively. The return value is the integer stored at **OFFSET** of size **BITS** from the string **EXPR**. The function can also be assigned to which modifies the value of the element you have specified. For example, using the database example above, you might use the following code to populate an "option" string:

```
vec($optstring, 0, 1) = $print   ? 1 : 0;
vec($optstring, 1, 1) = $display ? 1 : 0;
vec($optstring, 2, 1) = $delete  ? 1 : 0;
print length($optstring),"\n";
```

The **print** statement at the end of the code displays the length, in bytes, of the string. It should report a size of one byte. We have managed to store three Boolean values within less than one real byte of information.

The number of bits allows you to specify larger numbers: Perl supports values of 1, 2, 4, 8, 16, and 32 bits per element. You can therefore store four 2-bit integers (up to an integer value of three, including zero) into a single byte.

Obviously the **vec** function is not limited to storing and accessing your own bitstrings; it can be used to extract and update any string, providing you want to modify 1, 2, 4, 8, 16, or 32 bits at a time. Perl also guarantees that the first bit, accessed with

```
vec($var, 0, 1);
```

will always be the first bit in the first character of a string, irrespective of whether your machine is little endian or big endian. Furthermore, this also implies that the first byte of a string can be accessed with:

```
vec($var, 0, 8);
```

The **vec** function is most often used with functions that require bitsets, such as the **select** function. You'll see examples of this in later chapters.

Working with Strings

Creating a new string scalar is as easy as assigning a quoted value to a variable:

```
$string = "Come grow old along with me\n";
```

We have already seen in Chapter 2 the operators that can be used with strings. The most basic that you will need to use is the concatenation operator. This is a direct replacement for the C **strcat()** function. The problem with the **strcat()** function is that it is inefficient and it requires constant concatenation of a single string to a single variable. Within Perl you can concatenate any string, whether it has been derived from a static quoted string in the script itself, or in scripts exported by functions. The code fragment

```
$thetime = 'The time is ' . localtime() . "\n";
```

assigns the string, without interpolation; the time string, as returned by **localtime**; and the interpolated newline character. The concatenation operator is the single period between each element.

It is important to appreciate the difference between concatenation and lists. The **print** statement

```
print 'The time is ' . localtime() . "\n";
```

produces the same result as

```
print 'The time is ', localtime(), "\n";
```

But in the first example the string is concatenated first before being printed; in the second, the **print** function is printing a list of arguments. The second is more efficient because it doesn't have to copy the string before it is output.

However, there are times when concatenation is required because the function does not support a list of arguments. The **length** function returns the length, in bytes, of the supplied string:

```
length EXPR
length
```

The function only accepts a single argument (or it returns the length of the **$_** variable if none is specified), so attempting to find the length of the above string using

```
length 'The time is ', localtime(), "\n";
```

won't work. The Perl parser should produce an error when it sees this statement because it recognizes that there are too many arguments. To achieve what we want, we need to use concatenation:

```
length 'The time is ' . localtime() . "\n";
```

Simple String Modifications

There are some simple modifications built into Perl as functions that may be more convenient and quicker than using the regular expressions we will cover later in this chapter. The four basic functions are **lc**, **uc**, **lcfirst**, and **ucfirst**. They convert a string to all lowercase, all uppercase, or only the first characters to lower- or uppercase, respectively:

```
lc EXPR
lc
lcfirst EXPR
lcfirst
uc EXPR
uc
ucfirst EXPR
ucfirst
```

In each case the **$_** variable is modified if you do not specify an expression. The most obvious use of these functions is to change the case of a supplied expression when displaying or formatting text. You can also use the **lc** and **uc** functions to "normalize" a string so that when you are doing comparisons, or using a variable as the key to a hash element, every string is the same upper- or lowercase. We'll see examples of this in Chapter 7.

When you read in data from a filehandle using a **while** or other loop and the **<FH>** operator, the trailing newline on the file remains in the string that you import. It's often the case that you are processing the data contained within each line and do not want the newline character. The **chop** function can be used to strip the last character off of any expression:

```
while(<FH>)
{
    chop;
...
}
```

The only danger with the **chop** function is that it strips the last character from the line irrespective of what the last character was. The **chomp** function works in combination with the **$/** variable when reading from filehandles. It is the record separator that is attached to the records you read from a filehandle, which is by default set to the newline character. The **chomp** function works by removing the last character from a string only if it matches the value of **$/**. To do a safe strip from a record of the record separator character, just use it in place of **chop**:

```
while(<FH>)
{
    chomp;
...
}
```

This is a much safer option as it guarantees that the data of a record will remain intact, irrespective of the last character type.

Substrings

Within many languages a string is stored as an array of characters. To access an individual character within a string, you need to determine the location of the character within the string and access that element of the array. Perl does not support this option because often you are not working with the individual characters within the string, but the string as a whole.

Two functions, **index** and **rindex**, can be used to find the position of a particular character or string of characters within another string:

```
index STR, SUBSTR, POSITION
index STR, SUBSTR
rindex STR, SUBSTR, POSITION
rindex STR, SUBSTR
```

The **index** function returns the first position of **SUBSTR** within the string **STR** or –1 if the string cannot be found. If the **POSITION** argument is specified, then the search starts from that many characters in the string (from the beginning). The **rindex** function returns the opposite of the **index** function—the last occurrence of **SUBSTR** in **STR** or –1 if the substring could not be found. If **POSITION** is specified, then it starts from that many characters from the end of the string.

Note *In both cases the **POSITION** is actually calculated as the value of the **$[** variable plus (**index**) or minus (**rindex**) the number specified. The use of the **$[** variable is now deprecated, since there is little need when you can specify the value directly to the function anyway. There are further examples throughout the book of the deprecated use of this variable, and in all cases it's because a better solution has been introduced.*

The **substr** function can be used to extract a substring from another string based on the position of the first character and the number of characters you want to extract:

```
substr EXPR, OFFSET, LENGTH, REPLACEMENT
substr EXPR, OFFSET, LENGTH
substr EXPR, OFFSET
```

The **EXPR** is the string that is being extracted from. Data is extracted from a starting point of **OFFSET** characters from the start of **EXPR** or, if the value is negative, that many characters from the end of the string. The optional **LENGTH** parameter defines the number of characters to be read from the string. If it is not specified, then all characters to the end of the string are extracted. Alternatively, if the number specified in **LENGTH** is negative, then that many characters are left off the end of the string. For example, the script

```
$string = 'The cat sat on the mat';
print substr($string,4),"\n";
print substr($string,4,3),"\n";
print substr($string,-7),"\n";
print substr($string,4,-4),"\n";
```

should print

```
cat sat on the mat
cat
the mat
cat sat on the
```

The last example is equivalent to

```
print substr($string,4,14),"\n";
```

But it may be more effective to use the first form if you have used the **rindex** function to return the last occurrence of a space within the string.

You can also use **substr** to replace segments of a string. You can either use **substr** as an **lvalue**, or use the four argument version to replace the range specified with the REPLACEMENT text. For example, these two lines are identical:

```
substr($string,4,3) = 'dog';
substr($string,4,3,'dog');
```

should print "the dog sat on the mat" because we replaced the word "cat," starting at the fourth character and lasting for three characters.

The assignment works intelligently, shrinking or growing the string according to the size of the string you assign, so you can replace "dog" with "computer programmer" like this:

```
substr($string,4,3) = 'computer programmer';
print "$string\n";
```

Specifying values of zero allows you to prepend strings to other strings by specifying an **OFFSET** of zero, although it's arguably easier to use concatenation to achieve the same result. Appending with **substr** is not so easy; you cannot specify beyond the last character, although you could use the output from **length** to calculate where that might be. In these cases a simple

```
$string .= 'programming';
```

is definitely easier.

Regular Expressions

Using the functions we've seen so far for finding your location within a string and updating that string are fine if you know precisely what you are looking for. Often however what you are looking for is either a range of characters or a specific pattern, perhaps matching a range of individual words, letters, or numbers separated by other elements. These patterns are impossible to emulate using the **substr** and **index** functions because they rely on using a fixed string as the search criteria.

Identifying patterns instead of strings within Perl is as easy as writing the correct regular expression. A *regular expression* is a string of characters that define the pattern or patterns you are viewing. Of course, writing the correct regular expression is the more difficult part. There are ways and tricks of making the format of a regular expression easier to read, but there is no easy way of making a regular expression easier to understand!

The syntax of regular expressions in Perl is very similar to what you will find within other regular expression—supporting programs, such as **sed**, **grep**, and **awk**, although there are some differences between Perl's interpretations of certain elements.

The basic method for applying a regular expression is to use the pattern binding operators **=~** and **!~**. The first operator is a test and assignment operator. In a test context (called a *match* in Perl) the operator returns true if the value on the left-hand side of the operator matches the regular expression on the right. In an assignment context (substitution) it modifies the statement on the left based on the regular expression on the right. The second operator, **!~**, is for tests only and is the exact opposite: it returns true only if the value on the left does not match the regular expression on the right.

The statements on the right-hand side of the two test and assignment operators must be regular expression operators. There are two regular expression operators within Perl—**m//** (match) and **s///** (substitute). The match operator, **m//**, is used to match a string or statement to a regular expression. For example, to match the word "foo" against the scalar **$bar**, you might use a statement like this:

```
if ($bar =~ m/foo/)
```

Providing the delimiters in your statement with the **m//** operators are forward slashes, you can omit the leading **m**:

```
if ($bar =~ /foo/)
```

However, you must use **m//** if you want to specify delimiters other than the forward slash. This can be useful if your regular expression contains the forward slash that would otherwise need escaping.

For example, let's imagine you want to check on whether the **$dir** variable contains a particular directory. The delimiter for directories is the forward slash and would look messy if you had to escape each occurrence:

```
if ($dir =~ /\/usr\/local\/lib/)
```

By using a different delimiter, you can use a much clearer regular expression:

```
if ($dir =~ m(/usr/local/lib))
```

You can in fact use any character as a delimiter—even letters and numbers. Just remember that the aim is to make the code easier to understand!

It's also worth noting that the entire match statement (including the **$~**) actually returns all of the elements that match in the regular expression. The example below attempts to match a time specified in hours, minutes, and seconds using colons as separators:

```
my ($hours, $minutes, $seconds) = ($time =~ m/(\d+):(\d+):(\d+)/);
```

This example uses grouping and a character class to specify the individual elements. The groupings are the elements in standard parentheses, and each one will match (we hope) in sequence, returning a list that has been assigned to the hours, minutes, and seconds variables. The rest of this chapter will cover all the details of this.

There is also a simpler version of the match operator—the **?PATTERN?** operator. This is basically identical to the **m//** operator except that it only matches once. To match the same pattern/operator sequence again, you must use the **reset** operator. The operator works as a useful optimization of the matching process when you want to search a set of data streams, but only want to match once within each stream.

The substitution operator, **s///**, is more complex than the match operator, although the basic principles remain the same. The first "argument" within the delimiters is the regular expression that we are looking for. The second argument to the delimiters is a specification for the text or regular expression that we want to replace the found elements with. For example, you may remember from the **substr** definition above that you could replace a specific number of characters within a string by using assignment, as in

```
$string = 'The cat sat on the mat';
$start  = index($string,'cat',0);
$end    = index($string,' ',$start)-$start;
substr($string,$start,$end) = 'dog';
```

You can achieve the same result with a regular expression:

```
$string = 'The cat sat on the mat';
$string =~s/cat/dog/;
```

Note that we have managed to avoid the process of finding the start and end of the string we want to replace. This is a fundamental part of understanding the regular expression syntax. A regular expression will match the text anywhere within the string. You do not have to specify the starting point or location within the string, although it is possible to do so if that's what you want. Taking this to its logical conclusion, we can use the same regular expression to replace the word "cat" with "dog" in any string, irrespective of the location of the original word:

```
$string = 'Oscar is my cat';
$string = ~s/cat/dog;
```

The **$string** variable now contains the phrase "Oscar is my dog," which is factually incorrect, but it does demonstrate the ease with which you can replace strings with other strings.

Here's a more complex example that we will return to later. In this instance we need to change a date in the form 03/26/1999 to 19990326. Using grouping again, we can change it very easily with a regular expression:

```
$date = '03/26/1999';
$date =~ s#(\d+)/(\d+)/(\d+)#\3\1\2#;
```

This example demonstrates the fact that you can use delimiters other than the forward slash for substitutions too. Just like the match operator, the character used is the one immediately following the "s." Alternatively, if you specify a naturally paired delimiter such as a brace, then the replacement expression can have its own pair of delimiters:

```
$date = s{(\d+)/(\d+)/(\d+)}
         {\3\1\2}x;
```

There are also some functions that accept regular expressions as arguments. In these instances the format is the same as for a match operator without the leading "m," for example:

```
my @words = split(/ /,$sentence);
```

The delimiters are still required to tell Perl that the argument is a regular expression. The regular expression also uses exactly the same format as the operators, and this is what we'll examine next.

Regular Expression Elements

The regular expression engine is responsible for parsing the regular expression and matching the elements of the regular expression with the string supplied. Depending on the context of the regular expression, different results will occur: a substitution replaces character sequences, for example.

The regular expression syntax is best thought of as a little language in its own right. It's very powerful, and an incredible amount of ability is compacted into a very small space. Like all languages though, a regular expression is composed of a number of discrete elements, and if you understand those individual elements, you can understand the entire regular expression.

A Note About Regular Expression Coverage

On the topic of regular expressions in other books, you will often see reference to two aspects of regular expressions I do not cover here. First, I do not cover the "rules" of pattern matching since the sequence and exact method of matching should become apparent as we examine the regular expression operators.

The second aspect I have deliberately ignored is that of the type of operation. Many books will class individual regular expression operators as being one of a number of different types. However, once again the effects of the different operators will often imply how they are interpreted within the expression. Where there is a special case, I have mentioned it.

For most characters and character sequences the interpretation is literal, so a substitution to replace every occurrence of "cat" with "dog" can be as simple as

```
s/cat/dog/;
```

Additional functionality is provided by a number of metacharacters. These have special meaning within the context of a regular expression, and they are summarized in Table 4-1.

Metacharacter(s)	Description
\	Treats the following metacharacter as a real character, ignoring any associations with a Perl regexp metacharacter. Known as the escape character.
^	Matches from the beginning of the string (or the line if **/m** modifier in place).
$	Matches from the end of the string (or the line if **/m** modifier in place).
.	Matches any character except the newline character.
|	Allows you to specify alternate matches within the same regexp. Known as the OR operator.
()	Groups expressions together.
[]	Looks for a set of characters.

Table 4-1. *Regular Expression Metacharacters*

The first metacharacter is the backslash. If it is followed by an alphanumeric character, it has special meaning, which we'll examine shortly. If what follows is a metacharacter, the backslash acts as an escape and forces the regular expression engine to interpret the following character as a literal. To insert a backslash, for example, you would use a double backslash:

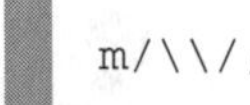

```
m/\\/;
```

The ^ metacharacter matches the beginning of the string. The line below would only return true if the character sequence "cat" were present at the beginning of **$string**:

```
if ($string =~ /^cat/)
```

Note that I've used "character sequence" in the description above. This is because regular expressions take the characters specified literally as they are written. So the above test would not only match "cat is a furry animal" but also "cationic surfactant" and "caterpillar," and indeed, any string whose first three characters are "c," "a," and "t." You'll see later how to refine the search.

The **$** operator matches the end of the string:

```
if ($string =~ /cat^/)
```

So the above example only matches when the "cat" character sequence is at the end of the string being matched.

The **.** (period) character is a wildcard and matches any single character (except the newline) in a string. The expression

```
if ($string =~ /c.t/)
```

would therefore match any sequence of "c" followed by any character and then "t." This would, for example, match "cat" or "cot," or indeed, words such as "acetic" and "acidification."

The **|** character is just like the standard bitwise OR within Perl. It specifies alternate matches within a regular expression or group. For example, to match "cat" or "dog" in the expression, you might use

```
if ($string =~ /cat|dog/)
```

You can group individual elements of an expression together in order to support complex matches. Searching for two people's names could be achieved with two separate tests like this:

```
if (($string =~ /Martin Brown/) ||
    ($string =~ /Sharon Brown/))
```

You could write this more efficiently in a single regular expression like this:

```
if ($string =~ /(Martin|Sharon) Brown/)
```

The use of grouping here is vital. By using a group the code looks for "Martin Brown" or "Sharon Brown" because the OR operation simply works on either side of the | metacharacter. Had you written

```
if ($string =~ /Martin|Sharon Brown/)
```

the regular expression would match either "Martin" or "Sharon Brown," which may or may not be what you want. In general the use of grouping with the | metacharacter follows the same rules as the logical operators elsewhere in Perl.

Finally, as you've already seen above, groupings have special results when used with both the match and substitution operators. In either case, each grouping is given a number, in the sequence of each leading open parenthesis. With a match operator, the resulting match for each group is returned as a list:

```
my ($hours, $minutes, $seconds) = ($time =~ m/(\d+):(\d+):(\d+)/);
```

Each group is also recorded in the special variables **$1**, **$2**, **$3**, and so on, so the above example could be rewritten as

```
$time =~ m/(\d+):(\d+):(\d+)/;
my ($hours, $minutes, $seconds) = ($1, $2, $3);
```

In the case of substitution, each matched group is also available within the replacement string using the same syntax. So, using the date string example above:

```
$date = '03/26/1999';
$date =~ s#(\d_)/(\d+)/(\d+)#$3$1$2#;
```

Each element of the date is placed into the temporary variables, so the month (group one) is in **$1**, the day is group 2, and the year is in group 3. To convert to the number format, you just need to specify each element in the desired order—in this example, year, month, day. The resulting string is "19990326." The matched groups are perpetual—that is, you can also access each matched group outside of the substitution expression. Obviously, the next regular expression executed resets all of the values.

When it comes to nested groups, you must remember that the numbering system keys on the first opening parenthesis, as demonstrated by the code below:

```
$date = '03/26/1999';
$date =~ s#((\d+)/(\d+)/(\d+))#Date $1 = $4$2$3#;
print "$date\n";
```

This prints

```
Date 03/26/1999 = 19990326
```

The first parenthesis matches the whole date string; the nested parentheses then match the individual year, month, and day of the date.

The final metacharacter(s) are the [] (square brackets). These allow you to specify a list of values for a single character. This can be useful if you want to find a name that may or may not have been specified with a leading capital letter:

```
if ($name =~ /[Mm]artin/)
```

Within the [] brackets you can also specify lists, such as "a-z" for all lowercase characters, "0-9" for numbers, and so on. If you want to specify a hyphen, use a backslash within the class to prevent Perl from trying to produce a range. If you want to match a right square bracket (which would otherwise be interpreted as a character class), use a backslash or place it first in the list, for example **[[]**.

Beyond the metacharacters above, you can also use special backslashed character sequences to specify assertions and specific characters for the regular expression. For example, there are sequences to match the beginning and end of a word, and also sequences to match alphanumeric and nonalphanumeric characters. The sequences are shown in Table 4-2.

Many of the entries in Table 4-2 should be self-explanatory, although some warrant special consideration.

The **\w** and **\W** sequences match alphanumeric characters and nonalphanumeric characters, respectively. So, to split up a string on its words, you might use a regular expression like this:

Sequence	Purpose
\w	Matches an alphanumeric character (including _).
\W	Matches a nonalphanumeric character.
\s	Matches a white-space character (spaces, tabs).
\S	Matches a non-white-space character.
\d	Matches a digit.
\D	Matches a nondigit character.
\b	Matches a word boundary.
\B	Matches a non–word boundary.
\A	Matches only the beginning of a string.
\Z	Matches only at the end of a string.
\G	Matches where previous m//g operation left off (only works with /g modifier).
\t	Matches tab.
\n	Matches newline.
\r	Matches carriage return.
\f	Matches form feed.
\a	Matches alarm (bell).
\e	Matches escape.
\b	Matches backspace (only within the [] character class).
\033	Matches octal character.
\x1B	Matches hex character.
\c[	Matches control character.
\l	Makes next character lowercase.
\u	Makes next character uppercase.
\L	Specifies lowercase till \E.
\U	Specifies uppercase till \E.
\E	Ends case modification.
\Q	Quotes (disables) regexp metacharacters till \E.

Table 4-2. *Regular Expression Character Patterns*

```
($worda, $wordb, $wordc) = $string =~ /(\w+)\W+(\w+)\W+(\w+)/;
```

This checks for an alphanumeric string of one or more characters followed by a string of nonalphanumeric characters. The nonalphanumeric string matches spaces, punctuation, tabs; and by specifying a multiplier, you can catch any number of these in sequence.

If you want to match white space—that is, spaces and tabs—use the **\s** sequence. This is best used when trying to import the contents of a text file that has fields separated by multiple spaces, tabs, or a combination of both. The inverse will catch anything that is not white space, even punctuation.

The **\d** sequence forces identification of the character as a digit. The match is strict, such that if you want to match periods or commas often used to separate elements of numbers, then you must specify them additionally within a set:

```
if ('23,445.33' =~ m/([\d,.]+)/)
```

A *word boundary* is defined as any character that would, in your locality, act as a word boundary. In English this means spaces and punctuation but does not include hyphens or underscores.

In many of the examples above you'll see a quantifier—a special character or sequence that defines the number of times the previous sequence or character appears. Using a quantifier you can specify that a sequence must appear a minimum or maximum number of times, or that a character can repeat indefinitely until the next regexp element. Table 4-3 shows the supported quantifiers.

Maximal	Minimal	Purpose
*	*?	Matches 0 or more items.
+	+?	Matches 1 or more items.
?	??	Matches 0 or 1 items.
{n}	{n}?	Matches exactly n times.
{n,}	{n,}?	Matches at least n times.
{n,m}	{n,m}?	Matches at least n times but no more than m times.

Table 4-3. *Regular Expression Pattern Quantifiers*

The * and + operators match 0 or more, or 1 or more items. By using a pattern of **/.*/**, you can match everything (although this seems rather pointless), or with **/.+/**, you can match nothing or everything. The brace specifications allow you to specify a range of repetitions. Some examples and equivalencies are shown below:

```
m/.{0}/;     #Matches no characters
m/.{1,}/;    #Matches any character at least once, equivalent to
/.+/
m/\d{2,4}/; #Matches any digit at least two and a maximum of four
times
```

In Table 4-3 entries in the left-hand (Maximal) column will match the maximum number of times. This means that the quantifier will soak up all the characters it can before it attempts the next match in the regexp. The Minimal column shows the sequence that will match the minimum number of times before the next element of the regular expression is matched. The code below demonstrates the effect:

```
$string = "There was a food shortage in foodham";
print "Maximal:",($string =~ /(.*)foo/),"\n";
print "Minimal:",($string =~ /(.*?)foo/),"\n";
```

If you run this, the result is

```
Maximal:There was a food shortage in
Minimal:There was a
```

You can modify the overall effect of the regular expression match using a number of modifiers. Some apply to both the match and substitution operators and are shown in Table 4-4.

Although referred to here as **/x** modifiers, they do of course follow the characters used to parenthesize the entire expression. For example, the regular expression "s#/#:#x" may use a hash character for separation, but it still has the **/x** modifier invoked.

The **/g** modifier forces a match or substitution to occur globally within the string. For example, using **s/foo/bar/g** will replace all occurrences of "foo" with "bar." Without this operator, only the match for "foo" will be replaced with "bar." In a list context the **m//g** returns a list of values matched by any parenthesized elements of the regexp, or if no parentheses are specified, then it returns a list of all the matches.

In a scalar **m//g** statement this means that the pattern match iterates through the string and returns true (the value of the match). Repetitive matches using the same regexp and string return each occurrence of the match. If you modify the string in any way, the start position is reset to the beginning of the string. You can use the **pos**

Modifier	Description
g	Matches/replaces globally every occurrence within a string, not just the first.
i	Makes the match case insensitive.
m	Specifies that if the string has newline or carriage return characters, the ^ and $ operators (in Table 4-1) match the start and end of the string, rather than individual lines.
o	Evaluates the expression only once.
s	Allows use of **.** to match a newline character.
x	Allows you to use white space in the expression for clarity.
e	Evaluates replacement string as an expression (substitution only).

Table 4-4. *Perl Regular Expression Modifiers for Matching and Substitution*

function to return the position of where the last **m//g** match left off. Here's an example that counts sentences ending in a period, question mark, or exclamation mark:

```
$/ = "";
while ($para = <>)
{
    while ($para =~ /[a-z]['")]*[.!?]+['")]*\s/g)
    {
        $sentences++;
    }
}
print "Sentence count: $sentences\n";
```

The **/i** modifier ignores case in the regular expression search. Thus the expression **/foo/i** will match "foo," "FOO," and indeed, "Foo." For a more specific case match, use the set, **[]**, expression, as in **/[fF]oo/**, which will match only "Foo" and "foo."

If the string you are trying to match contains multiple lines, it should be classed as a multiline string using the **/m** modifier. Without this specification, the **^** and **$** metacharacters will match the beginning and end of the entire string. With this modifier, they match the beginning and end of individual lines within the string. If you still want to match the beginning and end of the entire string, use the **\A** and **\Z** qualifiers.

If the match pattern that you specify includes variables, they will be interpolated as normal into the regular expression each time the pattern is evaluated. You can restrict the evaluation of the pattern to occur only once with the **/o** modifier. This lets you tell Perl that you will not be modifying the values of the variables during the script. This can improve performance since it avoids run-time compilations of the expression. The problem is that with this modifier, even if you do change the values, Perl won't take any notice of them. You should therefore make sure that the value you are interpolating will not change, otherwise you may not get the response you expect.

By default the **.** metacharacter does not match a newline character in a string. In most cases this is the behavior you want. However, if you are matching a multiline string, perhaps with the **/m** modifier as well, then you may want the period to match a newline character. The **/s** operator enables this behavior.

The final modifier that affects both matches and substitution is the **/x** modifier. Regular expressions can be very complicated when written down as a single line. For example, it's not immediately obvious what this regular expression is doing:

```
$matched =
/(\S+)\s+(\S+)\s+(\S+)\s+\[(.*)\]\s+"(.*)"\s+(\S+)\s+(\S+)/;
```

However, by specifying the **/x** modifier, you can insert white space and even newlines and comments into the regular expression to make the expression clearer and easier to understand. The above example actually processes a standard web log and could be rewritten as

```
matched = /(\S+)      #Host
           \s+        #(space separator)
           (\S+)      #Identifier
           \s+        #(space separator)
           (\S+)      #Username
           \s+        #(space separator)
           \[(.*)\]   #Time
           \s+        #(space separator)
           "(.*)"     #Request
           \s+        #(space separator)
           (\S+)      #Result
           \s+        #(space separator)
           (\S+)      #Bytes sent
          /x;
```

Although it takes up more editor and page space, it is much clearer what you are trying to achieve.

The **/e** modifier allows you to specify a replacement text that will be evaluated as an expression (a standard Perl expression, not a regular expression). This is basically equivalent to an **eval**, but the expression is syntax checked at compile time rather than at execution time. By using a combination of grouping and the expression modifier, you can perform specific functions on individual elements of a string. The example below is a typical regular expression used to extract the "quoted" elements of a URL during CGI programming. Quoted elements within a URL are expressed as the ASCII value of the character to be quoted, preceded by a percent sign:

```
$value =~ s/%([a-fA-F0-9][a-fA-F0-9])/pack("C", hex($1))/eg;
```

Note the use of the **$1** group match within the replacement function call to pass the value of the matching group.

Extensions and Variables

The regular expression engine also allows you to specify a number of additional extensions, called *assertions*, within the main expression. These extensions enable more specific matches to take place without the match affecting the variables and/or groupings that are in place. These work in combination with the grouping facilities within the regular expression and the global variables that are affected by regular expression matches. These include **$,** which contains whatever the last grouping match matched; **$&** contains the entire matched string; **$'** contains everything before the matched string; and **$′** contains everything after the matched string.

*Use of the **$'** and **$′** variables induces a significant overhead within your program, since the first time you use them Perl then starts to populate the variables for each regular expression executed. Avoid using them if you can. Grouping will often give you the same result without the same overhead. The **$&** also adds overhead, but since version 5.005, the performance hit is not as high as that induced by **$′**.*

The code below demonstrates the result,

```
$string = "The food is in the salad bar";
$string =~ m/foo/;
print "Before: $'\n";
print "Matched: $&\n";
print "After: $'\n";
```

which prints the following when executed:

```
Before: The
Matched: foo
After: d is in the salad bar
```

The assertions are summarized in Table 4-5, and we'll examine some pitfalls and traps shortly.

For example, here's a regular expression match using the **(?{code})** assertion:

```
use re 'eval';
$_ = '<A href="/index.shtml">';
m<
     (?{ $cnt = 0 })
     \<A.*"
     (.(?{ local $cnt = $cnt + 1;}))*
     "\>
     (?{ $res = $cnt })
     >x;

print $res," words\n";
```

It counts the number of letters between the double quotes in the HTML reference specified in **$_**. This is a fairly simplistic example, since the likelihood is that you'll

Assertion	Meaning
(?#text)	Comment—text within the brackets is ignored.
(?:pattern)	Identical to grouping, but does not populate **$1**, **$2**, and so on, on a match.
(?imsx:pattern)	Identical to grouping, but does not populate **$1**, **$2**, and so on, on a match; embeds pattern match modifiers for the duration of the specified pattern, according to Table 4-4.
(?=pattern)	Matches if the regular expression engine would match **pattern** next, without affecting the result of the match. For example, the expression **\w+(?=\t)/** would match a tab following a word without the tab being added to the value of **$&**.

Table 4-5. *Regular Expression Assertions*

(?!pattern)	Matches if the regular expression engine would not match **pattern** next. For example, the expression **\foo($!bar)/** would match only if there was an occurrence of "foo" not followed by "bar."
(?<=pattern)	Matches the next statement only if **pattern** would have matched with the following expression, but without placing the result of **pattern** into the **$&** variable. For example, to test for a word following a tab, but without placing the tab into **$&**, you would use **/(?<=\t)\w+/**.
(?<!pattern)	Matches the next statement only if **pattern** would not have matched with the following expression, but without placing the result of **pattern** into the **$&** variable. For example, to match any occurrence of "foo" that isn't following "bar," you might use **/(?<!bar)foo/**.
(?{ code })	Experimental—the intended use for this is for **code** to be executed, and if it returns true, then the result is considered as a match along the same lines as the **(?:pattern)**assertion. The **code** does not interpolate variables. This assertion only works if you have the **use re 'eval'** pragma in effect.
(?>pattern)	Matches the substring that a stand-alone **pattern** would match if the **pattern** was anchored at the current position. For example, the regexp /^(?>a*)ab/ will never match since the assertion **(?>a*)** will match all characters "a" at the beginning of the string, effectively removing the "a" required to match "ab."
(?(condition) yes-pattern | no-pattern) **(?(condition) yes-pattern)**	Conditional expression—the **(condition)** element should either be an integer in parentheses or an assertion.
(?imsx) **(?-imsx)**	Embedded pattern match modifiers, according to Table 4-4. Useful when you want to embed an expression modifier within a variable, which may then be used in a general regexp that does not specify its own modifiers. Anything following a – switches off the modifier for the duration, or until another embedded modifier is in place.

Table 4-5. *Regular Expression Assertions* (continued)

want to perform some sort of test (perhaps via a function call) within the **(?{code})** assertion, but you can see the general idea.

Supporting Functions

When you've performed a match, you can find the location within the string at the point where the regular expression stopped checking for new matches within an **m//g** regexp:

```
pos SCALAR
pos
```

The **pos** function returns the location for **SCALAR** if specified or **$_** if no scalar is specified. For example,

```
$string = "The food is in the salad bar";
$string =~ m/foo/g;
print pos($string),"\n";
```

should print a value of seven—the number of characters read before the match operator stopped looking for new entries (because there weren't any).

In Table 4-2 you should have noticed the **\Q** sequence, which prevented the regular expression engine from interpreting metacharacters or sequences as special values within a regular expression. This effect is actually achieved by the general Perl function **quotemeta**:

```
quotemeta EXPR
quotemeta
```

The function replaces any nonalphanumeric (not matching [a-zA-Z0-9]) character with a backslash version. For example, the string

```
print quotemeta "[Foobar!]";
```

will return

```
\[Foobar\!\]
```

If you do not specify an expression, then the value of **$_** will be quoted instead.

study

If you expect to perform a number of pattern matches on a large scalar, you may find that the regular expression process is very slow. To increase the performance of the regular expression system, you can use the **study** function:

```
study EXPR
study
```

The special **$_** is used if you do not specify a scalar to examine. The **study** function works by building a linked list of all the characters within the scalar. This enables the regular expression engine to identify where all of the x characters are, for example. When a search is requested, the character that occurs least in the search string is used to choose the starting point for the pattern search.

You will need to check the speed of the search process with and without the **study** function; for many cases you may find there is little or no difference. Unfortunately, only one scalar can be studied at any one time. The moment you specify a new scalar for the function to examine, it replaces the information stored on the previous scalar.

Translation

Translation is similar, but not identical, to the principles of substitution. The idea has been taken from the **sed** translation operation and the Unix command line **tr** utility. The translation operators are

```
tr/SEARCHLIST/REPLACEMENTLIST/cds
y/SEARCHLIST/REPLACEMENTLIST/cds
```

The translation replaces all occurrences of the characters in **SEARCHLIST** with the corresponding characters in **REPLACEMENTLIST**. For example, using the original version of the string we have been using in this chapter:

```
$string =~ tr/a/o/;
print "$string\n";
```

The script prints out "The cot sot on the mot." Standard Perl ranges can also be used, allowing you to specify ranges of characters either by letter or numerical value. To change the case of the string, you might use

```
$string =~ tr/a-z/A-Z/;
```

in place of the **uc** function. The **tr** operator only works on a scalar or single element of an array or hash; you cannot use it directly against an array or hash (see **grep** or **map** in Chapter 7). You can also use it with any reference or function that can be assigned to –. For example, to convert the word "cat" from the string to uppercase, you could do

```
substr($string,4,3) =~ tr/a-z/A-Z/;
```

In both s/// and tr/// expressions, the **SEARCHLIST** and **REPLACEMENTLIST** arguments to the operator do not need to use the same delimiters. As long as the **SEARCHLIST** is naturally paired with delimiters such as parentheses or braces, the **REPLACEMENTLIST** can use its own pair. This can make some expressions easier to read:

```
$string =~ s(cat)/dog/;
```

The same feature can be used to make certain character sequences seem clearer, such as the one below, which converts an 8-bit string into a 7-bit string, albeit with some loss of information:

```
tr [\200-\377]
   [\000-\177];
```

Three modifiers are supported by the **tr** operator, as seen in Table 4-6.

The **/c** modifier changes the replacement text to be the characters not specified in **SEARCHLIST**. You might use this to replace characters other than those specified in the **SEARCHLIST** with a null alternative, for example,

Modifier	Meaning
c	Complement **SEARCHLIST.**
d	Delete found but unreplaced characters.
s	Squash duplicate replaced characters.

Table 4-6. *Modifiers to the tr Operator*

```
$string = 'the cat sat on the mat.';
$string =~ tr/a-zA-Z/-/c;
print "$string\n";
```

replaces any noncharacter with a hyphen.

The **/d** modifier deletes the characters matching **SEARCHLIST** that were not replaced by the characters in **REPLACEMENTLIST**. For example,

```
$string = 'the cat sat on the mat.';
$string =~ tr/a-z/b/d;
print "$string\n";
```

deletes any characters from "a-z" but not "b," giving a resultant string of:

```
b b  b.
```

The last modifier, **/s**, removes the duplicate sequences of characters that were replaced; so

```
tr/a-zA-Z/ /cs;
```

replaces any nonalphanumeric characters with a single space.

If you do not specify the **REPLACEMENTLIST**, Perl uses the values in **SEARCHLIST**. This is most useful for doing character-class-based counts, something which cannot be done with the **length** function. For example, to count the nonalphanumeric characters in a string:

```
$cnt = $string =~ tr/a-zA-Z0-9//cs;
```

In all cases the **tr** operator returns the number of characters changed (including those deleted).

The Complete Reference

Part II

Advanced Perl Programming

The Complete Reference

Chapter 5

Subroutines, Packages, and Modules

Everything covered so far makes up the basics of programming Perl. We've looked at how to communicate with the users, how to manipulate basic data types, and how to use the simple control statements that Perl provides to control and manage the flow of execution in a program.

One of the fundamentals of any programming language is that there are often repeated elements in your programs. You could cut and paste from one section to another, but this is messy. What happens when you need to update that sequence you just wrote? You would need to examine each duplicated entry and then make the modifications. In a small program this might not make much of a difference, but in a larger program with hundreds of lines, it could easily double or triple the amount of time you require.

Duplication also runs the risk of introducing additional syntactic, logical and typographical errors. If you forget to make a modification to one section, or make the wrong modification, it could take hours to find and resolve the error. A better solution is to place the repeated piece of code into a new function, and then each time it needs to be executed, you can make a new call to the function. If the code needs modifying, you modify it once, and all instances of the function call use the same piece of code.

This method of taking repeated pieces of code and placing them into a function is called *abstraction*. In general, a certain level of abstraction is always useful—it speeds up the programming process, reduces the risk of introducing errors, and makes a complex program easier to manage. For the space conscious, the process also reduces the number of lines in your code.

Now that you have a suite of functions, you want to be able to share information among the functions without affecting any variables the user may have created. By creating a new *package*, you can give the functions their own *name space*—a protected area that has its own list of global variables. Unless defined directly, the variables defined within the package name space will not affect any variables defined by the main script.

You can also take this abstraction a stage further. Imagine you have created a suite of functions that extend the standard mathematical abilities of Perl for use in a single script. What happens when you want to use those same functions in another script? You could cut and paste, but we already know that's a bad solution. Imagine what would happen if you updated the original script's function suite—you would need to do the same for each script that used the same set of functions.

The solution is yet another stage in abstraction: you move the function suite from the original file and place it into a new file with the same name as that of the package the functions belong to. In Perl, this process is called creating a new *module*. Each script that wants to use the functions defined in the module can import them and use them just like the functions that Perl has built in. You import the functions from a module with the **use** command. The examples of **use** you have seen up to now are all importing modules and promoting code reuse.

In this chapter we'll be looking at how to create new functions for use within your Perl scripts and how to group functions and variables to create new packages. Then we'll examine how to convert a package into a module before moving on to the differences between the available methods for importing and using packages and modules within your scripts.

Functions

A function is a named code block that is generally intended to process specified input values into an output value, although this is not always the case. For example, the **print** function takes variables and static text and prints the values on the screen.

You can define functions anywhere within a program, including importing them from external files or having them generated on the fly using an **eval** statement. Furthermore, you can generate *anonymous subroutines*, which are functions that are attached, by reference, to a variable. This enables you to treat a subroutine as any other entity within Perl, even though you may consider it to be a fundamental part of the blocks that make up the Perl language.

A subroutine can be declared as follows:

```
sub NAME;
sub NAME (PROTO);
sub NAME BLOCK
sub NAME (PROTO) BLOCK
```

The first form is a "forward definition"—it reserves the **NAME** in the Perl name space, although the statements that make up the function have not been defined. The second form allows you to specify a prototype. C programmers will be familiar with this format, as it is regularly used in header files to define the function name and required/expected arguments. We'll return to this topic later.

The third format shows how you would declare the function name and the associated code block that should be executed as a result of calling the function. The last example shows a function being given a prototype and its definition block.

Function or Subroutine?

The two terms *function* and *subroutine* are used interchangeably in Perl. If you want to be strict on the semantics, small pieces of named blocks of code that accept arguments and return values are called subroutines. The built-in subroutines in Perl are called functions, because they provide additional functionality. In reality though, there is little difference between the two, and most agree that the term function is clearer than subroutine.

To call a function, you can use one of the following formats:

```
NAME(LIST);
NAME LIST;
&NAME;
```

The first two examples are the simple versions and are preferred. You can ignore the parentheses if the function has been predeclared or included via an external module; otherwise the parentheses signify to Perl that **NAME** is a function, not a static value. The last example explicitly defines that you are calling a function called **NAME**—the leading ampersand is the equivalent of the **$** or **%** signs on scalars and hashes. Without any parentheses and the leading ampersand, the current @_ array is passed to the function as the list of arguments.

Arguments and Return Values

Perl has a very simple attitude toward function arguments. In C, Pascal, and others the specification of a function is fixed, both in the form of the data types that can be supplied and the total number of arguments. Although C supports the 'varargs' option, this is the exception, rather than the rule. Within Perl you can pass any argument and any number of arguments to a function. (Actually, there is an exception to this rule—see "Prototypes" later in the chapter.) For most situations this is an incredibly practical solution to the problem of argument passing. Like all lists, passing an array or hash will cause the values to be interpolated into the flattened version of the argument list. There are ways around this, but in many cases this is probably the effect you want anyway.

The supplied arguments are accessible within the function using the special @_ array variable. Therefore, you can access the individual elements using the normal array notation:

```
sub add
{
    $first_num  = $_[0];
    $second_num = $_[1];
```

Although this is considered messy, a simpler solution is just to use the list operators in Perl to extract the elements:

```
sub add
{
    ($first_num, $second_num) = @_;
```

You can also extract an array in this way (or indeed, any number of scalars and an array):

```
sub add
{
    ($first_num, $second_num, @rest_of_nums) = @_;
```

Any arguments passed to the function that are not extracted using one of the techniques we'll examine shortly are simply ignored—if you only take the first 2 arguments out of the 20 supplied, that's your business.

Passing hashes is a special case. Although it is possible to pass them directly, as you can with scalars and arrays, care should be taken to ensure that you are receiving what you expect. Perl will interpolate arguments supplied as lists alternately into the keys and values of the hash you specify. For entire hashes passed as arguments, this shouldn't cause a problem, but if you accidentally supply a scalar or array into the function arguments, you could end up with a corrupted hash.

Return values are similarly easy. Perl allows you to return as many or as few return scalars as you desire. Returning arrays and hashes have the same caveats as those supplied as arguments to the original function; hashes and arrays are flattened to a simple list. It is up to the caller to assign the returned flattened list to the correct variable types. Perl takes the value of the last evaluated statement from the function as the return value, or you can use the special **return** keyword to specify the values you want returned. The example below shows a function for adding two numbers together that returns the final value:

```
sub add
{
    ($first_num, $second_num) = @_;
    $first_num + $second_num;
}
```

Of course, this is pointless, since the **+** operator already does what we want, but you get the idea.

Passing Typeglobs and References

It should be apparent by now that there are two problems with argument passing in Perl. First of all, there are some types that you cannot seem to pass easily. A filehandle cannot be distinguished from any other variable, since it has no leading character to identify it as a filehandle. You can get around this by using the typeglob symbol, *, to pass the symbol table entry to the function. It's then up to Perl to choose the correct variable format for the supplied typeglob when it is first used. For example, you may want to define a new read that returns a separated list of values, instead of the normal read function that returns a scalar:

```
sub myread
{
    (*FILE) = @_;
    $line = <FILE>;
    split(/:/, $line);
}

open(MYHANDLE, 'db') or die "File open Error, $!";
print join(' ',myread(*MYHANDLE));
```

The argument **MYHANDLE** is passed as a typeglob; in fact, typeglobs are passed to the function as a scalar value that represents all of the objects of that name, including any scalar, array, hash, filehandle, format, or subroutine. Whenever you assign a value to a typeglob, the typeglob sets up its own name to be an alias to the typeglob value that was assigned to it. In the example above the assignation is applied at the point the function arguments are resolved to the ***FILE** typeglob. In this case the value passed is a filehandle, and Perl allows us to use it as such in the rest of the function.

The second problem with argument passing is related to the method with which you pass variables. It's often the case that you want to supply an array or hash to a function. This is fine for small arrays, but for large arrays, it means that Perl must copy the elements of the array being passed into the argument list. Then it needs to copy the values from the argument list into the variables defined within the function. The solution is to use references. A *reference* is a pointer to a Perl entity (variable, function, object, etc.). Passing a reference to the function has two benefits. First of all, it enables you to edit the values in the variable in place, rather than copying the values each time. Second, by passing a reference to an array or hash, you can specify more than one hash in the same function call.

To pass a reference, instead of the variable, you place a backslash in front of the variable name. In the function, the reference is assigned to a scalar. To use the reference in its correct form, you place the special character for the variable in front of the reference scalar. The example below will make the process clearer. The function combines two arrays, sorts the values, and returns the new list:

```
sub combisort
{
```

```
    my ($alist, $blist) = @_;
    sort @$alist,@$blist;
}

@plants = qw/rose iris orchid/;
@animals = qw/lion aardvark zebra/;

print join(' ',combisort(\@plants, \@animals));
```

The same is true for hashes. You can use a function to merge a second hash into the first hash, ignoring elements that already exist in the first:

```
sub mergehash
{
    my ($ahash, $bhash) = @_;
    foreach (keys %$bhash)
    {
        $$ahash{$_} = $$bhash{$_} unless (defined($$ahash{$_}));
    }
}
```

In fact, the typeglob method supports the same functionality, since a typeglob passes a reference to the symbol table for the required argument. You could therefore rewrite the last line of the above example as

```
print join(' ',combisort(*plants, *animals));
```

Furthermore, you do not need to specify scalars as references; changing an element of the @_ array will modify the original scalar variable that was passed. So the script

```
sub square
{
    $_[0] *= $_[0];
}
$base=256;
square($base);
print "$base\n";
```

prints 65536.

When it comes to return values, the original rules apply. You can only return a list of scalars; you cannot specify that the return value is composed of multiple arrays or hashes. Most people make mistakes like this:

```
(%c, %d) = transpose(%a, %b);
```

If you want to support this sort of functionality, the only solution is to return references, either specifically or simply by returning the references extracted at the point the arguments were determined. For example:

```
sub transpose
{
    ($a, $b) = @_;
    return($b, $a)
}
($c, $d) = transpose(\%a, \%b);
print join(' ',keys %$a),"\n";
print join(' ',keys %$b),"\n";
```

Or for a tidier solution, you can combine references with typeglobs to produce a solution that makes using the returned values significantly easier:

```
sub transpose
{
    local (*ahash, *bhash) = @_;
    return(\%bhash,\%ahash);
}
(*a, *b) = transpose(\%hasha, \%hashb);
print join(' ',keys %a),"\n";
print join(' ',keys %b),"\n";
```

Because typeglobs are used here for the symbol table references, instead of direct references, you have to use **local** instead of **my** variables (see "Scoping" later in the chapter).

Anonymous Subroutines

An anonymous subroutine is one that has been defined without a name and then assigned to a variable. In its simplest form it looks like this:

```
$hw = sub { print "Hello World\n" };
&$hw;
```

The newly created variable now contains a reference to the function, which we can access by dereferencing the scalar and telling Perl what data type to identify the reference as; in this case we use & to signify a function call. An anonymous subroutine can only be composed on one line—you cannot have multiline blocks in an anonymous subroutine definition. This limits their usefulness to simple statements, but they are used for many tricks such as signal handlers. See Chapter 7 for some further examples of anonymous subroutines.

Contexts

The *context* of a function or statement is defined as the return value that is expected. This allows you to use a single function that returns different values based on what the user is expecting to receive. For example, the two calls below to the **getpwent** function return a list or a scalar, according to what was used in the assignation:

```
$name = getpwent();
($name, $passwd, $uid, $gid, $quota,
 $comment, %gcos, $dir, $shell) = getpwent();
```

In the first case the user expects a scalar value to be returned by the function, because that is what he is expecting to assign the return value to. In the second case, the user expects an array as the return value, again because he has specified a list of scalars for the information to be inserted into.

This can be confusing, since most other languages support only one type of return value. In fact it's very practical, because it reduces the amount of code required to achieve different results. Here's another example, again from the built in Perl functions that shows the flexibility:

```
my $timestr = localtime(time);
```

In this example, the value of **$timestr** is now a string made up of the current date and time. Conversely, the statement:

```
($sec,$min,$hour,$mday,$mon,$year,$wday,$yday,$isdst) =
localtime(time);
```

Now the individual variables contain the corresponding values returned by **localtime**. We can now use these values to build our own string, instead of relying on the default value returned in a scalar context.

In order to discover the context in which a function has been called, you use the **wantarray** function. This returns true if the function has been called in a list context, false otherwise. Consider the script below, which prints a scalar or list-based message, according to how the **hw** function was called:

```
sub hw
{
    if (wantarray)
    {
        return('Hello','World',"\n");
    }
    else
    {
        return "Hello World\n";
    }
}

$scalarmsg = hw();
$listmsg = join('--',hw());

print "Scalar is $scalarmsg\n";
print "List is $listmsg\n";
```

The list context is implied here because the **join** function expects a list as the second argument. If you run this program, you get

```
Scalar is Hello World
List is Hello--World--
```

which we know to be correct and is the result we expected.

Specifying a hash implies a list context, since a hash is just a structured list anyway. There is no equivalent **wanthash** function. Perl assumes that if you are playing with hashes, you will know when you want to return a hash to a caller.

You can force a function to return a scalar value with the **scalar** keyword. This forces the context of the function to be recognized as a scalar, not a list value. To use, just place the **scalar** function before the statement or expression that you want to be forced into scalar context:

```
my $time = scalar localtime;
```

Prototypes

The dictionary defines *prototype* as "an original type, form, or instance that serves as a model on which later stages are based or judged." Within Perl, the act of prototyping a function tells Perl (or a programmer, if he's looking) what arguments the function expects or requires. As with other elements of the Perl process, the arguments passed can also imply the format of the information returned by the function. For example, the built-in **syswrite** function could be declared like this:

```
sub syswrite($$$;$)
```

The prototype is used by Perl to make decisions about the number or type of arguments that are supplied to the function. The prototypes only affect function calls in the "new" form, that is, without a leading ampersand. If it looks like a built-in function, Perl will treat it as such. If you call a function using the "old" ampersand style, prototypes are ignored. In all cases, Perl only checks at compile time, so the function and calls must be visible at the time the functions are compiled.

You specify the function arguments by using the special characters that precede normal variables as indicators of the variable type expected. In the example above, the dollar signs signify that scalar values are expected. The @ and % characters, as expected, specify arrays and hashes. However, except in the case noted below, unbackslashed entries gobble up all the remaining arguments, regardless of the rest of the prototype. In addition, the **$** implies a scalar context, and **@** or **%** imply list context accordingly.

An ampersand requires an anonymous subroutine that can be specified without the **sub** keyword or the trailing comma if specified as the first argument. An * character specifies a typeglob, typically used to supply filehandles.

Any backslash quoted character signifies that the argument absolutely must start with that character—for example, **\@** would require that the function call specify a list as the first argument. A semicolon separates the required arguments from optional arguments in the prototype. The semicolon is used to distinguish between the arguments that are required and those that are optional. Table 5-1 shows some examples taken from the **perlsub** man page.

In the last three examples in Table 5-1 Perl treats the declarations slightly differently. The **mygrep** function is passed as a true list operator, interpreting the following arguments as elements of a list and not as further arguments to the original **mygrep** function. The **myrand** function behaves like a true unary operator, and the **mytime** function is treated as a function with no arguments at all. This means you can get away with statements like

```
mytime +2
```

and you'll end up with the return value of **mytime** added to the static value, instead of Perl calling **mytime** with an argument of **+2**.

You should be careful when specifying prototypes, since many of the options imply the context in which the function should return and, in turn, the function-specific

Declaration	Example Call
sub mylink ($$)	mylink $old, $new
sub myvec ($$$)	myvec $var, $offset, 1
sub myindex ($$;$)	myindex &getstring, "substr"
sub mysyswrite ($$$;$)	mysyswrite $buf, 0, length($buf) - $off,
sub myreverse (@)	myreverse $a, $b, $c
sub myjoin ($@)	myjoin ":", $a, $b, $c
sub mypop (\@)	mypop @array
sub mysplice (\@$$@)	mysplice @array, @array, 0, @pushme
sub mykeys (\%)	mykeys %{$hashref}
sub myopen (*;$)	myopen HANDLE, $name
sub mypipe (**)	mypipe READHANDLE, WRITEHANDLE
sub mygrep (&@)	mygrep { /foo/ } $a, $b, $c
sub myrand ($)	myrand 42
sub mytime ()	mytime

Table 5-1. *Sample Prototype Declarations*

utilities such as **wantarray**. In general, therefore, you should use prototypes only on new functions, rather than retrofitting them to functions you have already written. This will prevent the effects of imposing a scalar context on a function that is expecting to return in a list context. For example, consider a function with a single argument:

```
sub printmsg($)
{
    print "Message: ", shift, "\n";
}
```

Calling this function with an argument that returns a single element list wouldn't produce the same results. The call

```
printmsg(@message);
```

would actually print a value of 1, since the scalar prototype has imposed that the list argument supplied be converted to a scalar.

In the case of a list, the scalar value of a list variable is the number of elements in the list. Worse, using a function such as **split**, which uses the context in which it is called to determine where it puts its results, would cause a more serious problem. If used as the argument to the prototype function, **split** would execute in the scalar context, messing up your @_ argument list.

Indirect Function Calls

The reference facility, seen earlier in this chapter for passing the reference to a variable instead of the variable itself, can also be used when calling a function. Instead of using the normal methods for calling a function, you can specify the function name in a variable and then prepend the **&** character to signify that you are making a function call of the name specified by the variable, not accessing the contents of the variable.

For example, if we wanted to be perverse, we could call the **add** function we defined earlier like this,

```
my $function='add';
print &$function(2,2),"\n";
```

which would print the desired result of 4. The ampersand notation simply tells Perl to interpret whatever follows as the name of a function, not an evaluated expression.

You can even use blocks to generate a function name. For example:

```
print &{ 'add' }(2,2),"\n";
```

This example works because the last element in a code block is used as the return value, so the return value of the statement 'add' becomes the value to be used as a function name.

A more sensible use for this feature is to support the calling of functions at run time, based on the input from a user. The example below was taken from a network server that supports five basic commands. Each user command that is supported is defined by the key in a hash; the corresponding real function is defined in the value. So when a user connects to the server and types in one of the supported commands, the Perl code looks up the real function that should be called, checks for its existence, and calls the subroutine:

```
my %commandlist = (
                      'DISK'  => 'disk_space_report',
                      'SWAP'  => 'swap_space_report',
                      'STORE' => 'store_status_report',
                      'GET'   => 'get_status_report',
```

```
                'QUIT'   => 'quit_connection',
                );
...
            my ($command, @args) = split(' ');
            $command=uc($command);
            if (defined($commandlist{$command}))
            {
                my ($function) = $commandlist{$command};
                die "No $function()" unless defined(&$function);
                &$function(*CHILDSOCKET, @args);
            }
            else
            {
                return_error(*CHILDSOCKET,
                             "Error: Not a valid command\n");
            }
```

All of the code surrounding the additional code has been trimmed for clarity. Note that you can check the existence of the function within the script by using the **defined** function on the function variable. This type of script process is called a *dispatch table* and can make many operations that would otherwise need complicated and difficult-to-read **if** or **unless** statements very much simpler and quicker.

This trick of indirect function calling plays a part in many of the core aspects of Perl, including signal handlers and the methods that operate on Perl objects. It is certainly a topic we will return to a number of times throughout the rest of the book.

Packages

The main principle behind packages in Perl is to protect the name space of one section of code from another, therefore helping to prevent functions and variables from overwriting each other's values. Despite what you may have seen up to now, there is no such thing as a global variable—all *user* variables are created within the realms of a package. If no package name is specified, the package name is **main**.

You can change the current package to another by using the **package** keyword. The current package determines what symbol table is consulted when a user makes a function call or accesses a variable. The current package name is determined at compile and run time. This is because certain operations such as dereferencing require Perl to know what the "current" package is. Any **eval** blocks are also executed at run time, and the current package will directly affect the symbol table to which the **eval** block has access.

All identifiers (except those declared with **my** or with an absolute package name) are created within the symbol table of the current package. The package definition remains either until another package definition occurs or until the block in which the package was defined terminates. You can intersperse different package names in the same file and even specify the same package multiple times within multiple files. The **package** declaration only changes the default symbol table. For example, in the code below both the **add** and **subtract** functions are part of the **Basemath** package, even though the **square** function has been inserted within a **Multimath** package:

```
package Basemath;

sub add { $_[0]+$_[1] }

package Multimath;

sub square { $_[0] *= $_[0] }

package Basemath;

sub subtract { $_[0]-$_[1] }
```

The above example is probably not a good example of when a **package** is normally defined. Normally, the first statement within a new file would be used to define the package name for a module that would be imported via the **use** or **require** statement. Of course, there is nothing to stop you from using a **package** statement anywhere you would use any other statement.

You can reference a symbol entry from any package by specifying the full package and symbol name. The separator between the package and symbol entry is the double colon. You could refer to the **add** function above as **Basemath::add**. If you are referring to a variable, you place the character for the variable type before the package name, for example, **$Basemath::PI**. The main package can either be specified directly, as in **$main::var**, or you can ignore the name and simply use **$::var**.

Note *Perl4 and below used the ' symbol. This is currently still supported, but longer term, you should move to the :: notation. It's easier to read for a start, and editors that try to match quotes and parentheses don't fall over when you use double colons.*

You can also nest package names in order to create a package hierarchy. Using the math module again, you might want to split it into three separate packages. The main **Math** package contains the constant definitions, with two nested packages **Math::Base** and **Math::Multi**. The hierarchy does not introduce any additional symbol tables, so the variable **$Math::Multi::var** is not simply accessible as **$Multi::var**. You either need to change the current package with a **package** statement or refer to the variable with its full name.

The symbol table is the list of active symbols (functions, variables, objects) within a package. Each package has its own symbol table, and with some exceptions, all the identifiers starting with letters or underscore are stored within the corresponding symbol table for each package. This means that all other identifiers, including all of the special punctuation-only variables such as **$_**, are stored within the **main** package. Other identifiers that are forced to be within the **main** package include **STDIN**, **STDOUT**, **STDERR**, **ARGV**, **ARGVOUT**, **ENV**, **INC**, and **SIG**.

Finally, if you name any package with a name matching one of the pattern operators (**m//**, **s///**, **y///**, or **tr///**), you cannot use the qualified form of an identifier as a filehandle, as it will be interpreted as a pattern match, substitution, or translation.

Signals also need special care: when specifying a signal handler, you should ideally qualify the signal handler completely. See Chapter 10 for more information on specifying signal handlers.

Accessing Symbol Tables

The symbol table for a package can be accessed as a hash. For example, the **main** package's symbol table can be accessed as **%main::** or, more simply, as **%::**. Likewise, symbol tables for other packages are **%MyMathLib::**. The format is hierarchical so that symbol tables can be traversed using standard Perl code. The **main** symbol table includes a reference to all the other top-level symbol tables, so the nested example above could be accessed as **%main::Math::Base**.

The keys of each symbol hash are the identifiers of the symbols for the specified package; the values are the corresponding typeglob values. This explains the use of a typeglob, which is really just accessing the value in the hash for the corresponding key from the symbol table. The code below prints out the symbol table for the **main** package:

```
foreach $symname (sort keys  %main::)
{
    local *symbol = $main::{$symname};
    print "\$$symname is defined\n" if defined $symbol;
    print "\@$symname is defined\n" if defined @symbol;
    print "\%$symname is defined\n" if defined %symbol;
}
```

You can also use the symbol table to define static scalars, by assigning a value to a typeglob:

```
*C = 299792458;
```

You now cannot modify **$C**, the speed of light, since the variable **$C** does not really exist—Perl is just allowing us to access a typeglob as a scalar value. Note that uppercase is used for the constant, even though normally the speed of light is specified as "c." This is a convention in Perl. Constants and filehandles are typically in uppercase, variables and functions are lowercase, and package names are specified in title case. Although this is convention, Perl doesn't really care!

BEGIN and END

The **BEGIN** and **END** blocks in a package act as initializers and finalizers for the package. They are defined like this:


```
BEGIN { print "Start!\n" };
END   { print "End!\n"   };
```

A **BEGIN** block is executed as soon as possible after it has been defined. This overrides the parsing of the rest of the package. You can have multiple **BEGIN** blocks that are executed in the order they were defined. You can use a **BEGIN** block to import functions and values from other modules so that the objects required by the rest of the package are defined at the point the block is parsed. This can be especially useful if you are using the function prototyping and declarations seen earlier in this chapter. If a function has been defined such that it is interpreted as an operator, or with a specific prototyping format, then it will need to exist before Perl interprets the rest of the package.

An **END** routine is the opposite: it is executed as late as possible. In practice this means that an **END** block is executed at the point the parser and interpreter are about to exit to the calling process. This is the case even if the reason for the failure is a **die** function or the result of an exception raised due to the nonexistence of a required system call. You can use this facility to help print error messages or close filehandles cleanly in the event of an error. Of course, in a well-written Perl script, you should be able to find cleaner ways of handling exceptions and errors.

END blocks are executed in reverse order—that is, the last **END** block specified will be the first to be executed. The following program doesn't do quite what we want, although it's pretty close:

```
BEGIN { print "Eanie\n" }
die "Meanie\n";
END { print "Miney\n" }
END { print "Mo\n" }
```

You should not assume that the main program code has been executed in an **END** block. Care is needed to ensure you don't try to use a variable or function in an **END** block that has not otherwise been defined, although you should be doing this kind of checking in the main body of the script anyway.

Modules

A module is just another name for a package that has been moved to a separate file with the same name as the package, with the extension ".pm" attached. All of the extensions available within the standard Perl distribution are supplied as modules. There are two preferred ways to use a module: via either the **use** or the **require** statement. You can also import functions using the **do** and **eval** functions, although the use of these is deprecated, since both **use** and **require** do their own error checking at the time your program is parsed, rather than blindly accepting the supplied statements in **eval** or **do** as gospel at run time. Error checking still occurs, but because of the dynamic nature, it will occur within the execution cycle of your program.

In all cases, irrespective of how the module is imported into your program, it must return a true value, otherwise the import process assumes there was an error. You can do this in a number of different ways—complex modules may wish to decide on the status of other elements before they return a successful import. The most usual solution however is to place

```
1;
```

at the end of your module.

By default a module does not export its symbols to the symbol table of the package using it. However, you can configure this operation by using the **Exporter** module. Most exporter modules rely on this module, so it is a good base from which to learn the principles of the export process. To export the symbols from a module, you might use a header like this:

```
package MyMathLib;
require Exporter;
@ISA       = qw/Exporter/;
@EXPORT    = qw/add subtract/;
@EXPORT_OK = qw/$exponent square/;
```

The second line from the above example incorporates the **Exporter** module. This is the first format available for importing modules into the current package. There are some differences between the effects of **require** and **use**, which will be covered shortly.

The **Exporter** module provides the necessary methods for exporting the symbols from the **MyMathLib** module to the calling package. The **@ISA** array specifies the list of modules on which the module we are exporting is based. This has little relevance in a nonobject instance, but it is used by the **Exporter** module to make decisions about what other modules (or, more correctly, classes) must be imported in order for the current module to operate correctly. The easiest way to think of this variable is that you are defining the classes that this class "is-a" member of. In this instance, the module we are exporting is a member of the **Exporter** class, because we need the methods and functions supplied to export the symbols we have defined in the **@EXPORT** and **@EXPORT_OK** arrays.

use and require

When you import a module, you can use one of two keywords: **use** or **require**. The difference between the two will be discussed shortly, but in essence, a **require** statement imports the functions and objects only within their defined packages, but **use** imports the functions and objects so they are available to the current package as if they were defined globally.

The format of the **require** statement is

```
require Module;
```

The specified module is searched for in the directories defined in **@INC**, looking for a file with the specified name and an extension of .pm. You can also specify the full file name (and location, if necessary) by inserting the file name in single quotes:

```
require 'Fcntl.pl';
```

Furthermore, the **require** function can be used to specify that a particular minimum version of Perl is required. For example, to specify a minimum version of 5.003:

```
require 5.003;
```

This can be especially useful if a module or script you have written requires the features or functions of a specific version of Perl. If the specification does not match the version of Perl being used to execute the script, it will fail at compilation time.

The **use** keyword accepts one of two forms:

```
use Module;
```

and

```
use Module LIST;
```

The first format imports all of the symbols that have been specified in the **@EXPORT** array. You can therefore think of the **@EXPORT** array as listing the symbols that should be exported by default. The **@EXPORT_OK** array lists the additional symbols that can only be exported when the user requests them via the second form. For example, the line

```
use MyMathLib qw/add square/;
```

would cause only the **add** and **square** functions to be exported from the **MyMathLib** module.

What actually happens when you use the **use** statement is that Perl calls the **import** method defined in the specified module. If one has not been defined, the **Exporter** module supplies this method for you. The process without the **use** statement would therefore look something like this:

```
BEGIN
{
    require "Module.pm";
    Module->import();
}
```

Alternatively, you may not wish to import any symbols from the module, in which case you can use

```
use MyMathLib ();
```

or its **require** equivalent:

```
BEGIN { require MyMathLib; }
```

You can see from the above example that important difference: the **require** statement reads in the specified module, but it does not call the **import** method. This has the effect that symbols defined within another package do not update the current package's symbol table. For example,

```
require Cwd;
$pwd = Cwd::getcwd();
```

as opposed to:

```
use Cwd;
$pwd = getcwd();
```

One other significant difference between **require** and **use** is that **use** statements are interpreted and executed at the time the file is parsed and compiled. But **require** statements import modules at run time, which means you can supply a variable name to a **require** statement based on other elements of your program. This can be useful for dynamically selecting a different module to import, outside of the usual dynamic loading capabilities of the Perl module system.

The dynamic loading and autoloading features are generally used when you are extending Perl using external code written in C or Pascal or even Java. It's normally up to the module you import to autoload the external modules it requires. We'll look at the specifics of the autoloading process at the end of this chapter. Refer to Chapters 16, 17 and 20 for more details on using external C procedures within Perl.

You'll also notice from many of the latter examples that we are not specifying the full file name. By specifying a file name, we imply the full name and location of the file. If you do not specify the name in quotes, and leave off the extension, both **require** and **use** imply the .pm extension. The path used to determine the location of the files imported this way is the **@INC** array. This can be updated to allow other paths to be taken into account. The paths specified are the top directories. You can further subdivide modules into other subdirectories for clarity, in which case you must specify the relative pathname for the module you want to import, using the double colon notation in place of your operating system's pathname separator. For example,

```
use File::Basename;
```

actually imports the **File/Basename.pm** module on a Unix machine.

One final use of the **use** and **require** statements is to function as pragma mechanisms for affecting the behavior of the Perl compiler. This is something we will be examining in more detail in Chapter 16.

no

The **no** statement is the complete opposite of the **use** statement. It "unimports" meanings that have been imported via the **use** statement. It does this by calling a corresponding **unimport** method, if one has been defined, for a specified module. If no **unimport** method has been defined, Perl quits with a fatal error. Generally, **no** is only really required to switch off compiler pragmas, and we'll look at the use of the function in Chapter 16.

do

The **do** statement is rather like a cross between **eval** and the **require** and **use** functions, although it is neither as practical or user friendly as any of these functions. The format for the command is

```
do EXPR
```

where **EXPR** is the name of a file to be executed. The return value is taken as the evaluated value of the last statement in the file. If the file is not in the current directory, then the paths specified in the **@INC** array are searched instead.

The main difference between **do** and **require** is that the file specified by **do** will be executed each time it is called. The **require** function (and **use**), on the other hand, keeps track of the files it has imported and will only import a file once.

Scoping

Scoping affects the variables and functions that are available within a Perl package. You can control the scope of a variable in a number of different ways, some of which we have already seen. If you do not specify the scope, Perl assumes that the variable is a global value, within the current package.

To specify the scope of a variable, you use the **local** and **my** keywords to specify that a variable should be scoped within the specified block, subroutine, or **eval** statement. For example, consider the code below. Although a variable **$var** has been defined as global within the package, because a localized variable is defined within the function, it is the value of that variable that is printed:

```
$var = "Hello World\n";

sub hw
{
    my $var = "Hello Core\n";
    print $var;
}

hw();
print $var;
```

When run, this produces

```
Hello Core
Hello World
```

Also note that accessing the **$var** variable outside of the subroutine uses the global version again. Both **local** and **my** can be lvalues, so it is safe to assign a value to the specified variable or list of variables, as in the example above. If you do not specify a value, Perl initializes a scalar to the undefined value and an array or hash as an empty list.

There is a difference between the two keywords: **local** variables are dynamically scoped, and **my** variables are lexically scoped. Dynamically scoped variables are available both to the local block and to the functions called from within the block in which the variables are declared. Lexically scoped variables are truly localized to the current block—the variable is truly hidden from the outside world. This is true even if the function calls itself; a new localized variable is created for use by the new instance of the function.

In both cases the variable is cleared (deleted) from the symbol table when the block in which it was declared exits. As a general rule you should use **my** over **local**. The **my** keyword produces the result most people expect when they are localizing variables, and variables declared with **my** are also faster than those declared with **local**.

One advantage of **local** is that it can be used to modify the scope of an existing global variable. A commonly used trick is to localize the record separator variable in order to allow you to read the entire contents of a file into a scalar variable:

```
{ local $/; $file = <DATA>; }
```

Finally, the **my** keyword can be used in place to declare a variable within loops and other functions and operators. For example, you may want to localize the loop variable:

```
foreach my $key (keys %hash)
```

The **$key** variable will be localized to the **foreach** block, which guarantees that the **$key** variable you are accessing within the block is the one you want, not a variable defined elsewhere.

Autoloading

There are times when what you really want to do is use a subroutine that hasn't been defined. If a subroutine with the magic name **AUTOLOAD** has been defined within a package then any unknown subroutine calls are sent to this subroutine. The **AUTOLOAD** subroutine is called with all the same arguments as the unknown routine, and the fully qualified subroutine name is placed into the **$AUTOLOAD** variable.

This is traditionally used in combination with the **AutoSplit** module to automatically load functions from external script files where each file contains a single subroutine. What actually happens is that the **AUTOLOAD** subroutine uses **do**, **require** or **eval** to import and parse the external function into the current namespace. The **AUTOLOAD** subroutine then calls the special format of the **goto** function to make Perl (and the autoloaded subroutine) think that it was the function that loaded afterall.

This is effectively identical to the process used to load external C functions into the current namespace, however this is called dynamic loading and is handled by the **DynaLoader** module. However, the **DynaLoader** imports whole function suites, not single functions, and is generally used to import entire modules (and even base classes) at one time.

The **AUTOLOAD** module can also be used directly within a Perl script to add blanket functionality to a script without requiring you to create many subroutines. Here's an example that employs the **AUTOLOAD** routine as a way of introducing constants looked up from a hash:

```
BEGIN
{
    $constants{"PI"} = 3.141592654;
}

use subs keys %constants;
print "The value of PI is ",PI;

sub AUTOLOAD
{
    my $constant = $AUTOLOAD;
    $constant =~ s/.*:://;
    return $constants{"$constant"};
}
```

We actually use a few tricks here. First of all we create the **%constants** hash table in a **BEGIN** block to ensure it's defined as early as possible. The main reason for this is that we use the keys of this hash to the **use subs** pragma in order to predeclare the subroutines (or in this case, constants) that we want to use. By predeclaring them we set up Perl to allow us to use the 'functions' without requiring parentheses. See Chapter 16 for more details on this pragma.

Finally, we use the **AUTOLOAD** subroutine to lookup the value in the **%constants** hash and return the value.

The Complete Reference

Chapter 6

Managing Files, Users, Groups, and Time

It is almost impossible to make good use of a programming language without at some point having to access information about files. Accessing the information in a file is relatively easy, but unless you know the exact name of the file, you are basically stuck. Perl supports a number of ways of extracting the list of files, either by using the familiar wildcard operations that you use within a shell, or by reading individual file names directly from the directory.

You can also glean more information about the file you are using. You may need to find out the file size or perhaps the file permissions to test whether you can access a file. We will also take a look in this chapter at ways of controlling files, including deleting files, and creating and accessing symbolic and hard links.

Using files and filehandles effectively, particularly when using network sockets or providing an interactive user interface, also requires more complex controls on the abilities and data handling of individual filehandles. This can be achieved using **fcntl** and **ioctl**—two functions that provide an interface to the underlying operating system equivalents. Furthermore, in a complex installation you need to be able to handle data I/O between multiple files simultaneously. This can be achieved using a simple round-robin approach, but a more reliable and efficient method is to use the **select** function, which is examined in some detail in this chapter.

Accessing other external data structures is also covered in this chapter. We'll be investigating how to access the user and group information files under a Unix system. We'll also take the opportunity to look at how time information is stored in Perl and how to access this information and provide a more human version.

*All of the functions in this chapter are derived or descended from their operating system equivalents. It is vital that you check the return value of all the functions in this chapter, especially those that modify the execution environment for the script, such as **chdir** and **unlink**. In most cases, if there is an error, the error string is stored in the $! variable, which should be used with the **die** or **warn** function to report the error to the user. You'll see some examples of this.*

File Management

For most people the bulk of the data they want to process comes from the contents of a file. However, a significant amount of information is stored along with file data. The most obvious is the file's name, but this is often coupled with additional information about the file. This information is often called *metadata*, since it refers to metaphorical information about a file, rather than the file data itself. The exact specification of this information is reliant on the operating system, but it usually includes permissions (or attributes), ownership, and more trivial information such as modification times and the file size.

Perl provides an entire suite of functions for determining the metadata of a file. We'll start by looking at the basic test operators, **-X**, which return a Boolean response to simple queries about a specific file, such as whether the file can be read or written to. There is also a simple operator for finding the size, in bytes, of a specified file. We then move on to the **stat** and **lstat** functions, which return extended information from the directory entry for the specified file or link.

There is also a series of functions that enable you to create and manage files, including deleting files, creating hard and symbolic links, and obtaining the location of the file or directory that a particular link points to. We will also be examining methods for finding out the list of available files in a particular directory and how to access the entire directory contents.

Finally, we'll look at the more advanced operations available for control filehandles and I/O with a range of files using **fcntl**, **ioctl**, and the **select** function.

File Information

You can test certain features very quickly within Perl using a series of test operators known collectively as **-X** tests. The file test operators take either a file name or a filehandle, returning true, false, or a value, depending on the operator being used. The format of the operator is as follows:

```
-X EXPR
-X FILEHANDLE
-X
```

If you do not specify a file to get the information from, the operator uses the value of **$_** as a file name for all tests except **-t**, which instead uses **STDIN**. The full list of available tests is shown in Table 6-1.

For example, to perform a quick test of the various permissions on a file, you might use a script like this:

```
my (@description,$size);
if (-e $file)
{
    push @description, 'binary' if (-B _);
    push @description, 'a socket' if (-S _);
    push @description, 'a text file' if (-T _);
    push @description, 'a block special file' if (-b _);
    push @description, 'a character special file' if (-c _);
    push @description, 'a directory' if (-d _);
    push @description, 'executable' if (-x _);
    push @description, (($size = -s _)) ? "$size bytes" : 'empty';
    print "$file is ", join(', ',@description),"\n";
}
```

Operator	Description
-A	Age of file (at startup) in days since last access.
-B	Is it a binary file?
-C	Age of file (at startup) in days since last inode change.
-M	Age of file (at startup) in days since last modification.
-O	Is the file owned by the real user ID?
-R	Is the file readable by the real user ID or real group?
-S	Is the file a socket?
-T	Is it a text file?
-W	Is the file writable by the real user ID or real group?
-X	Is the file executable by the real user ID or real group?
-b	Is it a block special file?
-c	Is it a character special file?
-d	Is the file a directory?
-e	Does the file exist?
-f	Is it a plain file?
-g	Does the file have the setgid bit set?
-k	Does the file have the sticky bit set?
-l	Is the file a symbolic link?
-o	Is the file owned by the effective user ID?
-p	Is the file a named pipe?
-r	Is the file readable by the effective user or group ID?
-s	Returns the size of the file, with zero referring to an empty file.
-t	Is the filehandle opened by a TTY (terminal)?
-u	Does the file have the setuid bit set?
-w	Is the file writable by the effective user or group ID?
-x	Is the file executable by the effective user or group ID?
-z	Is the file size zero?

Table 6-1. *File Test Operators*

Note that after the first test I've used a special character, the underscore, which is a special filehandle. This is a buffer that holds the information from the last file name or filehandle test, or the last **stat** command. Using this special filehandle is more efficient than continually specifying the file, since this special filehandle stores all of the status information for the last file accessed. If you specify each file or filehandle individually, the physical device holding the file will be polled each time for the information.

Warning *Be careful of foreign language files with high-bit or special characters, such as characters with accents. They can sometimes be misinterpreted as a binary file when using -B or -T.*

Beyond this standard set of tests there is also a separate **stat** command that obtains further information about the file specified, including the physical device, underlying file system parameters such as the inode number, the owner and group permissions, and the access and modification times for the file. The information is returned by the function as a list:

```
($dev,  $inode, $mode,  $nlink, $uid,   $gid,     $rdev
 $rdev, $size,  $atime, $mtime, $ctime, $blksize, $blocks) = stat $file;
```

The full list of information supplied is shown in Table 6-2.

Element	Short Name	Description
0	dev	Device number of file system.
1	inode	Inode number.
2	mode	File mode (type and permissions).
3	nlink	Number of (hard) links to the file.
4	uid	Numeric user ID of file's owner.
5	gid	Numeric group ID of file's owner.
6	rdev	The device identifier (special files only).
7	size	File size, in bytes.
8	atime	Last access time since the epoch.
9	mtime	Last modify time since the epoch.
10	ctime	Inode change time (*not* creation time!) since the epoch.
11	blksize	Preferred block size for file system I/O.
12	blocks	Actual number of blocks allocated.

Table 6-2. *Data Returned by the stat Function*

Inodes

An *inode* is the name for a directory entry within a file system. The term inode comes from Unix, although all operating systems have a similar term for the inode. Both Macs and Windows use the term *directory entry*. Regardless of the operating system or file system type, the primary purpose for an inode or directory entry is to store the information about the physical location of the data that constitutes a file on the physical (or logical) device.

Because this is effectively a mapping structure between the data and the name the user gives the file, an inode is also used to store other information such as the ownership and security information and other data obtainable with the **stat** function. Inodes also play a part in the management of files.

The **stat** function uses the operating system **stat()** function to obtain information directly from the inode (see sidebar), returning the list. The information is very raw; for example, it returns user IDs rather than names, but using other functions seen elsewhere in this chapter, it's possible to extract the information to make it more usable.

The most complex procedure is the extraction of the permissions information, which is supplied back to use as a number, but needs to be treated as an octal value that many Unix programmers will be familiar with. The example below shows one method for extracting the information into a usable form using the logical **and** operator to compare known values against the value returned.

```
for $file (@ARGV)
{
     my ($mode,$nlinks,$uid,$gid,$size,$mtime) = (stat($file))[2..5,7,9];
     printf("%s %2d %-10s %-10s %8d %s  %s\n",extperms($mode),
                                                $nlinks,
                                                scalar getpwuid($uid),
                                                scalar getgrgid($uid),
                                                $size,
                                                scalar localtime($mtime),
                                                $file);
}


sub extperms ()
{
    ($mode) = @_;
    my $perms = '-' x 9;

    substr($perms,0,1) = 'r' if ($mode & 00400);
    substr($perms,1,1) = 'w' if ($mode & 00200);
    substr($perms,2,1) = 'x' if ($mode & 00100);
```

```
    substr($perms,3,1) = 'r' if ($mode & 00040);
    substr($perms,4,1) = 'w' if ($mode & 00020);
    substr($perms,5,1) = 'x' if ($mode & 00010);
    substr($perms,6,1) = 'r' if ($mode & 00004);
    substr($perms,7,1) = 'w' if ($mode & 00002);
    substr($perms,8,1) = 'x' if ($mode & 00001);
    substr($perms,2,1) = 's' if ($mode & 04000);
    substr($perms,5,1) = 's' if ($mode & 02000);
    substr($perms,8,1) = 't' if ($mode & 01000);

    $perms;
}
```


The script largely emulates the Unix **ls** command or, indeed, the Windows **dir** command. When run, it produces output similar to this:

```
rwxr-xr-x  7 root  root  512 Fri Jun 12 10:00:50 1998  /usr/local/atalk
rwxr-xr-x  2 root  root 1536 Tue Nov  3 22:17:09 1998  /usr/local/backups
rwxr-xr-x  4 root  root 3584 Wed Feb 17 12:12:32 1999  /usr/local/bin
rwxr-xr-x  3 root  root  512 Fri Jun 12 10:03:19 1998  /usr/local/com
rwxrwxrwx 15 root  root 1024 Sat Feb 20 06:57:26 1999  /usr/local/contrib
rwxr-xr-x  2 root  root  512 Sat Feb 20 07:04:19 1999  /usr/local/cpan
rwxrwxrwx  5 root  root  512 Wed Feb 17 13:08:56 1999  /usr/local/etc
rwxrwxrwx 10 root  root  512 Tue Jan 19 20:56:41 1999  /usr/local/http
rwxr-xr-x  6 root  root  512 Thu Aug 27 21:31:21 1998  /usr/local/include
rwxr-xr-x  2 root  root 4096 Mon Feb  8 10:14:58 1999  /usr/local/info
rwxr-xr-x 11 root  root 1024 Wed Jan 20 16:39:53 1999  /usr/local/lib
rwxr-xr-x  4 root  root  512 Fri Jun 12 10:30:39 1998  /usr/local/libexec
rwx------  2 root  root 8192 Thu Jun 26 13:31:45 1997  /usr/local/lost+found
rwxr-xr-x 16 root  root  512 Wed Jan 20 16:39:35 1999  /usr/local/man
rwxr-xr-x 11 root  root  512 Thu Jan 21 09:56:08 1999  /usr/local/nsr
rwxr-xr-x 10 root  root  512 Wed Feb 17 12:27:15 1999  /usr/local/qmail
rwxr-xr-x  6 root  root  512 Tue Jun 16 22:27:18 1998  /usr/local/samba
rwxr-xr-x  8 root  root  512 Tue Jun 16 23:52:46 1998  /usr/local/share
```

When accessing a symbolic link on a Unix system, the information returned by **stat** is that of the file the link points to, rather than the link itself. To return the information for the link (rather than the file it points to), you need to use the **lstat** function:

```
lstat EXPR
```

This returns exactly the same information as **stat**. (Refer to Table 6-2 for the list of information returned.) If your system does not support symbolic links, a normal **stat** operation is done instead.

Basic File Management

Under Unix, files are created on a file system by creating a link to an inode (see the earlier sidebar), which creates the necessary directory entry that links to the file data. Many of the functions for managing files therefore have a direct effect on the inode information without requiring you to access the file. The **rename** function is the first of these. It changes the registered name for a file:

```
rename OLDNAME, NEWNAME
```

The **OLDNAME** is the specification of the old file, and **NEWNAME** is the new name for the file. The function fails if it is unable to find the file or unable to change the file name (perhaps because it is open).

The next few functions all directly affect the existence, creation, or information about a link. The first is the **link** function. This creates a "hard" link to an existing file. A hard link is a new inode that points to an existing data stream—that is, it's a duplicate directory entry for an existing file. The duplicate has a different name and different permissions and access times. Only the inode field (from the **stat** function) is identical to the original:

```
link OLDNAME, NEWNAME
```

Creation of a new hard link updates the link count (the number of links to a file); the significance of this will be seen shortly. If the function fails, it returns a value of zero and sets the error string in **$!**. Note that you cannot create hard links across file systems because the new directory entry must refer to the inode of a file on the same file system; use symbolic links instead.

Since the notion of a duplicate directory entry for an existing file is a Unix feature, other operating systems are unlikely to support this option. They may however support symbolic links via the **symlink** function. Certainly MacOS and Windows support symbolic links in the form of aliases and shortcuts, respectively. A symbolic link is similar in principle to a hard link; however, rather than duplicating the information about an existing inode, a symbolic link contains a reference (the path) to the file you want to link to:

```
symlink OLDNAME, NEWNAME
```

Because a symbolic link is a reference to a file, rather than a physical pointer to a real file, you can create a symbolic link on any file system and have it point to any other file system.

Symbolic links do not update the link count either. This is significant because the link count of an inode is used by the file system to determine whether a file is to be deleted completely. The **unlink** function deletes a link from a file system. If you a delete a link, you are only deleting the directory entry that relates the file name you see in the file list to the physical file. By deleting a link, you effectively remove access to the file.

For most files you create, there will be only one link to the file (the name you originally gave it). Once the link count in the inode reaches zero, the file system deletes the file in question. In effect, therefore, the **unlink** function does not actually delete a file; it only decrements the link count for the inode number to which the directory entry relates.

```
unlink LIST
```

The function accepts a list of files to be deleted, or it uses the value of **$_** if you do not specify a list. Because the file globbing operator and functions return lists, that means all three of the examples below will work:

```
unlink $file;
unlink @files;
unlink <*.o>;
```

To delete directories, use the **rmdir** function. Although Perl supports the deletion of a directory via **unlink** (providing you are root and have specified the **-U** option on the command line), it's not advised. Removing the directory entry/inode for a directory without also deleting the files that refer to that directory can cause serious file system problems—probably not the effect you want.

Once you have created (or indeed identified) a symbolic link, any references to the link actually return the file contents that the link points to. This is sensible, since the link itself contains no valid information. However, you can find out the pathname of the file that the symbolic link points to using the **readlink** function:

```
readlink EXPR
```

The function returns the location of the file pointed to by the symbolic link **EXPR**, or **$_** if none is specified. If the value cannot be determined, or if **EXPR** is not a symbolic link, the function returns **undef**.

Also be aware that symbolic links can be relative to the location of the link, rather than a full pathname. The value returned to you will only be of any use if you are currently in the same directory as the link you are reading.

You may remember the access permissions information returned by **stat** earlier in this chapter. The access permissions (mode) of a file can also be set using the **chmod** function:

```
chmod MODE, LIST
```

The **MODE** should be the numerical value associated with a specific file mode. Normally, this information is represented as an octal value (as seen earlier). For example, to change the permissions of a file to be readable by everybody:

```
chmod 0444, $file;
```

The most common mistake when using this command is to specify a decimal rather than octal number. Remember that Perl identifies octal numbers by a leading zero, or you can use the **oct** function to convert a decimal value to its octal equivalent.

The **LIST** is the list of file names whose mode you want to change, and the function returns the number of files that successfully had their modes changed. To find out which files have not been successfully modified, you will either need to use a loop or use the **grep** function to identify the files in a list. For example:

```
@failure = grep { not chmod 0444, $_ } @files;
warn "Unable to change the mode of @failure" if @failure;
```

To change the user and group ownership of a file, you need to use the **chown** function:

```
chown USERID, GROUPID, LIST
```

The **USERID** and **GROUPID** are the numerical IDs of the user and group, and **LIST** is the list of files whose ownership you want to change. For example:

```
chown 1000,1000,@files;
```

Like the **chmod** function, it returns the number of files actually changed. You may want to use the **chmod** trick above if you are modifying a number of files.

Note that the user and group information must be specified numerically. You may want to use the **getpwnam** and **getgrnam** functions to obtain the IDs of user and group names, as in:

```
chown scalar getpwnam($user), scalar getgrnam($group), @files;
```

You'll see further examples of obtaining user and group information later in this chapter.

To modify the last access and modification time for a file, you need to use the **utime** function:

```
utime ATIME, MTIME, LIST
```

The **ATIME** and **MTIME** arguments specify the access and modification times you wish to set. The values should be specified as the number of seconds that have elapsed since the epoch. See the section "Time" at the end of this chapter for details on converting between the epoch value and date format.

For the example below the time specified is taken from the **time** function, which returns the number of seconds since the epoch at the time executed; so this script effectively emulates the Unix **touch** command:


```
$now = time;
utime $now, $now, @files;
```

Note in this example that the time is assigned to a variable before being set. This prevents two different times being set between invocations and also reduces the number of system calls. If you fail to specify a value, the corresponding time for the file is not modified. Like the previous two commands, the function returns the number of files that were successfully modified.

When creating a file using **open**, **sysopen**, or other functions, the mode of the file is determined by a combination of the mode specified the current umask. The umask is an octal permissions mask that specifies the permissions bits that cannot be set when a file is created. For example, with a umask of 0077, the read, write, and execute bits for group and other users cannot be set, even if the function creating the file specifies them.

```
umask EXPR
umask
```

The function returns the current mode, and if you do not specify **EXPR**, there is no modification of any kind to the umask.

Accessing Directory Entries

If you do not already know the name of the file you are trying to access, or if you want to specify a list of files but don't know where to get the list, you can use one of three methods. The first is similar to the filehandle operator:

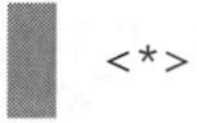

```
<*>
```

The pattern between the brackets is matched against the list of files in the current directory, or that specified within the pattern.

The pattern supports the standard file pattern matching of many shells on the Unix platform. Users of Mac and NT platforms may be unfamiliar with these, although they follow guidelines similar to the basic pattern matching supported by Perl regular expressions. The supported formats are very basic, and they only support the use of * as a wildcard for any number of characters and **?** as a wildcard for a single character. For example, to get a list of all of the files ending in ".c":

```
@files = <*.c>;
```

Other patterns that you may be familiar with within the shell, such as braces (for multiple options) and square brackets (for a single character from a set), are not supported. However, this is not a problem since you can use the **grep** function (discussed in the next chapter) to select a more specific list of files.

You can also use the standard variable interpolation to use a scalar variable as the pattern, but don't do

```
@files = <$pattern>;
```

since Perl will assume you're referring to an indirect filehandle (one specified by a variable, rather than a static tag). Instead either use braces to force interpretation as a file name glob,

```
@files = <${pattern}>;
```

or use the **glob** function, which is actually what calling the **<PATTERN>** operator does anyway. The **glob** function is also clearer: it is obvious to any reader that you are trying to do a file name glob, not access a filehandle.

The format for the **glob** function is identical to the operator. The above C source file example can be restated as

```
@files = glob("*.c");
```

Whether you use the operator or function, the return value in a scalar context is the next entry matching the specified pattern. If you don't assign the value returned to a variable in a **while** loop, the value is assigned to **$_**, so you can do

```
while (<*.c>)
{

}
```

Both the operator and function method for file name globbing invoke a subshell in order to expand the pattern supplied to a suitable file list. For quick searches this is not a major issue, but because you are using an external application to produce the list, you may run into a combination of both performance and memory allocation problems. This is definitely the case if your shell does not support large argument lists (and most shells don't).

To get around this problem, you can use the **opendir** function set. This facility is an interface to the underlying routines that the operating system supports, and it functions rather like a directory-specific filehandle. In fact you access it in a similar way, using a directory handle:


```
opendir   DIRHANDLE, EXPR
readdir   DIRHANDLE
rewinddir DIRHANDLE
telldir   DIRHANDLE
seekdir   DIRHANDLE, POS
closedir  DIRHANDLE
```

To use **opendir**, first you need to open the directory handle and associate it with the directory you want to examine. The **EXPR** should be a directory name, not a file specification, since the function set does not handle file name globbing. Once opened, subsequent reads to **readdir** on the specified filehandle return the next file name in the directory in a scalar context. In a list context the entire directory contents are returned. Once you have finished reading the directory names, you need to close the directory handle.

To list the contents of the directory:

```
opendir (DIR, '.') or die "Couldn't open directory, $!";
while ($file = readdir DIR)
{
    print "$file\n";
}
close DIR;
```

This circumvents all of the memory problems associated with the globbing operator and function, since each entry of the directory is retrieved individually.

Because the process of reading in from a directory is associated with a specific directory handle, you can have multiple handles open simultaneously. You can also record your position within a directory handle using the **telldir** function. The return value is an integer representing the current location within the directory list held within the instance of the directory handle. Unfortunately, even over short periods of time, this value is not guaranteed to actually return you to the location it originally indicated. This is because the number of directory entries may increase or decrease in size between the time you obtain the position information and when you attempt to move to that position using the **seekdir** function.

The best solution in these instances is to record not the theoretical position within an arbitrary directory list, but instead the actual pathname and file name you want to store. If all you want to do is start reading the directory entry list again, you can use the **rewinddir** function. This resets the pointer within the directory handle to the start of the list without the file pattern being reevaluated. Due to the nature of the directory handle system, a more reliable method for processing the same list of files a number of times is to use an array—providing, as ever, that the list size is not so great that it starts eating up too much memory in the process.

To emulate the globbing features of the **glob** function, you will need to check each individual file name or pass the list returned by **readdir** through the **grep** function. You can also use the opportunity to sort the list returned, since the **readdir** function does not return a sorted list. For example, to print the list of C source code files, you might use

```
opendir(DIR, '.') or die "Couldn't open directory, $!";
foreach (sort grep(/^.*\.c$/,readdir(DIR)))
{
    print "$_\n";
}
closedir DIR;
```

We'll be looking at the **sort** and **grep** functions in more depth in the next chapter.

Managing Directories

All programs are aware of their current directory. This is either the directory they reside in or the current directory of the application (such as a shell) that called the program. The system **chdir()** function is supported within Perl in order to change the current directory for the current process.

```
chdir EXPR
chdir
```

If you do not specify a directory to change to, Perl changes to the home directory for the current user. Under Unix this information is derived from the user's entry in the /etc/passwd file, and under NT it's the home directory defined in the environment variable **%HOME%**. On the Mac, if you do not specify a directory, it simply changes to the current directory (which means that it does nothing!). The function returns false if the function failed, or true if it succeeded:

```
chdir or die "Couldn't change back to the home directory, $!";
```

Perl does not support a built-in function for discovering the working directory. What is provided however is the **Cwd** module as part of the standard Perl library:

```
use Cwd;
print getcwd(),"\n";
```

The method used to discover the current working directory is basically the one that works on your system. In practice, most OSs support a **getcwd** function; others support a **pwd** command that returns the current directory. The **Cwd** module simply chooses the one that works each time **getcwd** is called.

For security reasons it can sometimes be necessary to create your own directory structure that contains a reduced set of devices and utilities, or you may want to restrict a user-defined function or process to a similar environment. Under Unix you also have the ability to change the root directory—the directory from which all "/" references are taken. This is not implemented under either the MacOS or Windows versions.

By changing the "root" of the current process to another directory, such as /etc/miniroot, you can guarantee that a call to a program of the form /sbin/shutdown actually executes /etc/miniroot/sbin/shutdown. The user may be unaware of the restricted directory structure and will be unable to access any directories above the one configured as the new root. For example, here's a line taken from a Perl-based web server. Without the restriction of the **chroot** function, it would be possible for a cracker to access the web page /etc/passwd—not the level of access we want to provide.

```
unless (chroot("/users/martinb"))
{
    warn "You are not root!\n" if ($>);
    die "Cannot change to root directory, $!";
}
```

You can only use the **chroot** function if you are root, and once set, there is no way to unset the root directory change (since all new references are relative to the previous **chroot** function call). The effect is inherited both by the current function and by any children, including those generated by **fork**, implicitly or otherwise.

You can make a new directory using the **mkdir** function:

```
mkdir EXPR, MODE
```

The **EXPR** is the name of the directory you would like to create, with the permissions specified by the octal **MODE**. If your operating system does not support a **mkdir** function within the C library, the command line **mkdir** program will be called, with

ADVANCED PERL PROGRAMMING

EXPR as the argument; so be wary of creating a large number of directories with this function if this is the case. Calling the external program puts extra overhead on the system, as it executes an additional program.

To remove a directory, use the **rmdir** function:

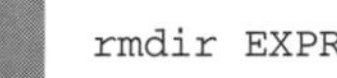

```
rmdir EXPR
```

The directory must be empty for the function to work. If an error occurs, the return value will be zero, and the **$!** variable will be populated with the error message. If the directory is not empty, the message is usually something like "File Exists"; so you may want to test specifically for this during execution, as in the example below:

```
unless (rmdir($dir))
{
    if ($! =~ /File Exists/i)
    {
        warn "Error removing directory: The directory is not empty";
    }
    else
    {
        warn "Error removing directory: $!";
    }
}
```

If you fail to specify an expression, the directory to remove will be taken from the **$_** variable, which may not be the desired result.

File Control with fcntl

The **fcntl** function is the Perl interface to the system **fcntl()** function, which enables certain file control operations on your files that are not supported by other functions. Typically, these are specific to an operating system, although many features are available across a number of different platforms.

```
fcntl FILEHANDLE, FUNCTION, SCALAR
```

The function performs the function specified by **FUNCTION**, using **SCALAR** on **FILEHANDLE**. **SCALAR** either contains a value to be used by the function or is the variable used to store any information returned by the corresponding **fcntl** function. To use **fcntl** effectively, you will probably want to import the **Fcntl** module with a

```
use Fcntl;
```

For all subfunctions of the **fcntl** function, the return value is slightly different in Perl from that returned by the operating system. A value of **–1** from the operating system is returned as **undef** by Perl, while a value of zero from the system is returned by Perl as **0 but true**. This equates to true in a test condition, but zero when evaluated as a number. For all other values the return values are the same for the operating system and Perl.

Since the **fcntl** functions are operating system specific, no details will be given on the **fcntl** function at this stage, but see Table 6-3 for some sample functions and Table 6-4 for a description of many of the constants you will need. You'll need to refer to your operating system documentation for details on the **fcntl()** functions supported on your system. Or examine the **Fcntl** module, which will contain a summarized list of the functions as a list of constants for use when using the command. We will be using some of the functions later in this chapter and elsewhere in the book.

If your system does not support **fcntl()**, a fatal error will occur.

Function	Description
F_DUPFD	Duplicates the supplied file descriptor, returning the lowest numbered file descriptor not currently in use. This is roughly equivalent to the ">&FH" format with the Perl **open** function.
F_GETFD	Returns the **FD_CLOEXEC** flag (see below) for the specified filehandle.
F_SETFD	Sets the state of the **FD_CLOEXEC** flag on the filehandle.
F_GETFL	Gets the current flags for the specified filehandle. These flags are identical to those you can specify during a **sysopen** function (see Table 6-4 for more information).
F_SETFL	Sets the flags for the specified filehandle (see Table 6-4 for suitable values).
F_GETLK	Gets the lock status for a specified filehandle; used to test whether a particular lock can be set on a file (see "File Locking" later in the chapter).
F_SETLK	Sets or clears a file segment lock (see "File Locking").
F_SETLKW	Identical to **F_SETLK**, except that the process will block until a read or write lock can be set on the specified filehandle (see "File Locking").

Table 6-3. *Example Functions for fcntl*

Constant	Description
FD_CLOEXEC	The close-on-exec flag—if set on a filehandle (it's set by default), it will be closed if its file descriptor number is greater than 2 (that is, not **STDIN**, **STDOUT**, or **STDERR**) when a new process is forked.
O_APPEND	File opened in append mode.
O_BINARY	File opened in binary mode.
O_TEXT	File opened in text mode.
O_NDELAY	Non-blocking I/O.
O_NONBLOCK	Non-blocking I/O.
O_RDONLY	File opened in read-only mode.
O_RDWR	File opened in read/write mode.
O_WRONLY	File opened in write-only mode.

Table 6-4. *Filehandle Flags for Use with fcntl*

I/O Control with ioctl

The **ioctl** function is similar in principle to the **fcntl** function. It too is a Perl version of the operating system equivalent **ioctl()** function.

```
ioctl FILEHANDLE, FUNCTION, SCALAR
```

The **ioctl** function is typically used to set options on devices and data streams, usually relating directly to the operation of the terminal. You will need to include the system **ioctl.h** header file, available in a Perl version, by doing

```
require 'ioctl.ph';
```

This will provide you with the necessary constants to use the **ioctl** function. A value of **–1** from the operating system is returned as **undef** by Perl, while a value of zero from the system is returned by Perl as **0 but true**. This equates to true in a test condition, but zero when evaluated as a number. For all other values the return values are the same for the operating system and Perl.

As a general rule, calls to **ioctl** should not be considered portable. When using terminals for a Perl interface, you may want to consider using a more portable module such as **Tk** to do the portability work for you. We'll be examining the use of the terminal and the **Tk** module in Chapter 13.

select

The second form of the **select** function (you may remember the first one was defined in Chapter 3 and set the "default" filehandle for **print**) is an interface to the system **select()** function. This function is for determining whether the filehandles you have specified are ready to accept input, supply output, or report an exceptional condition.


```
select RBITS, WBITS, EBITS, TIMEOUT
```

The **RBITS**, **WBITS**, and **EBITS** are bitmasks specifying the file descriptors that you want to monitor for reading, writing, and exceptional status, respectively. You can specify any of these as **undef** if you are not interested in the value. The bitsets are created by placing a value of 1 in each bit, with each bit number being equal to the file descriptor number (obtainable with **fileno**) that you want to monitor. You can create this structure using **vec**, for example:

```
vec($rbits,fileno(DATA),1) = 1;
```

The **TIMEOUT** specifies the interval to wait for the selection to complete. The **select** function will block until the time-out expires. If **TIMEOUT** is zero, the effect is the same as polling in a round-robin fashion—simply returning the current status without waiting.

The return value from the function is the number of filehandles that are waiting to be accessed, or on some platforms, it will return the number of filehandles and the time remaining on the time-out value:

```
($nfound, $timeleft) = select($rout=$rin, $wout=$win, $eout=$ein, $timeout);
```

The function also replaces the supplied scalar bitmasks with bitmasks defining the list of filehandles that require attention. The above example shows the best method for using the values of the bitmasks **$rin, $win**, **$ein** while returning the information into **$rout**, **$wout**, and **$eout**.

The problem with using most filehandles is that in order to monitor and read or write information from or to them, you need to "poll" each filehandle to see if it's ready. This is time consuming, especially with multiple files when a good proportion of them may not be ready. This is further complicated if your filehandles or network sockets are blocking (the default status). A blocking filehandle will cause a **<FH>**

operator or a **sysread** function to halt execution of the program until some data is ready to be read. The opposite is also true: if a filehandle or network socket is not ready to accept data, a **print** or **syswrite** function will also wait until it is ready. In some situations this is ideal; in others, particularly if you are handling multiple filehandles or a user interface, this is far from ideal.

The solution is to use **select**, which reports the status of the filehandle without attempting to access it, thereby ignoring the blocking state. A better alternative is to set a non-blocking operation on the filehandle using **fcntl**. Non-blocking I/O with **select** works as follows: First you need to open one or more filehandles—either genuine files, pipes, or network sockets—and then set them to be non-blocking using **fcntl**:

```
use Fcntl;
open(DATA,"ls|") or die "Couldn't open pipe, $!";
if ((fcntl(DATA,&F_GETFL,0) & O_NONBLOCK) != O_NONBLOCK)
{
    die "Can't set non-blocking status"
        unless fcntl(DATA,&F_SETFL,(fcntl(DATA,&F_GETFL,0) & ~O_NONBLOCK));
}
else
{
    die "Couldn't get non-blocking status";
}
```

Then, once the files are open and ready for access, you need to create the necessary bitsets for use with the **select** function. Since we're only reading from a pipe, we really only need to create the **RBITS** bitset, but the example below shows creation of all three for clarity:

```
$rbits = $wbits = $ebits = '';

vec($rbits, fileno(DATA), 1) = 1;
vec($wbits, fileno(DATA), 1) = 1;

$ebits = $rbits | $wbits;
```

You're now ready to start checking the status of the filehandles you want to monitor. Typically of course you'd do this in a loop as part of the main execution process, but for this example, we'll simply check the status once:

```
$nfound = select($rreq = $rbits, $wreq = $wbits, $ereq = $ebits, 0);
print "$nfound filehandle(s) waiting for input\n";
print "Expecting input from 'ls' command\n" if ($rreq && fileno(DATA));
```

If you put the above example together, and assuming there are no problems opening the **ls** command or setting non-blocking on the filehandle, you should get a result like this:

```
1 filehandle(s) waiting for input
Expecting input from 'ls' command
```

We'll return to the topic of using **select** on non-blocking I/O in Chapter 9, when we examine different methods for reading and writing network sockets.

File Locking

Using files in a single script environment does not often cause any sort of file access problems. But if you want to access a file that may be in use by another process (or another invocation of the same script), you need to support file locking. By "locking" a file, you can prevent it from being updated by another process at the same time you are using it. Furthermore, it can be used to stop other processes' even reading from the file, allowing you to update a file before it needs to be read by another process.

Note *When locking DBM databases, there is no built-in method for locking in the generic ODBM/NDBM/SDBM implementations. In these situations you must use **flock** or something similar. If you can use GDBM or Berkeley DB, these provide built-in file locking capabilities as part of the implementation. See Chapter 8 for more information.*

The main method for locking within Perl is the **flock** function.

```
flock FILEHANDLE, OPERATION
```

This supports file locking on the specified **FILEHANDLE** using the system **flock()**, **fcntl()** locking, or **lockf()**, in that order of preference. The exact implementation used is dependent on what your system supports. **OPERATION** is one of the static scalar values defined in Table 6-5, which can be obtained from the **Fcntl** module, although you must specify the symbols you want to import:

```
use Fcntl qw/LOCK_SH LOCK_EX LOCK_UN LOCK_NB/;
```

Here is an example of locking a mailbox before writing:

```
use Fcntl;
flock DATA, LOCK_EX;
print DATA $message;
flock DATA, LOCK_UN;
```

Operation	Result
LOCK_SH	Set shared lock.
LOCK_EX	Set exclusive lock.
LOCK_UN	Unlock specified file.
LOCK_NB	Set lock without blocking.

Table 6-5. *Locking Operations*

Note that **flock** will block process execution until such time as the requested lock can be achieved. The way to get around this is to use **$LOCK_NB**, which attempts to lock the filehandle without blocking. However, caution should be used here: you must make sure you test the result of the lock before you start using the file. When using **$LOCK_NB**, the result from **flock** will be true, irrespective of whether the lock succeeded.

In nearly all cases file locking is generally advisory, that is the fact the lock has been set does not guarantee that another application will not be able to access or overwrite the file. This is because all applications that use the file need to use the same file-locking mechanism. This is especially true if the underlying implementation is through the **flock()** function because of the way in which **flock()** sets its locks. You should also be aware that it is unlikely that **flock** will work over a networked file system. If you want to force the use of **fcntl**, you will need to use it directly; so the equivalent of the above example becomes

```
use Fcntl qw/F_SETLK LOCK_EX LOCK_UN/;
fcntl(DATA,F_SETLK,LOCK_EX);
print DATA $message;
fcntl(DATA,F_SETLK,LOCK_UN);
```

Another alternative is to use a separate file with a .lck or similar extension and check for that during execution. This only works if all processes are aware of the method of locking you are using. Both **flock** and **fcntl** have the advantage that they are operating system functions, so the information and locks are shared across the whole operating system.

In theory this means that a C program that uses file locking will also be aware of the locks imposed by a Perl script. It also means that all the operating system commands will also be aware of the locks imposed on different files. Of course, the exact system you use will often rely on the supported options for the platform you are using; **fcntl** is the most supported cross-platform solution.

Users and Groups

For most situations the built-in variables initialized at execution time provide the basic user and group information for the current script. To recap, the relevant variables are summarized in Table 6-6. Note that all of this information and the functions in this chapter are only really relevant on a Unix machine. Neither MacOS nor Windows have the same facilities, although the information about users and groups on each platform can be gained via platform-specific modules. See Chapters 21, 22, and 23 for details on the differences between the three main platforms and the modules available on each.

The most basic function for determining your current user name is the **getlogin** function, which returns the current user name (not uid) of the current process.

```
getlogin
```

The next two functions, **getpwuid** and **getpwnam**, return, in a list context, the user information as a list of scalar values based on the uid or user name supplied. These provide an interface to the equivalent system functions, which just return the information stored in the /etc/passwd file.

Variable	Description
$<	The real user ID (uid) of the current process. This is the user ID of the user who executed the process, even if running **setuid** (see Chapter 11).
$>	The effective user ID (uid) of the current process. This is the user ID of the current process and defines what directories and features are available.
$(	The real group ID (gid) of the current process. Contains a space-separated list of the groups you are currently in if your machine supports multiple group membership. Note that the information is listed in group IDs, not names.
$)	The effective group ID (gid) of the current process. Contains a space-separated list of the groups you are currently in if your machine supports multiple group membership. Note that the information is listed in group IDs, not names.

Table 6-6. *Perl Variables Containing Group and User Membership*

```
getpwuid EXPR
getpwnam EXPR
```

This returns the following:

```
($name,$passwd,$uid,$gid,$quota,$comment,$gcos,$dir,$shell) =
getpwnam EXPR;
```

In a scalar context each function returns the most useful value. That is, **getpwuid** returns the user name, while **getpwnam** returns the user ID. The details of the contents of each element are summarized in Table 6-7. Note that names are advisory; you can assign the details to any scalar.

By using these functions you can easily print the user name, as seen in the earlier example for printing directory entries. As another example, you can obtain the user name for the current user by using

Element	Name	Description
0	$name	The user's login name.
1	$passwd	The user's password, in its encrypted form. See "Password Encryption" later in this chapter for more details on using this element.
2	$uid	The numerical user ID.
3	$gid	The numerical primary group ID.
4	$quota	The user's disk storage limit, in kilobytes.
5	$comment	The contents of the comment field (usually the full name).
6	$gcos	The user's name, phone number, and other information. This is only supported on some Unix variants. Don't rely on this to return a useful name; use the **$comment** field instead.
7	$dir	The user's home directory.
8	$shell	The user's default login shell interpreter.

Table 6-7. *Information Returned by getpwent, getpwname, and getpwuid*

```
$name = getlogin || (getpwuid($<))[0] || 'Anonymous';
```

To read the entire contents of the /etc/passwd file, you could read and process the individual lines yourself. An easier method however is to use the **getpwent** function set:

```
getpwent
setpwent
endpwent
```

The first call to **getpwent** returns the user information (as returned by **getpwnam**) for the first entry in the /etc/passwd file. Subsequent calls return the next entry, so you can read and print the entire details using a simple loop:

```
while(($name,$dir)=(getpwent)[0,7])
{
    print "Home for $name is $dir\n";
}
```

In a scalar context the **getpwent** function only returns the user name. A call to **setpwent** resets the pointer for the **getpwent** function to the start of the /etc/passwd entries. A call to **endpwent** indicates to the system that you have finished reading the entries, although it performs no other function. Neither **setpwent** nor **endpwent** return anything.

Along with the password entries, you can also obtain information about the groups available on the system:

```
getgrgid EXPR
getgrnam EXPR
```

In a scalar context you can therefore obtain the current group name by using

```
$group = getgrgid($();
```

Or if you are really paranoid, you might try this:

```
print "Bad group information" unless(getgrnam(getgrgid($()) == $();
```

The **getgrgid** and **getgrnam** functions operate the same as the password equivalents, and both return the same list information from the /etc/group or equivalent file:

```
($name,$passwd,$gid,$members) = getgruid($();
```

The **$members** variable will then contain a space-separated list of users who are members of the group **$name**. The elements and their contents are summarized in Table 6-8.

There is also a **getgrent** function set for reading the entire group information in a loop:

```
while(($name,$members)=(getgrent)[0,3])
{
    print "$name has these members: $members\n";
}
```

Like the equivalent password functions, **setgrent** resets the point to the beginning of the group file, and **endgrent** indicates that you have finished reading the group file.

Password Encryption

All passwords on Unix are encrypted using a standard system function called **crypt()**. This uses an algorithm that is one-way—the idea being that the time taken to decode the encrypted text would take more processing power than is available in even the fastest computer currently available. This complicates matters if you want to compare a password against the recorded password. The operation for password checking is to encrypt the user-supplied passwords and then compare the encrypted versions with each other. This negates the need to even attempt decrypting the password.

The Perl encryption function is also **crypt**, and it follows the same rules. There are two arguments—the string you want to encrypt and a "salt" value. The salt value is

Element	Name	Description
0	$name	The group name.
1	$passwd	The password for gaining membership to the group. This is often ignored. The password is encrypted using the same technique as the login password information. See "Password Encryption" for more details.
2	$gid	The numerical group ID.
3	$members	A space-separated list of the user names (not IDs) that are members of this group.

Table 6-8. *Elements Returned by the getgrent, getgrnam, and getgrgid Functions*

an arbitrary string used to select one of 256 different combinations available for the encryption algorithm on the specified string. Although the rules say the size of the salt string should be a maximum of two characters, there is no need to reduce the string used, and the effects of the salt value are negligible. In most situations you can use any two-character (or more) string.

For example, to compare a supplied password with the system version:

```
$realpass = (getpwuid($<))[1];
die "Invalid Password" unless(crypt($pass,$realpass) eq $realpass);
```

The fact that the password cannot be cracked means the encryption system is useless for encrypting documents. For that process it is easier to use one of the many encryption systems available via CPAN.

Time

Date and time calculations are based around the standard epoch time value. This is the number of seconds that have elapsed since a specific date and time: 00:00:00 UTC, January 1, 1970 for most systems; 00:00:00, January 1, 1904 for MacOS. The maximum time that can be expressed in this way is based on the maximum value for an unsigned integer, 2^{-31} –1, which equates to Tue Jan 19 03:14:07 2038—a little more precise than the year 2000 rollover problem!

Note that this means Perl is completely Year 2000 compliant.

gmtime and localtime

To obtain the individual values that make up the date and time for a specific epoch value, you use the **gmtime** and **localtime** functions. The difference between the two is that **gmtime** returns the time calculated against the GMT or UTC time zones, irrespective of your current locale and time zone. The **localtime** function returns the time using the modifier of the current time zone.

```
localtime EXPR
localtime
```

In a list context both functions convert a time specified as the number of seconds since the epoch. The time value is specified by **EXPR**, or is taken from the return value of the **time** function if **EXPR** is not specified. Both functions return the same nine-element array:

```
# 0    1    2     3     4    5     6     7     8
($sec,$min,$hour,$mday,$mon,$year,$wday,$yday,$isdst) = localtime(time);
```

The information is derived from the system **struct tm** time structure, which has a few traps. The ranges for the individual elements in the structure are shown in Table 6-9.

Since the value returned is a list, you can use subscript notation to extract individual elements from the function without having to create useless temporary variables. For example, to print the current day, you might use

```
print (qw(Sun Mon Tue Wed Thu Fri Sat Sun))[(localtime)][6];
```

In a scalar context this returns a string representation of the time specified by **EXPR**, roughly equivalent to the value returned by the standard C **ctime()** function:

```
$ perl -e 'print scalar localtime,"\n";'
Sat Feb 20 10:00:40 1999
```

Element	Range	Notes
$sec	0..59	
$min	0..59	
$hour	0..23	
$mday	1..31	
$mon	0..11	This has the benefit that an array can be defined directly, without inserting a junk value at the start. It's also incompatible with the format in which dates may be supplied back from the user.
$year	0..	All years on all platforms are defined as the number of years since 1900, not simply as a two-digit year. To get the full four-digit year, add 1900 to the value returned.
$wday	0..6	This is the current day of the week, starting with Sunday.
$yday	0..366	
$isdst	0..1	Returns true if the current locale is operating in daylight savings time.

Table 6-9. *Ranges for the gmtime and localtime Functions*

The Perl module **Time::Local**, which is part of the standard distribution, can create an epoch value:

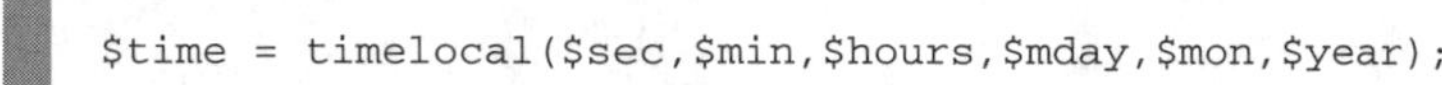

```
$time = timelocal($sec,$min,$hours,$mday,$mon,$year);
```

In most situations you should use **localtime** over **gmtime**, since **localtime** probably returns what you want. The only time to use the **gmtime** function is in a situation where a naturalized time is required for comparison purposes across time zones.

time Function

The **time** function returns the number of seconds elapsed since the epoch (see Chapter 21). You use this value to feed the input of **gmtime** and **localtime**, although both actually use the value of this function by default.

```
time
```

In addition, since it returns a simple integer value, you can use the value returned as a crude counter for timing executions:

```
$starttime=time;
for (1..100000)
{
   log(abs(sin($_)))*exp(sin($_));
}
$endtime=time;
print "Did 100,000 calculations in ",$endtime-$starttime, "seconds\n";
```

The granularity here is not good enough for performing real benchmarks. For that either use the **times** function, discussed next, or the **Benchmark** module, which in fact uses the **times** function.

Comparing Time Values

When comparing two different time values it is easier to compare epoch calculated times, i.e. the time values in seconds, and then extract the information accordingly. For example, to calculate the number of days, hours, minutes and seconds between dates:

```
($secdiff,$mindiff,$hourdiff,$ydaydiff)
        = (localtime($newtime-$oldtime))[0..2,7]
```

The **$secdiff** and other variables now contain the corresponding time value differences between **$newtime** and **$oldtime**.

times Function

The **times** function

```
times
```

returns a four-element list giving the CPU time used by the current process for user-derived and system-derived tasks, and the time used by any children for user- and system-derived tasks:

```
($user, $system, $child, $childsystem) = times;
```

The information is obtained from the system **times()** function, which reports the time in seconds to a granularity of a hundredth of a second. This affords better timing options than the **time** command, although the values are still well below the normal microsecond timing often required for benchmarking. That said, for quick comparisons of different methods, assuming you have a suitable number of iterations, both the **time** and **times** functions should give you an idea of how efficient, or otherwise, the techniques are.

Here's the benchmark example above, using **times**:

```
$starttime=(times)[0];
for (1..100000)
{
   log(abs(sin($_)))*exp(sin($_));
}
$endtime=(times)[0];
print "Did 100,000 calculations in ",$endtime-$starttime, "seconds\n";
```

sleep Function

You can pause the execution of a script by using the **sleep** function.

```
sleep EXPR
sleep
```

The function sleeps for **EXPR** seconds, or for the value in **$_** if **EXPR** is not specified.

The function can be interrupted by an alarm signal (see "Alarms" below). The granularity of the functions is always by the second. The accuracy of the function is entirely dependent on your system's **sleep** function. Many may calculate the end time as the specified number of seconds from when it was called. Alternatively, it may just add **EXPR** seconds to the current time and drop out of the loop when that value is reached. If the calculation is made at the end of the second, the actual time could be anything up to a second out, either way.

If you want a finer resolution for the **sleep** function, you can use the **select** function with undefined bitsets, which will cause **select** to pause for the specified number of seconds. The granularity of the **select** call is hundredths of a second, so the call

```
select(undef, undef, undef, 2.35);
```

will wait for 2.35 seconds. Because of the way the count is accumulated, the actual time waited will be more precise than that achievable by **sleep**, but it's still prone to similar problems.

Alarms

By using signals, you can set an alarm. This is another form of timer that waits for a specified number of seconds while allowing the rest of the Perl script to continue. Once the time has elapsed, the **SIGALRM** signal is sent to the Perl script, and if a handler has been configured, the specified function will execute. This is often used in situations where you want to provide a time-out for a particular task. For example, here's a user query with a default value—if the user does not respond after 10 seconds, the script continues with the default value:

```
print "What is your name [Anonymous]?\n";
eval
{
    local $SIG{ALRM} = sub { die "Timeout" };
    alarm 10;
    chomp($answer = <STDIN>);
    alarm 0;
};
if ($@ and $@ =~ /Timeout/)
{
    $answer = "Anonymous";
}
print "Hello $answer!\n";
```

The **eval** block is required so that the **die** statement which forms the signal handler drops out of the **eval**, setting the value of **$@**. You can then test that and decide how to proceed. Of course, the user provides some input; then the alarm is reset to zero, disabling the alarm timer and allowing you to drop out of the **eval** block normally.

We'll be looking in more detail at signals and signal handlers in Chapter 10, and at the use of the **eval** function in Chapter 11.

The Complete Reference

Chapter 7

Using Data Structures

A data structure is defined as the shape and layout of information and how pieces of information relate to each other. Within Perl, you have lots of options for creating data structures, and this chapter looks at both the simple base structures of arrays and hashes and the more complex nested structures, references, and objects.

The most basic of the available structures (beyond a simple scalar) is the array, which provides a list of scalar variables that use a sequential index. This also gives rise to lists, which are the arrays used to pass information between functions and operators.

You can also access binary data structures, such as those created by C, by using the **unpack** function to convert the binary format back into a list of scalars that you can access in Perl. Furthermore, using the **pack** function, you can convert a list of scalars back into the binary format. This is useful not only for communicating with the outside world, but also for storing data in fixed-length fields. This is actually covered in Chapter 8, but you may find the discussions in this chapter helpful.

A hash provides features similar to those of arrays except that you can refer to individual elements within the hash by a string, instead of an index number. This can be used to provide instantaneous access to a particular piece of information. Better still, it can be used to form records, where each element of the hash is the name of an array.

This is all very useful, but what if you want to use these record structures to create a set of records that are composed of individual hashes? In that case, you need to know about references—how to create them and how to use them. A reference is a pointer to another data structure and is stored in a scalar. Using references, you can create complex structures by storing a list of reference scalars in an array, or a hash, in order to produce arrays of hashes, or hashes of arrays, or arrays of arrays, or even hashes of hashes.

Furthermore, once you know how to use references, you can create objects, and objects open doors to all sorts of possibilities. The last section of this chapter deals with one particular use of objects, and that's to create associations between a particular variable type and a set of functions. You **tie** a particular variable to a corresponding class, and that class defines the individual methods used to access and update variables. The methods can provide access to anything—external data, complex internal structures, and even DBM databases.

Handling Arrays and Lists

The array data type, signified by a leading @ sign, is a list of scalars. Individual elements of the arrays can be referenced by a number, with the first element being identified as element zero, and further elements are referenced with a sequential numerical reference. When populating an array, you can either do it individually,

```
$users[0] = 'Bob';
$users[1] = 'Martin';
$users[2] = 'Phil';
```

or you can populate it directly using a list:

```
@users = ('Bob', 'Martin', 'Phil');
```

Note that the above list is signified by the enclosing parentheses. Each value from the list will be assigned to the elements of the **@users** array in order, such that **$users[0]** has a value of 'Bob'.

The option also works in reverse. A list on the left side of an equal sign assigns the individual values of the array to the individual scalars:

```
($bob, $martin, $phil) = @users;
```

If you don't specify enough scalars, then the rest of the array contents is discarded. Alternatively, you can use an array:

```
($bob, @rest) = @users;
```

The **@rest** array now contains two elements, 'Martin' and 'Phil'.

Individual elements of the array are accessed using "subscript" notation: the square brackets define that you want to extract a single element or a group of elements. Element references always start at zero. You can also specify a list of values in the square brackets, separated by commas, and you can use the range notation to specify both a range of elements and individual elements. This is a commonly used feature of arrays and is called slicing:

```
@selectusers = @allusers[0,4,5..10,14..17,20];
```

The above example would return a new list, consisting of the name elements and element ranges. The new array will contain 13 elements, irrespective of whether the **@allusers** array contains elements at the specified index values.

Note that when you access a single element, you use a **$** prefix to signify that you are expecting a scalar; but when splicing, you use the **@** prefix to show that you are expecting an array. Also note the value returned is a list, such that you can shorten the earlier **@rest** assignment to

```
@rest = @users[1..2];
```

A list is the structure returned when a list of scalars, or an array, is returned by a function. For example, the **getpwent** function, which you saw in Chapter 6, returns a list of information. Lists can be handled much like arrays, although there are some minor differences between the two. Whenever an array is placed on the right side of an equal sign, the value returned is a list. This feature enables you to concatenate arrays into a single array:

```
@users     = qw/Bob Martin Phil/;
@moreusers = qw/Bruce Tracy Adam/;
@allusers  = @users, @moreusers;
```

The **@allusers** array now contains all six array elements. The above example uses the **qw** operator, which allows you to automatically quote and separate bare words into list elements. Finally, to concatenate an array, you assign the array with its own value plus the new values. So in the previous example, to add **@moreusers** to **@users**:

```
@users = @users, @moreusers;
```

Returning to the **getpwent** function, and indeed any function that returns a list, you can extract elements from the list returned by using subscript notation. You can therefore shorten the following code

```
@userinfo = getpwent();
$name = $userinfo[0];
$uid  = $userinfo[2];
```

to:

```
($name, $uid) = (getpwent())[0,2];
```

You must use an additional pair of parentheses around the function call to ensure that Perl recognizes that you are treating the function call's return value as a list and that you want to access the individual elements of that list. If you forget this, the interpreter reports an error, so it should become second nature over time.

Of course, you already know that many functions also accept a list of values, which can be supplied as a comma-separated list of scalars, or you can pass an entire array to a function. We'll see some more examples of this later in this chapter. Because a list can be accepted by or returned by a function, you can use a number of function calls together in order to simplify a process that would otherwise take many lines and create many array structures:

```
foreach (reverse sort keys %hash)
```

This returns a list of the keys from the **%hash** structure, sorts them, puts them into reverse order, and passes the list on to **foreach**, which will then assign each element to the **$_** variable. We'll examine these functions, and others, in more detail throughout this chapter.

When writing your own subroutines, you can identify whether the caller is expecting a list using the **wantarray** function, which returns true if this is the case. If you want to force scalar context onto a particular function, you can use the **scalar** function to impose the scalar context. This will cause **wantarray** to return false, instead of true.

Incidentally, the value returned when you request the scalar value of an entire array (or list) is the number of elements. Note that this value is one more than the value of **$#array**, which returns the highest element index. Using the **@allusers** array:

```
print scalar @allusers, "\n";
print "$#allusers\n";
```

This prints a value of six and five, respectively.

The previous examples all use static numerical indexes. Perl also supports the use of functions and expressions within the **[]**, for example:

```
$value = $array[$index+2];
$value = $array[myindex('Timmy')];
$rand  = $array[int(rand(@array))-1];
```

Note in this example the nested reference. The scalar value of **@array** is passed to the **rand** function, which implies the maximum range.

Stacks

One of the most basic uses for an array is as a stack. If you consider that an array is a list of individual scalars, it should be possible to treat it as if it were a stack of papers. Index zero of the array is the bottom of the stack, and the last element is the top. You can put new pieces of paper on the top of the stack (**push**), or put them at the bottom (**unshift**). You can also take papers off the top (**pop**) or bottom (**shift**) of the stack.

There are in fact four different types of stacks that you can implement. By using different combinations of the Perl functions, you can achieve all the different combinations of LIFO, FIFO, FILO, and LILO stacks, as shown in Table 7-1.

Acronym	Description	Function Combination
LIFO	Last in, first out	**push/pop**
FIFO	First in, first out	**unshift/pop**
FILO	First in, last out	**unshift/shift**
LILO	Last in, last out	**push/shift**

Table 7-1. *Stack Types and Functions*

pop and push

```
pop ARRAY
pop
```

Returns the last element of **ARRAY**, removing the value from the list. If you don't specify an array, it pops the last value from the **@ARGV** special array when you are within the main program. If called within a function, it takes values from the end of the @_ array instead.

The opposite function is **push**:

```
push ARRAY, LIST
```

This pushes the values in **LIST** on to the end of the list **ARRAY**. Values are pushed onto the end in the order supplied.

shift and unshift

```
shift ARRAY
shift
```

Returns the first value in an array, deleting it and shifting the elements of the array list to the left by one. Like its cousin **pop**, if **ARRAY** is not specified, it shifts the first value from the @_ array within a subroutine, or the command line arguments stored in **@ARGV** otherwise.

The opposite is **unshift**, which places new elements at the start of the array:

```
unshift ARRAY, LIST
```

This places the elements from **LIST**, in order, at the beginning of **ARRAY**. Note that the elements are inserted strictly in order, such that the code

```
unshift @array, 'Bob', 'Phil';
```

will insert 'Bob' at index zero and 'Phil' at index one.

Note that **shift** and **unshift** will affect the sequence of the array more significantly (because the elements are taken from the first rather than last index). Therefore, care should be taken when using this pair of functions.

However, the **shift** function is also the most practical when it comes to individually selecting the elements from a list or array, particularly the **@ARGV** and @_ arrays. This is because it removes elements in sequence: the first call to **shift** takes element 0, the next takes what was element 1, and so forth.

The **unshift** function also has the advantage that it inserts new elements into the array at the start, which can allow you to prepopulate arrays and lists before the information provided. This can be used to insert default options into the **@ARGV** array for example.

Splicing Arrays

The normal methods for extracting elements from an array leave the contents intact. Also, the **pop** and other statements only take elements off the beginning and end of the array or list, but sometimes you want to copy and remove elements from the middle. This process is called splicing and is handled by the **splice** function.

```
splice ARRAY, OFFSET, LENGTH, LIST
splice ARRAY, OFFSET, LENGTH
splice ARRAY, OFFSET
```

The first argument is the array that you want to remove elements from, and the second argument is the index number that you want to start extracting elements from. The **LENGTH**, if specified, removes that number of elements from the array. If you don't specify **LENGTH**, it removes all elements to the end of the array. If **LENGTH** is negative, it leaves that number of elements on the end of the array.

Finally, you can replace the elements removed with a different list of elements, using the values of **LIST**. Note that this will replace any number of elements with the new **LIST**, irrespective of the number of elements removed or replaced. The array will shrink or grow as necessary. For example, in the code below the middle of the list of users is replaced with a new set, putting the removed users into a new list:

```
@users = qw/Bob Martin Phil Dave Alan Tracy/;
@newusers = qw/Helen Dan/;
@oldusers = splice @users, 1, 4, @newusers;
```

This sets **@users** to

```
Bob Helen Dan Tracy
```

and **@oldusers** to

```
Martin Phil Dave Alan
```

join

When you use the **print** function to print an array, the value of **$,** is used to separate the individual elements:

```
$, = '::';
print @array,"\n";
```

The default value for **$,** is nothing, and you should be aware that if you specify the array within double quotes, the value used is always a space.

When you want to create a new scalar containing a list of separated elements, you have to use the **join** function:

```
join EXPR, LIST
```

This combines the elements of **LIST**, returning a scalar where each element is separated by the value of **EXPR** to separate each element. Note that **EXPR** is a simple expression, not a regular expression. If you want to join elements using a regular expression, try **awk**:

```
print join(', ',@users);
```

Of course, **join** is a more practical solution if you don't want to constantly modify the value of **$,**, but you could also argue that **join** uses more processor cycles. There's actually very little difference between the two, since they both use the same internal function.

split

The **split** function is not strictly for handling arrays, but it does return an array and is essentially the opposite of the **join** function. The **split** function separates a scalar or other string expression into a list, using a regular expression.

```
split /PATTERN/, EXPR, LIMIT
split /PATTERN/, EXPR
split /PATTERN/
split
```

By default, empty leading fields are preserved, and empty trailing fields are deleted.

If you do not specify a pattern, then it splits **$_**, using white space as the separator pattern. This also has the effect of skipping the leading white space in **$_**. For reference, white space includes spaces, tabs (vertical and horizontal), line feeds, carriage returns, and form feeds.

The **PATTERN** can be any standard regular expression. You can use quotes to specify the separator, but you should instead use the match operator and regular expression syntax.

If you specify a **LIMIT**, then it only splits for **LIMIT** elements. If there is any remaining text in **EXPR**, it is returned as the last element with all characters in text. Otherwise, the entire string is split, and the full list of separated values is returned. If you specify a negative value, Perl acts as if a huge value has been supplied and splits the entire string, including trailing null fields.

For example, to split a line from the /etc/passwd file by the colons used to identify the individual fields:

```
while (<PASSWD>)
{
    @fields = split /:/;
}
```

You can also use all of the normal list and array constructs to extract and combine values

```
print join(" ",split /:/),"\n";
```

and even extract only select fields:

```
print "User: ",(split /:/)[0],"\n";
```

If you specify a null string, it splits **EXPR** into individual characters, such that

```
print join('-',split(/ */, 'Hello World')),"\n";
```

produces:

```
H-e-l-l-o--W-o-r-l-d
```

Note the inclusion of the space in the outputted string.

In a scalar context, the function returns the number of fields found and splits the values into the @_ array using **??** as the pattern delimiter, irrespective of supplied arguments; so care should be taken when using this function as part of others.

grep

The **grep** function works the same as the **grep** command does under Unix, except that it operates on a list rather than a file. However, unlike the **grep** command, the function is not restricted to regular expression searches, even though that is what it is usually used for.

```
grep BLOCK LIST
grep EXPR, LIST
```

The function evaluates the **BLOCK** or **EXPR** for each element of the **LIST**. For each statement in the expression or block that returns true, it adds the corresponding element to the list of values returned. Each element is parsed to the expression or block as a localized **$_**. A search for the word "text" on a file can therefore be performed with:

```
@lines = <FILE>;
print join("\n", grep { /text/ } @lines);
```

A more complex example, which returns on the elements that exist in a corresponding hash, is shown below:

```
print join(' ', grep { defined($hash{$_}) } @array);
```

In a scalar context, the function just returns the number of times the statement matched.

map

The **map** function performs an expression or block expression on a list. This enables you to bulk modify a list without the need to explicitly use a loop.

```
map EXPR, LIST
map BLOCK LIST
```

The individual elements of the list are supplied to a locally scoped **$_**, and the modified array is returned as a list to the caller. For example, to convert all the elements of an array to lowercase:

```
@lcarray = map { lc } @array;
```

This is itself just a simple version of:

```
for(my $i=0; $i<@array;$i++)
{
   $array[$i]=lc($array[$i]);
}
```

Note that because **$_** is used to hold each element of the array, it can also modify an array in place, so you don't have to manually assign the modified array to a new one. However, this isn't supported, so the actual results are not guaranteed. This is especially true if you are modifying a list directly rather than a named array, such as:

```
@new = map {lc} keys %hash;
```


sort

With any list it can be useful to sort the contents. Doing this manually is a complex process, so Perl provides a built-in function that takes a list and returns a lexically sorted version. For practicality, it also accepts a function or block that can be used to create your own sorting algorithm.

```
sort SUBNAME LIST
sort BLOCK LIST
sort LIST
```

Both the subroutine and block (which is an anonymous subroutine) should return a value—less than, greater than, or equal to zero—depending on whether the two elements of the list are less than, greater than, or equal to each other. The two elements of the list are available in the **$a** and **$b** variables.

For example, to do a standard lexical sort:

```
sort @array;
```

Or to specify an explicit lexical subroutine:

```
sort { $a cmp $b } @array;
```

To perform a reverse lexical sort:

```
sort { $b cmp $a } @array;
```

All the preceding examples are case-specific, differentiating between upper- and lowercase. You can use the **lc** or **uc** functions within the subroutine to ignore the case of the individual values. The individual elements are not actually modified; it only affects the values being compared during the sort process:

```
sort { lc($a) cmp lc($b) } @array;
```

If you know you are sorting numbers, you need to use the **<=>** operator:

```
sort { $a <=> $b } @numbers;
```

Alternatively, to use a separated routine:

```
sub lexical
{
    $a cmp $b;
}
sort lexical @array;
```

Of course, to sort a more complex structure, you can be more specific. We'll look at some examples of this when we look at complex structures later in this chapter.

reverse

On a sorted list you can use **sort** to return a list in reverse order by changing the comparison statement used in the sort. Alternatively for sorted and unsorted lists it is generally more practical to use the **reverse** function.

```
reverse LIST
```

In a list context the function returns the elements of **LIST** in reverse order. This is often used with the **sort** function to produce a reverse sorted list:

```
foreach (reverse sort keys %hash)
{
...
}
```

In a scalar context it returns a concatenated string of the values of **LIST**, with all bytes in opposite order. This also works if a single element list (or a scalar!) is passed, such that

```
print scalar reverse("Hello World"),"\n";
```

produces:

```
dlroW olleH
```

Accessing Structures

When storing information, and especially when exchanging information, it is essential to use a standardized format. The only recognized standardized format is binary, but converting textual and numerical data into a binary format is a difficult process to get right. Perl supports two functions that will do the conversion for you: **pack** converts a list into a binary structure, and **unpack** converts it back into a list.


```
pack EXPR, LIST
```

The **EXPR** is the template for the binary structure you want to create. The format is specified using the characters shown in Table 7-2.

Character	Description
@	Null fill to absolute position.
a	An ASCII string, will be null padded.
A	An ASCII string, will be space padded.
b	A bit string (ascending bit order).
B	A bit string (descending bit order).
c	A signed char value.
C	An unsigned char value.
d	A double-precision float in the native format.
f	A single-precision float in the native format.
H	A hex string (high nibble first).
h	A hex string (low nibble first).
i	A signed integer value.
I	An unsigned integer value.

Table 7-2. *pack Format Characters*

Character	Description
l	A signed long value.
L	An unsigned long value.
N	A long in "network" (big endian) order.
n	A short in "network" (big endian) order.
p	A pointer to a null-terminated string.
P	A pointer to a structure (fixed-length string).
s	A signed short value.
S	An unsigned short value.
u	A uuencoded string.
V	A long in "VAX" (little endian) order.
v	A short in "VAX" (little endian) order.
w	A BER compressed integer
x	A null byte.
X	Back up a byte.

Table 7-2. *pack Format Characters* (continued)

Each element of the list is packed according to the corresponding template. Each template character can be followed by a number specifying that the particular value type should be repeated that number of times.

Note that each specification applies to each element, so the format "a20" packs a single element to a null-padded size of 20 characters. The format "a20a20" packs two elements, each null padded and each 20 characters in size.

However, the repeat for individual character types applies only to the "a," "A," "b," "B," "h," "H," and "p," "P," types. For "a" and "A," it packs a string to the specified length. For "b" and "B," it packs a string that many bits long; for "h" and "H," that many nibbles (a nibble is 4-bits) long. For all other types, the function gobbles up that number of elements, such that the template "i20" will pack 20 elements as signed integers. If you specify "*" as the repeat count, then it gobbles up all the remaining elements in the list.

The floating-point packed values are not platform independent, so don't rely on these values for exchanging information between different platforms. You might try using a packed string instead and let Perl handle the conversion of the string into a platform-dependent double value. Also be aware that Perl uses doubles internally for floating-point numbers, so packing a double into a float and then unpacking again may not yield the same value.

Values can be unpacked with the **unpack** function:

```
unpack FORMAT, EXPR
```

This returns a list of values extracted using the specified **FORMAT** from the packed binary string **EXPR**.

The **pack** and **unpack** functions are primarily used for converting between different number formats, for creating fixed-length records for use internally and in external databases, and also for accessing stored C structures within Perl.

The first use makes use of the different number formats supported by the **pack** function. For example, to convert a 32-bit binary string into a number:

```
print unpack('I',pack("B32",'0' x 24 . '00001111')),"\n";
```

This should print 15—the value of 1111 in binary.

The second use makes use of the fact that you can specify field widths and store these fixed-width fields in a file. There are other issues surrounding this, so the information on this and other database methods in Perl are discussed in Chapter 8.

The third use is more complex, but uses many of the core principles you already know. All you need to do is know how to read a C structure and then use the **pack** and **unpack** functions to convert Perl lists to and from the specified format. For example, the **utmp** structure, which is used to store information about logins, has the following structure definition:

```
struct utmp {
    char ut_user[8];              /* User login name */
    char ut_id[4];                /* /etc/inittab id */
    char ut_line[12];             /* device name */
    short ut_pid;                 /* process ID */
    short ut_type;                /* type of entry */
    struct exit_status ut_exit; /* The exit status of a process */
                                  /* marked as DEAD_PROCESS. */
    time_t ut_time;               /* time entry was made */
};
```

This can be modeled within a pack template as "a8a4a12ssssl." Below is a script that outputs the information stored in the /var/adm/wtmp file, which uses the native format of the above structure:

```
my $packstring = "a8a4a12ssssl";
my $reclength = length(pack($packstring));
my @ut_types = qw(EMPTY RUN_LVL BOOT_TIME OLD_TIME
                  NEW_TIME INIT_PROCESS LOGIN_PROCESS
                  USER_PROCESS DEAD_PROCESS ACCOUNTING);

open(D,"</var/adm/wtmp") or die "Couldn't open wtmp, $!";

while(sysread(D,my $rec,$reclength))
{
    my ($user,$userid,$line,$pid,$type,$eterm,$eexit,$time)
        = unpack($packstring,$rec);
    print("$user, $userid, $line, $pid, $ut_types[$type], ",
          "$eterm, $eexit, ", scalar localtime($time),"\n");
}

close(D) or die "Couldn't close wtmp, $!";
```

The **unpack** function takes the binary string created by the C structure and returns it as a list, which you can then use to print out the information.

There are other uses for the **pack** and **unpack** functions, and we'll see some examples of these in the next few chapters.

You can also use the **unpack** function to provide a checksum for a given byte stream. The format is to prefix the packed type with **%number**, where **number** is the number of bits to use for the checksum. For example, to calculate the checksum for a character string:

```
$checksum = unpack("%32C*", $string);
```

The same trick can be used to count the number of set bits in a bit vector (such as that created by **vec**):

```
$bits = unpack("%32b*", $bitset);
```

Handling Hashes

Hashes work much the same as arrays, except that instead of a numerical (and also sequential) index, you can refer to individual scalars within the hash by a unique string value instead of a number. A hash is also known as an associative array, because there is an association between the string key and the corresponding value. You can populate hashes in two ways, either by explicitly defining the relationship, as in

```
$hash{'Bob'} = 'Manager';
$hash{'Sam'} = 'Tealady';
$hash{'Tim'} = 'Villager';
```

or by using the implicit form:

```
%hash = ('Bob', 'Manager', 'Sam', 'Tealady', 'Tim', 'Villager');
```

Perl interprets the first element of the list as the first key and the next element as the value. Subsequent key/value pairs are assumed according to pairs of elements. To make this process easier, you can use the **=>** operator, which is merely an alias for the comma:

```
%hash = ('Bob' => 'Manager',
         'Sam' => 'Tealady',
         'Tim' => 'Villager'
        );
```

This makes it clearer to the reader as to what you are attempting to do, although it makes no difference to Perl.

When used in a hash context, the reverse of the above assignment occurs. The hash is resolved into a simple list with keys and values appearing as pairs of elements. You can also use the **each**, **keys**, and **values** functions to extract pairs and individual sequences of information from a hash. However, it should be noted that a hash has no formal order. There is no guarantee that two accesses to the same hash will return elements in the same order. This shouldn't matter, however, since you do not access elements of a hash by using a numerical index value.

In a scalar context, a hash returns a string that defines the number of allocated blocks (called buckets) and used blocks in the entire hash structure. If you want to obtain the number of elements in the hash, imply scalar context on the **keys** functions. For example, the script

```
%hash = glob('/usr/lib/*');

print scalar %hash,"\n";
print scalar keys %hash,"\n";
```

returns:

```
64/128
105
```

On my machine, this indicates that there are 105 key/value pairs, but 64 out of 128 buckets have been used to store the information.

Hashes also accept expressions within the {} braces, just like indexes within arrays:

```
print $hash{lc($key)];
print $hash{"key-$field-$record"};
```

each

Because a single element of a hash consists of two strings, the key and the value, you cannot use the same functions or tricks with hashes that you can with arrays. For that reason there are a number of functions that support accessing key/value pairs individually, or obtaining entire lists of all the keys or values in a hash.

```
each HASH
```

The **each** function allows you to iterate over all the key/value pairs in a hash sequentially. There is no facility for sorting, and the information is returned in a random order. Since it only returns two arguments, it can be used to iterate through very large lists in a loop without Perl creating large temporary lists to store keys or values. When the end of the hash is reached, it returns a null list and is therefore safe to be used within loops. For example:

```
while (($key, $value) = each(%hash))
{
    print "$key=$value\n";
}
```

Alternatively, in a scalar context, it returns only the key:

```
while ($key = each(%hash))
{
    print "$key=$hash{$key}\n";
}
```

The same iterator (and therefore sequence and position within the hash) is used for every call to **each**. If you want to start back at the beginning of a hash, you must re-evaluate the entire hash, which is easiest to do with the **keys** function:

```
keys %hash;
```

Or you can use the **values** function, but note that in both cases the evaluation should be in scalar rather than list context:

```
scalar values %hash;
```

While within the iterator loop, you shouldn't add elements to the hash, since this will only confuse the **each** function. You can, however, delete elements from the list using **delete**.

keys

The **keys** function returns a list of all the keys in a hash.

```
keys HASH
```

The order of the keys returned is random, actually sharing the same order as the **each** function. The typical use is within a loop:

```
foreach (keys %hash)
{
    print "$_=$hash{$_}\n";
}
```

Since the function returns a simple list of the keys, you can use the **sort** function to sort the list of keys (and therefore, presumably, the information stored therein). This is usually employed directly within a loop:

```
foreach (sort keys %hash)
```

However, don't be tempted to do this

```
foreach (sort keys %oldhash)
{
```

```
        $newhash{$_} = $oldhash{$_};
    }
```

and expect **%newhash** to contain an ordered list of key/value pairs. It won't. It will just contain a copy of **%oldhash** and will return a random list of key/value pairs when accessed again.

Either way, you should always be careful when using the **keys** function on large hashes (such as a DBM file), since it will return a suitably large list. This may cause a problem if you are running short of memory. In this case it's probably best to use **each**, although be aware that you can't sort **each** pairs.

values

The equivalent of **keys** for the values stored in the hash is the **values** function.

```
values HASH
```

This returns a list of all the values within a hash. The order is the same as that returned by the **keys** and **each** functions. Note that accessing the values does exactly that: the key/value pair works in one direction; the key refers to the value. You cannot determine the key related to an individual value.

If you want to sort on the values within a hash, you must use the block or subroutine format of the **sort** command and compare the values of the hash. The **$a** and **$b** variables refer to the two keys of the hash being compared in the following example:

```
foreach (sort { $hash{$a} cmp $hash{$b} } keys %hash)
```

Or if you are comparing numerical values:

```
foreach (sort { $hash{$a} <=> $hash{$b} } keys %hash)
```

exists

The **defined** function (see Chapter 4) returns true if the value of a variable contains a valid value string, number, or reference. When used on an entire hash, it returns true if the hash contains any data (keys and/or values). When used on a hash element, it returns true only if the corresponding value for the element contains valid information. This does not make it useful if you are trying to determine whether a key exists, since a key could refer to the undefined value.

You can, however, use the **exists** function to determine whether a specified key exists:

```
exists EXPR
```

It returns true if the key exists, irrespective of the underlying value.

delete

If you have a hash and want to delete a hash element, the immediate temptation is to use the undefined value:

```
$hash{'key'} = undef;
```

However, all this does is assign the undefined value to the key "key". The key still exists within the hash, and it will still be returned by the **each** and **keys** functions. To delete the key/value pair, you need to use the **delete** function:

```
delete LIST
```

This deletes the hash elements specified by **LIST**, removing both the keys and their corresponding values.

For example, to empty the entire hash, you could use:

```
while ($key = each %hash)
{
    delete $hash{$key};
}
```

although it's quicker just to empty it with a simple assignment:

```
%hash = ();
```

If you use **delete** on elements of **$ENV** hash, then it modifies the current environment. This can be useful to remove environment variables for the current process, which will also affect all called and forked commands via functions such as **open** or **system**.

If you use **delete** on hash elements of a hash tied to an external DBM database (or other tied structure), the data is permanently removed from the tied source. See the section "Using **tie**" later in this chapter.

Hash Tricks

Because a hash uses string-based keys, you can use a hash for a number of functions that would otherwise require a complex function and array. The most useful of these is to dedupe a list of information. For example, imagine you have a list of keywords and you want to resolve the list, removing any duplicates. You can do this with a normal loop and array, but it's easier with a hash:

```
sub dedupe
{
    (@keywords) = @_;
    my %hash = ();
    foreach (@keywords)
    {
        $hash{$_} = $_;
    }
    return keys %hash;
}
```

This works because you cannot place the same keyword into a hash twice. You overwrite the old value with the new value, even though they are effectively the same. Because it adds no new values, two identical keywords will appear only once within the hash.

For a proper deduplication, you might want to consider including the use of the **lc** or **uc** function so that the case of the individual keywords is ignored. You could rewrite the above as:

```
sub dedupe
{
    (@keywords) = @_;
    my %hash = ();
    foreach (@keywords)
    {
        $hash{lc($_)} = $_;
    }
    return values %hash;
}
```

This retains the case of the original (and indeed first) keyword, and further keywords are ignored if they match an existing hash element. The hash keys are stored in lowercase format, but the values retain the original case. Because the values rather than the keys now retain the original keyword case, you must use **values** to supply the deduped list back to the caller.

Finally, here's the above script one last time. The change here is that it is the first occurrence of the keyword that is retained. In the previous example, had we supplied "Tachyon" and "TAchyon," the value returned would have been the latter, not the former.

```
sub dedupe
{
    (@keywords) = @_;
    my %hash = ();
    foreach (@keywords)
    {
        $hash{lc($_)} = $_ unless (defined($hash{lc($_)}));
    }
    return values %hash;
}
```

The trick is to test the existence of the value with **defined** before making the final assignment.

Another use for a hash is as a string to data reference. Right at the start of this book, in Chapter 2, you saw an example of this. The following array and hash cross-reference each other. If you access **$month[3]**, it returns "March," and if you access **$months{March}**, it returns 3:

```
@month = (JUNK, 'January', 'February', 'March', 'April', 'May',
           'June', July', 'August', 'September', 'October',
           'November', 'December');
%months = ('January'   => 1,
            'February'  => 2,
            'March'     => 3,
            'April'     => 4,
            'May'       => 5,
            'June'      => 6,
            'July'      => 7,
            'August'    => 8,
            'September' => 9,
            'October'   => 10,
            'November'  => 11,
            'December'  => 12);
```

You could use this to help convert dates into the different formats, using the array to produce a pretty version and the hash reference to produce a number. It seems trivial, but compared to the lookup table systems you would require in other languages, it's remarkably easy.

Other tricks with hashes center around the creative use of keys. This is a subject more akin to database design and development, so we'll look at that in Chapter 8. You can also use hashes as parts of more complex structures, and this will be covered later in this chapter.

References

A reference is, exactly as the name suggests, a reference or pointer to another object. That's essentially as complicated as it gets. References actually provide all sorts of abilities and facilities that would not otherwise be available. For C programmers using Perl for the first time, a reference is exactly like a pointer, except within Perl it's easier to use and, more to the point, more practical.

Before we examine the details of references, it's worth covering some of the terminology. There are two types of references: symbolic and hard. A symbolic reference enables you to refer to a variable by name, using the value of another variable. For example, if the variable **$foo** contains the string 'bar', the symbolic reference to **$foo** refers to the variable **$bar**. We'll look at more examples later.

A hard reference refers to the actual data contained in a data structure. However, the form of the data structure to which it points is largely irrelevant. Although a hard reference can refer to a single scalar, it can also refer to an array of scalars, a hash, a subroutine, or a typeglob.

There are several ways to create references to different structures, and we'll examine these later. The act of extracting information from these structures is called dereferencing. When you dereference a scalar reference, you are in fact referring to the original data structure. The act of dereferencing information must be explicit. There is no implicit dereferencing supported within Perl on any structure.

A reference is contained within a scalar, and because all other data structures within Perl are essentially based on a scalar or extensions of a scalar, you can create complex data structures. By using references, you can create complex, nested structures, including arrays of arrays, arrays of hashes, hashes of arrays, and hashes of hashes. The structures you create do not have to be two dimensional; you can have as many dimensions as you like. There is no restriction for you to create an array of hashes. Remember that the array contains references, so individual elements of the array could refer to an array, or hash, or indeed, an array of arrays, a hash of hashes, and so on. This enables you to create incredibly complex data structures with relative ease.

Creating Hard References

The unary backslash operator is used to create a reference to a named variable or subroutine, for example:

```
$foo = 'Bill';
$fooref = \$foo;
```

The **$fooref** variable now contains a hard reference to the **$foo** variable. You can do the same with other variables:

```
$array = \@ARGV;
$hash  = \%ENV;
$glob  = \*STDOUT;
```

To create a reference to a subroutine:

```
sub foo { print "foo" };
$foosub = \&foo;
```

Of course, because you are assigning this to a scalar, there is no reason why you can't place the information into any other scalar-based structure (which basically means everything!). For example:

```
$foo = 'Bill';
$bar = 'Ben';
$xyz = 'Mary';
@arrayofref = (\$foo, \$bar, \$xyz);
```

The **@arrayref** array now contains an array of scalars, and each scalar contains a reference to the three scalar variables.

Anonymous Arrays

When you create a reference to an array directly—that is, without creating an intervening named array—you are creating an anonymous array. The scalar contains a reference that does not have its own name. These are useful for creating complex structures, since you can create an array, hash, or combination within the confines of a named variable within a simple statement. This reduces the time it takes to code and also the time it takes for the program to run (although the differences are pretty small for small, simple structures).

Creating an anonymous array is easy:

```
$array = [ 'Bill', 'Ben, 'Mary' ];
```

This line assigns an array, indicated by the enclosing square brackets instead of the normal parentheses, to the scalar **$array**. The values on the right side of the assignment make up the array, and the left side contains the reference to this array. The significance of this description is that you could put other data structures on the left side of the assignment. We'll examine examples of these later in this chapter when we look at more complex data structures.

Remember that the significant element here is the use of square brackets around the list of scalars to indicate an array, not a list. Thus you can create more complex structures by nesting arrays:

```
@arrayarray = ( 1, 2, [1, 2, 3]);
```

The array now contains three elements; the third element is itself another array of three elements. Furthermore, you can use the same basic notation to create an array of arrays in a single reference:

```
$arrayarray = [ 1, 2, [1, 2, 3]];
```

Note as well that as with all other arrays, you could equally have used expressions or variables as elements to the arrays.

Anonymous Hashes

Anonymous hashes are similarly easy to create, except you use braces instead of square brackets:

```
$hash = { 'Man'   => 'Bill',
          'Woman' => 'Mary,
          'Dog'   => 'Ben'
        };
```

The same arguments for the anonymous array composer also apply here. You can use any normal element here—a string literal (as above), an expression, or a variable—to create the structure in question.

Note that this composition procedure only works when Perl is expecting a term—that is, usually when making an assignment or expecting a hash or reference as an element. Braces are not only used for creating anonymous hashes, but they are also responsible for selecting hash subscript elements and for defining blocks within Perl. This means you must occasionally explicitly specify the creation of an anonymous hash reference by preceding the hash creator with a **+** or **return**:

```
$envref = +{ %ENV };
sub dupeenv{ return { %ENV } };
```

Anonymous Subroutines

An anonymous subroutine is used in many key situations within Perl. We'll see perhaps the most common examples in Chapter 10 when we examine the methods available for handling signals. Again, the method for creating a reference to an anonymous subroutine is very straightforward:

```
$hw = sub { print "Hello World!\n" };
```

The new **$hw** variable now contains a reference to the anonymous subroutine, which prints the "Hello World!" message on the screen.

The important thing to remember when creating an anonymous subroutine is that you must have a trailing semicolon to end the declaration expression, unlike a typical subroutine definition.

In essence, what this does is create a reference to a piece of code, which you can execute directly using the reference. If you access the reference, then the subroutine code you supplied will be executed, almost as if it was parsed by a **do{}** or **eval{}** block.

For example, the single line

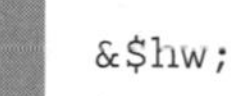

```
&$hw;
```

actually prints the "Hello World!" message. This is an example of dereferencing, and we're getting slightly ahead of ourselves, so we'll take a step back and instead look at another feature of anonymous subroutines before we look properly at the process of using hard references.

Closures

A closure is a Lisp term, where an anonymous subroutine can be created, and the resulting subroutine will execute within the same context as when it was created. This only works with lexically scoped variables (those created with **my**), and the results can provide you with some interesting facilities that provide alternative ways for introducing and using information within an anonymous subroutine.

Consider the code below, in which an anonymous subroutine is created as the return value from a function:

```
sub formatlist
{
    my @list = @_;
    return sub
           {
               my $title = shift;
               print "$title: ", join(' ',@list),"\n";
           }
}

$arguments = formatlist(@ARGV);

&$arguments('Command line');
```

If you run this within a script, you might get this:

```
Command line: -w -o file.txt
```

You'll note that the contents of the **@ARGV** array, which was determined and populated when the anonymous sub was created, are also available when you dereference the function later.

This has a number of uses, although to many this is actually the kind of behavior you would expect.

Filehandles/Typeglobs

Creating a reference to a filehandle is a case of passing a reference to the corresponding typeglob. This is in fact the best way to pass filehandles to or from subroutines, since it has the optical effect of removing the ambiguity of the typeglob:

```
writelog(\*LOG);

sub writelog
{
    my $LOG = shift;
    print $LOG scalar(localtime(time)),":",@_;
}
```

The alternative is to use a filehandle object and pass the object around instead. We'll see more on objects later in the chapter.

Dereferencing

The most direct way of dereferencing a reference is to prepend the corresponding data type you are expecting in front of the scalar variable containing the reference. For example, to dereference a scalar reference **$foo**, you would access the data as **$$foo**. Other examples are

```
$array = \@ARGV;
$hash  = \%ENV;
$glob  = \*STDOUT;
$foosub = \&foo;

push (@$array, "From humans");
$$array[0] = 'Hello'
```

```
$$hash{'Hello'} = 'World';
&$foosub;
print $glob "Hello World!\n";
```

It's important to get the semantics correct here. In the above **$$array[0]** and **$$hash{'Hello'}** lines, the corresponding structures are not actually being dereferenced; in fact, you are dereferencing the scalar to which the corresponding elements refer. We'll return to this in a moment. Also note that you do not explicitly dereference a filehandle, since a reference to a typeglob is merely a pointer into the symbol table, which is essentially what a typeglob is anyway (see Chapter 5).

References and dereferences execute in order. A reference (**$foo**) to a string of the form **"hello"** can be dereferenced using **$$$$foo**. However, it's unlikely you'll be using individual scalar references in this form. When it comes to more complex structures, there are different methods available, and these also get around some of the difficulties surrounding the dereferencing of entire structures rather than the individual scalars of which they are composed.

The second alternative is to use a **BLOCK**. Since the last statement in a block gives the block its return value, by putting a reference as the only statement in a block, you end up returning the data type to which the reference points. All you need to do is instruct Perl on how to interpret the returned data. You can therefore rewrite the examples above as follows:

```
${$foo} = "Hello World";
push (@{$array}, "From humans");
${$array}[0] = 'Hello'
${$hash}{'Hello'} = 'World';
&{$foosub};
```

Using the block notation is trivial in these cases, but it makes more sense when you want to identify a particular structure as a complete data type, not an element of a data type. For example, the line

```
foreach $key (keys %$hash)
```

looks a bit cryptic compared to

```
foreach $key (keys %{$hash})
```

which is a little clearer.

This notation really comes into its own, however, when you are using nested structures. Let's assume, for the moment, that you have a hash of hashes. If you try to access the keys of the hash in one of the parent hash elements like this,

```
foreach $key (keys %$hash{'hash'})
```

Perl will report an error, because it interprets the hash element first and therefore returns a scalar, not a hash reference. Instead, you need to write it as:

```
foreach $key (keys %{$hash}{'hash'})
```

Finally, the other alternative is to use the arrow operator, **->**. This works only on arrays or hashes, since the arrow operator (more correctly known as the infix operator) provides an easier method for extracting the individual elements from both structures. The benefit of the infix operator is that it does not require you to explicitly dereference the original scalar. Therefore you can rewrite the statements

```
$$array[0] = 'Hello'
$$hash{'Hello'} = 'World';
```

and

```
${$array}[0] = 'Hello'
${$hash}{'Hello'} = 'World';
```

as

```
$array->[0] = 'Hello'
$hash->{'Hello'} = 'World';
```

This is clearer than the other methods, but as usual, care should be taken to ensure you are actually extracting or using the correct element from the array or hash.

The statements

```
$array[0];
```

and

```
$array->[0];
```

do not equal the same thing. The first is accessing the first element of the **@array** variable, while the second is accessing the first element of the array pointed to by **$array**. The **$array** could point to any array, named or anonymous. This makes the infix notation practical and clear when using references directly within a subroutine that potentially needs to access the information for a supplied reference.

To use one of the previous methods, you might use a subroutine like the one below to print the first element of an array passed by reference:

```
sub first
{
    $array = shift;
    print ${$array}[0],"\n";
}
```

This is a little fussy and certainly less than clear, while this

```
sub first
{
    print ${$_[0]}[0],"\n";
}
```

looks suspiciously like line noise, although it achieves the desired result. Using the infix operator, the subroutine looks far clearer:

```
sub first
{
    print $_[0]->[0],"\n";
}
```

Although still a little complex, it's clearer that you are trying to access the first element of the first argument passed to the function.

Determining a Reference Type

You can determine the type of variable that a particular reference points to by using the **ref** function.

```
ref EXPR
ref
```

The function returns a true value (actually a string) if **EXPR**, or **$_**, is a reference. The actual string returned defines the type of entity the reference refers to. The built-in types are

```
REF
SCALAR
ARRAY
HASH
CODE
GLOB
```

For example, the code

```
$scalar = "Hello World\n";
$ref    = \$scalar;
print ref $ref,"\n";
```

prints:

```
SCALAR
```

Alternatively, the string value of a reference is a combination of the reference type and its memory location. For example, if you print the above reference, instead of dereferencing it,

```
print "$ref\n";
```

it will print out something like "SCALAR(0xaa472b4)," which doesn't make a lot of sense.

Symbolic References

If you refer back to the start of this section, you will remember that a symbolic reference was defined as the use of a scalar value as a string, which in turn gives a variable its name. For example:

```
$var = "foo";
$$var = "bar";
```

Because **$var** is not a reference, the act of dereferencing a nonexistent reference is to create a new variable with the name of the variable's contents. So in the example above, you have set the value of **$foo** to "bar." In essence, you've done:

```
$"$var" = "bar";
```

The above doesn't work, and the eventual result should be clear. The use of symbolic references makes the system very powerful: you can name a variable or subroutine based on a variable piece of information.

However, the problem with symbolic references is that it only takes a simple mistake for you to inadvertently create a symbolic rather than a hard reference. It is therefore important (if not imperative) that you check what you are doing or, better still, ask Perl to do it for you. The **use strict** pragma configures this. If you only want to check references, then use

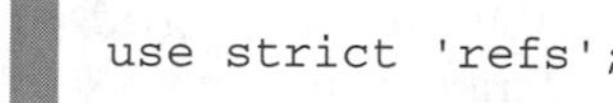

```
use strict 'refs';
```

in your script. See Chapter 16 for more information on pragmas.

Hashes and References

You must be careful when using references with hash keys. You cannot use a hard reference as a hash key, because the hard reference will be converted to a string for the benefit of the hash's key. It's unlikely that you will want a hash key of "SCALAR(0xaa472b4)", and even if you do, you cannot dereference the string into the original variable anyway.

The only time this feature is useful is when you want to create a unique key within a hash. The reference is guaranteed to be unique, since you can't have two data types at the same location. What you can't do is dereference the key back to its original variable.

Complex Structures

Beyond the normal constraints of arrays and hashes, you can also create complex structures made up of combinations of the two. These are nested, or complex, structures and can be used to model complex data in an easy-to-use format.

What actually happens with a nested structure is that Perl stores the nested data type as a reference to an anonymous variable. For example, in a two-dimensional array, the main array is a list of references, and the subarrays are anonymous arrays to which these references point. This means that an "array of arrays" actually means an array of references to arrays. The same is true of all nested structures, and although it seems complex, it does provide a suitably powerful method for creating complex, nested structures.

You can create any number of dimensions in an array or hash, simply by extending the existing notation. Perl will handle the rest of the work for you. There are of course some complexities and tricks associated with accessing and using these complex structures, and we'll look at the four basic types: arrays of arrays, hashes of hashes, arrays of hashes, and hashes of arrays.

Arrays of Arrays

An array of arrays is a two-dimensional structure and the most basic of those available. We'll be using the array of arrays as a core reference point for many of the nested structures, including how to access them, use them directly, and use arrays and array references to access the entire array and array elements. If you want to use nested structures, you should read this section first. We'll cover the differences and abilities of the other nested structures later.

An array of arrays can be used to hold any list of nested information. For example, users on a system have a list of individual users. The first dimension is the main array, and the second dimension is the array of group members. Another alternative is to think about the classic "battleships" game. Individual squares on the battleships grid can be referred to by an X,Y reference. You could use an array of arrays to hold this information.

Populating a list of lists is a case of including anonymous arrays or existing arrays within an existing array structure. For our example, we'll use a tic-tac-toe (or Noughts and Crosses, depending on your nationality) board:

```
@tictactoe = ( ['X','O','O'],
               ['O','O','X'],
               ['O','X','X']
             );
```

This creates a nested set of arrays within a parent array, **@tictactoe**. To print out the bottom right corner:

```
print $tictactoe[2][2];
```

Alternatively, you can place the whole lot into a reference:

```
$tictactoe = [ ['X','O','O'],
               ['O','O','X'],
               ['O','X','X']
             ];
```

Note the use of the square brackets around the nested arrays, which indicates to Perl that you are creating an anonymous array and you need to return a reference to it. You assign the reference to the **$tictactoe** scalar, and to access the bottom right corner:

```
print $tictactoe[2][2];
```

Note the semantics here. Shouldn't you have dereferenced **$tictactoe** somehow?

Perl automatically assumes you are dereferencing if you use pairs of brackets together. Perl knows that this indicates a structure to a list of references, whether that's a hash or an array, so the infix operator (or block names) are implied. This doesn't prevent you from using them if you want to. The following lines are all equal:

```
print $tictactoe[2][2];
print $tictactoe->[2][2];
print $tictactoe[2]->[2];
print $tictactoe->[2]->[2];
```

Like many other similar features, this is a direct attempt to improve the overall readability of the code. The first format looks cleaner, and should appeal to C programmers, since this is the same format used in C for multidimensional arrays. The other formats would perhaps make more sense to a hardened Perl programmer, and they help if you are particularly bothered about the notation of one reference point to another.

We'll need a more complex source for our next examples. I've used the /etc/passwd file here, since it's the most readily available for most people. However, the principles will apply to any data you want to map into an array of arrays. The individual "rows" of our array (the first dimension) will be each record; the individual fields will form the columns (the second dimension).

Below is a script that populates our database. I've assumed that the file is already open.

```
while(<PASSWD>)
{
    chomp;
    push @passwd,[ split /:/ ];
}
```

This creates an array **@passwd**, and each field contains a reference to an array, the contents of which is the list of values returned by **split**. Note the notation again here—the square brackets indicate that you are returning a reference to an array.

To put the information directly into an array reference:

```
open(PASSWD,"/etc/passwd");
while(<PASSWD>)
{
    push @{$passwd}, [ split /:/ ];
}
```

You could also set it more explicitly:

```
while(<PASSWD>)
{
    chomp;
    foreach $field (split /:/)
    {
        push @{$passwd[$index]},$field;
    }
    $index++;
}
```

This demonstrates another important point that carries through all nested references. The call to **push** requires an array as its first element, and it must begin with @; so you must quote the reference to the nested array using block notation. Furthermore, note the location of the index for the array reference: it's contained within the block quotes. This is because Perl would see the subscript reference and assume it was returning a scalar, not an array, irrespective of the leading character you have supplied.

What the example does show is the addition of fields, individually, to the row of an array. It uses **push** again, but there's no reason why you can't also track your location in the nested array:

```
while(<PASSWD>)
{
    chomp;
    @fields = ();
    @fields = split /:/;
    foreach $field (0..@fields)
    {
        $passwd[$index][$field] = $fields[$field];
    }
    $index++;
}
```

You need to make sure you empty the array before you fill it with the information from **split**. This prevents you from putting undefined data into the structure, since the assignment will only update fields, not actually empty them. Then it's a case of assignments to the array of arrays.

Another point to note here is that if you create an entry in an index that doesn't currently exist within the structure (as with any other array), Perl will create the intervening elements, filling them with **undef** as it goes. For example:

```
$passwd[120][0] = 'martinb';
```

Assuming **$passwd** has not already been defined or populated, it now contains a reference to an array 121 elements in size, the first 120 of which contain **undef**.

Now, if you turn to accessing the information, there are also complications. You can't do this

```
print @passwd;
```

for the original form, or

```
print $passwd;
```

because you'll get a list of hash references, and a reference to a hash back as a string value. This is one of the most common mistakes when using nested structures or just references in general. Perl doesn't dereference for you, so you need to use a loop to progress through the parent array.

Try using the simpler array, rather than reference to an array, first

```
foreach $array (@passwd)
{
    print join(':',@$array);
}
```

or

```
foreach $array (@{$passwd})
{
    print join(':',@$array);
}
```

Both of these work because the individual elements of the parent array are references, which you can dereference using the correct prefix. If you want to step through the child array as well, then you might use something like this:

```
foreach $x (0..@{$passwd})
{
    foreach $y (0..@{$passwd[$x]})
    {
        print "$x, $y = $passwd[$x][$y]\n";
    }
}
```

The same rules for previous constructs apply here to. You must use the block notation to ensure you get the correct array returned in the **foreach** statement. The reference to the subarray requires you to insert the subscript operation in the block, not outside of it.

Finally, you need to think about accessing the individual slices of a nested array. If you were to use

```
@new = @passwd[0..4];
```

the **@new** array would contain the first five references contained in **@passwd**. If you want to slice the fields for an individual record, you can either use loops, or use a block to indicate the array you are extracting from:

```
print @{$passwd[0]}[4..7];
```

To obtain a slice in the opposite direction—that is, the entire column from your structure—you have to use loops. The following doesn't work:

```
print @{{$passwd}[0..7]}[0];
print @{$passwd[0..7]}[0];
print @($passwd}[0..7][0];
```

Instead, you need to use a loop:

```
@users = ();
foreach $x (0..@{$passwd})
{
    push @users,$passwd[$x][0];
}
```

Or to create a completely nested array of arrays consisting of a two-dimensional slice, you either need to use two nested loops, or use the slice notation used above:

```
@userhome = ();
foreach $x (5..20)
{
    push @userhome, [ @{$passwd[$x]}[0,6] ];
}
```

The remainder of the nested structures use the same techniques you've seen here, albeit with some minor modifications.

Hashes of Hashes

Earlier in this chapter you saw how information in a hash could be handled and accessed almost immediately. With some clever use of the key strings you can also emulate a simple database system internally within a hash, but handling the keys is complex. By using a hash of hashes, you make the structures easier to use and more practical when storing and accessing the information.

The format for creating a hash of hashes is much the same as that for arrays of arrays. In the example below, I've created a hash of hashes that describes a company organization. The primary keys are the departments, and the nested keys are the employee names. The values then contain the corresponding employee's job title.

```
%company = ('Sales'       => {
                               'Brown'  => 'Manager',
                               'Smith'  => 'Salesman',
                               'Albert' => 'Salesman',
                             },
            'Marketing'   => {
                               'Penfold' => 'Designer',
                               'Evans' => 'Tea-person',
                               'Jurgens' => 'Manager',
                             }
            'Production' => {
                               'Cotton' => 'Paste-up',
                               'Ridgeway' => 'Manager',
                               'Web' => 'Developer',
                             }
           );
```

You can also use the nested format, which is also the way you would access the individual data types:

```
$company{'Sales'}{'Brown'}             = 'Manager';
$company{'Sales'}{'Smith'}             = 'Salesman';
$company{'Sales'}{'Albert'}            = 'Salesman';
$company{'Marketing'}{'Penfold'}       = 'Designer';
$company{'Marketing'}{'Evans'}         = 'Tea-person';
$company{'Marketing'}{'Jurgens'}       = 'Manager';
$company{'Production'}{'Cotton'}       = 'Paste-up';
$company{'Production'}{'Ridgeway'}     = 'Manager';
$company{'Production'}{'Web'}          = 'Developer';
```

Here's a more practical example, which reads in the contents of the file and then outputs the contents in a formatted form using a hash of hashes to store the information. Because you read the entire file into a hash of hashes, you can then sort and manipulate the information before you report. This would be difficult using any of the previous methods you have seen. This example uses the /etc/passwd file, not only because it is easily available, but also because it can be useful to sort the file into a more friendly format. Let's look at the output first:

```
root:x:0:1:Martin Brown:/:/sbin/sh:
smtp:x:0:0:mail daemon user:/::
daemon:x:1:1:0000-Admin(0000):/::
bin:x:2:2:0000-Admin(0000):/usr/bin::
sys:x:3:3:0000-Admin(0000):/::
adm:x:4:4:0000-Admin(0000):/var/adm::
uucp:x:5:5:0000-uucp(0000):/usr/lib/uucp::
nuucp:x:9:9:0000-uucp(0000):/var/spool/uucppublic:/usr/lib/uucp/uuc
ico:
listen:x:37:4:Network Admin:/usr/net/nls::
lp:x:71:8:0000-lp(0000):/usr/spool/lp::
mc:x:1000:1000:Martin C Brown:/users/mc:/usr/local/bin/bash:
martinb:x:1000:1000:Martin C
Brown:/users/martinb:/usr/local/bin/bash:
alias:*:7790:2108::/usr/local/qmail/alias:/bin/true:
qmaild:*:7791:2108::/usr/local/qmail:/bin/true:
qmaill:*:7792:2108::/usr/local/qmail:/bin/true:
qmailp:*:7793:2108::/usr/local/qmail:/bin/true:
qmailq:*:7794:2107::/usr/local/qmail:/bin/true:
qmailr:*:7795:2107::/usr/local/qmail:/bin/true:
qmails:*:7796:2107::/usr/local/qmail:/bin/true:
nobody:x:60001:60001:uid no body:/::
noaccess:x:60002:60002:uid no access:/::
```

And here's the script:

```
open(DATA,"</etc/passwd") || die "Couldn't open file properly";
my (%passwd, $ref);

while(<DATA>)
{
    chomp;
    @fields = split /:/;
    $login = shift @fields;
```

```
    $passwd{$login}{'passwd'} =  shift @fields;
    $passwd{$login}{'uid'}    =  shift @fields;
    $passwd{$login}{'gid'}    =  shift @fields;
    $passwd{$login}{'name'}   =  shift @fields;
    $passwd{$login}{'home'}   =  shift @fields;
    $passwd{$login}{'shell'}  =  shift @fields;
}

close(DATA) || die "Couldn't close file properly";

foreach (sort { $passwd{$a}{'uid'}
                       <=> $passwd{$b}{'uid'} } keys %passwd)
{
    print "$_:";
    foreach $field (qw/login passwd uid gid name home shell/)
    {
        print "$passwd{$_}{$field}:";
    }
    print "\n";
}
```


There are some important parts of this script that we need to cover. A standard **sort** block statement is used, but you want to sort on the nested hash, not the numerical sequence used to store each record. The **sort** statement works because the comparison will return the sorted primary key (as selected via the **$a** and **$b** sort variables), even though what you are actually sorting on is the value of the nested hash.

If you wanted to sort the primary hash keys, you could use a much simpler statement:

```
foreach (sort keys %passwd)
```

And if you wanted to sort on the nested hash keys in the nested loop:

```
foreach (sort keys %{passwd}{$_})
```

You must use the block method for selecting a variable name. The statement

```
foreach (sort keys %passwd{$_})
```

will report an error during compilation because Perl identifies the variable **%passwd** as a hash, but the fragment **$passwd{$_}** as a hash element. Therefore the entire

%passwd{$_}** is bogus, since you must reference a hash element with a leading **$ to indicate a scalar value.

Here's a different example of the same printing loop that sacrifices sorting for a more memory-efficient method:

```
while ($key = each %passwd)
{
    print "$key:";
    foreach $field (keys %{$passwd{$key}})
    {
        print "$passwd{$key}{$field}:";
    }
    print "\n";
}
```

Because the above example does not use temporary lists, you could safely use it on large structures without fear of running out of memory.

Arrays of Hashes

The previous example used an array of arrays to store information contained in the password file. A hash of hashes was used to access individual information for a specific user without having to search through the hash. As an alternative, an array of hashes could have been used. Each element of the array would be a record and could therefore be accessed in the traditional record number format. The value of the array element is a reference to a hash, and the hash structure consists of the normal key/value pairs, with the key being the field name and the corresponding value the field contents.

Let's take a look at the corresponding array of hashes script for the /etc/passwd file:

```
open(DATA,"</etc/passwd") || die "Couldn't open file properly";
my (%passwd, $ref);

while(<DATA>)
{
    chomp;
    @fields = split /:/;
    $aref = {};
    $aref->{'login'}  =  shift @fields;
    $aref->{'passwd'} =  shift @fields;
    $aref->{'uid'}    =  shift @fields;
    $aref->{'gid'}    =  shift @fields;
    $aref->{'name'}   =  shift @fields;
```

```
    $aref->{'home'}    =  shift @fields;
    $aref->{'shell'}   =  shift @fields;
    push @passwd,$aref;
}

close(DATA) || die "Couldn't close file properly";

foreach $ref (sort { $$a{'uid'} <=> $$b{'uid'} } @passwd)
{
    foreach $field (qw/login passwd uid gid name home shell/)
    {
        print $$ref{$field},":";
    }
    print "\n";
}
```


The array of hashes structure is built very simply. You create a new reference to an anonymous hash in **$aref**, then populate it with the correct key/value pairs. The new anonymous reference is then pushed onto the global **@passwd** array, just the same as any array element. The result is a fully populated array of anonymous hash references.

For sorting, you have a slightly different problem. You want to sort the records by the **uid** field of the record. You therefore need to use a sorting expression that will access the underlying hash element contents, returning a sorted list of array references from the **@passwd** array. You do this by dereferencing the **uid** key from the hash, using the hash references stored in the **$a** and **$b** variables used by the **sort** function.

For a simpler, nonsorted result, you could just use

```
foreach $record (@passwd)
{
    foreach $field (qw/login passwd uid gid name home shell/)
    {
        print $record->{$field},":";
    }
    print "\n";
}
```

Again, it's important to remember that the **$record** variable contains a reference to an anonymous hash. If all you did was print that value, Perl would report:

```
HASH(0xcfaf8)
```

If you wanted to access all the keys of the referenced hashes, you would have to use a slightly different method. Here's the remodeled original:

```
foreach $ref (sort { $$a{'uid'} <=> $$b{'uid'} } @passwd)
{
    foreach $field (keys %$ref)
    {
        print $$ref{$field},":";
    }
    print "\n";
}
```

And here's a record number alternative that uses less memory:

```
foreach $id (0..$#passwd)
{
    foreach $field (keys %{$passwd[$id]})
    {
        print $passwd[$id]{$field},":";
    }
    print "\n";
}
```

Note that this example uses a more direct method of accessing an individual within a record, although the eventual result is the same.

Using this method of record organization allows you to have different fields for individual records. You could even use separate keys in the hash, or you could use **pack** and a suitable "packstring" stored in hash keys to store complex structures. See Chapter 8 for more details on planning and using databases with Perl's internal and external structures.

Hashes of Arrays

A hash of arrays is best used when you want to store and use an array and want to access it by name. We'll use the /etc/group file, a cousin to the /etc/passwd file, for this demonstration. The file is essentially made up of a list of group names, and against each group name is a list of group members. Here's a sample /etc/group file:

```
root::0:root,dummy,martinb
other::1:dummy,martinb
bin::2:root,bin,daemon
sys::3:root,bin,sys,adm
```

```
adm::4:root,adm,daemon
uucp::5:root,uucp
mail::6:root
tty::7:root,tty,adm
lp::8:root,lp,adm
nuucp::9:root,nuucp
staff::10:
daemon::12:root,daemon
sysadmin::14:
nobody::60001:
noaccess::60002:
shared::1000:MC,SLP
qmail:*:2107:
nofiles:*:2108:
```


By modeling it within a hash of arrays, you can access a list of group members by referring to the group by name. The script below builds the **%group** hash. We'll deal with the printing separately.

```
open(DATA,"</etc/group") || die "Couldn't open file properly";
my (%passwd, $ref);

while(<DATA>)
{
    chomp;
    ($groupname,$members) = (split /:/)[0,3];
    $group{$groupname} = [ split /,/,$members ];
}

close(DATA) || die "Couldn't close file properly";
```

You build the group list by creating an anonymous array, which is generated by the list returned by separating the member list with **split**. When printing, you can very quickly print the results because there are no complicated structures to handle aside from the parent hash:

```
foreach (sort keys %group)
{
    print "$_: ", join(' ' ,@{$group{$_}}),"\n";
}
```

Note, as in previous examples, the most critical part is that the hash value contains a reference to an anonymous array; so to access it as a complete array, you need to use a block reference.

The example below sorts the list of groups by the number of elements in the subarray:

```
foreach (sort { @{$group{$a}} <=> @{$group{$b}} } keys %group)
{
    print "$_: ", join(' ' ,@{$group{$_}}),"\n";
}
```

And for a simpler, structured output, you can access the array by its individual index elements:

```
foreach (sort keys %group)
{
    print "$_ \n";
    for $i (0..$#{$group{$_}})
    {
        print "  $i = $group{$_}[$i]\n";
    }
}
```

Finally, the example below is a less memory intensive version, although you lose the ability to sort the list of names.

```
while (($key, $array) = each(%group))
{
    print "$key: ", join(' ', @$array),"\n";
}
```

This time you can dereference the hash value directly, rather than using block quotes.

Beyond Two Dimensions

The preceding examples still assume a relatively strict structure around your data. Depending on your point of view when it comes to data modeling, this may be a good or a bad thing. There is no reason why you can't extend the above examples beyond two dimensions. Consider the following nested hash of arrays of hashes, which emulates a database that supports multiple tables.

```
%db = (
        contacts => [
                           { 'name'  => 'Martin',
                             'email' => 'mc@mcwords.com' },
                           { 'name'  => 'Bob',
                             'email' => 'bob@bob.com' },
                           ],
        appointments => [
                              { 'Date'  => '22/3/98',
                                'Time'  => '10:30',
                                'Title' => 'Dentist' },
                              { 'Date'  => '5/5/98',
                                'Time'  => '00:00',
                                'Title' => 'Birthday' },
                              ]
        );
```


To make the process of building complex structures easier, you can also copy references so that a particular element points to some other part of the structure. For example, you might want to create a new appointment and add a new field—an array of contacts who will attend the meeting:

```
%appt = ( 'Date' => '4/5/1999',
          'Time' => '10:30',
          'Title' => 'Production Meeting',
          'Members' => [ $db{'contacts'}[0], $db{'contacts'}[1] ]
          );

push @{$db{'appointments'}}, \%appt;
```

The new 'Members' element of the hash contains an array, which has two references to the two contacts created above. You can access their email addresses directly with:

```
print ${$db{appointments}[2]{Members}[0]}{email},"\n";
```

But note that because it's a reference, an assignation like this

```
${$db{appointments}[2]{Members}[0]}{email} = 'foo@goo.bar';
```

updates the value of the contact's record directly, so that both

```
print ${$db{appointments}[2]{Members}[0]}{email},"\n";
```

and

```
print $db{contacts}[0]{email},"\n";
```

print out the new 'foo@goo.bar' email address.

There isn't any reason to store only literal values either. Arrays and hashes store lists of scalars, and a scalar can be a reference to a wide range of different entities, including subroutines (anonymous and named), filehandles, other hashes and arrays, and any combination thereof.

Here's another example—this time the creation of a hash with references to subroutines:

```
my %commandlist = (
                        'DISK'  => \&disk_space_report,
                        'SWAP'  => \&swap_space_report,
                        'STORE' => \&store_status_report,
                        'GET'   => \&get_status_report,
                        'QUIT'  => \&quit_connection,
                        );
```

You could now call the function directly, without

```
&{$commandlist->{STORE}};
```

and with arguments:

```
&{$commandlist->{STORE}}(@values);
```

This type of table is called a dispatch table and is often used in situations where a program receives a string or command from a user or remote process. Perl allows you to call the function desired directly, without having to use a long and complicated **if..elsif..else** statement.

Finally, here's a filehandle hash. The keys are the names of the files you have open, and the value is a reference to a filehandle, passed, as usual, by a typeglob:

```
%files = { 'source.txt'  => \*SOURCE,
           'report.out'  => \*REPORT,
           'scratch.tmp' => \*SCRATCH
         };
```

You can now print to a filehandle by using the file name, instead of the filehandle directly:

```
print { $files->{'report.out'}} "This is a report\n";
```

Note that you need braces around the indirect typeglob dereference.

Objects

In the early 1990s object-oriented programming was seen as the heralding of a new age in programming methods. Rather than dealing with data and functions as two separate entities, an object combines the two elements into a single, er…, object. An object knows what kind of thing it is, and furthermore knows what it can do based on what kind of thing it is. In programming terms, an object is a data structure that has a number of functions associated with it that act upon the object's data.

A classic example of object-oriented programming is the definition of animals. You might create a cat object. The object knows it is a cat and therefore knows its abilities. When you tell a cat object to move, the object will decide that because it has four legs, it should walk. However, a fish object would know that because it has fins it should swim when you ask it to move.

In theory, using objects to create programs reduces the amount of code you need to program, promotes code reuse, and allows you to program in terms of "I want to…" rather than "To do…, I need to …". This is certainly the tack applied by C++ and Java—two languages that heavily promote, and even require, the use of objects for programming.

The practice, however, is very different. Many programs do not need object-orientation technology to work effectively. There are instances where it is useful—GUI programming, for example, benefits from object methods. There are also instances where object-oriented programming takes significantly longer than the nonobject method.

Within Perl the philosophy is simple: use objects where it makes sense to use objects, and avoid them where it doesn't. Within the realm of packages and modules, object-oriented programming in Perl requires that you know how to create packages and modules. Object classes are another form of abstraction that use the abilities of packages. This means that object classes can cross the boundaries associated with individual files and modules.

Object Basics

Before covering the semantics of objects within Perl, it should be noted that you need to know how to create packages, and how to create and use references. Refer to Chapter 5 and the section on references earlier in this chapter for more information. Once again, it's worth covering terminology that will be used in this section before proceeding to the details of creating and using objects. There are three main terms, explained from the point of view of how Perl handles objects. The terms are object, class, and method.

- Within Perl, an *object* is merely a reference to a data type that knows what class it belongs to. The object is stored as a reference in a scalar variable. Because a scalar only contains a reference to the object, the same scalar can hold different objects in different classes. When a particular operation is performed on an object, the corresponding method is called, as defined within the class.
- A *class* within Perl is a package that contains the corresponding methods required to create and manipulate objects.
- A *method* within Perl is a subroutine, defined with the package. The first argument to the method is an object reference, or a package name, depending on whether the method affects the current object or the class.

Creating and Using Objects

When creating an object, you need to supply a *constructor*. This is a subroutine within a package that returns an object reference. The object reference is created by *blessing* a reference to the package's class. For example:

```
package Vegetable;
sub new
{
    my $object = {};
    return bless $object;
}
```

The code above creates a new package, **Vegetable**, with a single method, **new**, which is the default name for an object constructor. The **new** method returns a reference to a hash, defined in **$object**, which has been blessed using the **bless** function into an object reference.

You can now create a new **Vegetable** object by using this code:

```
$carrot = new Vegetable;
```

Note here that a hash is used as the base data type for the object. This is not required. You could use any of the available data types as the base for an object. Hashes are the normal receptacle only because you are usually constructing records where you want to be able to identify individual fields by name.

The use of **bless** defines the difference between a normal reference and an object reference. An object is a reference that has been blessed into a particular class, whereas a reference is just a reference to another entity.

If you want to initialize the object with some information before it is returned, you can put that into the subroutine itself (the example below takes the data from the supplied arguments),


```
sub new
{
    my $object = {@_};
    return bless $object;
}
```

which can now populate when you create a new object:

```
$carrot = new Vegetable('Color' => 'Orange',
                        'Shape' => 'Carrot-like');
```

You don't have to use the information supplied to the **new** method as a hash. The subroutine can take any arguments and process them as you require. Here's the same constructor, but this time it assumes you are supplying the information in the arguments to the constructor function:

```
sub new
{
    my $object = {};
    $object->{'Color' => $_[0],
               'Shape'  => $_[1]
              };
    bless $object;
    return $object;
}
```

Normally of course you'd check the contents of the arguments before you started blindly filling in the details, but the process is essentially the same.

If you want to call your own initialization routine on a newly blessed object:

```
sub new
{
    my $object = {};
    bless $object;
    $object->_define();
    return $object;
}
```

The use of a leading underscore on the method **_define** is a convention used to indicate a private rather than public method. Here's a quick example of the function:

```
sub _define
{
    my $self = shift;
    $self->{'State'}       = 'Raw';
    $self->{'Composition'} = 'Whole';
}
```

Don't worry too much about the semantics for a second, we'll cover that shortly.

For inheritance purposes, you will need to use a two-argument call to **bless**. The second argument should be the class into which you are blessing the object, and you can derive this from the first argument to the constructor method. For example, to explicitly define the above object into the **Vegetable** class:

```
sub new
{
    my $class = shift;
    my $object = {};
    return bless $object, $class;
}
```

The reason you need this is that methods execute within the confines of their base class, not their derived class. Thus if you were to create a new class **Fruit**, which inherited methods from **Vegetable**, a call to the **new** constructor would bless an object into the **Vegetable** rather than the **Fruit** class. Using the above format with the two-argument version of **bless** ensures that the new object is part of the **Fruit** method.

Methods

We'll start with a reminder: an object is a blessed reference, but a reference is just a pointer to a data structure. When writing methods, it's important to understand this distinction. Within the confines of the class package and corresponding methods, you use the object as if it was a reference (which it is), but outside the class package, you use it as an object.

There is no special way within Perl to define a method, since a method is just a function defined within the class package. The only difference between a normal subroutine and a method is that the method should accept at least one argument, the contents of which will be the object you want to manipulate. There are no complications to creating the method. All you need to do is define the function, and Perl will handle the rest. See the later section "Classes and Inheritance" for some exceptions, but otherwise this definition stands.

There are two types of methods—class and instance. A *class* method is one that affects the entire class. You've already seen some examples of this: the constructor subroutine is an example of a class method. The first argument a class method receives is the name of the class. This is ignored by most functions since they already know to which class (package) they belong. However, as you've already seen in the previous section, it is sometimes necessary to identify the class.

An *instance* method is a function that operates on a specific object. It should accept at least one argument, which is the object on which you want to operate. For example, the **boil** method for our **Vegetable** object modifies the 'State' element of the object's hash to 'Boiled':

```
sub boil
{
    my $self = shift;
    $self->{'State'} = 'Boiled';
}
```

You take the first argument off with **shift** and then modify the object's contents. Note that the name of the variable that you store the reference in is called **$self**. This is an accepted standard, although there is no reason why you can't call it something else. The use is convention, rather than law. Remember that an object is just a reference to a particular data type, so you can modify the hash "object" just as you would any other reference.

To use this method, you use the infix operator to select the method to use on a particular object, for example:

```
$carrot = new Vegetable('Color' => 'Orange', 'Shape' =
'Carrot-like');
$carrot->boil;
```

The 'State' field of the hash has now been updated!

You can also accept arguments to the method,

```
sub boil
{
    my $self = shift;
    $self->{'State'} = 'Boiled';
    if (@_ == 1)
    {
        $self->{'Composition'} = shift;
    }
}
```

thus allowing you to define how the vegetable will be before it's boiled:

```
$carrot->boil('Chopped');
```

You can also create a method that behaves differently based on what information it is supplied in that first argument. The way to do this is to use **ref** to identify whether the method was supplied a reference to an object or not.

```
sub new
{
    my $self = shift;
    my $type = ref($self) || $self;
    return bless {}, $type;
}
```

If the return value of the **ref** is a valid reference, then it's safe to assume you should be blessing an object. If **ref** returns false, then the argument is not an object but a class name.

Method Calls

There are two ways of invoking a method. The first format looks like this:

```
METHOD CLASS_OR_INSTANCE LIST
```

This is the format you've used for creating objects, for example:

```
new Vegetable('Color' => 'Orange', 'Shape' = 'Carrot-like');
```

In this case, **new** is the method, **Vegetable** is the class (and indicates to Perl the package to search for the **new** method), and list is the optional list of arguments that will be passed to the method after the initial class name. The same format can be used for methods on existing objects:

```
boil $carrot 'Chopped';
```

This actually makes more sense (providing your methods and classes are suitably defined). The above line is equal to the earlier example, which uses the second syntax format:

```
CLASS_OR_INSTANCE->METHOD(LIST)
```

For our carrot, this means using this line to get it chopped and boiled:

```
$carrot->boil('Chopped');
```

Note that this second method requires parentheses around the arguments to the method because this syntax cannot be used as a list operator. This means you must be careful with the first format. It assumes that the first parenthesis defines the start of the arguments, and the matching closing parenthesis ends the argument list.

Note also that in both cases you can explicitly define the method/class you want to use with the normal qualification:

```
$carrot->Vegetable::boil('Chopped');
```

Finally, you can use a scalar variable to hold the name of a method to call, providing you use the infix operator form of the method call:

```
$method = 'boil';
$carrot->$method('Chopped');
```

It won't work with other constructs, so don't attempt to use a function call or other expression here. It won't be parsed properly, and Perl will report an error.

Accessing Object Data

At the risk of repeating myself yet again, an object is just a reference that knows what class it belongs to. This means you can access an element of the object by using reference notation. For example, to print the status of one of our **Vegetable** objects, you could use a line like this:

```
print $carrot->{'State'},"\n";
```

The same is true of any other data structure you decide to use. There is no need to create a subroutine to do it for you. However, if you want to use this method of accessing fields via methods, then you can use autoloading. See Chapter 5 for more details on autoloading, and for an object-specific example, see below:

```
sub AUTOLOAD
{
    my $self = shift;
    my $type = ref ($self) || croak "$self is not an object";
    my $field = $AUTOLOAD;
    $field =~ s/.*://;
    unless (exists $self->{$field})
    {
        croak "$field does not exist in object/class $type";
    }
    if (@_)
    {
        return $self->($name) = shift;
    }
    else
    {
        return $self->($name);
    }
```

So you can print a value,

```
print $carrot->state();
```

or set a value:

```
$carrot->state('Peeled');
```

Classes and Inheritance

A class is just a package. You can inherit methods from a parent class in a new class through the use of the **@ISA** array. Note that you cannot automatically inherit data. Perl leaves that decision to you. Since an object is a reference, you should be able to copy the information over easily, or just copy references in the new object to allow access to the inherited object's data. Since the normal base data type for an object is a hash, copying "fields" is a case of accessing the corresponding hash elements. See the sections above for more information.

You may remember in the "Modules" section of Chapter 5 that **@ISA** was said to define the list of base classes on which the package relies. This is in fact the array used for inheriting methods. When you call a method on an object, Perl first looks for it within the package class. It then follows the inheritance tree based on the root classes (packages) defined in **@ISA**. For each class (package) defined in the array, Perl follows the inherited classes defined in that package's **@ISA** array, and so on, until the complete tree has been followed. It then moves on to the next one. This allows you to inherit, almost by assumption, the methods defined in the packages specified in the **@ISA** array and, in turn, any methods defined within the base classes of those packages.

This is how you can identify the list of packages specified in **@ISA** as base classes, and how the interpretation of the **@ISA** array becomes "is-a," since a new object "is-a" member of the specified base classes.

The full path followed for method inheritance is actually slightly more complex, and the full list is shown below:

1. Perl searches the class of the specified object for the specified object.
2. Perl searches the classes defined in the object class's **@ISA** array.
3. If no method is found in steps 1 or 2, then Perl uses an **AUTOLOAD** subroutine, if one is found in the **@ISA** tree.
4. If a matching method still cannot be found, then Perl searches for the method within the **UNIVERSAL** class (package) that comes as part of the standard Perl library.
5. If the method still hasn't been found, then Perl gives up and raises a run-time exception.

You can force Perl to examine the base class's **@ISA** list first by specifying the **SUPER** pseudoclass within the base class package, as in,

```
$carrot->SUPER::fry();
```

which would automatically force Perl to look in the **@ISA** classes, rather than the local class, for the **fry** method. This can only be used within the base class package. You cannot use it on an object outside of the base class; so it's only of any use to object programmers, rather than object users.

Destructors and Garbage Collection

If you have programmed using objects before, then you will be aware of the need to create a "destructor" to free the memory allocated to the object when you have finished using it. Perl does this automatically for you as soon as the object goes out of scope.

You may want to provide your own destruction mechanism, however. This is sometimes necessary if you are using objects to define network connectivity or to update tied persistent data (see "Using **tie**" later in the chapter), or if you are using other objects that access external information. You will need to close the connections to these external sources politely, and for that, you need to define a special method called **DESTROY**. This method will be called on the object just before Perl frees the memory allocated to it. In all other respects, the **DESTROY** method is just like any other, and you can do anything you like with the object in order to close it properly.

A **DESTROY** method is absolutely essential in situations where you have objects that refer to nested structures (objects within objects), or when you have inherited information from another class. In these instances you will need to destroy the nested references yourself as part of the special **DESTROY** method.

Comparing Perl Objects to Other Languages

Perl objects have some very specific features and advantages that make them easy to use within a Perl script. The lack of a distinct compartment for object-oriented programs may seem like a problem for programmers used to the confinement of Python or C++. In fact, it makes programming with objects and normal structures much more fluid and intelligent—you can use objects when the need requires it without having to make the decision before starting to program. Let's have a look at some other differences between the object implementation on Perl and other languages.

Python

Python is an object-oriented language. All data structures are created within an object environment and the individual structures such as lists and dictionaries (which are like Perl's hashes) can all be accessed using a consistent object interface. The external libraries also have an object interface. Although this all appears to be restrictive, in fact Python makes it very easy and straightforward and you never feel as confined as you do with say, C++ or Java. As such, Python is an excellent language for learning OO techniques, and although it is more structured than Perl, the fluidity of the environment will appeal to Perl programmers.

The main difference between Python and Perl is that Perl does not impose the structure. Perl also supports objects based on scalars, arrays, or hashes. Python only supports objects using dictionaries (hashes).

C++/Java

C++ and Java are very similar when it comes to their internal representation and treatment of objects and so we can comfortably lump the two together when we make a comparison back to Perl.

Perhaps the most significant difference is that Perl is much more relaxed about its object implementation. C++ (and Java) require you to explicitly declare a new class (using the **class** keyword), and you must explicitly specify a function as separate from a method using the **static** keyword. You must also declare your classes separately from their implementations, and the class goes in a header file and the implementation in a separate file, except in the case of inline definitions.

C++ also requires you to specify the privacy of a method, object, or class explicitly. There is no such feature within Perl. If you need to protect the privacy of a method or function, don't advertise it. If you want to protect a variable, then use a lexically scoped one instead. You can also get away with using a constructor with any name—you don't have to create a constructor with the same name as the class you are creating. Although we typically use **new** in Perl, this is a convention, rather than a restriction.

Finally, because C++ (and indeed Java) are compiled languages, the class information (that is the definition, supported methods, inheritance etc.) must be known at compile time. Perl allows the definition of everything at run time. We can even modify the inheritance hierarchy by making modifications to the **@ISA** array, whilst simultaneously making changes to the methods and even format dynamically.

Using tie

Within Perl (versions 5 and up) you can "tie" a variable type to a particular class. The class implements the core methods that create, access, update, and destroy the elements of the underlying data type they are tied to. You can tie a scalar, array, or hash to any external data source. The most obvious use is for DBM files. You can tie a hash to an external DBM file (which uses a hashing system to store data in a physical file) and then use the normal hash constructs to access the keys and values within the external file.

The tie system uses objects and classes to associate a variable with the underlying object methods that support the interface between the Perl data type and the external data source. The base function is **tie**:

```
tie VARIABLE, CLASSNAME, LIST
```

The **VARIABLE** is just a normal variable that you will use to access the information in the tied resource. **CLASSNAME** defines the name of the package that supports the required class methods to tie the variable. Note that **CLASSNAME** is a string, not a bare word or other value. It can come from a variable, but that variable must contain the string to a valid class package.

The package that contains the class definition must have been imported via **use** or **require**. The **tie** function doesn't do this for you. The **LIST** is passed on directly to the class constructor at the point when the variable is tied.

Also note that the underlying class never gets passed the variable. The **tie** function creates the association, not the method class. The actual constructor name is the only way a package can determine what type of variable is being tied. If you **tie** a scalar, then it calls **TIESCALAR** as the constructor. With an array, it's **TIEARRAY**, and **TIEHASH** is used if it's a hash variable. In addition, in each case, the constructors are identical in all other respects to a typical object constructor. They just return a reference to the correct object; the constructor has no way of determining whether it was called from **tie**.

If you want to determine the name of the class to which a variable is tied, you use the **tied** function:

```
tied VARIABLE
```

This returns a reference to the object underlying the tied **VARIABLE**.

Once you have finished with the variable, you need to disassociate the variable from the underlying class methods, and for this you use **untie**:

```
untie VARIABLE
```

This breaks the binding between a variable and a package, undoing the association created by the **tie** function. It calls the **DESTROY** method, if it has been defined.

Creating New tie Classes

In this section we'll look at the creation of new base classes for tying different variable types. In each case, the base class must define a number of methods in order for the tie operation to work. Three methods are constant across all three variable types: **FETCH**, for reading the value of a tied variable, **STORE**, for assigning a value to a tied variable, and **DESTROY**, which deletes the tied variable when you call **untie**.

The **FETCH** and **STORE** methods are used to provide an interface to the variable that has been tied, not the underlying object. Accessing the object directly doesn't invoke these methods. The object reference is available either by using **tied** or by capturing the value returned by **tie**, which will be a reference to the underlying object being used.

Tying Scalars

We'll use the methods for tying scalars as our base reference, examining the entire process from start to finish. For this we'll use the example of file ownership, supported by the **FileOwner** package. When you tie a scalar using the methods in the **FileOwner** class, the variable tied contains the name of the file. Accessing the tied variable returns the owner (name, or user ID if the name cannot be resolved). Assigning a value to the tied variable sets the file's ownership, accepting a user ID or name accordingly.

For example, consider the script:

```
use FileOwner;

tie $profile, 'FileOwner', '.bash_profile';

print "Current owner is: $profile\n";
$profile = 'mcslp';
print "New owner is: $profile\n";
```

When the **tie** function is called, what actually happens is that the **TIESCALAR** method from **FileOwner** is called, passing '.bash_profile' as the argument to the method. This returns an object, which is associated by **tie** to the **$profile** variable.

When **$profile** is used in the print statements, the **FETCH** method is called. When you assign a value to **$profile**, the **STORE** method is called, with 'mcslp' as the argument to the method. If you can follow this, then you can create tied scalars, arrays, and hashes, since they all follow the same basic model. Now let's examine the details of our new **FileOwner** class, starting with the **TIESCALAR** method:

```
TIESCALAR CLASSNAME, LIST
```

The **TIESCALAR** is a class method and, as such, is passed the name of the class, which you'll use when blessing the new object you create, and the list of additional arguments passed to the **tie** function. For our example there is only one argument—the name of the file to use for determining and setting file ownership. The method should return an object, blessed accordingly. The contents of the scalar object is the name of the file you supplied when the object was created. Thus you get a method like this:

```
sub TIESCALAR
{
    my $class = shift;
    my $file = shift;
```

```
    unless (-e $file)
    {
        carp("File $file does not exist");
        return undef;
    }

    return bless \$file,$class;
}
```

Note that you must make sure the file exists before you continue. You can't create an object that refers to a file that doesn't exist. The method returns an undefined object if the file does not exist, and this will be picked up by **tie**. You also report an error via the **carp** function, defined in the **Carp** module, which supports a more package friendly way of raising errors.

In essence, the object you have created is anonymous, since you return the reference to the **$file** variable directly. **tie** does what it needs to with the returned object.

```
FETCH THIS
```

The **FETCH** method is called every time the tied variable is accessed. It takes only one argument, **THIS**, which is a reference to the corresponding object that is tied to the variable. Because we're working with scalars, the dereferencing is easy. The complex part is the determination of the owner of the file and the resulting resolving process to convert the user ID returned into a user name.

```
sub FETCH
{
    my $self = shift;

    local $! = 0;
    my $userid = (stat($$self))[4];
    if ($!) { croak("Can't get file owner: $!") }
    local $! = 0;
    my $owner = getpwuid($userid);
    $owner = $userid unless (defined($owner));
    return $owner;
}
```

The return value from this method is the user name or user ID. Because of this, you have no way of raising an error exception to the calling script, so you have to use **croak** to indicate a serious problem when determining the owner of the file.

```
STORE THIS, VALUE
```

The **STORE** method is called whenever an assignation is made to the tied variable. Beyond the object reference that is passed, **tie** also passes the value you want stored in the scalar variable you are tied to.

```
sub STORE
{
    my $self = shift;
    my $owner = shift;

    confess("Wrong type") unless ref $self;
    croak("Too many arguments") if @_;

    my $userid;

    if ($owner =~ /$[a-zA-Z]+/)
    {
        $userid = getpwnam($owner)
    }
    else
    {
        $userid = $owner;
    }

    local $! = 0;
    chown($userid,$$self);
    if ($!) { croak("Can't set file ownership: $!") }
    return $owner;
}
```

The only thing of note here is that you return the new assigned value, since that's the return value of any other assignment.

```
DESTROY THIS
```

The **DESTROY** method is called when the associated object is disassociated, either because it's gone out of scope, or when **untie** is called. Generally, this method shouldn't be used, since Perl will do its own deallocation and garbage collection. However, as mentioned earlier, this method can be used when you want to close opened files, disconnect from servers cleanly, and so on. In the realms of a scalar this is seldom required.

Tying Arrays

Classes for tying arrays must define at least three methods: **TIEARRAY**, **FETCH**, and **STORE**. You may also want and/or need to define the **DESTROY** method. At the present time the methods for tied arrays do not cover some of the functions and operators available to untied arrays. In particular, there are no equivalent methods for the **$#array** operator, nor for the **push**, **pop**, **shift**, **unshift**, or **splice** functions.

Since you already know the basics surrounding the creation of the tied objects, we'll dispense with the examples and cover the details of the required elements of the methods required.

```
TIEARRAY CLASSNAME, LIST
```

This method is called when the **tie** function is used to associate an array. It is the constructor for the array object and, as such, accepts the class name and should return an object reference. The method can also accept additional arguments, used as required. See the **TIESCALAR** method above.

```
FETCH THIS, INDEX
```

This method will be called each time an array element is accessed. The **INDEX** argument is the element number within the array that should be returned.

```
STORE THIS, INDEX, VALUE
```

This method is called each time an array element is assigned a value. The **INDEX** argument specifies the element within the array that should be assigned, and **VALUE** is the corresponding value to be assigned.

```
DESTROY THIS
```

This method is called when the tied object needs to be deallocated.

Tying Hashes

Hashes are the obvious (and most complete) of the supported **tie** implementations. This is because the **tie** system was developed to provide more convenient access to DBM files, which themselves operate just like hashes.

```
TIEHASH CLASSNAME, LIST
```

This is the class constructor. It needs to return a blessed reference pointing to the corresponding object.

```
FETCH THIS, KEY
```

This returns the value stored in the corresponding **KEY** and is called each time a single element of a hash is accessed.

```
STORE THIS, KEY, VALUE
```

This method is called when an individual element is assigned a new value.

```
DELETE THIS, KEY
```

Removes the key and corresponding value from the hash. This is usually the result of a call to the **delete** function.

```
CLEAR THIS
```

This empties the entire contents of the hash.

```
EXISTS THIS, KEY
```

The method called when **exists** is used to determine the existence of a particular key in a hash.

```
FIRSTKEY THIS
```

The method triggered when you first start iterating through a hash with **each**, **keys**, or **values**. Note that you must reset the internal state of the hash to ensure that the iterator used to step over individual elements of the hash is reset.

```
NEXTKEY THIS, LASTKEY
```

Triggered by a **keys** or **each** function. This method should return two values—the next key and corresponding value from the hash object. The **LASTKEY** argument is supplied by **tie** and indicates the last key that was accessed.

```
DESTROY THIS
```

The method triggered when a tied hash's object is about to be deallocated.

The Complete Reference

Chapter 8

Database Systems

Up to now, all of the chapters have concentrated on the process of utilizing information within the Perl environment and the Perl script you have invoked. However, it is often desirable, if not essential, to create, update, and access information for external databases. This process is called *object persistence*, since the data is created and is persistently (or permanently) available.

There are many different types of database systems. Some of them will be familiar to many of you, as you probably already use them using different methods. In fact databases take two basic forms: flat file and relational. With a flat file database, the information is stored in a fixed format, and the information stored is considered to be isolated or complete. For example, the /etc/passwd file on a Unix machine is an example of a flat file database. The information is stored in its entirety in a format that is easy to understand, and it does not need to be linked to another database for the information to make sense.

A relational database, on the other hand, uses a number of separate "tables." Each table contains a list of information, and links between the tables enable you to store information in a structured and relative way. For example, imagine a record database. It might have two tables—one lists the artists and the other lists the individual albums and records they have made. You can access all of the records for a particular artist by examining the link between the two tables.

When it comes to accessing and using databases, there are other problems to contend with. First of all you must decide how you are going to store the information within a file. Using a single- or multicharacter delimiter is a fairly common system and one that Unix uses in many different places. By using a tab or colon or some other character, you can separate the individual fields within a record. The return character is often used to separate the individual records within the entire file.

The problem with this method is that if you want to store information that may possibly contain one of these delimiting characters, you may experience some corruption of data or even complete loss of information. A better solution in this instance is to use a fixed-length record system. Rather than delimiting the individual fields and records, fixed-length systems specify the maximum length of a particular field. Provided you know the format (field sizes and types), you should be able to read entire records from the file and determine the individual fields. This is wasteful on space for databases with very large fields. In a database with 16K records you can easily eat up a lot of space. A record with 1K of useful data still takes up 16K of storage space.

Even once you have broached these problems, there are other considerations. Text databases are great for accessing sequential information or for storing a stream of information that will be processed by a program at a later time. What they are not so good at is random access. Searching through a large text database can be a time-consuming task, since you will need to read in each individual record to determine whether it is the one you want. There are ways around this: you can use an index system to point to the records you want, but the chances are this also uses a text format, and you are back at square one.

To get around this particular problem, you need to investigate a system that automatically handles the indexing and searching of your database in a timely manner but still provides you with a simple interface for extracting the individual records and fields from the database files. The easiest solution is to use the DBM system (the precise expansion of the acronym has been lost, but it probably stands for database management). This is a hashing database using the same key/value pair system as Perl's internal hash variable.

The more complex database implementations, especially those relying on relational features, either require more complex use of the text or DBM database systems or require the use of an external database implementation. Perl supports access to all of the major database systems, and many of the smaller systems, through a number of extensions provided by the DBI toolkit, a third-party module available from CPAN. Interfaces are available for use with the DBI toolkit for accessing Oracle, Sybase, Msql, PostgreSQL, and the ODBC (Open Database Connectivity). ODBC is rapidly becoming an accepted standard, and is now available on Windows and Unix platforms.

Since the DBM database is the most accessible, it's the one we will investigate most fully in this chapter. However, as an introduction, we'll look at the use of text databases, and we'll follow up by examining the use of external databases via the DBI toolkit.

Text Databases

Although the most basic of the database systems, text databases provide a reliable and safe location for storing information. Many log systems using either delimited or fixed-length records; many of the files that you take for granted on Unix and Windows systems are actually text based, and only imported or reported on when required.

If you look at a typical /etc/passwd file, you will notice that it has records—one per line—where the individual fields are separated by colons, for example:

```
root:x:0:1:0000-Admin(0000):/:/sbin/sh
daemon:x:1:1:0000-Admin(0000):/:
bin:x:2:2:0000-Admin(0000):/usr/bin:
sys:x:3:3:0000-Admin(0000):/:
adm:x:4:4:0000-Admin(0000):/var/adm:
lp:x:71:8:0000-lp(0000):/usr/spool/lp:
smtp:x:0:0:mail daemon user:/:
uucp:x:5:5:0000-uucp(0000):/usr/lib/uucp:
nuucp:x:9:9:0000-uucp(0000):/var/spool/uucppublic:/usr/lib/uucp/uucico
listen:x:37:4:Network Admin:/usr/net/nls:
nobody:x:60001:60001:uid no body:/:
noaccess:x:60002:60002:uid no access:/:
martinb:x:1000:1000:Martin C Brown:/users/martinb:/usr/local/bin/bash
```

There is a problem with the type of layout shown above if you start using this technique for more complex databases. What happens if the data you are trying to store contains a colon? As far as the Perl script is concerned, the colon specifies the end of one field and the beginning of the next. An additional colon would only upset the information stored in the "record." Even worse, what would happen if you wanted to record multiple lines of text in the database? Individual records are often stored on individual lines; multiline fields would confuse the script again. You could use separate record delimiters that don't rely on the newline character, but again this adds more complexity.

There are ways around these problems. You could use a different character for the field and record separators, although this is still open to the same abuse and possible results. You could just remove the field and record separator characters from the source before you put them in the database, but this reduces the utility of being able to store the information in the first place. The simplest solution is to ignore any field or record separators and instead use fixed-length records to store the information. The use of fixed-length records implies that you know the maximum size of the data that you are storing before you place it into the database, and therefore you need to know the format of the database before you write to and from it.

Using fixed-length records would allow you to store any sort of information in the database, including multiple-line text, without worrying about how the data may affect the database layout. The only problem with fixed-length databases is that you not only restrict the amount of information you can store but also increase the size of the data file for small records, as the individual fields are "padded" to make up the fixed lengths. To complicate matters further, you may have trouble choosing a padding character that won't affect the contents of the fields you are storing. Null characters, for example, produce all sorts of results when they are included as the text within a browser window when writing CGI programs. In these situations you can usually augment the fixed-length structure by also specifying the field length for each field in each record. But this too increases the size of the database.

To add more complexity, you will also need to overcome the problems of searching the file if you are using it as a random access database. If you know the record number you want to access, then with either form of text database you should be able to move to the location relatively quickly. But if you don't, the time taken to find the data will be a factor of the database size. This is why, practically, text databases are only good for small-scale installations or in situations where the information flow is basically one-way.

Using a text database for storing log information is an example of a one-way information flow. One or more programs will add data to the file, without referring back to the data they have written. Another script will be responsible for taking in the raw data and producing a summary report of the information contained in it. Again, the information flow is one-way: the data comes from the database but is not updated or modified.

In the following sections we'll look at the techniques for reading from and writing to textual databases, including some example scripts of how to use them. We'll also examine the methods you will need to employ if you need to update, rather than read from or append, information in a text database.

Delimited Databases

Accessing delimited databases is a case of using the **split** and **join** functions to extract fields from and combine fields into the records used to store the information. For example, to access the password file on a Unix system, which uses colons for the field delimiters and newlines for record delimiters, you can use a very simple script:

```
open(D,"</etc/passwd") || die "Can't open file, $!";
while(<D>)
{
    chomp;
    @fields = split /:/;
    print join(' ', @fields),"\n";
}
close(D) || dir "Couldn't close file, $!";
```


Of course, in this instance it's easier to use the **getpwent** and other functions to read the file in a more reliable and safe format, but the principles remain the same.

If you want to import and export records using a different record separator, you can use the **$/** and **$** variables. You can set the values of the input and output field values when you call the **split** and **join** functions. You may also want to investigate the **DBI::CSV** module at the end of this chapter.

Many of the remaining technicalities surrounding the use of delimited text files also apply to fixed-length databases, so we'll examine these problems in the next section.

Fixed-Length Records

Using fixed-length records is also a case of using an existing function set that you already know about. The **pack** and **unpack** functions, which you saw in the previous chapter, can be used to create fixed-length records that can be written to a file. Because the byte-string generated by **pack** is (within reason) architecture independent, using **pack** and **unpack** can be a reliable method for storing and exchanging information across platforms.

Below, we look at three simple scripts: one to add data to a task list, one to report from it, and one to update the information in a task list. The first is relatively simple. We will compose the information from that supplied on the command line and append a packed byte-string to the end of the file.

```
my ($taskfile) = "tasks.db";
my ($taskformat) = "A40LL";

my ($sec,$min,$hour,$mday,$mon,$year) = (localtime(time))[0..5];
```

```
$mon++;
$year += 1900;

die "Usage: $0 title required-date\n" if (@ARGV<2);

($mday,$mon,$year) = split '/',$ARGV[-1];
$reqdate = ($year*10000)+($mon*100)+$mday;

open(D,">>$taskfile") || die "Couldn't open the task file, $!\n";
print D pack($taskformat,$ARGV[0],$reqdate,0);
close(D);
```

The only important note is that we convert the date into a numerical format. The reason for this, which will be more important in the next script, is that the numerical version can be more easily sorted via the standard Perl functions.

Reporting from the database is almost as simplistic. Once again we employ the **unpack** function to extract the individual records in turn:

```
use Getopt::Std;

my $taskfile   = "tasks.db";
my $taskformat = "A40LL";
my $tasklength = length(pack($taskformat,));
my $ref=0;

getopts('drc');

open(D,"<$taskfile") || die "Couldn't open the task file, $!\n";

while(read(D,$_,$tasklength))
{
    ($title,$reqdate,$compdate) = unpack($taskformat,$_);
    $lref{$ref} = $title;
    $lref{$ref} = "$reqdate" if ($opt_r);
    $lref{$ref} = "$compdate" if ($opt_c);
    $ltitle{$ref} = $title;
    $lreqdate{$ref} = $reqdate;
    $lcompdate{$ref} = $compdate;
    $ref++;
}
```

```
close(D);

printf("%-40s  %-10s  %-10s\n","Title","Req. Date","Comp. Date");

foreach $key (sort_values(\%lref))
{
    $lreqdate{$key} =~ s#(....)(..)(..)#$3/$2/$1#;
    if ($lcompdate{$key}>0)
    {
        next if ($opt_d);
        $lcompdate{$key} =~ s#(....)(..)(..)#$3/$2/$1#;
    }
    else
    {
        $lcompdate{$key}="";
    }
    printf("%-40s %10s %10s\n",$ltitle{$key},
                     $lreqdate{$key},$lcompdate{$key});
}

sub sort_values
{
    my $lref = shift;

    if ($opt_r || $opt_c)
    {
        sort {$lref{$a} <=> $lref{$b}} keys %$lref;
    }
    else
    {
        sort {$lref{$a} cmp $lref{$b}} keys %$lref;
    }
}
```

The final script is more complicated. Updating information in either a delimited or fixed-length database requires that you know the location of the data that you want to update. With a delimited database the data can potentially be of any length, and so you need to copy the existing information from the current database into a new file, substituting the updated information in the new file before continuing the copy process. It's not possible to "insert" data into the file—you cannot move data within a physical file without moving the information somewhere else first. You could do it in memory, but for large databases this wouldn't be practical. Instead, the better solution is to use external files for the process.

With a fixed-length database the process is slightly easier. The length of all the records in the database is the same, so updating a record is as easy as overwriting the updated and packed record in the same physical location within the file. To do this you use the **seek** and **tell** functions. This is a cyclical process in which you read in each record until you find the one you want, remembering the location of the start of the record in each case. Then, once the information has been updated, you go back to the start of the record and rewrite the packed record.

Here's the script that updates our earlier task file entries:

```
use Fcntl;

my ($taskfile) = "tasks.db";
my ($taskformat) = "A40LL";
my $tasklength = length(pack($taskformat,));

die "Usage: modtask.pl title completed-date\n" if (@ARGV<2);

open(D,"+<$taskfile") || die "Couldn't open the task file, $!\n";

while(read(D,$_,$tasklength))
{
    ($title,$reqdate,$compdate) = unpack($taskformat,$_);
    last if (($title eq $ARGV[0]) && ($compdate eq 0));
    $lastseek=tell(D);
}

if ($lastseek >= (-s $taskfile))
{
    die "Couldn't find the task specified\n";
}

($mday,$mon,$year) = split '/',$ARGV[-1];
$compdate = ($year*10000)+($mon*100)+$mday;

seek(D,$lastseek,SEEK_SET);

print D pack($taskformat,$title,$reqdate,$compdate);

close(D) || die "Couldn't close the database\n";
```

To use all three scripts, first call **addtask.pl** (the first script) to create and add a record to the database, and then update the task you have added by specifying a completion date:

```
$ perl -w addtask.pl 'Phone Richard' 25/3/1999
$ perl modtask.pl 'Phone Richard' 26/3/1999
$ perl listtask.pl
Title                                         Req. Date    Comp. Date
Phone Richard                                 25/03/1999   26/03/1999
```


DBM Databases

For simple structures such as single-record databases, and especially for a sequential series of data, text files are exceedingly practical. However, they suffer from performance issues if you want to access the information on a random access basis, or where the amount of information you wish to store becomes unmanageable in a text database. A better solution is to store the information in a real database where the information can be recorded and extracted using identified and unique keys. This enables you to ignore the searching and storage mechanisms that are required for text databases and instead to concentrate on writing the code for using, rather than the code for accessing, the database.

The standard database under Unix is a system called DBM, which is based on a simple key/value pair, much like Perl's own hash data type. Each entry within the database will have a unique key, and attached to this will be the piece of data you want to store. To extract information from the database, you simply request the data associated with a particular key.

Although it sounds complicated, it is really no different from the way hash variables are stored within Perl. You access a hashed variable entry within Perl by specifying a textual key. With some careful programming and the use of well-worded keys, you can store information in a DBM file in the same way you would store information in any off-the-shelf database.

DBM files are an integral part of the Unix operating system. Many of the standard components use DBM files for their own storage. Sendmail, for example, uses DBM to store aliases in a time-efficient manner. The alias file is converted, using the **newalias** command, into a DBM database. This is quicker than manually trawling through the text-based alias file—something that is vitally important when processing a large number of email messages. As a demonstration of the power of the DBM system, it is also the storage format for the Network Information Service (NIS, formally called the Yellow Pages), a networked version of many of the core OS configuration files for everything from user data to hostnames and IP addresses.

Over the years, the original DBM system has been improved and has gone through a number of different incarnations, although the original specification remains the same. Most of the different DBM systems are compatible with each other, but to a greater or lesser extent, compatibility depends on the platform and implementation involved. It should be noted as well that DBM files are nonportable. The storage format used is specific to a particular hardware platform and operating system. In some cases, even different versions of the same OS have incompatible DBM systems. Furthermore, the format used by DBM is very wasteful of space compared to even a fixed-length text database. Because of this, copying a DBM file across file systems on the same machine can be problematic.

Depending on the implementation, a DBM database is composed of either two files or a combined single file. In the two-file combination, one is a directory table containing a bit-based representation of the buckets and their index location and has .dir as its suffix. The second file contains all the data and has .pag as its suffix. The data file is often full of "holes," where storage space has been allocated but not used or the key has been deleted. In these instances the area within the file actually contains no useful information, although it will be reused when new data is added to the file.

The downside to this method is that some implementations allocate too much storage space, thereby generating a file that is reported to be 10, 100, or even 1,000 times the amount of useful information stored within the file. There is, unfortunately, no clear method for compacting the information into a smaller version of the database. Even using Perl to copy the contents of the database into a new one will not necessarily provide you with a suitable solution to the problem. Of course, the flip side to all of this is that the speed of access, even for a very large database, is very quick.

There is a limitation on the storage size of each key/value pair, which is known as the bucket size. Creating entries larger than this will either crash you out of Perl or just truncate the information you attempt to store, depending entirely on how the database has been implemented at C level. The maximum bucket size is dependent on the DBM implementation being used, and the information is summarized in Table 8-1.

The following sections describe common DBM implementations and their advantages, disadvantages, and differences from the range available.

DBM/ODBM

The generic term for the original DBM toolkit on which all the newer toolkits are based is DBM/ODBM. Although included as standard in most Unix variants, it has been replaced almost entirely by NDBM as the DBM implementation of choice. Perl refers to ODBM as "Old DBM." The supported bucket size is 1K on most platforms, but it may be as high as 2K on some. The database files are created with .dir and .pag extensions, although you only specify the prefix name when opening the file.

NDBM

The "new" replacement for the original DBM, with some speed and storage allocation improvements, is NDBM. This has replaced the standard DBM libraries and in some cases is the only implementation available. Depending on the OS, the bucket size is anything from 1K to 4K. The database files are created with .dir and .pag extensions,

Implementation	DBM/ ODBM	NDBM	SDBM	GDBM	Berkeley DB
Module	ODBM_File	NDBM_File	SDBM_File	GDBM_File	DB_File
Bucket Limit	1–2K	1–4K	1K (none)	None	None
Disk Usage	Varies	Varies	Small	Big	Big
Speed	Slow	Slow	Slow	OK	Fast
Data Files Distributable	No	No	Yes	Yes	Yes
Byte-order Independent	No	No	No	No	Yes
User Defined Sort Order	No	No	No	No	Yes
Wildcard Lookups	No	No	No	No	Yes

Table 8-1. *DBM Modules in Perl*

although you only specify the prefix name when opening the file. NDBM should, in theory, be compatible with files created using the DBM/ODBM implementations, although this isn't guaranteed. You should use this in place of ODBM if it is available.

SDBM

Substitute/Simple DBM is a speed- and stability-enhanced version of DBM. Included as standard with the Perl distribution, it's supported on all Perl platforms except MacOS. The SDBM system supports a default bucket size of 1K, but this can be modified at compile time. The database files are created with .dir and .pag extensions, although you only specify the prefix name when opening the file.

GDBM

The GNU/FSF implementation of DBM is faster than all implementations except Berkeley DB. GDBM has also been ported to a larger number of platforms than other implementations. Unlike other systems, it also supports an unlimited bucket size and has built-in file locking within the GDBM module. This eliminates a lot of the complexity surrounding the normal responsibilities of file locking. Unlike other DBM implementations, the entire hash table is stored in a single file, rather than two separate files.

Berkeley DB

Berkeley DB is a public domain C library of database access methods, including B+Tree, Extended Linear Hashing, and fixed/variable length records. The DB_File Perl module puts a DBM-like wrapper around the B-Tree and hash implementations, enabling them to be used as DBM replacements. The fixed/variable length record implementation also has a Perl array wrapper for direct use within Perl scripts.

Berkeley DB libraries also support relational database system facilities such as multiuser updates and transactions and the ability to recover corrupt database files. We'll take a look at using the additional features of Berkeley DB beyond simulating DBM files later in this chapter.

DBM Functions

Perl 4 used a system of functions to access DBM files. The process was basically identical to the process used for any normal file, and the result was very similar to the **tie** solution we will see shortly. In each case, the **dbmopen** function creates a relation between a Perl hash and an external DBM database. Using these functions, only one type of DBM implementation is supported, and that's usually the standard for your operating system (NDBM, ODBM) or the Perl-supplied SDBM if these are not available.

```
dbmopen HASH, EXPR, MODE
```

This binds the database file specified by **EXPR** to the hash **HASH**. If the database does not exist, then it is created using the mode specified by **MODE**. The file **EXPR** should be specified without the .dir and .pag extensions.

For example, to associate the aliases database on a Unix machine to a hash called **%aliases**:

```
Use Fcntl;
dbmopen %aliases,'/etc/aliases',O_RDWR;
foreach (keys %aliases)
{
    print "$_: $aliases{$_}\n";
}
```

Once you have finished using the DBM database, you must disassociate the hash from the underlying DBM file with the **dbmclose** function:

```
dbmclose HASH
```

Using Tied DBM Databases

Using the **tie** function, which you saw in the last chapter, provides an object-oriented interface to DBM databases and is now the preferred method within Perl 5. By using **tie**, you can create a connection between a standard Perl hash and a DBM database. Since DBM databases use the same key/value system as Perl hashes, there is no complex handling of the information. Accessing a key in the hash automatically provides you with the correct key/value pair in the DBM database. Creating new entries and deleting them similarly updates the DBM file. The access and control is instantaneous, and it eliminates so much of the complexity of using a DBM database that it's very easy to forget you are even using an external file instead of an internal structure.

The format of the **tie** function with DBM files is as follows:

```
tie %hash, DBMTYPE, FILENAME, MODES, FILEMODE;
```

The **DBMTYPE** element should be the name of a DBM implementation from which to inherit the necessary methods for the **tie** function. For example, to create a new database using GDBM, you might use

```
tie %db, 'GDBM_File', 'database.db', O_CREAT|O_RDWR, 0644;
```

You will need the definitions from the Fcntl module for the specification of the different modes for opening and closing the files. The different modes available for all DBM implementations are shown in Table 8-2. Both GDBM and Berkeley DB have their own additional modes, which we will examine separately.

Once opened, the DBM file can be accessed using the hash it has been tied to. For example, the code fragment below opens a text file and creates a DBM database of the contents. The first line of the text file is assumed to be the list of fields to be used as keys in the rest of the database.

```
#!/usr/local/bin/perl5 -w

use NDBM_File;
use Fcntl;

my ($dbfile,%db,$i,@fieldnames,@fields,$key,$n);

die "Usage:\n$0 source\n" if (@ARGV<1);
```

```
$dbfile = $ARGV [0];

open(D,"<$dbfile") || die "Can't open $dbfile, $!";

(tie %db, NDBM_File, $dbfile, O_RDWR|O_CREAT|O_EXCL, 0666)
      || die "$0: Error creating $dbfile: $!\n";
$_ = <D>;
chomp;
s/,//;
@fieldnames = split "\t";

$db{fieldlist} = join(",",@fieldnames);

while(<D>)
{
    chomp;
    @fields = split "\t";

    for($n=0;$n<=@fields;$n++)
    {
        if (defined($fields[$n]))
        {
             $key = $fieldnames[$n] . "-$i";
             $db{$key} = $fields[$n];
        }
    }
    $i++;
}

$db{seqid} = $i;
close(D) || die "$0: Couldn't close source, $!\n";
untie %db || die "$0: Couldn't close db, $!\n";

print "Read $i records\n";
```

Other hash functions, such as **each**, **keys**, and **delete**, work the same way on a DBM file as on a hash. The changes are immediate: if you delete an entry in the hash tied to the DBM database, it has been deleted forever; recovery is impossible. You can also check for the existence of a key within the database using the normal **exists** function, and you can check the value of a specific key using **defined**. The **tie** object interface performs all the necessary checks and other operations for you on the actual DBM file.

Flag	Description
O_APPEND	Appends information to the given file.
O_CREAT	Creates a new file if it doesn't already exist.
O_EXCL	Causes the open to fail if the file already exists when used with **O_CREAT**.
O_NDELAY	Opens the file without blocking. Reads or writes to the file will not cause the process to wait for the operation to be complete.
O_NONBLOCK	Behaves as **O_NDELAY**.
O_RDONLY	Opens the file read-only.
O_RDWR	Opens the file for reading and writing.
O_TRUNC	Opens the file, truncating (emptying) the file if it already exists.
O_WRONLY	Opens the file write-only.

Table 8-2. *File Access Flags*

Also note that the **keys** and **values** functions should be used sparingly if the DBM file is particularly large. Perl will quite happily create an internal temporary array to contain the list of information. Unless you are producing a sorted list of the contents, it's best to avoid the use of functions altogether. In most cases you will be accessing individual key/value pairs from the database, and this should not then be a problem. However, when searching (perhaps when building a list of records to display), use the **each** function (see Chapter 7) to prevent Perl from creating such large temporary structures.

Converting Between DBM Formats

Because Perl 5 now uses the **Tie** module to create a link between a hash and a DBM object, you can use Perl to convert from one DBM implementation to another. The example below converts an NDBM_File database into a GDBM_File database:

```
use NDBM_File;
use GDBM_File;
use Fcntl;
```

```
die "Usage:$0 old new\n" if (@ARGV<2);

my($old,$new) = @ARGV;

tie (%oldhash, 'NDBM_File', $old, O_RDONLY, 0444)
    || die "$0: Error opening source $old: $!\n";
tie (%newhash, 'GDBM_File', $new, O_CREAT|O_RDWR|O_EXCL, 0666)
    || die "$0: Error opening dest $new: $!\n";

%newhash = %oldhash;

untie %oldhash || die "$0: Error closing old DBM file, $!\n";
untie %newhash || die"$0: Error closing new DBM file, $!\n";
```

Given our earlier concerns, you may want to use a less-memory-intensive process for copying the records. Here's the same example using **each** to extract the information before writing it into the new database:

```
use NDBM_File;
use GDBM_File;
use Fcntl;

die "Usage:$0 old new\n" if (@ARGV<2);

my($old,$new) = @ARGV;

tie (%oldhash, 'NDBM_File', $old, O_RDONLY, 0444)
    || die "$0: Error opening source $old: $!\n";
tie (%newhash, 'GDBM_File', $new, O_CREAT|O_RDWR|O_EXCL, 0666)
    || die "$0: Error opening dest $new: $!\n";

while(($key, $value) = each(%oldhash))
{
    $newhash{$key} = $value;
}

untie %oldhash || die "$0: Error closing old DBM file, $!\n";
untie %newhash || die"$0: Error closing new DBM file, $!\n";
```

Using AnyDBM_File

If you are not worried about the DBM implementation you are using, you can use the AnyDBM_File module to include a DBM implementation from those available. It selects a class from the implementations, choosing the first valid one from the following list: NDBM_File, DB_File, GDBM_File, SDBM_File, and ODBM_File. In the unlikely event that all of these modules are unavailable, the **use** statement will fail.

When using AnyDBM_File, you should be aware that the implementation selected may differ from the one you require if you are attempting to open an existing DBM database. If you do not know the format of the database you are trying to open, you will have to try and work it out. In general, any DBM file set ending in .dir or .pag will be an NDBM or ODBM database. If you know these are not supported on your system, then it's probably an SDBM database (except on MacOS, where SDBM is not supported). If the DBM database is stored in a single file, the most likely implementation is GDBM, but it's possible that Berkeley DB is also supported.

GDBM Features

The GDBM_File implementation, if available on your system, provides some additional benefits over the standard DBM implementations. Although the GDBM library supports DBM/NDBM compatibility, you cannot use the GDBM_File module to open existing databases. If you need to do this and don't have DBM/NDBM, try the SDBM module that comes with Perl.

The biggest benefit with the GDBM implementation of the DBM database system is that there is no limit on the bucket size. This, theoretically, means you can store arbitrary pieces of data in a single key/value pair. The size of the GDBM files that are created is slightly larger than traditional files—about 24K for a "blank" database is about average. I've successfully used the GDBM system to store large data structures within a database file, even, in one case, the graphics used for a website.

```
use GDBM_File;
tie %db, 'GDBM_File', 'db', &GDBM_WRCREAT, 0640;
untie %db;
```

You can use the modes ordinarily supplied by the Fcntl module, or you can instead use a set of modes defined by GDBM_File, as listed in Table 8-3.

In addition, you can specify the **GDBM_FAST** mode when opening a file for read/write. This forces disk synchronization with the memory version of the hash only when the file is closed. This improves performance, but it may produce unpredictable results if the script exits ungracefully.

Mode	Description
GDBM_READER	Open for read-only.
GDBM_WRITER	Open for read/write.
GDBM_WRCREAT	Open for read/write, creating a new database if it does not already exist, using the mode specified.
GDBM_NEWDB	Open for read/write, creating a new database even if one already exists, using the mode specified.

Table 8-3. *GDBM-Specific Modes*

Berkeley DB Features

The Berkeley DB system is a more involved and enhanced version of the base DBM implementation. The module provides a number of different database formats, accessed and used by means of the same **tie** function. The modules are the standard key/value pair database supported by other DBM systems (**DB_HASH**); a B-Tree-based system, accessible via a hash (**DB_BTREE**); and a record number system using arrays (**DB_RECNO**).

Standard Hash Database

A **DB_HASH** is identical in most respects to Perl's internal hash structure, only the key/data pairs are stored in data files, not memory. The functionality provided is basically identical to that provided by the other DBM-style database engines. DB_File uses its own hashing algorithm for storing and retrieving the key/data pairs, but you can supply your own system if you prefer.

```
use DB_File ;
[$X =] tie %hash,  'DB_File', $filename, $flags, $mode, $DB_HASH;
```

The value of **$flags** is identical to that of other databases and refers to the mode in which the file will be opened. The **$mode** is the octal mode with which the file should be created or accessible. The final item is actually a reference to a hash; I've used a predefined reference in the synopsis above. We'll return to the configuration options available via this hash shortly.

The **$DB_HASH** reference supports a number of configurable options, specified as a hash. The options are listed in Table 8-4.

Hash Key	Description
bsize	Defines the hash table bucket size. The default is 256 bytes, and you may want to increase this if you know you are storing information larger than this size. Remember that the size defined here will apply to all new entries created in the database. Arbitrarily increasing this may degrade performance and increase the storage space used by the database.
ffactor	Indicates the density of information. The value assigned becomes the number of keys that will accumulate within a single bucket allocation. The default is 8, and therefore a maximum of 8 key/value pairs of 32 bytes each could be stored in a single bucket. Reducing the value to 1 will increase the file size by the bucket size (defined in **bsize**) for each record. Specifying too large a value may decrease performance.
nelem	An estimation of the final size of the hash table (number of buckets or the number of elements divided by **ffactor**). If you know the number of elements you are going to store, you can use this to achieve a slight increase in performance. The value set is not restrictive; the database will automatically grow in size if you set a value that is too low. The default value is 1.
cachesize	The maximum size in bytes of physical memory to allocate as a buffer between the in-memory database and the physical file store. Specifying a large value will increase performance, since more of the database will be kept in memory. But it may also cause a synchronization error if there is a crash or other problem, since there may still be data in the cache that has not been written to a file. A value of 0 lets the system choose a reasonable value for you.
hash	A reference to a user-defined function that returns a 32-bit quantity suitable for ordering and referencing a hash. See the example in the text using the **hash** element for more details.
lorder	The byte order to be used for storing integers within the metadata in the file. The number specified should represent the order as an integer (that is, 4321 is big endian, and 1234 is little endian). If a value of 0 (the default) is specified, the current host order is used instead. If the file you are using already exists, the format used within that file is always used. This can help with compatibility across platforms if you are sharing a database file on multiple systems that support different byte orders.

Table 8-4. *Customizable Elements for DB_HASH Databases*

For example, to create a database with a bucket size of 1,024 bytes:

```
$options = new DB_File::HASHINFO;
$options->{'bsize'} = 1024;
tie %db, 'DB_File', "file.db", O_RDWR, 0644, $options;
```

The **hash** element should point to a function that you want to use for creating a hash value.

B-Tree Hash Database

The B-Tree hash is architecturally identical to the standard hashing system used on most other DBM systems. The difference is that the keys are stored in an ordered format using a binary tree. This allows you to use a hash database in an ordered form without having to resort to the use of **sort** to order the data before it is used.

```
use DB_File ;
tie %hash,  'DB_File', $filename, $flags, $mode, $DB_BTREE;
```

As before, the **$flags** and **$mode** are identical to other DBM databases. The **$DB_TREE** is a reference to a default hash that supports a number of configurable options, specified as a hash. The options are listed in Table 8-5.

Hash Key	Description
flags	A value that should be composed of values **or**'d together. Two values are currently available, **R_DUP** and **R_NOOVERWRITE**. The value **R_DUP** allows duplicate keys to be entered into the database. The **R_NOOVERWRITE** prevents you from overwriting existing keys. You cannot specify the two flags together, since they effectively cancel each other out.
cachesize	The maximum size in bytes of physical memory to allocate as a buffer between the in-memory database and the physical file store. Specifying a large value will increase performance, since more of the database will be kept in memory. But it may also cause a synchronization error if there is a crash or other problem, since there may still be data in the cache that has not been written to a file. A value of 0 lets the system choose a reasonable value for you.

Table 8-5. *Options for DB_TREE Databases*

Hash Key	Description
maxkeypage	The maximum number of keys that will be stored in a single page. This currently has no effect on the process within Perl.
minkeypage	The minimum number of keys that will be stored in a single page. This value defines which keys will be stored on overflow rather than main pages. The default value is 2, and this value will be selected if you try to define a value of 0.
psize	The size, in bytes, of the pages used to store nodes of the B-Tree structure. The minimum page size is 512 bytes and the maximum is 65,535 (64K). Ideally, you should choose a size that matches your data and the **minkeysize** value, or a value that matches the underlying size of your operating system allocation blocks.
compare	A reference to a function that operates the comparison between keys that will be used when storing the information. (See the discussion of the comparison function in this section for more information.) If none is specified, or if the **undef** value is used, then a default function that uses lexical comparisons. This function is basically alphanumeric, with shorter keys considered as being less than longer keys.
prefix	A reference to a function that returns the number of bytes necessary to determine whether the second key supplied is greater than the first key. The basic point behind the function is to optimize the size of the search tree used to find key/value pairs. For lexical comparisons, the built-in function should suffice. See the discussion of the **prefix** option for more information.
lorder	The byte order to be used for storing integers within the metadata in the file. The number specified should represent the order as an integer (that is, 4321 is big endian, and 1234 is little endian). If a value of 0 (the default) is specified, the current host order is used instead. If the file you are using already exists, the format used within that file is always used. This can help with compatibility across platforms if you are sharing a database file on multiple systems that support different byte orders.

Table 8-5. *Options for DB_TREE Databases* (continued)

The method for defining these flags is identical to the

```
$options = new DB_File::BTREEINFO;
$options->{'cache'} = 16384;
tie %db, 'DB_File', "file.db", O_RDWR, 0644, $options;
```

The comparison function should accept and compare two keys, returning a numerical value depending on how key1 compares to key2. The function should return 0 if the two keys are equal, -1 if key1 is less than key2, and 1 if key1 is greater than key2. For example, to use the default Perl string comparisons, you might use the following functions:

```
sub compare
{
    my ($key1, $key2) = @_;
    return 0  if ("\L$key1" eq "\L$key2");
    return -1 if ("\L$key1" lt "\L$key2");
    return 1  if ("\L$key1" gt "\L$key2");
}
```

More simply, you could just use the **cmp** operator:

```
sub compare
{
    my ($key1, $key2) = @_;
    "\L$key1" cmp "\L$key2";
}
```

Note in both examples that you convert the keys to lowercase to ensure that the comparison works in proper alpha order rather than the normal ASCII order that would be implied otherwise.

The **prefix** option allows you to specify the number of bytes that should be used when making comparisons between keys. The value should simply return the number of bytes used to make the comparison. This works with the comparison function to decide at what size a specific key is given priority over another key in the sorting process.

Record Number Database

The **DB_RECNO** option enables you to store fixed-length or variable-length records within a database file. The format used is basically text based. If you want to open and use a comma-separated file (CSV), you can use the **DB_RECNO** system to open and then use the database. Alternatively, you can make use of the fixed length we looked at, at the start of this chapter.

Unlike other systems, the database is tied to a standard array rather than a hash, and individual records are accessed by their record number using the standard index you would use with any normal hash:

```
use DB_File ;
tie @array, 'DB_File', $filename, $flags, $mode, $DB_RECNO ;
```

The **$DB_RECNO** is the reference to a default hash, with the options for specifying your own hash shown in Table 8-6.

Hash Element	Description
flags	This is a value based on **or**'d predefined flags, and three values are currently defined: **R_FIXEDLEN**, **R_NOKEY**, and **R_SNAPSHOT**. The **R_FIXEDLEN** flag signifies that the records are of fixed length rather than being byte delimited. Use the **reclen** option to specify the length of the record and **bval** to specify the character to be used for padding the record to the specified size. Records are automatically padded if you supply a record with a length less than that specified. The **R_NOKEY** flag forces the routines and methods that are used to access the database not to include the key information. This allows you to access records that are at the end of the database without having to read in the intervening records. The **R_SNAPSHOT** flag specifies that a snapshot of the file's contents be taken when the file is opened.
cachesize	The maximum size in bytes of physical memory to allocate as a buffer between the in-memory database and the physical file store. Specifying a large value will increase performance, since more of the database will be kept in memory. But it may also cause a synchronization error if there is a crash or other problem, since there may still be data in the cache that has not been written to a file. A value of 0 lets the system choose a reasonable value for you.

Table 8-6. *Options for DB_RECNO Databases*

Hash Element	Description
psize	Records from a **DB_RECNO** database are stored in memory in a B-Tree format. The **psize** specifies the number of pages to be used for the nodes of the B-Tree structure.
lorder	The byte order to be used for storing integers within the metadata in the file. The number specified should represent the order as an integer (that is, 4321 is big endian, and 1234 is little endian). If a value of 0 (the default) is specified, the current host order is used instead. If the file you are using already exists, the format used within that file is always used. This can help with compatibility across platforms if you are sharing a database file on multiple systems that support different byte orders.
reclen	The length, in bytes, of a fixed-length record.
bval	The value of the character to be used to mark the end of a record in a variable-length database, and the character to use for padding in a fixed-length database. If no value is specified, then a newline is used to specify the end of a record in a variable-length database, and spaces are used to pad fixed-length records.
bfname	The name of the B-Tree file to be used for the B-Tree structure of the in-memory record number database. If none is specified, the hash is stored entirely in memory.

Table 8-6. *Options for DB_RECNO Databases* (continued)

For example, to set the record length in a fixed-length database:

```
$options = new DB_File::BRECNOINFO;
$options->{'reclen'} = 1024;
tie @db, 'DB_File', "file.db", O_RDWR, 0644, $options;
```

If you want, you can use the array as a stack. Versions of Perl newer than 5.004_57 can use the normal **pop**, **push**, **shift**, and **unshift** functions directly with the tied array. Older versions will need to use the object methods for the object reference returned when the database is first opened, for example:

```
$DBX = tie @db, 'DB_File', "file.db", O_RDWR, 0644, $DB_RECNO;
```

You can then use the methods shown in Table 8-7 to push, pop, shift, and unshift information from the stack.

In-Memory Databases

You can use the features of the Berkeley DB databases for in-memory databases. This can be useful if you want to use a hash with information stored in an ordered format (as with **DB_BTREE**) but don't want to create a file in the process. To do this, you specify the **undef** value as the name of the database file. For example:

```
tie %db, 'DB_File', undef, O_CREAT|O_RDWR, 0666, $DB_BTREE;
```

Or for the standard hash:

```
tie %db, 'DB_File', undef, O_CREAT|O_RDWR, 0666, $DB_HASH;
```

If you want to use an in-memory standard hash, the above line can be shortened to

```
tie %db, 'DB_File';
```


Storing Complex Data in a DBM Database

The simplest model for storing information in a DBM database is identical to the model used for a Perl hash. You have a unique key of information and use that key to refer to a single piece of data. However, this is a fairly flat model if you want to store complex pieces of information in a structured format. Instead, you can use the key/value pairs to store the more traditional records used in a database system.

Method	Description
$DBX->push(list)	Pushes the elements of **list** onto the end of the tied array.
$DBX->pop	Pops the last element of the array.
$DBX->shift	Removes and returns the first element of the array.
$DBX->unshift(list)	Pushes the elements of **list** onto the start of the tied array.
$DBX->length	Returns the number of elements in the array.

Table 8-7. *Object Methods for DB_RECNO Databases*

By using a formatted key or value, you can store the information for individual fields within a DBM file. The entire record can be stored either in multiple keys or within a single key with a structure value. For example, imagine the simple record structure below:

```
Firstname, 10 characters
Lastname, 10 characters
Email, 40 characters
```

You could use a formatted key value of the form **field-id**, such that a single record could be entered into the database as

```
$db{'firstname-1'} = 'Martin';
$db{'lastname-1'} = 'Brown';
$db{'email-1'} = 'mc@mcwords.com';
```

The first name of the next person in the table would be stored in the key **firstname-2**, the last name in **lastname-2**, and so on. Although this seems like a practical method, it is a relatively complex system to implement, and it is wasteful of database keys, which will need to be processed individually.

An alternative solution is to use one of the methods described earlier for text-based databases. By using delimiters or fixed-length records, an entire record can be stored within a single key/value pair. Using delimiters, the above information could be written into the database and then recovered from it using the following Perl code:

```
use Fcntl;
use GDBM_File;

tie %db, 'GDBM_File', 'Test_GDBM', O_CREAT|O_RDWR, 0644
     || die "Can't open DB File, $!";;

$db{'1'} = join(',',qw/Brown Martin mc@mcwords.com/);
$db{'2'} = join(',',qw/Foo Bar foo@foobar.com/);
$db{'3'} = join(',',qw/Bar Foo bar@barfoo.com/);

foreach $id (sort keys %db)
{
    ($lastname, $firstname, $email) = split(/,/,$db{$id});
    print "$id: lastname: $lastname\n";
    print "$id: firstname: $firstname\n";
    print "$id: email: $email\n";
}

untie %db || die "Can't close DB File, $!";
```

In this example the database is populated using a simple numeric key, with the data added via a **join** using a comma as the delimiter. To print the information you've just stored, you work through the database and, using **split**, place the fields data into individual variables, which you then print.

As you know, however, delimited text requires very careful selection of the delimiter to ensure that the information is stored correctly. Here is the same result using **pack** and fixed-length records, which gets around this problem.

```
use Fcntl;
use GDBM_File;

tie %db, 'GDBM_File', 'Test_GDBM', O_CREAT|O_RDWR, 0644
     || die "Can't open DB File, $!";

$db{'email-pstr'}    = 'a10a10a30';
$db{'email-fields'} = join(',', qw/Lastname Firstname Email/);

$db{'email-1'} = pack($db{'email-pstr'},qw/Brown Martin mc@mcwords.com/);
$db{'email-2'} = pack($db{'email-pstr'},qw/Foo Bar foo@foobar.com/);
$db{'email-3'} = pack($db{'email-pstr'},qw/Bar Foo bar@barfoo.com/);

@fieldnames = split(/,/,$db{'email-fields'});

foreach $id (sort grep(/^email-[0-9]+/,keys %db))
{
    @fields = unpack($db{'email-pstr'},$db{$id});
    for($i=0;$i<@fields;$i++)
    {
        $id =~ s/email\-//;
        print "$id: $fieldnames[$i]: $fields[$i]\n";
    }
}

untie %db || die "Can't close DB File, $!"
```

Note in this example that you also manage to keep track of the field names and sizes by recording this information into keys within the database. This makes the format of the database and its contents completely database defined. Also note that I've used a prefix in the base keys. Although it's relatively useless here, it can be useful if you want to store multiple tables within a single database file. Each table has its own name and in turn its own **pack** string, field list, and sequence.

There is still a problem with this particular solution. It is even more wasteful of space than a flat text file using fixed-length records. This is because of the internal storage method used for DBM databases and the problems associated with fixed-length records. In this example every record will take up at least 60 bytes. A more complex record structure will take up significantly more.

Of course, Perl allows you to do more than just use simple key/value pairs. In Chapter 7 we looked at the complex data structures you can create to model information using nested Perl variables such as hashes of hashes and arrays of hashes.

```
use Fcntl;

use GDBM_File;

tie %db, 'GDBM_File', 'Test_GDBM', O_CREAT|O_RDWR, 0644;
     || die "Can't open DB File, $!";

$db{1} = 'Record';
$db{1}{lastname} = 'Brown';
$db{1}{firstname} = 'Martin';
$db{1}{email} = 'mc@mcwords.com';

$db{2}{lastname} = 'Foo';
$db{2}{firstname} = 'Bar';
$db{2}{email} = 'foo@foobar.com';

$db{3}{lastname} = 'Bar';
$db{3}{firstname} = 'Foo';
$db{3}{email} = 'bar@barfoo.com';

foreach (sort keys %db)
{
    foreach $field (sort keys %{$db{$_}})
    {
        print "$_: $field: $db{$_}{$field}\n";
    }
}

untie %db || die "Can't close DB File, $!"
```

Unfortunately, you cannot use normal DBM implementations to create nested hashes of hashes and hashes of arrays. If we return to our first solution, we can expand this by using a hash of hashes to store the data in a more structured format.

However, the **MLDBM** module by Gurusamy Sarathay (available from CPAN) uses existing DBM modules and the **Data::Dumper** module to convert such complex references into a simple format that can be stored within an ordinary hash file. It uses the same basic idea, using the **tie** function to associate a hash with hash file—the **MLDBM** object handles all of the complexity for you:

```
use GDBM_File;
use MLDBM qw(GDBM_File);
use Fcntl;
tie (%db, 'MLDBM', 'Test_MLDBM', O_CREAT|O_RDWR, 0644) || die $!;
```

This overcomes all the previous problems. The data is stored in a structured format, which can be accessed simply using standard hash techniques. Furthermore, the storage space used for this system is significantly lower than the fixed-length database example shown earlier. The storage space is still slightly higher than the delimited system due to the use of a secondary level key, but it overcomes the problem of choosing a suitable delimiter.

Relational Databases with DBM

The *relational* element of a relational database that most people think of is actually the automatic lookup of information. When you report from a database that is composed of many tables, you can choose to print out the "merged" information from all of the linked tables in order to produce the desired set of results. The clever bit is the linking between the individual tables, and this is something that is actually possible to do manually using any database system—text, DBM, or otherwise. With DBM, you have the advantage over text databases of convenient random access, which is the only practical way of achieving a "flat" relational system.

You can model relational data in any database system. The only requirement for using it is that you are able to access all of the tables simultaneously. The actual method of linking between the tables can be done automatically or manually. With the **tie** interface, you can have as many physical DBM databases open at any one time as you like (operating system limits permitting). Through the use of the principles you saw in the previous section, there is no reason why you couldn't actually model the information in a single database with structured key/value pairs.

The most critical part of the development of a relational system is the modeling of the data. Once you have decided on the format of the information and how it is going to be linked, you also need to consider how the links will work. Let's look briefly at a relational system for storing multiple contact information for multiple people using a DBM database. The list below shows the information we need to store, extracted from a raw text file.

The first list (and therefore table) is the list of contact names. This has three fields—first name, last name, and a list of record numbers for the second table, numbers.

The numbers table has two fields—the number type and the number itself. "Number" can mean pager, phone, fax, mobile, email, and so on.

The first table might be populated like this:

```
$db{'contact-1'} = "Martin;Brown;1,3,4";
$db{'contact-2'} = "Bob;Smith;2,5";
```

The key is made up of the table name and a unique ID within that table. The information is stored using delimited text fields in the value portion of the key/value pair. Note that semicolons separate the individual fields, but commas separate the link data in the third field.

The numbers table could be populated with the following information:

```
$db{'numbers-1'} = "Email;mc@mcwords.com";
$db{'numbers-2'} = "Email;bsmith@foobar.com";
$db{'numbers-3'} = "Fax;01234 456789";
$db{'numbers-4'} = "Phone;09876 543210";
$db{'numbers-5'} = "Mobile;0789 123456";
```

To access the complete contact information for Martin Brown, you need to access record number one of the contact table and then access the related information listed in field three of that record. In this case this is records 1, 3, and 4 from the numbers table. To dump the information from the database in a formatted formation, you might use a script like this:

```
use Fcntl;
use GDBM_File;

tie %db, 'GDBM_File', 'Test_Rel', O_CREAT|O_RDWR, 0644
     || die "Can't open DB File, $!";;

foreach $id (sort grep(/^contact-[0-9]+/,keys %db))
{
    ($lastname, $firstname, $relations) = split(/;/,$db{$id});
    print "$firstname $lastname\n";
    foreach $subid (sort split(/,/,$relations))
    {
        ($type,$num) = $db{"numbers-$subid"}
            if (exists($db{"numbers-$subid"}));
        print "    $type: $num\n";
    }
```

```
}

untie %db || die "Can't close DB File, $!";
```

The method is basically very similar to the tricks you saw in the previous section for modeling complex data structures within a DBM database. When run on the database above, it produces the following:

```
Brown Martin
    Email: mc@mcwords.com
    Fax: 01234 456789
    Phone: 09876 543210
Smith Bob
    Email: bsmith@foobar.com
    Mobile: 0789 123456
```


If you want to use some of the earlier techniques for including information in the database about the database, you can even begin to drive the links using formatted structures. I've developed a simple relational database system originally designed for complex contact management, using this type of relational system. It needed to be ultimately portable to a variety of platforms, and the client wanted to keep away from proprietary database systems.

Before that I used a simple NDBM database within Perl 4 (before the **tie** function) to develop a relational system for configuring Hewlett-Packard Unix workstations and servers online. The database system itself is still in use now and can be found on Hewlett-Packard's website.

Database File Locking

Without at least some file locking, it will be possible for two processes, Perl based or otherwise, to access and update the database file at the same time. For reading from the database this is not an issue; there is no reason (normally) to lock people out from the database if all they want to do is look up a value. When updating, however, the end results could be disastrous. With more than one person updating different lines, sections, and key/value pairs in the different database types, you could end up with at best a corrupt database and, at worst, one that is completely unreadable.

The best solution is to use the Perl **flock** function, which uses the best of the underlying locking mechanisms (**flock**, **lockf**, or **fcntl**). You may also want to consider using a separate file to indicate the lock condition. See the example in Chapter 6 for information on using and checking the file locks with the **flock** function.

You will need to take care about how you implement the locking mechanism. With a text file database, you can use **flock** directly on the filehandle you use to access the database. With DBM databases, the system is more complex, since the actual file is hidden from you via the **tie** object interface. For the ODBM_File, NDBM_File, and SDBM_File, this will mean checking and imposing locks on both files used to store the DBM data. For GDBM_File, you only need to check the locks on one file.

For DB_File, you can use a method applied to a DB_File object in order to discover the file descriptor, and then use the duplication notation with the **open** function to assign it to a filehandle that can be used with **flock**. For example:

```
use Fcntl qm/:flock:/;
use DB_File;

$dbobj = (tie(%db, 'DB_File', 'dbfile.db', O_RDWR, 0644)
        || die "Can't tie database to hash, $!";

$fileno = $dbobj->fd;
open(DBHANDLE, "+<&=$fileno") || die "Can't open FH, $!";
unless (flock(DBHANDLE, LOCK_EX|LOCK_NB)) { die "Can't lock: $!" }
...
# Update the database
...
flock(DBHANDLE, LOCK_UN);
close(DBHANDLE);
untie %db;
```

This only sets and releases a lock for update. You'll also need to include the necessary tests to ensure that the file is not already locked.

Other Database Systems

The CPAN archives contain a range of different modules capable of accessing different databases. Although there are advantages and disadvantages to all of them, the most practical, especially if you are using multiple database systems, is the DBI toolkit. We'll look at the features of this system briefly before we leave the topic of databases completely.

The DBI Toolkit

The DBI toolkit is a database interface to a range of different databases, including Oracle, Sybase, and other RDBMSs (relational database management systems). The base interface to querying and updating the database is SQL (Structured Query Language), which is the standard method used on many of the database systems. In addition, you can use SQL to query ODBC and even CSV databases using the DBI toolkit. This makes it a practical solution for accessing a wide variety of databases while using the same core code. You can write a program that reports from a SQL database, and the DBI toolkit will take of the interface to whatever database is available on the platform you are using.

The system is modular, so you have the base DBI module, which provides a consistent interface and the necessary glue code to interface to the interface modules. Accessing different data sources is as easy as using a different interface module, which is specified within the code as an option to the **open** and **close** functions. Each underlying database driver (DBD) may implement a different method for accessing the database. This may lead to some problems when using a mixture of databases, as the error codes returned by each DBD are not consistent across the whole DBI toolkit.

The problem with developing an interface to a commercial database is that although the SQL standard is well adhered to, the different C APIs (Application Programming Interfaces) that are used to access the information differ enormously. Until recently there was no accepted standard. Microsoft bridged the gap on the Wintel machines by creating the ODBC initiative, which attempts to standardize on the frontend used to access relational databases. The underlying access is still SQL; only the interface to the SQL interpreter on the required database platform has been standardized. The ODBC system has now been accepted by a number of other RDBMS developers as a suitable interface to their database systems. The original targets of ODBC were the Microsoft database tools, including SQL Server, Access, and even Excel spreadsheets.

To retain some compatibility with our earlier examples, the CSV interface for the DBI toolkit will be used to demonstrate the base features of the system. This uses a set of modules specially adapted for modifying text files rather than connecting to another database system using the usual network or shared memory interfaces.

The DBI toolkit supplies all the functions and constructs required for creating, reporting, and editing information in the database. The CSV functions are written in C for speed, and these functions are interfaced to the Perl CSV module. The DBI module, which supplies the base SQL interface, supplies SQL commands to the DBD::CSV module, which in turn passes control to another SQL interpretation module. The CSV DBD uses the system **flock** function to lock the underlying CSV files, thereby solving one of our earlier concerns. A DBI-managed CSV file will be multiuser compatible without requiring any additional code.

The CSV module overcomes many of the problems associated with both text-delimited files and the fixed-length files you have already seen. Furthermore, the DBI toolkit, via the SQL interface, provides you with a standard way of retrieving the information that doesn't require sifting through the file looking for the record you want. Speed is still an issue, however, but it may solve an immediate problem or allow you to develop SQL software without access to a SQL database.

Using the CSV DBI Interface

Depending on your point of view, it may be a bit perverse to consider using a CSV file through as complex an interface as the DBI toolkit. In fact, it makes perfect sense if the file you need to read has originated from a less-than-friendly format. Most database systems and many spreadsheets and other tools provide the ability to export to a CSV file, and you could easily use the file supplied in its native format using this interface. Furthermore, you could use the CSV source as the basis for creating a live SQL database in a real RDBMS.

In the example below I've duplicated the functionality of our earlier scripts for recording tasks, using the DBI toolkit in place of our own functions. The scripts are noticeably shorter than the variable or fixed record length equivalents, because the DBI module is doing all the work behind the scenes.

The most complicated part of the process when using the DBI toolkit with any DBD interface is writing the correct SQL statement to access and update the data. I'll leave that particular avenue of investigation to the reader.

CREATING A CSV DATABASE WITH THE DBI TOOLKIT The method for using the DBI module is to create a new database handle, and the creation of the handle implies the database type you are connecting to. In this first script we use a SQL statement to create a new table, which in the case of the CSV toolkit implies the creation of a new file. The file name is the table name that you have selected; thus you can make multiple tables as you would with any SQL database by creating multiple files. The SQL support is advanced enough that you can even create links and joins between separate CSV files to create the impression of, or to emulate, a real RDBMS. The field size and definition information, which is required when creating a table within a SQL environment, is ignored by the CSV interface, which again helps to retain compatibility with RDBMS databases.

Once the table has been created, you can use a simple **INSERT** SQL statement to enter the data into the table. Note that you must use the **quote** method to the database handle to ensure that strings and values are correctly interpreted when inserted into the database.

```
#!/usr/local/bin/perl

use DBI;

my ($reqdate);
die "Usage: $0 title required-date\n" if (@ARGV<2);

($mday,$mon,$year) = split '/',$ARGV[-1];
$reqdate = ($year*10000)+($mon*100)+$mday;
```

```
my ($table) = "csvtasks";

my($dbh) = DBI->connect("DBI:CSV:");

unless (-e $table)
{
    $dbh->do("CREATE TABLE $table (title CHAR(40),
             reqdate CHAR(8), compdate CHAR(8))")
         || die "Couldn't create table " . dbh->errstr();
}

$dbh->do("INSERT INTO $table VALUES (" .
    $dbh->quote($ARGV[0]) . "," .
    $dbh->quote($reqdate) . "," .
    $dbh->quote(0) . ")")
    || die "Couldn't add record, " . $dbh->errstr();
```


To use this, you need to specify the task you want to add on the command line:

```
$ addcsv.pl 'Phone Richard' 25/3/1999
```

REPORTING FROM A CSV DATABASE WITH THE DBI TOOLKIT Reporting from a CSV database is more complex. You need to extract the information from the database into a variable or structure that Perl can use effectively. The DBI toolkit supplies a number of methods for extracting data from a DBI-connected database, but the most practical, and the one we use here, is to convert a single row of data into a hash, with each key of the hash referring to one of the fields.

One benefit of using a SQL database is that the complex parts, such as sorting and searching for the information, are conducted by the SQL interface. The information extracted from the database will be in the order you specify in the SQL statement and should consist only of the information you were looking for—provided, of course, that you wrote the correct SQL statement to access the information.

```
#!/usr/local/bin/perl5

use DBI;
use Getopt::Std;

my ($reqdate,$compdate);
my ($mday,$mon,$year,$key);
```

```
etopts('drc');

my ($table) = "csvtasks";

my($dbh) = DBI->connect("DBI:CSV:");

my ($query) = "SELECT * FROM $table";

$query .= " WHERE compdate = 0" if ($opt_d);

if ($opt_r)
{
    $query .= " ORDER BY reqdate";
}
elsif ($opt_c && !($opt_d))
{
    $query .= " ORDER BY compdate";
}
else
{
    $query .= " ORDER BY title";
}

my ($sth) = $dbh->prepare($query)
           || die "prepare: " . $dbh->errstr();

$sth->execute() || die "execute: " . $dbh->errstr();

printf("%-40s  %-10s  %-10s\n","Title","Req. Date","Comp. Date");

while ($row = $sth->fetchrow_hashref)
{
    $row->{'reqdate'} =~ m/(....)(..)(..)/;
    $reqdate = "$3/$2/$1";

    if ($row->{'compdate'}>0)
    {
       $lcompdate{$key} =~ m/(....)(..)(..)/;
       $compdate = "$3/$2/$1";
    }
    else
    {
```

```
        $compdate="";
    }
    printf("%-40s  %10s  %10s\n",$row->{'title'},
                                  $reqdate,$compdate);
}
```

If you use this script to report on the information you just inserted into the database with the last script:

```
$ listcsv.pl
Title                                       Req. Date    Comp. Date
Phone Richard                               25/03/1999
```


UPDATING A CSV DATABASE WITH THE DBI TOOLKIT Like the earlier creation example for inserting information, updating it is a case of writing the correct SQL statement. Here's the script:

```
#!/usr/local/bin/perl

use DBI;

die "Usage: $0 title completed-date\n" if (@ARGV<2);

my ($mday,$mon,$year) = split m:/:,$ARGV[-1];
my ($compdate) = ($year*10000)+($mon*100)+$mday;

my ($table) = "csvtasks";

my($dbh) = DBI->connect("DBI:CSV:");

my($query) = "UPDATE $table SET compdate = " .
              $dbh->quote($compdate) .
             " WHERE title = " . $dbh->quote($ARGV[0]);

$dbh->do($query) || die "Unable to update, " . $dbh->errstr();
```

Although the principles here are directly attributed to the CSV toolkit, they can just as easily be applied to any of the database systems supported by the DBI toolkit, and all demonstrate the power of this particular module.

Using ODBC Under Windows

Although you can use the ODBC interface with the DBI toolkit, it's also possible to use the separate **Win32::ODBC** module that is part of the Windows port of Perl. It follows a similar approach to the DBI system, with a connection being opened, a SQL statement executed, and then the information reported and extracted from the database.

```
use Win32::ODBC;
$dbname = "Floorpoints";
$dbhandle = new Win32::ODBC($dbname);
if dbhandle->Sql("select ID, device from floorpoints")
{
 print 'Error: ", $dbhandle->Error(), "\n";
 $dbhandle->Close();
 exit(1);
}
```

We'll look at the features of the **Win32::ODBC** module in more detail as part of the general discussion on Win32 modules in Chapter 22.

The Complete Reference

Chapter 9

Networking

Before we examine the processes behind using network connections in Perl, it's worth understanding the background of how networks are supported in the modern world, and from that we can glean the information we need to network computers using Perl.

Most networking systems have historically been based on the OSI/ISO (Open Systems Interconnection/International Standards Organization) seven-layer model. Each layer defines an individual component of the networking process, from the physical connection up to the applications that use the network. Each layer is dependent on the layer it sits on top of to provide the services it requires.

More recently the seven-layer model has been dropped in favor of a more flexible model that follows the current development of networking systems. You can often attribute the same layers to modern systems, but it's often the case that individual protocols lie over two of the layers in the OSI model, rather than conveniently sitting within a single layer.

Irrespective of the model you are using, the same basic principles survive. You can characterize networks by the type of logical connection. A network can either be connection oriented or connectionless. A connection-oriented network relies on the fact that two computers that want to talk to each other must go through some form of connection process, usually called a handshake. This handshake is similar to using the telephone: the caller dials a number and the receiver picks up the phone. In this way the caller immediately knows whether the recipient has received the message, because the recipient will have answered the call. This type of connection is supported by TCP/IP (Transmission Control Protocol/Internet Protocol) and is the main form of communication over the Internet and local area networks (LANs).

In a connectionless network, information is sent to the recipient without first setting up a connection. This type of network is also a datagram or packet-oriented network because the data is sent in discrete packets. Each packet will consist of the sender's address, recipient's address, and the information, but no response will be provided once the message has been received. A connectionless network is therefore more like the postal service—you compose and send a letter, although you have no guarantee that the letter will reach its destination, or that the information was received correctly. Connectionless networking is supported by UDP/IP (User Datagram Protocol/Internet Protocol).

In either case, the "circuit" is not open permanently between the two machines. Data is sent in individual packets that may take different paths and routes to the destination. The routes may involve local area networks, dialup connection, ISDN routers, and even satellite links. Within the UDP protocol the packets can arrive in any order, and it is up to the client program to reassemble them into the correct sequence—if there is one. With TCP the packets are automatically reassembled into the correct sequence before they are represented to the client as a single data stream.

There are advantages and disadvantages to both types of networks. A connectionless network is fast, because there is no requirement to acknowledge the data or enter into any dialogue to set up the connection to receive the data. However, a connectionless network is also unreliable, because there is no way to ensure the information reached its destination. A connection-oriented network is slow (in comparison to a connectionless network) because of the extra dialogue involved, but it guarantees the data sequence, providing end-to-end reliability.

The IP element of the TCP/IP and UDP/IP protocols refers to the Internet Protocol, which is a set of standards for specifying the individual addresses of machines within a network. Each machine within the networking world has a unique IP address. This is made up of a sequence of 4 bytes typically written in dot notation, for example, 198.10.29.145. These numbers relate both to individual machines within a network and to entire collections of machines.

Because humans are not very good at remembering numbers, a system called DNS (Domain Name System) relates easy-to-remember names to IP addresses. For example, the name www.mcgraw-hill.com relates to a single IP address. You can also have a single DNS name pointing to a number of IP addresses, and multiple names point to the same name. It is also possible to have a single machine that has multiple interfaces, and each interface can have multiple IP addresses assigned to it. However, in all cases, if the interfaces are connected to the Internet in one form or another, then the IP addresses of each interface will be unique.

The specification for communication does not end there. Many different applications can be executed on the same machine, and so communication must be aimed not only at the machine, but also at a port on that machine that relates to a particular application. If the IP address is a telephone number, the port number is the equivalent of an extension number. The first 1024 port numbers are assigned to well-known Internet protocols, and different protocols have their own unique port number. For example, HTTP (Hypertext Transfer Protocol), which is used to transfer information between your web browser and a web server, has a port number of 80. To connect to a server application, you need both the IP address (or machine name) and the port number on which the server is "listening."

The BSD socket system was introduced in BSD 4.2 as a way of providing a consistent interface to the different available protocols. A socket provides a connection between an application and the network. You must have a socket at each end of the connection in order to communicate between the machines. One end must be set to receive data at the same time as the other end is sending data. As long as each side of the socket connection knows whether it should be sending or receiving information, then the communication can be two-way.

There are many different methods for controlling this two-way communication, although none is ultimately reliable. The most obvious is to "best-guess" the state that each end of the connection should be in. For example, if one end sends a piece of information, then it might be safe to assume it should then wait for a response. If the opposite end makes the same assumption, then it can send information after it has just received some. This is not necessarily reliable, because if both ends decide to wait for information at the same time, then both ends of the connection are effectively dead. Alternatively, if both ends decide to send information at the same time, the two processes will not lock; but because they use the same send-receive system, once they have both sent information, they will both return to the wait state, expecting a response.

A better solution to the problem is to use a protocol that places rules and restrictions on the communication method and order. This is how SMTP and similar protocols work. The client sends a command to the server, and the immediate response from the server tells the client what to do next. The response may include data and will definitely include an end-of-data string. In effect, it's similar to the technique used when communicating by radio. At the end of each communication you say, "Over" to indicate to the recipient that you have finished speaking. In essence, it still uses the same best-guess method for communication. Providing the communication starts off correctly, and each end sends the end-of-communication signal, the communication should continue correctly.

Although generally thought of as a technique for communicating between two different machines, you can also use sockets to communicate between two processes on the same machine. Communicating between processes on a single machine (IPC—interprocess communication) allows you to control and cooperatively operate several different processes. Most servers use IPC to manage a number of processes that support a particular service.

We'll be looking at the general techniques available for networking between processes, either on the machine or across a network to a different machine. Techniques include those using the built-in Perl functions and those using modules available from CPAN that simplify the process for communicating with existing protocol standards.

If you want more information on networking with sockets and streams under TCP, UDP, and IP, then I can recommend *The UNIX System V Release 4 Programmers Guide: Networking Interfaces* (1990, Englewood Cliffs, NJ: Prentice Hall), which covers the principles behind networking, as well as the C source code required to make it work.

Obtaining Network Information

The first stage in making a network connection is to get the information you need about the host you are connecting to. You will also need to resolve the service port and protocol information before you start the communication process. Like other parts of the networking process, all of this information is required in numerical rather than name format. You therefore need to be able to resolve the individual names into corresponding numbers. This operation is supported by several built-in functions.

Hosts

In order to communicate with a remote host, you need to determine its IP address. The names are resolved by the system, either by the contents of the /etc/hosts file, or through a naming service such as NIS or DNS. The **gethostbyname** function calls the system-equivalent function, which looks up the IP address in the corresponding tables, depending on how the operating system has been configured.

```
gethostbyname NAME
```

In a list context this returns the hostname, aliases, address type, length, and physical IP addresses for the host defined in **NAME**. They can be extracted like this:

```
($name, $aliases, $addrtype,
 $length, @addresses) = gethostbyname($host);
```

The **$aliases** scalar is a space-separated list of alternative aliases for the specified name. The **@addresses** array contains a list of addresses in a packed format, which you will need to extract with **unpack**. In a scalar context, the function returns the host's IP address. For example, you can get the IP address of a host as a string with

```
$address
    = join('.',unpack("C4",scalar gethostbyname "www.mchome.com")));
```

It's more normal, however, to keep the host address in packed format for use in other functions.

```
gethostbyaddr ADDR, ADDRTYPE
```

In a list context this returns the same information as **gethostbyname**, except that it accepts a packed IP address as its first argument. The **ADDRTYPE** should be one of **AF_UNIX** for Unix sockets and **AF_INET** for Internet sockets. These constants are defined within the **Socket** module. In a scalar context it just returns the hostname as a string.

```
gethostent
endhostent
sethostent
```

The **gethostent** function iterates through the /etc/hosts file and returns each entry in the form:

```
($name, $aliases, $addrtype, $length, @addresses) = gethostent;
```

Each subsequent call to **gethostent** returns the next entry in the file. This works in the same way as the **getpwent** function you saw in Chapter 6.

The **sethostent** function resets the pointer to the beginning of the file, and **endhostent** indicates that you have finished reading the entries. Note that this is identical to the system function, and the operating system may or may not have been configured to search the Internet DNS for entries. Using this function may cause you to start iterating through the entire domain name system, which is probably not what you want.

Protocols

You will need to resolve the top-level names of the protocols supporting a specific set of transmission protocols. Examples include the TCP and UDP protocols that you already know about, as well as AppleTalk, SMTP, and ICMP (Internet Control Message Protocol). This information is traditionally stored on a Unix system in /etc/protocols, although different systems may store it in different files, or even internally.

```
getprotobyname NAME
```

This translates a specific protocol **NAME** into a protocol number in a scalar context, or returns the following in a list context:

```
($name, $aliases, $protocol) = getprotobyname('tcp');
```

Alternatively, you can resolve a protocol number into a protocol name with the **getprotobynumber** function.

```
getprotobynumber NUMBER
```

This returns the protocol name in a scalar context, and the same name, aliases, and protocol number information in a list context:

```
($name, $aliases, $protocol) = getprotobyname(6);
```

Alternatively, you can also step through the protocols available using the **getprotoent** function:

```
getprotoent
setprotoent
endprotoent
```

The information is the same as that returned by **getprotobyname** in a list context. The **setprotoent** and **endprotoent** functions reset and end the reading of the /etc/protocols file.

Services

The services are the names of individual protocols used on the network. These relate to the individual port numbers used for specific protocols. The **getservbyname** function resolves a name into a protocol number by examining the /etc/services file, or the corresponding networked information service table:

```
getservbyname NAME, PROTO
```

This resolves **NAME** for the specified protocol **PROTO** into the following fields:

```
($name, $aliases, $port, $protocol_name) = getservbyname 'http',
'tcp';
```

The **PROTO** should be either 'tcp' or 'udp', depending on what protocol you want to use. In a scalar context, the function just returns the service port number.

```
getservbyport PORT, PROTO
```

This resolves the port number **PORT** for the **PROTO** protocol, returning the same fields as **getservbyname**:

```
($name, $aliases, $port, $protocol_name) = getservbyport 80, 'tcp';
```

In a scalar context it just returns the protocol name.

```
getservent
setservent
endservent
```

You can step through the contents of the /etc/services file using **getservent**, which returns the same fields again, and **setservent** resets the pointer to the beginning of the file. The **endservent** indicates to the system that you've finished reading the entries.

Networks

A network is a collection of machines logically connected together. The logical element is that networks are specified by their leading IP addresses, such that a network of machines can be referred to by "198.112.10"—the last digits specifying the individual machines within the entire network. This information is stored, mostly for routing purposes, within the /etc/networks file. Just like the hosts that make up the network, a network specification is composed of both a name and a corresponding address, which you can resolve using the **getnetbyname** and **getnetbyaddr** functions.

```
getnetbyname NAME
```

This returns, in a list context:

```
($name, $aliases, $addrtype, $net) = getnetbyname 'loopback';
```

In a scalar context, it returns the network address as a string. You can also do the reverse with the **getnetbyaddr** function:

```
getnetbyaddr ADDR, ADDRTYPE
```

The **ADDRTYPE** should be **AF_UNIX** or **AF_INET**, as appropriate.

As before, you can step through the individual entries within the network file using the **getnetent** function:

```
getnetent
setnetent
endnetent
```

The **getnetent** function returns the same information as **getnetbyaddr** in a list context. The **setnetent** function resets the current pointer within the available lists, and **endnetent** indicates to the system that you have finished reading the entries.

The Socket Module

The **Socket** module is the main support module for communicating between machines with sockets. It provides a combination of the constants required for networking as well as a series of utility functions that you will need for both client and server socket systems. It is essentially a massaged version of the socket.h header file that has been converted with the **h2ph** script. The result is a module that should work on your system irrespective of the minor differences that OSs impose on constants.

The exact list of constants, including those that specify the address (**AF_***) and protocol (**PF_***), are system specific, so it's pointless to include them here. Check the contents of the Socket.pm file for details.

Address Resolution and Conversion

The **inet_aton** and **inet_ntoa** functions provide simple methods for resolving and then converting hostnames and numbers to the packed 4-byte structure required by most of the other socket functions. The **inet_aton** function accepts a hostname or IP address (as strings) and resolves the hostname and returns a 4-byte packed structure. Thus

```
inet_aton("www.mcwords.com");
```

and

```
scalar gethostbyname("www.mcwords.com");
```

return identical values. In fact, **inet_aton** returns only the first IP address resolved; it doesn't provide the facility to obtain multiple addresses for the same host. This function is generally more practical than the **gethostbyname** or **gethostbyaddr** function since it supports both names and numbers transparently. If a hostname cannot be resolved, the function returns **undef**.

The **inet_ntoa** function takes a packed 4-byte address and translates it into a normal dotted-quad string, such that

```
print inet_ntoa(inet_aton("198.112.10.10"));
```

prints 198.112.10.10.

Address Constants

When setting up a socket for serving requests, you need to specify the mask address used to filter out requests from specific addresses. Two predefined constants specify all addresses and no addresses. They are **INADDR_ANY** and **INADDR_NONE**, respectively. The value of **INADDR_ANY** is a packed 4-byte IP address of 0.0.0.0. The **INADDR_NONE** is a packed 4-byte IP address of 255.255.255.255.

The **INADDR_BROADCAST** constant returns a packed 4-byte string containing the broadcast address to communicate to all hosts on the current network.

Finally, the **INADDR_LOOPBACK** constant returns a packed 4-byte string containing the loopback address of the current machine. The loopback address is the IP address to which you can communicate back to the current machine. It's usually 127.0.0.1, but the exact address can vary. The usual name for the local host is **localhost**, and is defined within the /etc/hosts file or the DNS or NIS systems accordingly.

Socket Structures

Socket functions within Perl call the system equivalents, which themselves use structures to store the information for communicating with remote hosts. For Internet communication (that is, within the **AF_INET** domain), the structure is **sockaddr_in**, and for Unix communication (within the **AF_UNIX** domain), the structure is **sockaddr_un**. Although you could create your own Perl versions of the structures using **pack**, it's much easier to use the functions supplied by the **Socket** module.

The primary function is **sockaddr_in**, which behaves differently according to the arguments it is passed and the context in which it is called. In a scalar context, it accepts two arguments—the port number and packed IP address:

```
$sockaddr = sockaddr_in PORT, ADDRESS
```

This returns the structure as a scalar. To extract this information back, you call the function in a list context:

```
($port, $address) = sockaddr_in SOCKADDR_IN
```

This extracts the port number and packed IP address from a **sockaddr_in** structure.

As an alternative to the above function, you can use the **pack_sockaddr_in** and **unpack_sockaddr_in** functions instead:

```
$sockaddr = pack_sockaddr_in PORT, ADDRESS
($port, $address) = unpack_sockaddr_in SOCKADDR_IN
```

A similar set of functions pack and unpack addresses to and from the **sockaddr_un** structure used for sockets in the **AF_UNIX** domain:

```
sockaddr_un PATHNAME
sockaddr_un SOCKADDR_UN
pack_sockaddr_un PATHNAME
unpack_sockaddr_un SOCKADDR_UN
```

Line Termination Constants

The line termination for network communication should be \n\n. However, because of the differences in line termination under different platforms, care should be taken to ensure that this value is actually sent and received. You can do this by using the octal values \012\012. Another alternative is to use the constants **$CR**, **$LF**, and **$CRLF**, which equate to \015, \012, and \015\012, respectively.

These are exported from the **Socket** module only on request, either individually or with the **:crlf** export tag:

```
use Socket qw/:DEFAULT :crlf/;
```

Socket Communication

There are two ends to all socket connections, the sender and the receiver.

Connecting to a Remote Socket

The process for communicating with a remote socket is as follows:

1. Create and open a local socket, specifying the protocol family (**PF_INET** or **PF_UNIX**), socket type, and top-level protocol number (TCP, UDP, etc.).
2. Determine the IP address of the remote machine you want to talk to.
3. Determine the remote service port number you want to talk to.
4. Create a **sockaddr_in** structure based on the IP address and remote service port.
5. Initiate the connection to the remote host.

This all sounds very complicated, but in fact, it is relatively easy. Many of the functions you need to use have already been discussed in this chapter. To speed up the process, it's a good idea to use something like the function **connectsocket** below:

```
use Socket;

sub connectsocket
{
    my ($SOCKETHANDLE, $remotehost_name,
        $service_name, $protocol_name) = @_;
    my ($port_num, $sock_type, $protocol_num);
    my ($remote_ip_addr, $remote_socket);

    $protocol_num = getprotobyname($protocol_name);
    unless ($protocol_num)
    {
        $error = "Couldn't find protocol $protocol_name";
        return;
    }
```

```
    $sock_type =  $protocol_name eq 'tcp'
                                ? SOCK_STREAM : SOCK_DGRAM;

    unless (socket($SOCKETHANDLE, PF_INET, $sock_type,
$protocol_num))
    {
        $error = "Couldn't create a socket, $!";
        return;
    }

    if ($service_name =~ /^\d+$/ )
    {
        $port_num = $service_name;
    }
    else
    {
        $port_num = (getservbyname($service_name,
                                   $protocol_name))[2];
        unless($port_num)
        {
            $error = "Can't find service $service_name";
            return;
        }
    }

    $remote_ip_addr = gethostbyname($remotehost_name);
    unless ($remote_ip_addr)
    {
        $error = "Can't resolve $remotehost_name to an IP address";
        return;
    }
    $remote_socket = sockaddr_in($port_num, $remote_ip_addr);
    unless(connect($SOCKETHANDLE, $remote_socket))
    {
        $error = "Unable to connect to $remotehost_name: $!";
        return;
    }
    return(1);
}
```

I've used a variable, **$error**, to indicate the type of error, thus allowing you to return true or false from the function to indicate success or failure. The bulk of the function's code is given over to identifying or resolving names and/or numbers for service ports and other base information. The core of the function's processes is the **socket** function, which associates a filehandle with the relevant protocol family. The synopsis of the **socket** function is

```
socket SOCKET, DOMAIN, TYPE, PROTOCOL
```

The **SOCKET** is the name of the filehandle you want to use to communicate over this network connection. The **DOMAIN** is the corresponding domain type, which is typically one of **PF_UNIX** for the Unix domain and **PF_INET** for Internet communication. The **TYPE** is the type of communication, either packet stream or datagram.

A simple test is used in the above function to see if the top-level protocol (TCP, UDP, etc.) is 'tcp', in which case it's safe to assume that you are doing stream communication. Valid values can be extracted from the **Socket** module, but it's likely to be one of **SOCK_STREAM** (for stream-based connections such as TCP) and **SOCK_DGRAM** for datagram connections such as UDP. The final argument, **PROTOCOL**, is the protocol number, as determined by the **getprotobyname** function.

The next part of the function is responsible for looking up the numeric equivalents of the service port and hostname, before you build the **sockaddr_in** structure within the **sockaddr_in** function. You then use the newly created structure with the **connect** function in order to associate the socket you have created with the communications channel to a remote machine. The **connect** function's synopsis looks like this:

```
connect SOCKET, NAME
```

The **SOCKET** is the socket handle created by the **socket** function, and **NAME** is the scalar holding the **sockaddr_in** structure with the remote host and service port information.

Armed with this function, you can create quite complex systems for communicating information over UDP, TCP, or any other protocol. As an example, here's a simple script for obtaining the remote time of a host, providing it supports the **daytime** protocol (on service port 13):

```
use Ssockets;

my $host = shift || 'localhost';
```

```
unless(connectsocket(*TIME, $host, 'daytime', 'tcp'))
{
    die $Ssockets::error;
}

$_ = <TIME>;
print "Time on $host is $_";
close(TIME);
```

For convenience the **connectsocket** function has been inserted into its own package, **Ssockets**. This is actually the module used in Chapter 5 of the *Perl Annotated Archives* book (see Appendix A).

The **daytime** protocol is pretty straightforward. The moment you connect, it sends back the current, localized date and time of the remote machine. All you have to do is connect to the remote host and then read the supplied information from the associated network socket.

Listening for Socket Connections

The process of listening on a network socket for new connections is more involved than creating a client socket, although the basic principles remain constant. Beyond the creation of the socket, you also need to bind the socket to a local address and service port, and set the socket to the "listen" state. The full process is therefore as follows:

1. Create and open a local socket, specifying the protocol family (**PF_INET** or **PF_UNIX**), socket type, and top-level protocol number (TCP, UDP, etc.).
2. Determine the local service port number on which you want to listen for new connections.
3. Set any options for the newly created socket.
4. Bind the socket to an IP address and service port on the local machine.
5. Set the socket to the listen state, specifying the size of the queue used to hold pending connections.

You don't initiate any connections or, at this stage, actually accept any connections. We'll deal with that particular part later. Again, it's easier to produce a simple function to do this for you, and the **listensocket** function below is the sister function to the earlier **connectsocket**:

```
use Socket;

sub listensocket
{
    my ($SOCKETHANDLE, $service_name,
        $protocol_name, $queuelength) = @_;
    my ($port_num, $sock_type, $protocol_num, $local_socket);

    $protocol_num = (getprotobyname($protocol_name))[2];
    unless ($protocol_num)
    {
        $error = "Couldn't find protocol $protocol_name";
        return;
    }
    $sock_type = $protocol_name eq "tcp"
                            ? SOCK_STREAM : SOCK_DGRAM ;

    if( $service_name =~ /^\d+$/)
    {
        $port_num = $service_name;
    }
    else
    {
        $port_num = (getservbyname($service_name,
                                   $protocol_name))[2];
        unless($port_num)
        {
            $error = "Can't find service $service_name";
            return;
        }
    }

    unless(socket($SOCKETHANDLE, PF_INET,
                  $sock_type, $protocol_num))
    {
```

```
        $error = "Couldn't create a socket: $!";
        return;
    }
    unless(setsockopt($SOCKETHANDLE,SOL_SOCKET,
                      SO_REUSEADDR,pack("l",1)))
    {
        $error = "Couldn't set socket options: $!";
        return;
    }
    $local_socket = sockaddr_in($port_num, INADDR_ANY);
    unless(bind($SOCKETHANDLE, $local_socket))
    {
        $error = "Failed to Bind to socket: $!";
        return;
    }
    unless(listen($SOCKETHANDLE, $queuelength))
    {
        $error = "Couldn't listen on socket: $!";
        return;
    }
    return(1);
}
```

Again, the bulk of this function is given over to determining the numerical versions of the IP addresses, protocols, and service ports that you want to use. Most of the function is therefore identical to the **connectsocket** function. The only difference is the setting of some socket options, which we'll return to later in this chapter, and the use of the **bind** and **listen** functions.

The **bind** function attaches your newly created socket to a local IP interface and service port. This is essentially the same as the **connect** function used to connect to a remote port, except that you are attaching the socket to a local port instead.

```
bind SOCKET, ADDRESS
```

The port definition does not have to be a specific IP address (although it could be). Instead you use the predefined **INADDR_ANY** to allow the connection to be accepted on any of the local configured IP interfaces. On a machine with a single interface this will obviously mean only one interface, but on a machine with multiple interfaces it allows you to accept the connection on any of them.

The **listen** function switches the new socket into listen mode. Without this function the socket will never accept new connections. It accepts two arguments—the socket handle and something called the **queue** length:

```
listen SOCKET, LENGTH
```

The **LENGTH** parameter is the maximum number of connections that will be held in a queue by the operating system before the remote hosts receive an "unable to connect" response. This allows you to control the server loading and response times. It doesn't affect the number of connections that can be open at any one time, since that is controlled (we hope) by the server application. For example, with a web server, since the response time for an individual request is quite small, you may want to specify a relatively high value so the time between individual **accept** calls will be relatively low. Setting the queue length to a low value will affect performance, since the OS may be refusing connections even when your server is not very busy.

It's also worth keeping in mind the type of communication you expect. With a web server you tend to get a high number of relatively short requests in a short space of time. If you consider that a typical web page consists of one HTML file and ten images, then you could easily get 11 requests within a few seconds and should therefore set the queue length to a higher value. With an FTP server, you tend to get a smaller number of concurrent connections, but with longer times to service the actual requests. This would tend to indicate a lower value, thus helping to reduce the overall loading of your server.

It's always important to remember that your server can run as many child processes as it likes, and so you should also have other safeguards, such as connection counters or load monitors, to ensure that you are not accepting and servicing more requests than you can handle. The queue length will make no difference here. If the time to accept a connection and spawn a new process is one second, you could get 100 requests every second and end up with 100 child processes. On a small server this could kill it, no matter how small the individual requests might be.

Once your socket is ready and listening, you need to accept new connections as they are made by clients. The **accept** function handles this, blocking the current process until a new connection is made and accepted.

```
accept NEWSOCKET, SOCKET
```

The function monitors **SOCKET**, opening the **NEWSOCKET** filehandle on the accepted connection. It returns the packed address of the remote host that made the connection, or the false value if the connection failed.

This is usually used in combination with **fork** (see Chapter 10) to support multiple simultaneous connections from remote hosts. For example, here is a very simple web server (supporting HTTP) written entirely in Perl. It uses the **listensocket** function above and demonstrates the simplicity of the network server once you have gotten past the complexities of creating the original, listening socket.

```
use Ssockets;
use FileHandle;
use Cwd;
use Getopt::Std;
use Socket;
getopts('d');

$SIG{'INT'} = $SIG{'QUIT'} = \&exit_request_handler;
$SIG{'CHLD'} = \&child_handler;

my ($res);
my ($SERVERPORT) = 80;

unless(listensocket(*SERVERSOCKET, $SERVERPORT, 'tcp', 5))
{
    die "$0: ", $Ssockets::error;
}

autoflush SERVERSOCKET 1;

chroot(getcwd());
die "$0: Couldn't change root directory, are you root?"
    unless (getcwd() eq "/");

print "Changing root to ", getcwd(), "\n" if $opt_d;

print "Simple HTTP Server Started\n" if $opt_d;

while(1)
{
  ACCEPT_CONNECT:
    {
        ($remaddr = accept(CHILDSOCKET, SERVERSOCKET))
            || redo ACCEPT_CONNECT;
    }
```

```
    autoflush CHILDSOCKET 1;
    my $pid = fork();
    die "Cannot fork, $!" unless defined($pid);
    if ($pid == 0)
    {
        my ($remip)
            = inet_ntoa((unpack_sockaddr_in($remaddr))[1]);
        print "Connection accepted from $remip\n" if $opt_d;
        $_ = <CHILDSOCKET>;
        print "Got Request $_" if $opt_d;
        chomp;

        unless (m/(\S+) (\S+)/)
        {
            print "Malformed request string $_\n" if $opt_d;
            bad_request(*CHILDSOCKET);
        }
        else
        {
            my ($command) = $1;
            my ($arg) = $2;
            if (uc($command) eq 'GET')
            {
                if (open(FILE, "<$arg"))
                {
                    while(<FILE>)
                    {
                        print CHILDSOCKET $_;
                    }
                    close(FILE);
                }
                else
                {
                    bad_request(*CHILDSOCKET);
                }
            }
        }
        close(CHILDSOCKET);
        exit(0);
    }
    close(CHILDSOCKET);
}
```

```
sub bad_request
{
    my ($SOCKET) = shift;

    print $SOCKET <<EOF;
<html>
<head>
<title>Bad Request</title>
</head>
<body>
<h1>Bad Request</h1>
The file you requested could not be found
</body>
</html>
EOF
}

sub child_handler
{
    wait;
}

sub exit_request_handler
{
    my ($recvsig) = @_;
    $SIG{'INT'} = $SIG{'QUIT'} = 'IGNORE';
    close(SERVERSOCKET);
    close(CHILDSOCKET);
    die "Quitting on signal $recvsig\n";
}
```

The main loop of this program will continue forever, either until a fatal error occurs or the program receives the **SIGINT** or **SIGQUIT** signal. This operation is dealt with by signal handlers, which we'll cover in more detail in Chapter 10.

The main acceptance loop is here,

```
ACCEPT_CONNECT:
    {
        ($remaddr = accept(CHILDSOCKET, SERVERSOCKET))
            || redo ACCEPT_CONNECT;
    }
```

where you just cycle around for as long as it takes until you get a valid connection. Remember that **accept** blocks process execution, so it's not a major concern that you'll be continually looping through this section. In fact, you should only ever **redo** the block if the accepted connection could not be opened properly.

Once you have opened a valid connection, you fork a new child process to handle the communication using the newly created **CHILDSOCKET** filehandle. Since you are forking a new process each time, you don't have to worry about the fact that the filehandle name is identical. You close the filehandle in the parent immediately after the child process has been forked.

There are a couple of other important notes here. First of all, you use a command line option to handle the printout of additional debugging information. Second, you use **chroot** to change the root directory of the script to the current directory. This guarantees the security of the web server by restricting the files that can be served to the files within the current directory and all its subdirectories. Even attempts to access files or directories associated by symbolic links will fail.

Finally, note the communication method employed. Because of the complexities of two-way communication over a single socket, you have to make some assumptions about the process involved. For HTTP the client sends a single-line request and then waits for the server to send the reply, sending **EOF** or closing the connection as appropriate. The information returned by the server must be text based and can consist of HTTP header information and the actual body of data. We'll look at some examples of this in Chapters 14 and 15.

Using IO::Socket

The standard Perl distribution actually includes a module that provides a simpler interface to the built-in socket functions, much like the scripts above. If you are not designing a custom solution, you might find that the distributed module better suits your needs. It's also more likely to be updated regularly than my own solution, and as part of the standard Perl distribution, it should work on a wide range of platforms without any modifications to your scripts.

Client Side

Initiating a client network connection with the **IO::Socket** module is very simple and actually follows a similar model to the **connectsocket** function:

```
use IO::Socket;
$sock = new IO::Socket::INET (PeerAddr => 'twinspark',
                              PeerPort => 4003,
                              Proto    => 'tcp'
                             );
```

The **$sock** scalar now contains a reference to a filehandle that you can use to transfer information to a remote host.

Server Side

The server side initialization follows a similar model:

```
use IO::Socket;
$sock = new IO::Socket::INET (LocalHost => 'twinspark',
                              LocalPort => 4003,
                              Proto     => 'tcp',
                              Listen    => 5,
                              Reuse     => 1
                             );
```

This follows the same fundamental idea as the **listensocket** function. This creates a socket and binds to the address and port specified by **LocalHost** and **LocalPort**. The **listen** queue is set to the value of the **Listen** element of the passed hash, and you set the **SO_REUSEADDR** option with the **Reuse** hash element.

Once the socket is created, you can use it as before, although many of the functions are now available as methods to the newly created socket object. Thus you can accept new requests on a server socket with statements like this:

```
$new_sock = $sock->accept();
```

Note how the client- and server-side object constructing methods are identical. The type of socket to be created is determined by the keys passed to the constructor.

Getting Socket Addresses

When connecting with a remote socket, you might take it for granted that you know the remote IP address of the machine you are talking to. In fact, you can't necessarily guarantee it's the one you expect. It's possible for a single name to resolve to a number of IP addresses, and the exact one you have connected to may not be obvious.

When acting as a server, the same problem occurs if you forget to use the IP address returned by the **accept** function. In both cases, you can use the **getpeername** function to return the IP address of the remote machine you are talking to:

```
getpeername SOCKET
```

The function returns the packed **sockaddr_in** structure of the remote socket connection. You'll need to extract the real address with something like this:

```
print "Remote: ",inet_ntoa((unpack_sockaddr_in(getpeername
SOCKET))[1]),"\n";
```

The opposite is true when you are acting as a server. If you specified one of the wildcard addresses such as **INADDR_ANY** as the address to bind to, then you may not know what you have bound to on a multiple interface host. You can find out that information with **getsockname**:

```
getsockname SOCKET
```

This returns the same information as **getpeername**, except that it's for the local machine, rather than the remote one.

Note that in both cases the functions only work on open and connected sockets. You can't create a socket and bind it or connect to it in order to get the current IP address of the local or remote machine. Until a connection has been accepted or connected, the socket is not attached to any local or remote IP address.

Closing Sockets

Because Perl treats a socket just like any other filehandle, the obvious (and natural) way to close a socket is to use the **close** function. However, you can use the **shutdown** function to provide a controlled shutdown of a connected socket.

```
shutdown SOCKET, HOW
```

The **SOCKET** is the filehandle of the open socket. The **HOW** value defines how the socket should be shut down. If **HOW** is zero, you cannot use the socket to receive more information. If **HOW** is one, you cannot use the socket for sending information. If **HOW** is two, the socket cannot be used for either sending or receiving information. Note that this doesn't actually close the socket connection; it just indicates to the system that the full-duplex nature of a socket has been modified.

This is perhaps most useful when you are creating a pair of sockets at each end of a connection—one socket purely for sending and one for receiving information. Although it doesn't automatically redirect it for you, it will make sure you do not send data to a remote socket that won't be listening for it anyway, thus preventing deadlocking.

Socket Options

You can specify certain options on individual sockets to improve facilities or performance. For example, the **SO_SNDBUF** option sets the buffer size when sending information via a network socket, while the **SO_REUSEADDR** allows you to reuse an existing address/port if a previous connection is still shutting down. Without setting this option, new connections will fail, even if you know that you've closed down the previous socket connection.

To set a particular option, you use

```
setsockopt SOCKET, LEVEL, OPTNAME, OPTVAL
```

The **LEVEL** is the level within the networking model that you want the option to affect. Most of the time this will be **SOL_SOCKET**, to directly affect the BSD network sockets. The **OPTNAME** is one of the constants, exported by the **Socket** module, and summarized in Table 9-1. Note that the list here is for guidance only. The exact options available will depend both on your operating system and the level of the connection that you are configuring.

The **OPTVAL** is the value that you want to assign to the particular option. Because each option can have a specific value, you cannot combine multiple options into the same **setsockopt** call; you must set the options individually. For options that can be enabled or disabled, zero indicates that the option should be disabled, and 1 indicates that it should be enabled.

For example, to switch **SO_REUSEADDR** on:

```
setsockopt(SOCKET, SOL_SOCKET, SO_REUSEADDR, 1);
```

Option	Description
SO_DEBUG	Enable/disable recording of debugging information.
SO_REUSEADDR	Enable/disable local address reuse.
SO_KEEPALIVE	Enable/disable keep connections alive.
SO_DONTROUTE	Enable/disable routing bypass for outgoing messages.
SO_LINGER	Linger on close if data is present.
SO_BROADCAST	Enable/disable permission to transmit broadcast messages.
SO_OOBINLINE	Enable/disable reception of out-of-band data in band.
SO_SNDBUF	Set buffer size for output.
SO_RCVBUF	Set buffer size for input.

Table 9-1. *Socket Options Under Solaris 2.4*

On some systems you may need to pack the setting into a long integer using **pack**:

```
setsockopt(SOCKET, SOL_SOCKET, SO_REUSEADDR, pack('l',1));
```

To get the current options, use **getsockopt**:

```
getsockopt SOCKET, LEVEL, OPTNAME
```

This returns the current setting for **OPTNAME**, or undefined if the value cannot be determined. Note that once again you must request each option value individually; it's not possible to request all of the currently set options.

Data Transfer

Transferring information over a network is problematic because of line termination and other issues to contend with. However, providing you are careful, you shouldn't have any difficulties while using the normal **print** function and **<FILEHANDLE>** operator. Since Perl treats sockets like filehandles, there is no reason why you shouldn't use any of the available functions and operators that work with filehandles for transferring information.

To avoid getting into a deadlocked situation when communicating between hosts on a single socket, you will need to design a suitable protocol that tells each end of the network link what state it should be in. For simple communication it should be enough to use a simple flip-flop situation. For example, the server end sits waiting for data while the client sends information, and once transfer is complete, the end toggles. Now the client waits for data while the server sends it. This is the basic idea behind protocols such as HTTP and SMTP. However, if you are using one of these protocols for transfer, then you might find one of the CPAN modules, such as Graham Barr's excellent **libnet** bundle, significantly easier to use.

A possible alternative solution, as already discussed, is to open two sockets at each end of the connection. The client uses **shutdown** to disable sending on socket A while disabling receiving on socket B. The server, on the other hand, disables receiving on socket A while disabling sending on socket B. Although this improves the situation, you can still enter a deadlocked state if you are expecting to receive data on both ends of the connection.

You cannot even use **select** to solve the problem. Many people mistakenly believe that **select** eliminates the deadlocking situation. It doesn't; all it does is provide a method for a single threaded process to communicate on more than one socket semi-simultaneously. If both ends of the connection are listening, when one of them should be sending, all **select** does is monitor multiple sockets very efficiently for no data.

If you are transferring fixed blocks of information, particularly binary data or fixed-length records, then you might find the **send** and **recv** functions to be more practical. You may also find that your operating system does not support the use of **print** and other filehandle constructs for sending information. In these instances you will have to use the **send** and **recv** functions.

The **send** function sends a message on a socket handle, just like the **send()** system function:

```
send SOCKET, MSG, FLAGS [, TO]
```

The **MSG** argument is the data string that you want to send. Since Perl automatically knows the length of a string, you do not need to supply this information. The **FLAGS** specify particular operations to be configured for this transmission. Only two are generally supported—**MSG_OOB** and **MSG_DONTROUTE**. **MSG_OOB** allows you to send the **MSG** as out-of-band data. This is generally only supported on Internet streams. The **MSG_DONTROUTE** flag switches on the **SO_DONTROUTE** option for the duration of the transfer (see "Socket Options" above). The **TO** argument, if specified, should be a suitable **sockaddr_in** structure to send the data to if the socket has not already been connected to a remote socket.

```
recv SOCKET, SCALAR, LEN, FLAGS
```

The **recv** function accepts information from **SOCKET**, placing it into **SCALAR**. It accepts up to a maximum of **LEN** bytes from the socket, and **SCALAR** will be shrunk or grown accordingly to hold the received information. The function returns the IP address of the host from which the data was received, or **undef** on error.

CPAN Modules

Graham Barr supports the **libnet** bundle, which consists of a large number of modules that support communication over a network with existing TCP/IP servers and protocols such as HTTP, FTP, SMTP, and NNTP. Because the complexities of the protocols have been determined for you, the difficulties associated with communicating using these protocols is virtually eliminated. The interfaces provided are object based, and if you are familiar with the protocols, then using the modules and the classes provided is very easy. Even if you don't understand the protocols, simplified top-level functions are provided for the most common tasks.

For example, here's a script that expands an email address, first by resolving the MX (mail exchanger) hosts for the email address's domain, and then by communicating directly with the mail server to expand the email address. This script also uses the

Net::DNS module by Michael Fuhr, which provides an interface to the DNS name-resolving system. Again, it's object based and is very easy to use. See Appendix F for details on the networking modules that are available from CPAN, or use Appendix A to locate your local CPAN mirror.

```
#!/usr/local/bin/perl5

use Net::SMTP;
use Net::DNS;

while (@ARGV)
{
    my $email = shift;
    my ($user, $host) = split '@', $email;
    my $res = new Net::DNS::Resolver;
    my @mx = mx($res, $host);

    if (@mx)
    {
        print "Expansions for $email\n";
        foreach my $rr (@mx)
        {
            my ($mxhost) = $rr->exchange;
            print "Checking $mxhost\n";
            my $smtp = Net::SMTP->new($mxhost);
            unless($smtp)
            {
                warn "Couldn't open connection to $host";
                next;
            }
            my $realrecipient = $smtp->expand($email);
            print "$realrecipient\n" if $realrecipient;
            $smtp->quit();
        }
        print "\n";
    }
    else
    {
        print "Couldn't find any MX hosts for $host\n";
    }
}
```

You can see from this sample how easy it is both to resolve an address using DNS and to communicate with an SMTP server. The complexities of opening the remote connection and handling the protocol and communication have been eliminated, and something that would otherwise take hundreds of lines is resolved to just 34 lines. To use, just specify an address on the command line:

```
Expansions for mc@mcwords.com
Checking mcwords.com
<mcwords@prluk.demon.co.uk>
```

The example below downloads messages from an NNTP (Network News Transfer Protocol) server. Individual articles from Usenet are downloaded into a directory structure that corresponds to the individual newsgroups, and the current status is recorded so future executions download only the new messages from the Usenet server.

```
use Getopt::Long;
use Net::NNTP;

$SIG{'INT'} = $SIG{'QUIT'} = \&clean_exit;

my ($newgroup, $debug, $oldgroup, $server, $usage, $annotate);
my ($force, $directory, $recurse);

GetOptions("n=s" => \$newgroup,
           "g"   => \$debug,
           "r=s" => \$oldgroup,
           "s=s" => \$server,
           "h"   => \$usage,
           "a"   => \$annotate,
           "d=s" => \$directory,
           "c"   => \$recurse,
           "f"   => \$force
           );

print_usage() if $usage;

$annotate = 1 if $debug;
$directory = $directory || "./";
$server = $server || "news.foo.bar";
```

```
my $nntp = Net::NNTP->new($server, Debug => $debug ? 1 : 0);
die "Couldn't open connection" unless $nntp;

my (%groups);

init_group_table();

init_new_group($newgroup) if $newgroup;
delete $groups{$oldgroup} if $oldgroup;

foreach my $group (sort keys %groups)
{
    get_group_mesgs($group, $groups{$group}, $directory, $recurse);
}

update_group_table();

sub get_group_mesgs
{
    my ($group, $first, $directory, $recurse) = @_;
    my @groupinfo = $nntp->group($group);
    my $last=$groupinfo[2];

    print "Retrieving $group (messages $first to $last)\n"
        if $annotate;

    if (($recurse) && ($last-$first++))
    {
        mkdir ("$directory/$group", 0700)
            unless (-d "$directory/$group");
    }

    for (my $id=($first);$id<=$last;$id++)
    {
        print "Getting article $id\n" if $annotate;
        my $lines = $nntp->article($id);
        next unless $lines;
        my ($filespec) = $recurse ? ">$directory/$group/$id" :
            ">$directory/$group.$id";
```

```
if (open(D, $filespec))
        {
            print D @$lines;
            close(D);
        }
        else
        {
            warn "Couldn't create $filespec\n";
        }
        $groups{$group} = $id;
    }
}

sub init_new_group
{
    my ($group) = @_;

    if (exists($groups{$group}))
    {
        warn "$group is already in table\n" if $annotate;
        return unless ($force);
        warn "Resetting $group\n" if $annotate;
    }
    my @groupinfo = $nntp->group($group);
    if (@groupinfo)
    {
        $groups{$group} = $groupinfo[1]-1;
        print "Added $group starting msgno $groupinfo[1]\n"
            if $annotate;
    }
    else
    {
        warn "Group $group is not available on this server";
    }
}

sub init_group_table
{
    unless (open(GROUPS, "<autonntp.rc"))
    {
        warn "Couldn't open an existing group file\n";
        warn "A new file will be created\n";
```

```
        return;
    }
    while(<GROUPS>)
    {
        chomp;
        my ($group, $lastid) = split ', ';
        $groups{$group} = $lastid;
    }
    close(GROUPS);
}

sub update_group_table
{

    open(GROUPS, ">autonntp.rc")
        || die "Couldn't update the group table\n";

    foreach my $key (sort keys %groups)
    {
        print GROUPS "$key, $groups{$key}\n";
    }
    close(GROUPS);
}

sub clean_exit
{
    my ($sig) = @_;

    $SIG{'INT'} = $SIG{'QUIT'} = 'IGNORE';
    update_group_table;
    $nntp->quit() if (defined($nntp));
    die "Asked to quit on $sig";
}

sub print_usage
{
    print <<EOF
Usage:
        $0 [-d] [-n|-r group] [-s server] [-h] \
              [-f] [-c] [-d directory]
Where:
```

```
-a            Annotate download
-g            Show debugging information (implies annotate)
-n group      Add new group to the download list
-r group      Delete group from the download list
-f            Resets the message ids for an existing group
-d directory Save files/structure in specified directory
-c            Store messages as group/msgid not group.msgid
-s server     Specify a different NNTP server

-h            Show this help information
EOF
    ;
    exit(0);
}
```

I've used this script for synchronizing a remote NNTP host with a local copy of Usenet messages on announcements and other lists, which were then processed by another Perl script for use within an intranet. It may seem less practical than a solution based on threads or message IDs, but if you are synchronizing, you are only interested in receiving all the messages from a specific newsgroup anyway.

The Complete Reference

Part III

Execution Enhancements

The Complete Reference

Chapter 10

Interprocess Communication

Interaction with other processes is often an essential part of the programming process. Interaction can take many forms. Sometimes it is as simple and straightforward as calling an external program. At other times, you may want to control the process's priority, send a particular signal, or even exchange information with it.

All of these operations can be classed as a form of interprocess communication. Before you fully appreciate the need for interprocess communication, however, you must understand how to create additional processes. Some of the methods in this chapter will be familiar, as we've used them in earlier chapters; but here we'll be specifically looking at the complexities of creating and communicating with these additional processes.

We have already covered one form of interprocess communication—the use of standard network sockets. There is nothing to stop you from connecting to yourself over a network socket, and more importantly, you have the benefit of also being able to communicate over a network with few changes to the original script.

There are better ways, however, that don't require the use of what is primarily a network communication rather than process communication system. Most of these center around pipes—a unidirectional communication path between two processes. Unix users will be familiar with the use of pipes, and, once again, it's something that we looked at, albeit briefly, within Chapter 3 when examining the **open** function.

In this chapter we'll look at all the different functions and instances where interprocess communication is useful, beneficial, and in some cases vital. Furthermore, we'll be looking at many of the additional functions used to support interprocess communication and at methods for creating and controlling additional processes within a Perl script.

Processes

Processes are the individual programs that are running on your machine. Some of these are obvious to you, like the applications and utilities that you use. Others are hidden from view and control different parts of the OS operation. On a Unix machine these include everything from the core operating system and scheduler right through to the shell you use to run other programs.

Under Windows, the core operating system is hidden, but there are still references to the underlying applications and background processes used to support different services. You can view the individual processes using the Task Manager. The same effect can be seen under MacOS, although you will be unable to see the background processes without a special application— the usual About This Macintosh window won't show them.

Note that most of the functions in this section do not work under the MacOS, although the actual interpretation under Windows NT and Unix should be more or less identical because of the common **POSIX** support on both platforms. The only feature with processes that does work under MacOS is the value of the **$$** variable, which is in fact always 1.

Controlling Perl Execution

You already know about the statements and the operators that can help to control the execution of a Perl program. You also know about **die** and **warn**. The **die** function reports an error to **STDERR** and quits the program, while **warn** just reports an error to **STDERR**.

However, there are times when you want to exit a program without triggering an error message to **STDERR**, or when you want to trigger an installed signal handler (see "Signal Handlers" later in this chapter). In these instances, the solution is to use the **exit** function:

```
exit 1;
```

This immediately causes the script to exit, passing a value of **1** back to the caller. If you do not specify a value, then a value of zero is returned, which is generally accepted as indicating a successful completion.

You should really only use **exit** within the main part of a script, because using it within a subroutine is bad practice. What you should do is call **return**, passing a suitable value back to the caller to deal with. Furthermore, if you want to trap the execution of a block, use **die** within **eval** to trap the error.

Process Information

The process ID of the current script is permanently available within the **$$** variable. Since this value will be different for each execution, you cannot rely on this number to store persistent information. On the other hand, the process ID can be used as part of a random identification number if combined with date, time, and even a random number.

If you want to get the process ID of the parent process, you need to use the **getppid** function:

```
print "The parent of $$ is ",getppid,"\n";
```

This information is useful if you want to modify process groups or send the parent process a signal. Under Unix, your parent process ID should be greater than one; a parent process ID of one indicates that the parent has died and that you've been adopted by the **init** process.

Process Groups

A collection of processes is logically grouped into process groups. For example, all the programs run within a shell belong to the same process group, providing they don't elect to change the process group. You can obtain the process group of a process using the **getpgrp** function:

```
print "Group of current($$): ", getpgrp(0),
        ", parent(",getppid,"):", getpgrp(getppid),"\n";
```

If you do not specify a process, or use a process ID of 0, then it returns the process group of the current process.

You can "daemonize" a process—that is, make it act like a typical Unix daemon process that runs in the background without a controlling terminal—by calling the **setpgrp** function. A daemon process is one that is running in the background, and by using **setpgrp**, you can emulate a Unix command line like this:

```
$ script.pl &
```

To do this, you need to change the process group for the current process to zero. This needs to be done after forking a new process to ensure that you are not automatically a member of an existing process group:

```
my $childpid = fork;
exit if $childpid;
setpgrp(0, $$);
```

Because you are starting a daemon process, it's also a good idea to ensure that the new process you are creating is safe and well behaved. For example, you should consider redirecting **STDIN**, **STDOUT**, and **STDERR** either to /dev/null or to an external log file. You'll see some more examples of this later in this chapter when we look at the **fork** function in more detail.

Process Priority

You can obtain and set the priority of a given process, process group, or user, using the **getpriority** and **setpriority** functions:

```
getpriority WHICH, WHO
setpriority WHICH, WHO, PRIORITY
```

The value of **WHICH** should be one of **PRIO_PROCESS** for an individual process, **PRIO_PGRP** for a process group, and **PRIO_USER** for an individual user. The **WHO** value should then be the corresponding process ID, process group ID, or user ID (all numerical) that you want to obtain or set the priority for. The current priority will be returned by the **getpriority** function, and you can set it by supplying a new priority value in **PRIORITY**.

Note that the priorities are arbitrary values, and different values will have different meanings on different operating systems. For most instances, however, the priority is in reverse order. The higher the priority number, the lower the actual priority of the process. All users can decrease the priority of a process (just as they can with **nice**), but only the superuser can increase the priority (by setting a lower value).

Signals

Signals do exactly what the name suggests. They provide a method for signaling a particular process. Since a single signal is not very practical, there are a whole range of signals that indicate different events to the process. Some signals are generated by the operating system and signify some problem with the current execution process. Other signals can be user generated. Almost all signals can be trapped, both by other processes and by Perl scripts. The list of **POSIX** signals is shown in Table 10-1.

POSIX Name	Perl Name	Description
SIGABRT	ABRT	Abnormal termination.
SIGALRM	ALRM	The timer set by the **alarm** function has expired.
SIGFPE	FPE	Arithmetic exceptions, for example, divide overflow or divide by zero.
SIGHUP	HUP	Hangup detected on the controlling terminal or death of a controlling process.
SIGILL	ILL	Illegal instruction indicating a program error.
SIGINT	INT	Interrupt signal (special character from the keyboard or signal from another application).
SIGKILL	KILL	Termination signal; cannot be caught or ignored.

Table 10-1. *POSIX Signals*

POSIX Name	Perl Name	Description
SIGPIPE	PIPE	Attempt to write to a pipe with no application reading from it.
SIGQUIT	QUIT	Quit signal (special character from the keyboard or signal from another application).
SIGSEGV	SEGV	Attempt to access an invalid memory address.
SIGTERM	TERM	Termination signal (from another application or OS).
SIGUSR1	USR1	Application- (user) defined signal.
SIGUSR2	USR2	Application- (user) defined signal.
SIGCHLD	CHLD	A child process terminated or stopped.
SIGCONT	CONT	Continue the process if currently stopped.
SIGSTOP	STOP	Stop signal. Stops the specified process.
SIGTSTP	TSTP	Stop signal from special character from keyboard.
SIGTTIN	TTIN	A read was attempted from the controlling terminal by a background process.
SIGTTOU	TTOU	A write was attempted to the controlling terminal by a background process.

Table 10-2. *POSIX Signals* (continued)

Different Perl implementations will support a different range of signals. On most Unix systems the list will be longer than that shown in Table 10-1 to cater to the OS-specific entries supporting features such as threads and resource limits. Under Windows NT there is a subset of the full **POSIX** list, which includes most of the **POSIX** and therefore Unix signals. Under the MacOS implementation there is a very short subset, since the MacOS does not treat or handle processes in the same way as Unix or Windows. Refer to Chapter 24 for more information on the list of signals supported under different operating systems, or use this simple script:

```
foreach $signal (sort keys %SIG)
{
    print "$signal\n";
}
```

Signal Handlers

If you have used signal handling systems within C before, then you will find the signal handling abilities of Perl something of a shock. Perl provides an incredibly simple interface to signal handling using a single **%SIG** hash. The individual keys of the **%SIG** hash are the signal names (as seen in the second column of Table 10-1), and the corresponding value indicates the operation that should be performed when that signal is received by the script. For example:

```
$SIG{INT} = sub { print "Got SIGINT" };
```

The above example sets up a signal handler to an anonymous subroutine, which will print a message when an interrupt signal is received. This is a fairly impractical example, as we don't do anything with the signal once we've caught it. Usually, you'd create a special signal handling function:

```
sub sig_int
{
    my $signal = shift;
    print "Got the signal $signal\n";
    $SIG{$signal} = \&sig_int;
}

$SIG{INT} = \&sig_int;
```

The above example has a number of advantages. First of all, the signal handler is now a separate function, which means you can use the same handler for a number of signals. Furthermore, it ensures that the signal is reset to the current signal handler after it has been received, which guarantees that the handler will always be in place. Also note from this example that the first argument given to a signal handler is the name of the signal received.

It's important to remember that you should be passing a reference to the desired signal handler function, not simply a bare word, which could be misinterpreted, or the return value from a function call itself. The following are bad examples that you should try to avoid:

```
$SIG{INT} = sig_int;
$SIG{INT} = sig_int();
```

Both could cause problems. The bare word doesn't guarantee that the function will be called correctly. The function call is positively lethal—the value of the signal handler is now the value returned by the **sig_int** function.

Care should be taken with signal handlers. Since a signal can be received at any time, it's possible to receive a signal while another signal handler is executing. It's unusual, for example, to do this:

```
sub sig_int
{
    my $signal = shift;
    print "Got the signal $signal\n";
    do_some_work();
    $SIG{$signal} = \&sig_int;
}

$SIG{INT} = \&sig_int;
```

The obvious solution is to keep the contents of the signal handler as short as possible. Alternatively, you can set the condition of a signal (or signals) to **IGNORE** during the signal handler. This setting will cause Perl to ignore the specified signal until a new signal handler has been installed, thereby allowing you to work uninterrupted (if you'll excuse the pun).

```
sub sig_int
{
    my $signal = shift;
    $SIG{$signal} = IGNORE;
    do_some_work();
    $SIG{$signal} = \&sig_int;
}

$SIG{INT} = \&sig_int;
```

An alternative solution is to use Perl's **local** keyword to inherit the signal hash from the enclosing block. This will allow you to set an alternative handler, or **IGNORE** status on signals within the current handler, while retaining the handler information for the parent block, as in:

```
sub sig_int
{
    my $signal = shift;
    local $SIG{$signal} = 'IGNORE';
    do_some_work();
```

```
    $SIG{$signal} = \&sig_int;
}

$SIG{INT} = \&sig_int;
```

To reset a signal to its original state (before you started installing your own handlers), you can set the signal value to **DEFAULT**:

```
$SIG{INT} = 'DEFAULT';
```

A common use for the alarm signal (**ALRM**) is as a time-out system for different operations. This can be used for many things, just as setting file options, file locking, networking communication, or, as in the example below, for accepting input and setting a default value:

```
print "Your name is? :\n";
eval
{
    local $SIG{ALRM} = sub { die "Timeout"; };
    alarm 10;
    $name = <STDIN>;
    chomp $name;
    alarm 0;
};
if ($@ and $@ =~ /Timeout/) { $name = 'Anonymous' }
print "Hello $name!\n";
```

The action you want to place a time-out on is put within the **eval** block, and the signal handler calls **die** when the alarm time has been exceeded. This causes the **eval** block to drop out, and you check the return status with the **$@** variable, setting a default name if the user hasn't supplied one.

Note *Not all signals can be trapped or ignored. You'll need to check your operating system for the exact list. Typical signals that cannot be trapped include **KILL** and **STOP**.*

Using Signals with warn and die

There are two special signals that will not appear directly within the **%SIG** hash. These are the special tokens **__WARN__** and **__DIE__**. If you install signal handlers for these two "signals," then you can trap a call to **warn** or **die**, respectively. This is useful in situations where you want to write the warnings out to an alternative file, or close down sockets and other active resources when **die** is called.

The **__WARN__** handler is called when a warning message is about to be printed, and the normal printing of the message passed to **warn** is suppressed. However, you can still extract the warning message, as it is passed as the first argument to the signal handler function:

```
sub warn_handler
{
    print "!!!!Trapping a warning:\n$_[0]";
}

$SIG{__WARN__} = \&warn_handler;

print "Hello World\n";
warn "Whoops, something isn't right...\n";
print "Blimey, that was close!\n";
```

If you run this, you get

```
Hello World
!!!!Trapping a warning:
Whoops, something isn't right...
Blimey, that was close!
```

For the **__DIE__** handler, the result is slightly different. The signal handler is called, but you cannot stop the normal **die** message being printed unless the handler calls **goto** or **exit**. It's usual therefore to do something like this:

```
sub die_handler
{
    print STDERR "Panic:$_[0]Trying to exit nicely\n";
    goto &close_everything;
}

sub close_everything
{
    exit 1;
}

$SIG{__DIE__} = \&die_handler;

print "Hello World\n";
die "Whoops, something isn't right";
print "Blimey, that was close!\n";
```

The second **print** statement in the main package will never be reached, and, presumably, you would put some **close** and other statements into **close_everything** to ensure that you shut down properly.

Note that in both cases, the **__WARN__** and **__DIE__** signals are disabled explicitly by the interpreter when the signal handler is called. This allows you to use **die** within either handler without the risk of inducing recursion on the signal handler. For example:

```
sub die_handler
{
    print LOG "Panic: $_[0]";
    die $_[0];
}

$SIG{__DIE__} = \&die_handler;

die "Whoops, something isn't right";
```

This assumes, of course, that **LOG** is open and pointing to a suitable file, but the effect should be obvious.

Sending Signals

You can send signals to other processes using the **kill** function, which actually just calls the Unix **kill()** function. For example, to call the **SIGINT** handler within the function, you could use

```
kill('INT', $$);
```

You can use short names or numbers as the first argument to the function, and the second argument should be the process ID or process group to which you are sending the signal. To send the signal to all of the processes in the specified signal group, prefix the process ID with a minus sign:

```
kill INT => -$$;
```

Note here that the hash notation has also been used to define the signal. Since the **=>** operator is just an alias for the comma, this works perfectly. It also has the advantage of automatically quoting the signal number to send, which makes more sense if you think about the process logically. In the above example you are sending the signal **INT** to the process group **-$$**.

By sending the signal number zero to a process, you can determine whether it is currently running, or whether it's possible to send a valid signal. Since you can only send a signal to processes you own, this is a good way to test whether a specific process is still running and whether it is still yours. It is particularly useful when forking and subsequently monitoring a child process.

For example, the following checks that the schedule is running on a Solaris (and indeed most other Unix flavors) machine:

```
unless (kill 0 => 0)
{
    die "Panic: Scheduler not running!\n";
}
```

Pipes

Pipes are a one-way communication channel that can be used to transfer information between processes. Because they are one-way, they can only be used to communicate information to or from a process, although there are ways to get around this. The most typical use of pipes is within the **open** function when you want to read from and write to a particular command, instead of a typical file. This class of pipe is called an anonymous pipe. You can also have named pipes (within Unix only) that provide a method for two unconnected processes to communicate with each other.

There are other methods available using pipes, but these are only practical when used with child processes, so we'll cover these at a later stage. For now, let's concentrate on the basics of opening and reading from and writing to pipes.

Anonymous Pipes

An anonymous pipe is one implied through the use of the pipe symbol at the beginning or end of an **open** statement. For example, to read the output from **gzcat**, which decompresses a Gzipped file to the standard input:

```
open(COMPRESSED, "gzcat file.gz|") or die "Can't fork: $!";
while(<COMPRESSED>)
{
    print;
}
close(COMPRESSED) or die "Error in gzcat: $!";
```

Alternatively, to write information and have it immediately compressed, you can pass input directly to the **gzip** command:

```
open(COMPRESS, "|gzip - >file.gz") or die "Can't fork: $!";
print COMPRESS "Compressed Data";
close(COMPRESS) or die "Gzip didn't work: $!";
```

When using pipes, you must check the return status of both **open** and **close**. This is because each function returns an error from a different element of the piped command. The **open** function forks a new process and executes the specified command. The return value of this operation trapped by **open** is the return value of the **fork** function. The new process is executed within a completely separate process, and there is no way for **open** to obtain that error. This effectively means that the **open** will return true if the new process could be forked, irrespective of the status of the command you are executing. The **close** function, on the other hand, picks up any errors generated by the executed process because it monitors the return value received from the child process via **wait** (see "Creating Child Processes" later in this chapter).

Therefore, in the first example, you could actually read nothing from the command, and without checking the return status of **close**, you might assume that the command failed to return any valid data.

In the second example, where you are writing to a piped command, you need to be more careful. There is no way of determining the status of the opened command without immediately calling **close**, which rather defeats the purpose. Instead, you can use a signal handler on the **PIPE** signal. The process will receive a **PIPE** signal from the operating system if the piped command fails.

Two-Way Communication

As convenient as it may seem, you can't do the following:

```
open(MORE, "|more file|");
```

This is because a pipe is unidirectional—it either reads from or writes to a piped command. Although in theory this should work, it can result in a deadlocked process where neither the parent nor piped command know whether they should be reading from or writing to the **MORE** filehandle.

The solution is to use the **open2** function that comes as part of the **IPC::Open2** module, which is part of the standard distribution:

```
use FileHandle;
use IPC::Open2;
$pid = open2(\*READ, \*WRITE, "more file");
WRITE->autoflush();
```

You can now communicate in both directions with the **more** command, reading from it with the **READ** filehandle and writing to it with the **WRITE** filehandle. This will receive data from the standard output of the piped command and write to the standard input of the piped command.

There is a danger with this system, however, in that it assumes the information is always available from the piped command and that it is always ready to accept information. But accesses either way will block until the piped command is ready to accept or to reply with information. This is due to the buffering supported by the standard **STDIO** functions. There isn't a complete solution to this if you are using off-the-shelf commands; if you are using your own programs, then you'll have control over the buffering, and it shouldn't be a problem.

The underlying functionality of the **open2** function is made possible using the **pipe** function, which creates a pair of connected pipes, one for reading and one for writing:

```
pipe READHANDLE, WRITEHANDLE
```

We'll look at an example of this when we look at creating new child processes with **fork**.

Named Pipes

A named pipe is a special type of file available under Unix. It resides, like any file, in the file system but provides two-way communication between two otherwise unrelated processes. This system has been in use for some time within Unix as a way of accepting print jobs. A specific printer interface creates and monitors the file while users send data to the named pipe. The printer interface accepts the data, spools the accepted file to disk, and then spawns a new process to send it out to the printer.

The named pipe is treated as a FIFO (see Chapter 7) and is sometimes simply called a FIFO. You create a named pipe using the **mknod** or **mkfifo** command, which in turn creates a suitably configured file on the file system. The following example, therefore,

```
system('mknod', 'myfifo', 'p');
```

is identical to this one:

```
system('mkfifo', 'myfifo');
```

Once created, you can read from or write to the file just like any normal file, except that both instances will block until there is a suitable process on the other end. For example, here is a simple script that accepts input from a FIFO and writes it into a permanent log file:

```
my $fifo = 'logfifo';
my $logfile = 'logfile.txt';

unless (-p $fifo)
{
    unlink $fifo;
    if (system('mkfifo','logfifo'))
    {
        die "Can't create FIFO: $!";
    }
}

open(FIFO, "<$fifo") or die "Can't open fifo for reading: $!";
open(LOG, ">>$logfile") or die "Can't append to $logfile: $!";
while(<FIFO>)
{
    my $date = localtime(time);
    print LOG "$date: $_"\n;
}

close(FIFO) or die "Can't close fifo: $!";
close(LOG) or die "Can't close log: $!";
```


Here's the corresponding log reporter, which takes input from the command line and writes it to the FIFO:

```
my $fifo = 'logfifo';

die "No data to log" unless @ARGV;

open(FIFO,">$fifo") or die "Can't open fifo for writing: $!";
print FIFO @ARGV;
close(FIFO) or die "Can't close fifo: $!";
```

If you run the "server" and then call the client, you should be able to add an entry to the log file. Note though that the server will quit once it has accepted one piece of information, because the "client" closes the pipe (and therefore sends **eof** to the server) when it exits. If you want a more persistent server, call the main loop within a forked subprocess. See the discussion of **fork** later in "Creating Child Processes" for more information.

Safe Pipes

You may remember Chapter 3 briefly discussed the different methods you can use to open pipes with the **open** command. Two of these options are **-|** and **|-**, which imply a fork and pipe, providing an alternative method for calling external programs. For example:

```
open(GZDATA,"-|") or exec 'gzcat', 'file.gz';
```

This example forks a new process and immediately executes **gzcat**, with its standard output redirected to the **GZDATA** filehandle. The method is simple to remember. If you open a pipe to minus, then you can write to the filehandle, and the child process will receive the information in its **STDIN**. Opening a pipe from minus enables you to read information that the child sends to its **STDOUT** from the opened filehandle.

This can be useful in situations where you want to execute a piped command when running as a setuid script. More useful in general though is the fact that you can use this in combination with **exec** to ensure that the current shell does not parse the command you are trying to run. Here's a more obvious version of the above example that also takes care of the setuid permission status:

```
$child = open(GZCAT, "-|");
if ($child)
{
    while(<GZCAT>)
    {
        print $_;
    }
    close(<GZCAT>);
}
else
{
    ($EUID, $EGID) = ($UID, $GID);
    exec 'gzcat', 'file.gz';
}
```

Here, the **exec**'d program will be sending its output (a decompressed version of file.gz) to the standard output, which has in turn been piped through the **GZCAT** filehandle in the parent. In essence this is no different from a standard piped **open**, except that you guarantee that the shell doesn't mess with the arguments you supply to the function.

Executing Additional Processes

There are times when you want to run an external program but are not interested in the specifics of the output information, or if you are interested, you do not expect vast amounts of data that needs to be processed. In these situations a number of avenues are open to you. It's also possible that you want to create your own subprocess, purely for your own use. You've already seen some examples of this throughout this book. We'll look at both techniques in this section.

Running Other Programs

To run an external command, you can use the **system** function:

```
system LIST
```

This **fork**s a new process and then executes the command defined in the first argument of **LIST** (using **exec**), passing the command any additional arguments specified in **LIST**. Execution of the script blocks until the specified program completes.

The actual effect of **system** depends on the number of arguments. If there is more than one argument in **LIST**, the underlying function called is **execvp()**. This bypasses the current shell and executes the program directly. This can be used when you do not want the shell to make any modifications to the arguments you are passing. If there is only one argument, it is checked for shell metacharacters. If none are found, the argument is split into individual words and passed to **execvp()** as usual. If any metacharacters are found, the argument is passed directly to /bin/sh -c (or the current operating system equivalent) for parsing and execution.

Note that any output produced by the command you are executing will be displayed as usual to the standard output and error unless you redirect it accordingly (although this implies metacharacters). If you want to capture the output, use the **qx//** operator or a piped **open**. For example:

```
system("rm","-f","myfile.txt");
```

The return value is composed of the return status of the **wait** function used on the **fork**'d process and the exit value of the command itself. To get the exit value of the command you called, divide the value returned by **system** by 256.

You can also use this function to run a command in the background, providing you are not dependent on the command's completion before continuing:

```
system("emacs &");
```

The above example works on Unix, but other operating systems may use different methods.

The **system** function has one other trick. It can be used to let a command masquerade as a login shell or otherwise hide the process's name. You do this by using a slightly modified version of the command:

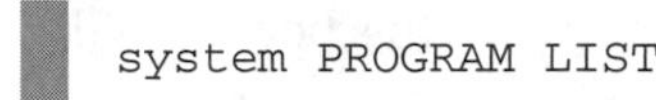

```
system PROGRAM LIST
```

The first argument is an indirect object and should refer to the actual program you want to run. The entries in **LIST** then become the values of the called program's **@ARGV** array. Thus, the first argument becomes the masquerading name, with remaining arguments being passed to the command as usual. This has the added benefit that **LIST** is now always treated as a list, even if it contains only one argument. For example, to execute a login shell:

```
system {'/bin/sh'} '-sh';
```

A more convenient method for executing a process, especially if you want to capture the output, is to use the **qx//** quoting operator:

```
my $hostname = qx/hostname/;
```

This is probably better known as the backticks operator, since you can also rewrite this as:

```
my $hostname = `hostname`;
```

The two are completely synonymous. It's a question of personal taste which one you choose to use. Backticks will be more familiar to shell users, since the same characters are used. The string you place into the `` or **qx//** is first interpolated, just like an ordinary double-quoted string. Note however that you must use the backslash operator to escape characters, such as **$** and **@**, that would otherwise be interpreted by Perl. The command is always executed via a shell, and the value returned by the operator is the output of the command you called.

Also note that like other quoted operators, you can choose alternative delimiter characters. For example, to call **sed** from Perl:

```
qx(sed -e s/foo/bar/g <$file);
```

Note as well in this example that **$file** will be parsed by Perl, not the shell.

In the previous examples, for instance, you assign a variable **$hostname** to the output of the **hostname** command. If the command is called in a scalar context, then the entire output is placed into a single string. If called in a list context, the output is split line by line, with each line being placed into an individual element of the list. The list is split using the value of **$/**, so you can parse the output automatically by changing the value of **$/**.

The return value of the command you called is placed in the special **$?** variable directly. You do not need to parse the contents in any way to determine the true exit value.

The function used to support the **qx//** operator is **readpipe**, which you can also call directly:

```
readpipe EXPR
```

Replacing the Current Script

You can replace the currently executing script with another command using the **exec** function. This works exactly the way the **system** command works, except that it never returns. The command you specify will completely replace the currently executing script. No **END** blocks are executed, and any active objects will not have their **DESTROY** methods called. You need to ensure therefore that the current script is ready to be replaced. It will be, and should be treated as, the last statement in your script.

```
exec LIST
```

All the constructs noted for **system** apply here, including the argument list handling. If the call fails for any reason, then **exec** returns false. This only applies when the command does not exist and the execution was direct, rather than via a shell. Because the function never returns, Perl will warn you (if you have warnings switched on) if the statement following **exec** is something other than **die**, **warn**, or **exit**.

Note that the masquerading system also works:

```
exec {'/bin/sh'} '-sh';
```

Creating Child Processes

It is common practice for servers and other processes to create "children." These subprocesses can be controlled from the parent (see the "Processes" section at the start of this chapter). You do this by using **fork**, which calls the **fork()** system call. **fork** creates a new process that is identical in nearly all respects to the parent process. The only difference is that the subprocess has a new process ID. Open filehandles and their buffers (flushed or otherwise) are inherited by the new process, but signal handlers and alarms, if set, are not:

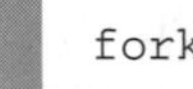

```
fork
```

The function returns the child process ID to the parent and 0 to the child process. The **undef** value is returned if the **fork** operation fails.

Use of the **fork** function needs some careful consideration within the Perl script. The execution contents of the new process are part of the current script; you do not call an external script or function to initiate the new process (you are not creating a new thread—see Chapter 11). For example, you can see from the comments in the code below where the boundaries of the child and parent lie:

```
#Parent Process

print "Starting the parent\n";

unless ($pid = fork)
{
#Start of Child Process
    sleep 2;
    for (1..10)
    {
        print "Child, Count $_\n";
        sleep 1;
    }
    exit 0;
}
#End of Child

#Continuation of Parent
for (1..5)
{
    print "Parent, Count $_\n";
    sleep 2;
}

waitpid($pid,0);

#End of Parent
```

As soon as the **fork** function returns, the child starts execution, running the script elements in the following block. You can do anything within this block. All the functions, modules, and variables are inherited by the child. However, you cannot use an inherited variable to share information with the parent. We'll cover the method for that shortly.

Also note that execution of the parent continues as soon as the **fork** function returns; so you get two simultaneously executing processes. If you run the above script, you should get output similar to this:

```
Starting the parent
Parent, Count 1
Child, Count 1
Parent, Count 2
Child, Count 2
Child, Count 3
Parent, Count 3
Child, Count 4
Child, Count 5
Parent, Count 4
Child, Count 6
Child, Count 7
Parent, Count 5
Child, Count 8
Child, Count 9
Child, Count 10
```

You can therefore use **fork** as a quasi-multithreading solution. Many HTTP, FTP, and other servers use this technique to handle more than one request from a client at the same time (see the simple web server example in Chapter 9). Each time a client connects to the server, it spawns a new process solely for servicing the requests of the client. The server immediately goes back to accepting new requests from new clients, spawning additional processes as it goes.

Open filehandles are inherited; so had you redirected **STDOUT** to a different file, the child would also have written to this file automatically. This can be used for parent-child communication, and we'll look at specific examples of this in the "Communicating with Children" section below.

As you fork new processes and they eventually die, you need to wait for the child processes to exit cleanly to ensure they do not remain as "zombies" within the process table. Child processes send the **SIGCHLD** signal to the parent when they exit, but unless the signal is caught, or the processes are otherwise acknowledged, they remain within the process table. They are called zombies because they have completed execution but have not been cleared from the table.

In order to acknowledge the completion of the child process, you need to use one of the two available functions, **wait** and **waitpid**. Both functions block the parent process until the child process (or processes) have exited cleanly. This should not cause problems if the functions are used as part of a signal handler, or if they are called as the last function within a parent that knows its children should have exited, probably because it sent a suitable signal.

```
wait
waitpid PID, FLAGS
```

The **wait** function simply waits for a child process to terminate. It's usually used within a signal handler to automatically reap child processes as they die:

```
$SIG{CHLD} = sub { wait };
```

This should guarantee that the child process completes correctly. The other alternative is to use the **waitpid**, which enables you to wait for a specific process ID and condition.

Valid flags are defined in the **POSIX** module, and they are summarized here in Table 10-2.

Of course, there are times when you specifically want to wait for your children to exit cleanly.

Communicating with Children

It's possible to do one-way communication between a parent and its children using the |- and -| methods to the **open** command. However, this is a one-way transfer, and the

Flag	Description
WIFEXITED	Wait for processes that have exited.
WIFSIGNALED	Wait for processes that received a signal.
WNOHANG	Non-blocking wait.
WSTOPSIG	Wait for processes that received STOP signal.
WTERMSIG	Wait for processes that received TERM signal.
WUNTRACED	Wait for processes stopped by signals.

Table 10-2. *Flags for waitpid*

fork is implied by the **open** command, which reduces your flexibility somewhat. A better solution is to use the **pipe** function to create a pair of filehandles.

```
pipe READHANDLE, WRITEHANDLE
```

Information written to **WRITEHANDLE** is immediately available on **READHANDLE** on a simple first in, first out (FIFO) basis. Since a **fork**'d process inherits open filehandles from the parent, you can use a pair of filehandles for communicating between the child and parent and reading from and writing to the corresponding filehandle. The example below creates a new subprocess which accepts calculations that are then evaluated by **eval** to produce a result.

```
use IO::Handle;
pipe(PARENTREAD, PARENTWRITE);
pipe(CHILDREAD, CHILDWRITE);

PARENTWRITE->autoflush(1);
CHILDWRITE->autoflush(1);

if ($child = fork)      # Parent code
{
    close CHILDTREAD;  # We don't need these in the parent
    close PARENTWRITE;
    print CHILDWRITE "34+56;\n";
    chomp($result = <PARENTREAD>);
    print "Got a value of $result from child\n";
    close PARENTREAD;
    close CHILDWRITE;
    waitpid($child,0);
}
else
{
    close PARENTREAD;  # We don't need these in the child
    close CHILDWRITE;
    chomp($calculation = <CHILDREAD>);
    print "Got $calculation\n";
    $result = eval "$calculation";
    print PARENTWRITE "$result\n";
    close CHILDREAD;
    close PARENTWRITE;
    exit;
}
```

You can see that the calculation is sent to **CHILDWRITE**, which is then read by the child from **CHILDREAD**. The result is then calculated and sent back to the parent via **PARENTWRITE** where the parent reads the result from **PARENTREAD**. Note that you must use newlines as terminators when communicating between the parent and the child to identify the end of the communication. You could have used any string (see Chapter 9), but newlines are the natural choice, since it's what you use elsewhere.

Another alternative is to use sockets, and you saw many examples of this in Chapter 9. There is, however, one trick particularly relevant to communication between parents and children. This is the **socketpair** function, which is only supported on a small number of platforms. It works in a similar way to **pipe**, except that you can use just two filehandles to communicate between the two processes. Here's the above example, this time using **socketpair**:

```
use IO::Handle;
use Socket;
socketpair(CHILD, PARENT, AF_UNIX, SOCK_STREAM, PF_UNSPEC)
    or die "socketpair failed: $!";

PARENT->autoflush(1);
CHILD->autoflush(1);

if ($child = fork)      # Parent code
{
    close PARENT;
    print CHILD "34+56;\n";
    chomp($result = <CHILD>);
    print "Got a value of $result from child\n";
    waitpid($child,0);
    close CHILD;
}
else
{
    close CHILD;
    chomp($calculation = <PARENT>);
    $result = eval "$calculation";
    print PARENT "$result\n";
    close PARENT;
    exit;
}
```

Note that this works slightly differently, although the basic theory is the same. The **socketpair** function creates a pair of network sockets where information sent to **CHILD** is readable on **PARENT**, and vice versa. So you write information to the **CHILD** filehandle in the parent, but read it from **PARENT** in the child. This is the same as the **PARENTWRITE** and **PARENTREAD** filehandles in the **pipe** example above, except that you have only one filehandle in each to deal with.

Note the importance of the **close** statements in both this and the previous example. The filehandles will remain open if you do not explicitly close them correctly in the child and parent. You must make sure all filehandles in both the parent and child are closed correctly. This is less important in the **pipe** version since Perl will close them for you, but in the **socketpair** version you run the risk of either child or parent assuming that the connection is still open.

Other Function Calls

Although not strictly a method of IPC, Perl does provide a mechanism for calling functions that are part of the system library, but not available as a directly supported function. In order for this to work, you'll need to create the syscall.ph Perl header file using the **h2ph** script:

```
h2ph /usr/include/sys/syscall.h
```

This will install the Perl header file into the Perl library structure so it's available via a normal **require** statement.

```
require syscall.ph;
syscall(&SYS_chown,"myfile",0,0);
```

You can supply up to 14 arguments to be passed to the function, and they are interpreted according to their types. If the scalar is numeric, it is passed to the system function as an **int**; otherwise a pointer to a string is passed. If the system call populates a variable, then you may supply a suitable variable, but make sure it's large enough to contain the returned value.

The **syscall** function always returns the value returned by the function you have called. If the call fails, the return value is –1, and the **$!** variable is populated accordingly.

A better solution if you regularly make use of a system function not supported within Perl is to create an XSUB definition for it. See Chapter 17 for more information.

System V IPC

The System V flavor of Unix introduced a number of different methods for interprocess communication. It centers around three basic premises: messages, semaphores, and shared memory. The messaging system operates a simple message queue for the exchange of information. Semaphores provide shared counters across processes and are usually used to indicate the availability of shared resources. Shared memory allows for segments of memory to be shared among processes.

From my point of view, as well as a practical one, sockets provide a much better system for communicating and transferring information between processes, both locally and remotely. For a start, they are supported on far more platforms than the System V IPC. Furthermore, they are far more practical in most instances than the methods shown here, which restrict you, necessarily, to a few minor facilities. System V IPC is not supported on many Unix flavors and certainly not under MacOS or Win32 systems. If you want to use this system, I suggest you refer to the man pages for more information on these functions. The information provided here simply outlines the Perl interface to the underlying system.

Note that in all cases below you will need to incorporate the **IPC::SysV** module. This is a replacement for the ipc.ph, msg.ph, shm.ph, and the sem.ph Perl header files.

Messages

The messages system allows for the simple exchange of messages, stored in fixed structures between processes. Messages are placed into a message queue, and each queue is given its own unique queue ID. When placing a message into the queue, first you create a unique message queue ID with the **msgget** function. You can then push a message onto the desired queue ID. Other processes can then extract messages from the specified queue, and the system works on a FIFO basis. To get the message of the desired queue, you use the **msgrcv** function. You can control the contents of the queue with the **msgctl** function.

The structures used in the queueing system can be determined from your header files. The sample below was taken from the header files for a Solaris system.

```
struct msqid_ds {
        struct ipc_perm msg_perm;        /* operation permissions */
        struct msg      *msg_first;      /* ptr to first message on queue */
        struct msg      *msg_last;       /* ptr to last message on queue */
        ulong           msg_cbytes;      /* current # bytes on queue */
        ulong           msg_qnum;        /* # of messages on queue */
        ulong           msg_qbytes;      /* max # of bytes on queue */
        pid_t           msg_lspid;       /* pid of last msgsnd */
        pid_t           msg_lrpid;       /* pid of last msgrcv */
```

```
        time_t          msg_stime;      /* last msgsnd time */
        long            msg_pad1;       /* reserved for time_t expansion */
        time_t          msg_rtime;      /* last msgrcv time */
        long            msg_pad2;       /* time_t expansion */
        time_t          msg_ctime;      /* last change time */
        long            msg_pad3;       /* time expansion */
        kcondvar_t      msg_cv;
        kcondvar_t      msg_qnum_cv;
        long            msg_pad4[3];    /* reserve area */
};
```

The control function is **msgctl**:

```
msgctl ID, CMD, ARG
```

This calls the system function **msgctl()** function; **ID** should be the ID of the message queue you want to control. The **CMD** should be a predefined constant. Valid values are **IPC_STAT**, which places individual queue information into the scalars or array supplied as **ARG**. You'll need to use **unpack** in combination with the above structure detail to read the queue information. The **IPC_SET** allows you to define values for the queue using the structure contained in **ARG**. The **IPC_RMID** constant indicates that you want to remove the queue specified in **ID**.

```
msgget KEY, FLAGS
```

Returns the message queue ID matching the numerical **KEY** using the supplied **FLAGS**.

```
msgrcv ID, VAR, SIZE, TYPE, FLAGS
```

Places the next message from queue **ID**, into **VAR**, up to a maximum size of **SIZE**.

```
msgsnd ID, MSG, FLAGS
```

Places the message **MSG** onto the queue **ID**.

Semaphores

Semaphores provide a simple method of indication between processes. Each semaphore has its own ID and its numerical value. They are typically used to indicate the current status of a particular resource. Within your program you attribute a particular resource with a unique semaphore ID. You can then increase the value of the semaphore while it is in use and decrease it when you have finished using it.

```
semctl ID, SEMNUM, CMD, ARG
```

Controls a specific semaphore **ID**.

```
semget KEY, NSEMS, FLAGS
```

Gets **NSEMS** matching **KEY** from the semaphore table.

```
semop KEY, OPSTRING
```

Performs the option on the semaphore identified by **KEY** using the information in **OPSTRING**. The **OPSTRING** should be a packed value composed of three short integers and consisting of the semaphore number, semaphore operation, and semaphore flags.

On a Win32 system you may have more success with the **Win32::Semaphore** module. See Chapter 22 for more information.

Shared Memory

Perl provides an interface to the shared memory system supported under System V compatible systems. Shared memory can be used to share simple, small amounts of information between processes. Access to the shared memory areas follows the basic interface for messages.

```
shmctl ID, CMD, ARG
```

Controls the shared memory segment **ID**, using the command **CMD**. Valid constants are shown in Table 10-3.

```
shmget KEY, SIZE, FLAGS
```

Returns the shared memory segment ID for the segment identified by **KEY**. If **SIZE** and **FLAGS** are specified, then it creates a new segment of the specified **SIZE**.

```
shmread ID, VAR, POS, SIZE
```

Command	Description
IPC_STAT	Places the current value of each member of the data structure associated with **ID** into the scalar **ARG**.
IPC_SET	Sets the value of the following members of the data structure associated with **ID** to the corresponding values found in the packed scalar **ARG**.
IPC_RMID	Removes the shared memory identifier specified by **ID** from the system and destroys the shared memory segment and data structure associated with it.
SHM_LOCK	Locks the shared memory segment specified by **ID** in memory.
SHM_UNLOCK	Unlocks the shared memory segment specified by **ID**.

Table 10-3. *Control Commands for the **shmctl** Function*

Reads the shared memory segment **ID**, starting at byte **POS** within that segment, up to a maximum of **SIZE** bytes, placing the data read into **VAR**.

```
shmwrite ID, STRING, POS, SIZE
```

Writes the data **STRING** into the shared memory segment **ID**, starting at **POS** for **SIZE** bytes.

The Complete Reference

Chapter 11

Advanced Execution Methods

The term "advanced" is perhaps a little over the top, but in this chapter we'll look at alternative methods for executing Perl subroutines and scripts beyond the normal direct interpretation of a file.

The main consideration is the options that are available on the command line. You already know from previous chapters that you can specify options on the command line to Perl that change, or modify, the behavior of the Perl interpreter. The **–w** option, for example, turns on "warnings"—a list of possible problems that may be in your script. There are other tricks though: you can use Perl on the command line as an advanced editor, and you can even use it for copying files between directories.

You also know you can execute Perl statements within a separate Perl interpreter via the **eval** function. This trick has been used in many of the previous chapters where an **eval** block was used to act as an exception handler for statements that could cause problems if executed within the main part of the script.

Multithreading is a relatively recent invention in computer science and currently an experimental feature of the Perl interpreter. Although not available on all platforms, threads allow you to execute multiple subroutines simultaneously. The result is a multitasking script that can take advantage of the fact it can service the requests of many different users at the same time.

Finally, we consider the security implications of using Perl and how to get around them using the standard Perl distribution. Perl has always supported a "tainting" mechanism, which highlights variables and information Perl considers possibly unsafe. Or, for a more secure environment, you can use the Safe module to create a new, unique compartment where you can restrict the list of available opcodes (the smallest executable part of a Perl script). This can reduce the resources and methods available to a script, preventing it from using functions or even operators that you do not want it to run.

Perl on the Command Line

During the normal execution process, Perl looks for a script in one of the following places, in this order:

1. On the command line (via the **–e** option).
2. Contained in the file specified by the first non-option argument to the Perl interpreter.
3. Piped in to the interpreter via the standard input. This works either if there are no arguments or if there is a command line argument.

Perl supports a number of command line options. These can either be specified on the actual command line if you are manually executing Perl, or they can be specified within the **#!** line at the start of the script. The **#!** line is always processed by Perl, irrespective of how the script is invoked. If you are using this method, be aware that some Unix systems place a limit on the size of the line—usually 32 characters. You will therefore need to make sure you place the most significant of the command line options early in the arguments. Although there are no hard-and-fast rules, the **–T** (taint checking) and **–I** arguments should be placed as early as possible in the command line options irrespective of where they are specified.

Whether they are specified on the command line or within the **#!** line, command line options can either be selected individually, as in

```
$ perl -p -i.bak -e "s/foo/bar/g"
```

or they can be combined:

```
$ perl -pi.bak -e "s/foo/bar/g"
```

-a

Turns on autosplit mode (implies the **split** function); fields are split into the **@F** array. The use of the **–a** option is equivalent to

```
while (<>)
{
    @F = split(' ');
}
```

This is generally used with the **–F**, **–n** or **–p** option to automatically split and/or summarize a group of input files.

-c

Checks the syntax of the script without executing it. Only **BEGIN** and **END** blocks and **use** statements are actually executed by this process, since they are considered an integral part of the compilation process.

-d[:module]

Without the optional **module**, this invokes the Perl debugger after your script has been compiled and places the program counter within the debugger at the start of your script. If **module** is specified, the script is compiled, and control of the execution is passed to the specified module. For example, **-d:Dprof** invokes the Perl profiling system.

-Dflags

Specifies the debugging options defined by **flags**, as seen in Table 11-1. Note that options can be selected either by their letter combination or by specifying the decimal value of the combined options. For example, to switch on taint checks and memory allocation, you would use **–Dmu** or **–D2176**.

You will need to have compiled Perl with the **–DDEBUGGING** compiler directive for these debugging flags to work. See Chapter 18 for more details on debugging Perl scripts.

Number	Letter	Description
1	p	Tokenizing and parsing.
2	s	Stack snapshots.
4	l	Context (loop) stack processing.
8	t	Trace execution.
16	o	Method and overloading resolution.
32	c	String/numeric conversions.
64	P	Print preprocessor command for **-P**.
128	m	Memory allocation.
256	f	Format processing.
512	r	Regular expression parsing and execution.
1024	x	Syntax tree dump.
2048	u	Tainting checks.
4096	L	Memory leaks (you need to have used the **–DLEAKTEST** directive when compiling Perl).
8192	H	Hash dump.
16384	X	Scratchpad allocation.
32768	D	Cleaning up.
65536	S	Thread synchronization.

Table 11-1. *Debugging Flags*

-e commandline

The **commandline** will be interpreted as a single-line Perl script. For example,

```
$ perl -e 'print 4+5,"\n";'
```

will print 9.

-F regex

Specifies the pattern to use for splitting when the **–a** command line option is in use. By default the value used is a single space. The **regex** can be specified including any of the normal delimiters allowed by **split**, that is **''**, **""**, and **//**.

-h

Prints the Perl usage summary but does not execute the Perl interpreter.

-iext

Edits the file "in place"—that is, edits are conducted and written straight back to the file. The optional **ext** defines the extension to append to the old version of the file. Actually, what happens is that the file is moved to the "backup" version, and then the file and edits are written back into the original. If **ext** is not specified, a temporary file is used. Note that you must append the extension including a period if desired, Perl does not add any characters to the backup file except those specified.

This is generally used with the **–p** and **–e** options to edit a series of files in a loop. For example, the command line

```
$ perl -pi.bak -e "s/foo/bar/g" *
```

replaces every occurrence of "foo" with "bar" in all the files in the current directory.

-Idir

Prepends the directory **dir** to the list used to search for modules (**@INC**) and the directories used to search for include files included via the C preprocessor (invoked with **–P**). See also the **use lib** pragma in Chapter 16 and the **PERLLIB** and **PERL5LIB** environment variables later in the chapter.

-l[char]

Sets the character **char** that will automatically be appended to all printed output. The specification should be via the octal equivalent. By default no characters are automatically added to printed lines. If **char** is not specified, this makes the value of the output record separator (**$**) equal the value of the input record separator (**$/**).

-mmodule and -Mmodule

Includes the module specified by **module** before executing your script and allows you to specify additional options to the **use** statement generated. For example, the command line

```
$ perl -MPOSIX=:fcntl_h,:float_h
```

is equivalent to:

```
use POSIX qw/:fcntl_h :float_h/;
```

The **–M** form also allows you to use quotes to specify the options. For example, the above line could be written as:

```
$ perl -M'POSIX qw/:fcntl_h :float_h/'
```

In both cases, a single hyphen as the first character after **-M** or **-m** indicates that **no** should be used in place of **use**.

-n

Causes Perl to assume the following code around your script for each file specified on the command line:

```
while(<>)
{
}
```

Note that the contents of the files are not printed or otherwise output during execution, unless specified within the script itself. Any files in the list of those to be opened that cannot be opened are reported as errors, and execution continues to the next file in the list.

-p

Causes Perl to assume the following code around your script for each file specified on the command line:

```
while(<>)
{
}
continue
{
    print or die "-p destination: $!\n";
}
```

As you can see, an error during printing/updating is considered fatal. The **–p** option overrides the **–n** option.

Any files in the list of those to be opened that cannot be opened are reported as errors, and execution continues to the next file in the list.

-P

Invokes the C preprocessor on the script before it is parsed by the Perl interpreter. Care should be taken when using comments in the original C source, since lines starting with a # character and a keyword such as **if** or **define** will be interpreted as a preprocessor directive.

-s

Enables basic command line switching. Once this option has been set, any command line options specified after the script name are interpreted as the names of variables, with their value being set to true within the script. For example,

```
$ perl -s t.pl -true
```

will create a variable **$true** within the current invocation of t.pl.

A more advanced system is to use the Getopt::Long or Getopt::Std modules.

-S

Uses the **$PATH** environment variable to find the script. It will also add extensions to the script being searched for if a lookup on the original name fails.

-T

Switches on "taint" checking. Variables and information that originates or derives from external sources are considered to be "unsafe" and will cause your script to fail when used in functions such as **system**. This is most often used when a script is executed on behalf of another process, such as a web server. You should specify this option at the start of the command line options to ensure that taint checking is switched on as early as possible. See the section "Security" later in this chapter for more information.

-u

Causes Perl to dump the program core of the interpreter and script after compilation (and before execution). In theory this can be used with an **undump** program to produce a stand-alone executable. The Perl-to-C compiler has superseded this option. See Chapter 19 for more information on these and other methods for generating stand-alone Perl binaries.

-U

Allows the Perl script to do unsafe operations. These currently include only the unlinking of directories when you are superuser, or when running setuid programs. This option will also turn fatal taint checks into warnings, providing the **-w** option is also specified.

-v

Prints the version and patch level of the Perl interpreter, but does not execute the interpreter.

-V[:var]

Prints the version and configuration information for the Perl interpreter. If the optional **var** is supplied, it prints out only the configuration information for the specified element as discovered via the Config module. Here is the default output from the function:

```
perl -V
Summary of my perl5 (5.0 patchlevel 5 subversion 53) configuration:
  Platform:
    osname=solaris, osvers=2.4, archname=sun4-solaris
    uname='sunos twinspark 5.4 generic_101945-59 sun4c sparc '
    hint=previous, useposix=true, d_sigaction=define
    usethreads=undef useperlio=undef d_sfio=undef
  Compiler:
    cc='gcc -B/usr/ccs/bin/', optimize='-O', gccversion=2.8.1
    cppflags='-I/usr/local/include'
    ccflags ='-I/usr/local/include -DDEBUGGING'
    stdchar='unsigned char', d_stdstdio=define, usevfork=false
    intsize=4, longsize=4, ptrsize=4, doublesize=8
    d_longlong=define, longlongsize=8, d_longdbl=define, longdblsize=16
    alignbytes=8, usemymalloc=y, prototype=define
  Linker and Libraries:
    ld='gcc -B/usr/ccs/bin/', ldflags =' -L/usr/local/lib'
    libpth=/usr/local/lib /lib /usr/lib /usr/ccs/lib
    libs=-lsocket -lnsl -lgdbm -ldb -ldl -lm -lc -lcrypt
    libc=/lib/libc.so, so=so, useshrplib=false, libperl=libperl.a
  Dynamic Linking:
    dlsrc=dl_dlopen.xs, dlext=so, d_dlsymun=undef, ccdlflags=' '
    cccdlflags='-fPIC', lddlflags='-G -L/usr/local/lib'


Characteristics of this binary (from libperl):
  Compile-time options: DEBUGGING
  Built under solaris
  Compiled at Mar 18 1999 08:15:07
  @INC:
    /usr/local/lib/perl5/5.00553/sun4-solaris
    /usr/local/lib/perl5/5.00553
    /usr/local/lib/perl5/site_perl/5.00553/sun4-solaris
    /usr/local/lib/perl5/site_perl/5.00553
    .
```

-w

Prints out warnings about possible typographical and interpretation errors in the script.

See Chapter 18 for more details on debugging Perl scripts, and Chapter 16 and Appendix D for more information on the warning messages and internals of the Perl compiler and interpreter that generate them.

-x[dir]

Extracts the script from an email message or other piped data stream. Perl will ignore any information up to a line that starts with **#!** and contains the word **perl**. Any directory name will be used as the directory in which to run the script, and the command line switches contained in the line will be applied as usual. The script must be terminated either by an EOF or an **__END__** marker.

This option can be used to execute code stored in email messages without first requiring you to extract the script element.

-0[val]

Specifies the initial value for the input record separator **$/**.

Special Handling

When running Perl via the command line there are some special treatments of some of the functions and operators we have already seen. In general these only affect Perl when you have called it with the **–p** and/or **–i** options. For example:

```
$ perl -pi.bak -e "print" *
```

As we already know, it's puts a notional loop around the single **print** statement to iterate through the files on the command line. In fact, the loop is slightly more complex, and more correctly actually looks like this:

```
while($ARGV = shift)
{
    open(ARGV, $ARGV) or warn "Can't open $ARGV: $!\n";
    while(<ARGV>)
    {
    }
    continue
    {
        print or die "-p destination: $!\n";
    }
}
```

The special filehandle **ARGV** is attached to the current file within the list of files supplied on the command line. The effect of the **eof** function is now changed slightly. The statement:

```
eof();
```

Only returns the end of file of the last file in the list of files supplied on the command line. You have to use **eof(ARGV)** or **eof** (without parentheses) to detect the end of file for each file supplied on the command line.

Perl Environment Variables

The effects of certain elements of Perl and Perl functions can be modified by environment variables. Many of these variables are set automatically by your shell. In the case of MacPerl these values can be configured within the MacPerl environment.

HOME

The home directory for the script. Used by **chdir** if no argument is specified.

LOGDIR

Used by **chdir** if no argument is specified and the **HOME** environment variable is not set.

PATH

This is the list of directories searched when invoking a command via **system**, **exec**, backticks, or other external application callers. This is also the directory list searched with the **–S** command line option.

PERLLIB

The colon-separated list of directories used to look for the modules and libraries required for the Perl script. Note that this list overrides the values defined within the interpreter. This variable is ignored if **PERL5LIB** has been set.

PERL5LIB

The colon-separated list of directories used to look for the modules and libraries required for the Perl script. Note that this list overrides the values defined within the interpreter.

The values here can be added to or overridden entirely using the **use lib** pragma (see Chapter 16) and the **–I** command line option (see above). Note that only the **use lib** pragma is supported when taint checking is in effect.

PERL5OPT

Allows you to predefine any of the **DIMUdmw** command line switches for every invocation of the Perl interpreter. The variable is ignored when taint checking is in effect.

PERL5DB

The command used to load the debugger code when the **–d** option is specified on the command line. The default value is

```
BEGIN {require 'perl5db.pl' }
```

You can use this variable to permanently enable profiling or use an alternative debugger (including those with windowed interfaces).

PERL5SHELL

This is specific to the Win32 port of Perl (see Chapter 22). It specifies the alternative shell that Perl should use internally for executing external commands via **system** or backticks. The default under Windows NT is to use the standard **cmd.exe** with the **/x/c** switches. Under Windows 95 the **command.com /c** command is used.

PERL_DEBUG_MSTATS

This option causes the memory statistics for the script to be dumped after execution. It only works if Perl has been compiled with Perl's own version of the **malloc()** function. You can use

```
$ perl -V:d_mymalloc
```

to determine whether this is the case. A value of **define** indicates that Perl's **malloc()** is being used.

PERL_DESTRUCT_LEVEL

Controls the destruction of global objects and other references, but only if the Perl interpreter has been compiled with the **–DDEBUGGING** compiler directive.

Perl in Perl (eval)

A favorite function of many Perl programmers is **eval**. This function provides a great number of facilities, the most useful of which is the ability to execute Perl source code at run time, rather than using the code supplied as part of a script. Because it executes the code effectively in a separate instance of the interpreter, it also provides a useful method for checking the existence of modules, functions, and other elements that would normally cause a break in execution during the compilation stage of the main script.

The basic format for the former method of execution with **eval** is

```
eval EXPR
```

The expression is evaluated as a separate Perl program, but within the confines of the enclosing Perl script. This enables the variables and functions that are defined within the parent to be available to the **eval** block as well.

The process of execution is quite simple: the code is parsed and compiled just like an ordinary script. The **EXPR** will be parsed and interpreted each time the **eval** function is called, so the value of **EXPR** can change. This also means there is a small performance degradation as the code is compiled and parsed each time. This has the advantage that errors and other actions can be trapped at run time rather than compile time.

The other form is to use a **BLOCK**. This differs only from an **EXPR** invocation in that the **BLOCK** is parsed at the same time as the rest of the script, rather than at run time. This is generally used to trap nonfatal exceptions, or to trap exceptions at compile time. It is also faster than the first method, although it does not provide all the same abilities.

Any error returned by the parsing process, or from a **die** function, is placed directly into the **$@** variable, and execution of the expression ends. Note though that any error messages normally printed to **STDERR** continue to be printed. Also note that although **die** errors are passed to **$@**, the statements from **warn** are printed normally. If there are no errors, then the value of **$@** is guaranteed to be null and therefore false when checked with **if** or other conditionals.

You can, however, use the **$SIG{__WARN__}** signal handler to interrupt the normal **warn** execution and update the **$@** variable if necessary. See Chapter 10 for more information.

You can also return any value from the **eval** block, either by a **return** or through the last evaluated statement in the **EXPR** or **BLOCK**, as with any normal subroutine. The **wantarray** function also functions normally and indicates the required return values from the function.

A good example is the use of **eval** to test whether a particular module or function is available. For example, you might check for the existence of the **Thread** module (our next major topic) with code like this:

```
print "Checking for Threads\n";

eval "use Thread;";

warn "Thread module not found:\n   $@" if ($@);

print "Non-thread execution...\n";
```

Note that you have to use the **EXPR** rather than **BLOCK** format here. If you used a **BLOCK**, it would be parsed and an error produced during the compile time, and the final **print** statement would actually never be reached. This is obviously not the desired result. Note as well that if the module specified is found, it is imported as usual and is then available to the enclosing script.

If you have installed the **__DIE__** signal handler, you need to take care if you use the **die** function within an **eval** block. If you do not want the signal handler to be called when the **die** function is used, you can localize the **$SIG{__DIE__}** function, which effectively disables the main signal handler for **die** (if installed) for the duration of the **eval** statement. This is as easy as placing the localize statement within the **eval** block.

This becomes even more useful if you actually make use of the localized signal handler within the confines of the **eval** sequence. Since the signal handler is cyclical, once the localized signal handler has completed, you can call **die** again to exit the **eval** block, thereby producing a customized error message. The example below prepends some information to the error message produced:

```
{
    local $SIG{'__DIE__'} =
          sub { die "Fatal Error: $_[0]"; };
    eval { die "Couldn't open...." };
    print $@ if ($@);
}
```

Threads

A recent addition to the abilities of Perl, and still considered to be in the developmental stages, is a thread interface to any underlying threading ability in the operating system. Support is currently limited to a few choice operating systems, although further support is promised in the future.

The best way to think of a thread is as a separate, small process that is part of the larger component of the main script. A normal script is only capable of following a predefined sequence of events. The main idea behind threads is that to effectively multitask between a number of different jobs you must be able to do more than one thing at the same time, and threads allow you to do this.

You can use polling systems to progress through a series of choices, but this is still following a specific path. If there are 30 items in your list of things to poll, a single process may have to wait for 29 polls before it can continue operation.

With threads, you can create new processes based on predefined subroutines. They execute simultaneously with the parent script and can therefore be used for a variety of tasks that would either require complex polling systems or simply wouldn't be possible. For example, you could use threads to handle multiple requests within a Perl-based network server. Alternatively, you could use a multithreaded system to act as a mail server where multiple threads watch and monitor a number of different queue folders.

Of course, multithreading systems introduce their own range of problems. It is likely, for example, that you want to share information, either between threads or between children and the parent process. But allowing multiple threads to update a single variable without some type of locking is liable to introduce all sorts of corruption and errors. You also need some way of controlling the execution of a thread and deciding how and when it should execute. All of these problems are handled by the **Thread** module.

The thread system is object based, and rather than centering around a complex "assumption," such as the **fork** function, you create a new **Thread** object, which actually runs a predefined or anonymous Perl function. Other functions then support the control of individual threads and control the individual variables that may be used by the threads to communicate.

Creating a New Thread

To create a new thread, import the **Thread** module and then create a new **Thread** object. For example, to create a new **thread** that uses the subroutine **process_queue**:

```
use Thread;
$thread = new Thread \&process_queue,"/usr/local/queue";
```

You can supply arguments to be sent to the function as additional arguments to the new object creation. The **$thread** variable in the above example contains a reference to the newly created thread and will provide a link from the main program to the thread.

The thread can obtain a reference to itself with the **self** method:

```
$me = Thread->self;
```

Each thread is given its own unique thread ID. The main program has a thread ID of 0, and subsequent threads are given a sequential thread number up to a current maximum of 2^{32}-1. You can discover the thread ID using the **tid** method:

```
$tid = $thread->tid;
```

Or for a thread to find its own ID:

```
$mytid = Thread->self->tid;
```

You can also get a list of all the running and finished threads (providing the thread has not been **join**ed—see the next section) by using the **list** method:

```
@threads = Thread->list;
```

You'll need to process the information yourself, but the list of object references should be enough.

If all you want is a unique identifier for a thread (perhaps for tracking or logging purposes), the best solution is to use the **Thread::Specific** module, which creates a thread-specific key. To use, call the **key_create** function within a thread:

```
use Thread::Specific;
my $k = key_create Thread::Specific:
```

If you want to create a thread to an anonymous subroutine, you can use the special **async** function, which accepts a **BLOCK** and executes it as a separate thread, for example:

```
async
{
...
};
```

Note that the block is treated as an anonymous subroutine and must be terminated by a closing semicolon. It returns a thread object, just like the **new** function/constructor.

Controlling a Thread

There are three basic methods for controlling a thread once created and one function for controlling the processor cycles available to each thread. The **detach** method explicitly detaches a thread so that it runs independently.

The **join** method waits for a thread to end, returning any values the thread returned during the process of execution:

```
$result = $thread->join;
```

This can be used either to force the thread to block until the specified thread has finished, or to get a return value from the thread at the end of execution. If the specified thread exited as a result of a **die** function, then the error returned during the **die**, as would be trapped by **$@**, is returned instead. Since the **join** effectively combines the two threads, care will need to be taken if the specified thread **die**s after the **join** method has been called. If you want to prevent the calling thread from also **die**ing, then you should enclose the **join** method call in the **eval** statement.

The **eval** method on a thread automatically wraps an **eval** function around the **join** method. Return values from the thread are placed into **$@** as usual.

The **yield** function gives up processor cycles for the current function and redistributes them to other threads. This provides a crude method for prioritizing individual threads and assigning them processor time.

Controlling Variables

Sharing variables across threads is as dangerous and prone to error as sharing a database file across many processes (see Chapter 8). The basis for controlling access to the variables is much the same. You set a "lock" on the variable to indicate its status.

Also, like the file locks that are available, the variable locks are advisory. Although you can lock a variable, there is nothing to prevent a thread from accessing or updating it. It is entirely up to the programmer to check the lock status and decide whether the variable should or should not be used. The main function for locking a variable is the **lock** function:

```
lock($var);
```

The lock set on the variable lasts as long as the scope of the current block. If a lock is already set on the variable by another thread, then the **lock** function will block execution of the current thread until the other has finished using it. Note that the lock is on the entity, not the contents, so a call such as

```
lock(@var);
```

only sets the lock on the **@var** variable, not the individual elements of the array. Therefore, another call to **lock($var[0])** will not block. Also, references are only followed to one level such that a reference to lock **\$var** will work, but **\\$var** will not work.

In addition, since subroutines are just other objects, you can also lock them using the **lock** function. Again, this blocks execution only if another thread tries to lock the subroutine.

Once a variable is locked, you can control the unlocking process with three separate functions: **cond_wait**, **cond_signal**, and **cond_broadcast**. The **cond_wait** function is the main one. It unlocks the variable and blocks until another thread does a **cond_signal** or **cond_broadcast** call for the variable. The function therefore enables you to wait until another process indicates (either through the **cond_signal** or **cond_broadcast** function) that the thread has finished using the variable. Once the **cond_wait** unblocks, the variable is locked again.

The **cond_wait** function takes one argument—a locked variable—and unblocks a random thread that is waiting for the variable via **cond_wait**. It is not possible to specify which thread is unblocked. You can unblock all waiting threads using the **cond_broadcast** function, which also takes a single (locked) variable as an argument.

This is a very complicated description of what is basically a simple process of indicators and signals that allow you to control access to a variable. Consider that you have two threads, A and B, and they both want to update a variable **$var**. Thread A locks the variable with **lock** and then starts its update. Meanwhile, thread B decides that it needs to update the variable, so it calls **cond_wait($var)**, effectively halting the B thread until A has finished.

Once A has completed the update, it calls **cond_signal($var)**, indicating to thread B that it has finished with the variable. The **cond_wait** function called from thread B then locks the variables for its own use and continues execution. This process of waiting and signaling the status of locked variables allows you to control access to them and prevent the corruption that could occur if two threads were to update the variable at the same time.

Fortunately, in the example, there are only two threads, and so the locking method is relatively straightforward. In a multithreaded process, controlling access to a single variable may be more difficult. You may want to try using either the queuing or semaphore methods for divining information about the variables that you want to share among processes.

Queues

Although you can use ordinary variables for exchanging information between running threads, it often requires careful use of the **lock** function to ensure you are using the right value at the right time. If all you want to do is exchange simple information between threads, a better method is to use a simple stack. However, you can't use a simple scalar array, since that will exhibit the same (if not more complex) problems that you already know about regarding the **lock** and other functions.

Instead, the Perl thread system supports a message queue object. This is basically a standard array, except that it is thread compatible and handles additions and removals from the list safely without the normal risk of corruption to the variables. To create a new queue:

```
use Thread::Queue;
my $queue = new Thread::Queue;
```

The list operates strictly on a LILO (last in, last out) format, so new entries are added to the end of the list, and entries are removed and returned from the start of list. The **enqueue** method adds a list of values to the end of the queue:

```
$thread->enqueue('Martin', 'Brown');
```

The **dequeue** function returns and removes a single scalar from the beginning of the queue:

```
$value = $thread->dequeue;
```

If the queue is empty, the thread blocks until there is an entry in the queue. To immediately return from a **dequeue** operation, you use the **dequeue_nb**, which does not block; it simply returns **undef** if the list is empty.

Finally, you can use the **pending** method to find out how many items are left on the queue. Note that this information is correct at the time the method was called, but this does not guarantee this is the actual value if multiple threads are accessing and using the queue simultaneously. To get around this, you can use the **lock** function seen earlier to lock the object so that its state is consistent between the **pending** method and when you use it.

Semaphores

A semaphore is defined in the dictionary as a system of signaling. In the realm of threads a semaphore can be used to indicate a particular occurrence to a thread. The information is provided in the form of a number, and this number can be increased or decreased accordingly. The method for employing the semaphore is to use the **Thread::Semaphore** module and create a new object:

```
$sema = new Thread::Semaphore;
```

The default value is one, or you can specify the initial value:

```
$sema = new Thread::Semaphore(256);
```

Two methods, **up** and **down**, then increase or decrease the value, either by the default value of one, or by the amount specified. For example, the code

```
$sema->up;
$sema->down(256);
```

will set the value of the **$sema** semaphore back to one.

How you use the semaphore value is entirely up to you. The usual method is to create a semaphore that relates to the available quantity of a specific resource.

Signals

Because signals could interrupt the normal execution process of the script, and even more so when working with threads, it can be a good idea to create a separate thread just for handling signals. This is practical not only for multithreaded applications, but also for applications that make use of pipes, non-blocking I/O, and even networking. Of course, by creating a new thread for signals, your script is now multithreaded, but it doesn't mean you have to create additional threads.

To create a new signal-handling thread, all you do is import the **Thread::Signal** module:

```
use Thread::Signal;
```

This automatically generates a new thread and causes all signals to the program to be handled within this thread. There is no difference in the way you set up signal handlers.

They can be assigned to existing functions or handled by anonymous subroutines, as usual. The difference is that the signal handlers execute within the realm of a new thread. This allows execution of the current process to continue when a signal is received.

There are some traps in this. Using **die** within a signal handler executed in the signal thread will cause the thread to exit, but won't necessarily cause the main thread to quit. This also means you will have problems when using **exit** within an extension, since this too will affect the signal handler thread and not the main program.

Security

The security of the script you are running may be an issue, whether running a secure service or when you are using Perl as the CGI interface on a web server. There are two basic threats. The first is that of introducing bogus or dangerous information from the outside world into the data structures within a Perl script. The second threat is from the execution of a specific feature of Perl that might otherwise make it unsafe. These two elements, although seemingly innocuous, can potentially cause all manner of problems.

Solving the first problem is a case of checking and marking the information so that it can be recognized as possibly being dangerous. Perl will do this automatically for you by "tainting" the data that has come from external sources such as the command line or environment. However, using "tainted" information in functions that statements that run an external could be dangerous. Imagine, for example, getting an email address from a user, entered on the command line. If you passed this, unchecked, to the **sendmail** program, it could potentially send back any information or even modify information in the system files through the use of pipes. The taint mode gets around this problem.

The second problem is more difficult to solve, but a method is also provided with the standard Perl distribution. Execution of certain functions and even some operators could be a potential problem. Using the **Safe** module (which also makes use of the **Opcode** module), you can enable and disable different functions and operators and then execute a Perl script within this restricted environment.

Using Taint Mode

Perl provides a facility called *taint checking*. This option forces Perl to examine the origin of the variables used within a script. Information gleaned from the outside world is tainted, or marked as possibly unsafe, depending on the context in which it's used. Further, variables derived from tainted variables are also tainted. Perl then examines where the variables are used, and in what context, to decide whether the code breaks any of the prebuilt rules.

Some of the checks are relatively simple, such as verifying that the directories within a given path are not writable by others. Some are more complex and rely on Perl's compiler and syntax checker to accept or reject the statement.

The rule is straightforward: you cannot use any data from the outside world that may directly or indirectly affect something outside of your program. In essence, this means you can use external variables internally for everything except specific system calls, subshell executions, or destinations for data files. The following code fragment shows the results of running some statements with taint checking switched on:

```
$cmd = shift;                # tainted - its origin is the command line
$run = "echo $cmd";          # Also tainted - derived from $cmd
$alsoran = 'echo Hello';     # Not tainted
system "echo $cmd";          # Insecure - external shell with $cmd
system "$alsoran";           # Insecure - until $PATH set
system "/bin/echo", $cmd;    # Secure - doesn't use shell to execute
```

If you try to execute this as a script, with taint checking switched on, you will receive errors similar to "Insecure dependency" or "Insecure $ENV{PATH}" for lines 4 and 5.

Also note that anything that implies the use of an external command or function also makes the data insecure. Therefore anything that accesses the environment (via **%ENV**), calls to file globbing routines (**glob** or **<*.c>**), and some **open** constructs also returns tainted information. Finally, any system functions, such as **umask**, **unlink**, **link** and others, when used with tainted variables, are also considered insecure. In each case, there are some exceptions.

With the environment, if you modify the environment from Perl before accessing it, then the information is not tainted (Perl "remembers" that you made the modification); so the code

```
$ENV{'PATH'} = '/bin:/usr/bin';
$path = $ENV{'PATH'};
```

does not taint **$path**, since its source was actually internal.

With the **open** command, reads from tainted file names are allowed, since reading is nondestructive. However, writes to files referred to by tainted variables are not allowed; thus the code

```
$file = shift;
open(DATA,">$file");
```

will generate an error, since the **$file** variable has come from an external source.

Using pipes is also an insecure option if the command or data you are using with a command has come from an external source, such that

```
$file = shift;
open(FOO,"gunzip -c $file|");
```

is considered unsafe, since you must call a shell in order to interpret the entire command line. You can get around this by using the alternative pipe notation,

```
$file = shift;
open(FOO,"-|") or exec 'gunzip', '-c', $file;
```

which is considered safe, because you do not use a shell to execute the command.

To switch on taint checking, you must specify the **–T** option on the command line. This works for Unix and Windows NT. Taint checking with MacPerl is not strictly available, and even if it were, it wouldn't make a huge difference since the MacOS is not capable of executing external programs. In any case, it is not prone to the same security breaches as a Unix or NT system.

Taint checking is also automatically enabled by Perl if you attempt to run a script that is running with different real and effective user and group IDs. If the setuid or setgid bit has been set on a Unix system, this automatically implies taint checking. Once switched on, taint checking is enabled for the rest of your script; you cannot switch it off until the script ends.

To detect whether a variable is tainted, you can use the function **is_tainted** from the **tainted.pl** script supplied in the standard library of the Perl distribution. The only way to untaint variables is to reference substring regular expression matches. For example, for an email address you might use the following code fragment to extract an untainted version of the address:

```
If ($addr =~ /^([-\@\w.]+)$/)
{
   $addr = $1;
}
else
{
   die "Bad email address";
}
```

Obviously, running an expression match on every tainted element defeats the object of taint checking in the first place. You can switch this untainting behavior off by using the **re** pragma,

```
use re 'taint';
```

which means that all regular expressions taint data if their source data is already tainted.

Because variables from CGI scripts are tainted (they come from either an external environment variable or the standard input), tainting Perl CGI scripts is a good idea.

The Safe and Opcode Modules

The **Safe** module makes use of Perl's ability to run code within a separate compartment. Normally this is done via the **eval** function. The difference with the **Safe** module is that the compartment can be configured to allow only certain internal Perl functions to execute. This allows you to disable or enable functions that you want to allow or prevent the use of in the script you want to execute.

The new compartment is completely restrictive. You cannot access subroutines or variables outside of the compartment, regardless of the methods you try to use. In fact, the only variables that are shared between the main script and the safe compartment are **$_**, **@_**, **%_**, and the _ special filehandle. You can place variables into the compartment for the main script if you need to.

The method for creating the new compartment is to create a new **Safe** object and then, optionally, create a new opcode mask that limits the list of available opcodes that form the basis of any Perl script (see Chapters 16 and 17):

```
$safe = new Safe;
```

You can create a new name space to use for the new compartment by specifying it as an argument:

```
$safe = new Safe("Compartment");
```

By default the value is **Safe::Root0**, and it is incremented for each new compartment created within the scope of the current script.

There are five main methods for controlling the compartment once it has been created:

```
$safe = new Safe;
$safe->permit(OP,...);
$safe->permit_only(OP,...);
$safe->deny(OP,...);
$safe->deny_only(OP,...);
$safe->share(NAME,...);
```

The **permit** and **deny** methods add opcodes to the lists of allowed and restricted opcodes for the new compartment, respectively. Thus, additional calls to these methods add or remove the specified opcodes from the list of those that can be used. The **permit_only** and **deny_only** methods explicitly define the entire list of allowed and restricted opcodes for the compartment.

The **share** method specifies the list of variables and subroutines from the enclosing script that can be shared with the compartment. The **NAME** should include the variable type (**$foo**, **@foo**, and so on), and all the main object types are allowed. All the shared items are assumed to be in the calling package. Alternatively, you can use the **share_from** method to specify the package from which you want to share the symbols:

```
$safe = new Safe;
$safe->Share_from('main',['calc_sin', '$PI']);
```

Once you have completed the mask and specified the opcodes that you want to enable (or disable), you run a Perl script either by supplying a text string or by using the **reval** method:

```
$safe = new Safe;
$safe->reval($script);
```

Or you can point execution to an external file with the **rdo** method:

```
$safe = new Safe;
$safe->rdo($file);
```

For the list of available opcodes on your machine, refer to the **Opcode** module for your platform. The available list of opcodes is specific both to your platform and the current version of Perl, so a list here would be useless without the cross-reference of the specific module for your platform.

Part IV

Enhancing the User Interface

Chapter 12

Making Perl More User Friendly

The title of this chapter is a bit of a misnomer, but the practicalities are clear. All the uses of Perl discussed so far have centered around the specifics of the Perl language. When using Perl in the wide world, however, there are some niceties that can make the use of Perl easier for both the programmer and the user. The most basic of these is to allow the user to supply information and instructions to a Perl script on the command line. Most users will be familiar with command line arguments to programs, under both Windows and Unix. Command line arguments can consist of either straight information (usually a file, or hostname) or a series of options, signified by a preceding hyphen. A number of methods, both manual and automatic, can help to extract the information from the command line, and we'll look at them in the beginning of this chapter.

If you are a programmer, you may have already encountered the problems associated with reporting information in a formatted format. The most obvious method is to use the **printf** function to arrange the output data into a normalized format, but it suffers from numerous problems. The most fundamental of these is that information may stretch beyond the width of an element specified in the **printf** format definition. This means using regular expressions and/or functions to extract a specific number of characters from the data.

This is all too complex and still doesn't get around the difficulties presented by producing a report, such as accounting for page length and printing headers (and footers) on a page. The solution to this with Perl is to use the Perl reporting mechanism (otherwise known as Formats). This allows you to define a fixed output format for printed information. The format allows you to specify the justification (left, right, or centered) and even the template that should be used when printing floating point numbers. Formats also automatically handle page sizes, line numbers, and headers, although you will need to work out a method for printing footers for yourself.

Although seen as a programmer's weakness, documentation is one of the most important elements of releasing your script or module to the world at large. It should be up there right underneath the entry for testing your script and module before it is released.

The final section in the chapter deals with documenting your Perl scripts and modules using the Perl Plain Old Documentation (POD) format. POD documents are straightforward text-tag-based documents that can be converted (using modules and scripts) into a variety of host-friendly formats, including the Unix man page and HTML. There is a knack, however, to doing this properly, and hints and tips are given about the format and layout of POD documents that you should be aware of.

Processing Command Line Arguments

Command line arguments are available to any script via the **@ARGV** array. You can access this directly, either by referencing individual elements or by using the **shift** and

pop functions. The important thing to remember about the **@ARGV** array is that unlike many other languages (most notably C/C++), element zero is not the name of the script. This is contained in the **$0** variable. This means that the first argument is at index zero, and therefore you can print out the entire command line argument list by printing the array:

```
print join(' ',@ARGV),"\n";
```

You can also use **shift** to take off individual arguments in sequence:

```
$filein = shift;
$fileout = shift;
```

Note though that this technique only works when you use **shift** in the main script block; calling it within a subroutine takes values off the @_ array instead.

It can also sometimes be necessary to put arguments back onto the command line before it is processed, perhaps to insert default or required options. Because the command line arguments are simply available as the **@ARGV** array, you can **push** or **unshift** elements onto the command line. For example:

```
unshift @ARGV,qw/-v --/ if (@ARGV == 0);
```

Refer back to Chapter 7 if you want more information on the manipulation of arrays.

If you want to process command line arguments, rather than doing it yourself, the best method is to use either the standard or extended options supported by the **Getopt::Std** and **Getopt::Long** modules, respectively.

*Both **Getopt::Std** and **Getopt::Long** support functions that process the individual elements of the **@ARGV** array looking for command line options. When the function finds a valid argument, it removes it from the array. Any elements of the **@ARGV** array that cannot be identified as options remain in the **@ARGV** array, so you can continue to use the values supplied in your script.*

Getopt::Std

The **Getopt::Std** module provides a very simple interface for extracting options from the command line arguments. Each option can only be specified with a single letter, for example:

```
$ script.pl -ol file.in
```

There are two functions, **getopt** and **getopts**:

```
use Getopt::Std;

getopt('ol');
getopts('ol:');
```

Both functions require a single argument that specifies the list of single-letter arguments you would like to identify on the command line.

In the case of the **getopt** function, it assumes that all arguments expect an additional piece of information, such that the example above would accept the following line:

```
$ script.pl -o -l
```

But it would incorrectly assume that "-l" was the data for the **-o** option. With the **getopts** function each character is taken to be a Boolean value. If you want to accept arguments with additional information, then append a colon. This means that the above example will accept,

```
$ script.pl -o -l file.input
```

correctly identifying the **-l** as a simple switch.

The **getopts** function supports combined options, for example,

```
$ script.pl -eafl
```

which would correctly be recognized as four individual options, setting the values of **$opt_e**, **$opt_a**, **$opt_f**, and **$opt_l** to one.

Both **getopt** and **getopts** create new variables starting with a prefix of **$opt_**. The above script would create two variables: **$opt_o** will have a value of one, and **$opt_l** will have a value of "file.input." If a letter defined to the function is not found, then no variable will be created. In addition, for either function you can also supply a second argument, which should be a reference to a hash:

```
getopts('i:',\%opts);
```

Each supplied argument will be used as the key of the hash, and any additional information supplied will be placed into the corresponding values. Thus a script with the above line when called,

```
$ getopts -i Hello
```

will place the string "Hello" into the **$opts{'i'}** hash element.

If you have the **use strict 'vars'** pragma in effect (see Chapter 16/Appendix E), you will need to predefine the **$opt_** and hash variables before they are called. Either use a **my** definition before calling the function, or, better still, predeclare them with **use vars**.

Getopt::Long

The **Getopt::Std** module is suitable for simple scripts and argument passing. However, it falls over if you try to do more complex processing, or want to place the extracted information into specific variables and structures. The **Getopt::Long** module implements a more advanced system. The function is identical in operation to the one that is defined as part of the POSIX standard, and is therefore suitable for use in scripts that require **POSIX** compliance.

POSIX compliance allows not only the standard single-character matching supported by the **Getopt::Std** module, but also string arguments. For example:

```
$ script.pl --inputfile=source.txt
```

The command line option in this case is **--inputfile**. Note that long names as arguments are supported by both the single and double hyphen, although the double hyphen is the **POSIX** default. The older, single-hyphen style is still supported, but you cannot support the combined options, such that,

```
$ script.pl -eafl
```

is interpreted as a single argument, "eafl."

The module uses a different format from the previous functions in the **Getopt::Std** module to support the extended functionality. The specification for the command line arguments is passed to the **GetOptions** functions in one of two ways. The first is to supply a hash. The keys of the hash specify the command line arguments to accept, and the value should be a reference to the variable in which you want to store the value.

The code below sets the value of **$verbose** to one if the word "verbose" is found as a command line argument:

```
use Getopt::Long;
GetOptions("verbose" => \$verbose);
```

The alternative is to supply a reference to a hash as the first argument. As with the **Getopt::Std** module, each further argument to the function is then treated as a command line argument to match. The name specified will be used as the key, with the value, if supplied, being inserted into the corresponding value:

```
use Getopt::Long;
GetOptions(\%options, "verbose");
```

The default interpretation for all arguments is as Boolean values. However, like the **getopts** function in the **Getopt::Std** module, you can signify that additional values can be supplied on the command line. The module supports two constructs for specifying values: you can either use a space separator or an equal sign, for example:

```
--inputfile source.txt
--inputfile=source.txt
```

The **+** *sign is also supported, but the use of this is deprecated and not part of the* ***POSIX*** *specification.*

The list of available modifiers, which should be specified, is given in Table 12-1.

For example, to set debugging in a script from a value on the command line, you might use

```
use Getopt::Long;
GetOptions("debug:i" => \$debug);
```

This allows you both to use

```
$ script.pl -debug
```

to simply set debugging, or

```
$ script.pl -debug 256
```

to specify a debug level.

Option	Description
!	The option does not accept an optional piece of information and may be negated by prefixing **no**. For example, **opt!** will set the value of an option **--opt** to one, and **--noopt** to zero.
+	The option does not accept an additional piece of information. Each appearance in the command line options will increment the corresponding value by one, such that **--opt --opt --opt** will set a value of three, providing it doesn't already have a value.
=s	The option requires a mandatory additional string argument. The value of the string will be placed into the corresponding variable.
:s	The option accepts an optional string argument. The value of the string will be placed into the corresponding variable.
=i	The option requires a mandatory integer argument. The value will be placed into the corresponding variable.
:i	The option accepts an optional integer argument. The value will be placed into the corresponding variable.
=f	The option requires a mandatory real number argument. The value will be placed into the corresponding variable.
:f	The option accepts an optional real number argument. The value will be placed into the corresponding variable.

Table 12-1. *Options for the **Getopt::Long** Module*

The function also allows you to use a single hyphen, which will be treated as a valid argument with the corresponding entry name as the empty string. The **--** double hyphen (on its own) will be interpreted by the **GetOptions** function as the termination of the command line arguments.

Linkage

When using a hash reference as the first argument to the **GetOptions** function, there are additional facilities available to you for processing more complex command lines. By default, the operation is identical to the **getopts** function, that is,

```
GetOptions(\%options, "file=s");
```

will perform the equivalent of the assignment below:

```
$options{file} = "source.txt";
```

By using a trailing @ sign,

```
GetOptions(\%options, "files=s@");
```

you can process command lines like this:

```
$ script.pl --files source.txt --files sauce.txt
```

The result is an assignment to the hash, as follows:

```
$options{files} = ['source.txt', 'sauce.txt'];
```

Finally, you can process more complex "name=value" command line assignments by using a trailing % in the definition:

```
GetOptions(\%options, "users=s%");
```

Thus you can now process a command line,

```
$ script.pl --users Bob=Manager --users Fred=Salesman
```

which is roughly equivalent to:

```
$options{users} = { 'Bob' => 'Manager', 'Fred' => 'Salesman' };
```

If you do not specify a hash reference as the first argument, the function will instead create a new variable of the corresponding type, using the argument name prefixed by **opt_**. Thus the above examples could be translated as follows:

```
$opt_file = "source.txt";
@opt_files = ('source.txt', 'sauce.txt');
%opt_users = ( 'Bob'  => 'Manager',
               'Fred' => 'Salesman' );
```

Providing you supplied a function call like this,

```
GetOptions("file=s","files=s@","users=s%");
```

you can also use the hash argument feature to update your own variables directly:

```
GetOptions("file=s"   => \$file,
           "files=s@" => \@files,
           "users=s%" => \%users);
```

This last specification method also supports a function that will handle the specified option. The function will receive two arguments—the true option name (see the next section) and the value supplied.

Aliases

You can support alternative argument names by using | characters to separate individual names. For example:

```
GetOptions("file|input|source=s");
```

The "true" name would be "file" in this instance, placing the value into **$opt_file**. This true name is also passed to a function if specified (see above).

Callback Function

If **GetOptions** cannot identify an individual element of the **@ARGV** array as a true argument, then you can specify a function that will handle the option. You do this by using a value of <> as the argument name, for example:

```
GetOptions("<>" => \&nonoption);
```

Remember that the **GetOptions** function removes identifiable arguments from **@ARGV** and leaves the remainder of the elements intact if you don't use this facility. You can then process the arguments as you wish after **GetOptions** has completed successfully.

Identifying Errors

The **GetOptions** function returns true (1) if the command line arguments could be identified correctly. If an error occurs (because the user has supplied a command line argument the function wasn't expecting), the function returns false and uses **warn** to report the bad options.

If the definitions supplied to the function are invalid, then the function calls **die**, reporting the error.

Perl's Reporting Mechanism

Using your own custom reporting mechanisms for complex structures such as arrays and hashes can be a practical way of outputting information in a formatted fashion. However, if you are reporting simpler structures, or you want to produce reports that would be reported and formatted using the **printf** function, then you use a specially designed feature of Perl to format the output for you. The Perl mechanism actually inherits much of its functionality from a variety of sources, including FORTRAN and BASIC.

The Perl mechanism (otherwise called Formats) is a complete reporting environment that is very similar to many systems in commercial database-oriented packages such as those used for accounting and contacts systems. The Perl reporting mechanism keeps track of all the different parameters that affect a report, including the number of lines on the page, the page number you are currently printing to, and even the production of formatted page headers for each generated page. The format for a format definition is as follows:

```
format NAME =
FORMLIST
.
```

A format is treated like another core structure within Perl, and so it can be defined anywhere in your script, just like a subroutine or package declaration. Just like other structures, a format also has its own name space, so a format called **Foo** can coexist with a function called **Foo**. The tradition is for format names to be uppercase and usually have the same name as the filehandle to which they are output. The default format name is **STDOUT**, for example.

The **FORMLIST** portion is just like a subroutine definition, but without the brace enclosure, and is made up of three types of information: a comment, a "picture," or an "argument" line. A comment is signified by a **#** character in the first column and is treated just like any other comment within Perl.

The picture line is a text string that specifies how the information will be output. It is printed verbatim, apart from the field definitions that are used to print out the information you want to output. Special characters, as summarized in Table 12-2, specify the individual field formats for the pictures.

Using the information in Table 12-2, you can create definitions accordingly. For example,

```
format STDOUT =
@<<<<<<<< @|||||| @####.## @>>>>
$prodid,  $type,  $cost,   $instock
.
```

prints out each line with an eight-character, left-justified product ID; a centered type; a cost, printed as a formatted floating point value; and a right-justified stock level. The repetition of the individual format characters specifies the field width; so in the example of the cost field, it is printed as four digits, a decimal point, and two more digits.

Note that this format is used for *each* line in the printed report. How you treat and refer to this line is entirely dependent on how you decide to use the reporting mechanism. For most uses the individual line will be a record of information. We'll return to the significance of this shortly.

Picture Character	Description
@	Defines a field picture.
<	Specifies left justification; the number of repetitions specifies the field width.
>	Specifies right justification; the number of repetitions specifies the field width.
|	Specifies centered justification; the number of repetitions specifies the field width.
#	Specifies numbered justification; usually used for floating point fields. See the example in the text.
^	Defines a split field; information will be printed at the specified width, but will span multiple lines.
~	Indicates that blank lines in a format should be ignored. This means that if you specify multiple ^ fields but the information does not fill all the lines, then blanks won't be printed instead.

Table 12-2. *Field Formats*

Note that the above example also includes the third type of line, the argument line, which specifies the information that will be printed on each line. This is defined quite simply using a list of variables, separated by commas. Each variable is printed using each format, in order. The actual values supplied are evaluated at run time, so the values can also be functions and even arrays and hash references.

You can define multiline records by specifying a multiline format. So you can modify the above example to

```
format STDOUT =
Product: @<<<<<<<<
         $prodid
Type:    @||||||
         $type
Cost:    \$@####.##
         $cost
Stock:   @>>>>
         $instock
.
```

Note that in each case, for each output line, you have to specify the value you want printed on the next line. This means that although the above format is eight lines long, the report will only produce four lines for each record of output.

There are a number of ways of producing reports that output a single variable or record on multiple lines. The first method is to use the ^ field definition. This allows you to specify a justified format for a field, and each invocation of the picture and the variable that goes with it will produce an additional string of information extracted from the variable supplied. Perl puts as much information as possible into the field, removing the information each time the picture format is called.

To get a clearer idea, let's add a description to the above example, printed next to the existing details:

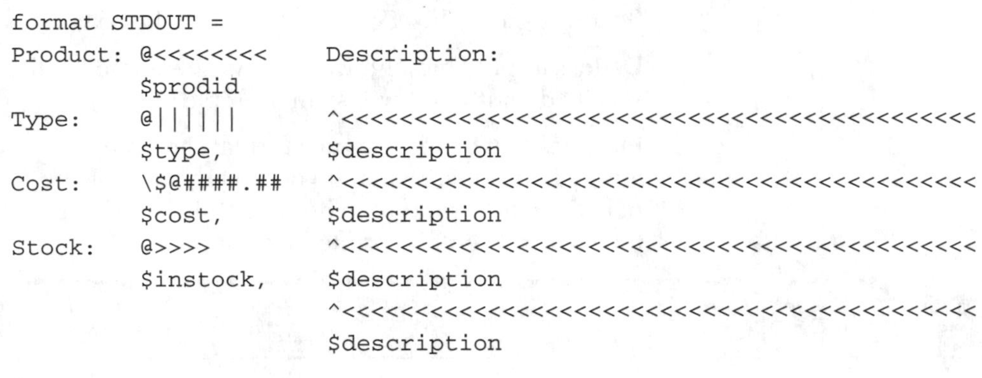

```
format STDOUT =
Product: @<<<<<<<<    Description:
         $prodid
Type:    @||||||      ^<<<<<<<<<<<<<<<<<<<<<<<<<<<<<<<<<<<<<<<<<<<
         $type,       $description
Cost:    \$@####.##   ^<<<<<<<<<<<<<<<<<<<<<<<<<<<<<<<<<<<<<<<<<<<
         $cost,       $description
Stock:   @>>>>        ^<<<<<<<<<<<<<<<<<<<<<<<<<<<<<<<<<<<<<<<<<<<
         $instock,    $description
                      ^<<<<<<<<<<<<<<<<<<<<<<<<<<<<<<<<<<<<<<<<<<<
                      $description
.
```

Unfortunately, this process means that the variable itself is modified during the reporting procedure. If you want to preserve the contents of the data, you should use a temporary variable to hold the information. The individual lines are correctly separated so that words do not cross line boundaries. You can also change the list of characters that Perl considers it sensible to break a line on by modifying the value of the **$:** variable.

Also note that the above method presents a very different problem. The above example uses a field width of 44 characters. If the data contained in **$description** is longer than 176 characters (4 x 44), then it will be truncated; and if it is shorter, you will get a blank line printed where you probably don't want one.

The latter problem is easier to solve. You just insert a ~ character anywhere on the line. This indicates that the line should be ignored if it contains no useful information. The first problem is more complex, since you have to get around the problem of printing an infinitely long text field. There are two ways to get around this. The first is to use a double ~ on a line, which indicates that the line should be repeated until the corresponding variable is empty. The other option is to use the special @* format. This prints multiline values without truncating them, but it also reduces your ability to specify a maximum width or any justification for the item and is therefore less useful and practical than the ~~ method.

Once you have written your format, it's then up to you to process the results and call **write** for each set of values that you want to report. To complete the above example, you might use something like the following:

```
format STDOUT =
Product: @<<<<<<<<     Description:
         $prodid
Type:    @||||||       ^<<<<<<<<<<<<<<<<<<<<<<<<<<<<<<<<<<<<<<<<<<<<<
         $type,        $description
Cost:    \$@####.##    ^<<<<<<<<<<<<<<<<<<<<<<<<<<<<<<<<<<<<<<<<<<<<<
         $cost,        $description
Stock:   @>>>>         ^<<<<<<<<<<<<<<<<<<<<<<<<<<<<<<<<<<<<<<<<<<<<<
         $instock,     $description
                       ^<<<<<<<<<<<<<<<<<<<<<<<<<<<<<<<<<<<<<<<<<<<<<
                       $description
.
open(DATA,"<datafile.db") or die "Can't open database";
while(<DATA>)
{
    chomp;
    ($prodid, $type, $cost, $instock, $description) = split /:/;
    write;
}
close(DATA);
```

This does the absolute minimum to produce a report from the information supplied in an external file. For each input line from the file, the data is extracted and the **write** function is called. This tells the reporting mechanism to build the line, according to the specified format, and then output. In this case the output is **STDOUT**, but it could have been any open filehandle, providing you named the format accordingly.

Headers and Footers

If you want to print a header for each page of output, you can create a format with the same name as the main format with **_TOP** attached. The information contained in this format will be printed at the top of every page (see "Format Variables" later in this chapter). This can be helpful both for printing column headers and for printing titles and page numbers.

For example, the two formats for printing a columnar version of the above report might look like this:

```
format STDOUT_TOP =
Product   Type    Cost      Stock  Description
-------   ------  --------  -----  ------------------------------------
.
format STDOUT =
@<<<<<<<< @||||||  @####.## @>>>>  ^<<<<<<<<<<<<<<<<<<<<<<<<<<<<<<<<<<<
$prodid,  $type,   $cost,   $instock,$description
                                   ^<<<<<<<<<<<<<<<<<<<<<<<<<<<<<<<<<<<~~
.
```

Footers are more difficult because there is no built-in device for printing a footer on each page. The best method is to check the value of the **$-** (**$FORMAT_LINES_LEFT** when the **English** module is used) and then print out the new footer before calling writing. Note, however, that you will need to update the value of **$-** to account for the number of lines you have added to the current page. Setting **$-** to zero triggers the generation of a new page.

Format Functions

The format process makes use of three main functions: **format**, **formline**, and **write**. The **format** function you already know about. The **formline** function takes a **PICTURE** specification and a list of values and places the value into the accumulate variable, **$^A**. It is this variable that is printed to the filehandle when **write** is called. For example, the function call

```
formline "@<<<<<<<< @|||||| @####.##", $prodid, $type, $cost;
write;
```

is equivalent to:

```
format STDOUT =
@<<<<<<<< @|||||| @####.##
$prodid, $type, $cost
.
write;
```

You can think of **formline** as the reporting mechanism's own version of **printf**. Note as well that because the **$^A** variable is populated during the process, you can create a function that returns a **formline** formatted string:

```
sub sformline
{
    my $picture = shift;
    $^A = '';
    formline($picture,@_);
    return $^A;
}
```

Care should be taken, of course, to ensure that you don't unwittingly overwrite the values currently stored in the accumulator using this method.

The **write** function populates the **$^A** accumulator variable (using **formline** and the predefined format). It then writes the contents of **$^A** to the current output filehandle, or to the filehandle specified:

```
write FILEHANDLE
write
```

Note that the format used changes when you specify a different filehandle. This is not normally a problem, since it's unlikely that for most installations you'll be using more than one filehandle with more than one type of format.

Format Variables

The main format variables, including their **English** module names and their descriptions, are shown in Table 12-3.

Use of any of these variables affects the currently selected default filehandle (defined using the **select** function). However, if you want the effects to be felt on a different filehandle, you will either have to change filehandles with the **select** function, or use the **FileHandle** module, which provides methods for all of the special variables. For example, to specify the format name for the **REPORT** filehandle:

```
use FileHandle;
REPORT->format_name("Financial_Report");
```

Perl Documentation

Perl documentation is supplied in a simple format called POD, short for Plain Old Documentation. This is a text-based format designed to be processed simply by a Perl script into a variety of destination formats. Like HTML, the POD format uses tags to

Variable	English	Description
$~	$FORMAT_NAME	Current format name.
$^	$FORMAT_TOP_NAME	Current top-of-form format name.
$%	$FORMAT_PAGE_NUMBER	Current page number (within current format).
$=	$FORMAT_LINES_PER_PAGE	Number of printable lines on a current page.
$-	$FORMAT_LINES_LEFT	Number of printable lines left on the page.
$^L	$FORMAT_FORMFEED	String to be output before each top of the page (except the first).

Table 12-3. *Variables Used by the Format System*

describe the individual features of the document; but unlike HTML, POD documents have a stricter structure and are geared more specifically to the process of producing destination documentation formats.

Because POD is a very simple, textual format, it can be easily converted into other, more familiar formats. This enables a POD document to be converted into man pages for easy use on Unix machines and HTML for any platform. The MacPerl implementation reads and displays POD documentation directly. Translators are supplied with the Perl distributions for making HTML, man, TeX/LaTeX, and even plain text files, and we'll examine this later in this chapter (see the section "Conversion to Other Formats").

POD documentation can also be embedded into Perl files (scripts, packages, etc.). The Perl interpreter will ignore the POD definitions, and POD readers/converters will ignore the Perl scripting elements. This provides a facility for supplying a single file that will be supported both as a script and as documentation, with all the flexibility of both.

Documentation Components

A POD document is made up of three different types of paragraph: verbatim, command, and ordinary text. Each type of paragraph is translated and handled differently, according to the output format of the translator.

In addition to these paragraph types, there are also escape sequences, which allow you to specify an alternative printed format for a word or sentence. This includes things like boldfacing and underlining text, as well as introducing references and links to other parts of the document. All of these elements are translated by the conversion scripts into suitable destination formats.

There is no standard format or layout for a POD document, but different translators place certain levels of significance on different elements within the source POD file. We'll examine a "standard" POD document later in this section, but be aware that many of the constructs we discuss here can be used, as with any normal word processing document, to create very simple documentation.

Command Paragraph

A command paragraph specifies that some special element or formatting should be applied to the supplied word, sentence, paragraph, or section. It is typically used to insert headings, subheadings, and lists into the document. All command paragraphs start with an equal sign and a keyword that specifies the formatting to be applied. The paragraph may include an additional keyword or reference. For example, the paragraph

```
=head1 This is a main heading
```

creates a level-one heading, the text of which is "This is a main heading."

The full list of available command paragraphs is in Table 12-4.

Ordinary Text Paragraph

Ordinary paragraphs of text are converted by the translation program into justified and filled paragraphs, according to the destination format. How the justification takes place is entirely dependent on the translator and the reader of the file that it creates. For example, if the conversion is to HTML, then the browser handles paragraph formatting; so an ordinary text paragraph will simply be copied to the destination file.

Verbatim Paragraph

A verbatim paragraph will be reproduced within the final document exactly; you cannot use formatting escapes, and the translator won't make any assumptions about the contents of the paragraph. A verbatim paragraph is identified by indentation in the source text, either with spaces or tabs. Probably the best use for a verbatim paragraph is to reproduce code within the document to ensure that it appears as working code within the final document. Without this facility the code would be justified and filled just like any other paragraph.

Escape Sequences

Escape sequences are recognized within both ordinary text and command paragraphs. The escape sequences allow you to specify that a block of text is to be displayed as

Command	Result
=head1 text	Applies first-level heading, using "text" as the description.
=head2 text	Applies second-level heading, using "text" as the description.
=over n	Starts a section for the generation of a list. The value of *n* specifies the number of characters to indent the paragraphs.
=item text	Specifies the title for an item in a list. The value of text will be interpreted differently, according to the translator.
=back	Ends a list/indentation.
=for format	Allows you to specify that the following paragraph should be inserted exactly as supplied, according to the specified format. For example, **=for html <font size=+1>Heading</font>** would be inserted into the translated file only by an HTML translator.
=begin format **=end format**	Acts similarly to **=for**, except that all the paragraphs between **=begin** and **=end** are included by the specified format translator as preformatted text.
=pod	Specifies the start of a POD document. It is best used when the documentation is included as part of a script. The **=pod** command paragraph tells the compiler to ignore the following text.
=cut	Specifies the end of a **=pod** section.

Table 12-4. *POD Command Paragraphs*

italicized, boldfaced, underlined, and so on. An escape sequence consists of a single letter and a pair of angle brackets that contain the text to be modified. For example, the POD fragment

```
B<Hello World!>
```

specifies that the string should be boldfaced, producing

Hello World!

A note: The resulting format must support this sort of text formatting!

The full list of escape sequences supported by the POD standard is shown in Table 12-5. The sequences will not always be transferred correctly to the destination format, and then the sequence is open to interpretation by the resulting file-viewing mechanism.

<table>
<tr><th>Sequence</th><th>Description</th></tr>
<tr><td>I<text></td><td>Italic text</td></tr>
<tr><td>B<text></td><td>Boldfaced text</td></tr>
<tr><td>S<text></td><td>Text with nonbreaking spaces (spaces within text that will not be used to wrap or split lines)</td></tr>
<tr><td>C<code></td><td>Literal code fragment (for example, the C <printf()> function)</td></tr>
<tr><td>L<name></td><td>A link or cross-reference to another section, identified by name. Links are further subdivided as follows:</td></tr>
<tr><td>   L<name></td><td>   Manual page</td></tr>
<tr><td>   L<name/ident></td><td>   Item or section within a manual page</td></tr>
<tr><td>   L<name/"sec"></td><td>   Section in other manual page</td></tr>
<tr><td>   L<"sec"></td><td>   Section within the current manual page (quotes are optional, as in L<name>)</td></tr>
<tr><td>   L</"sec"></td><td>   Same as above</td></tr>
<tr><td>   L<text|name>
    L<text|name/ident>
    L<text|name/"sec">
    L<text|"sec">
    L<text|/"sec"></td><td>   Same as above, but destination is identified by name but displayed as text; the text element cannot contain | or ></td></tr>
<tr><td>F<file></td><td>Used for file names</td></tr>
<tr><td>X<index></td><td>An index entry</td></tr>
<tr><td>Z<></td><td>A zero-width character</td></tr>
<tr><td>E<escape></td><td>A named character (similar to HTML escapes):</td></tr>
<tr><td>   E<lt></td><td>   A literal <</td></tr>
<tr><td>   E<gt></td><td>   A literal ></td></tr>
<tr><td>   E<n></td><td>   Character number (in ASCII)</td></tr>
</table>

Table 12-5. *POD Escape Sequences*

Embedding Documentation in Scripts and Modules

You can embed documentation into a Perl script simply by starting the POD section with **=head1** and ending it with **=cut**. The compiler ignores the POD documentation between the two command paragraphs. A POD translator ignores any code outside of the command paragraphs. In this way, you can place both script and documentation within a single file, allowing the compiler and translator to interpret the corresponding sections. For example, the script

```
=head1 NAME

HelloWorld.pl

=cut

print "Hello World!";

=head1 SYNOPSIS

This program prints Hello World! on the screen.

=cut
```

when parsed with the compiler, produces

Hello World!

and, when parsed with a POD viewer, produces

NAME

HelloWorld.pl

SYNOPSIS

This program prints Hello World! on the screen.

Suggested Elements

Different resulting formats have different requirements and restrictions on what can and can't be incorporated within a POD source document. At first glance, this would appear to have an effect on the cross-platform nature of the POD format, but in fact it helps to standardize the base POD documents.

The translated format that has the most stringent rules is the **man** format because the Unix manual format places certain restrictions and requirements on a manual page so that the information can be indexed and displayed in standard format. Within the confines of POD documentation, this restriction aids in the formatting and layout of nearly all the documents that are produced.

The format of a manual page consists of the elements outlined in Table 12-6. Element titles are historically shown in uppercase, although this is not a requirement, and each should be the reference with the **=head1** element. Subheadings can be included in **=head2** elements.

Element	Description
NAME	Mandatory comma-separated list of the functions or programs documented by the man page.
SYNOPSIS	Outline of the function's or program's purpose.
DESCRIPTION	Longer description/discussion of the program's purpose.
OPTIONS	The command line options or function arguments.
RETURN VALUE	What the program returns if successful.
ERRORS	Any return codes, errors, or exceptions that may be produced.
EXAMPLES	Examples of the program's or function's use.
ENVIRONMENT	The environment or variables used by and modified by the program.
FILES	The files used.
SEE ALSO	Other entries to refer to.
NOTES	Any additional commentary.
CAVEATS/ WARNINGS	Anything to be aware of during the program's use.
DIAGNOSTICS	Errors or messages produced by the program and what they mean.
BUGS	Things that do not work as expected.
RESTRICTIONS	Items that are built-in design features and limitations.
AUTHOR	Who wrote the function or program.
HISTORY	The source or origin of the program or function.

Table 12-6. *Elements of a POD man Page*

Conversion to Other Formats

Perl comes with its own set of conversion scripts that will convert either raw POD documents or embedded POD documentation into a variety of formats. The actual translation is done inside a variety of modules under the **Pod** directory within the standard Perl library. We'll look mainly at the scripts that handle this conversion here; refer to Appendix E for more details on the modules.

Text

If you do not want to view formatted output from a POD document, you can convert it into textual format. The resulting output is not completely without format, but it does strip links and styled text that require some form of configurable display device. If Termcap is supported on your machine or terminal, then this will be used to display boldfaced and italicized text. Otherwise, Perl will attempt to use backspaces.

```
$ pod2text [-a] [-width] script.pl
```

The **pod2text** script is the command line interface for converting documents to text format. It primarily takes one argument—the document to convert (it will use the standard input if you don't specify one). You can optionally supply two arguments: **-a** defines an alternative output format (which makes fewer assumptions about the destination format capabilities). The second optional argument specifies the maximum width of the generated text. Since the conversion formats the individual paragraphs and does its own word wrapping, this figure will affect the length of individually formatted lines.

The output is always sent to the standard output, so you will need to redirect the output to a new file unless you want to view it interactively.

The functionality of the **pod2text** script is actually just a wrapper around the **pod2text** function that is part of the **Pod::Text** module, which you can examine in more detail in Appendix E.

HTML

The most compatible destination format (especially across platforms) is HTML. The **pod2html** script works in the same way as the **pod2text** script:

```
$ pod2html script.pl
```

Output is also sent to the standard out, so you will need to redirect the generated HTML to a file if you want to install it on a web server or view it with a browser. It also accepts a number of command line options, as shown in Table 12-7.

Again, the **pod2html** script is a wrapper around the **Pod::Html** module. See Appendix E for more information.

Option	Description
--flush	Flushes the contents of the item and directory caches created during the parsing of a POD document.
--help	Prints out a help message.
--htmlroot	The base directory from which you reference documents relatively. This is required if you expect to install the generated HTML files onto a web server. The default is /.
--index	Generate an index of **=head1** elements at the top of the HTML file generated (default).
--infile	The file name to convert. You don't have to use this element; the first nonhyphenated argument is taken as a file name. If you don't specify a file by either method, then it will accept input from standard input.
--libpods	A colon-separated list of pages searched when referencing **=item** entries. These are not the file names, just the page names, as they would appear in **L<>** link elements.
--netscape	Use Netscape-specific browser directives when necessary.
--nonetscape	Prevents the use of Netscape-specific browser directives (default).
--outfile	The destination file name for the generated HTML. Uses standard output if none is specified.
--podpath	A colon-separated list of directories containing POD files and libraries.
--podroot	The base directory prepended to each entry in the **podpath** command line argument. The default is . (dot) and the current directory.
--noindex	Don't generate an index at the top of the HTML file generated.
--norecurse	Don't recurse into the subdirectories specified in the **podpath** option.
--recurse	Recurse into the subdirectories specified in the **podpath** option (this is the default behavior).
--title	The contents of the **<TITLE>** tag in the created HTML document.
--verbose	Produces status and progress messages during production.

Table 12-7. *Options for the **pod2html** Script*

man Pages

The online documentation on Unix is stored in ***roff** format, using the **man** macro extensions. This is a special formatting system that has been part of Unix and, many years ago, part of full-scale print production systems. To create a man page from raw POD source, you use the **pod2man** script:

```
$ pod2man script.pl
```

The formatted output is sent to the standard out, so you will need to redirect the output. The conversion process will highlight different entities correctly. Headings, page headers and footers, and formatting will all be translated to the manual pages. The script converts the references to other manual pages such that interactive man page readers such as **emacs** can access the linked pages correctly.

Manual pages are stored and organized into different sections. Unless you have special needs, you should let the Perl Makefile and the **MakeMaker** utility decide where to put the final documents. For reference, the different manual sections for SVR4 Unix variants are listed in Table 12-8. If you use BSD, you may have a slightly different specific layout. Although most of the numbered sections are the same, the alphanumeric subsections may be different.

Typically, the Perl-specific manual pages are installed in the **man** directory of the main Perl library directory. The location of this depends on the version of Perl you are using and on the platform. Again, you should let **MakeMaker** sort this out for you.

PostScript/PDF

The PostScript format is a common format created to direct printing to a PostScript-capable printer. You can also view PostScript files on screen, either directly if you have a PostScript viewer such as Display PostScript on SunOS/Solaris and others, or via the GNU Ghostscript application. Another option is to convert the complex PostScript format into the simpler, screen-optimized Portable Document Format (PDF).

Acrobat PDFs are a special type of formatted document allowing you to generate a printer-ready document that cannot (easily) be modified. The main advantages of a PDF are that it is generally smaller than a PostScript file and it is cross-platform independent. For most situations the best solution for generating a PDF is to build it from a PostScript file. There are two options here: either use the commercial Adobe Acrobat product, or use the GNU Ghostscript package, which provides facilities for converting simple PostScript files into PDF documents. For professional use, you should consider the commercial package, which also provides other facilities such as incorporating links and indexes and thumbnail images of the finished pages.

The methods for creating PostScript files vary across platforms. On Solaris, and other platforms, you can use the **dpost** program, which takes formatted output from

Section	Contents
1	User Commands
1C	Basic Networking Commands
1F	FMLI Commands
1M	Administration Commands
2	System Function Calls
3	BSD Routines
3C	C Library Functions
3E	ELF Library Functions
3G	Libgen Functions
3M	Math Functions
3N	Network Services Functions
3S	Standard I/O Functions
3X	Specialized Libraries
4	File Formats
5	Miscellaneous
6	Games
7	Special Files
8	System Maintenance Procedures
9	Device-Driver Interface/Driver-Kernel Interface (DDI/DDK)

Table 12-8. ***man*** *Page Sections*

troff (not **nroff**, which is normally used for man pages) and produces raw PostScript. Because most POD documentation does not make use of the ***roff** table or equation formats, you can use a very simple command to create a PostScript file:

```
pod2man script.pl|troff -man|dpost >script.ps
```

Under any platform, if you have access to a web browser, your easiest solution is to convert a POD document to HTML. Then generate a PostScript file (if you want to convert it into a PDF) or print it directly to the desired printer.

Alternatively, you can use the **pod2latex** converter, which outputs TeX documents that can be translated into printable documents for your printer, and into PostScript. There are TeX programs for Unix (Linux comes with the TeX package as standard) and Windows NT. Under MacOS, the only solution I'm aware of is OzTeX. Although this is an old application, it still produces good-quality PostScript from TeX source.

If you are planning to release a script or module that consists of POD documentation (which it should), you should leave it in this format. This will guarantee that users can read and convert it into a suitable format, providing, of course, they have Perl installed.

Chapter 13

Advanced User Interfaces

Designing an effective user interface is a difficult task. There are the complexities of designing the interface elements: the display boxes, buttons, menus, and general layout of the interface. More difficult is the implementation. There is no single user interface toolkit (although Tk does a pretty good job), and depending on your platform, you may choose a number of different possible solutions.

For an operating system that supports a text-based interface, the difficulties are even more significant. Many would argue that the number of people actually using text interfaces is very small, and few would disagree. Although Windows and Unix have had windowed environments for many years, both still support a text interface, and many well-known programs rely heavily on that interface as their way of supporting functionality. Two of the best applications under Unix are emacs, an editor, and Lynx, a web browser.

Working directly with a terminal to control an interface is not a step to be taken lightly. It only really affects Unix and Win32 systems, since the Mac does not support a text-based interface anyway. Irrespective of the platform, you will need to "drive" the terminal directly. Although toolkits and modules are available (such as **Term::Cap** for Unix and **Win32::Console** for Windows), you will still need to design and manage your own on-screen elements, such as menus, buttons, and text areas, and none of it is easy, even with a simplified toolkit.

Generally, if you're developing an application in any programming language, it's highly likely you're planning on building a GUI environment for your application. There is no standard toolkit for designing GUI interfaces, but Tk is a good choice. It removes a lot of the complexity of implementing an interface, although the individual design is still your responsibility.

The other option for GUI interfaces, although perhaps less flexible, is to design a web interface to your application. For years Perl has been the programming language behind many popular and successful websites (see Chapter 1 for some examples).

We'll be looking at using Tk within Perl in this chapter; and the next two chapters, 14 and 15, deal with the complexities and vagaries of web development within the Perl environment. However, before we write off the text-based terminal as dead, we'll take a look at some of the most common things you can do within the basic Perl environment to communicate with the outside world.

Working with a Terminal

Most terminal interfaces rely on the use of the special escape code sequences that the terminal driver supports for moving the cursor around the screen, changing the text to inverse, and so on. The information is held in a central database, and it's the accessibility of this database that causes problems within Perl.

In the early years of Unix development, editing was handled by **ed**. The **ed** program was advanced for its time, allowing you to edit individual lines of a document. You could even search for text and replace it. Unfortunately, working on a document more than ten lines long becomes tedious when you can only view and edit one line at a time.

Editors progressed in the late 1970s with the introduction of **vi**, the visual version of **ed**. The same basic functionality remained; what was different was that you were able to view multiple lines of the document and move around them in a way never before possible. This presented something of a problem for the developer of **vi**, Bill Joy. The problem was that different terminals used different sets of control characters and control codes to perform even basic tasks like moving the cursor around the screen. Out of the **vi** project grew the termcap terminal capabilities database. This described the abilities of each terminal, and a set of functions allowed a programmer to access the functions in a standard way.

The termcap system was eventually improved upon and became the curses package. This package offered the same basic functionality, but with some higher-level and more complex functions added to take advantage of the clever features being introduced to the newer terminals. The next development phase was carried out by the Unix Systems Group (USG), which improved upon the curses package to produce terminfo. Like curses before it, terminfo provided the same basic interface to the terminal as termcap, albeit via a different set of functions. Also like curses, terminfo was intended to eliminate some of the shortcomings of the termcap system.

The result is that we now have two basic systems for using terminals. The termcap system is found largely on BSD-based Unix variants. The terminfo package is found mainly on System V–based Unix variants. Some Unix systems, such as Solaris, SunOS, and HP-UX, supply both termcap and terminfo.

Within Perl the **Term::Cap** module provides an interface to the termcap system. It's beyond the confines of this book to go into detail about the processes behind the termcap system and how to make the best use of it. The **Term::Cap** module should provide you with everything you need to access and control your terminal. Since the bulk of the development effort concentrates on Tk GUI interfaces, we'll move straight onto using that for building user interfaces.

Using Tk

Although there are other toolkits for building GUIs, Tk has become the most respected of the available toolkits, largely because of its feature list and the professional-looking quality of the windows and interfaces it builds. The history of Tk is somewhat checkered, but this has not affected the overall development of Tk as an interface system.

Tk was originally developed by Dr. John Ousterhout, who was originally at the University of California, Berkeley, before moving to Sun Microsystems. Ousterhout, Tk, and its sister scripting language Tcl are now part of a commercial development effort called Scriptics. The original Tcl and Tk projects are still free, while Scriptics also develops commercial products such as Tcl Pro.

The role of Tk is to make the process of designing a user interface significantly easier. In essence, most windowing systems such as Microsoft Windows, MacOS, and X Windows (as used on Unix) are very simple. The core of the windowing system provides the methods and basis for simple operations and events such as opening windows and drawing lines and accepting input and actions from the keyboard and mouse.

Creating even a simple on-screen element such as a button or simple text pane originally involved hundreds of lines of code. The result was the development of individual elements of a GUI environment called widgets. A single widget can define a core element of the interface such as a button or scroll bar and even more complex elements such as scales and hierarchical lists, which themselves can be composed of other simpler widgets. Within Unix and the X Windows system a number of different widget toolkits have been produced, including Motif, Athena, OpenWindows, and, of course, Tk.

Because of the natural relationship between widgets and objects, developing GUIs within a scripting language is incredibly easy, and Tk was originally developed in cooperation with the Tcl language. Tcl (short for Tool Command Language) is essentially a macro language for making development of complex programs within the shell easier. (See Chapter 1 for a summary of other Tcl features.) However, Tcl is itself difficult to use in comparison to Perl, Python, and other scripting languages, so efforts were made to support the Tk widgets directly within these languages.

The first real system was designed by Malcolm Beattie, who embedded a Tcl interpreter within a Perl layer to enable a connection between Perl and Tk. Nick Ing-Simmons developed the now standard Perl/Tk interface by stripping the Tk system of its Tcl-specific code. On top of the base Tk functionality was built a generic porting layer, called pTk, which is now the basis for a number of Tk interfaces to scripting languages, including Perl, Python, Scheme, and Guile.

The result is Perl/Tk—an interface system that you access within Perl as the Tk module. This has been successfully supported on Unix for a number of years. At Sun, Tcl and Tk were ported to Windows and MacOS, and although the Windows version of Perl/Tk has been available for some time, a Mac version has yet to materialize. Of course, it's almost worth arguing that the interface to the underlying OS is so good under MacPerl that you don't need Tk. The reality is that the features supported are no match for a proper development environment such as Tk. The other problem is that it doesn't solve cross-platform compatibility problems.

In this chapter, we'll look at the basics of creating user windows and widgets with Perl/Tk, although the exact layouts and other design details are left to the reader. I would be the first to admit that user interfaces are not my strong point.

If you are serious about developing interfaces with Tk, or any other system, I suggest for the benefit of you and your users that you read a suitable human-computer interface book. I can heartily recommend all of Apple's texts; they are the basis for many of the best interfaces you will find. You may also want to check Alan Cooper's *About Face: The Essentials of User Interface Design*, or the excellent introductory guide *The Elements of User Interface Design*, by Theo Mandel.

Hello from Tk

Developing a user interface with Tk is a case of creating a number of nested objects. The first object you create is the main window for your application. The nested objects are the individual widgets that make up the user interface. A widget is a button, text box, menu, or a variety of other components used to build up your interface within your window.

Once you have defined the individual widgets that make up the window, the script then goes into a loop, called the event loop. The script accepts events from the user and performs the commands and actions that were defined when the widgets were created. This is different from most other Perl scripts, which follow a logical process. However, unlike many Perl scripts, users control the execution and choose a number of different options, according to which button, text box, or other widget they manipulate.

Here is a very quick Perl/Tk script that demonstrates this idea:

```
use Tk;

$main = MainWindow->new();
$main->title("Hello World!");

$label = $main->Label(text => 'Hello from Tk!');
$button = $main->Button();

$icon = $button->Photo(-file => 'icon.gif');

$button->configure(image => $icon,
                   command => sub { exit; }
                   );

$label->pack(side => 'left');
$button->pack(side => 'left',
              padx => 5
              );

MainLoop();
```

The example shows the basic process of building a Perl/Tk application, which can be summarized like this:

1. Create a window to hold all of your objects. The main window is generally known as *main* or *top-level*. This is handled in the preceding script by the **MainWindow->new()** function call, which returns a new window object.

2. Create a number of widgets, defining their contents, actions, and other elements. In this example, we create a label to hold a simple message and a button, which when pressed will exit the script.
3. Display and arrange the widgets within the window. This is controlled with the **pack** function, which controls the orientation and spacing of the widgets within the window. In essence, though, the **pack** function does the work itself, almost like instructing a kitchen cupboard how best to stack its cans. Luckily, as in this script, you also get the opportunity to specify some additional options on how to lay out the individual widgets.
4. Start the event loop. The main execution of the script has now finished, and the rest of the script will be driven by the events configured for individual widgets. Our script has only one event: when the button is clicked, you exit the script.

The result, when run, looks like Figure 13-1 on a Windows machine. You can see the effects of the script quite clearly. As a comparison, you can see the same script executed on a Redhat Linux machine in Figure 13-2. The insides of the two windows are identical. It is only the window manager dressing for resizing the window, minimizing or maximizing the window, or closing it altogether that are different. The window decorations are specific to the platform and window manager, and any window you create within Tk will have these decorations.

It's possible to create a number of different "main" windows within the same application; you are not restricted to only one window. Note, though, how the widgets are created: they are children of the parent main window. It's also possible to use widgets that contain their own nested widgets. The **Frame** widget, for example, is used for creating multiple areas within the same window, while a Tk menu can consist of familiar menu items as well as buttons and check boxes.

The purpose of the **pack** method is to physically construct and lay out the widgets within their parent window. If you do not call the **pack** method, the widget will never be displayed within the window. We'll return to the **pack** method, and the purpose and methods available to you for managing the geometry of the widgets within a window, later in this chapter.

Figure 13-1. *The "Hello from Tk" window under Microsoft Windows*

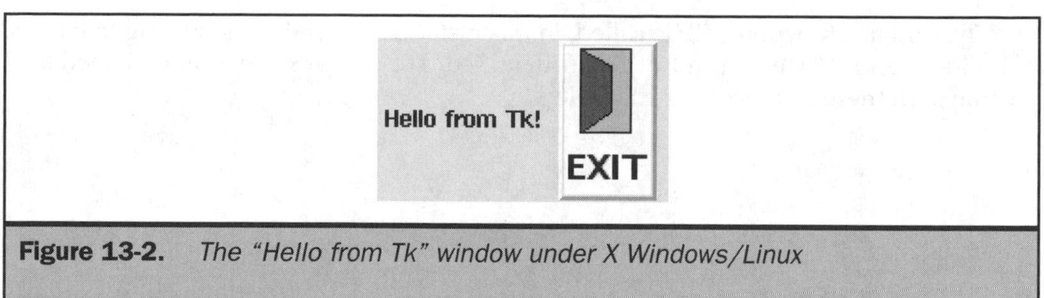

Figure 13-2. *The "Hello from Tk" window under X Windows/Linux*

Event Loops

The **MainLoop** function executes a simple loop that dispatches requests from the underlying windowing system to the corresponding widgets. For each event, the function defined in the **command** property is executed. However, it's the responsibility of the called function to perform its job and relinquish control as soon as possible, so as to allow other waiting events to execute.

For complex systems that are CPU intensive, you will also need to make sure that you can effectively multitask between the different threads of execution so that you don't lock up the process while servicing an earlier event loop. For some applications and some systems, this will require you to manually divide a task into manageable chunks. This will allow the event loop to send requests to other callback functions. An alternative solution is to use a multithreaded application model.

The main thread handles the interface, and callbacks initiate new threads according to their needs. This is the method employed by many operating systems and applications. Most notably, the BeOS operating system does this multithreading for you. As yet, Perl and Tk have not been ported to the BeOS, although it makes for an interesting and advanced development environment.

Any system call that blocks is generally a bad idea within a GUI interface, since events in the event stack will not be processed while the system blocks. The best method is to use something like **select**, which will do the job of multiplexing between open filehandles for you. Unfortunately, this doesn't get around the problem of handling GUI and file events for you.

The **MainLoop** function is not configurable; it's impossible to supply your own version. The loop only exits when users click on the close box within their windowed environment, or when a call to **exit** is made. Without multithreaded support there will be no way for you either to use the **select** function or to handle the data. The solution is to use the **fileevent** function. This notifies a callback function when the specified filehandle is ready to accept or supply data. You use it much like you use any other callback function within the Tk environment:

```
open(DATA, "file.txt) or die "Can't open $!";
$label->fileevent(DATA, "readable", \&accept_data);
```

The callback function will be called, in this instance, when data is waiting to be read from the file, and when an end-of-file is identified. The callback function will need to handle both these instances, for example:

```
sub accept_data
{
    if (eof(DATA))
    {
        $label->fileevent(DATA, "readable", undef);
        return;
    }
    else
    {
        $text .= <DATA>;
    }
}
```

Of course, this doesn't guarantee that the operator or function you have chosen will not block the process if there isn't as much information as it was expecting. You should be using non-blocking I/O for this sort of process anyway. See Chapter 6 for more information.

Event Bindings

Beyond the basic event bindings handled by the **command** property, it is possible to bind specific events, such as keypresses and mouse clicks, to other functions. This is how you make keys equate to specific function calls and provide shortcuts to commands and functions. Tk provides the **bind** function, which allows you to map these low-level events to corresponding functions. It is also the method employed by individual widgets when you define the **command** property. The format for the function is

```
$widget->bind(event, callback);
```

The **event** is the name of the event you want to bind and can include keypresses or a mouse click (which is defined as a press and release). The **bind** function also supports more complicated events, such as a mouse click and drag, general mouse motion, or the mouse pointer entering or leaving the windows, and whole window events, like resizing and iconifying.

The **event** is defined as a string containing the sequence you want to map, which can be made up of one or more individual events called event sequences. For example, the code

```
$widget->bind("<z>", \&pressed_z);
```

maps the user pressing the Z key, without any modifier, to the function. Other possible values for **event** are

```
$widget->bind("<Control-z>", \&undo);
```

which occurs when the CTRL key and Z are pressed at the same time, and

```
$widget->bind("<Escape><Control-z>", \&redo);
```

which would call **redo** when the ESC key was pressed, followed by CTRL and Z. For mouse clicks you would use

```
$widget->bind("<Button1>", \&redo);
```

Individual events are grouped into different classes called modifiers, types, and details. A modifier is a special key such as *Escape*, *Control*, *Meta*, *Alt*, and *Shift*. Mouse buttons are also grouped into this class, so you get *Button1*, *Button2*, *Double* (for a double click), and *Triple* (for a triple click). There is also a special modifier, *Any*, which matches all of the modifiers, including none. The type of event is one of *KeyPress*, *KeyRelease*, *ButtonPress*, *ButtonRelease*, *Enter*, *Leave*, and *Motion*. The detail class is only used for keyboard bindings and is a string defining the character that has been pressed. In addition, it also supports *Enter*, *Right*, *Delete*, *Backspace*, *Escape*, *F1*, and so on.

Tk also supports abbreviations of common keypresses so that **<KeyPress-z>** can be specified simply as **<z>** and **<Button1-ButtonPress>** as **<1>**.

In addition, the text and canvas widgets allow an even finer granularity on individual bindings, allowing you to attach a binding to a specific tag. The format of **bind** changes accordingly: the first argument now defines the tag to identify, and the second and third arguments define the binding and function to be called. Thus you can create a binding for pressing the second button on a piece of tagged text:

```
$text->bind('word', '<2>', \&synonym_menu);
```

Obtaining Event Details

Since it's possible to bind any key or button sequence to a function, it's also possible to assign multiple bindings to a single handler. In these instances, the handler must be able to determine what key or button was pressed and where the cursor was at the time the event occurred. To obtain the event details, you use the **Ev** function, which extracts the information from the event itself, since it is the event that records the information about what was pressed and where.

The **Ev('k')** call returns the keycode that triggered the event, as previously defined, and **Ev('x')** and **Ev('y')** return the x and y coordinates of the mouse pointer when the event was received. To use, you need to supply an array as the value to the function-binding argument:

```
$widget->bind("<Button1>", [\&redo, Ev('k')]);
```

The first element of the array reference is the function to be called, and further elements are the arguments to be passed to the function.

Widgets

To understand how the system works, we'll take a brief look at the most commonly used widgets. There are many exceptions that are not listed, due to space constraints. If you want more information, check the well-organized and voluminous documentation supplied with the Perl/Tk package.

Properties

The configuration of individual widgets is controlled through a series of properties. All widgets have a set of properties that define everything from the existence of borders and colors, through to font styles and sizes. Individual specialized widgets also have properties for the unique elements that make up that widget. For example, a **MenuButton** widget has a property called **state**, which indicates whether the menu is active or disabled (there is also a **normal** setting).

When you define a widget, you set the properties by specifying the property name and value as part of the hash that you supply to a widget method called **configure**. For example:

```
$label->configure(text = "Hello World!\n", foreground = 'red');
```

The generic properties that are configurable for all widgets are shown in Table 13-1. Note that although the properties shown here are without leading hyphens (as required by Tk normally), you may need to add them. The Perl/Tk interface allows you to use specifications both with and without the hyphen prefix.

All widgets also support a number of methods for controlling and configuring their options. There are two basic methods. The first is **configure**, which allows you to set multiple properties on a widget object at once:

```
$label->configure(text  => 'Hello World!', foreground => 'red');
```

Property	Description
font	The font name in X or Windows format.
background, bg	The color of the background, specified either by name or hexadecimal RGB value.
foreground, fg	The color of the foreground, specified either by name or hexadecimal RGB value.
text	The string to be displayed within the widget, using the foreground and font values specified.
image, bitmap	The image or bitmap file to be displayed within the widget.
relief	The style of the widget's border, which can be either raised, sunken, flat, ridge, or groove.
borderwidth	The width of the relief border.
height	The height of the widget; specified in the number of characters for labels, buttons, and text widgets, and in pixels for all other widgets.
width	The width of the widget; specified in the number of characters for labels, buttons, and text widgets, and in pixels for all other widgets.
textvariable	The name of a variable to be used and/or updated when the widget changes.
anchor	Defines the location of the widget within the window, or the location of the text within the widget. Valid values are n, ne, e, se, s, sw, w, nw, or center.

Table 13-1. *Generic Widget Properties*

The second, **cget**, returns the value of a specific property:

```
$color = $label->cget('foreground');
```

SPECIFYING FONTS Font values are traditionally specified in the XLFD (X Logical Font Description) format. This is a complex string consisting of 14 fields, each separated by a hyphen. Each field defines a different property. For example, the string

```
-sony-fixed-medium-r-normal--16-120-100-100-c-80-iso8859-1
```

defines a font from the "sony" foundry, the "fixed" family, of medium weight. It's a regular (rather than italic) font, and the width is normal. The size of the font is 16 pixels high and 12 points high (point size is specified in tenths of a point, so the size specified is 120 rather than 12). The next two fields specify the resolution—in this instance 100 pixels wide and 100 pixels high—with an overall character width of 80. The last field is the registry or character locale name.

Usually, however, you can get away with specifying an asterisk or question mark as wildcards in particular fields so that you can request a more general font, and then let the Tk and windowing interface determine the correct font. You should be able to get away with specifying the foundry, family, weight, slant, and points fields. For example, to use 12-point Helvetica, you might use:

```
$label->configure(font =>
'-adobe-helvetica-medium-r-*--*-120-*-*-*-*-*');
```

Under Windows and MacOS platforms you should be able to use the simpler Windows style, which just defines the font name, point size, and weight; for example:

```
$label->configure(font => 'Helvetica 12 regular');
```

SPECIFYING COLORS The X Windows system supports a file called rgb.txt, which maps red, green, and blue intensities to color names. This allows you to specify a color with a simple name. Here's a short extract from the beginning of a sample rgb.txt file:

```
255 250 250             snow
248 248 255             ghost white
248 248 255             GhostWhite
245 245 245             white smoke
245 245 245             WhiteSmoke
```

Within Tk you can use these values to specify colors within properties. Alternatively, you can specify the RGB values precisely in the form **#RGB**, **#RRGGBB**, **#RRRGGGBBB**, and **#RRRRGGGGBBBB**, where the **R**, **G**, and **B** refer to an individual hexadecimal digit of the corresponding color's intensity.

IMAGES AND BITMAPS Certain widgets support the use of images rather than text. For example, you can use an image in place of the text that would normally appear on a button. There are essentially two types of images—a two-color bitmap and a multicolored pixmap. In an effort to help improve performance, Tk considers an image to be a unique element. If it needs to be displayed in more than one place, you render it once and use the rendered image object as the source for the widget image. This means there are two steps to using an image within a widget.

The first step is to create the rendered image object. You use a different function to render individual image formats, although the return value from each function is always of the same type. To create an image object from X Bitmap (XBM):

```
$image = $label->Bitmap(file => 'icon.xbm');
```

For an X Pixmap (XPM):

```
$image = $label->Pixmap(file => 'icon.xpm');
```

And for a GIF or Portable Pixmap (PPM) format, you need to use the **Photo** constructor:

```
$image = $label->Photo(file => 'icon.gif');
```

When you want to configure a particular widget with an image object, use the **image** property:

```
$label->configure(image => $image);
```

For bitmaps, the **foreground** and **background** properties of the widget control the foreground and background color of the bitmap.

Labels

A **Label** widget is the basic widget and provides a simple way of displaying a small text label within a window. It supports all the basic properties shown in Table 13-1.

Buttons

Button widgets are essentially just labels with an additional property, **command**, which is a reference to a function to be called when the button is pressed. The list of additional properties and methods beyond the base list are shown in Table 13-2.

You saw an example of both the label and button in the introductory script.

Radio Buttons

The **Radiobutton** widget is used to provide either a simple on/off button, or to act as a toggle between several different options. The valid properties and methods for a radio button are shown in Table 13-3.

Property	Description
command	A reference to the Perl function to be called when button is clicked with mouse button 1.
Method	
flash	Flashes the button briefly by reversing and resetting the foreground and background colors.
invoke	Starts the subroutine defined in the **command** property.

Table 13-2. *Properties and Methods for Buttons*

Property	Description
command	A reference to the Perl function to be called when button is clicked with mouse button 1. The variable referred to by the **variable** property is updated with the value in the **value** property before the referenced subroutine is invoked.
variable	Takes a reference to a variable and updates with the **value** property when the button is clicked. When the value of the referenced variable matches the **value** property, the button is selected automatically.
value	Specifies the value to store within the variable pointed to by the **variable** property when the button is selected.
Method	
select	Selects the radio button and sets the **variable** to **value**.
flash	Flashes the button briefly by reversing and resetting the foreground and background colors.
invoke	Starts the subroutine defined in the **command** property.

Table 13-3. *Properties and Methods for Radio Buttons*

For example, the script below shows a very simple radio button that allows you to choose between different names:

```
use Tk;

$name = 'martin';

$main = MainWindow->new();

$main->Radiobutton(text  => 'Martin',
                   value => 'martin',
                   variable => \$name)->pack(side => 'left');
$main->Radiobutton(text  => 'Sharon',
                   value => 'sharon',
                   variable => \$name)->pack(side => 'left');
$main->Radiobutton(text  => 'Wendy',
                   value => 'wendy',
                   variable => \$name)->pack(side => 'left');

MainLoop();
```

Note that the same variable is used in each property definition, and so the information is shared. A change to the value will update the corresponding radio button family with the correct selection. The resultant window is shown here:

Check Buttons

A **Checkbutton** widget, perhaps better known as a check box, depending on your background, is like a radio button, except that it is normally used to allow the user to select multiple check boxes for a single option. The possible properties and methods for a **Checkbutton** widget are shown in Table 13-4.

Text

A **Text** widget is a simple text box used for displaying multiple lines of text, unlike a label, which is really only useful for a small number of words on a single line. A **Text** widget becomes an editable entry box for information. It supports the **emacs** keyboard shortcuts for data entry and for moving around the box. In addition to the editing

Property	Description
command	A reference to the Perl function to be called when the button is clicked with mouse button 1. The variable referred to by the **variable** property is updated with the value in the **value** property before the referenced subroutine is invoked.
variable	Takes a reference to a variable and updates with the **value** property when the button is clicked. When the value of the referenced variable matches the **value** property, the button is selected automatically.
onvalue	Specifies the value to store within the variable pointed to by the **variable** property when the button is selected.
offvalue	Specifies the value to store within the variable pointed to by the **variable** property when the button is not selected.
indicatoron	If false (zero), then rather than displaying the check box indicator, it toggles the **relief** base property of the entire widget, effectively making the whole widget the check box.
Method	
select	Selects the check button and sets the **variable** to **value**.
flash	Flashes the button briefly by reversing and resetting the foreground and background colors.
invoke	Starts the subroutine defined in the **command** property.
toggle	Toggles the selection state and values of the button on and off.

Table 13-4. *Properties and Methods for Check Buttons*

features of a **Text** widget, you can also "tag" individual pieces of text and change their properties. This allows you to create a fully featured text editor with multiple font, point size, and color support without any additional programming.

Text widget methods take one or more index specifications as arguments. An argument can be an absolute number (base) or a relative number (base and modifier), and both are specified as strings. Supported base index specifications are shown next. Items in italics indicate the components of the index specification that you can modify. Anything else is a keyword.

```
line.char
```

Indicates the character at **char** characters across (left to right) and **line** lines down (top to bottom). The specification starts at zero for characters within a line, and 1 for lines within a text box.

```
end
```

The end of the text, as defined by the character just after the last newline.

```
insert
```

The location of the insertion cursor.

```
mark
```

The character just after the marker whose name is **mark**.

```
tag.first, tag.last
```

Used to specify the first and last characters of a tag.

These index specifications can also be qualified with an additional modifier:

```
+count chars, -count chars, +count lines, -count lines
```

Adjust the base index specification by the **count** characters or lines.

```
wordstart, wordend, linestart, lineend
```

Adjust the index to point to the first character on the word or line specified by the index (**wordstart**, **linestart**) or to the character immediately after the word or line.

A sample of supported properties and methods is shown in Table 13-5.

For example, to insert a piece of text at the end of a text box:

```
$text->insert('Beginning!', 'end');
```

Or to insert the same piece of text at character 20 on line 5:

```
$text->insert('Beginning!', '5.20');
```

Property	Description
tabs	The list of tab stops for the **Text** widget. Specification should be as a reference to a list of strings. Each string should be composed of a number defining the character location within the line, followed by **l**, **c**, or **r** for left, center, or right justification for the specified tab.
state	One of **normal** for a standard editable text box, or **disabled** for a nonmodifiable text box.
Method	
insert(index [,string [,tag]] ...)	Insert one or more strings with an optional tag at the specified **index**.
delete(index1 [,index2])	Delete the character at **index1** or the text from **index1** to **index2**.
get(index1 [,index2])	Get the character at **index1** or the text from **index1** to **index2**.
index(index)	Returns an absolute index for the corresponding **index** supplied.
see(index)	Returns true if the text at **index** is visible.
markSet(markName, index)	Gives a logical bookmark name to **index**.
markUnset(markName)	Unsets a bookmark.

Table 13-5. *Properties and Methods for **Text** Widgets*

To specify and configure the tags, you need the methods and properties shown in Table 13-6.

For example, to create a simple tag:

```
$text->tagAdd('tagged', '1.0', '3.0');
```

This creates a tag called "tagged" from lines 1 through 3 inclusive. The tag name should be unique because you need it when configuring the options on an individual

Method	Description
tagAdd(tagName [,index1[.index2]] ...)	Adds a tag at the position specified in **index1** or bounded by **index1** and **index2**.
tagRemove(tagName [,index1[.index2]] ...)	Removes the tag from the specified area, but does not delete the actual tag definition.
tagDelete(tagName)	Removes and deletes the tag.
tagConfigure	Configures one or more properties for a tag.
Property	
-foreground, -background, -fgstipple, -bgstipple, -font	As for the basic properties.
-justify	Justification for the tagged text, one of **center**, **left**, and **right**.
-relief, -borderwidth	The border width and relief style.
-tabs	As for basic text properties, but applies only if the first character in that line also belongs to the same tag. You cannot add "subtabs" to a tagged block.
-underline	Underlines the tagged text.

Table 13-6. *Tag Methods and Properties*

tag. Therefore, to change the text tagged with the name "tagged" to 24-point Times, boldfaced:

```
$text->tagConfigure('tagged', font => 'Times 24 Bold');
```

You can also use the **tie** function with a **Text** widget to tie the text box contents to a filehandle. Once tied, you can print and read from the text widget just like any other filehandle. Thus you can create a very simple text file viewer with code like this:

```
use Tk;
```

```
$main = MainWindow->new();
$main->title("Text Viewer");

$maintext = $main->Scrolled('Text');

open(SOURCE, "t.pl") or die "Can't open source";
tie(*TEXT, 'Tk::Text', $maintext);
print TEXT <SOURCE>;
close (SOURCE);

$maintext->pack();

MainLoop();
```

Entry

An **Entry** widget is essentially a single-line text box, and it inherits many of the same features and methods from the **Text** widget. However, because it's only a single line, the indexing and methods are much simpler. The indexing options are as follows:

```
number
```

An index into the widget's contents, starting with zero as the first character.

```
end
```

The end of the text.

```
insert
```

The position immediately after the insertion cursor.

```
sel.first, sel.last
```

Indicates the first and last character of a tag.

The supported properties and methods are shown in Table 13-7.

List Boxes

A **Listbox** widget enables you to create a list, from which you can select an individual item. It displays a list of strings, one per line, and all the strings displayed have the same characteristics. When creating the list, the easiest way to populate it is to create

Property	Description
show	A simple Boolean option. If set, it displays * for each character entered, and is primarily used for password entry. Note that although the characters are displayed in this manner, copying and pasting the contents of a "hidden" field will reveal the real contents.
Method	
get(index)	Gets the string starting at **index**.
insert(index, string)	Inserts **string** at **index**.
index(index)	Returns an absolute index from a relative one.
selectionFrom(index)	Sets the selection from **index** to the end of the field.
selectionTo(index)	Sets the selection from the beginning of the field to **index**.
selection(from, to)	Sets the selection to the characters starting at **from** and ending at **to**.
selectionClear	Clears the selection.
selectionPresent	True if a selection is currently active.

Table 13-7. *Properties and Methods for the **Entry** Widget*

the widget and then use the **insert** method to add items to the list. The **width** and **height** properties for the **Listbox** widget define the width of the list box and the height in characters. Or you can specify values of zero, which will cause the list box to grow to display all of the objects.

Here is an extended example of the **Checkbutton** widget:

```
use Tk;

$main = MainWindow->new();

$list = $main->Listbox(height => 5,
                        width => 0)->pack();

$list->insert('end', qw/Martin Sharon Wendy Sharon Chris/);
```

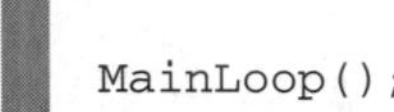

```
MainLoop();
```

The result is shown below. Note that you will need to use the **bind** method shown earlier in this chapter to bind a particular operation, such as a double click, to a function. Within the function, you'll need to use the **get** method to obtain the current selection.

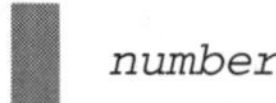

```
number
```

The index of the row, starting with zero for the first element.

```
end
```

Indicates the end of the current row.

```
active
```

Where the location cursor is currently positioned, and the active location appears underlined in the list view.

```
anchor
```

The anchor point of the selection.

The properties and methods supported by the **Listbox** widget are shown in Table 13-8.

Menus

Menus are logically split into **MenuButton** widgets, which are the menu names. The **MenuButton** widget then becomes a container that holds the individual menu item

Property	Description
height, width	The height and width of the list in rows and characters. If either is zero, then the widget resizes to incorporate all of the list elements.
selectMode	Defines the selection mode of the list, one of **single**, **browse**, **multiple**, or **extended**.
Method	
get(index)	Gets the string, starting at **index**.
insert(index, string)	Inserts **string** at **index**.
delete(index [, last])	Deletes the row at **index**, or the rows between **index** and **last**.
see(index)	Brings the element **index** into the current view.
selectionFrom(index)	Selects all the rows from **index** to the end of the list.
selectionTo(index)	Selects all the rows from the beginning of the list to **index**.
selection(from, to)	Selects the rows starting at **from** and ending at **to**.
selectionClear()	Clears the selection.
selectionPresent()	Returns true if there is an active selection.
curselection()	A list of the index values of all the selected items.

Table 13-8. *Properties and Methods Supported by the **Listbox** Widget*

widgets, which are split into different types to allow you to add normal menu items (actually just labels), buttons, check boxes, and radio buttons to your menus.

The normal method for a creating a menu is as follows:

1. Create a menu bar frame, using the **Frame** widget, to hold individual menu buttons.
2. Create the individual menu buttons within the new frame.
3. Use the **MenuButton** widget methods to create the individual menu items.

Every method of the **MenuButton** widget supports a now familiar index format, although the index refers to the individual menu item:

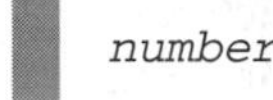

```
number
```

The index of the menu item, starting at zero for the first item. When the menu is configured for tear-off, the first entry is a separator automatically inserted by the widget.

```
end, last
```

Indicates the last entry.

```
active
```

Where the location cursor is currently active.

```
none
```

Indicates that none of the menu options are active.

```
pattern
```

A pattern to be matched against all entries. This only matches exactly; regular expressions are supported.

Properties and methods for the **MenuButton** widget are shown in Table 13-9.

The configurable **options** supported for the methods in Table 13-9 work like all other properties and are listed in Table 13-10. Note that because you can have hierarchical menus, individual items can use further methods from Table 13-9.

Property	Description
indicatorOn	If true, shows a small diamond to the right of the menu.
state	The state of the menu—one of **normal**, **active**, or **disabled**.

Table 13-9. *Properties and Methods Supported by the* ***MenuButton*** *Widget*

Property	Description
Method	
menu	Returns the underlying menu associated with this menu button.
command(options)	Creates the corresponding type of menu item. This is the normal type for a standard menu entry.
separator(options)	A separator.
radiobutton(options)	A radio button menu item.
checkbutton(options)	A check button menu item.
cascade(options)	Inserts a new cascading (hierarchical) menu.
add(type, options)	Adds a new menu of **type** with **options**.
delete(index1 [, index2])	Deletes the menu item **index1** or the items from **index1** to **index2**.
insert(index1, type, options)	Inserts a menu item of **type** with **options** into the location **index1**.
entryconfigure(index, options)	Changes the properties of the menu item pointed to by **index**.
entrycget(index)	Gets the configuration options for the menu item at **index**.

Table 13-9. *Properties and Methods Supported by the **MenuButton** Widget* (continued)

Property	Description
indicatorOn	If true, places a small diamond next to the menu option, which allows an option to be toggled on and off by a menu.
selectColor	The color of the indicator, if **indicatorOn** is true.

Table 13-10. *Configurable **options** Supported for the **MenuButton** Widget Methods*

Property	Description
tearOff	If true, the first element of the menu is a separator. Clicking on the separator "tears off" the menu into a separate top-level window. This is not always supported on all implementations.
foreground, **background**, **font**, **image**, **indicatorOn**	The base properties.
label	The text to use for the menu item. This should be used in place of the normal **text** property.
underline	The index of a character to underline. This is used in combination with the **accelerator** property to indicate which keyboard shortcut should be used for this menu.
accelerator	Shows the string to be displayed, right justified, as the keyboard equivalent for the menu option. This doesn't bind the key to the command for you; you'll have to do that separately.
state	Status is **normal**, **active**, or **disabled**.
command	The reference of a subroutine to call when the menu item is selected.
value	The value of the attached radio button (see Table 13-3).
variable	The variable used to store **value**.
onvalue, **offvalue**	Identical to the options in Table 13-4 for check button style entries.

Table 13-10. *Configurable* ***options*** *Supported for the* ***MenuButton*** *Widget Methods* (continued)

For example, to create a simple Help menu, you might use a script like this:

```
use Tk;

$main = MainWindow->new();

$menu = $main->Frame()->pack(side => 'top');
```

```
$help_menu = $menu->Menubutton(text        => 'Help',
                               relief      => 'raised',
                               borderwidth => 2,
                               )->pack(side => 'left',
                                       padx => 2
                                       );

$help_menu->command('-label'    => 'About',
                    accelerator => 'Meta+A',
                    underline   => 0,
                    command     => sub { print "All about me\n" }
                    );

$help_menu->separator();

$help_menu->command('-label'    => 'Help Index',
                    accelerator => 'Meta+H',
                    underline   => 0,
                    command => \&draw_help_window(),
                    );

$help_menu->command('-label' => 'Help on Help',
                    command   => sub { print "Try Help Index\n" }
                    );

MainLoop();
```

The result can be seen in Figure 13-3.

Frame

A **Frame** widget is simply a container for other widgets. It's used when you need to create a complex layout that requires more advanced geometry management than you can normally do with the available tools. The way it works is that you divide individual areas of the window into frames and pack the collection of objects into the frame. For example, you might create a new frame that contains the menu bar, which you gravitate to the top of the window, while the actual menu buttons within the menu bar are arranged horizontally. We'll see an example later in this chapter when we look at the **Scale** widget.

Scroll Bars

Scroll bars are available either as separate widgets, in which case you are responsible for managing the corresponding widget you are scrolling, or they can be automatically added to any suitable widgets. We'll deal with the automatic scroll bars first. To create an

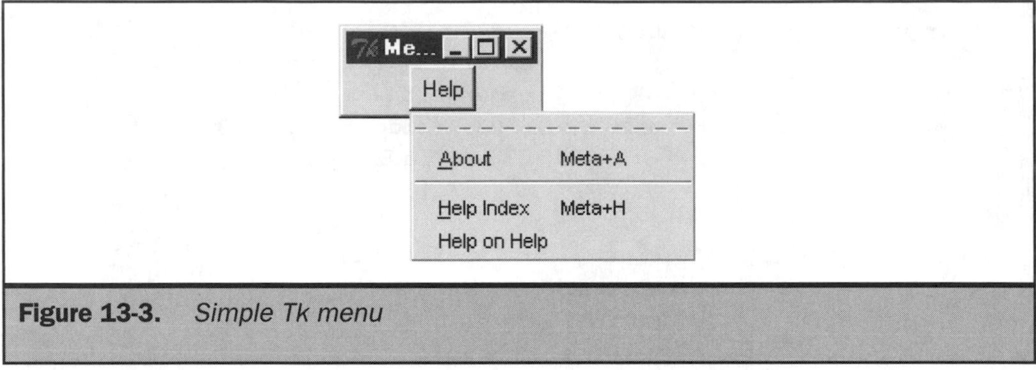

Figure 13-3. *Simple Tk menu*

automatically scrolled widget, you use the special **Scrolled** widget method, and then specify the type of widget to create with a scroll bar.

For example, here's the line from the text viewer that creates a scrolled **Text** widget:

```
$maintext = $main->Scrolled('Text');
```

Internally, this creates a **Frame** widget that contains the main **Text** widget and the horizontal (and vertical) scroll bars. The reference returned actually refers to the newly created **Frame** widget.

Alternatively, you can create and manage your own scroll bars using the methods and properties in Tables 13-11 and 13-12. The methods in Table 13-11 allow you to set

Property	Description
command	A reference to a subroutine used to change the view in the widget.
Method	
set(first, last)	Indicates the current view. The **first** and **last** elements should be fractions between 0 and 1. For example, a value of 0.1 and 0.2 should indicate that the area between 10 percent and 20 percent of the item should be shown.
get	Returns the current scroll bar settings.

Table 13-11. *Properties and Methods for Scroll Bars*

the current view within the widget to which you want to associate the scroll bar. The **set** function controls the current view, and the **command** property is called when the scroll bar is moved.

All widgets that are scrollable also support the methods and properties shown in Table 13-12. The properties define the functions and increments that the scroll bars control. The scroll bar automatically calls the specified method (**xview** or **yview**) on the widget.

Many of the properties and methods of the scroll bar are shared by the **Scale** widget.

Scale

Scales are like thermometers. You define a size and range, and the widget displays a horizontal or vertical slider. The slider automatically has a label (if you've defined one)

Property	Description
xscrollincrement, **yscrollincrement**	The scrolling, x and y, will be down in the specified increments.
xscrollcommand, **yscrollcommand**	A reference to the function used to reposition the widget when the scroll bar is moved.
Method	
xview('moveto', fraction) **yview('moveto', fraction)**	Changes the view, where **fraction** indicates the leftmost, or topmost, character or pixel.
xview('scroll', number, what) **yview('scroll', number, what)**	Indicates that the view should be moved up or down, or left or right, for **number** increments. If **what** is "units," then it is scrolled according to the increment in the **xscrollincrement** and **yscrollincrement** properties. If **what** is "pages," then the widget is scrolled **number** pages.

Table 13-12. *Properties and Methods for **Scrollable** Widgets*

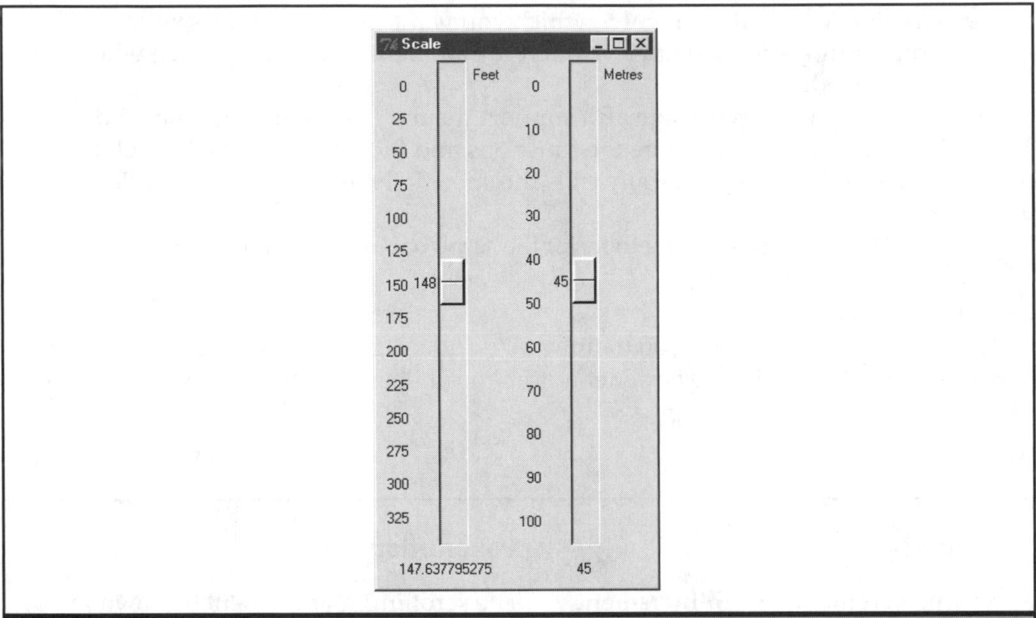

Figure 13-4. *A **Scale** widget for converting feet into meters*

and tick marks to indicate individual divisions. You can see a sample in Figure 13-4, and we'll look at the code required to build this application shortly.

The supported properties and methods are shown in Table 13-13.

Property	Description
command	Reference to a subroutine, called when the scale's value is changed.
variable	Reference to a variable to be updated whenever the slider moves. Works like **variable** base property; updating this value will also set the slider position.
width, **length**	The width and length of the scale in pixels (not characters).
orient	Allows you to select **horizontal** or **vertical** orientation.

Table 13-13. *Properties and Methods for **Scale** Widgets*

Property	Description
from, to	The real range of values that the widget should scale **from** and **to**.
resolution	The value displayed and set into **variable** will always be a multiple of this number. The default is 1.
tickinterval	The spacing, in real values, between tick marks on the scale.
label	The label to be displayed to the top (horizontal) or left (vertical) scale.
Method	
set(value)	Identical to modifying the value of **variable**.

Table 13-13. *Properties and Methods for* ***Scale*** *Widgets* (continued)

Here's the script that generated Figure 13-4. It provides a simple tool for converting feet into meters and vice versa.

```
use Tk;

my ($feetscale, $metrescale) = (0,0);

$main = MainWindow->new();

$feetframe = $main->Frame()->pack(side => 'left');

$feetframe->Scale(command     => \&update_feet,
                  variable     => \$feetscale,
                  width        => 20,
                  length       => 400,
                  orient       => 'vertical',
                  from         => 0,
                  to           => 328,
                  resolution   => 1,
                  tickinterval => 25,
                  label        => 'Feet'
                  )->pack(side => 'top');

$feetframe->Label(textvariable => \$feetscale)->pack(side => 'top',
                                                     pady => 5);
```

```
$metreframe = $main->Frame()->pack(side => 'left');

$metreframe->Scale(command      => \&update_metre,
                   variable     => \$metrescale,
                   width        => 20,
                   length       => 400,
                   orient       => 'vertical',
                   from         => 0,
                   to           => 100,
                   resolution   => 1,
                   tickinterval => 10,
                   label        => 'Metres'
                   )->pack(side => 'top');

$metreframe->Label(textvariable => \$metrescale)->pack(side => top,
                                                        pady => 5);

MainLoop();

sub update_feet
{
    $metrescale = $feetscale/3.280839895;
}

sub update_metre
{
    $feetscale = $metrescale*3.280839895;
}
```

A **Frame** widget is used to specify two frames, side by side, and then within each frame the scale and the floating-point value are shown one above the other.

Controlling Window Geometry

Throughout this chapter you've seen examples of the **pack** function, and you already know it is a required element of the window-building process. However, there are some tricks you can do with **pack** to aid in the arrangement of individual widgets within a window. Tk also supports two other methods of arranging widgets: the placer and the grid. You must use the same geometry manager within a single parent, although it's possible to mix and match individual geometry managers within a single window to suit your needs.

The placer requires some careful planning to use properly, since you must specify the location of each widget within the window using x, y coordinates. This is the same system used within the Bulletin Board widget under Motif and Visual Basic, so people moving from these systems may be more comfortable with this system. The grid geometry manager uses a simple table layout, as you might use within a word processor or when designing web pages with HTML. Each widget is placed into a table cell, and you specify its location by defining the row and column in which the widget should appear. Individual widgets can span multiple rows and columns if necessary. As with the placer geometry manager, you will need to give some careful thought to how to lay out your widgets in this system.

The packer geometry manager is the one we've been using in this chapter, and it's the most practical if you do not want to think too much about the geometry management process. If you want details on the systems, please see the documentation that comes with the Perl/Tk module.

Packer

The packer geometry manager is similar to Motif's Form widget and uses a much simpler system for defining the location of widgets within a frame of a window. Remember that the **pack** function is just that—it only provides the algorithm used to organize the layout of widgets. Individual calls to the **pack** method pack the corresponding widget into the next available space within the frame or window. This means that widgets are added to the window or frame in the order they are packed. This is similar to how you would pack a bag, or fill a shelf: you start from a single point and add items until the space is all used up.

The algorithm works like this:

1. Given a frame, the packer attaches a widget to a particular side (top, bottom, left, or right).
2. The space used up by the widget is taken off from the space available in the frame. This area is called the parcel. If the widget does not fill the parcel completely (if it is wider or taller than the area sliced for the widget), then that space is essentially wasted. This is in fact the reason for supporting additional **Frame** widgets to make the best of the space.
3. The next widget is then placed into the remaining space, and once again the widget can attach itself to the top or bottom of the available space.
4. Note that all widgets that specify a particular anchor point will be grouped together and share that space. Thus, if you specify multiple widgets with "left" anchor, they will be organized left-to-right within the frame. Once again, if you want to do more complex layouts (as in the **Scale** widget example), you will need to create separate frames.

The available options to the packer method are shown in Table 13-14. Like other elements of the Tk system, options are specified as a hash to the **pack** method.

Property	Description
side	The side of the frame to which the widget should be added. Should be one of **left**, **right**, **top**, or **bottom**.
fill	Specifies whether the widget should fill up the space in the parcel in the **x** or **y** direction accordingly. You can also specify **both**, to fill in both directions, or **none**, to prevent filling altogether. The **ipadx** or **ipady** options can be used to specify some additional blank padding space around the widget within the parcel.
expand	Specifies whether the widget should expand to take up all of the remaining space after the other widgets have been placed. This is useful for **Textbox** widgets where you are defining an outer menu and toolbar and want the main widget to take up all the remaining space.
padx, pady	The number of pixels to use as spacing between widgets.
ipadx, ipady	The number of pixels to use as spacing around a widget that is "filling" the space provided by the parcel.

Table 13-14. *Options to the* ***pack*** *Function*

If you do not specify an option, the packer geometry manager inserts widgets from top to bottom.

Easing the Process

If you are designing a static window for your Perl script rather than one with many dynamic elements, you may find the **SpecPerl** application of some use. It's the Perl/Tk version of **SpecTcl**, a GUI designer, which is itself written in Tcl and Perl. With the **SpecPerl** application, you can lay out widgets of static pages by simply dragging and dropping the individual elements into a window and configuring the properties such as fonts and colors from familiar lists, instead of hand coding everything. **SpecPerl** creates all the Perl/Tk code for you; all you need to do is supply the rest of the code to go with it.

It's primarily aimed at producing simple form-based windows for data entry and other similar static window development, although it may also provide you with enough base code to start you on your way with Tk development. **SpecPerl** development is handled by Mark Kvale, and you can download the latest version from http://www.keck.ucsf.edu/~kvale/specPerl.

The Complete Reference

Part V

Perl for the Web

Chapter 14

The Web Environment

Perl has for a long time had aproven track record within the development of website, largely because of its ease of use, speed of development, and advanced text processing facilities. Things that we take for granted within Perl, such as splitting up lines and performing regular expressions, are difficult within other languages. Although it's unfair to tar Perl as being purely a web programming language (see Chapter 25), it's also true that Perl's web strengths are probably the one aspect of the language that has helped to propel it into the forefront of many web development projects.

Understandably, with all this history, Perl has a lot of modules and scripts that can be used for all sorts of web-related tasks. The standard Perl distribution comes with a number of modules for dealing with CGI requests, and CPAN contains innumerable modules for all sorts of web programming tricks. We'll be examining many of these modules and some sample scripts in this and the next chapter.

Specifically for this chapter, however, I want to concentrate on the environment in which Perl scripts are executed. We'll start by looking at the issues surrounding the basics of web development. The first section covers HTML, the language of the web, and includes some of the easier ways to generate HTML within Perl. For a brief diversion, we'll look into URLs, the Uniform Resource Locators that are used to address machines, web pages, and other resources on the Internet. There are some traps when using them and some tricks for easing the process.

We'll then move on to the physical environment of a web application. Web-based applications work differently from just about every other application. They are not strictly stand-alone or client-server applications. Although information can flow both ways, the methods used to transfer information between the user's browser and the web server are not immediately obvious. We'll be looking, therefore, both at the environment in which a web script runs and how to access and control the information flow between the browser and the server.

The scripts and principles here have been made as generic as possible, although there are some differences between the different platforms when installing and using Perl scripts on your web server. Please see Chapters 21 through 24 for more information.

HTML

The core of any web application is HTML (Hypertext Markup Language). Despite what design agencies and professional web authors tell you, it is not difficult to learn and use. What is difficult, however, is ensuring that the HTML you have generated does what you want and displays correctly. A lot of the complexity comes from the coding required to produce the format and layout of the HTML you are writing; a much smaller but perhaps more significant proportion comes from the semantics of the HTML itself.

I don't really want to get into the precise details on how HTML is formed. If you want more information on how to write good HTML, refer to the www.w3c.org

website, which gives full details. Alternatively, visit a bookstore and select almost any HTML title off the shelf. HTML is a simple text format that uses tags to format text in different point sizes and type styles. For example,

```
<b>Hello World!</b>
```

would produce a boldfaced "Hello World!" within a web browser window. The tags are the <b> at the beginning of the text section and the </b> at the end.

This format is used throughout HTML coding; so the fragment

```
<i>Hello World!</i>
<u>This is a test message</u>
```

would produce "Hello World!" in italics and "This is a test message" underlined. This tagging technique has developed over the years, and actually it borrows a lot from the principles of typesetting systems where they used tags within a document to indicate how the manual typesetter should lay out a document. It's interesting to see that the old techniques are still practical, even though the technology that uses them has moved on.

One very useful tag is <a>, which is short for "anchor" or "address." It denotes the hypertext links that allow you to jump from one HTML document to another. Another significant tag is <img…, which allows you to incorporate graphics into your pages. Unlike the other links discussed so far, there is no closing tag, since you are simply inserting another element into the web page.

Creating HTML is normally a case of using **print** or a here document to output text with the tags as part of the quoted strings. The danger is that you could generate HTML that is missing tags or contains badly formed tags that don't produce what you expect. The problem is not a lack of knowledge, just a typographical error like those you can introduce into any piece of typed text.

As an alternative, you can use a number of modules to produce "clean" HTML for you. They do this not by checking and cleaning the HTML as it is produced, but instead through the use of functions to generate the individual textual elements. For example, the **CGI** module, which is part of the standard Perl distribution, provides a number of functions that add the correct tags around a piece of text to format it within HTML. For example,

```
h1('All About Me');
```

correctly produces

```
<H1>All About Me</H1>
```

You don't have to worry about ensuring that the tags are correct, or that they are opened, closed, or terminated properly. It is all done for you. We'll be looking at other features of the **CGI** module throughout this and the next chapter. You might also want to view the reference information contained in Appendix E.

Uniform Resource Locators

Before we continue, we need to take a slight detour to ensure that you understand the basic principles of how the Internet, and more specifically the World Wide Web, is used. Everybody who uses the Internet uses Uniform Resource Locators. A URL is an address for a resource on the Internet that consists of the protocol to be used, the address of the server, and the path to the file that you want to access. For example, the address

```
http://www.mcwords.com/index.shtml
```

indicates that you want to use the HTTP protocol, that you are connecting to the machine known as www.mcwords.com, and that you want to retrieve the file index.shtml.

URLs can also incorporate login names, passwords, and optional service port number information:

```
http://anonymous:pass@ftp.mcwords.com:1025/cgi/sendme.pl?info.zip
```

The example above shows downloading information from the server ftp.mcwords.com, using service port 1025, with a login of **anonymous** and a password of **pass**.

Also shown in the example above is the feature that we are particularly interested in with respect to Perl. Although it's difficult to tell with any certainty from the URL above, it looks like you're accessing a Perl script called sendme.pl. Rather than the server returning the contents of the Perl script, it will instead be executed. You've supplied it some information—in this case the name of a file (info.zip)—although exactly what the script does is not clear.

This demonstrates, from the browser end, how an end-user executes a script on a server. The user accesses a URL. The file path that he supplies is parsed by the web server, which identifies the file that the user has requested as, in fact, a script, and executes. What the script is, what it does, or indeed what language it is written in are completely hidden from the user. Although by convention Perl scripts terminate in .pl, this does not guarantee that the script you are accessing is a Perl script.

Now let's take a wider look at the whole process, including how the script interacts with the web server software.

Web Operation Overview

At the start of this chapter I stated that a web-based application using a Perl script is not really a client-server application. In fact, a web application (written in Perl or any other language) exhibits many traits of a client-server application, even though the connection is not permanent. The definition of a client-server application is one that makes use of the client to act as a user interface to a server, which hosts the information and runs the application. The client does not store any data, and the server does not provide any user interface.

In some systems, both ends can do some form of processing on the information. In the case of a web application, the browser supports a certain amount of processing. You can select check boxes and pop-up lists. If you need more complex systems, you can use JavaScript or even Java to provide a more interactive client interface.

What the server provides is a communications channel for exchanging information between the stored information and the client. With a web server, the information includes the HTML files, graphics, animations, and other downloadable elements. It also includes any other data sources that can be accessed via an application, and this is where CGI scripts are used.

Here's the normal execution sequence of a user accessing a script on a web server:

1. The user's browser (the client) opens a connection to the server.
2. The user's browser requests a URL from the server.
3. The server parses the URL and determines whether a file is to be returned, or whether it needs to run an external application. For this run-through we'll assume the latter.
4. The external application is called. This can be a binary executable, a batch file, a shell script, an **awk** script, or perhaps one written in Python. For us though, we're only interested in Perl scripts.
5. Any additional information supplied by the user's browser, such as that from a form, is supplied to the application, either using an environment variable, or by passing the data as a stream to the application's standard input.
6. Any output produced by the application is sent back directly to the user's browser.

This is a very simplified outline of how the process works, but it does show the basic process. The steps we are interested in are 4, 5, and 6.

In step 4, you need to think about the environment in which an application is executed. The environment defines the physical and logical confines of the Perl script you want to run. In addition to the standard environment variables such as **PATH**, there is also some web-specific information. In step 5, you have to extract any information supplied by the browser, either from one of the environment variables, which is called the **GET** method, or from the standard input, which is called the **POST** method. In step 6, you have to know how to communicate information back to the user's browser.

We'll take a look at each of these issues separately in the next few sections of this chapter.

The Environment

The environment in which a script is run does not directly affect the script's execution, but it will affect the information that is available to your script, both that supplied by the user, and that related to the specifics of the web script itself. What you really need to know is the environment variables that are available within the confines of your script. You can see a list of the most useful environment variables in Table 14-1.

Environment Variable	Description
DOCUMENT_ROOT	The root document directory for this web server.
GATEWAY_INTERFACE	The interface name and version number.
HTTP_ACCEPT	The formats accepted by the browser. This information is optionally supplied by the browser when it first requests the page from the server. In our the example, the default types accepted include all of the major graphics types (GIF, JPEG, X bitmap), as well as all other MIME types (*/*).
HTTP_ACCEPT_CHARSET	The character sets accepted by the browser.
HTTP_ACCEPT_ENCODING	Any special encoding formats supported by the browser. In our the example, Netscape supports Gzip-encoded documents; they will be decoded on the fly at the time of receipt.
HTTP_ACCEPT_LANGUAGE	The languages accepted by this browser. If supported by the server, then only documents of a specific language will be returned to the browser.

Table 14-1. *Web Server Environment Variables for CGI Scripts*

Environment Variable	Description
HTTP_CONNECTION	Any HTTP connection directives. In our example, the only directive is "Keep-Alive," a typical directive that forces the server to keep a web server process and the associated network socket dedicated to this browser until a defined period of inactivity.
HTTP_HOST	The server host (without domain).
HTTP_USER_AGENT	The name, version number, and platform of the remote browser. In our the preceding example output, this was Mozilla (Netscape—actually Microsoft Internet Explorer) v4.5b2, for Macintosh PPC. Don't be fooled into thinking that the name Mozilla applies only to Netscape; other browsers, including Microsoft Internet Explorer, also report themselves as being Mozilla browsers; this helps with compatibility, even though all browsers render HTML differently.
PATH	The PATH for the CGI script.
QUERY_LENGTH	The length of the query information. It's available both for **GET** and **POST** requests, and it can help with the security of the scripts you produce.
QUERY_STRING	The query string, used with **GET** requests.
REMOTE_ADDR	The IP address of the browser.
REMOTE_HOST	The resolved name of the browser.
REMOTE_PORT	The remote port of the browser machine.
REQUEST_METHOD	The request method, for example, **GET** or **POST**.

Table 14-1. *Web Server Environment Variables for CGI Scripts* (continued)

Environment Variable	Description
REQUEST_URI	The requested URI (Uniform Resource Identifier).
SCRIPT_FILENAME	The full path to the CGI script.
SCRIPT_NAME	The name of the CGI script.
SERVER_ADMIN	The email address of the web server administrator.
SERVER_NAME	The fully qualified name of the server.
SERVER_PORT	The server port number.
SERVER_PROTOCOL	The protocol (usually HTTP) and version number.
SERVER_SOFTWARE	The name and version number of the server software that is being used. This can be useful if you want to introduce a single script that makes use of specific features of multiple web servers.
TZ	The time zone of the web server.

Table 14-1. *Web Server Environment Variables for CGI Scripts* (continued)

The exact list supported depends on your web server, and also on the instance in which the URL was requested. For pages that are displayed as the result of a referral, you will also get a list of "referrer" information—the site from which the reference to the requested URL was made. You can find out this information using a CGI script like the one below. Don't worry too much about the detail of this script at this stage.

```
print "Content-type: text/html\n\n";

print "<font size=+1>Environment</font><p>\n";

foreach (sort keys %ENV)
{
    print "$_: $ENV{$_}<br>\n";
}
```

On my web server, which is Apache 1.2.6 running under Solaris 2.4, the following ends up being displayed within a browser window (Microsoft Internet Explorer for Mac 4.5):

```
DOCUMENT_ROOT: /usr/local/http/webs/disobedience
GATEWAY_INTERFACE: CGI/1.1
HTTP_ACCEPT: image/gif, image/x-xbitmap, image/jpeg, image/pjpeg,
image/xbm, image/x-jg, */*
HTTP_ACCEPT_LANGUAGE: en
HTTP_CONNECTION: Keep-Alive
HTTP_EXTENSION: Security/Remote-Passphrase
HTTP_HOST: disobedience.mchome.com
HTTP_IF_MODIFIED_SINCE: Sat, 01 May 1999 10:25:34 GMT
HTTP_UA_CPU: PPC
HTTP_UA_OS: MacOS
HTTP_USER_AGENT: Mozilla/4.0 (compatible; MSIE 4.5; Mac_PowerPC)
PATH: /usr/sbin:/usr/bin
QUERY_STRING:
REMOTE_ADDR: 198.112.10.134
REMOTE_HOST: sulaco
REMOTE_PORT: 2546
REQUEST_METHOD: GET
REQUEST_URI: /cgi/webenv.cgi
SCRIPT_FILENAME: /usr/local/http/webs/disobedience/cgi/webenv.cgi
SCRIPT_NAME: /cgi/webenv.cgi
SERVER_ADMIN: webmaster@mchome.com
SERVER_NAME: disobedience.mchome.com
SERVER_PORT: 80
SERVER_PROTOCOL: HTTP/1.1
SERVER_SOFTWARE: Apache/1.2.6
TZ: GB
```

You can glean lots of useful information from this that you can use in your script. For example, the **SCRIPT_NAME** environment variable contains the name of the CGI script that was accessed by the client. The most important fields as far as a CGI program are concerned, however, are the **REQUEST_METHOD**, which defines the method used to transfer the information (request) from the browser, through the web server, to the CGI application.

The **QUERY_LENGTH** defines the number of bytes contained in the query when using the **POST** method. This is useful primarily for verifying that some data has been supplied (and therefore needs processing). However, if used properly, it can also be used to aid in the security of your web scripts. See "Security" later in this chapter for more information. The **QUERY_STRING** is the environment variable used to store the data from the client's browser when using the **GET** method.

The Common Gateway Interface

The Common Gateway Interface, or CGI, is a set of standards that define how information is exchanged between the web server and a script. In fact, web applications are often called CGI scripts, but don't make the mistake of calling a CGI script simply "CGI." The term CGI refers to the standards and isn't the name of an application.

The part of the process you need to worry about at this stage is the transfer of information from the browser, through the web server, to the CGI script. The reason you need to accept information is to enable you to process information entered into an HTML form. For example, the form shown in Figure 14-1 comes from my own site and is used to accept book errors.

Each of the fields in the form can contain free-form data or, in the case of the "Type" and "Book Title" fields, the information in the pop-up menus. The information and definition of the form is done in HTML. Although in this case a static file supplies the definition, there is no reason why it couldn't be script driven.

When the user clicks the Send button, the information will be transferred to the web server and then on to the CGI script. The CGI script to be used is defined within the HTML definition for the form. The information is transferred using one of two main

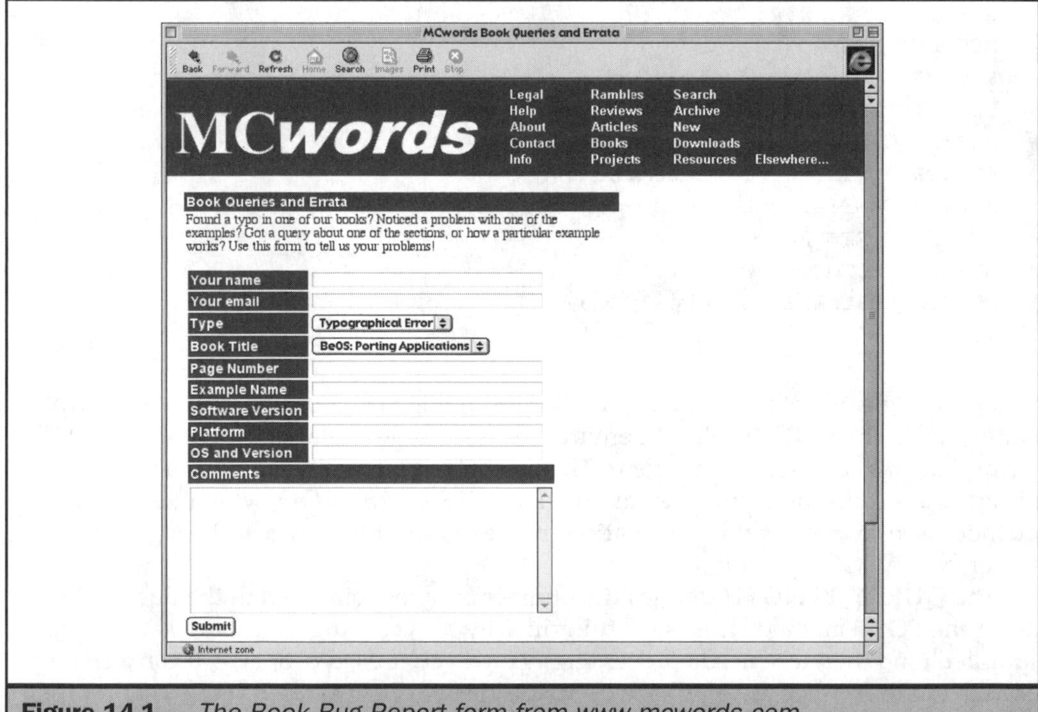

Figure 14-1. *The Book Bug Report form from www.mcwords.com*

methods, **GET** and **POST**. The difference between the two methods is directly attributable to how the information is transferred. With the **GET** method, the information is placed into the **QUERY_STRING** environment variable, and with the **POST** method, the information is sent to the standard input of the application that has been called. There are other methods supported for transferring information, but these are the main two that are used.

There are advantages and disadvantages to both methods. The **GET** method supports two ways of transferring information from the client. With **GET** you can supply information either through HTML forms or through the use of an extended URL. If you remember, back at the start of this chapter we looked at the following URL:

```
http://anonymous:pass@ftp.mcwords.com:1025/cgi/sendme.pl?info.zip
```

The sendme.pl is the name of a script, and the question mark indicates the start of the information that you want to supply to the script. This has major benefits because you can generate new URLs and include the information as links in normal HTML pages, thus saving time. The limitation is that the **GET** method has a limited transfer size. Although there is officially no limit, most people try to keep **GET** method requests down to less than 1K (1,024 bytes). Also note that because the information is placed into an environment variable, your OS might have limits on the size of either individual environment variables or the environment space as a whole.

The **POST** method has no such limitation. You can transfer as much information as you like within a **POST** request without fear of any truncation along the way. However, you cannot use a **POST** request to process an extended URL. For the **POST** method, the **QUERY_LENGTH** environment variable contains the length of the query supplied, and it can be used to ensure that you read the right amount of information from the standard input.

No matter how the field data is transferred, there is a format for the information that you need to be aware of before you can use the information. The HTML form defines a number of fields, and the name and contents of the field are contained within the query string that is supplied. The information is supplied as name/value pairs, separated by ampersands (**&**). Each name/value pair is then also separated by an equal sign. For example, the query string below shows two fields, **first** and **last**:

```
first=Martin&last=Brown
```

Splitting these fields up is easy within Perl. You can use **split** to do the hard work for you.

One final note, though, is that many of the characters you may take for granted are encoded so that the URL is not misinterpreted. Imagine what would happen if my name contained an ampersand or equal sign!

The encoding, like other elements, is very simple. It uses a percent sign, followed by a two-digit hex string that defines the ASCII character code for the character in question. So the string "Martin Brown" would be translated into

```
Martin%20Brown
```

where 20 is the hexadecimal code for ASCII character 32, the space. You may also find that spaces are encoded using a single "+" sign—the example below accounts for both formats.

Armed with all this information, you can use something like the **init_cgi** function below to access the information supplied by a browser. The function supports both **GET** and **POST** requests:

```
sub init_cgi
{
    my $length = $ENV{QUERY_LENGTH};
    my $query = $ENV{QUERY_STRING};
    my (@assign);

    if (defined($query))
    {
        @assign = split('&',$query);
    }
    elsif (defined($length) and $length > 0 )
    {
        sysread(STDIN, $_, $length);
        chomp;
        @assign = split('&');
    }
    foreach (@assign)
    {
        my ($name,$value) = split /=/;
        $value =~ tr/+/ /;
        $value =~ s/%([a-fA-F0-9][a-fA-F0-9])/pack("C", hex($1))/eg;
        if (defined($formlist{$name}))
        {
            $formlist{$name} .= ",$value";
        }
```

```
            else
            {
                $formlist{$name} = $value;
            }
        }
    }
```

The steps are straightforward, and they follow the description. First of all you access the query string, either by getting the value of the **QUERY_STRING** environment variable or by accepting input up to the length specified in **QUERY_LENGTH**, from standard input using the **sysread** function. Note that you must use this method rather than the **<STDIN>** operator because you want to ensure that you read in the entire contents, irrespective of any line termination. HTML forms provide multiline text entry fields, and using a line input operator could lead to unexpected results. Also, it's possible to transfer binary information using a **POST** method, and any form of line processing might produce a garbled response. Finally, it acts as a security check. Many "denial of service" attacks prey on the fact that a script accepts an unlimited amount of information while also tricking the server into believing that the query length is small or even unspecified. If you arbitrarily imported all the information provided, you could easily lock up a small server.

Once you have obtained the query string, you split it by an ampersand into the **@assign** array and then process each field/value pair in turn. For convenience, you place the information into a hash. The keys of the hash become the field names, and the corresponding values become the values as supplied by the browser. The most important trick here is the line

```
$value =~ s/%([a-fA-F0-9][a-fA-F0-9])/pack("C", hex($1))/eg;
```

This uses the functional replacement to a standard regular expression to decode the **%xx** characters in the query into their correct values.

To encode the information back into the URL format within your script, the best solution is to use the **URI::Escape** module by Gisle Aas. This provides a function, **uri_escape**, for converting a string into its URL escaped equivalent. You can also use the **uri_unescape** to convert it back. See Appendix E for more information.

Using the above function you can write a simple Perl script that reports the information provided to it by either method:

```
#!/usr/local/bin/perl -w
```

```
print "Content-type: text/html\n\n";

init_cgi();
print("Form length is: ", scalar keys %formlist, "<br>\n");

for my $key (sort keys %formlist)
{
    print "Key $key = $formlist{$key}<br>\n";
}
```

If you place this on a server and supply it a URL such as

```
http://www.mcwords.com/cgi/test.cgi?first=Martin&last=Brown
```

the browser window reports back:

```
Form length is: 2
Key first = Martin
Key last = Brown
```

Success!

Of course, most scripts do other things besides printing the information back. Either they format the data and send it on in an email, or search a database, or a myriad of other tasks. What has been demonstrated here is how to extract the information supplied via either method into a suitable hash structure that you can use within Perl. How you use the information depends on what you are trying to achieve.

The process detailed here has been duplicated many times in a number of different modules. The best solution, though, is to use the facilities provided by the standard **CGI** module. This comes with the standard Perl distribution and should be your first point of call for developing web applications. We'll be taking a closer look at the **CGI** module in the next chapter.

Communicating Information Back

Communicating information back to the user is so simple, you'll be looking for ways to make it more complicated. In essence, you print information to **STDOUT**, and this is then sent back verbatim to the browser.

The actual method is more complex. When a web server responds with a static file, it returns an HTTP header that tells the browser about the file it is about to receive. The header includes information such as the content length, encoding, and other information. It then sends the actual document back to the browser. The two elements—the header and the document—are separated by a single blank line. How the browser treats the document it receives is then a combination of the information supplied by the HTTP header and the extension of the file it receives. This allows you to send back a binary file (such as an image) directly from a script by telling the application what data format the file is encoded with.

When using a CGI application, the HTTP header is not automatically attached to the output generated, so you have to generate this information yourself. This is the reason for the

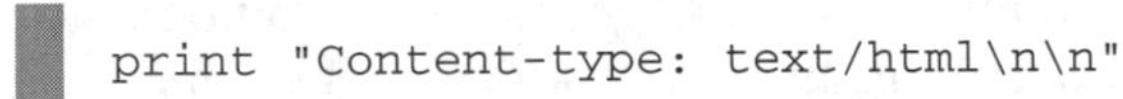

```
print "Content-type: text/html\n\n";
```

lines in the previous examples. This indicates to the browser that it is accepting a file using **text** encoding in **html** format. There are other fields you can return in the HTTP header, which we'll look at now.

HTTP Headers

The HTTP header information is returned as follows:

```
Field: data
```

The case of the **Field** name is important, but otherwise you can use as much white space as you like between the colon and the field data. A sample list of HTTP header fields is shown in Table 14-2.

Field	Meaning
Allow: list	A comma-delimited list of the HTTP request methods supported by the requested resource (script or program). Scripts generally support **GET** and **POST**; other methods include **HEAD, POST, DELETE, LINK,** and **UNLINK**.
Content-Encoding: string	The encoding used in the message body. Currently the only supported formats are Gzip and compress. If you want to encode data this way, make sure you check the value of **HTTP_ACCEPT_ENCODING** from the environment variables.

Table 14-2. *HTTP Header Fields*

Field	Meaning
Content-type: string	A MIME string defining the format of the file being returned.
Content-length: string	The length, in bytes, of the data being returned. The browser uses this value to report the estimated download time for a file.
Date: string	The date and time the message is sent. It should be in the format 01 Jan 1998 12:00:00 GMT. The time zone should be GMT for reference purposes; the browser can calculate the difference for its local time zone if it has to.
Expires: string	The date the information becomes invalid. This should be used by the browser to decide when a page needs to be refreshed.
Last-modified: string	The date of last modification of the resource.
Location: string	The URL that should be returned instead of the URL requested.
MIME-version: string	The version of the MIME protocol supported.
Server: string/string	The web server application and version number.
Title: string	The title of the resource.
URI: string	The URI that should be returned instead of the requested one.

Table 14-2. *HTTP Header Fields* (continued)

The only required field is Content-type, which defines the format of the file you are returning. If you do not specify anything, the browser assumes you are sending back preformatted raw text, not HTML. The definition of the file format is supplied by a MIME string. MIME is short for Multipurpose Internet Mail Extensions and is a slash-separated string that defines the raw format and a subformat within it. For example, text/html says the information returned is plain text, using HTML as a file format. Mac users will be familiar with the concept of file owners and types, and this is the basic model employed by MIME.

Other examples include application/pdf, which states that the file type is application (and therefore binary) and that the file's format is pdf, the Adobe Acrobat file format. Others you might be familiar with are image/gif, which states that the file is a GIF file, and application/zip, which is a compressed file using the Zip algorithm.

This MIME information is used by the browser to decide how to process the file. Most browsers will have a mapping that says they deal with files of type image/gif so that you can place graphical files within a page. They may also have an entry for application/pdf, which either calls an external application to open the received file or passes the file to a plug-in that optionally displays the file to the user. For example, here's an extract from the file supplied by default with the Apache web server:

```
application/mac-binhex40        hqx
application/mac-compactpro      cpt
application/macwriteii
application/msword              doc
application/news-message-id
application/news-transmission
application/octet-stream        bin dms lha lzh exe class
application/oda                 oda
application/pdf                 pdf
application/postscript          ai eps ps
application/powerpoint          ppt
application/remote-printing
application/rtf                 rtf
application/slate
application/wita
application/wordperfect5.1
application/x-bcpio             bcpio
application/x-cdlink            vcd
application/x-compress
application/x-cpio              cpio
application/x-csh               csh
application/x-director          dcr dir dxr
```

It's important to realize the significance of this one, seemingly innocent, field. Without it, your browser will not know how to process the information it receives. Normally the web server sends the MIME type back to the browser, and it uses a lookup table that maps MIME strings to file extensions. Thus when a browser requests image.gif, the server sends back a Content-type field value of image/gif. Since a script is executed by the server rather than sent back verbatim to the browser, it must supply this information itself.

Other fields in Table 14-2 are optional, but they also have useful applications. The Location field can be used to automatically redirect a user to an alternative page without using the normal **RELOAD** directive in an HTML file. The existence of the Location field automatically instructs the browser to load the URL contained in the field's value. Here's another script that uses the earlier **init_cgi** function and the Location HTTP field to point a user in a different direction:

```
init_cgi();

respond("Error: No URL specified")
    unless(defined($SCGI::formlist{url}));

open(LOG,">>/usr/local/http/logs/jump.log")
    or respond("Error: A config error has occurred");

print LOG (scalar(localtime(time)),
           " $ENV{REMOTE_ADDR} $SCGI::formlist{url}\n");
close(LOG)
    or respond("Error: A config error has occurred");

print "Location: $SCGI::formlist{url}\n\n";

sub respond
{
    my $message = shift;
    print "Content-type: text/html\n\n";
    show_debug();
    print <<EOF;
<head>
<title>$message</title>
</head>
<body>
$message
</body>
EOF
    exit;
}
```

This is actually a version of a script used on a number of sites I have developed that allows you to keep a log of when a user clicks onto a foreign page. For example, you might have links on a page to another site, and you want to be able to record how many people visit this other site from your page. Instead of using a normal link within your HTML document, you could use the CGI script:

```
<a href="/cgi/redirect.pl?url=http://www.mcwords.com">MCwords</a>
```

Every time users click on this link, they will still visit the new site, but you'll have a record of their leap off of your site.

Document Body

You already know that the document body should be in HTML. To send output, you just print to **STDOUT**, as you would with any other application. In an ideal world, you should consider using something like the **CGI** module to help you build the pages correctly. It will certainly remove a lot of clutter from your script, while also providing a higher level of reliability for the HTML you produce. Unfortunately, it doesn't solve any of the problems associated with a poor HTML implementation within a browser.

However, because you just print the information to standard output, you need to take care with errors and other information that might otherwise be sent to **STDERR**. You can't use **warn** or **die**, because any message produced will not be displayed to the user. While this might be what you want as a web developer (the information is usually recorded in the error log), it is not very user friendly.

The solution is to use something like the function shown in the previous redirection example to report an error back to the user. Again, this is an important thing to grasp. There is nothing worse from a user's point of view than this displayed in the browser:

```
Internal Server Error

The server encountered an internal error or misconfiguration and
was unable to complete your request.
Please contact the server administrator, webmaster@mchome.com and
inform them of the time the error occurred, and anything you might
have done that may have caused the error.
```

Security

The number of attacks on Internet sites is increasing. Whether this is due to the meteoric rise of the number of computer crackers, or whether it's just because of the number of companies and hosts who do not take it seriously is unclear. The fact is, it's incredibly easy to ensure that your scripts are secure if you follow some simple guidelines. However, before we look at solutions, let's look at the types of scripts that are vulnerable to attack:

- Any script that passes form input to a mail address or mail message
- Any script that passes information that will be used within a subshell
- Any script that blindly accepts unlimited amounts of information during the form processing

The first two danger zones should be relatively obvious: anything that is potentially executed on the command line is open to abuse if the attacker supplies the right information. For example, imagine an email address passed directly to **sendmail** that looks like this:

```
mc@foo.bar;(mail mc@foo.bar </etc/passwd)
```

If this were executed on the command line as part of a **sendmail** line, the command after the semicolon would mail the password file to the same user—a severe security hazard if not checked. You can normally get around this problem by using taint checking to highlight the values that are considered unsafe. Since input to a script is either from standard input or an environment variable, the data will automatically be tainted. See Chapter 11 for more details on enabling and using tainted data.

There is a simple rule to follow when using CGI scripts: don't trust the size, content, or organization of the data supplied.

Here is a checklist of some of the things you should be looking out for when writing secure CGI scripts:

- Double-check the field names, values, and associations before you use them. For example, make sure an email address looks like an email address, and that it's part of the correct field you are expecting from the form.
- Don't automatically process the field values without checking them. As a rule, come up with a list of ASCII characters that you are willing to accept, and filter out everything else with a simple regular expression.
- Check the input size of the variables or, better still, of the form data. You can use the **$ENV{CONTENT_LENGTH}** field, which is calculated by the web server, to check the length of the data being accepted on **POST** methods. Some web servers supply this information on **GET** requests, too.
- Don't assume that field data exists or is valid before use; a blank field can cause as many problems as a field filled with bad data.
- Don't ever return the contents of a file unless you can be sure of what its contents are. Arbitrarily returning a password file when you expected the user to request an HTML file is open to severe abuse.
- Don't accept that the path information sent to your script is automatically valid. Choose an alternative **$ENV{PATH}** value that you can trust, hardwiring it into the initialization of the script. While you're at it, use **delete** to remove any environment variables you know you won't use.
- If you are going to accept paths or file names, make sure they are relative, not absolute, and that they don't contain **..**, which leads to the parent directory. An attacker could easily specify a file of ../../../../../../../../etc/passwd, which would reference the password file from even a deep directory.

- Always validate information used with **open**, **system**, **fork**, or **exec**. If nothing else, ensure any variables passed to these functions don't contain the characters **;| ()**. Better still, think about using the **fork** and piped **open** tricks you saw in Chapter 10 to provide a safe interface between an external application and your script.
- Ensure your web server is not running as **root**, which opens up your machine to all sorts of attacks. Run your web server as **nobody**, or create a new user specifically for the web server, ensuring that scripts are readable and executable only by the web server owner, and are not writable by anybody.
- Use Perl in place of **grep** where possible. This will negate the need to make a system call to search file contents. The same is true of many other commands and functions, such as **pwd** and even **hostname**. There are tricks for gaining information about the machine you are on without resorting to calling external commands. For a start, refer back to Table 14-1. Your web server provides a bunch of script-relevant information automatically for you. Use it.
- Don't assume that hidden fields are really hidden—users will still see them if they view the file source. And don't rely on your own encryption algorithms to encrypt the information supplied in these hidden fields. Use an existing system that has been checked and is bug free, such as the **DES** module available from your local CPAN archive.
- Use taint check, or in really secure situations, use the **Safe** or **Opcode** module. See Chapter 11 for more details.

If you follow these guidelines, you will at least reduce your risk from attacks, but there is no way to completely guarantee your safety. A determined attacker will use a number of different tools and tricks to achieve his goal.

Again, at the risk of repeating myself: don't trust the size, content, or organization of the data supplied.

Chapter 15

Web Programming

In the previous chapter you saw some of the principles behind programming in Perl for the web. In this chapter, we'll be taking a closer look at the programming process and some of the techniques you will need to use when programming for the web. Since you already know how to obtain information supplied on a web form, we will instead concentrate on the semantics and process for the script contents. In particular, we'll examine the **CGI** module, web cookies, the debug process, and how to interface to other web-related languages.

We'll start by taking a look at the use of the standard **CGI** module for generating HTML documents and for producing and processing the contents of web forms. The **CGI** module removes a lot of the complexities of writing good HTML and reduces (but doesn't solve) the problems related to writing syntactically correct web pages.

Then we'll move on to cookies. A cookie is a small data structure used to store information between individual accesses to a web server. These are the storage holders used when you visit sites for e-commerce or those that provide a customized page based on preferences you have previously supplied. The actual cookie data is stored in the user's browser, not on the server, and so the information is valid across a number of script invocations from the same machine and browser.

Then we'll look at the methods required for debugging and testing CGI applications. An extra level of complication has been added now; you can't use **warn** or **die**, and the Perl debugger won't help either. You therefore need a different system for debugging your scripts. The final section gives a brief overview of the processes involved in cooperating with other languages, such as Java and JavaScript.

The CGI Module

The **CGI** module started out as a separate module available from CPAN. It's now included as part of the standard distribution and provides a much easier interface to web programming with Perl. As well as providing a mechanism for extracting elements supplied on a form, it also provides an object-oriented interface to building web pages and, more usefully, web forms. You can use this interface either in its object-oriented format or with a simple functional interface.

Along with the standard CGI interface and the functions and object features supporting the production of "good" HTML, the module also supports some of the more advanced features of CGI scripting. These include the support for uploading files via HTTP and access to cookies—something we'll be taking a look at later in this chapter. For the designers among you, the **CGI** module also supports cascading style sheets and frames. Finally, it supports server push—a technology that allows a server to send new data to a client at periodic intervals. This is useful for pages and especially images that need to be updated. This has largely been superseded by the client-side **RELOAD** directive, but it still has its uses.

For example, you can build a single CGI script for converting Roman numerals into integer decimal numbers using the following script. It not only builds and produces the

HTML form, but also provides a method for processing the information supplied when the user fills in and submits the form.

```
#!/usr/local/bin/perl -w

use CGI qw/:standard/;

print header,
       start_html('Roman Numerals Conversion'),
       h1('Roman Numeral Converter'),
       start_form,
       "What's the Roman Numeral number?",
       textfield('roman'),p,
       submit,
       end_form,p,hr,p;

if (param())
{
    print(h3('The value is ',
            parse_roman(uc(param('roman')))),p,hr);
}

sub parse_roman
{
    $_ = shift;
    my %roman = ('I' => 1,
                 'V' => 5,
                 'X' => 10,
                 'L' => 50,
                 'C' => 100,
                 'D' => 500,
                 'M' => 1000,
                 );
    my @roman = qw/M D C L X V I/;
    my @special = qw/CM CD XC XL IX IV/;
    my $result = 0;

    return 'Invalid numerals' unless(m/[IVXLXDM]+/);

    foreach $special (@special)
    {
        if (s/$special//)
```

```
        {
            $result += $roman{substr($special,1,1)}
                           - $roman{substr($special,0,1)};
        }
    }
    foreach $roman (@roman)
    {
        $result += $roman{$roman} while s/$roman//;
    }
    return $result;
}
```

The first part of the script prints a form using the functional interface to the **CGI** module. It provides a simple text entry box, which you then supply to the **parse_roman** function to produce an integer value. If the user has provided some information, you use the **param** function to check this; the information is printed after a new form has been provided. You can see what a sample screen looks like in Figure 15-1.

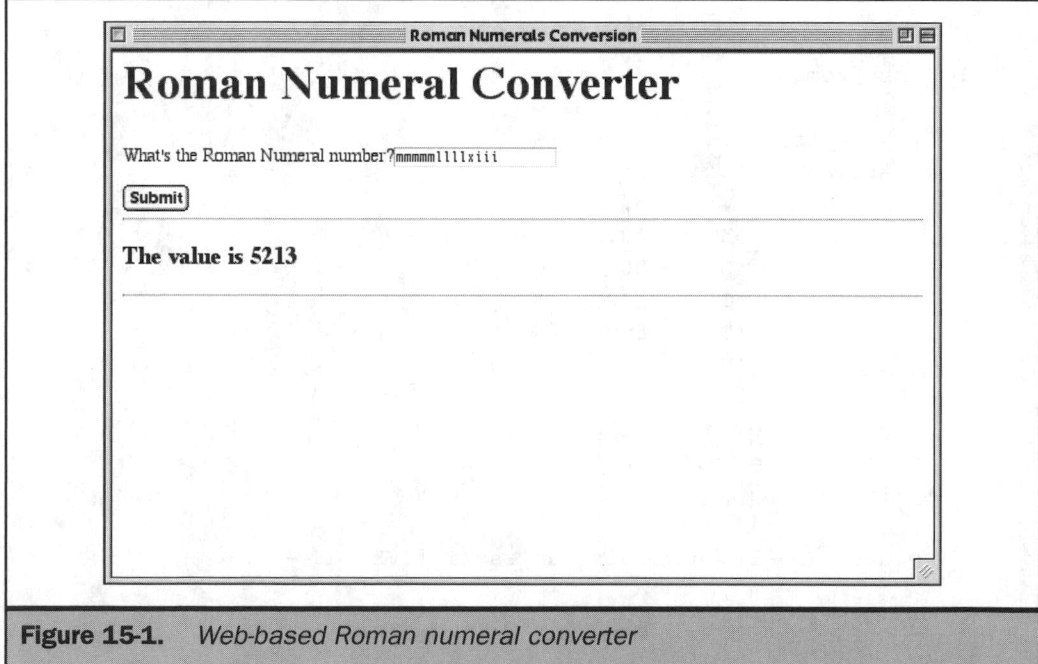

Figure 15-1. *Web-based Roman numeral converter*

Because you are using the functional interface, you have to specify the routines or sets of routines that you want to import. The main set is **:standard**, which is what is used in this script. See Appendix E for a list of other supported import sets. Let's look a bit more closely at that page builder:

```
print header,
      start_html('Roman Numerals Conversion'),
      h1('Roman Numeral Converter'),
      start_form,
      "What's the Roman Numeral number?",
      textfield('roman'),p,
      submit,
      end_form,p,hr,p;
```

The **print** function is used, since that's how you report information back to the user. The **header** function produces the HTTP header (see Chapter 14). You can supply additional arguments to this function to configure other elements of the header, just as if you were doing it normally. You can also supply a single argument that defines the MIME string for the information you are sending back, for example:

```
print header('text/html');
```

If you don't specify a value, the text/html value is used by default. The remainder of the lines use functions to introduce HTML tagged text. You start with **start_html**, which starts an HTML document. In this case it takes a single argument—the page title. This returns the following string:

```
<HTML><HEAD><TITLE>Roman Numerals Conversion</TITLE>
</HEAD><BODY>
```

This introduces the page title and sets the header and body style. The **h1** function formats the supplied text in the header level-one style.

The **start_form** function initiates an HTML form. By default, it assumes you are using the same script—this is an HTML/browser feature rather than a Perl CGI feature, and the **textfield** function inserts a simple text field. The argument supplied defines the name of the field as it will be sent to the script when the Submit button is pressed. To specify additional fields to the HTML field definition, you pass the function a hash, where each key of the hash should be a hyphen-prefixed field name; so you could rewrite the above as:

```
textfield(-name => 'roman')
```

Other fields might include **–size** for the size of the text field on screen and **–maxlength** for the maximum number of characters accepted in a field.

Other possible HTML field types are **textarea**, for a large multiline text box, or **popup_menu**, for a menu field that pops up and provides a list of values when clicked. You can also use **scrolling_list** for a list of values in a scrolling box, and check boxes and radio buttons with the **checkbox_group** and **radio_group** functions. See Appendix E for details.

Returning to the example script, the **submit** function provides a simple Submit button for sending the request to the server, and finally the **end_form** function indicates the end of the form within the HTML text. The remaining functions **p** and **hr** insert a paragraph break and horizontal rule, respectively.

This information is printed out for every invocation of the script. The **param** function is used to check whether any fields were supplied to the script, either by a **GET** or **POST** method. It returns an array of valid field names supplied, for example:

```
@fields = param();
```

Since any list in a scalar context returns the number of elements in the list, this is a safe way of detecting whether any information was provided. The same function is then used to extract the values from the fields specified. In the example there is only one field, roman, which contains the Roman numeral string entered by the user.

The **parse_roman** function then does all the work of parsing the string and translating the Roman numerals into integer values. I'll leave it up to the reader to determine how this function works.

This concludes our brief look into the use of the **CGI** module for speeding up and improving the overall processing of producing and parsing the information supplied on a form. Admittedly, it makes the process significantly easier. Just look at the previous examples to see the complications involved in writing a non-**CGI**–based script. Also, check out the script at the end of this chapter, where we look at how Perl can be used for writing JavaScript applications. It uses here documents. Although you can argue that it works, it's not exactly neat. But to be fair, the bulk of the complexity centers around the incorporation of the JavaScript application within the HTML document that is sent back to the user's browser.

Cookies

A cookie is a small discrete piece of information used to store information within a web browser. The cookie itself is stored on the client, rather than server, end and can therefore be used to store state information between individual accesses by the browser, either in the same session or across a number of sessions. In its simplest form, a cookie might just store your name; in a more complex system, it provides login and password information for a website. This can be used by web designers to provide customized pages to individual users.

In other systems, cookies are used to store the information about the products you have chosen in web-based stores. The cookie then acts as your "shopping basket," storing information about your products and other selections.

In either case, the creation of a cookie and how you access the information stored in a cookie are server-based requests, since it's the server that uses the information to provide the customized web page, or that updates the selected products stored in your web basket. There is a limit to the size of cookie, and it varies from browser to browser. In general, a cookie shouldn't need to be more than 1,024 bytes, but some browsers will support sizes as large as 16,384 bytes, and sometimes even more.

A cookie is formatted much like a CGI form field data stream. The cookie is composed of a series of field/value pairs separated by ampersands, with each field/value additionally separated by an equal sign. The contents of the cookie is exchanged between the server and client during normal interaction. The server sends the cookie updates back as part of the HTTP headers, and the browser sends the current cookie contents as part of its request to the server.

Besides the field/value pairs, a cookie has a number of additional attributes. These are an expiration time, a domain, a path, and an optional secure flag.

- The expiration time is used by the browser to determine when the cookie should be deleted from its own internal list. As long as the expiration time has not been reached, the cookie will be sent back to the correct server each time you access a page from that server.
- The definition of a valid server is stored within the domain attribute. This is a partial or complete domain name for the server that should be sent to the cookie. For example, if the value of the domain attribute is .foo.bar, then any server within the foo.bar domain will be sent the cookie data for each access.
- The path is a similar partial match against a path within the web server. For example, a path of /cgi-bin means that the cookie data will only be sent with any requests starting with that path. Normally, you would specify "/" to have the cookie sent to all CGI scripts, but you might want to restrict the cookie data so it is only sent to scripts starting with /cgi-public, but not to /cgi-private.
- The secure attribute restricts the browser from sending the cookie to unsecure links. If set, cookie data will only be transferred over secure connections, such as those provided by SSL.

The best interface is to use the **CGI** module, which provides a simple functional interface to updating and accessing cookie information. For example, you can create a cookie like this:

```
$cookie = cookie(-name => 'SiteCookie',
                 -value => \%webvalues,
                 -expires => '+24h',
                 -path => '/',
                 -domain => '.foo.bar'
                );
```

If you update the values of the cookie, then it must be supplied back to the user as part of the HTTP header, like this:

```
print header(-cookie => $cookie);
```

To access the values, call the **cookie** function without the **–values** argument:

```
my %cookie_values = cookie(-name => 'SiteCookie');
```

Since the use of the cookie information is related to the standard CGI field information, there is little I can add to the process. Anything you can do with Perl can be done with a CGI script, and anything you can do with a CGI script can be augmented with cookies.

See the end of this chapter for an example use of a cookie, albeit using JavaScript rather than Perl, that demonstrates some of the flexibility of the cookie system.

Debugging and Testing CGI Applications

Although it sounds like an impossible task, sometimes you need to test a script without requiring or using a browser and web server. Certainly, if you switch warnings on and use the **strict** pragma, your script may well **die** before reporting any information to the browser if Perl finds any problems. This can be a problem if you don't have access to the error logs on the web server, which is where the information will be recorded.

You may even find yourself in a situation where you do not have privileges or even the software to support a web service on which to do your testing. Any or all of these situations require another method for supplying a query to a CGI script and alternative ways of extracting and monitoring error messages from your scripts.

The simplest method is to supply the information that would ordinarily be supplied to the script via a browser using a more direct method. Because you know the information can be supplied to the script via an environment variable, all you have to do is create the environment variable with a properly formatted string in it. For example, for the **phone.pl** script you might use the following lines for a Bourne shell:

```
QUERY_STRING='first=Martin&last=Brown'
export QUERY_STRING
```

This is easy if the query data is simple, but what if the information needs to be escaped because of special characters? In this instance, the easiest thing is to grab a **GET**-based URL from the browser, or get the script to print a copy of the escaped query string, and then assign that to the environment variable. Still not an ideal solution.

As another alternative, if you use the **init_cgi** from the previous chapter, or the **CGI** module, you can supply the field name/value pairs as a string to the standard input. Both will wait for input from the keyboard before continuing if no environment query string has been set. It still doesn't get around the problem of escaping characters and sequences, and can be quite tiresome for scripts that expect a large amount of input.

All of these methods assume that you cannot (or do not want) to make modifications to the script. If you are willing to make modifications to the script, then it's easier, and sometimes clearer, just to assign sample values to the form variables directly; for example, using the **init_cgi** function:

```
$SCGI::formlist{name} = 'MC';
```

Or if you are using the **CGI** module, then you need to use the **param** function to set the values. You can either use a simple functional call with arguments,

```
param('name','MC');
```

or you can use the hash format:

```
param(-name => 'name', -value => 'MC');
```

Just remember to unset these hard-coded values before you use the script; otherwise you may have trouble using the script effectively!

For monitoring errors there are a number of methods available. The most obvious is to use **print** statements to output debugging information (remember that you can't use **warn**) as part of the HTML page. If you decide to do it this way, remember to output the errors *after* the HTTP header; otherwise you'll get garbled information. In practice, your scripts should be outputting the HTTP header as early as possible anyway.

Another alternative is to use **warn**, and in fact **die**, as usual, but redirect **STDERR** to a log file. If you are running the script from the command line under Unix using one of the previous techniques, you can do this just by using the normal redirection operators within the shell; for example:

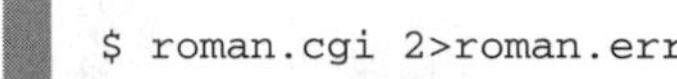

```
$ roman.cgi 2>roman.err
```

Alternatively, you can do this within the script by restating the association of **STDERR** with a call to the **open** function:

```
open(STDERR, ">>error.log") or die "Couldn't append to log file";
```

Note that you don't have to do any tricks here with reassigning the old **STDERR** to point elsewhere; you just want **STDERR** to point to a static file.

One final piece of advice: if you decide to use this method in a production system, remember to print out additional information with the report so that you can start to isolate the problem. In particular, consider stacking up the errors in an array just using a simple **push** call, and then call a function right at the end of the script to dump out the date, time, and error log, along with the values of the environment variables. I've used a function similar to the one below to dump out the information at the end of the CGI script. The **@errorlist** array is used within the bulk of the CGI script to store the error lines:

```
sub error_report
{
    open (ERRORLOG, ">>error.log") or die "Fatal: Can't open log $!";
    $old = select ERROR;
    if (@errorlist)
    {
        print scalar localtime,"\n\n";
        print "Environment:\n";
        foreach (sort %ENV)
        {
            print "$_ = $ENV{$_}\n";
        }
        print "\nErrors:\n";
        print join "\n",@errorlist;
    }
    select $old;
}
```

That should cover most of the bases for any errors that might occur. Remember to try to be as quick as possible, though—the script is providing a user interface, and the longer users have to wait for any output, the less likely they are to appreciate the work the script is doing. I've seen some, for example, that post information on to other scripts and websites, and even some that attempt to send email with the errors in. These can cause both delays and problems of their own. You need something as plain and simple as the **print** statements and an external file to ensure reliability; otherwise you end up trying to account for and report errors in more and more layers of interfaces.

Remember as well that any additional modules you need to load when the script initializes will add seconds to the time to start up the script: anything that can be avoided should be avoided. Alternatively, think about using the **mod_perl** Apache module. This provides an interface between Apache and Perl CGI scripts. One of its major benefits is that it caches CGI scripts and executes them within an embedded Perl interpreter that is part of the Apache web server. Additional invocations of the script do not require reloading. They are already loaded, and the Perl interpreter does not need to be invoked for each CGI script. This helps both performance and memory management.

Interfacing to Other Web Languages

There are two main web languages, Java and JavaScript. Java is a full developmental language in its own right and works with separate applets that provide information and applications as part of a web page. They are included within the page just like images. Because of their self-contained nature, there is little you can do within the realms of a CGI script that isn't already handled by the interaction methods you already know about.

Java has its own communications toolbox for using TCP/IP as a communications medium, so you might consider using Perl as a backend to a Java development. If so, look at Chapter 9 rather than here for more information. If your Java application uses calls to URLs and CGI scripts, you already know how to extract information and process it in order to give replies back. It's up to the Java applet to make sense of what it receives.

For JavaScript, the interface is slightly different. JavaScript programs are included within the HTML of the page itself. This means you can "write" JavaScript applications within Perl. All you have to do is output the JavaScript elements as part of the HTML response. Here's a very simple (and slightly messy) example:

```
#!/usr/local/bin/perl -w

use ConfigDB;

print "Content-type: text/html\n\n";

my @currs = sort get_currency_list();

print <<EOF;
<HTML>
<HEAD>
<TITLE>Systems Configurator - Which product family?</TITLE>
```

```
 <SCRIPT language="JavaScript">

  <!-- Hide from older browsers
  var bikky = document.cookie;

var currency = new blankArray(20);
EOF

for(my $i=0;$i<@currs;$i++)
{
    print 'currency[',$i,']="',$currs[$i],'";',"\n";
}

print <<EOF;
  function getCookie(name) {
    var index = bikky.indexOf(name + "=");
    if (index == -1) return null;
    index = bikky.indexOf("=", index) + 1;
    var endstr = bikky.indexOf(";", index);
    if (endstr == -1) endstr = bikky.length;
    return unescape(bikky.substring(index, endstr));
  }

function deleteCookie (name) {
  if (getCookie(name)) {
    document.cookie = name + "=" + "; expires=Thu, 01-Jan-70 00:00:01 GMT";
  }
}
  var today = new Date();
  var expiry = new Date(today.getTime() + 28 * 24 * 60 * 60 * 1000);

  function setCookie(name) {
    document.cookie = eval('"' + name + '=" + escape(' + name + ') + "; expires=' +
           expiry.toGMTString() + '"');
    bikky = document.cookie;
  }

  function blankArray(arrayLength) {
    this.length = arrayLength;
    for (var i=0; i < this.length; i++)
      this[i] = "";
  }

  function defineCookie(newData) {
    Choice01 = newData[0];
    for (var i=1; i < newData.length; I++)
```

```
      Choice01 += "!" + newData[i];
    setCookie("Choice01");
  }

  function resetCurrency() {
  deleteCookie("Choice01");
  history.go(0);
  }

// data[0] = bgcolour; data[1] = userName; data[2] = headCount
  var Choice01 = getCookie("Choice01");
  if (Choice01 == null)
    Choice01 = "UD";

  var numVars = 1;
  var start = Choice01.indexOf("!") + 1;
  while (start != 0) {
    numVars++;
    start = Choice01.indexOf("!", start) + 1;
  }
  var data = new blankArray(numVars);
  for (var i=0; i < data.length; i++) {
    var end = Choice01.indexOf("!", start);
    if (end == -1) end = Choice01.length;
    data[i] = Choice01.substring(start, end);
    start = end + 1;
  }
  // Stop hiding -->


</SCRIPT>
</HEAD>

<SCRIPT>
//document.write("Current Currency: " + currency[data[0]] + "<br>");

if (currency[data[0]] == null)
{
document.write("<FORM name=\\"ChoiceTest\\" METHOD=POST> \\
<br>\\
Please choose the currency in which you would like to see prices displayed:<br>  \\
<br> \\
<table><tr><td width=10><br></td><td width=428> \\
<center> \\
<select name=data0 size=9> \\
```

```
EOF

foreach $currency (sort @currs)
{
    print "<option>$currency \\\n";
}

print <<EOF;
</select> \\
<br><br> \\
<input type=button value=\\"Continue...\\" onClick=\\" \\
  with (this.form) { \\
    data[0] = data0.selectedIndex; \\
    data[1] = currency[data0.selectedIndex]; \\
  } \\
  defineCookie(data); \\
  history.go(0);\\
 \\"><br><br> \\
</center></tr></table> \\
</FORM>     \\
");
}
else
{
var mycur = currency[data[0]];
var curtext = mycur.split(" ").join("+");

document.write(" \\
Click on the product you're interested in:<br> \\
<H3><A HREF=\\"/cgi-bin/
config.pl?range=workstation&curr="+curtext+"\\">Workstations</A></H3><BR> \\
<H3><A HREF=\\"/cgi-bin/
config.pl?range=server&curr="+curtext+"\\">Servers</A></H3><BR> \\
<H3><A HREF=\\"/cgi-bin/
config.pl?range=notebook&curr="+curtext+"\\">Notebooks</A></H3><BR> \\
<h3><A HREF=\\"JavaScript: resetCurrency();\\">Respecify Currency</a></h3><br>\\
");
}
</script>

</BODY>
</HTML>
EOF
```

I developed this for a client (Hewlett-Packard) as part of an exercise in developing the existing Computer Systems Buyer's Guide. The idea was to use a cookie to store users' currency choices when they wanted to configure a particular computer. The different currencies were supported as part of a larger DBM database using a roughly relational structure. The list of available currencies depended on the status of the workstation servers and other equipment available in each country. The problem encountered was how to populate the JavaScript application (which created, updated, and accessed the cookie, building the page as it went) with the "current" list of currencies based on the contents of the database.

The result is the previous script. The first screen produced by the script can be seen in Figure 15-2. It provides a list of currencies currently configured and active in the database.

Once the user selects a currency and clicks the Continue button, a cookie with the selected currency is created. If the user has a cookie, the information provided is a list of links with the built-in currency selection, as seen in Figure 15-3.

As a very early beta version, it has some rough edges, and JavaScript actually accounts for much more of the generated HTML page than Perl. There is no reason

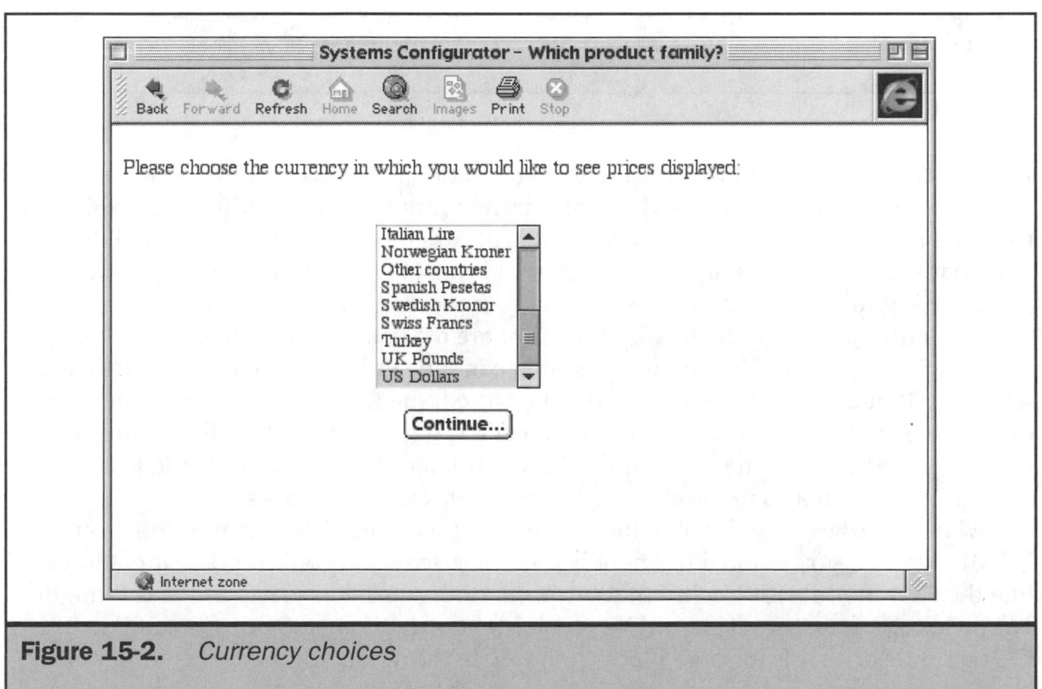

Figure 15-2. *Currency choices*

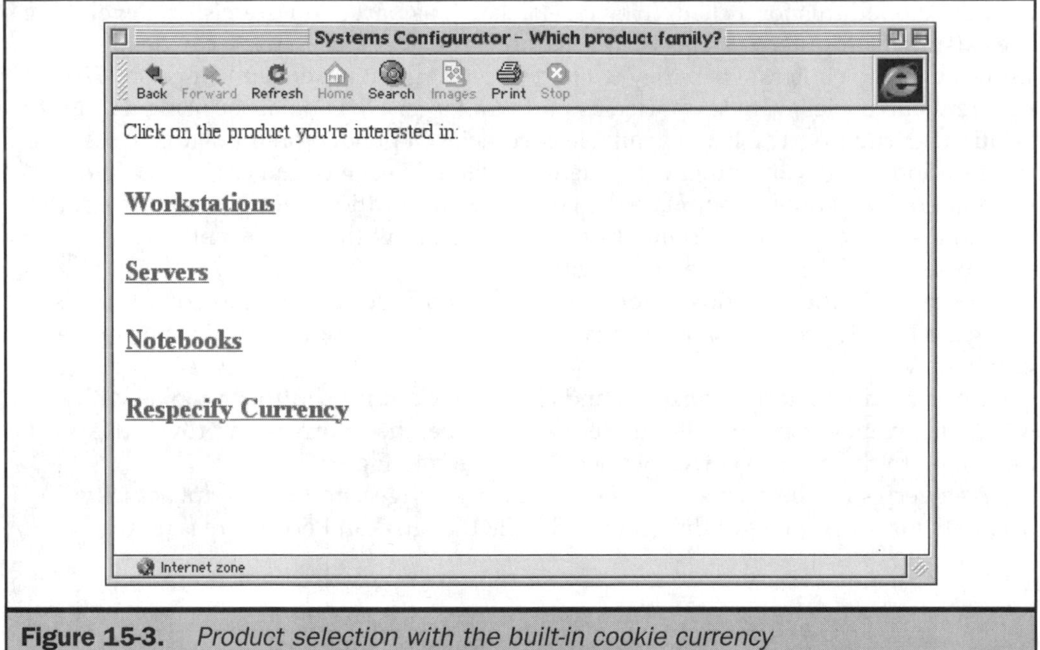

Figure 15-3. *Product selection with the built-in cookie currency*

why I couldn't have used Perl for the cookie creation. There's certainly no reason why the CGI scripts used to provide the configuration forms for the products couldn't have used the methods for accessing cookies shown earlier in this chapter to divine the information. The only reason I chose this route was to try to eliminate the problems associated with modifying the existing configuration scripts.

The important things to note in this script are the backslashes. These are a vital part of a JavaScript program, which uses them to combine individual lines into single lines. Also note that the double quotes need to be backslashed. This is not a Perl requirement, but a JavaScript requirement, since HTML code is written out within the confines of the JavaScript. Indeed, the method required is no different from producing the HTML within Perl, which also requires backslashed quotes in some places.

What Perl doesn't do is solve the problem of producing JavaScript within your HTML pages. If you wanted to, there is no reason why you couldn't develop a toolkit like the **CGI** module for exactly that purpose. With some well-designed and thought out JavaScript functions it should be possible to create a general-purpose toolkit. The **CGI** module does this in some places to improve the quality of the forms it builds.

As a postscript—and as is always the way—the script as seen here was never used. In fact the whole project for improving the system was dropped.

The Complete Reference

Part VI

Getting "Inside" Perl

Chapter 16

Under the Hood

For many people, their understanding of Perl extends up to this point, if you have followed this book sequentially. However, there is a lot more to the language, even within the realms of writing a simple program. Some of it has been hinted at already—pragmas, the different processes in the execution of a Perl script, and some of the internal structures used by Perl to represent information.

In this chapter we'll lift the hood of the Perl engine and have a look at how the language works at its lowest level and how we can affect that behavior. Our first goal is to examine the individual components that make up the Perl interpreter. By examining each component of the system, you should gain an insight into how the entire application works. Armed with this information, we'll then dig further and follow the execution process of a script from the time it has finished being written to the point at which it completes its execution cycle, including all the intervening steps.

Next, we'll look at Perl pragmas—instructions to the interpreter that change the behavior of either the interpreter or the elements that make up a Perl program, including the variables, functions, and even the regular expression engine. Some of the pragmas can become a vital part of the programming process, and by using many of them in every script, you can learn how to write better, more efficient code, without relying on the Perl interpreter to assume too much about what you are trying to achieve.

Since you know the internal processes involved in interpreting and executing a Perl program, it makes sense to examine how some common errors are introduced in scripts. By using the same information, you can also speed up the execution of your scripts. These investigations will include examining the reasons why some statements are more efficient than others, and why you might prefer the inefficient version to the optimized version.

Perl Internals

There comes a time for most programmers when they want to understand how a particular application works. For many commercial applications, this information is just not available. But for open source projects such as Perl, anybody can go along and read the source code for the application. The more inquisitive may even go off and do their own thing (see the sidebar, "Every Hacker's Goals"). In this chapter, the aim is really to take a step back from that level of detail and instead look at the architecture and process involved in interpreting and executing a script.

My intention is not to dissuade you from examining the source code if you want to. The code is available, and despite the fact that it's largely uncommented and is composed of a number of complex macros and optimizations, it's still readable by a hardened C programmer. My best suggestion is to get the latest source and start by examining the source code for the different variable types (hv.c for hash values and so on). Once comfortable with the concepts there, you should then move on to the op.c and doop.c, which handle the opcode (see the "Opcodes" section), before finally examining the execution process in run.c, preferably with a debugger such as **gdb** or the debugger that comes with Microsoft's Developer Studio Product.

Every Hacker's Goals

It has been said, by others as well as me, that the ultimate dream of all serious computer programmers is to achieve three simple goals in their lifetime:

- Write their own computer language
- Write their own operating system
- Build their own computer from individual components (microchips, resistors, and so on)

I'm pleased to say that I've managed to achieve all three, although for the last two I'm not sure that an embedded computer for controlling a model lift is what one would call a real achievement.

I should probably add at this point that you should not confuse the term "hacker" with the term "cracker." A hacker is someone who enjoys toying with computers and, often, programming them. A cracker is a malicious individual who tries to break in (crack) to a secure program, website, nuclear facility, and so on. Don't get the two mixed up; you'll offend a hacker by calling him a cracker!

If want to skip the technicals and examine the lexical process of converting the written Perl script into the internal structures and opcodes, then look at perly.y. This is a **yacc** definition file that outlines the main components and structures for the Perl language. Some of the more complex lexical analysis is hand coded within the other source files, most notably toke.c. For regular expressions, Perl uses a modified standard regular expression library, although all of the functionality has actually been from scratch. The regular expression compiler and executor are in the regcomp.c and regexec.c files, respectively.

If you want to avoid the source code, or perhaps just cannot follow it, three tools are available on CPAN (see Appendix A) that provide access to the internal structures within Perl. The **Devel::Peek** module allows you to dump the internal information associated with a variable, while **Devel::Symdump** will dump the symbol table. (See "Accessing Symbol Tables" in Chapter 5 for another method of accessing symbol tables.) The **Devel::RegExp** module can examine and monitor regular expressions.

We'll be examining other ways of monitoring the execution process of a Perl script in the coming sections, but first you need to understand how the Perl interpreter works.

Architecture

You can see from Figure 16-1 the basic architecture for the entire Perl interpreter. The shaded blocks show the internal components of the Perl interpreter, including the internal data structures and the execution components. Some of the components can

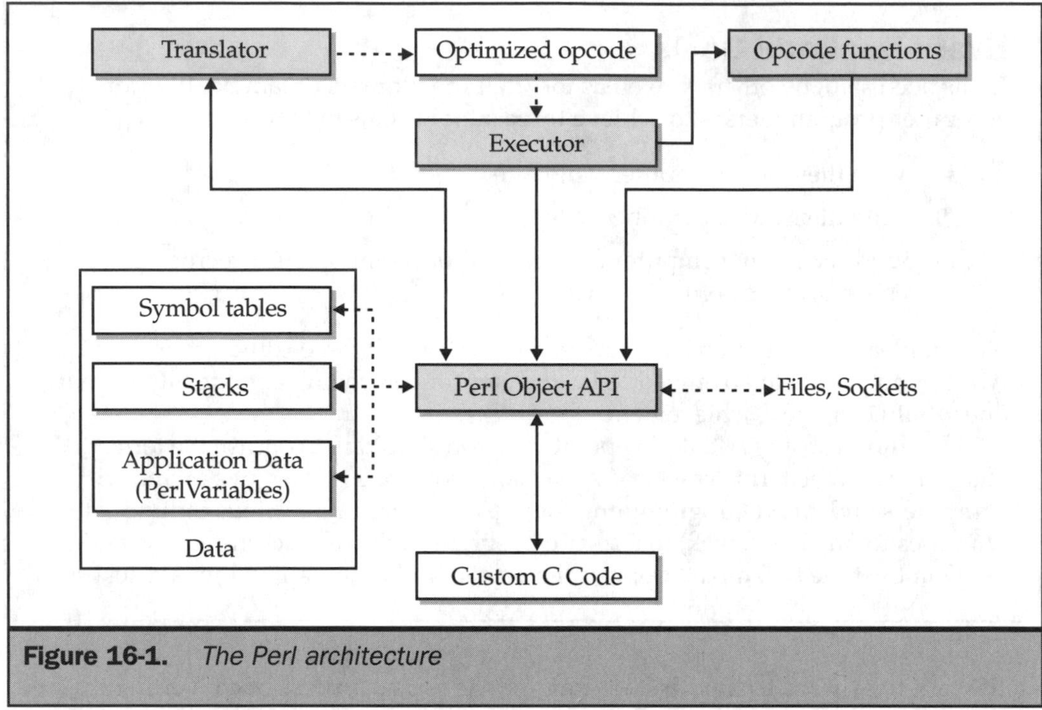

Figure 16-1. *The Perl architecture*

have multiple instances (we'll cover this later). The unshaded blocks on the diagram are the compiled C source code.

Some of you will recognize the diagram as looking mildly similar to the virtual machine diagram often used to describe the operation of the Java language. There are some similarities between the two languages: Perl uses the optimized opcodes (the smallest executable component of a compiled Perl script) in combination with the Executor component to actually run the Perl script. We'll look at these similarities more closely as we examine the execution process.

Internal Objects

The Perl Object API in Figure 16-1 represents the functions and structures used to support the four main internal data structures for any Perl program, variables, symbol tables, stacks, and external data streams.

The data formats supported by Perl are familiar by now. We'll examine the gory details of these variable types and how to use them in Chapter 17. For now, a summary of the supported types is all we'll need. Each variable can be identified by a two-letter acronym, as seen in Table 16-1.

The scalar value can also be further subclassed as an IV (integer value), PV (string value), and DV (double value). Other internal data structures, such as the symbol

Acronym	Full Name
SV	Scalar value
AV	Array value
HV	Hash value
CV	Code value
GV	Glob value (typeglobs)
RV	Reference value

Table 16-1. *Internal Perl Data Type Acronyms*

tables and stacks, are also represented by these core value types, which are strictly managed and controlled with efficient memory management.

Perl's internal symbol tables (see Chapter 5) are actually just HVs. Identifiers are stored as the keys, and the corresponding data value is a pointer to a GV.

Temporary information (including that passed to functions as arguments), the current location within a script, and variables used to store temporary data are all held on stacks. These are AVs, which are treated as simple stacks similar to the principles you saw in Chapter 7. When function **foo** wants to call function **bar** with arguments, the arguments are pushed onto the argument stack and the **bar** is called. The first operation performed by **bar** internally is to pop the arguments off the stack and populate the function's @_ array.

Other individual stacks are used to hold the other temporary variables such as local variables, loop iterators, and control information for the Perl interpreter. We'll be examining the stack and how it can be accessed and modified within a C program in the next chapter.

External data streams are handled by the I/O abstraction API. This is a suite of functions that provide a thin porting layout for the standard **stdio** and **sfio** libraries. We'll look at the Perl I/O API system briefly in Chapter 17. For most people there is no need to refer to the I/O abstraction, even when producing new C-derived Perl functions, but it can be useful background information.

Translator

The translator converts the Perl script into a series of opcodes, which we'll take a closer look at shortly. The opcodes are listed in a tree format to allow for branching,

Multiple Simultaneous Interpreters

The Perl executable can optionally be compiled with **-DMULTIPLICITY**. When embedding Perl into a C program, you can create multiple instances of **PerlInterpreter()**—the main interpreter function. Each instance will have its own "global" name space, rather than the normal shared name space that uses global C variables to store the main data structures. Unless you have a real need for multiple interpreter instances, you should use the single instance. This is faster (because the data structures do not need to be copied around), and you can create separate packages to separate most user variables.

In a secure installation there may well be a need for isolating instances of the Perl interpreter in your programs. You can also use the **Safe** module to create a secure environment for script execution. See Chapter 11 for more information on this module.

argument passing, and for a structured logical progression through the original script. The translator is made up of a combination of the **yacc**-based parser file, a hand-coded lexical analyzer, and the actual opcode generator. This is also the point that regular expressions are compiled (assuming they can be compiled at compilation time) using a customized regular expression engine.

Opcodes

An opcode is the smallest executable component within a Perl program. There are opcodes for all of the built-in functions and operators in the Perl language. During the execution stage it is the opcodes, and the functions on which they rely, that are executed by the Perl interpreter. It is at this point that Perl begins to resemble the Java-style virtual machine.

However, within Java, all operations are resolved down a machine-code–like format, not vastly dissimilar to the assembly language for a RISC (reduced instruction set computer) processor. RISC processors use a small number of instructions, with more complex operations being based on collections of the reduced set of instructions. When you execute a Java program, you are effectively emulating a RISC processor and all of the baggage that goes with it. This has some advantages, since it makes building a hardware-based Java processor as easy as building any other processor.

However, this is where the similarities between Java and Perl end. In Perl, the level of abstraction is much higher. Many of the functions in Perl that you use at a scripting level are in fact entire opcodes. Even functions as seemingly complex as the **grep** function are handled by a single opcode. The current distribution defines 347 opcodes. The source code for the opcode is hand optimized, which explains why Perl code executes so fast. When you "interpret" a Perl script, you are almost running native C code, just written (nay, translated) from Perl.

The use of such high-level opcode abstraction, and the hand-coded and optimized C source code that executes it, is why building a Perl compiler, which creates very fast stand-alone executables, is so easy. It also explains why the difference between interpreted Perl scripts and the generated executables is often minimal; in fact, I've often seen the so-called interpreted version working faster than the compiled version. This could be due to the effects of loading the wrapper that sits around the opcodes in order to make the run, or it could just be a complete fluke.

An opcode is defined by a C structure called **op** in the op.h header file. The important fields for any opcode are defined as follows:

```
OP*          op_next;
OP*          (*op_ppaddr)();
OPCODE       op_type;
```

The **op_next** field is a pointer to the next opcode to be executed when the current opcode has completed. The **op_type** field defines the type of opcode that will be executed. Different opcodes require different additional fields in order to define their execution. The list of opcode types can be determined from the **opcodes.pl** script, which is itself executed during the compilation of the interpreter. This file also conveniently lists all of the opcodes.

The **op_ppaddr** field contains the pointer to the function that will actually be executed. The functions are defined in the pp.c, pp_ctl.c, pp_sys.c, and pp_hot.c source files in the distribution tree. The first three define a range of opcode functions that support the standard operators and functions, but the last is the most important from a speed point of view.

The pp_hot.c file contains all of the opcode functions that are hand optimized and are expected to be executed a number of times in a typical Perl script. The opcodes defined in this file include those related to assignments, regular expressions, conditional operators, and functions related to handling and converting scalar and list values.

It's also worth noting that there are opcodes for defining and obtaining different variables and constants. Even the definition of a constant within a Perl script is actually handled by an opcode. The significance of this will become apparent very shortly.

Remember that I described the opcode sequence as being a tree? This is because certain opcode functions require calls to additional opcodes for their information. Consider the Perl script:

```
$a = $b + 2;
```

There are four opcodes in this statement. There are two operators—one is the assignment of the expression to the **$a** scalar, and the other is the addition of the **$b** scalar and the constant. There are also two values—one, the **$b** scalar and the other, the constant value of 2. Each of these operators and values is an opcode.

You can view the opcodes produced by the statement if your version of Perl has been built with the **–DDEBUGGING** option. The opcode tree is reproduced when you execute a Perl program using the **-Dx** command line option. For example, the command

```
perl -Dx -e '$a = $b +2;'
```

produces

```
{
8   TYPE = leave  ===> DONE
    FLAGS = (VOID,KIDS,PARENS)
    {
1       TYPE = enter  ===> 2
    }
    {
2       TYPE = nextstate  ===> 3
        FLAGS = (VOID)
        LINE = 1
    }
    {
7       TYPE = sassign  ===> 8
        FLAGS = (VOID,KIDS,STACKED)
        {
5           TYPE = add  ===> 6
            TARG = 1
            FLAGS = (SCALAR,KIDS)
            {
                TYPE = null  ===> (4)
                  (was rv2sv)
                FLAGS = (SCALAR,KIDS)
                {
3                   TYPE = gvsv  ===> 4
                    FLAGS = (SCALAR)
                    GV = main::b
                }
            }
            {
4               TYPE = const  ===> 5
                FLAGS = (SCALAR)
                SV = IV(2)
            }
        }
```

```
            {
                TYPE = null  ===> (7)
                  (was rv2sv)
                FLAGS = (SCALAR,KIDS,REF,MOD,SPECIAL)
                {
6                   TYPE = gvsv  ===> 7
                    FLAGS = (SCALAR)
                    GV = main::a
                }
            }
        }
    }
```

You can follow the execution through the opcode tree by following the opcode numbers. Each pair of braces defines the information about a single opcode, and nested braces show the parent-child relation between the opcodes. Execution starts at opcode number one, which simply passes execution to opcode number two, which actually just passes execution to number three after initializing the statement as being part of the first line (and only line) of the script. Opcode number three gets the scalar value of the **main::b** variable and places it onto the stack.

Execution is then passed to opcode number four, which places the static integer value of 2 onto the stack, which then passes execution to opcode number five, the "add" opcode. It takes the two arguments from the stack and adds them together, placing the result back on the stack for opcode six, which obtains the reference for the variable named **main::a** and places it on the stack. Then opcode seven assigns **main::a** the value of addition placed on the stack in opcode five. This is the end of the script.

The tree structure can be seen from this description. The assignation opcode has two siblings: the variable to which the value is to be assigned, and the value. The value is calculated from the result of the addition, which as a binary operator has two children: the values it is adding together. You can see this opcode structure more clearly in Figure 16-2.

Obviously, the more complex the statement, the more complex the opcode tree. And once you examine the output from a multiline script, you'll begin to identify just how efficient and complex the Perl opcode system is.

Compilation

The actual compilation stage is a multipass process that first processes the basic Perl script using the **yacc** parser. Language parsed by **yacc** is actually processed from the bottom up—the most complex expressions within single statements are processed first. So the nodes at the deepest points (leaves) of an execution tree are populated first, before the higher opcodes (twigs and branches) are finally produced. Once all of the entire

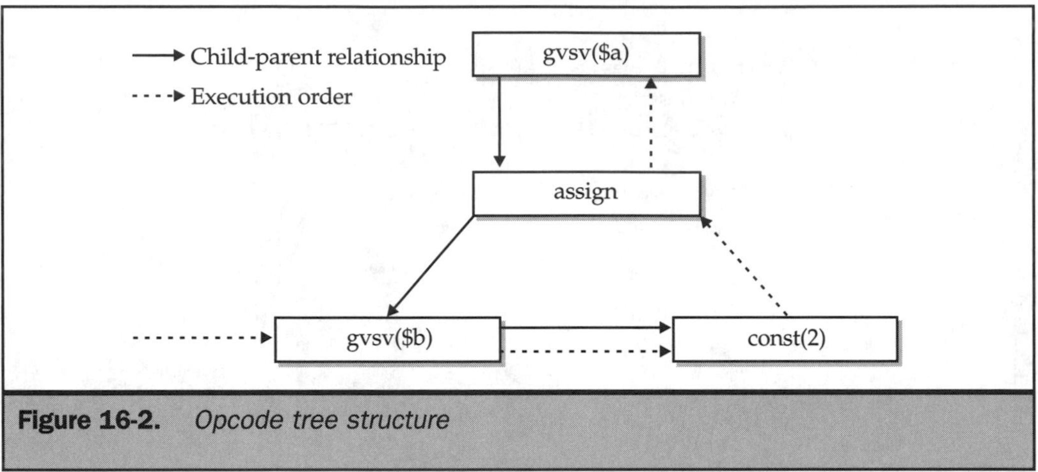

Figure 16-2. *Opcode tree structure*

statements have been passed, you can follow the execution line by line, by examining the trunk of the opcode tree.

Once all the opcodes have been produced, the compiler then goes over a number of optimization processes. The first is called *constant folding* and identifies entries that can be executed at the point of compilation. For example, the statement

```
$a = 4 + 5;
```

can be reduced from four opcodes to three by instead creating a parent opcode that assigns a value of 9 to the **$a** variable:

```
$a = 9;
```

You can see the effect of this by comparing the opcode tree for the more complex statement with the variable and constant tree you saw earlier:

```
{
6   TYPE = leave  ===> DONE
    FLAGS = (VOID,KIDS,PARENS)
    {
1       TYPE = enter  ===> 2
    }
    {
2       TYPE = nextstate  ===> 3
        FLAGS = (VOID)
```

```
            LINE = 1
        }
        {
5           TYPE = sassign  ===> 6
            FLAGS = (VOID,KIDS,STACKED)
            {
3               TYPE = const  ===> 4
                FLAGS = (SCALAR)
                SV = IV(9)
            }
            {
                TYPE = null  ===> (5)
                  (was rv2sv)
                FLAGS = (SCALAR,KIDS,REF,MOD,SPECIAL)
                {
4                   TYPE = gvsv  ===> 5
                    FLAGS = (SCALAR)
                    GV = main::a
                }
            }
        }
    }
```

The next optimization process is *context propagation*, which is the act of defining the context to a specific opcode and its children. You are used to the terms scalar or list context when creating and using functions. Internally, Perl also supports contexts for void, Boolean, and lvalue statements. Context propagation works top down—that is, parent opcodes are examined first, and the context requirement is then propagated down to child opcodes.

The final optimization stage is a process of reduction and is handled by the peephole optimizer. This process effectively executes the opcode tree, but without actually doing anything. The purpose is to look ahead to future opcodes in the tree and reduce them as much as possible. At the moment, the lookahead is only two statements, which means that a maximum of three statements could be reduced to just one statement.

Any larger figure would slow down the optimization process to the point that any gains made in optimizing the opcode tree would be lost in the optimization process itself. Remember that Perl is still essentially an interpreter, and unlike C or Java, the opcode tree is regenerated each time a script is executed. When you execute a Perl script, Perl doesn't simply reexecute the previous optimized opcode tree because Perl assumes the source file has changed (probably a good idea).

Ultimately, this makes individual executions of the same script slower than they might be if the peephole optimization was allowed to look ahead further. On the other hand, it ensures that every execution of a script is optimized to a reasonable point, even if you change just one character in the original script each time.

Unfortunately, there is no way of controlling the peephole process. You cannot specify, for example, that when creating a stand-alone executable the peephole lookahead value is greater than two, although this would be a great idea.

Execution

Once all three stages of the optimization have taken place, it's time to execute the code. The actual path of execution is not as sequential as it may have appeared earlier. All opcodes are numbered, and it's the value of the **op_next** (from the **op** structure) that defines the actual execution path. Since Perl supports conditional statements like **if** and loops like **while**, some opcodes may never be executed, or may be executed a significant number of times. Perl therefore relies on the value of **pp_next** returned by each opcode to decide which opcode to execute next.

For each opcode, Perl calls the corresponding function with the information on any child opcodes that are also required to call what the programmer recognizes as the original statement. Once all the opcodes in the desired execution path have been executed, the process ends, and Perl quits.

Opcodes and Safety

Many of the various methods for executing Perl in a safe manner rely on the ability of a single opcode to derive the source of its information. The taint checking mechanism uses opcodes to ensure that any variable derived from data external to the current program is marked as possibly dangerous. Because you can trace the flow of data within a program via the opcode tree, it's easy for the taint checking module to track external information.

If you want a very secure environment, you can use the **Safe** module, which we looked at briefly in Chapter 11 (see also Appendix E), to restrict the execution of code (rather than data) in a script. The **Opcode** module even allows you to restrict execution to a specific number of opcodes and then to execute a program within a safe compartment. If the compilation process creates an opcode tree that falls outside the environment you have specified, then an error is returned.

Without opcodes the tracking and filtering at this level would not be possible, and it's one reason Perl is considered a secure environment for many development and e-commerce applications.

Perl Pragmas

You can control the parsing and execution of a Perl script through a series of hints given to the Perl parser. These hints, called *pragmas*, control how the rest of the program is parsed and executed. The Perl **use** command defines these pragmas for the current Perl script or, in some cases, for the current block in which the pragma is specified. What actually happens in many cases though is that a Perl module is imported. The standard (supplied) pragma modules are listed here.

To turn off a specified pragma, you use the **no** keyword, which is the logical opposite of the **use** keyword. If you specify **no** at the same level as a previous **use** statement, then it acts as a toggle, switching off the earlier pragma until a new **use** statement is seen, or until the end of the block. If you use **no** within an enclosed block (a function or loop) inside a block with the corresponding **use** statement, then the pragma is disabled only for the duration of the enclosed block. For example:

```
use integer;
function intdivide
{
    print "67/3","\n"; #Uses integer math
}

function divide
{
    no integer;
    print "67/3","\n"; #Uses floating point math
}

print "67/3","\n"; #Integer math
no integer;
print "67/3","\n"; #Floating point math
```

Other pragmas work in similar ways, although some of the effects are dependent on other pragmas or on the specific implementation.

autouse

The **autouse** pragma postpones the loading of the **Module** until one of **funca** or **funcb** is actually used:

```
use autouse 'Module' => qw(funca funcb);
```

This is similar in principle, but not identical, to the **Autoload** module. Note that you must specify the functions that will trigger the **autouse** process; otherwise there is no way for the Perl interpreter to identify the functions that should be imported. The line above is therefore equivalent to the standard method for importing selected functions:

```
use Module qw(funca funcb);
```

You can also supply function prototypes to the **autouse** pragma to trap errors during the compilation rather than execution stage:

```
use Module qw(funca($$) funcb($@));
```

The effect of the **autouse** pragma reduces the loading and compilation time for a script and also reduces the number of modules that are loaded at startup in scripts where specific external functions are used only in certain execution trees. Unfortunately, the pragma also has the effect of delaying the loading of the module until execution time, thus bypassing the usual checks that are made when importing a module and shifting the responsibility of reporting any errors to the execution.

Problems can occur when there are bugs or typographical errors in the modules being autoused, since your program will fall over at the point of the module's import. Additionally, any module that relies on early initialization (say, within a **BEGIN {}** block) may fail, because it expects the initialization to occur during the initial compilation of the whole script.

You can get around the bugs in autoused modules during the development phase by placing a genuine **use** statement for the **autouse** modules. For example:

```
use File::Basename
use autouse 'File::Basename' => qw(basename dirname);
```

The first line masks the second; when you come to release your script and/or module to the public, just comment out the first line and let the **autouse** pragma do its work.

base

The **base** pragma establishes a relationship with a base class at compile (rather than execution) time. In effect, this is equal to adding the specified classes to the **@ISA** array during the module initialization, such that

```
package Object;
use base qw(Foo Bar);
```

is effectively equal to

```
BEGIN
{
    require Foo;
    require Bar;
    push @ISA, qw(Foo Bar);
}
```

You might also want to examine the **fields** pragma, which provides additional error checking to objects at compile time.

blib

The **blib** pragma forces Perl to look for modules in the blib directory structure, created by the **MakeMaker** module. This is especially useful for testing modules before you intend to publish them and make them available to the general Perl community. Ideally, it should be used only on the command line with the **-M** option:

```
perl -Mblib script
perl -Mblib=dir script
```

If **dir** is specified, it looks in that directory (and subdirectories) for the blib structure. If you do not specify **dir**, then it assumes you want to include the current directory.

You can also use

```
use blib;
use blib 'dir';
```

But this is not the preferred solution, since it requires modification of the script to disable the behavior.

constant

Although there are other techniques for introducing constant variables (for example, Chapter 5 demonstrates a method using typeglobs) the most practical solution is the **constant** pragma. The advantages of a constant are obvious—if you use the same constant value throughout all of your calculations and programs then you can be guaranteed that the values calculated will also remain constant.

The rule applies even when the constant is used over many different platforms. For example, the value of π can be endlessly calculated, and there are varying methods and degrees of precision used of the value. We can create a constant value to be used in all calculations like this:

```
use constant PI => 3.141592654;
```

The value can be any normal Perl expression, including calculations and functions, such that the following also works:

```
use constant PI   => 22/7;
use constant USER => scalar getpwuid($<);
```

Once defined you can use a constant directly; there is no need for a preceding character to denote the variable type:

```
$zero = (cos(PI/2));
```

The values supplied are evaluated in a list context, which allows you to define constant lists as well as scalars. Note the constants are lists, so you must use subscript, not array notation. Therefore the statement:

```
$quota = USERDATA[5];
```

will not work; you must use:

```
$quota = (USERDATA)[5];
```

Also note that constants can't be directly interpolated; you must use indirect notation:

```
print "I want to eat some @{[PI]}\n";
```

It's also worth noting that because constants are actually just subroutines you cannot use them in contexts where a bareword is automatically quoted, such as hashes. Instead, use an empty parenthesis or + character in front of the constant to force Perl to identify it as a function:

```
$hash{PI()};
$hash{+PI};
```

Although not essential, constants should have names composed only of uppercase characters to help distinguish them from normal variables. All constants must begin with a letter.

Constant definitions are package scoped rather than blocked scoped, so you can have different constant values within the confines of different packages, and you can also refer to constants using fully qualified names.

diagnostics

The **diagnostics** pragma inserts additional diagnostic capabilities into the Perl script. Although Perl normally outputs a fair number of errors and warnings when it discovers a problem, at both compile and run time, the messages are often very terse single-line descriptions. Even if you know what the error message signifies, the exact cause of the problem may be difficult to determine.

The **diagnostics** pragma prints out not only the terse one-line warnings but also the additional descriptive text that you find in the **perldiag** man page. Although this doesn't provide you with any further benefit than a more in-depth description of the problem, it can often highlight things you have overlooked.

To use, insert the **diagnostics** pragma at the top of the script you want to examine for problems, and then run the script (preferably with warnings switched on) and examine the extended output. The program below will produce a few errors:

```
use diagnostics;
print DUMMY 'Wont work';
```

When run, we get the following:

```
$ perl -w nodiag.pl
Name "main::DUMMY" used only once: possible typo at t.pl line 2 (#1)

    (W) Typographical errors often show up as unique variable names.
    If you had a good reason for having a unique name, then just mention
    it again somehow to suppress the message.  The use vars pragma is
    provided for just this purpose.

Filehandle main::DUMMY never opened at t.pl line 2 (#2)

    (W) An I/O operation was attempted on a filehandle that was never
    initialized. You need to do an open() or a socket() call, or call
    a constructor from the FileHandle package.
```

Alternatively, leave your script as it is and pipe the error output to a file. The **splain** program can then be used to analyze the errors and produce the full descriptions for the error messages and warnings:

```
perl -w nodiag.pl 2> nodiag.err
./splain <nodiag.err
```

Under MacPerl there is no separate **splain** application, but the pragma still works if specified within the script.

If you specify the **–verbose** option when specifying the pragma, the introduction from the **perldiag** man page will be printed out before the diagnostic warnings and extended information:

```
use diagnostics -verbose;
```

Once imported, you can control the behavior of individual elements of the script by switching the diagnostics messages on and off using the **enable** and **disable** functions:

```
enable  diagnostics;
disable diagnostics;
```

These changes only affect any run-time errors. It's not possible to switch off the diagnostics process during the parsing/compilation stage.

If your program is making use of the **$SIG{__WARN__}** and **$SIG{__DIE__}** handlers to trap errors in your program, you can still use them in conjunction with the **diagnostics** module. However, the **diagnostics::splainthis** function will be executed first.

If you want to examine exactly what the **diagnostics** module is doing, you can switch on "debugging" for the **diagnostics** modules by defining

```
BEGIN { $diagnostics::DEBUG =1 }
```

before the script starts the rest of the execution process.

fields

The **fields** pragma affects the compile time error checking of objects. Using the **fields** pragma enables you to predefine class fields, such that a call to a specific class method will fail at compile time if the field has not been specified. This is achieved by populating a hash called **%FIELDS**. When you access a hash with a typed variable holding an object reference, the type is looked up in the **%FIELDS** hash, and if the variable type exists, the entire operation is turned into an array access during the compilation stage. For example:

```
{
    package Foo;
    use fields qw(foo bar _private);
}
...
my Foo $var = new Foo;
$var->{foo} = 42;
```

If the specified field does not exist, then a compile time error is produced.

For this to work, the **%FIELDS** hash is consulted at compile time, and it's the **fields** and **base** pragmas that facilitate this. The **base** pragma copies fields from the base class definitions, and the **fields** pragma adds new fields to the existing definitions. Field names that start with an underscore character are private to a class; they are not even accessible to subclasses.

The result is that objects can be created with named fields that are as convenient and quick to access as a corresponding hash. You must access the objects through correctly typed variables, or you can use untyped variables, provided a reference to the **%FIELDS** hash is assigned to the 0th element of the array object. You can achieve this initialization with

```
sub new
{
    my $class = shift;
    no strict 'refs';
    my $self = bless [\%{"$class\::FIELDS"], $class;
    $self;
}
```

integer

Perl does all of its calculations in floating point by default. Although you can normally force integer results from specific calculations using the **int** function, it can be more useful to specify that all calculations are performed with integers only. For example:

```
use integer;
print 67/3,"\n";
```

The **use integer** pragma only lasts as long as the current block, so it can safely be used within individual functions without affecting the rest of the script. In addition, you can switch off the **integer** pragma with the **no** keyword:

```
use integer;
print 67/3,"\n";
no integer;
print 67/3,"\n";
```

You can also use **no** within an enclosed block to temporarily turn off integer math, as seen in the introductory example under "Perl Pragmas."

less

The **less** pragma is currently unimplemented.

```
use less;
```

The intention is to allow you to specify reductions for certain resources such as memory or processor space.

lib

When importing modules with **use**, the interpreter examines the **@INC** array for a list of directories to search for the modules to be imported. Since **use** statements are evaluated during the compilation process, you cannot insert additional directories in the main part of the script. You can of course use a **BEGIN {}** block:

```
BEGIN { unshift @INC, LIST }
```

Or you can use the **lib** pragma. The equivalent of the above block would be

```
use lib LIST;
```

Note that the directories are added before (using **unshift**) the standard directories to ensure that you use the local modules in preference to the standard ones. For all directories added in this way, the **lib** module also checks that a $dir/$archname/auto exists, where $archname is the name of the architecture of the current platform. If it does exist, then it is assumed to be an architecture-specific directory and is actually added to **@INC** before the original directory specification.

Once added, it is not normally necessary to remove directories. Furthermore, you shouldn't ever remove standard directories from the array. It's also worth remembering that you may affect the future operation of a later module if you remove a directory that contains a module on which it relies. Although you could argue that it is the module's responsibility to make sure it has access to the modules it needs, it's also sensible to assume that in the interests of good relations you shouldn't be removing directories anyway. There is no advantage to removing them; it doesn't take a considerable amount of extra memory or processing power for the interpreter to search for what it's looking for.

With all this in mind, you remove directories with a **no lib** pragma, which removes the first instance of the named directory from **@INC**. If you want to remove multiple instances, you will need to call **no lib** multiple times. You can also remove all the specified names from **@INC** by specifying ":ALL" as the first parameter of **no lib**. For example:

```
no lib qw(:ALL .);
```

For each directory, the opposite of the earlier process is executed. The architecture-specific directories are also searched for in the **@INC** array before they too are removed.

Although in practice you shouldn't need to, if you want to reinstate the original (standard) list of directories in **@INC**, you need to use

```
@INC = @lib::ORIG_INC;
```

locale

Perl supports the use of the locales defined in the POSIX standard. Locales affect certain internal operations and functions such as regular expressions, string comparisons, and sorts. To use the current locale:

```
use locale;
```

The default operation for Perl is to ignore locales, which means that most operations are actually in a quasi-C locale, which sorts and does comparisons based on the ASCII table. If you have switched locales on, you can switch them off with

```
no locale;
```

ops

The **ops** pragma switches off specific opcodes during the compilation process. The synopsis is as follows:

```
perl -Mops=:default
```

which enables only reasonably safe operations. Or you can specify opcodes to be removed from those available using

```
perl -M-ops=system
```

Note that the best way to use this option is via the command line incorporation; otherwise you open yourself up to abuse before the compilation process starts through the use of **BEGIN {}** statements.

The pragma actually makes use of the **Opcode** module, which we examined in Chapter 11.

overload

The **overload** pragma is probably the most complex of the modules that are listed as pragmas in the Perl distribution. It enables you to install alternative functions for the core operators defined in Perl. The main syntax is

```
use overload
     '+' => \&myadd,
     '-' => \&mysubtract;
```

The arguments are specified here as a hash, and each key/value pair assigns the operator defined in the key to use the function in the value, instead of using one of the built-in opcodes. The module operates on objects and classes, so the **myadd** function will be called to execute the statement **$a + $b** operator if **$a** is a reference to an object blessed into the current package, or if **$b** is a reference to an object in the current package.

You can overload the following operators and functions:

```
+ += - -= * *= / /= % %= ** **= << <<= >> >>= x x= . .=
<  <= >  >= == != <=>
lt le gt ge eq ne cmp
& ^ | neg ! ~
++ --
atan2 cos sin exp abs log sqrt
bool "" 0+
```

The pragma also supports three special operators: **nomethod**, **fallback**, and =.

In practice it's unlikely you will ever need to override any of the internal operators, since Perl provides you with many ways of generating your own methods, functions, and operators. See the **overload** man page for more information on the **overload** pragma.

re

The **re** pragma alters regular expression behavior. The pragma has three options: **taint**, **debug**, and **eval**. One additional pragma is really just a modification of an earlier one, called **debugcolor**. The only difference is in the color of the output.

The **taint** option ensures that variables modified with a regular expression are tainted in situations where they would be considered clean:

```
use re 'taint';
```

That is, in situations where matches or substitutions on tainted variables would ordinarily produce an untainted result, the results are in fact marked as tainted. See Chapter 11 for more information on tainted execution.

The **debug** and **debugcolor** options force Perl to produce debugging messages during the execution of a regular expression:

```
use re 'debug';
use re 'debugcolor';
```

This is equivalent to using the **–Dx** switch during execution if the **–DDEBUGGING** option was specified during the build process. The information provided can be very large, even on a relatively small regular expression. The **debugcolor** option prints out a color version if your terminal supports it. We'll return to the use of this pragma in Chapter 18.

The **eval** option enables regular expressions to contain the **(?{...})** assertions, even if the regular expression contains variable interpolation:

```
use re 'eval';
```

Ordinarily this is disabled because it's seen as a security risk, and the pragma is ignored if the **use re 'taint'** pragma is in effect.

Individual pragmas can be switched off with **no re**.

In all cases the **re** pragma applies to the entire file (it is not lexically scoped), and the effect is felt at both compile and execution time.

sigtrap

The **sigtrap** pragma enables simple signal handling without the complexity of the normal signal handling routines.

```
use sigtrap;
```

The pragma supports three handlers: two are supplied by the module itself (one provides a stack trace and the other just calls **die**), and the third is one that you supply yourself. Each option supplied to the module is processed in order, so the moment a signal name is identified, the signal handler is installed.

Without any options specified, the module defaults to the **stack-trace** and **old-interface-signals** options. The individual options are listed below.

```
use sigtrap qw/stack-trace HUP INT KILL/;
```

Generates a Perl stack trace to **STDERR** when the specified signals are received by the script. Once the trace has been generated, the module calls **dump** to dump the core.

```
use sigtrap qw/die HUP INT KILL/;
```

Calls **croak** (see Appendix E), reporting the name of the message that was caught.

```
use sigtrap 'handler' => \&my_handler, HUP, INT, KILL;
```

Installs the handler **my_handler** for the specified signals.

The pragma defines some standard signal lists. If your system does not support one of the specified signals, the signal is ignored rather than allowed to produce an error.

```
normal-signals
```

These are signals that might ordinarily be trapped by any program: **HUP, INT, PIPE, TERM**.

```
error-signals
```

These are the signals that indicate a serious error: **ABRT, BUS, EMT, FPE, ILL, QUIT, SEGV, SYS, TRAP**.

```
old-interface-signals
```

The list of signals that were trapped by default by the old **sigtrap** pragma. This is the list of signals that are used if you do not specify others and include **ABRT, BUS, EMT, FPE, ILL, PIPE, QUIT, SEGV, SYS, TERM, TRAP**.

```
untrapped
```

This special option selects from the following signal list or specification all the signals that are not otherwise trapped or ignored.

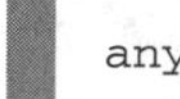

```
any
```

Applies handlers to all subsequently listed signals; this is the default.

strict

The **strict** pragma restricts those constructs and statements that would normally be considered as unsafe.

```
use strict;
```

In particular, it reduces the effects of assumptions Perl makes about what you are trying to achieve and, instead, imposes limits on the definition and use of variables, references, and bare words that would otherwise be interpreted as functions. These can be individually turned on or off using **vars**, **refs**, and **subs**.

Although it imposes these limits, the pragma generally encourages (and enforces) good programming practice. However, for casual scripts it imposes more restrictions than are really necessary. In all cases, the pragmas are lexically scoped, which means you must specify **use strict** separately within all the packages, modules, and individual scripts you create.

The **vars** option requires that all variables are predeclared before they are used, either with the **my** keyword, the **use vars** pragma, or through an absolute name, including the enclosing package.

```
use strict 'vars';
```

The **local** keyword is not sufficient, since its purpose is only to localize a variable, not to declare it. Therefore the following examples work:

```
use strict 'vars';
$Module::var = 1;
my $var = 1;
use vars qw/$var/;
```

But these will fail:

```
use strict 'vars';
$vars = 1;
local $vars = 1;
```

I recommend always using this pragma, even if you ignore the next two.

The **refs** pragma generates an error if you use symbolic references.

```
use strict 'refs';
```

Thus the following works:

```
use strict 'refs';
$ref = \$foo;
print $$ref;
```

but this does not:

```
use strict 'refs';
$ref = "foo";
print $$ref;
```

The **subs** pragma restricts the method with which you can refer to subroutines.

```
use strict 'subs';
```

Normally Perl allows you to use a bare word for a subroutine. This pragma disables that ability, best seen with signal handlers. The examples

```
use strict 'subs';
$SIG{QUIT} = "myexit";
$SIG{QUIT} = \&myexit;
```

will work, since we are not using a bare word, but

```
use strict 'subs';
$SIG{QUIT} = myexit;
```

will generate an error during compilation.

subs

The **subs** pragma predeclares **func** so that the function can be called without parentheses even before Perl has seen the full definition.

```
use subs qw(func);
```

This can also be used to override internal functions by predefining subroutines:

```
use subs qw(chdir);
chdir $message;
sub chdir
{
...
}
```

The overriding versions may be defined in the local file (as in the above example), or they may be imported from an external module, although it's possible to override functions from external modules by defining the function specifically to the import process, as in

```
use MyBuiltin 'chdir';
```

Obviously, you will need to define the **chdir** function in the **@EXPORT_OK** array as part of the module initialization. See Chapter 5 for more information.

vmsish

The **vmsish** pragma implies that the script should be executed with VMS-specific features.

```
use vmsish;
```

You can specify VMS features as follows:

```
use vmsish 'status';
```

Implies that the return values from backticks (in **$?**) and the value returned by **system** should return the VMS rather than the POSIX exit status value.

```
use vmsish 'exit';
```

A call to the function **exit** with a value of 1 returns a successful exit status (**SS$_NORMAL**) instead of indicating a failure, as it would be recognized by other platform implementations.

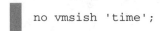

```
use vmsish 'time';
```

All times are returned in the local time size, rather than UTC or GMT.

You can also switch off features with **no**:

```
no vmsish 'time';
```

vars

The **vars** pragma predeclares the variables defined in the list, which has the effect of preventing typographical warnings for variables not yet created. It is also the best way to declare variables that are to be shared with other modules if you do not want to use the **local** keyword. The use of **my** variables won't work, since the variables will be localized strictly to the module. Since the variables are declared globally, it's also the easiest way to declare global variables that would otherwise trip up the **use strict** pragma.

```
use vars qw($scalar @array %hash);
```

Note that **vars** is not block scoped. The variables are truly global within the current file.

warnings

The **warnings** module is a pragma that can help to control the level of warnings that are produced (see Table 16-2).

You can switch on options with:

```
use warnings 'all';
```

Option	Description
all	All warnings are produced; this is the default if none are specified.
deprecated	Only deprecated feature warnings are produced.
unsafe	Lists unsafe warnings.

Table 16-2. *Options for **warnings** Pragma*

or you can switch off specific sets with **no**:

```
no warnings 'deprecated';
```

Language Differences

It's probable that you've migrated to Perl with some experience in other languages. In this section you will find some tips on making the migration from one language to Perl. Although I've done my best to cover all the bases, in most cases the information provided will only get you past certain common traps. Refer to one of the other chapters for specific information on a feature and how to use it within Perl.

Differences from awk

If you are moving to Perl from **awk**, or if you regularly use the two languages, then you may find the following list of hints and tips useful. You can convert an **awk** script to Perl script. (See the section "Language Conversion" in Chapter 12.)

- The **English** module in Perl allows you to use the full variable names as used by **awk** for variables as the record separator (**$RS** in **awk**, identical to **$RS** in the **English** module). See Chapter 2 for more information.
- Perl uses a semicolon to signify the end of a statement; the newline as used in **awk** is not sufficient.
- All blocks require braces, including those used with **if** and **while** statements.
- Variables in Perl begin with a prefix character—**$** for scalars, **@** for arrays (numeric indices), and **%** for hashes (string indices). Indexes in arrays and subscripts begin at zero, as do references to specific characters within strings.
- Numeric and string comparisons are different in Perl. Numeric comparisons use special characters, such as **!=** for not equal to. String comparisons use letters; the equivalent "not equal to" when comparing strings is **ne**.
- Input lines from files must be manually split using the **split** function. The results will go to the array you specify, or to the global @_ if you don't specify a destination (this also clobbers any function arguments). The current input line (or default pattern space) is **$_** in Perl; if you want the newline stripped, you must use **chop** or **chomp** (better).
- Once the fields have been split, you cannot access them using the **$1**, **$2**, and so on, variables to extract each field. These variables are only filled on a match or substitution of a regular expression with grouping.
- The pattern binding operator is **=~** in Perl, and the range operator is **..** not **,**. The exponential operator is ******.

- Field and record separators are not automatically added to arrays printed with **print**. Use the **$** (or **$OFS**) for the field separator and **$** (**$ORS)** for the record separator. If you want to concatenate variables, the concatenation operator is the period.
- Files must be opened before you can print to them.
- Within loop control, the keywords **next**, **exit**, and **continue** work differently.

The variables in **awk** are equivalent to those in Perl as shown in Table 16-3.

C Traps

Although at first glance Perl seems very like C, there are some minor differences that may catch out a C programmer who isn't concentrating.

awk	Perl
ARGC	**$#ARGV** or **scalar @ARGV**
ARGV[0]	**$0**
FILENAME	**$ARGV**
FNR	**$.** (for the current/last used filehandle)
FS	No equivalent; use **split** to split fields
NF	No equivalent; you could count the number returned by **split**, though
NR	**$.**
OFMT	**$#**
OFS	**$,**
ORS	**$**
RLENGTH	**length($&)**
RS	**$/** (can only be set to a string; patterns are not supported; try using **split**)
RSTART	**length($')**
SUBSEP	**$;**

Table 16-3. *awk/Perl Variable Differences*

All code blocks require curly brackets, {}. The statement

```
if (1) print "Hello";
```

will fail in Perl. You can, however, do

```
print "Hello" if (1);
```

if the statement you want to execute fits on one line.

There is no **switch** statement in C, although you can emulate it in a number of different ways in Perl. The most obvious is a messy **if..elsif..else** conditional block. Note that the secondary test is **elsif** in Perl, not **else if**. A better alternative for the **switch** statement, and also one that will look familiar, is

```
SWITCH:
{
    ($date == $today) && do {
                                print "Happy Birthday!\n";
                                last SWITCH;
                            }
    ($date != $today) && do {
                                print "Happy Unbirthday!\n";
                                last SWITCH;
                            }
    ($date == $xmas)  && do {
                                print "Happy Christmas!\n";
                                last SWITCH;
                            }
}
```

Note from this example that the keyword to break out from the statement is **last**, not **break**. The **last** and **next** keywords are direct replacements for the C **break** and **continue** keywords. However, be aware that the Perl versions do not work within a **do { } while** loop. (See Chapter 2 for other **switch** examples.)

Perl uses special characters to identify a variable (and its type). Variables start with **$**, **@**, and **%** in Perl and relate to scalars (normal variables), arrays, and hashes. Scalars can store numbers, characters, or strings. You cannot access a Perl string using the **$var[]** index notation; you must use the **substr** function instead. The **&** symbol in C takes the address of an object, but this is not supported in Perl, although you can use \ to pass a reference to an object instead of the object itself. Arguments to a Perl script, accessed via **$ARGV[0]**, start at zero, which refers to the first *argument* to the script, not the name of the script, which can instead be found in the **$0** special variable.

Here are some other differences between C and Perl to watch out for:

- The Perl **printf** function does not accept the * character in a format definition for inserting a variable field width. However, since Perl does support variable interpolation, you can insert the variable directly into the format and let Perl interpolate the value into the format string.
- Comments in Perl start with the hash sign and continue until the end of line. They do not need to be terminated as in the C **/*..*/** construct.
- The system call functions built into Perl (and indeed most functions) return non-zero for success and zero for failure. In cases where a zero would be a valid return result, the function returns **0 but true**, which evaluates to zero when interpreted as a number.
- When using a signal handler, Perl allows you to use the signal name (without the prefix **SIG**) instead of the signal numbers.

sed Traps

Much of the functionality for Perl, including a large bulk of the regular expression syntax, was inherited from **sed**. There are, however, some minor differences.

Logical groupings of regular expression elements are specified using unbackslashed brackets. The line

```
s/\([A-Z]+\)/\1/;
```

in **sed** should be written as

```
s/([A-Z]+)/$1/;
```

The same is true for the logical **or** operator, which is also unbackslashed. A backslashed bracket **or** | operator within a regular expression will be interpreted by Perl as a literal. Back references in substitutions should use **$1** instead of **\1**, although support for **\1** back references is still present—just don't bank on this situation continuing. See Chapter 4 for more details on the regular expression system in Perl.

Finally, when specifying a range of values in Perl, the **...** operator should be used instead of the comma. See Chapter 2 for more details.

Note that a translator is available to convert **sed** programs into Perl equivalents. See Chapter 12 for more details.

Emacs Traps

The regular expression syntax in **emacs** is more or less identical to the **sed** syntax. See the previous "**sed** Traps" section for details on the differences.

Shell Traps

The most fundamental difference between any shell and the Perl interpreter is that Perl compiles the program into a series of opcodes before execution; whereas a shell interprets lines (and sometimes blocks) at once, ignoring the remainder of the code until it reaches that point.

The interpolation of variables is different. Perl always interpolates variables into backticked and double-quoted strings and into angle brackets and search patterns, and the interpolation is only done once (not recursively).

Variables in Perl start with **$**, **@**, and **%**. You must specify the prefix character in Perl. You cannot get away with

```
var = "Hello"
```

as you can in shell script. To confuse matters, you can't do the reverse in shell script, either. The example

```
$var = "Hello"
```

will fail in most shells.

Three more differences are worth noting:

- All statements in Perl must end with a semicolon (except when the last statement is in a block).
- The command line arguments in Perl are available via the **@ARGV** array, not in the **$1**, **$2**, and so on, functions that the shell uses; Perl uses these for grouped regular expression matches.
- With particular reference to **csh**, return values from backticks in Perl are not parsed in any way.

Python Traps

Python and Perl are two very different languages, and since both are available on identical platforms, which one you use is likely to be driven by personal choice or the requirement of a client. However, necessity dictates all sorts of things, so here is a list of differences that may trip up a Python programmer trying to work in Perl. It's intended as a quick checklist of things you may have done wrong, not an entire list of all the differences, which would probably take up an entire book!

- All statements in Perl end in a semicolon, unlike Python, which effectively doesn't have a statement terminator other than the newline, and even then, it's only implied as the statement terminator.

- Variables in Python are free-form: there is no difference between creating a scalar, array, or hash. You must remember to specify your Perl variables by their type and to use the prefix of **$** for scalars (strings or numbers), **@** for arrays, and **%** for hashes (the Perl term for Python dictionaries).
- Accessing an element from an array or a hash changes the prefix character to a **$**. For example, to access the sixth element of an array:

```
print $array[5];
```

  Note that square brackets are still used to refer to the individual elements. With a hash you use braces:

```
print $hash{elem};
```

- When splicing elements from an array in Perl, you can either use the **splice** function, or use commas and list operators in the square brackets to define the elements to splice (similar to, and identically named, the subscript operator in Python). The **splice** function is the preferred option on named arrays; the subscript option should be used on the return values from lists.
- You must specify lists in Perl in surrounding brackets. The Python statement

```
a, b = 1, 2
```

  will not work in Perl, even if you add the semicolon and **$** prefix to make

```
$a, $b = 1, 2;
```

  What actually happens is that Perl sees three separate expressions in one large statement; only **$b** will actually be assigned a value. It should be rewritten as

```
($a, $b) = (1, 2);
```

- Variables within Perl are the actual storage containers of the data. Within Python all data storage is via a reference to an object. If you want to pass a variable reference to a function, you need to prefix the variable with a backslash to indicate to Perl that it is a reference. When dereferencing a variable, you need to specify the type of variable you are attempting to dereference. See Chapters 4, 5, and 7 for more information on this method.

- Perl supports a number of internal functions that provide a lot of the functionality that Python requires external modules for. These include functions for reading and writing files, using network sockets, handling arrays and hashes, and many other things. See Appendix B for a full list of the built-in functions and Appendixes E and F for a list of additional modules that are either distributed with Perl or are available from CPAN.
- Most notable of the external data that is available within Perl directly without the use of an imported module is the environment, available via the **%ENV** hash, and the command line arguments, available via the **@ARGV** array.
- External modules are imported via the **use** function in Perl, which is effectively equivalent to the **import** keyword in Python. However, once a module is imported in Perl, you do not have to use the full name to access the function:

```
use Cwd;
print getcwd();
```

- If you are using objects in Perl, then to call a method you use the **->** operator:

```
FILEHANDLE->autoflush(1);
```

- Strings are concatenated in Perl using a single period; the Python statement

```
"Hello" "World" "\n";
```

  in Perl, would become

```
"Hello" . "World" "\n";
```

  Also, Perl interpolates variables and escape sequences (such as the newline above) only in certain quotes. Unfortunately, this excludes single quotes; in Perl the value of

```
'\n'
```

  is a string composed of a backslash and the lowercase character "n." However, this does make **print** statements easier. You can place the variables straight into the double quotes, without having to specify a print format. If you want a formatted version of a string, use the **printf** function. See Chapter 3 for more information.

- Code blocks in Perl must be enclosed in braces. An **if** statement looks like this:

```
if ($test)
{
}
```

The block starts after the opening brace and ends before the last brace.

Perl Traps

Novice and experienced Perl programmers alike have certain blind spots when it comes to programming in Perl. I've listed below many of the most common ones seen on Usenet newsgroups and those I and others make frequently. If you are used to a different language, refer to the previous sections to identify potential problems between the various languages and Perl.

- Functions in Perl can return arrays or lists, depending on the context in which they are used. The context is defined by the type of value that the caller expects to receive. There is no way of determining from name alone which of the internal functions returns differently according to the context. Use Appendix B to identify those that do.
- Also remember that some functions use the value of **$_** and **@ARGV** if you fail to specify an alternative variable. Others, such as **split**, also update @_ if called in a scalar rather than a list context.
- Perl tries to evaluate bare words as functions first, then strings. Bare words are best avoided at all costs. If you want to insert a string, use quotes and leave bare words to functions (or, better still, use brackets to help Perl identify the word as a function).
- The **eval** keyword is a function and needs a closing semicolon even when using a code block. The fragment

```
eval
{
    local $SIG{ALRM} = sub { die "Timeout" };
    alarm 10;
    chomp($answer = <STDIN>);
    alarm 0;
}
```

will fail with a parser error. The same is also true for functions that take an inline block—that is, **map**, **grep**, and **sort**. They must have a terminating semicolon to define the end of the statement.

- Filehandles should be uppercase and composed only of alphanumeric characters. **<FH>** is not the name of the filehandle; **FH** is the name of the filehandle, and **<>** is the operator that does a **readline** operation on **FH**. It's also worth noting that the value of **<FH>** is not automatically assigned to **$_** when **<FH>** is the sole condition in a while loop. The line

```
<FH>;
```

  reads a line from the filehandle **<FH>** and discards it!

- The pattern binding operator for regular expressions is **=~**. The following lines do not do the same thing:

```
$string = /foo/;
$string =~ /foo/;
```

- You cannot use loop control keywords within a **do {}** statement: it isn't a loop. This has advantages and disadvantages (see the comments on **switch** statements in the "C Traps" section).

  The keywords **my** and **local** are not the same. Variables defined with **my** are local to the current block and any enclosed blocks. The **local** function merely gives a global variable local scope. This can, however, be used to give a predefined variable a local scope; so statements like

```
{ local $/; $file = <FH>; }
```

  can be used to slurp the entire contents of a file into a scalar variable. Use **my** for all variables that you can get away with (functions, packages, and so on). If using the **strict vars** pragma, use the **vars** pragma to define variables that can be published to the outside world.

Enhancing Performance

Despite all the optimization of the internal execution process of a Perl script, there are some ways in which you can improve the execution of your Perl script. Most of the time the solutions are obvious, but some solutions are more obscure. Because Perl supports many variables and data types that other languages do not, there are efficiencies that can be had just by using the correct variable type and function. Unfortunately, the reverse is also true. Certain operations are faster in other languages because of those very restrictions.

Some operations are slow in Perl, even accounting for both the efficiencies below and the optimization and native C code used to execute the opcodes your script is converted into. If you are still worried about the speed of execution in your program, you may want to rewrite your function in native C code and create an external module within Perl to use it. See Chapter 17 for more information.

The tips are split into two sections, "Increasing Speed" and "Reducing Memory." The contents of each should be obvious. For tips on producing tidy code suitable for distribution, refer to Chapter 20; and for guidelines on writing portable Perl code, refer to Chapter 24.

Increasing Speed

- Avoid using **goto** when a function or loop control statement will achieve the same result. Any call to **goto** causes the parser to search for the specified label; Perl doesn't keep an internal table.
- Use **print** in place of **printf** unless you absolutely have to print a specific format. Remember that variables can be interpolated directly into certain quoted strings (see Chapter 3 for more information).
- When working with regular expressions, avoid using the **$&**, **$'**, and **$'** variables. At the first point of use, Perl starts to track the information for every regular expression.
- Use hashes instead of arrays to hold information like keywords, which you would otherwise use an array and a search mechanism to find. Also remember that you can use hashes to remove duplicates from a list (see Chapter 7 for some examples).
- Don't use **eval** when you can use braces to expand information, such as variable names, inline. You can use something like

```
${$prefix . $var} = "String";
```

  Also, avoid using **eval** inside a loop, since this will cause Perl to run the parser over the **eval** statement for each iteration. Instead, put the iteration inside the **eval** so the block will only have to be parsed once.
- Using a logical **or**, ||, outside of a regular expression can sometimes be quicker than using the alternate within a regular expression. So use

```
$found = if /one/ || /two/;
```

  instead of

```
$found = if /one|two/;
```

- Within the context of a loop always place control statements as early as possible to prevent Perl from executing statements it then never uses. For example, the following code is wasteful:

```
while (<DATA>)
{
    chomp;
    next if /^#/;
...
}
```

  You don't have to take the newline off the end of the string in order for the regular expression test to match.

- Optimize regular expressions by reducing the number of quantifiers and assertions in a single expression, especially when using groupings, since this causes the regular expression engine to backtrack and populate the **$1** variables.
- Avoid using **substr** many times on a long string when a regular expression could perform the conversion or extraction quicker. For example, to extract the elements from a date in the form "19980326," using **substr**

```
$date = '19980326';
$year = substr($date,0,4);
$month = substr($date,4,2);
$day   = substr($date,6,2);
```

  is almost certainly quicker using a regular expression:

```
$date = '19980326';
($year, $month, $day) = $date =~ /(\d{1,4})(\d{1,2})(\d{1,2})/;
```

  Better still, use **pack** and **unpack** for strings. You could rewrite the above example as

```
($year, $month, $day) = unpack("c4c2c2",$date);
```

- Use **substr** to modify a string, rather than extracting the elements and concatenating the new version. Better still, use regular expression substitution.
- When testing a string a number of times with many regular expressions, group all the a's, all the b's, and so on. Perl works faster this way because the internal tables will have already been built.

- If the string is large and the regular expressions are complex, use the **study** function to improve performance.
- Avoid calling complex subroutines in large loops, especially those with few other steps. The overhead in copying arguments to the stack and back again will slow the process down. If you can, use references rather than static lists; or if it becomes a real problem, rewrite the function in C.
- Use **sysread**, not **getc**.
- Use **grep** and **opendir** for reading directory listings to avoid large lists being returned from the **glob** function.
- Replace **if..else** statements used to select from a range of single values with a logical **or**. You can always use

```
$login = getlogin || (getpwuid($<))[0] || "Anonymous";
```

- Use **my** instead of **local**.
- Use **tr///** instead of **s///g** to delete characters from a string.
- Use lists with functions that accept them in place of concatenating a string. Using concatenation with **print**, for example, involves copying each value into a new string before returning the concatenated version and moving on to the next element. Using a list speeds up the process considerably. Alternatively, try using **join** with a null separator value, since **join** will add each string to a new string, instead of performing multiple copies on each element.
- Pre-extending an array or string can save time, as it preallocates memory that Perl would otherwise attempt to allocate on the fly.
- Don't **undef** variables you may want to use again later for a different purpose. More specifically, don't create multiple variables when a single temporary variable will do. Better still, use **$_** if you can get away with it.
- Use the OS **mkdir** command (if supported) when creating multiple directories, instead of the built-in **mkdir**.
- Don't use **eof** when operators and functions detect **eof** automatically.
- Avoid making calls to operating system functions when the predefined variables built into every Perl script at execution time are likely to contain the information you want.
- Use the **Cwd** module instead of making an external call to **pwd**. Using **system** creates a subprocess and possibly a shell, which involves a lot of extra instructions and processor time you could do without.
- Use lists with **system** and **exec** instead of using one big string that you have to quote and format in order to get the right information.

- Avoid using default values for variables. Perl always initializes variables to zero or empty anyway.

Reducing Memory

- Use the **vec** function to store very small numbers. Use **pack** and **unpack** to store information efficiently in external files. Use **substr** to store small fixed-length strings in one larger string.

  You can also follow this through to arrays and hashes, which can be stored in a file if memory space is really tight. If necessary, use temporary files to store large arrays, and consider using a DBM file to store hash information out of memory. If you want to store small pairs of information in hashes, consider using the **Tie::SubstrHash** module (See Chapter 8), which will compact hash data much more tightly than the normal 1K (or larger) key/value pair size.

- Use **each** in place of **keys** for iterating through hashes when order is not important. It reduces the size of the temporary list passed to the loop control statement.
- In general, try to avoid any list operations that could be avoided; creating an array and then using it frequently uses a lot of temporary storage space, even on relatively small arrays.
- Use **undef** and **delete** to remove variables or hash elements that you no longer need.

The Complete Reference

Chapter 17

Extending and Embedding Perl

Perl is a very practical language, and for most people its built-in functions and features provide everything they need to work effectively. However, many people need access to the outside world, and this requires an interface between Perl and the C language. This process, called extension programming, provides a method for writing a simple mapping file that equates Perl functions with external C functions.

This is in fact how much of the functionality we take for granted is provided in Perl. The Perl distribution uses this system to provide an interface between Perl and network sockets, DBM databases such as **GDBM_File** and **DB_File**, and also the more advanced elements such as the Perl compiler.

For the end-user, extension programming provides you with unlimited flexibility to interface your Perl scripts with external C functions, whether self-written or provided by external libraries and systems. The CPAN archives contain countless examples of this sort of interface, from simple math libraries up to some of the more complex systems you have already seen. The DBI toolkit, for example, provides access to a wide range of external database systems through the use of C functions and the Perl extension interface.

For others, the practicalities and facilities provided by Perl are too attractive, and they want or need to embed the Perl interpreter within their C programs. This has some advantages, such as the ability to parse regular expressions within a C program more easily than many of the available libraries. Other people have also made good use of the features provided by embedding to improve facilities within their software. On CPAN, for example, there is a module called **mod_perl** that embeds a Perl interpreter within the Apache web server, enabling you to execute Perl CGI scripts much faster than you would otherwise be able to by calling an external Perl interpreter.

Finally, Perl also provides facilities for cooperating with other languages, either through the coercive use of Perl as a language producer or through the supplied scripts that provide you with facilities for converting programs written in other languages, such as **awk** and **sed**, into Perl scripts.

In this chapter, we'll attempt to cover all of these issues. We'll start by examining the core C functions available (and required) when writing extensions to Perl, and when calling Perl from C. We then move on to the specifics of writing extensions and embedding Perl within your C programs, before finally discussing the methods available for cooperating with languages other than C.

Perl's Internal Structures

For the processes of writing extensions to Perl and for embedding Perl within your C programs, you will need to understand the different structures used internally by the Perl interpreter. Although it's possible to skip this section, proper extension development requires that you know at least the basis of the different Perl data types and how they can be used with C functions rather than Perl functions and operators.

There are two core data structures that you need to consider: variables and the stack. Variables are the data storage entities that you are accustomed to using within Perl. The stack is a special type of array that is used to pass information to functions, and pass return values from functions back to the calling statement.

Note that the information here assumes you know C—at least well enough to know the basic structure of the program and how to call functions and handle variables. For some of the more complex elements, you will also need to understand C pointers. Although we are still talking about Perl in the literal sense, we will not be dealing with Perl source, only C.

If you prefer, you can skip this section and use it only as reference for the later parts of this chapter.

Variables

You already know that a number of different variables are available in Perl. At a base level these are scalars, arrays, and hashes. You're probably also aware that there are references, typeglobs, and objects. A reference is essentially just a scalar variable that refers to a particular entity. A typeglob is a special structure that is mapped to all of the variables of different types with the same common name. An object is a special, or "magic," variable type and is treated separately, even though it's essentially a scalar value.

In each case, the value is stored internally as a structure, which has been created as a new variable type with the **typedef** keyword. The name of each type is the two letters for the Perl data type; so a scalar value is stored in an **SV** structure, an array in an **AV** structure, and so on. There are two basic value types used in all the definitions: The **I32** is a signed integer that is guaranteed to be at least 32 bits wide, irrespective of the host platform. The **U32** value is an unsigned integer, also 32 bits wide. On a 64-bit machine the values will be 64 bits wide.

In this section we'll look at the macros that are defined within the Perl environment for accessing, modifying, and converting between the different variable types in their raw C format. We'll leave the use of these different functions to the remainder of this chapter.

Scalar Values

A scalar value, abbreviated **SV**, contains the contents of a scalar variable. Since a scalar variable can contain many different types of information, **SV**s are subclassified as integer values (**IV**), doubles (**NV**), strings (**PV**), and references (**RV**). The functions for using **AV**s are shown Table 17-1.

MORTALS When you initially create an **SV**, it is up to you to automatically delete it once you have finished using it. If you set a variable to be mortal with **sv_2mortal** or one of the other mortal functions, Perl will delete it at the end of the current scope, unless it is used by a reference. Once the reference count reaches zero, Perl will call **sv_free** for you to free the **SV**.

Function/Macro	Description
SV* newSViv(I32)	Creates a new **SV** from an integer value.
SV* newSVnv(double)	Creates a new **SV** from a float or double value.
SV* newSVpv(char *str, int len)	Creates a new **SV** from a string of length **len**. The length will be calculated if **len** is zero.
SV* newSVsv(SV *)	Duplicates the scalar value. Creating a new empty scalar value requires the use of the special **sv_undef** global scalar.
SV* newSVrv(SV* rv, char *pkgname)	Creates a new **SV** and points **rv** to it. If **pkgname** is not null, then it blesses **rv** into that package. This is the method used to create references to scalars.
SV* newRV_inc(SV* other)	Creates a reference pointing to any type of value, specified by **other**, incrementing the reference count of the entity referred to. Can be used to create references to any type of value.
SV* newRV_noinc(SV* other)	Creates a reference pointing to any type of value, specified by **other**, without incrementing the reference count of the entity referred to. Can be used to create references to any type of value.
SvIOK(SV*)	Returns true if the **SV** is an **IV**.
SvNOK(SV*)	Returns true if the **SV** is an **NV**.
SvPOK(SV*)	Returns true if the **SV** is a **PV**.
SvROK(SV*)	Returns true if the **SV** is a reference (**RV**).
SvOK(SV*)	Returns true if the **SV** is not **undef**.
SvTRUE(SV*)	Returns true if the **SV** is true.

Table 17-1. *Functions for Accessing and Using **SV**s*

Function/Macro	Description
SVTYPE(SV*)	Returns a value referring to the **SV** type. Macros exist for the following: **SVt_IV** (integer) **SVt_NV** (double) **SVt_PV** (string) **SVt_RV** (reference) **SVt_PVAV** (array) **SVt_PVHV** (hash) **SVt_PVCV** (code) **SVt_PVGV** (glob) **SVt_PVMG** (magic/blessed scalar)
IV SvIV(SV*)	Converts an **SV** to an **IV**. Returns zero if the **SV** contains a non-numeric string.
double SvNV(SV*)	Converts an **SV** to a **double**.
char* SvPV(SV*, int len)	Converts an **SV** to a pointer to a string, and updates **len** with the string's length.
SV* SvRV(SV*)	Dereferences a reference, returning an **SV**. This can then be cast to an **AV** or **HV** as appropriate.
sv_setiv(SV*, int)	Gives **SV** an integer value, converting **SV** to an **IV** if necessary.
sv_setiv(SV*, double)	Gives **SV** a double value, converting **SV** to an **NV** if necessary.
sv_setsv(SV* dest, SV* src)	Copies **dest** to **src**, ensuring that pointers **dest != src**.
sv_setpv(SV*, char *)	Gives **SV** a string value (assuming a null terminated string), converting **SV** to a string if necessary.

Table 17-1. *Functions for Accessing and Using **SV**s* (continued)

Function/Macro	Description
sv_setpvn(SV*, char *, int len)	Gives **SV** a string value of length **len**, converting SV to a string if necessary.
sv_catpv(SV*, char*)	Concatenates the string to the **SV**.
svcatpvn(SV*, char*, int len)	Copies **len** characters from the string, appending them to the **SV**.
svcatsv(SV* A, SV* B)	Concatenates the **SV B** to the end of **SV A**.
sv_setref_iv(SV* rv, char *classname, int value)	Creates a new **IV** with the value of **value**, and points **rv** to it. If **classname** is non-null, then bless **rv** into that package.
sv_setref_nv(SV* rv, char *classname, double value)	Creates a new **NV** with the value of **value**, and points **rv** to it. If **classname** is non-null, then bless **rv** into that package.
sv_setref_pv(SV* rv, char *classname, char* value)	Creates a new **PV** with the value of **value**, and points **rv** to it. If **classname** is non-null, then bless **rv** into that package.
svREFCNT_dec(SV*)	Decrements the reference count for **SV**, calling **sv_free** if the count is zero.
SV* sv_bless(SV *rv, HV* stash)	Blesses **rv** within the package represented by **stash**.
int sv_isa(SV*, char *pkgname)	Returns 1 if the **SV** inherits from the class **pkgname**.
int sv_isobject(SV*)	Returns 1 if the **SV** is an object.
SV* sv_newmortal()	Creates a new blank mortal **SV**. See the section "Mortals."
SV* sv_2mortal(SV*)	Marks an existing **SV** as mortal. See the section "Mortals."

Table 17-1. *Functions for Accessing and Using **SV**s* (continued)

Function/Macro	Description
SV* sv_mortalcopy(SV*)	Duplicates an existing **SV** and makes the duplicate mortal. See the section "Mortals."
SV* perl_get_sv(char *varname, int create)	Gets the variable name within a Perl script specified by **varname**, which should be a fully qualified reference. If **create** is set to 1, then it creates a new scalar variable of that name.
sv_dump(SV*)	Pretty-prints a Perl variable (**SV**, **AV**, **HV**, and so on.).

Table 17-1. *Functions for Accessing and Using* ***SVs*** (continued)

Warning *Do not call* ***sv_free*** *yourself; rely on the internal functions to do it for you.*

REFERENCES You can reference a reference using the **SvRV()** function, and this can be used in combination with the **SvTYPE()** function to obtain the type of value that is referenced. The code fragment

```
SvTYPE(SvRV(SV*)
```

will return a number relating to the value type. Refer to Table 17-1 for a list of definitions to use when identifying the type.

ACCESSING PERL VARIABLES BY NAME The **perl_get_sv** function obtains an **SV** by its fully qualified name within the script. For example, to get the value of **$foo** in the **main** package:

```
SV *foo = perl_get_sv("main::foo",0);
```

There shouldn't be any need to create a variable of a specified name using this function, although it is possible. If you want to pass information back to a Perl script, you should probably be using return values from a function anyway.

Array Values

An array is just a sequential list of scalar values. This is stored within Perl as an array of pointers to **SV**s. Entries in an **AV** can be referenced with an index, and adding new entries beyond the current maximum index number automatically increases the size of the **AV**. The functions for accessing **AV**s are summarized in Table 17-2.

Function/Macro	Description
AV* newAV()	Creates a new, empty **AV**.
AV* av_make(int num, SV **ptr)	Creates a new **AV** populated with the **SV**s contained in ****ptr**.
I32 av_len(AV*)	Returns the highest index of the array. Note that this is not the number of elements in the array; indexes start at zero, so the value is equivalent to **scalar(@array)-1**, or **$#array**.
SV av_fetch(AV *, I32 index, I32 lval)**	Returns a pointer to the **SV** at location **index** from an **AV**. Because a pointer is returned, you can use the reference to update as well as access the value stored. If **lval** is non-zero, then it replaces the value at **index** with **undef**.
SV av_store(AV*, I32 index, SV* val)**	Stores an **SV val** at **index** within an **AV** and returns the pointer to the new element.
void av_clear(AV*)	Deletes the references to all the **SV**s in an **AV**, but does not delete the **AV**.
void av_undef(AV*)	Deletes the **AV**.

Table 17-2. *Functions for Handling **AV**s*

Function/Macro	Description
void av_extend(AV*, int num)	Increases the size of the **AV** to **num** elements. If **num** is less than the current number of elements, it does nothing.
void av_push(AV*, SV*)	Pushes an **SV** onto the end of the **AV**. This is identical to the Perl **push** function.
SV* av_pop(AV*)	Pops an **SV** off the end of an **AV**. This is identical to the Perl **pop** function.
SV* av_shift(AV*)	Returns the first **SV** from an **AV**, deleting the first element. This is identical to the Perl **shift** function.
void av_unshift(AV*, I32 num)	Adds **num** elements to the end of an **AV**, but does not actually store any values. Use **av_store** to actually add the **SV**s onto the end of the **AV**. This is not quite identical to the operation of the **unshift** function.
AV* perl_get_av(char* varname, int create)	Gets the **AV** called **varname**, which should be a fully qualified name, without the leading @ sign. Creates an **AV** with the specified name if **create** is 1.

Table 17-2. *Functions for Handling **AVs*** (continued)

Hash Values

Hashes are only slightly more complex than **AV**s. A hash is a list of paired data consisting of a string key and a pointer to an **SV**. You cannot have two entries in a hash with the same key, trying to store a new value with an existing key will simply overwrite that value. The functions for accessing **HV**s are summarized in Table 17-3.

Function/Macro	Description
HV* newHV()	Creates a new, empty **HV**.
SV hv_store(HV* hash, char* key, U32 klen, SV* val, U32 hashval)**	Stores the pointer to **SV** against the **key**. You must supply the length of the key in **klen**. The value of **hashval** is the hash value used for storage. If it is zero, then the value is computed for you. The return value is a pointer to the location of the new value within the hash.
SV hv_fetch(HV* hash, char* key, U32 klen, I32 lval)**	Fetches an entry from an **HV**, returning a pointer to the value.
SV* hv_delete(HV* hash, char* key, U32 klen, I32 flags)	Deletes the element specified by **key**, returning a mortal copy of the value that was stored at that position. If you don't want this value, then specify **G_DISCARD** in the **flags** element.
void hv_clear(HV* hash)	Empties the contents of the hash, but does not delete the hash itself.
void hv_undef(HV* hash)	Empties the contents of the hash and then deletes it.
I32 hv_iterinit(HV* hash)	Returns the number of elements in the **HV**, and prepares for iteration through the hash.
SV* hv_iternextsv(HV* hash, char key, I32* pkeylen)**	Returns the value for the next element in the hash. The key is placed into the variable pointed to by **key**, the physical length of which is placed into the variable pointed to by **pkeylen**. This is the function used with the **keys**, **values**, and **each** functions within Perl.
HV* perl_get_hv(char* varname, int create)	Gets the hash named **varname**, which should be a fully qualified package name. If **create** is 1, the hash is created.

Table 17-3. *Accessing* ***HVs***

Glob Values

A typeglob or glob value (**GV**) relates real value types with a symbol table entry. This enables you to pass a typeglob in a Perl script and have the function use the correct type of value. Normally this is used for passing filehandles, but it can also be used for scalars, arrays, hashes, functions, and even formats. The result is that a single identifier, such as **value**, can be used as **$value**, **@value**, **%value**, and so on. What in fact happens is that the main identifier is referenced to each of the different value types through the glob value, which is an element in the symbol table hash. Strictly speaking, it's a stash, short for symbol table hash.

Some of the stash values are available directly within the C environment. These are **$_**, **$@**, **$&**, **$'**, and **$'** and relate to the C variables **defgv**, **errgv**, **ampergv**, **leftgv**, and **rightgv**, respectively.

The functions for accessing glob values are a modified subset of that used to access hash values, with functions closely tailored to the glob process. The functions are summarized in Table 17-4.

Function/Macro	Description
GvSV	Returns a pointer to an **SV**.
GvAV	Returns a pointer to an **AV**.
GvHV	Returns a pointer to an **HV**.
GvIO	Returns a pointer to a filehandle.
GvFORM	Returns a pointer to a format.
HV *gv_stashpv(char* name, int create)	Gets the corresponding **HV** for the glob named **name**, and creates it if **create** is equal to one.
HV *gv_stashsv(SV *, int create)	Gets the corresponding **HV** for the glob named by the **SV**, and creates it if **create** is equal to one.
HV *SvSTASH(SV* sv)	Gets the stash from a blessed object **sv**. You will need to use **SvRV(sv)** to dereference **sv** if it's a reference.
char* HvNAME(HV* stash)	Given a stash entry, returns the package name.

Table 17-4. *Accessing Values*

Other Values

Perl also supports objects and code values (**CV**) within the C environment. However, the methods for accessing these different elements are handled separately in this chapter. A **CV** can be accessed using a number of special functions, which are actually the functions used when you want to call Perl functions, and therefore covered under the "Embedding Perl" section later in the chapter.

The Stack

In Chapter 7 we looked at the use of a list or array as a stack. Data was pushed onto the top of the stack using **push**, and data was taken back using **pop**. The **push/pop** stack was classed as a LIFO stack, for last in, first out. The same principle is used within Perl to store the arguments that are passed to a function during a function call.

This is better understood with an example. When the **print** function is called with arguments, the strings and variables that are passed to it are pushed onto a stack. The internal function for **print** is then called, and its first action is to take the variables from the stack.

The actual sequence is slightly longer, since the Perl interpreter and the stack-handling system need to know when a function wants to examine the stack, and how many elements of the stack are actually destined for the function. The result is that there are two stacks. One is the real stack where the data is stored. The other is a stack of pointers, called the markstack, that shows where within the main stack the elements for a particular function start. You can see a sample diagram that demonstrates a simple function call, **add(2,2)**, in Figure 17-1.

You can see from the diagram that the arguments to the **add** function are stored in order from bottom to top. The function can determine how many arguments it has been passed by calculating the difference between the top of its stack, and the stack pointer information for the function in markstack.

The result is that the @_ array to the **add** function is populated with the contents of the stack. Within the realms of the Perl interpreter this happens automatically. Perl populates the stack when the **add** function is called, and populates the contents of @_ within the context of the **add** function for you to do with what you will. When the function exits, any return values are placed back on the Perl stack, so that the calling function can use the returned values. If the caller does not use the values, a special function is called, which removes the return values from the stack and also the corresponding markstack pointer.

When you are accessing the internals of the Perl interpreter via C, you need to do this stack manipulation manually. This is true whether you are calling Perl functions or creating Perl extensions. In both instances you will need to be able to exchange information between the Perl environment and the functions that make up the Perl interpreter.

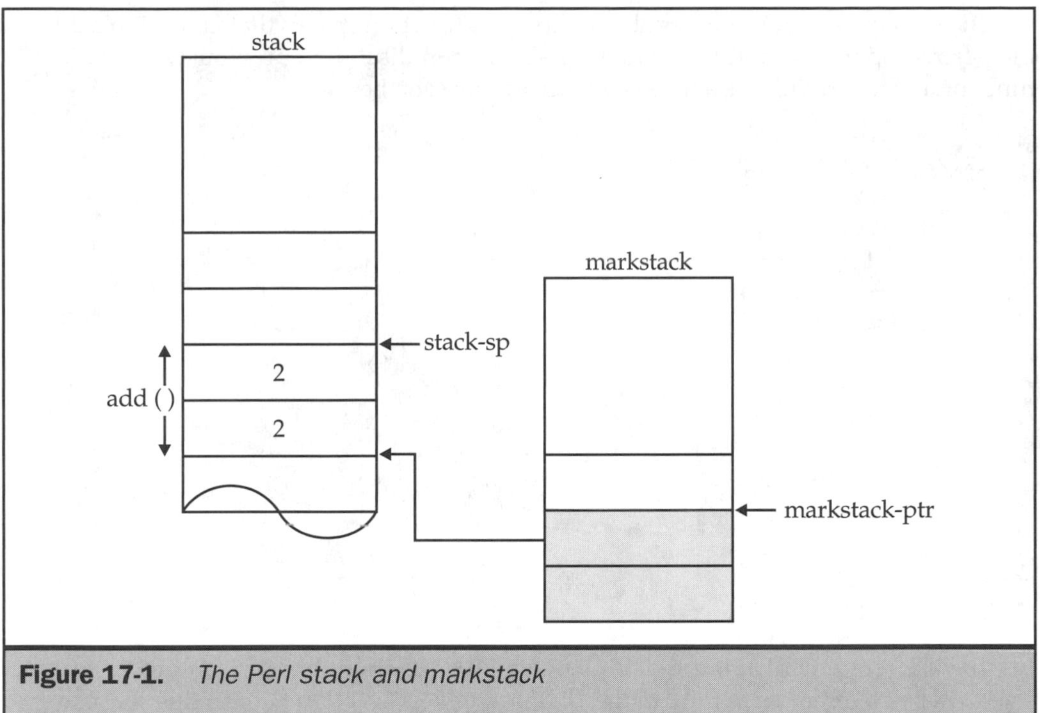

Figure 17-1. *The Perl stack and markstack*

There are some differences between the two environments that imply the need for this interface. Most significant of these is that Perl supports multiple values to be passed both to and from a function. Within C, a function can only return a single entity. Although this can include structures and unions, this feature is not supported in Perl. The use of a stack to hold the variables going in and out of a function supports the multiple value syntax that is one of the powerful features of Perl.

We'll deal with the use of the stack within a Perl extension first and then look at the effects of embedding Perl on the stack.

Stack Access Within Extensions

When a C function is called from Perl, the Perl stack is used to pass any arguments to the function. The process for retrieving arguments within the C code and then passing return values back is as follows:

1. Initialize the stack interface (**dXSARGS**).
2. Retrieve an argument from the stack into a variable (**ST**).
3. Place the return values back on the stack (**XSRETURN***).

The elements in parentheses above show the function macro that is used to achieve the desired operation. Returning to the **add** function discussed previously, the C function incorporating the above sequence can be seen below:

```
XS(XS_StatVFS_add)
{
    dXSARGS;
    if (items != 2)
        croak("Usage: StatVFS::add(a,b)");
    SP -= items;
    {
        int     a = (int)SvIV(ST(0));
        int     b = (int)SvIV(ST(1));
                XSRETURN_IV(a+b);
        PUTBACK;
        return;
    }
}
```

The **XS()** statement at the start defines a new C function for use with the XS system. This will be covered more fully in the "Extending Perl" section later in this chapter. The next call is to **dXSARGS**, which initializes a number of variables for use in the rest of the function. The most important is **items**, which specifies the number of arguments that were passed to the function. This is the value calculated by taking the value of the top of the stack pointer away from the pointer on markstack, and it is used in the next line to ensure that you have received the correct number of arguments to your function.

Next, the value of the stack pointer is reset to the beginning. You need to do this to ensure that any return values are not added on top of the arguments passed. When you access a value, it is not automatically removed from the stack. This is an optimization, since doing this deletion would add overhead that just isn't required if you manage the stack properly in the first place.

The next two lines actually extract the arguments from the stack. **ST()** is a special macro that accesses the stack directly. The first element, **ST(0)**, is equivalent to **$_[0]** within a Perl function. Note that the values are accessed in order, rather than popping them from the stack. This is to ensure that you receive the variables in the order that they were supplied in the code, not in the order they were pushed onto the stack.

The next line does the calculation by calling the **XSRETURN_IV()** macro. This macro places a new **IV** (integer) value onto the stack, ready to be returned to the caller. You can only use this, and its related functions, for passing back single variables to the caller. For returning lists you need to use a different method. See the section "Extending Perl" for more details.

The next line is not required. The **PUTBACK** macro is used to specify that you have finished placing values onto the stack. The **XS** stubs insert this function automatically, although if you are hand coding the function, you can get away without using it.

That's it. The function has been defined, and the arguments have successfully been taken from the stack and then put back. The available macros that you can use in this process are summarized in Table 17-5.

If you want to place more than one variable onto the stack to return to the caller, you will need to use a different method from the example above. Instead you will need to push values onto the stack, either with a push function or by accessing the stack elements directly using **ST()**. Either way, you should still, ideally, specify the number of elements

Macro	Description
dXSARGS	Defines the local variables used by other macros. Defines the **items** variable, which contains the number of items passed to the function via the stack.
SV* ST(n)	Retrieves element **n** from the stack as an **SV**. The first parameter is **ST(0)**.
XSRETURN(n)	Specifies the number of elements, **n**, you have left on the stack, adjusting the reference stored on the markstack.
XSRETURN_NO	Returns a value of **0**, and calls **XSRETURN(1)**.
XSRETURN_YES	Returns a value of **1**, and calls **XSRETURN(1)**.
XSRETURN_UNDEF	Returns a value of **undef**, and calls **XSRETURN(1)**.
XSRETURN_EMPTY	Returns a value of **0**, and calls **XSRETURN(1)**.
XSRETURN_IV()	Places a mortal **integer** on the stack, and calls **XSRETURN(1)**.
XSRETURN_NV()	Places a mortal **float** on the stack, and calls **XSRETURN(1)**.
XSRETURN_PV()	Places a mortal **char*** on the stack, and calls **XSRETURN(1)**.

Table 17-5. *Macros for Using the Stack Within Extensions*

you have pushed back onto the stack by calling **XSRETURN()**. For example, the lines below push both an addition and a subtraction calculation onto the stack:

```
XPUSHs(sv_2mortal(newSViv(a+b)));
XPUSHs(sv_2mortal(newSViv(a-b)));
XSRETURN(1);
```

The specification of these as mortal ensures that the values will be automatically freed at the end of the scope. See the earlier section "Scalar Values" for more information on marking them as mortal.

Stack Access for Embedded Perl

The process for calling a single Perl function with arguments is more or less identical to the previous extension example, except that the process is done in reverse. The process is as follows:

1. Initialize the environment (**dSP**).
2. Start the scope (**ENTER**).
3. Set up the environment such that temporary variables will be automatically deleted at the end of the scope (**SAVETMPS**).
4. Remember the current top of the stack (**PUSHMARK**).
5. Push arguments onto the stack (**XPUSHs**).
6. Signify the end of the arguments (**PUTBACK**).
7. Call the Perl function.
8. Signify the start of return value reclamation (**SPAGAIN**).
9. Get the values from the stack (**POP***).
10. Signify the end of return value reclamation (**PUTBACK**).
11. Free the temporary variables.
12. End the scope (**LEAVE**).

The same **add** function example will be used to demonstrate this sequence in practice. We'll assume the **add** function has already been defined within the Perl environment.

```
void perl_add(int a, int b)
{
    int retval;
    dSP;
    ENTER;
```

```
    SAVETMPS;
    PUSHMARK(sp);
    XPUSHs(sv_2mortal(newSViv(a)));
    XPUSHs(sv_2mortal(newSViv(b)));
    PUTBACK;
    retval = perl_call_pv("add", G_SCALAR);
    SPAGAIN;
    if (retval == 1)
        printf("Returned: %d\n",POPi);
    PUTBACK;
    FREETMPS;
    LEAVE;
}
```

If you followed the sequence at the start of this section, you should be able to follow the sequence in the code. The important parts are the calls to **XPUSHs**, which place the mortal values of the two arguments passed to the **perl_add** function onto the stack, and the **POPi** call. This pops the values placed onto the stack by the call to the Perl **add** function off of the stack. In this example, it's used in a **printf** statement.

The values popped off the stack in this way come off in the inverse order in which the values were placed onto the stack. That is, the last value in a list will be returned first. You'll need to account for this if you are accepting multiple values back from the Perl function.

The macros available when embedding Perl are summarized in Table 17-6.

Macro	Description
dSP	Sets up the environment for the following macros.
ENTER	Starts the scope of the call.
SAVETMPS	Marks all mortal variables created after this call to be deleted when **FREETMPS** is called.
PUSHMARK	Defines the start of the arguments to be pushed onto the stack.
XPUSHs	Pushes a scalar value onto the stack, extending the stack if necessary.

Table 17-6. *Macros Used When Embedding Perl Statements*

Macro	Description
XPUSHn	Pushes a double onto the stack, extending the stack if necessary.
XPUSHp	Pushes a string onto the stack, extending the stack if necessary.
XPUSHi	Pushes an integer onto the stack, extending the stack if necessary.
XPUSHu	Pushes an unsigned integer onto the stack, extending the stack if necessary.
PUSHs	Pushes a scalar value onto the stack. The stack must have room to accept the new value.
PUSHn	Pushes a double onto the stack. The stack must have room to accept the new value.
PUSHp	Pushes a string onto the stack. The stack must have room to accept the new value.
PUSHi	Pushes an integer onto the stack. The stack must have room to accept the new value.
PUSHu	Pushes an unsigned integer onto the stack. The stack must have room to accept the new value.
PUTBACK	Defines the end of the arguments placed on the stack.
SPAGAIN	Defines the start of the process for obtaining return values.
POPi	Pops an **int** value from the stack.
POPl	Pops a **long** value from the stack.
POPn	Pops a **double** value from the stack.
POPp	Pops a **pointer** value from the stack.
POPs	Pops a **char*** (string) value from the stack.
PUTBACK	Defines the end of the process for obtaining return values.
FREETMPS	Clears the variables marked as mortal.
LEAVE	Ends the scope.

Table 17-6. *Macros Used When Embedding Perl Statements* (continued)

Stack Size

The size of the stack is finite. Although you can normally add values to the stack without having to worry about its size, you may run into problems if you are passing a large number of variables between the C and Perl environments. The quickest way to increase the size of the stack is to use the **EXTEND** macro, as in

```
EXTEND(sp,10);
```

If you use the **XPUSHs** macro to place values onto the stack, and remember to reset the stack pointer to the beginning, you shouldn't need to use this, since **XPUSHs** increases the stack automatically. The XS interface resets the stack pointer for you when it creates the C code for the individual functions.

In practice, I've never had to use the **EXTEND** macro; but as a general rule, if you are returning or accepting more than ten elements, you may want to use this function to increase the available stack space. Remember, however, that increasing stack space also increases the memory footprint of your application.

Internals Summary

You should now be armed with all of the information (in fact, more information) than you will need for interfacing between C and Perl. The next two sections deal with the specifics of developing extensions to the Perl environment and the different methods for embedding Perl within an application.

Extending Perl

Writing a Perl extension is seen by many as a black art, only to be conducted by senior programmers in the recesses of their programming environments. Unlike modules, which only require a modicum of Perl knowledge to create, extensions require not only knowledge of C or C++, but also knowledge of the internals in order to make your extensions work within the Perl interpreter.

The process of creating an external C extension is actually more straightforward than you may think. An understanding of the internals of the Perl interpreter is not required, even by a relatively advanced extension programmer. You can write complex extensions using a small subset of the range that is available. That said, the introductory material provided in this and the previous chapter should prove invaluable to the understanding of the processes and conversions involved.

Once you are comfortable with the process we'll examine—or just because your curiosity gets the better of you—you can examine the Perl documentation for more in-depth detail. For reference, all the internals of the extension process and of the Perl interpreter itself are in the perlxs, perlxstut, and perlguts man pages. For further information, you might also want to refer to the perlcall and perlembed man pages, which contain information on the data interface between Perl and C, as well as details of how to embed a Perl interpreter into your C programs, which is also the next major topic in this chapter.

The process of developing the interface is made easier by two tools that eliminate much of the complexity involved: one is called the XS interface, and the other is called SWIG. The XS interface system is part of the standard Perl distribution and actually refers to the language used to define the interface. The Simplified Wrapper and Interface Generator (SWIG) is a third-party system written by Dave Beazley. It's also based on an intermediary language that defines the interface between the two language environments.

As you will notice as we progress through this section, much of the information here is not actually specific to producing extensions. The functions and methods explained will also apply to the process of calling the Perl interpreter from a C program. Conversion of information from C variables to the variable types used by the Perl interpreter, and therefore the Perl language, make up the bulk of the information provided, and the processes are vital for either extending or embedding Perl using C and C++.

The Extension Interface

The Perl interpreter has the ability to call external C functions. This is the basis of many of the built-in functions. When you call a function within Perl, it looks for the definition of the function. If it's a Perl function, it just jumps execution of the opcode tree to the start of the function definition. If it's a built-in function, it makes a call to the underlying C function, if necessary, or uses one of the data-handling functions you saw at the start of this chapter. If the function is neither built-in nor a Perl defined function, then it can be loaded from an external dynamic library. The development of an extension therefore requires you to build the library that Perl loads in order to execute your customized C function.

The actual process is slightly more complex than just creating a new function in C and installing it in the Perl directory hierarchy. There are some fundamental differences between the format of Perl data types and their C counterparts. C, for example, does not by default support hashes, whereas Perl does.

The development process must also create some code that interfaces between the internals of the Perl interpreter and the internals of a C function. This is called glue code and solves the two main differences between Perl and C—data types and memory management.

Data types in Perl are actually complex C structures. Some of the structure and complexity can be found at the beginning of this chapter where we looked at the different Perl variable types and the functions that enable you to access them. Most of the base data types, such as integers and strings, are handled automatically by both XS and SWIG. More complex structures and data types, including C structures and Perl objects, must have special typemapping code written for them so that both sides of the interface are able to access and use the information stored within them.

Perl handles all of its memory management automatically. When you create new variables and delete or undefine them, Perl automatically allocates and deallocates the necessary storage for each variable. C, on the other hand, expects you to do all of this explicitly. For simple variables this means specifying their size at the initialization stage, but for more complex or large variables you have to use the **calloc()** or **malloc()** function to allocate the memory, and **free()** to deallocate it when you've finished.

In addition, both interfaces solve two further problems—that of the specializations available in Perl and the glue code that is necessary to make the functions work. Specializations include the use of objects, packages, and multiple return values, which a Perl programmer takes for granted. The glue code is all of the necessary wrapper and interface code that makes a simple C function accessible within Perl.

XS Overview

The XS interface is part of the standard Perl distribution, and as such it is given more attention here than the third-party SWIG interface. XS, or XSUB, stands for eXternal SUBroutine. The term XS is usually taken to be the interface system, while XSUB specifies an individual function within the XS definition. Using the special language called XS, you specify the interface between a Perl module and the C functions you want access to. The actual layout is not hugely different from a typical C header file, except that the information is organized and structured to include the necessary links for the Perl side of the equation.

The XS file is then parsed by the **xsubpp** script, which processes the contents and spits out the C source code ready for compilation. The code includes all the necessary glue code and initialization procedures. You are expected to supply a suitable module for communicating between Perl and the underlying library, but otherwise, the process is completed.

Because of the similarity of the XS file to a header file, there is a tool, **h2xs**, that will convert existing header files into the XS format for you. This greatly simplifies the process of manually writing an interface to a C library by doing most of the work for you. In most cases, the converted file can be passed immediately onto **xsubpp**, and the resulting C source file is compiled without any further intervention.

SWIG Overview

The SWIG system takes a slightly different tack. SWIG itself was designed as an interface builder between C functions and a number of scripting systems. At the time of writing they include Perl, Python, Tcl, Guile, and Eiffel. A Java extension has also just been released that provides yet another tool for bringing Java to the desktop.

Like XS, SWIG uses an intermediary file that defines the interface between the C and the high-level language at which it is aimed. The result is two files—the glue code in a C file and the Perl module file that can be used to access it. This is more automated than the XS system, which requires you to develop your own module file if you are producing the XS file manually. With **h2xs**, of course, this is not an issue.

One big difference between SWIG and XS is that SWIG is capable of providing the necessary code to support the complex structures within C and objects within C++. The **h2xs** tool, on the other hand, is fairly dumb and can only handle simple data types and functions. Although you can design your own interface and typemap systems, it adds overhead to what is already a complex process.

I very rarely, however, find myself passing back structures or objects to Perl. Instead you use the other features such as hashes and multiple return values to return the information. If you consider the **getpwent** and similar functions, they all supply information back to the caller as structures when used in the C environment, but within Perl, the values are returned as a list.

Because of this generalized approach, SWIG is a much more practical solution if you are developing extensions to many scripting languages simultaneously. I've used it before for providing the same basic interface to a C library for both Python and Perl to suit the needs of two different clients at the same time. On a personal level, I actually prefer to use the XS system for Perl and SWIG for other languages if I'm developing for them in isolation. If I have to develop a library that will be practical for many languages, I use SWIG, if only to cut down on the headaches from developing on two different systems.

There is a school of thought that says XS is better than SWIG because it's a Perl-derived tool and can therefore take advantage of the Perl environment better than SWIG. I've never once found that to be the case. The two systems produce code that is almost identical, and unless you are doing something very Perl specific, it's likely that either tool will suit you well. The other thing to consider is that all of the modules on CPAN are provided as XS rather than SWIG extensions. If you ever plan to provide your module to the Perl community, use XS.

Using XS

For the process of designing an extension we'll be examining the creation of two sample modules. The first is our own interface to the standard C math library, which will help us to cover the basics of the XS process. The other is more complex and will demonstrate the advanced features of the XS interface as we develop a simple module that obtains the size of a file system using the **statvfs()** function that is available on many Unix platforms. The result will be a new Perl function. You supply the directory or file name, and the function will return a list of scalars, detailing the total size of the file system and the amount of space used and available.

Although this example could be classed as platform specific (it was generated on a Sun Solaris 2.4 machine), the principles learned here will easily translate to other functions and modules. Where necessary, we'll also be side-tracking to look at the other features and capabilities of the XS system.

The h2xs Converter

For all libraries there is a corresponding header file that contains the definitions of any constant values, structure definitions, and the prototypes of any functions contained within the library. Although the XS system does not handle C structures, you can use the **h2xs** utility to convert an existing header file into an XS file, suitable for producing the interface.

This command reads in the contents of the header file and produces an XS file that consists of all the basic definitions and function interface components to make the C functions available as an extension in Perl. The file produced is very basic and is only suitable for functions that return one of the basic data types. You will need to modify the file if you want to do more complex conversions, or if you want to return, say, the contents of a structure as a list of return values. The modification and production of this information makes up the bulk of this section of the chapter.

In addition, **h2xs** produces a module file with all the necessary code required to import the external C function and provide the necessary constants and other values to a Perl script. The module file also includes a bare template of some POD formatted documentation that you should modify if you plan on distributing the module to other people.

The other major component is a Perl Makefile called Makefile.PL. This contains the absolute minimum of definitions required to ensure that the **MakeMaker** module produces a Makefile suitable for building and installing the extension. This takes a lot of the guesswork out of the process of compiling the extension, as you will see. It's also the method used in the CPAN modules to automatically extract, build, and install the extension on any destination machine. See Chapter 20 for more information.

Finally, **h2xs** produces a test script and two documentation files. The test.pl file just calls each of the functions mentioned to make sure they could be loaded. Again, this file should be modified to include more complex tests to ensure that the extension can be used properly. By default, it's the script used to test the distribution when a **make test** command is run. The Changes file is provided for you to record any modifications, and the MANIFEST file lists the files that make up the core files required for the extension. These files are vital components of a typical CPAN module because they provide additional information to the user about the expected contents of the package they have downloaded.

Using, the **h2xs** script is very straightforward:

```
$ h2xs /usr/include/sys/statvfs.h
Writing Statvfs/Statvfs.pm
Writing Statvfs/Statvfs.xs
Writing Statvfs/Makefile.PL
Writing Statvfs/test.pl
Writing Statvfs/Changes
Writing Statvfs/MANIFEST
```

The file name and package name are title-cased, as per the usual Perl standards, and, depending on the source content, the files are written into a separate subdirectory. In theory, the files produced should be ready for compilation and installation. If you need to include additional libraries when using the functions, you should append the library names to the command line you supply.

There are also some options to the **h2xs** command, but refer to the man page for more information. The core of the XS system is the XS file, and although one is produced by the **h2xs** system, it is much more likely that you will want to build in some form of customization.

The .xs File

The XS file is the core of the XS system. It defines the interface between Perl and the underlying C functions you are providing an interface to. Although in some cases the file will be automatically produced by the **h2xs** utility, it's unlikely that it will perfectly match either the desired results or the interface you have come to expect between callers and functions in the Perl language.

Once the XS file has been created, it is parsed by a Perl script, **xsubpp**, which takes the information provided and produces the C source file with the necessary statements required to build the interface library.

The format of the file is as follows:

```
C includes

MODULE: Name PACKAGE: Name

OPTIONS

function definitions
```

The top section is passed verbatim onto the C source file that is generated. The headers you include at this point should consist of all the headers required for the functions you are using. The **PACKAGE** and **MODULE** definitions set the module and package names. There are then a number of options that affect the whole interface process, before you proceed to the function definitions.

The format of the function definitions is very strict. The return type is specified first, on its own line, followed by the name of the function and a list of argument names that can be supplied. Then, one per line, come the data type declarations for the argument names. These type declarations are also very strict. If you are defining a pointer to an argument (as in **char* string**), the asterisk must remain with the type, not the argument name. Finally, there are a number of function-specific options. We'll cover all these different aspects as we examine the different XS file complexities.

If we look at a real function definition for our math interface, you can see the format more clearly:

```
double
tan (value)
        double value
```

As you can see, the return value is specified on its own line, and the function's only argument is specified on its own line. This is actually all you need to do if the function is simple. In this case, the **tan()** function accepts and returns a simple value, so there is no need to do any conversion between, say, a structure and a list of return values for Perl. The XS interface system will handle everything else during the compilation process. It really is that simple and straightforward.

You need to understand that the functions you "define" within the XS file are merely function mappings between the function as it will appear in Perl, and the function call and arguments accepted within the C environment. In the above example, a map is created between the **tan** function in Perl and the **tan()** function in C. The definition of the passed and returned values helps the XS process identify the arguments supported by the Perl function and determine how they translate to the underlying C function. The actual conversion of the values is handled automatically by the XS system in conjunction with a predefined **typemap**.

Let's look at a more complex example—this time the **StatVFS** module, which we'll use to discuss the more advanced components of the XS file structure. The full file can be seen below. It defines two functions, **fsavail** and **fsstat**. The **fsavail** function is a simple one-shot function to find out the number of bytes available on a file system. It returns a long integer specifying the number of bytes. The **fsstat** function returns a list of values containing the total size, space used, and space available for a file system. In both cases, the functions take a single argument—a string containing a file path. The internal **statvfs** function uses this to determine which file system to return the space for.

```
#include "EXTERN.h"
#include "perl.h"
#include "XSUB.h"

#include <sys/types.h>
#include <sys/statvfs.h>

MODULE = StatVFS    PACKAGE = StatVFS

PROTOTYPES: DISABLE

long
fsavail (path)
        char *  path
```

```
        CODE:
              struct statvfs vfsrec;
              int statreturn;
              statreturn = statvfs(path,&vfsrec);
              if (statreturn == 0)
              {
                  RETVAL = (vfsrec.f_frsize * vfsrec.f_bavail);
              }
              else
              {
                  RETVAL = -1;
              }
        OUTPUT:
        RETVAL

void
fsstat (path)
        char *  path
        PPCODE:
        {
              struct statvfs vfsrec;
              int statreturn;
              statreturn = statvfs(path,&vfsrec);
              if (statreturn == 0)
              {
                  PUSHs(sv_2mortal(
                          newSViv(vfsrec.f_frsize *
                                  vfsrec.f_blocks)));
                  PUSHs(sv_2mortal(
                          newSViv((vfsrec.f_frsize *
                                  (vfsrec.f_blocks-vfsrec.f_bavail)))));
                  PUSHs(sv_2mortal(
                          newSViv((vfsrec.f_frsize *
                                   vfsrec.f_bavail))));
              }
        }
```

The important things to note with this file are the function definitions. For both functions, you are no longer mapping directly between the supported C function, **statvfs()**, and its identical cousin in Perl, **statvfs**. Instead, you are creating brand-new functions that act as wrappers around the underlying calls to the **statvfs()** C function. You no longer rely on XS to do the translation, because the underlying function you are calling returns a C structure, not a single value. C doesn't support multiple return values, so you need to do some manipulation of the information returned in order to translate it into a simple list of values.

For the **fsavail** function you rely on the XS system to convert between the **long** that you've stated as the return value, and a normal integer value within Perl. You assign the return value to a special variable, **RETVAL**, and then mark that variable with the **OUTPUT:** keyword as the value to be returned to Perl when this function is called.

For the **fsstat** function you do this conversion within a **PPCODE** block, which tells the XS interface builder that you are manipulating the contents of the Perl stack directly, rather than supplying a return value. The first few steps create the required C structures and then call the **statvfs()** library function to populate the structure with the information you want. In addition to the **PPCODE:** definition, you also need to ensure that the function is defined as **void**, since you are not directly returning any values from the function.

Then you push values onto the Perl argument stack with the **PUSHs** function, which you saw in the section "Stack Access for Embedded Perl" earlier in this chapter. This pushes a scalar value—in this case an integer—onto the stack. You could (and perhaps should) have used the **XPUSHs** function to ensure that the stack was extended accordingly. For only three values, we're probably safe with **PUSHs**.

Note that the calculated values are encapsulated within a call to **newSViv**, which creates a new integer scalar value, and **sv_2mortal**, which marks the scalar value as mortal, allowing it to be deleted when the whole process has finished. This helps to prevent memory problems by freeing up values after they have been used—you have no need for those temporary values in the calculation.

Also note that error checking is supported in the **fsstat** by returning an empty list, the default return value on an error; while **fsavail** returns -1 on an error, also the default operation when calling external system functions. Remember that you can't use zero as a return value, because that could equally indicate that there was no available space on the drive.

For reference, the format for the **statvfs** C structure is shown below:

```
typedef struct statvfs {
        u_long  f_bsize;        /* fundamental file system block size */
        u_long  f_frsize;       /* fragment size */
        u_long  f_blocks;       /* total # of blocks of f_frsize on fs */
        u_long  f_bfree;        /* total # of free blocks of f_frsize */
        u_long  f_bavail;       /* # of free blocks avail to non-superuser */
        u_long  f_files;        /* total # of file nodes (inodes) */
        u_long  f_ffree;        /* total # of free file nodes */
        u_long  f_favail;       /* # of free nodes avail to non-superuser */
        u_long  f_fsid;         /* file system id (dev for now) */
        char    f_basetype[FSTYPSZ]; /* target fs type name */
        u_long  f_flag;         /* bit-mask of flags */
        u_long  f_namemax;      /* maximum file name length */
        char    f_fstr[32];     /* filesystem-specific string */
        u_long  f_filler[16];   /* reserved for future expansion */
} statvfs_t;
```

Again, the process is relatively straightforward. If you know how to program in C, you should be able to create and access the necessary structures and use the techniques shown here to produce a customized interface to a C function. Of course, there is no reason to use and translate values determined by an external function; you could use the **CODE** or **PPCODE** block to define your C function without requiring an external function at all.

XS Keywords

You've already seen some of the keywords used by the XS system to indicate different operations and situations. The full list is given here, including all the currently supported keywords and operations.

As a general rule, all keywords with a trailing colon expect some form of argument, statement, or code block following them. Keywords without a trailing colon are generally assigned to (as with **RETVAL**) or assign values or options to an existing statement (as in **NO_INIT**). The exact location and use of these varies, so ensure you understand the descriptions and locations given.

ALIAS: You can specify additional unique Perl names for the current **XSUB** using the **ALIAS:** keyword. The format used is a simple assignation statement, where each individual name should be given an incremental integer value. When called, you can identify which name was used by the value of the **ix** variable, which will contain the number defined in the **XSUB**. If **ix** contains zero, then it was called by its original name. The example below shows that **fsavail** is also available as **spaceavail** and **fileavail**:

```
long
fsavail (path)
        char *  path
        ALIAS:
        spaceavail = 1
        fileavail  = 2
        CODE:
              struct statvfs vfsrec;
              int statreturn;
              statreturn = statvfs(path,&vfsrec);
              if (statreturn == 0)
              {
                  RETVAL = (vfsrec.f_frsize * vfsrec.f_bavail);
              }
              else
              {
                  RETVAL = -1;
              }
        OUTPUT:
        RETVAL
```

BOOT: This keyword defines the code to be added as part of the extension's bootstrap function, which is used to register the XSUB within the current Perl interpreter. The **xsubpp** program actually generates the bootstrap function, and the statements added with the **BOOT:** keyword will be appended to the standard bootstrap code. The keyword can be used at any time after the **MODULE** keyword, and a blank line will terminate the bootstrap code.

C_ARGS: This keyword allows you to define an alternate sequence for passing the arguments received to the underlying function. For example, if you were providing an interface to a program that calculated the power of a number,

```
int power(raise, number);
```

you might want to provide the function within Perl as

```
power(number, raise);
```

The definition you would use might be

```
int
power(number, raise)
    int number;
    int raise;
C_ARGS:
    raise, number
```

This negates the need to use the **CODE:** or **PPCODE:** keyword.

CASE: The **CASE:** keyword allows you to set up a multiple choice option list within an XSUB. The **CASE:** statement can switch via an XSUB parameter, via the **ix** variable, created via the **ALIAS:** keyword or through the **items** variable (see "Accepting Variable Length Argument Lists" below). The **CASE:** keyword must be the first entry in the XSUB definition, and it will swallow all remaining arguments to the current XSUB, regardless of their contents.

The format of **CASE:** is very similar to a typical **switch** statement within the standard Unix shell. For example, below is an alternative to the **ALIAS:** and **C_ARGS:** keywords. This time the **CASE:** keyword is used to allow both **power** (which raises **a** to the power of **b**) and **r_power** (which raises **b** to the power of **a**):

```
int
power(a, b)
```

```
CASE: ix == 1
    ALIAS:
    r_power = 1
    INPUT:
    int a
    int b
    CODE:
         RETVAL = power(a,b)
    OUTPUT:
    RETVAL
CASE:
    int a
    int b
    CODE:
         RETVAL = power(b,a)
    OUTPUT:
    RETVAL
```

Note that you place a conditional statement after the **CASE:** keyword to act as the matching value; the last **CASE:** becomes the default if you do not specify a conditional statement.

CLEANUP: This keyword enables you to define additional code to be called before the XSUB terminates. This keyword must follow a **CODE:**, **PPCODE:**, or **OUTPUT:** block. The defined code will be appended to the end of these blocks as the last statements within the XSUB.

CODE: The **CODE:** keyword supports the inclusion of additional wrapper code to be used when calling the function. See the **fsavail** definition above for an example. Note that the **RETVAL** is not automatically assumed to be the return value; you explicitly define this via the **OUTPUT:** keyword.

INCLUDE: You can use this keyword to specify the name of another file from which to import XS code:

```
INCLUDE: AddFuncs.xsh
```

You can also import the information from an external command by appending a | symbol:

```
INCLUDE: generatedXS.pl |
```

INIT: The **INIT:** keyword allows you to insert initialization code before the destination function is called. This can be used for initializing variables, allocating memory or inserting debugging statements. Unlike **CODE:**, **RETVAL** works as you expect.

INPUT: This keyword causes the input parameters to be evaluated later than normal within the function initialization. This is usually used in conjunction with the **PREINIT:** keyword and may be included multiple times within the XSUB definition.

INTERFACE: The **INTERFACE:** keyword allows you to define a mapping for a number of functions simultaneously. For example, when developing an interface to a suite of functions that all have the same argument list, such as **sin**, **cos**, **tan**, you could define them as

```
float
interface_s(value)
        float value
INTERFACE:
    sin cos tan
```

All three functions are now available as individual functions, but you have saved some time processing the directory.

INTERFACE_MACRO: This keyword allows you to define an **INTERFACE** (as defined above) using a predefined macro to extract a function pointer for the XSUB definition. The text following this function should be the names of the preprocessor macros that would extract and set a function pointer. The default macros are **XSINTERFACE_FUNC** and **XSINTERFACE_FUNC_SET**, and are used if you don't explicitly specify them. The extractor macro is given the return type, the **CV***code value pointer, and the **XSANY.any_dptr** pointer for the **CV***. The macro for setting the function is given **cv** (the code value) and the pointer to the correct function.

MODULE The **MODULE** keyword starts the XS definition section of the XS file:

```
MODULE = StatVFS
```

Everything before the **MODULE** keyword is taken as raw C code to be passed on to the C file created by **xsubpp**. The name specified will be used as the basis of the bootstrap function that will form the interface between Perl and the C functions. It will also be the name of the package that will use the function unless you specify differently with the **PACKAGE** keyword.

NO_INIT This keyword indicates that a function parameter is being used only as an output value, as in the case of a passed parameter being populated by the function and then used as the return value. This option prevents Perl from taking all the arguments from the argument stack and assigning them to C variables upon entry. For example:

```
bool_t
rpcb_gettime(host, timep)
    char *host;
    time_t &timep = NO_INIT
    OUTPUT:
    timep
```

OUTPUT: The **OUTPUT:** keyword indicates that a particular value within the function arguments has been updated, and the new values should be made available to Perl when the function terminates. This is useful for functions where you are passing the address of a structure to the C function. The C function updates the contents of the array or structure directly, but may actually return an unrelated value (usually an error code). By defining the passed variable or structure as the **OUTPUT:** value, Perl knows this is the information to return to the calling Perl script.

You should also use this keyword when it is unclear what value Perl should be returning. When you use a **CODE:** block, the **RETVAL** variable is not recognized as an output variable, and you would need to pass **RETVAL** to the **OUTPUT:** keyword to ensure that the XS interface returns the correct information.

Finally, an **OUTPUT:** keyword can be used to create an in-line typemap; so the output parameter can be mapped to a particular piece of code, just as it would in the standard typemap.

PACKAGE You can specify an alternative package name or the specific package name if it's part of a package hierarchy, using the **PACKAGE** keyword:

```
MODULE = StatVFS PACKAGE = StatVFS
```

It is always used with the **MODULE** keyword.

PPCODE: This defines a block of code, just like the **CODE:** block. However, the XS system expects you to update the contents of the Perl stack directly, rather than relying on return values. You also need to make the call to the underlying function yourself, which allows you to use a different function name from that of the XSUB. You will also need to handle errors and conversions within the **PPCODE:** block. This is also the only way you can support a function that returns multiple values.

PREFIX The **PREFIX** keyword should follow the **MODULE** and/or **PACKAGE** keywords and specifies a string that should be removed from the C function when it is requested within Perl:

```
MODULE = StatVFS PREFIX = prefix
```

For example, if the function is **rpcb_gettime()**, then you might specify a **PREFIX** of **rpcb_** so that function is available within Perl as **gettime()**.

PREINIT: The **PREINIT:** keyword enables you to declare additional variables before they are parsed through the typemap. This prevents the ordinary parsing of the supplied variable through the typemap when it is used within a **CODE:** block. You can use this keyword one or more times within the XSUB definition.

PROTOTYPE: You can specify a particular prototype for an individual function with this keyword. This overrides all other prototypes and keywords for the current XSUB. The prototype format follows the normal Perl conventions. See Chapter 5 for more details.

```
long
fsavail (path)
        char *  path
        PROTOTYPE: $
        CODE:
              struct statvfs vfsrec;
              int statreturn;
              statreturn = statvfs(path,&vfsrec);
              if (statreturn == 0)
              {
                  RETVAL = (vfsrec.f_frsize * vfsrec.f_bavail);
              }
              else
              {
                  RETVAL = -1;
              }
        OUTPUT:
        RETVAL
```

PROTOTYPES: Creates Perl prototypes for the XSUB functions. This overrides the **-prototypes** and **-noprototypes** options to the **xsubpp** compiler. Prototypes are enabled by default, so to explicitly enable them:

```
PROTOTYPES: ENABLE
```

Or to disable them (permanently):

```
PROTOTYPES: DISABLE
```

REQUIRE: This keyword allows you to specify the minimum version number of the XS interface and, more specifically, the **xsubpp** compiler that you want to use:

```
REQUIRE: 1.9507
```

SCOPE: This keyword enables scoping for a particular XSUB. To enable scoping:

```
SCOPE: ENABLE
```

This will cause the **ENTER** and **LEAVE** macros to be called automatically (see "The Stack" earlier in the chapter). You can switch it off with

```
SCOPE: DISABLE
```

VERSIONCHECK This enables or disables version checking and overrides the command line options to the **xsubpp** program. With version checking switched on (the default), the XS module will verify that its version number matches the version number of the host Perl module. To enable version checking:

```
VERSIONCHECK: ENABLE
```

And to disable:

```
VERSIONCHECK: DISABLE
```

XS Tricks

Using the above keywords and some other tricks, there are ways in which you can easily get around problems without resorting to additional C code within the XSUB definition.

INITIALIZING PARAMETERS When an argument from Perl is supplied to the underlying function you are mapping within XS, a typemap entry is used to convert the supplied Perl value (**IV**, **NV**, **SV**, and so on) into a suitable C data type. You can override the conversions supported within a typemap (see the section "Typemaps" below) by supplying your own initialization code as part of the XSUB definition. The method required is to use typemap code directly within the XSUB definition, as shown here:

```
long
fsavail (path)
        char *  path = (char *)SvPV($arg,PL_na);
        CODE:
              struct statvfs vfsrec;
              int statreturn;
              statreturn = statvfs(path,&vfsrec);
              if (statreturn == 0)
              {
                  RETVAL = (vfsrec.f_frsize * vfsrec.f_bavail);
              }
              else
              {
                  RETVAL = -1;
              }
        OUTPUT:
        RETVAL
```

The supplied code will be **eval**'d before it is parsed by the compiler, so care should be taken to ensure you backslash-quote any Perl variables. The special variables supported by the typemap system are also supported here, so you can use **$var**, **$arg**, and **$type** directly within the initialization code.

For more complex operations you can also use initialization strings that begin with **;** or **+** rather than the **=** used above. In the **=** and **;** cases, the supplied code overrides the code supplied by the typemap, while the **+** form is in addition to the typemap code, which is executed before the supplied code. Both the **;** and **+** forms output the initialization code after the arguments have been declared, in deference to the **=** format, where the initialization is placed on the same line.

DEFAULT VALUES Many Perl functions allow you to use them without specifying any arguments. For example, the **fsavail** function might be handy to use like this:

```
$rootfree = fsavail;
```

In order to do this you need to set a default value for this instance of a function call. The normal operation, of course, is for Perl to accept values of the argument stack and pass them to the XSUB. The value you assign will be used if the caller does not supply any values. The method for doing this is to specify the default value within the XSUB definition:

```
long
fsavail (path="/")
        char *  path
        CODE:
              struct statvfs vfsrec;
              int statreturn;
              statreturn = statvfs(path,&vfsrec);
              if (statreturn == 0)
              {
                  RETVAL = (vfsrec.f_frsize * vfsrec.f_bavail);
              }
              else
              {
                  RETVAL = -1;
              }
        OUTPUT:
        RETVAL
```

RETURNING undef IMPLICITLY You can return **undef** from the C function by using a **CODE:** block and setting the first return value to that returned by **sv_newmortal()**, which returns the undefined value default. You could therefore rewrite the **fsavail** function as

```
SV *
fsavail (path)
        char *  path
        CODE:
              struct statvfs vfsrec;
              int statreturn;
              statreturn = statvfs(path,&vfsrec);
              ST(0) = sv_newmortal();
              if (statreturn == 0)
              {
                  sv_setnv( ST(0),(vfsrec.f_frsize
                            * vfsrec.f_bavail));
              }
```

Note the other changes to the function definition. You are returning a scalar value directly, rather than relying on the XS system to do the conversion for you. This means a change to the return type, which is now a pointer to a scalar value, and a modification to the return value. You now have to set the value of **ST(0)**, the "top" entry within the stack, explicitly to an integer value with the **sv_setnv()** function.

RETURNING undef EXPLICITLY You can explicitly (rather than implicitly) return an undefined value by setting the return value to the address of **&PL_sv_undef**; so you can rewrite the above as

```
SV *
fsavail (path)
        char *  path
        CODE:
              struct statvfs vfsrec;
              int statreturn;
              statreturn = statvfs(path,&vfsrec);
              ST(0) = sv_newmortal();
              if (statreturn == 0)
              {
                  sv_setnv( ST(0),(vfsrec.f_frsize
                            * vfsrec.f_bavail));
              }
              else
              {
                  ST(0) = &PL_sv_undef;
              }
```

RETURNING EMPTY LISTS You have already seen an example of returning an empty list. It requires use of a **PPCODE:** block, to ensure that the XS system recognizes that you are manipulating the stack directly. To empty an empty list, you just neglect to push any values onto the stack.

ACCEPTING VARIABLE LENGTH ARGUMENT LISTS To accept a variable length of arguments from Perl to a C function, you need to specify an **...** (ellipsis) in the parameter list. This is the same structure as used by ANSI C to define a multiargument function within Perl. Once you have specified this within the function definition, you can examine the value of the **items** variable, supplied to all XSUBS, which specifies the number of arguments supplied.

Once you have determined how many arguments have been supplied, you can then take off the stack directly using **ST()**. You will need to convert the supplied argument yourself, using the correct function to convert from the internal Perl data type to the C equivalent.

Typemaps

The XS system handles the translation of most of the basic data types used in C and Perl automatically. For more complex entities such as structures and objects, you need to tell the XS system how to convert and translate between the different formats. The Perl distribution installs its own basic typemap, which is composed of, and converts between, most of the data types used as part of the standard libraries. For nonstandard libraries you will need to supply your own typemaps if you want XS to convert between structures and objects transparently. Obviously, if you are using a **CODE:** or **PPCODE:** block, then chances are you are doing your own conversion by returning a specific value or list of values to the caller; the typemap is only used for automatic conversions.

The default typemap is contained within the **ExtUtils** directory within your Perl library. Any typemap you define within the local XS directory will override the conversions available in the default typemap.

A typemap is split into three parts: **TYPEMAP**, **INPUT**, and **OUTPUT**. The **TYPEMAP** section contains instructions on how to translate between formats, using the definitions in the **INPUT** and **OUTPUT** sections. The **INPUT** section tells the XS system how to translate Perl values into C variables, and the **OUTPUT** section tells the XS system how to translate C values into Perl values.

The file is parsed by Perl, so the constructs and code should be Perl friendly, even though the resulting code within the typemap will be compiled as C source to perform the conversions. The value to be converted is in the **$arg** variable, and the **$var** variable is the destination of the translated value. Thus you can generate a simple typemap for converting integer values into Perl scalars and back again like this:

```
int                     T_IV
unsigned                T_IV
unsigned int            T_IV
long                    T_IV
unsigned long           T_IV
short                   T_IV
unsigned short          T_IV
INPUT
T_IV
        $var = ($type)SvIV($arg)
OUTPUT
T_IV
        sv_setiv($arg, (IV)$var);
```

The top of the example is the **TYPEMAP** section, which is implied if no section is specified. The definitions show the C type on the left and the corresponding **INPUT** or **OUTPUT** map to be used on the right. The definition, **T_IV** in this case, is then looked up in the corresponding section, depending on whether you are passing an argument to a C function, or returning a value from a C function. The corresponding code is then **eval**'d by Perl and used within the XSUB to do the conversion. Note that you can use the same definition for multiple **TYPEMAP** entries.

If you want to convert structures, you can use the predefined **T_PTROBJ** and **T_PTRREF**, which convert a structure to and from a blessed reference, or an unblessed reference, respectively. This allows you to interface directly, both to normal C structures and to C++ objects; the XS interface will handle the conversion for you.

For most situations, the use of a **PPCODE:** block, where you can return a list of values, is generally the best method, since it fits in with the style of the core Perl functions such as **getpwnam** and others.

The Extension Module

Provided you have used **h2xs** to create a base XS file and module, you should rarely need to make any modifications to it. However, it's worth looking at the code to understand the processes involved in loading and using your extension after it has been compiled.

```
package StatVFS;

use strict;
use Carp;
use vars qw($VERSION @ISA @EXPORT @EXPORT_OK $AUTOLOAD);

require Exporter;
require DynaLoader;
require AutoLoader;

@ISA = qw(Exporter DynaLoader);
# Items to export into callers namespace by default. Note: do
# not export names by default without a very good reason. Use
# EXPORT_OK instead.
# Do not simply export all your public functions/methods/constants.
@EXPORT = qw(
             fsavail
             fsstat
             );

$VERSION = '0.02';

sub AUTOLOAD {
```

```
    # This AUTOLOAD is used to 'autoload' constants from the
    # constant() XS function. If a constant is not found then
    # control is passed to the AUTOLOAD in AutoLoader.

    my $constname;
    ($constname = $AUTOLOAD) =~ s/.*:://;
    croak "& not defined" if $constname eq 'constant';
    my $val = constant($constname, @_ ? $_[0] : 0);
    if ($! != 0) {
        if ($! =~ /Invalid/) {
            $AutoLoader::AUTOLOAD = $AUTOLOAD;
            goto &AutoLoader::AUTOLOAD;
        }
        else {
                croak "Your vendor has not defined StatVFS macro
$constname";
        }
    }
    *$AUTOLOAD = sub () { $val };
    goto &$AUTOLOAD;
}

bootstrap StatVFS $VERSION;

# Preloaded methods go here.

# Autoload methods go after =cut, and are processed by the
# autosplit program.

1;
__END__
```

The most obvious item you will need to change in the module file is the names of the functions you have defined within the XS file. Of course, there is nothing to stop you from adding more Perl functions, variables, or statements to the generated file—it is, after all, just an ordinary module.

Two elements are omitted from the example. One is the list of constants that may or may not be defined within the header file from which the extension and module were produced. There are no constants required for the **StatVFS** module, so there was no **constant()** function to define within the XS file. However, for an example see the XS interface file from a typical math.h header file below. The method is to create a function called **constant()**, which accepts the name of the constant to look up. You then use C code and a **switch()** statement to identify the constant that was requested and return the correct value, which is itself taken from the macro values defined in the header file.

```
#include "EXTERN.h"
#include "perl.h"
#include "XSUB.h"

#include <math.h>

static int
not_here(char *s)
{
    croak("%s not implemented on this architecture", s);
    return -1;
}

static double
constant(char *name, int arg)
{
    errno = 0;
    switch (*name) {
    case 'A':
   break;
    case 'B':
   break;
    case 'C':
   break;
    case 'D':
   if (strEQ(name, "DOMAIN"))
#ifdef DOMAIN
       return DOMAIN;
#else
       goto not_there;
#endif
   break;
    case 'E':
   break;
    case 'F':
   break;
    case 'G':
```

```
   break;
    case 'H':
   if (strEQ(name, "HUGE"))
#ifdef HUGE
       return HUGE;
#else
       goto not_there;
#endif
   if (strEQ(name, "HUGE_VAL"))
#ifdef HUGE_VAL
       return HUGE_VAL;
#else
       goto not_there;
#endif
   break;
    case 'I':
   break;
    case 'J':
   break;
    case 'K':
   break;
    case 'L':
   break;
    case 'M':
   if (strEQ(name, "MAXFLOAT"))
#ifdef MAXFLOAT
       return MAXFLOAT;
#else
       goto not_there;
#endif
   if (strEQ(name, "M_1_PI"))
#ifdef M_1_PI
       return M_1_PI;
#else
       goto not_there;
#endif
   if (strEQ(name, "M_2_PI"))
#ifdef M_2_PI
       return M_2_PI;
#else
       goto not_there;
#endif
```

```
    if (strEQ(name, "M_2_SQRTPI"))
#ifdef M_2_SQRTPI
        return M_2_SQRTPI;
#else
        goto not_there;
#endif
    if (strEQ(name, "M_E"))
#ifdef M_E
        return M_E;
#else
        goto not_there;
#endif
    if (strEQ(name, "M_LN10"))
#ifdef M_LN10
        return M_LN10;
#else
        goto not_there;
#endif
    if (strEQ(name, "M_LN2"))
#ifdef M_LN2
        return M_LN2;
#else
        goto not_there;
#endif
    if (strEQ(name, "M_LOG10E"))
#ifdef M_LOG10E
        return M_LOG10E;
#else
        goto not_there;
#endif
    if (strEQ(name, "M_LOG2E"))
#ifdef M_LOG2E
        return M_LOG2E;
#else
        goto not_there;
#endif
    if (strEQ(name, "M_PI"))
#ifdef M_PI
        return M_PI;
#else
        goto not_there;
#endif
```

```
   if (strEQ(name, "M_PI_2"))
#ifdef M_PI_2
       return M_PI_2;
#else
       goto not_there;
#endif
   if (strEQ(name, "M_PI_4"))
#ifdef M_PI_4
       return M_PI_4;
#else
       goto not_there;
#endif
   if (strEQ(name, "M_SQRT1_2"))
#ifdef M_SQRT1_2
       return M_SQRT1_2;
#else
       goto not_there;
#endif
   if (strEQ(name, "M_SQRT2"))
#ifdef M_SQRT2
       return M_SQRT2;
#else
       goto not_there;
#endif
   break;
    case 'N':
   break;
    case 'O':
   if (strEQ(name, "OVERFLOW"))
#ifdef OVERFLOW
       return OVERFLOW;
#else
       goto not_there;
#endif
   break;
    case 'P':
   if (strEQ(name, "PLOSS"))
#ifdef PLOSS
       return PLOSS;
#else
       goto not_there;
#endif
```

```
   break;
    case 'Q':
   break;
    case 'R':
   break;
    case 'S':
   if (strEQ(name, "SING"))
#ifdef SING
        return SING;
#else
        goto not_there;
#endif
   break;
    case 'T':
   if (strEQ(name, "TLOSS"))
#ifdef TLOSS
        return TLOSS;
#else
        goto not_there;
#endif
   break;
    case 'U':
   if (strEQ(name, "UNDERFLOW"))
#ifdef UNDERFLOW
        return UNDERFLOW;
#else
        goto not_there;
#endif
   break;
    case 'V':
   break;
    case 'W':
   break;
    case 'X':
   break;
    case 'Y':
   break;
    case 'Z':
   break;
    case '_':
   if (strEQ(name, "_POSIX_C_SOURCE"))
#ifdef _POSIX_C_SOURCE
```

```
        return _POSIX_C_SOURCE;
#else
        goto not_there;
#endif
    break;
     }
     errno = EINVAL;
     return 0;

not_there:
     errno = ENOENT;
     return 0;
}


MODULE = Math       PACKAGE = Math


double
constant(name,arg)
    char *      name
    int     arg
```

The other element missing from our module is the documentation, written in POD format, for using the function. This is extracted and used to create man or HTML-formatted pages, depending on the platform. See Chapter 12 for more information on the documentation format, and see Chapter 20 for details on the installation process of a module.

Compiling and Testing Your Code

Assuming you've used **h2xs**, either on a genuine header file or a dummy one, the process for compiling your extension should be as easy as:

```
$ perl Makefile.PL
$ make
```

The Makefile.PL is essentially just a Perl script that uses the **MakeMaker** module to produce a Makefile for use with the **make** system. The **MakeMaker** module is complex and is the topic of Chapter 20. Chapter 20 also includes a good walk-through of the process of building and installing an extension, and the locations and methods used for the extension system.

Testing your extension is more critical. The rule often given is that if you divide the amount of time to develop and test a program, then 80 percent of that total time should be used for the testing process. In practice this is not always possible. A two-month project would take a further eight months just to test the result, making the total development time almost a year. What you can do, however, is test the ranges of the values that your extension accepts. By this I mean that you should test the function at the limits of its capabilities. For example, a mathematical function that returns true if the supplied value is even should be tested with values of zero, **-LONG_MAX** and **UNSIGNED_LONG_MAX**, the two definitions for the lowest and highest possible values within the confines of a **long int** and an **unsigned long int**.

For other more complex functions, you need to ensure that suitable test data is supplied that will stress the function to its limits. If you have written the extension (or indeed any program) correctly, it should trap errors before they cause problems, or process the arguments supplied as it should.

Once again, the **h2xs** system builds you a sample test file, but all it does is test that the module/extension you have tried to load actually loads and imports correctly. You will need to add custom tests to really stress your function.

The format to follow should match that of the test suite that comes with the Perl distribution. You need to print "OK" or "not OK" for each test you perform, remembering to sequentially number the tests so any errors can be identified. Here's the test script for the **StatVFS** module:

```
# Before 'make install' is performed this script should be runnable with
# 'make test'. After 'make install' it should work as 'perl test.pl'

######################## We start with some black magic to print on failure.

# Change 1..1 below to 1..last_test_to_print .
# (It may become useful if the test is moved to ./t subdirectory.)

BEGIN { $| = 1; print "1..3\n"; }
END {print "not ok 1\n" unless $loaded;}
use StatVFS;
$loaded = 1;
print "ok 1\n";

######################### End of black magic.

# Insert your test code below (better if it prints "ok 13"
# (correspondingly "not ok 13") depending on the success of chunk 13
# of the test code):
```

```
# If we don't get any sort of space reading from /
# we're probably in trouble

my ($total, $used, $free) = fsstat("/");

print ((($total+$used+$free) ? '' : 'not'),"ok 2\n");

# We should get a number >= 0

print (((fsavail("/")>=0) ? '' : 'not'), "ok 3\n");
```

The first thing you should do is check that the module, and therefore the XS library, can be loaded correctly. You do this by printing the preamble in a **BEGIN** block and printing an error via the **END** block if the module didn't load. This will be automatically generated for you if you use the **h2xs** script. Each individual test is then executed, printing "OK" or "not OK" accordingly.

Remember to create tests that are compatible. I could have equally requested the space on the /users file system, which is perfect for mine, but may not appear on other people's systems. This would have caused the functions to fail, even though the functions may be working perfectly.

Automating the Production/Compilation/Installation Process

The **h2xs** utility, which was covered near the start of this process, created a number of files, including one called Makefile.PL. This file is a Perl Makefile, similar in principle to the file used by **make** to build Perl in the first place. The contents of the file produced by the **h2xs** program is very basic, but it provides enough configuration information to the **MakeMaker** module to generate a Makefile for automatically building your extension.

In fact, the file produced will split your module into any component parts, generate the C source from your XS definition file, and compile the source code into a library suitable for use within your Perl scripts. It takes all the guesswork and trials out of the compilation process, automatically specifying the correct location of headers and libraries so that the extension compiles correctly. If you've written any documentation for your module, it will create the man file for the module, suitable for inclusion with the man pages for other modules and extensions.

Finally, **MakeMaker** provides all the necessary installation routines for copying your module, extension libraries, and documentation into the platform-specific directory of the machine you want to install the extension on. Better still, because the source definition for the Makefile is written in Perl, you can package the raw files—that is, the Makefile.PL, Module.pm, Module.xs, and any typemap file—and send them to another machine, or even other users, and they can install and compile the module for their machine. The process accounts for all of the platform specifics, such as file locations and the available C compiler, and installs your module and extension in the right place.

This is the way most of the modules on CPAN are supplied. Even some of the Perl extensions such as **NDBM_File** are supplied in this way within the Perl distribution. During the build process the main Perl Makefile runs the necessary commands to extract the Makefile for the module in question, before asking **make** to parse the file and produce and build the extension.

I frequently use the **h2xs** command on an empty header file. It provides a complete set of skeleton files for any XS development. All you have to do is fill in the blanks—something many people would argue is the complex part. This only adds more weight to the use of **h2xs**, as it takes all the guesswork out of the development process. Make a change to the XS file, and then just type **make** to produce and compile the library. Then use **make install** to install the library, ready for use.

Because the format of the Makefile.PL file can be customized to incorporate all sorts of features and abilities, it is the subject of Chapter 20, at the end of Part VI. Before you refer to that chapter, I should explain that the reason it is at the end is because it should be the last thing you do before supplying your extension to the world at large. Before then, you should ensure that your module is debugged (see Chapter 18), and you might want to investigate the Perl compiler, which provides other useful information and abilities (see Chapter 19).

Embedding Perl

In the previous chapter, you saw how the core of the Perl interpreter was actually handled by a single function call within Perl. The interpreter is obviously made up of a number of other functions, but at the frontend, the interface between the outside world and the interpreter is handled by a single function. Indeed, the main loop of the Perl binary actually calls this function itself. If you separate the idea of the Perl binary being the same as the Perl interpreter, then you could almost argue that the **perl** command has a Perl interpreter embedded within it. This is a feature of the "new" version 5 of Perl and provides the ability to embed a Perl interpreter within any C application.

There are a number of different ways and situations in which you may want to incorporate a feature from Perl, or the whole Perl interpreter, within your application. For example, you may want to make use of the regular expression features within Perl to parse certain statements. Another alternative is that you have created an extension to the Perl environment using the XSUB interface discussed earlier in this chapter. However, when an error occurs within the extension function, you want it to call not a C error handler, but a Perl one instead. Both these situations can be achieved by using a function that calls the internal Perl function directly.

A much more obvious reason is to provide an internal scripting system to an existing application. Many different applications already provide this functionality, albeit in many different forms. Microsoft applications use Visual Basic for Applications, a specialized version of the Visual Basic environment. Emacs, the editor of choice for many programmers, supports an internal scripting mechanism based on Lisp.

Other benefits also spring to mind. The text processing features of Perl are difficult to achieve directly within C without a lot of work. Using Perl to process a configuration file provides you with an instant configuration system without all the hassles normally associated with parsing a text file.

Strangely, the development of an embedded Perl environment is raw compared to the development of extensions. You are, more or less, left to your own devices when embedding Perl within your C programs. We'll look quickly at the methods both for embedding an entire interpreter into your C programs and for calling an individual function, whether built into the Perl interpreter or defined within the script or an external module.

Embedding the Perl Interpreter

In Chapter 16, Figure 16-1 showed the basic layout of the Perl interpreter. At the time, I mentioned that the possibility exists to embed a Perl interpreter within a C program. For a simple program, try the following:

```
#include <EXTERN.h>
#include <perl.h>

static PerlInterpreter *my_perl;

int main(int argc, char **argv, char **env)
{
    my_perl = perl_alloc();
    perl_construct(my_perl);
    perl_parse(my_perl, NULL, argc, argv, (char **)NULL);
    perl_run(my_perl);
    perl_destruct(my_perl);
    perl_free(my_perl);
}
```

This creates a simple Perl interpreter that accepts options from the command line. If you don't specify a Perl script on the command line, then just like the Perl interpreter, it reads the script from the standard input; so you can now do something like this within the shell:

```
$ myperl <<EOF
> print 56*35,"\n";
> EOF
1960
```

The individual components of the C source are quite straightforward. The **PerlInterpreter** is a structure that holds all of the vital information required for an instance of the Perl interpreter. The **perl_alloc()** and **perl_construct()** functions create an interpreter object. The **perl_parse()** function then does some initializations, including supplying the arguments supplied to the C program on the command line. The second argument is **NULL**, but you could equally put **xs_init** in there so it initializes the XS interface, or indeed any other initialization code you think you need. It also parses the script supplied on the command line (via **-e**) or from the standard input. The **perl_run()** function then executes the script, before you finally shut down and deallocate the memory allocated to the embedded interpreter with **perl_destruct()** and **perl_free()**.

To compile the above file, you can use the information provided via the **ExtUtils::Embed** function:

```
$ cc -o myperl myperl.c 'perl -MExtUtils::Embed -e ccopts -e ldopts'
```

Using a Specific Perl Function

If what you want to do is call a specific function, you need to use a slightly more complex method, and there are many different options available. The easiest method is to use the **perl_call_argv** function, which calls a specified function with an array of string arguments, as in the example below:

```
#include <EXTERN.h>
#include <perl.h>

static PerlInterpreter *my_perl;

main(int argc, char **argv, char **env)
{
  char *print_args[] = {"Hello ", "World!\n", NULL};
  my_perl = perl_alloc();
  perl_construct(my_perl);
  perl_parse(my_perl, NULL, argc, argv, env);

  perl_call_argv("print", G_DISCARD, print_args);

  perl_destruct(my_perl);
  perl_free(my_perl);
}
```

This calls the **print** function with the arguments supplied in **print_args**. The **G_DISCARD** option to the **perl_call_argv** function indicates that you want to discard any values returned by the Perl function. The list of possible C functions you can call is shown in Table 17-7.

You have already seen an example of the **perl_call_argv** function. The equivalent in **perl_eval_va** would be

```
perl_eval_va("print (qw/Hello World!\n/)", NULL);
```

Note the use of **qw** to quote the individual arguments, thus saving you from quoting quotes. You can do the same thing with **perl_call_va**:

```
perl_call_va("print","s","Hello","s","World!\n",NULL);
```

In all cases, the functions return the number of items returned by the Perl subroutine called, or **-1** on error.

The possible values for the **flags** argument of **perl_call_argv** are listed in Table 17-8.

Function	Description
perl_call_argv(char *sub, I32 flags, char **argv)	This calls a subroutine, **sub**, using the **flags** (see Table 17-8), passing the arguments to the called functions specified in **argv**.
perl_call_va(char *sub, [char *type, arg,] * ["OUT",] [char *type, arg,] * NULL)	Calls the subroutine **sub**, passing the arguments supplied by the argument pairs **type** and **arg**, which specify the argument type and value. If an argument "OUT" is seen, then all the arguments following that are taken to be return value pairs of type and variables.
perl_eval_va(char *str, [char *type, *arg], NULL)	Evaluates an arbitrary Perl statement, **str**, instead of calling a specific function. The **type** and **arg** arguments are pairs of return argument types and values.

Table 17-7. *C Functions for Calling Perl Subroutines*

Flag	Description
G_SCALAR	Calls the Perl subroutine in a scalar context.
G_ARRAY	Calls the Perl subroutine in a list context.
G_DISCARD	Forces Perl to remove any information placed onto the stack by the Perl subroutine.
G_NOARGS	Indicates that you are not passing parameters to the subroutine you are calling. This has the effect of not building or initializing the @_ array for the subroutine being called.
G_VOID	Calls the Perl subroutine in a void context, and removes any values placed onto the argument stack.
G_EVAL	This places an **eval{}** around the subroutine call. This enables a basic form of error checking around the subroutine you are calling, and also handles **die** calls accordingly. You will have to examine the value of the **$@** variable, just as you would within Perl, to ensure that the function executed correctly. See the reference information on accessing Perl variables at the start of this chapter for more details.
G_KEEPERR	This flag is meant to be used in conjunction with the **G_EVAL** flag. It indicates that the value of **$@** should be updated and/or reset by code that executes after the **eval{}** block. Setting this flag ensures that the contents of **$@** contain the return status of the **eval{}** block.

Table 17-8. *Execution Flags for Called Subroutines*

In all the cases so far, we have casually ignored any return values from the functions we have been calling. Using the **perl_call_argv** or **perl_call_va** functions, you could take off the values returned by using the stack manipulation functions that were covered at the start of this chapter. That said, you could also put argument values onto the stack in the same way and use a different method of calling the Perl subroutine.

If you look at the following code, it's complete C source for calling a Perl function called **add** that adds two numbers together:

```
#include <EXTERN.h>
#include <perl.h>
```

```
void perl_add(int a, int b)
{
    int retval;
    dSP;
    ENTER;
    SAVETMPS;
    PUSHMARK(sp);
    XPUSHs(sv_2mortal(newSViv(a)));
    XPUSHs(sv_2mortal(newSViv(b)));
    PUTBACK;
    retval = perl_call_pv("add", G_SCALAR);
    SPAGAIN;
    if (retval == 1)
        printf("Returned: %d\n",POPi);
    PUTBACK;
    FREETMPS;
    LEAVE;
}

int main (int argc, char **Argv, char **env)
{
    char *my_argv[] = { "", "add.pl" };
    my_perl = perl_alloc();
    perl_construct(my_perl);

    perl_parse(my_perl, NULL, 2, my_argv, (char **)NULL);
    perl_add(35, 53);

    perl_destruct(my_perl);
    perl_free(my_perl);
}
```

The **perl_add** C function calls a very simple function, **add**, defined in a file called add.pl. The bulk of the **perl_add** function is given over to the process of initializing and populating the Perl argument stack before calling the Perl function and then taking the single value returned by the Perl function back off the stack again.

Note that the **perl_parse** function has also been used with our own set of arguments. This is because you need to get the Perl interpreter to load the file that contains the Perl source, which looks like this:

```
sub add
{
```

```
    my ($a, $b) = @_;
    return(a+b);
}
```

The whole process runs like this:

1. Initialize a Perl interpreter.
2. Parse the external Perl script that you want to call from the C source code.
3. Call the C function that calls the actual Perl function you want to use. The execution path of that performs the following:

   Initialize the stack.

   Push the first argument onto the stack.

   Push the second argument onto the stack.

   Call the Perl subroutine.

   Pop the returned value back off the stack.

   Return to the **main** function within Perl.
4. Destruct and free the Perl interpreter object.

Multiplicity

In some rare cases it may be necessary to create multiple instances of the Perl interpreter within your C code. This is something that was mentioned back in Chapter 16 when we looked at the internal organization of the Perl interpreter. The problem with doing this normally is that the act of initializing any Perl interpreter may actually overwrite some of the values and structures created and required by the first interpreter.

To avoid this, you need to set the value of the global variable **PL_Perl_destruct_level** to one. This is set automatically if you have compiled your Perl distribution with the **-DMULTIPLICITY** preprocessor directive. Once set, you can create as many **PerlInterpreter** structures as you require, memory permitting, within your C source. Since all the functions you have already seen accept a first (and sometimes only) argument, which is the name of the **PerlInterpreter** object, it should be obvious that each instance should have its own name and object and be called accordingly.

XS Initialization

If you want to call external XSUB functions from C via a Perl interpreter, then you need to supply some initialization code. We touched on this briefly earlier. The reason you need it is that by default the embedded interpreter does not know how to import the extensions—you have to do it manually.

To do this, you must create a C function, traditionally called **xs_init()**, which calls the bootstrap function that the **xsubpp** script builds for you from the XS file you supply during the extension development process. Although you can write this yourself, a much easier method is to use the **ExtUtils::Embed** module to do it for you:

```
$ perl -MExtUtils::Embed -e xsinit -- -o xsinit.c
$ cc -c xsinit.c 'perl -MExtUtils::Embed -e ccopts'
$ cc -c myperl.c 'perl -MExtUtils::Embed -e ccopts'
$ cc -o myperl myperl.o xsinit.o 'perl -MExtUtils::Embed -e ldopts'
```

All you need to do is ensure that you call the **xs_init()** function, by placing it as the second argument to the **perl_parse()** function:

```
perl_parse(my_perl, NULL, argc, argv, env);
```

Cooperating with Other Languages

Interfacing with other languages is more complex. Since Perl is written in C, the interpreter and extension interface are closely integrated. Without this level of integration, and especially without the tools provided via the XSUB interface and the Perl internals, integration is difficult, but not impossible.

The Perl distribution comes with a number of tools that allow other languages and tools to be converted into a Perl script. Recent versions of Perl also enable you to convert the Perl script in a number of different formats, including some C source code that can be compiled into a stand-alone executable.

Of course, if you need to interact with another language, there are a number of options available. Perl makes an excellent source code producer, and with some work, you can create quite complex systems that interact with a program or language.

Converting Other Languages to Perl

As has been repeated in this and many other pieces of documentation over the years, Perl owes a lot of its functionality to the ideas and functionality of other programs. Because of its Unix roots, Perl used features from some of the most common and useful Unix command line utilities. It's no accident that the regular expression system looks like the one available within **sed**, or that some of the operators and semantics of the Perl language look similar to the **awk** language. Of course, Perl provides all the features of a great number of programs built into a single application.

If you have previously been developing one of these applications, then conversion to Perl can be a long and complex process. To speed up the process, the Perl distribution comes with three programs to convert **sed**, **awk**, and **find** programs and statements into Perl script. This can then either be used natively or modified to fit into an existing application or environment.

sed

Although not strictly a programming language, **sed** does provide a way of modifying files in a programmable fashion. The most significant part of the **sed** environment is the regular expression matching and substitution engine. This is similar to the same regular expression system in Perl, and many of the commands are identical in operation between **sed** and Perl.

The format of a **sed** "script" is a series of lines. Each one starts with a letter defining the operation that should take place, followed by a number of arguments. The name **sed** is short for stream editor, and each command is executed on each input line. The functionality can be modeled in Perl using a simple **while** loop.

The **s2p** command is a Perl script that takes a **sed** program and converts it into a Perl script using the **while** loop and some corresponding code to account for other features within the **sed** environment. The script is capable of turning any **sed** script into a Perl equivalent; it supports all of the functions and constructs of the **sed** language.

To use, specify the name of a **sed** script to the **s2p** command, or enter the script during standard input. The resulting Perl script is sent to the standard output. For example,

```
$ s2p
s/foo/bar/g
```

produces

```
#!/usr/local/bin/perl
eval 'exec /usr/local/bin/perl -S $0 ${1+"$@"}'
        if $running_under_some_shell;

while ($ARGV[0] =~ /^-/) {
    $_ = shift;
  last if /^--/;
    if (/^-n/) {
        $nflag++;
        next;
    }
    die "I don't recognize this switch: $_\\n";
}
```

```
$printit++ unless $nflag;

$\ = "\n";                  # automatically add newline on print

LINE:
while (<>) {
    chop;
    s/foo/bar/g;
    print if $printit;
}
```

The **s2p** command provides three options, supplied as arguments, as shown in Table 17-9.

It's true to say, of course, the resulting script is less than friendly, and it's likely that many of the features in Perl provide quicker and cleaner ways of achieving the same goal. In general, therefore, rewriting a **sed** script is probably more efficient than using the conversion program. Since most **sed** programs involve regular expression substitution, matching, or transliteration, the process should be relatively easy.

Option	Description
-Dx	Sets debugging, using a value of **x**. Depending on the value specified, it adds a number of additional statements to the Perl script that is produced to enable you to trace possible bugs and problems.
-n	Specifies that the **sed** script was always invoked with the **–n** switch. Functionality for this argument is normally built into the Perl script that is produced, but this option removes this code and sets the option on permanently.
-p	Specifies that the **sed** script was never invoked with the **–n** switch. Functionality for this argument is normally built into the Perl script that is produced, but this option removes this code and sets the option off permanently.

Table 17-9. *Options to the **s2p** Converter*

awk

The **awk** language was one of the few programming environments (other than the shell) that was provided as standard with the Unix operating system. Its original incarnation was fairly basic, and it was replaced with **nawk**. Most people come across the language as **gawk**, the GNU version developed solely by Arnold Robbins. Like Perl it exists on many different platforms, and also like Perl, its primary purpose is for parsing and processing text files. Some of the features of **awk**, and especially those of **nawk** and **gawk**, are not supported by Perl. They are too numerous to list here, but in general the more complex regular expressions and the use of regular expressions within certain functions (such as **join**) are not supported in Perl.

The **a2p** command that can be used to convert from an **awk** script is only compatible with **awk**, and your mileage may vary with **nawk** and **gawk**. Unlike the **sed** converter, **a2p** is written in C, although the basic operation is the same. It accepts the **awk** script, either from a file or from the standard input, and generates Perl script to the standard output. For example, this **awk** script sums up the values of the first column of an input file:

```
{ s += $1 }
END  { print "sum is", s, " average is", s/NR }
```

Looking at this, you can see some of the similarities between Perl and **awk**. The first line adds the value of **$1**, which **awk** has automatically interpreted as the first field in the input file, into a variable. The loop that proceeds through the input file is implied within **awk**, as is the automatic splitting of the input source into individual fields. Once the main block has completed, the **END** block is executed, and this prints out the sum and average of the numbers.

Running this through the converter produces

```
#!/usr/local/bin/perl
eval 'exec /usr/local/bin/perl -S $0 ${1+"$@"}'
    if $running_under_some_shell;
                        # this emulates #! processing on NIH machines.
                        # (remove #! line above if indigestible)

eval '$'.$1.'$2;' while $ARGV[0] =~ /^([A-Za-z_0-9]+=)(.*)/ && shift;
                        # process any FOO=bar switches

$, = ' ';               # set output field separator
$\ = "\n";              # set output record separator
```

```
while (<>) {
    ($Fld1) = split(' ', $_, 9999);
    $S += $Fld1;
}

print 'sum is', $S, ' average is', $S / $.;
```

Once again, the output produced is filled with a number of compatibility elements, including the ability to create new variables for use within the script's command line using an **eval** function. The main bulk of the actual script is the last five lines.

Also, like the **sed** converter, the Perl produced in this manner should be classed as compatible, rather than optimal. Rewriting the code in Perl, rather than using a converter, will produce better results, albeit at a slower pace.

The **a2p** program accepts four command line options that affect the script generated, as shown in Table 17-10.

find

The **find** command does not really have a language, but it does have a complex array of command line options that can specify, fairly expertly, the definition of the files you want to find. The **find2perl** script takes the command line options you would normally supply to the **find** command, and generates a Perl script that will perform the same function. The script produced actually makes use of the **File::Find** module, which

Option	Description
-Dx	Sets debugging, using a value of **x**. The value affects the output produced by the conversion process, and adds a number of additional statements to the script to output debugging information during the script's progress.
-Fc	Specifies that the **awk** script was always invoked with a **–F** switch, which changes the default input field separator to **c**.
-nfields	Specifies the names of the input fields, rather than automatically using a value of **$Fld1**, **$Fld2**, and so on. Fields can be separated by any of the normal separation characters.
-number	Forces **a2p** to assume that the input is always made up of the number of fields specified by **number**.

Table 17-10. *Command Line Options to the **awk** Converter*

provides a mechanism for parsing a directory tree, following all the subdirectories. For each file or directory found, a user-specified function is called, with the name and location of the current file being available via the **$_** variable, and some variables located within the **File::Find** module.

The result is that Perl has the ability not only to locate a file within the current directory structure, but also to do any number of other operations to convert, translate, summarize, and so on, the contents of the files found.

The **find2perl** script does the basics of the file specification process for you, producing a script that you can modify to your own ends. If you know how to use the **find** command, then using the **find2perl** script should be easy. The command

```
$ find2perl / -name '*bin*' -type d -print
```

produces

```
#!/usr/local/bin/perl
    eval 'exec /usr/local/bin/perl -S $0 ${1+"$@"}'
        if $running_under_some_shell;

require "find.pl";

# Traverse desired filesystems



&find('/');

exit;
sub wanted {
    /^.*bin.*$/ &&
    (($dev,$ino,$mode,$nlink,$uid,$gid) = lstat($_)) &&
    -d _ &&
    print("$name\n");
}
```

You can also specify more complex constructs directly to the **find2perl** script without having to modify the code. There are two options: one to create a **tar** file and the other to specify a Perl-specific evaluation for the file. The **–tar** option takes a file name and adds the necessary code to the Perl script to generate a file list to a piped **tar** command that then generates the **tar** file.

The **–eval** option takes a string that will be evaluated as a Perl statement, and if it returns true, the file will be considered as a match.

Converting Perl to Other Languages

With Perl 5 the facilities have been put in place to resolve a Perl script to its lowest common denominator—the string of optimized opcodes that are executed by the Perl interpreter proper. At the moment, two modules (**B** and **O**) provide a Perl interface to the internals of a Perl script. The result is that the internal opcode tree can be converted and parsed into a number of different formats, to provide a range of different pieces of information.

At the moment this is limited to more extensive debugging features and the cross-referencing abilities that are often available to other languages. The same interface also provides you with the ability to generate a file in binary format called bytecode. This binary code can then be executed directly by a special Perl interpreter. The code has already been parsed and optimized, and much of the typical interpretation process has already taken place. This makes the code execution much faster and also ensures, to a greater or lesser extent, that the Perl source is hidden from casual view.

The most interesting feature of the **B** and **O** modules, however, is that they can generate raw C code, which can then be compiled into a stand-alone executable. The final executable does not require Perl and cannot be reverse engineered. The performance benefits are debatable, but the distribution and security offered by the process are obvious advantages.

Because this is a significant part of the entire Perl environment, it's discussed more fully in Chapter 19.

Calling Other Languages from Perl

You have seen many times how Perl can call and interact with an external program. In some cases, the level of interaction has been as simple as calling the program with some specified options. There is no reason why, with the use of dual pipes, you couldn't call and interact with another program, or even another programming language.

The most obvious road to cooperating with another language from Perl, however, is to use Perl as a high-level environment that generates an optimized or customized program that can then be executed via a separate language. Perl has many features that make the manipulation of data, particularly strings, significantly easier; and if you want to produce customized or optimized code automatically, it makes sense to make use of a textual development environment to produce it.

You saw in Chapter 15, for example, how Perl can be used to generate JavaScript code. Although it was a fairly simplistic example, it did demonstrate the power of Perl as a tool for creating the source code for other languages. In that instance the contents of a DBM database was used to produce a list of available options that were then hard coded into the text of an HTML document, which was then passed back to the user's browser. In that instance, obtaining the information with JavaScript would have been impossible, and other options, such as static text files, would have made the process unmanageable.

The trick is to make the best use of the Perl environment and, especially, make use of the here document to create customized source code to be passed to the program or language interpreter in question. Although it is possible to make use of pipes, most languages accept an input file as their source. Remember that "compiled" languages such as C, C++, and Pascal will require an external compiler, as well as additional processes between code production and the final execution stages, but this should not present too much difficulty.

If it truly is interaction with another language that you require, then the obvious method is to set up some form of communication channel over which you can exchange requests and requirements. All modern languages, including Java, Python, Rebol, and of course Perl, provide the ability to open a network socket and exchange information. If you want to talk to a platform-specific language, such as AppleScript or Visual Basic, check out Part VII, which deals with the complexities of Perl on other platforms. Here you'll find information on the standard and CPAN modules that can provide interfaces to many of the platform-specific devices.

Chapter 18

Debugging

Identifying and removing bugs is an art. Some people would even consider the art of debugging an application to be more of a skill than writing the original program. This is because you need to be able to find the exact location of the problem and then find a suitable solution that doesn't introduce a new set of bugs. With your own scripts this should be relatively easy; you can quickly identify the bug and probably know the reason that the bug exists.

There are some situations, though, when even within your own programs the problem is difficult to trace. It's in these situations that you need to use some form of debugging. The easiest method is to insert **print** statements into your script that output the current status of different functions and variables as the script progresses. This is a fairly simplistic method, but often it can be quicker than using the full-blown debugger, albeit with less flexibility.

To help with the information that is printed, you can also use the **caller** function, which prints out the details of the calling function or package. Using this function you can monitor the execution of individual functions and when and where they are called. With some complex insertions, this can provide a detailed trace of the execution path of a script.

A better all-around solution is to use the debugger that is part of the Perl distribution. This is an external module that provides you with a wrapper interface for the underlying script and enables complete control of the execution of the script. You can stop the script at any point, monitor variables, and find the execution of the script. In fact, the **trace** function uses the **caller** function to find this information.

We'll be looking at all of these methods in this chapter. We'll also look at the debugging process for regular expressions, which is really a programming language in it's own right. Furthermore, we'll examine other available solutions that can help in the debugging process, while not actually being classed as debuggers themselves. These include the profiling system, which provides information on the execution times of individual subroutines.

Bug Prevention Is Better Than Cure

Preventing bugs before they occur is a more efficient method of eliminating them. Once a bug has been introduced, it is very difficult to trace and eliminate, which is of course why we have tools like debuggers and profilers. However, if you write the program as specifically, and tidily, as possible, you should prevent many of the most common bugs and problems seen in many scripts. It is also a good idea if you intend to release your code to the public to use comments, these will help clarify the process and methods you were using when you wrote the script.

Two standard features of the Perl interpreter can help you eliminate at least some of the uncertainty that can be introduced in a script: warnings and the **use strict** pragma. Warnings can pick up many typical typographical errors that can creep into your source code. The pragma imposes a more strict interpretation of the code you have written that should highlight many of the bugs introduced as part of the assumptions that Perl makes about how you've written your code.

We'll also look very briefly at how Perl uses memory and how, and indeed whether, this can affect the way you write Perl programs.

Warnings

Turning on warnings—that is, using the **-w** switch to the interpreter—is the best way to pick up many of the constructs that could potentially cause a problem. The exact list of warnings that are picked up is very long (see Appendix D for a list of error messages that are produced during the compilation stage).

Potential problems include bad variable names, missing variables, use of undefined variables, bare words, and undefined functions. The **-w** switch also picks up other more complex errors related to the structure, layout, and format of different statements, and examples of where Perl has made assumptions based on its own internal rules for how a particular statement should have been evaluated.

The use of warnings will not highlight specific bugs in your code, but it will highlight problems that may be related to your bugs. If you can eliminate all of the warnings for a script, you will have certainly removed some of the problems in your script.

Use the "Operators" section in Chapter 2 and the hints in Chapter 16 to resolve many of the problems. A full list of errors and warnings given by the interpreter can be found in Appendix D.

use strict

The **use strict** pragma discussed in Chapter 16 imposes some very strict rules on how individual constructs within Perl are written. These relate to three areas: subroutines, variables, and references.

Perl normally interprets bare words as functions, but the **subs** option to the **use strict** pragma removes this automatic interpretation. In fact, a compile-time error is generated if a bare word is used that is not a subroutine, unless the word appears in curly braces or on the left side of the **=>** operator used to separate the key and value for a hash.

The variables portion reports an error when a variable is used that has not previously been declared, either via the **use vars** pragma or with the **my** keyword. It also highlights variables that have been accessed without a fully qualified name.

The references element of the pragma causes an error if you use symbolic references. It imposes the use of implicit references,

```
$bar = \$foo;
print $$foo;
```

instead of the normally allowed

```
$bar ="foo";
print $$bar;
```

All three effects combined can help to eliminate some of the suspicion surrounding how Perl interprets different statements.

By rewriting the scripts to the specification imposed by the **use strict** pragma, many bugs in a script could be eliminated without making any other modifications to how the script works.

Thanks for the Memory

Many programmers take the memory handling within Perl for granted. Unlike other languages, and even other operating systems, Perl takes only as much memory as it thinks it needs to achieve its goals. The advantages are obvious: you can open a file, slurp the entire contents of the file into a variable, and then modify it. Perl handles the allocation of memory from what is available in the operating system (check the sidebar "MacOS Caveats" for the exception). This means, potentially, that a Perl script could soak up all the available memory on a machine without warning the user. This can, of course, cause problems: either Perl will fail (and cause a core dump) because it can no longer allocate any more memory, or the operating system or other applications will fail because there is no spare memory available.

However, unless you are handling very large structures, the chances of using all the memory are fairly slim. All of the memory management in Perl is handled automatically; you do not need to do any conscious management of the memory you are using.

If you do want to monitor the amount of memory you are using within Perl, you need to know that it supports two different methods: **PERL_DEBUG_MSTATS** and the **–DL** command line switch. The first, using the **PERL_DEBUG_MSTATS** environment variable, only works if you are using the Perl rather than the operating system–supplied **malloc()** memory allocation function. The **–DL** switch to the command

MacOS Caveats

Unlike virtually every other operating system I have come across, MacOS demands that all applications specify how much memory they will want to use at the time they are started. The amount of memory required/available to each application is configurable via the Info window for an application. If the application runs out of memory, that's it. It cannot request or demand any further memory from the available pool without the application being restarted.

For MacPerl this can cause some unexpected problems when you try to use a lot of memory in a script. The only solution is to make sure the MacPerl binary has enough memory allocated to it. The standard figure is about 3MB. If you know your script is likely to use a lot of memory, it's probably a good idea to use the tips from Chapter 16 on reducing memory requirements. Actually, it's probably a good idea to do this anyway.

See Chapter 23 for more information on using Perl on the MacOS.

line of the Perl interpreter is only available if Perl has been compiled with the **–DDEBUGGING** compiler directive. Both methods provide a mountain of information that you cannot make full use of unless you know about the internals of the Perl interpreter. See the **perldebug** man page for more details on using these two methods.

As a general rule, you can normally ignore this level of detail, even when debugging. Instead, if you are worried about the amount of memory you are using, refer to the hints in Chapter 16 for some examples of reducing the amount of memory used in your programs.

Debugging Methods

Different people swear by different methods of debugging their programs. Often there is no right or wrong way of debugging a script, only the way with which you are most comfortable. There are in fact two basic methods for reporting bugs. The first is to use simple **print** statements to output a progress message or variable contents, either to a file or to one of the standard filehandles. To aid in the process within Perl, you can also use the **caller** function, which provides information about the caller to the current subroutine.

The second method is to use a debugger that allows you to examine the execution of a program in real time. Perl provides this via a command line option and an external module that provides an interface to the debugging process. To aid in the process, there are a number of graphical interfaces to the underlying Perl debugger, and we'll briefly look at the **ptkdb** interface modules.

In addition, there is a noninteractive method for debugging that outputs raw debug information during the execution of the script.

Using print

To me, **print** statements have always seemed easier, and, providing you're careful, they can usually provide enough information for you to trace the bug. This is best used in combination with a global variable, perhaps set via the scripts command line, to enable or disable some simple debugging. The only place where they are often useless is within a loop because they produce a voluminous amount of information that needs to be processed manually after the execution is complete. On occasion the loop mechanism can prove useful if you want to continually monitor a single variable as it is processed, or when you want to monitor the input or output to a filehandle.

Usage is pathetically simple. Using a statement such as

```
print "Got here!\n";
```

you can trace the execution path of a program. Of course, it makes more sense to include a more detailed report, such that the output produced is as detailed as necessary. Here's the output from a **print** debugged script that processes a file. The output includes the contents of the variables that we are using to process the data:

```
$ foo.pl
Opened file (input.dat)
Read data (hello)
Read data (world)
Closed file
```

Other tricks using this method include the use of a debug variable that is often user configurable. If set, the debugging information is printed out, but by default the debugging information is ignored. This enables both the developer and the end-user to obtain extended debugging information when they discover a problem. This is the method usually employed by third-party modules: you set the value of a variable in the package at the initialization. For example, here is some output from a script that uses the **Net::FTP** module by Graham Barr (see Chapters 9 and 25 for more details):

```
grfile.pl ftp://martinb:foo@twinspark.mcslp.com/pub/filelist.txt
Net::FTP: Net::FTP(2.33)
Net::FTP:   Exporter
Net::FTP:   Net::Cmd(2.11)
Net::FTP:   IO::Socket::INET
Net::FTP:     IO::Socket(1.1603)
Net::FTP:       IO::Handle(1.1504)

Net::FTP=GLOB(0xb68ec)<<< 220 twinspark FTP server (UNIX(r) System V Release 4.0) ready.
Net::FTP=GLOB(0xb68ec)>>> user martinb
Net::FTP=GLOB(0xb68ec)<<< 331 Password required for martinb.
Net::FTP=GLOB(0xb68ec)>>> PASS ....
Net::FTP=GLOB(0xb68ec)<<< 230 User martinb logged in.
Net::FTP=GLOB(0xb68ec)>>> CWD /pub
Net::FTP=GLOB(0xb68ec)<<< 250 CWD command successful.
Net::FTP=GLOB(0xb68ec)>>> PORT 198,112,10,130,128,13
Net::FTP=GLOB(0xb68ec)<<< 200 PORT command successful.
Net::FTP=GLOB(0xb68ec)>>> RETR filelist.txt
Net::FTP=GLOB(0xb68ec)<<< 150 ASCII data connection for filelist.txt (198.112.10.130,32781)
(1328 bytes).
Net::FTP=GLOB(0xb68ec)<<< 226 ASCII Transfer complete.
Net::FTP=GLOB(0xb68ec)>>> QUIT
Net::FTP=GLOB(0xb68ec)<<< 221 Goodbye.
```

With all of these solutions, however, the output is printed to the **STDOUT** filehandle. You may need to use the trick from Chapter 3 to duplicate the **STDOUT** filehandle if you are developing an application that uses a text-based interface. To recap, you duplicate the filehandle and recreate the new **STDOUT** to point to a different file:

```
open(SECOUT,">&STDOUT");
open(SECERR,">&STDERR");
open(STDOUT,">stdlog.txt");
open(STDERR,">stderr.txt");
```

Now to print to the real standard output, you need to send output to **SECOUT**. Since you will have control over the device on which you provide the user interface, but not the filehandle used to print the debugging information from the contributed module, this is a more practical solution to the problem.

It's also possible, using this method, to create a log file of the debug output you create. This is especially useful when using an indirectly accessed script such as that used on a web server. Here, printing the debug information to the standard output will cause the information to be included as part of the document that is sent back to the user's web browser.

Using caller

Printing your own debug information requires a lot of manual entry if you are trying to trace the execution path through a program. For each **print** statement you include in your source, you will need to include a reference about the location of the statement in order for your debug output to make sense.

To ease the process, you can use the **caller** function, which returns the current context information for a subroutine. The information includes details about the subroutine (or **eval** or **require**) statement:

```
caller EXPR
caller
```

In a scalar context, it simply returns the package name. In a simple list context, the function returns the package name, file name, and line of the caller of the current subroutine, **eval**, or **require** statement:

```
($package, $filename, $line) = caller;
```

If **EXPR** is specified, **caller** returns extended information. The value of **EXPR** should be the number of frames on the stack to go back to before the current one. That is, if you specify a value of one, the parent subroutine information will be printed, a value of two will print the grandparent subroutine, and so forth. The information returned is

```
($package, $filename, $line, $subroutine,
 $hasargs, $wantarray, $evaltext, $is_require) = caller($i);
```

The **$evaltext** and **$is_require** values are only returned when the subroutine being examined is actually the result of an **eval()** statement.

As an example, examine the script below:

```
sub bar
{
    Top::top();
}

bar();

package Top;

sub top
{
    my $level = 0;
    print "Top of the world, Ma!\n";
    while ((($package, $file, $line,
             $subname, $hasargs, $wantarray) = caller($level++)))
    {
        $hasargs    = $hasargs    ? 'Yes' : 'No';
        if (defined($wantarray))
        {
            $wantarray = 'Yes';
        }
        else
        {
            $wantarray = 'No';
        }
        print <<EOF;
Stack:
           Package: $package
              File: $file
              Line: $line
        Subroutine: $subname
    Has Arguments?: $hasargs
```

```
    Wants Array?: $wantarray
EOF
    }
}
```

When executed, the resultant information shows the stack trace for the **top** function, including its original call from **main** and from the **bar** function:

```
Top of the world, Ma!
Stack:
           Package: main
              File: ././t.pl
              Line: 5
        Subroutine: Top::top
    Has Arguments?: Yes
      Wants Array?: No
Stack:
           Package: main
              File: ././t.pl
              Line: 8
        Subroutine: main::bar
    Has Arguments?: Yes
      Wants Array?: No
```

The information provided should enable you to pinpoint the location within a script. If you want to report the information to a log, you may want to introduce a wrapper function like this one:

```
sub callerlog
{
    my $reference = shift;
    open(DATA,">>caller.log") || return;
    print DATA join(' ',@_),":$reference\n";
    close(DATA);
}
```

Then to call the function, you would use a line such as

```
callerlog("Writing data",caller());
```

to report the information for the current stack trace. Note that you can't directly use the information from **callerlog**, since that will introduce its own frame of information at location zero within the stack. You could, however, use a modified form of the **callerlog** function that returns the stack trace from frame one onwards:

```
sub callerlog
{
    my $reference = shift;
    my $level = 1;
    while (((@data) = caller($level++)))
    {
        print join(' ',@data),":$reference\n";
    }
}
```

The information provided by **caller** is actually used by the Perl debugger in order to provide the tracing information used in the debugging environment.

Perl Debugger

With a standard application there are two situations when you need to use some form of debugging:

- *Postmortem debugging* is required when your program aborts the execution process. This normally results when the process is sent a specific signal due to some form of memory fault. A core dump of the process image is created, and the information in this image can then be used to trace where the problem occurred.
- *Debugging a live process* involves running the program within a wrapper program that monitors each stage of the execution process in real time. During execution you can monitor and change the values of variables. An online debugger will also allow you to set breakpoints where the normal execution of the program will halt and let you monitor the current state. You can trace variables back from these breakpoints and stop, start, and restart the application as you see fit.

Within Perl, postmortem debugging is not really applicable. Since Perl is the application, the script you are running is protected by the Perl interpreter. It's unlikely that the interpreter will create a core dump, and even if it did, the information provided would be in the form of the opcodes that make up the compiled version of the script, rather than the source of the script being interpreted.

The second option is available with Perl. It provides a debugger as part of the interpreter (actually it's an external module, but since it's part of the standard distribution, it should always be available). The debugger provides all the usual tools available in the normal symbolic debuggers plus additional facilities only available because Perl is an interpreted rather than a compiled language.

For example, the debugger allows you to execute Perl statements directly within the debugging environment, so you can test different versions of the same statement without having to modify the original source. Execution is via the **eval** function, so you have the abilities of the entire Perl interpreter and libraries at your disposal.

Debugging Commands

The debugger supports a wide range of commands. Anything not immediately identified as a command, or any input line beginning with a space, is interpreted as a Perl statement that is executed via an **eval** function.

h

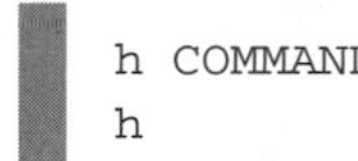

```
h COMMAND
h
```

Prints out help information for **COMMAND**, or general help if **COMMAND** is not specified. If you use the special **h h** command, a condensed version of the general help is printed—it should fit onto a standard screen without scrolling. You can use the pipe symbol to parse the output through a pager. See the **O** command later for details on how to change the default paging program.

p

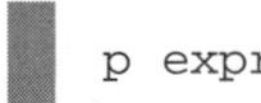

```
p expr
```

Prints the evaluated value of **expr** using the standard print built-in function. The value of **expr** can include variables and functions defined within the current script being debugged.

The usual rules to the print function apply—nested structures and objects will not be printed correctly. (See the **x** command for a more useful version of this.)

x

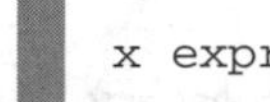

```
x expr
```

Evaluates its expression in list context and dumps out the result in a pretty-printed fashion. Nested data structures are printed out recursively, unlike the print function. See the options in Table 18-1.

V

```
V PACKAGE VARS
V PACKAGE
V
```

Displays the list of variables specified in **VARS** within the package **PACKAGE** if both are specified. If **VARS** is omitted, all variables for **PACKAGE** are printed. If no arguments are specified, it prints out all the variables for the **main** package. Information is intelligently printed, with the values of arrays and hashes and nested structures being formatted before output. Control characters are also converted into a printable format.

If you specify the variables, you should omit the variable type character (**$**, **@**, or **%**). You can also specify a pattern to match, or a pattern not to match, using **~PATTERN** and **!PATTERN** arguments.

X

```
X VARS
X
```

Same as **V VARS** for the current package.

T

```
T
```

Prints a stack backtrace, as determined by the **caller** function and the value of the current stack frame array. See the section "Debugger Interfaces" later in this chapter for some examples.

s

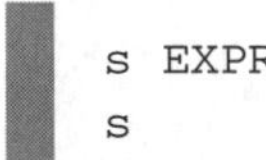

```
s EXPR
s
```

Executes only the next statement (single step), following subroutine calls if necessary. If **EXPR** is supplied, then executes **EXPR** once, descending into subroutine calls as necessary. This can be used to drop directly into a subroutine outside of the normal execution process.

n

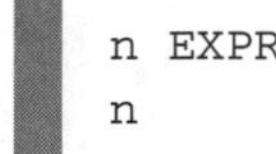

```
n EXPR
n
```

Single steps the next statement, but steps over the subroutines instead of stepping into them. If **EXPR** is specified, then any subroutines are stepped into.

Carriage Return

Repeats the last **n** or **s** command.

c

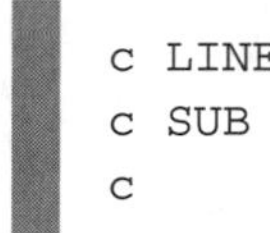

```
c LINE
c SUB
c
```

Continues execution (all statements) until the next configured breakpoint of the end of the script. If **LINE** or **SUB** is specified, then a breakpoint, active for one break only, is inserted before **LINE** or the subroutine **SUB**.

l

```
l
```

Lists the next page of lines for the current script from the current line.

```
l MIN+INCR
```

Lists **INCR+1** lines from the line specified by **MIN**.

```
l MIN-MAX
```

Lists the lines from line **MIN** to **MAX**.

```
l LINE
```

Lists the line **LINE**.

```
l SUB
```

Lists the first page of lines for the subroutine **SUB**.

-

Lists the previous page of lines.

w

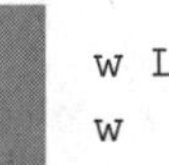

```
w LINE
w
```

Lists a page of lines surrounding the current line, or **LINE** if specified.

.

Returns the line pointer to the last line executed and prints it out.

f

```
f FILENAME
```

Changes the file currently being viewed to **FILENAME**. The value of **FILENAME** should match either the main script or the name of a file identifiable within the **%INC** variable. If still not found, then it is interpreted as a regular expression that should resolve to a file name.

/PATTERN/

Searches forward within the current file for the regular expression **PATTERN**.

?PATTERN?

Searches backward within the current file for the regular expression **PATTERN**.

L

Lists all the currently set breakpoints and actions.

S

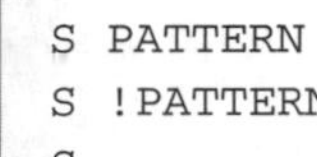

```
S PATTERN
S !PATTERN
S
```

Lists all subroutines, those matching the regular expression **PATTERN**. If **PATTERN** is preceded by an exclamation mark, then lists those not matching the regular expression **PATTERN**.

t

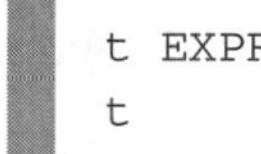

```
t EXPR
t
```

Toggles trace mode. Trace mode enables the printing of each statement as it is executed. If **EXPR** is specified, traces the execution of **EXPR**. See also the **AutoTrace** option in Table 18-1.

For example, the script

```
sub one { 1 };
sub two { 2 };
print one()*two();
```

only prints out the final value of two. With trace mode switched on, it also prints the statements

```
DB<1> r
main::one(t2.pl:1):    sub one { 1 };
main::two(t2.pl:2):      sub two { 2 };
2
```

b

```
b LINE CONDITION
b LINE
b CONDITION
b
```

Sets a breakpoint on the current line when no arguments are specified. If **LINE** is specified, then the breakpoint is set on the specified line. If **CONDITION** is specified, then each time the breakpoint is reached, it only breaks execution if the condition resolves to true. The **CONDITION** does not use an **if** statement; it is purely the test. If you use **/PATTERN/**, then the breakpoint only breaks if the statement matches the regular expression **PATTERN**.

```
b SUB CONDITION
b SUB
```

Sets a breakpoint on subroutine **SUB**, using **CONDITION** if specified.

```
b postpone SUB CONDITION
b postpone SUB
```

Sets a breakpoint on subroutine **SUB** only after it has been compiled.

```
b compile SUB
```

Sets a breakpoint on the first executable statement of the subroutine **SUB** after it has been compiled.

```
b load FILENAME
```

Sets a breakpoint at the first executed line of **FILENAME**.

d

```
d LINE
d
```

Deletes the breakpoint specified on **LINE**, or the breakpoint on the line that is about to be executed.

D

Deletes all the currently set breakpoints.

a

```
a LINE COMMAND
a COMMAND
```

Sets the action specified by **COMMAND** to be executed before the current line, or the line specified by **LINE**, is executed. For example, this can be used to print the value of a variable before it is used in a calculation.

A

Deletes all currently installed actions.

W

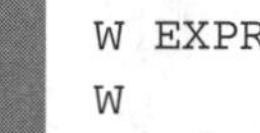

```
W EXPR
W
```

Sets a watch on the variable specified by **EXPR**. A change to the specified variable will be printed before the next line to be executed is printed. If **EXPR** is not specified, then all watchpoints are deleted.

O

```
O OPT?
O OPT=VALUE
O
```

The first form, **O OPT?**, prints the value of the option named **OPT**. The second format specifies the value for **OPT**; if no value is specified, it defaults to one. If no arguments are given, then the values of all the current options are printed. The option name can be abbreviated to the minimum identifiable name; for example, the **pager** option can be reduced to **p**.

A list of the most commonly used options is shown in Table 18-1. For others, refer to the **perldebug** man page.

The default values for the options can be obtained by typing **O** into a new debugger process:

```
perl -de 1

Loading DB routines from perl5db.pl version 1.0401
Emacs support available.

Enter h or 'h h' for help.

main::(-e:1):   1
  DB<1> O
           hashDepth = 'N/A'
          arrayDepth = 'N/A'
         DumpDBFiles = 'N/A'
        DumpPackages = 'N/A'
          DumpReused = 'N/A'
```

```
          compactDump = 'N/A'
          veryCompact = 'N/A'
                quote = 'N/A'
              HighBit = 'N/A'
           undefPrint = 'N/A'
            globPrint = 'N/A'
             PrintRet = '1'
            UsageOnly = 'N/A'
                frame = '0'
            AutoTrace = '0'
                  TTY = '/dev/tty'
                noTTY = ''
             ReadLine = '1'
              NonStop = '0'
             LineInfo = '/dev/tty'
          maxTraceLen = '400'
        recallCommand = '!'
            ShellBang = '!'
                pager = '|more'
            tkRunning = ''
            ornaments = 'us,ue,md,me'
          signalLevel = '1'
            warnLevel = '1'
             dieLevel = '1'
         inhibit_exit = '1'
        ImmediateStop = 'N/A'
        bareStringify = 'N/A'
```

<

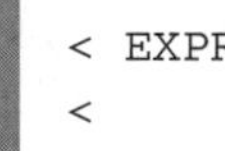

```
< EXPR
<
```

Sets a Perl command, specified in **EXPR**, to be executed before each debugger prompt. If **EXPR** is omitted, the list of statements is reset.

Option	Description
recallCommand	The character(s) used to recall a command.
ShellBang	The character(s) used to spawn a shell.
pager	The program to use for paging the output using the | command within the debugger. The value of the **PAGER** environment variable will be used by default.
tkRunning	Run Tk when prompting. (See "The ptkdp Debugger Interface" later in this chapter for a more complete Tk interface to the Perl debugger.)
signalLevel	The level of verbosity applied to signals. Default operation is to print a message when an uncaught signal is received. Set to zero to switch this off.
warnLevel	The level of verbosity applied to warnings. Default operation is to print a backtrace when a warning is printed out. Set to zero to switch this off.
dieLevel	The level of verbosity applied to warnings. Default operation is to print a backtrace when a warning is printed out. Set this option to a value of two to enable messages to be printed by surrounding **eval** statements. Set to zero to switch this off.
AutoTrace	Trace mode, identical to the **t** option on the command line. Set to zero to disable tracing.
LineInfo	The file or pipe to print line number information to. This is used by debugger interfaces with a pipe to enable them to obtain the information.
inhibit_exit	When set to zero, allows you to step to a point beyond the normal end of the script.
PrintRet	When set to zero, does not print the return value resolved when the **r** command is used. When set to one (the default), the return value is printed.

Table 18-1. *Internal Options for the Debugger*

Option	Description
frame	Controls how messages are printed during the entry and exit process from subroutines. The value is numeric, based against a bitset. If the value is zero, then messages are printed only on entry to a new subroutine. If bit 1 (value of 2) is set, then both entry and exit to the subroutine is printed. If bit 2 (4) is set, then the arguments to the subroutine are printed, and bit 4 (8) prints the values parsed to **tied** functions and methods. Bit 5 (16) also causes the return value from the subroutine to be printed. Thus, a value of 18 prints the entry and exit to a subroutine with the returned value.
maxTraceLen	The maximum number of arguments printed when bit 4 of the **frame** option is set.
arrayDepth	The maximum number of elements printed from an array. An empty string prints all elements.
hashDepth	The maximum number of keys and values printed from a hash. An empty string prints all keys.
compactDump	Sets the style of the array or hash dump. Short arrays may be printed on a single line.
veryCompact	Sets the style of the array or hash dump to be very compact.
globPrint	Sets whether the resolved file name globs are printed.
TTY	The TTY device to use for debugging I/O.
noTTY	If set, goes into a nonstop debugging mode, as if there is no controlling terminal. See the examples under the **O** command for more information.
ReadLine	When set to zero, disables readline support within the debugger, so that scripts that use ReadLine can be debugged.
NonStop	Automatically set by **noTTY**, sets the debugger into noninteractive mode.

Table 18-1. *Internal Options for the Debugger* (continued)

<<

```
<< EXPR
```

Sets a Perl command, specified in **EXPR**, to be executed before each debugger prompt.

>

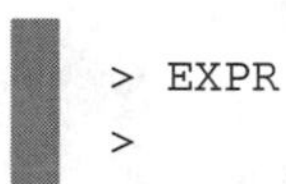

```
> EXPR
>
```

Sets the Perl command **EXPR** to be executed after each debugger prompt and after any command on the prompt has been executed. If **EXPR** is not specified, the list of commands is reset.

>>

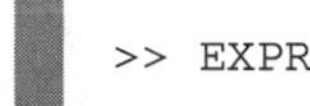

```
>> EXPR
```

Sets the Perl command **EXPR** to be executed after each debugger prompt and after any command on the prompt has been executed.

{

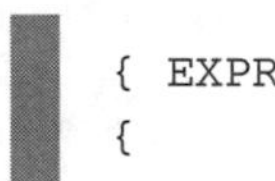

```
{ EXPR
{
```

Sets a debugger command, specified in **EXPR**, to be executed before each debugger prompt. If **EXPR** is omitted, the list of statements is reset.

{{

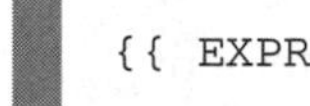

```
{{ EXPR
```

Sets a debugger command, specified in **EXPR**, to be executed before each debugger prompt.

!

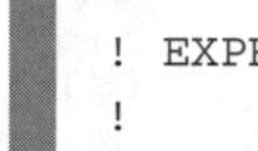

```
! EXPR
!
```

Redoes the previous command specified by the number **EXPR** (as shown in the debugger prompt), or the previous command if **EXPR** is not specified.

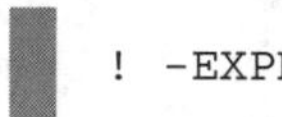

```
! -EXPR
```

Redoes the **EXPR** to the last command.

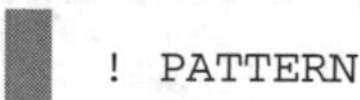

```
! PATTERN
```

Redoes the last command starting with **PATTERN**.

!!

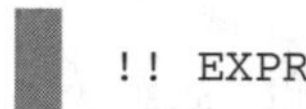

```
!! EXPR
```

Runs **EXPR** in a subprocess.

H

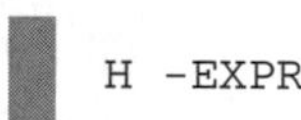

```
H -EXPR
```

Displays the last **EXPR** commands.

q or ^D

Quits from the debugger.

r

Returns immediately from the current subroutine. The remainder of the statements are ignored.

R

Restarts the debugger. Some options and history may be lost during the process, although the current specification allows for histories, breakpoints, actions, and debugger options to be retained. Also, the command line options specified by **-w**, **-I**, and **-e** are also retained.

|

```
|EXPR
```

Runs the command **EXPR** through the default pager.

||

```
||EXPR
```

Runs the command **EXPR** through the default pager, ensuring that the filehandle **DB::OUT** is temporarily selected.

=

```
= ALIAS EXPR
ALIAS
```

Assigns the value of **EXPR** to **ALIAS**, effectively defining a new command called **ALIAS**. If no arguments are specified, the list of current aliases is listed. Note that the aliases do not accept arguments, but you can simulate the effects of arguments by defining **EXPR** as a regular expression:

```
$DB::alias{'strlen'} = 's/strlen(.*)/p length($1)/';
```

This effectively reexecutes the original **strlen** command as **print length($1)**, where **$1** is the value of the first matching parentheses.

m

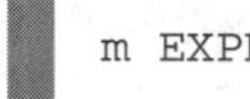

```
m EXPR
```

Evaluates expression and lists the currently valid methods that could be applied to it.

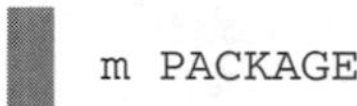

```
m PACKAGE
```

Lists the available methods defined in **PACKAGE**.

The Debugger's User Interface

To start the debugger, you need to specify the **–d** option on the command line to the Perl interpreter:

```
perl -d t.pl
```

Alternatively, it can be used with a dummy **–e** statement to drop you straight into a dummy debugger environment:

```
perl -de 1
```

Once invoked you are placed into the debugger at the first executable statement within the defined script:

```
Loading DB routines from perl5db.pl version 1.0401
Emacs support available.

Enter h or 'h h' for help.

main::(-e:1):   1
  DB<1>
```

The value in the angle brackets—one, in this example—is the number of the debugger command. This can be recalled with the **!** debugger command. The number of angle brackets shows the current depth of the debugger. Calling a new subroutine via an **s**, **n**, or **t** command will introduce a new set of brackets as a new execution path is created within the script. You can specify multiline commands by using the \ character, which has the effect of escaping the newline that would ordinarily end the command.

Rather confusingly, the line that is displayed before the prompt is the line that is *about* to be executed, rather than the line that has been executed. Therefore, on first entry into the debugger, no lines (other than compiler directives and package imports) have actually been executed.

The normal operation is to set a breakpoint on a line or statement that you want to monitor and then use the **T** command to produce a stack trace. For example:

```
    DB<4> b 16
    DB<5> r
Top of the world, Ma!
main::callerlog(t.pl:16):           print join(' ',@data),":$reference\n";
    DB<6> T
. = main::callerlog('Printed Message') called from file 't.pl' line 23
. = main::top() called from file 't.pl' line 5
. = main::bar() called from file 't.pl' line 8
```

The actual execution process for each line in the script is as follows:

1. Check for a breakpoint.
2. Print the line, using tracing if the **AutoTrace** option has been set.
3. Execute any actions defined.
4. Prompt the user if there is a breakpoint or single step.
5. Evaluate the line.
6. Print any modified watchpoints.

Once the execution has halted, you can step through the script, either by every line, using the **s** command, or by each line, stepping over subroutine calls using the **n** command.

Note that compile-time statements are not trapped by the debugger, which means that those enclosed in a **BEGIN** block, or statements such as **use**, are not stopped by the debugger. The best method for trapping them is to specify the value of the **$DB::single** variable that is part of the Perl debugger. Although it requires modification of the code, it does nothing if the debugger is not running. A value of one for the **$DB::single** variable is equivalent to having just typed **s** to the debugger. A value of two indicates that **n** should be used. Alternatively, you can monitor the status of the commands using the **AutoTrace** option.

You can set watchpoints, which display the value of a variable if it has been modified in the just executed statement. For example, in the script

```
while (<DATA>)
{
    chomp;
...
}
```

you could set a watchpoint for **$_**, which would print the value of **$_** for each iteration of the loop.

You can also run the debugger in a noninteractive mode. This enables you to print a stack trace, or watch variables, in much the same way as you might use **print** statements, but without requiring any modification to the code. To do this you need to set the value of the **PERLDB_OPTS** environment variable before running the debugger. The example below switches on full frame information for called subroutines and runs the debugger without human intervention, outputting the full trace to the standard output:

```
$ export set PERLDB_OPTS="N f=31 AutoTrace"
$ perl -d t.pl
Package t.pl.
8:      bar();
in  .=main::bar() from t.pl:8
 5:          top();
 in  .=main::top() from t.pl:5
  22:        print "Top of the world, Ma!\n";
Top of the world, Ma!
  23:        callerlog("Printed Message");
  in  .=main::callerlog('Printed Message') from t.pl:23
   12:       my $reference = shift;
   13:       my $level = 1;
   14:       while (((@data) = caller($level++)))
   15:       {
   16:           print join(' ',@data),":$reference\n";
main t.pl 5 main::top 1 :Printed Message
   14:       while (((@data) = caller($level++)))
   15:       {
   16:           print join(' ',@data),":$reference\n";
main t.pl 8 main::bar 1 :Printed Message
   14:       while (((@data) = caller($level++)))
   15:       {
  out .=main::callerlog('Printed Message') from t.pl:23
 out .=main::top() from t.pl:5
out .=main::bar() from t.pl:8
```

Customization

There are two ways of customizing the Perl debugger. The first is to specify the internal debugger options within the value of the **PERLDB_OPTS** environment variable, as you have already seen. The other option is to specify options and aliases and commands to be executed when the debugger starts by placing commands into the .perldb file, which is parsed at the time of execution by the debugger module.

The normal use for this file is to specify new aliases to the debugger, which you do by specifying the keys and values of the **%DB::alias** hash. The key is the name of the alias, and the value is the command that should be executed. See the = command in the earlier "Debugging Commands" section for details.

You can change options to the debugger by calling the **parse_options** function, which takes a single argument—a string such as would be specified in the **PERLDB_OPTS** variable. Note however that the definitions in .perldb are parsed before the string defined in the environment **PERLDB_OPTS** variable.

Debug Flags

On the command line, providing you have compiled the original source with the **-DDEBUGGING** compiler switch, are a number of debugging flags. Each flag specifies that a particular set of debug information is printed.

You saw the **-Dx** option in Chapter 16, and other options are shown in Table 18-2. Debug options can be specified either by specifying a list of letters or by specifying the

Bit	Letter	Meaning
1	p	Tokenizing and parsing.
2	s	Stack snapshots.
4	l	Context (loop) stack processing.
8	t	Trace execution.
16	o	Method and overloading resolution.
32	c	String/numeric conversions.
64	P	Print preprocessor command for **-P**.
128	m	Memory allocation.
256	f	Format processing.
512	r	Regular expression parsing and execution.
1024	x	Syntax tree dump.
2048	u	Tainting checks.
4096	L	Memory leaks (you need to have used the **–DLEAKTEST** directive when compiling Perl).
8192	H	Hash dump.
16384	X	Scratchpad allocation.
32768	D	Cleaning up.
65536	S	Thread synchronization.

Table 18-2. *Options for the **–D** Command Line Option*

sum of the bits. For example, to print out string/number conversions and hash dumps, you could use either **–DcH** or **–D8224**. The numerical value of the options is available via the **$^D** internal variable.

Debugger Interfaces

The **emacs** editor provides an interface to the Perl debugger that enables you to use the **emacs** editor as a complete development and debugging environment. There is also a mode available that allows **emacs** to understand at least some of the debugger commands that can be used during the debugging process.

There are also a number of modules available on CPAN that provide windows-based interfaces to the Perl debugger. The most friendly of the interfaces I have come across is the **ptkdb** interface.

The ptkdb Debugger Interface

The **ptkdb** debugger interface uses the Tk interface system to provide a windowed interface to the Perl debugger. All of the normal interface elements are available, with buttons and entry points for the most regularly used items. You invoke the **ptkdb** interface (once it has been installed) using the debug extension command line option:

```
$ perl -d:ptkdb t.pl
```

You can see a sample window for the chapter's example debug script in Figure 18-1. The left side of the window shows the listing of the original Perl script. The right panel displays variables, expressions, subroutines, and breakpoints for the current debugger invocation. The information printed is the same as that produced within the normal text-based debugger interface, albeit within a nice preformatted and windowed environment.

Other Debuggers and Methods

Perl is a very extensible language, and with version 5 the functions and hooks were provided to investigate many of the internals of the Perl interpreter. This information can be used to discover all sorts of information that may not normally be available via the debugging processes you have already seen.

The regular expression parser within Perl is a very complex programming language in its own right. There is a supported method within Perl for debugging regular expressions, which we'll cover shortly.

We'll also consider two other systems. One is based on a module available from CPAN that provides profiling and performance information. The other uses the compiler interface, which we'll look at in more detail in the next chapter. It provides additional checks and cross-referencing information. Both of these can be used to further enhance or reduce the errors and uncertainty in your script, as well as provide you with useful performance and cross-referencing information.

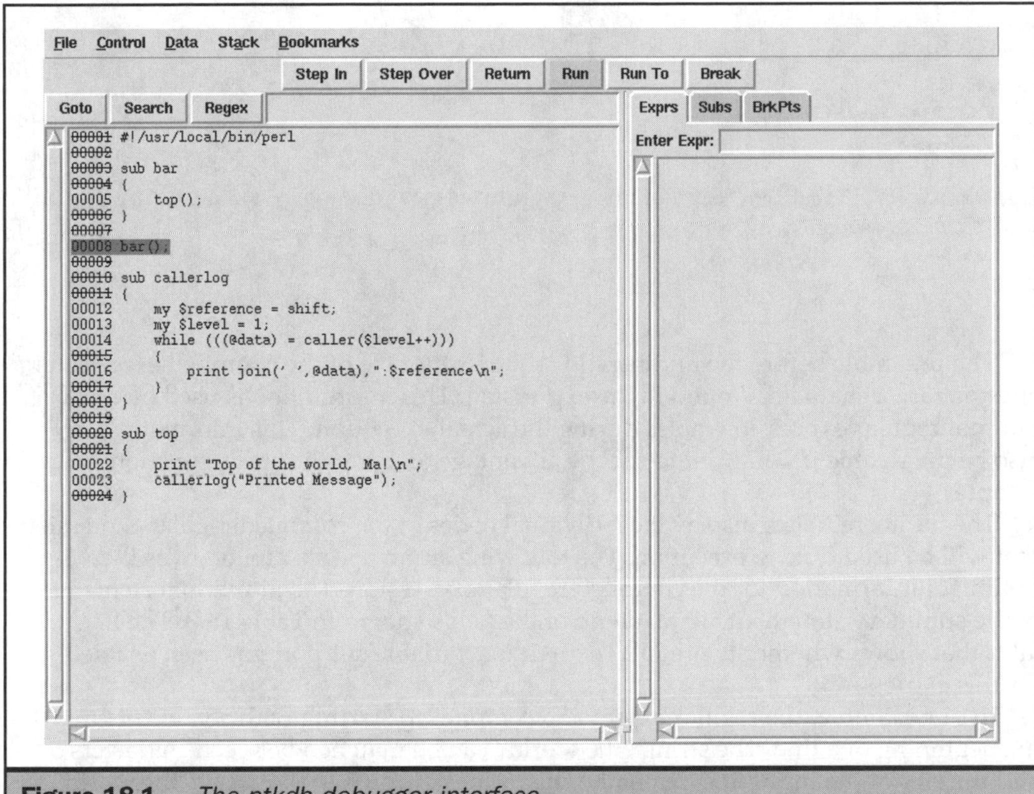

Figure 18-1. *The ptkdb debugger interface*

Debugging Regular Expressions

The **–Dr** command line option allows you to debug regular expressions, providing you have built the Perl interpreter with the **–DDEBUGGING** compiler directive. The same option can be enabled through the use of the **use re 'debug'** pragma. The result is an extensive list of the compile-time output for the regular expression engine. For example:

```
perl -Dr -e '/top[of]\s+the (world)/;'
compiling RE 'top[of]\s+the (world)'
size 26 first at 1
rarest char w at 4
rarest char p at 2
   1: EXACT <top>(4)
   4: ANYOF(14)
  14: PLUS(16)
  15:   SPACE(0)
```

```
   16: EXACT <the >(19)
   19: OPEN1(21)
   21:   EXACT <world>(24)
   24: CLOSE1(26)
   26: END(0)
anchored 'top' at 0 floating 'the world' at 5..2147483647 (checking floating) minlen 14
Omitting $' $& $' support.

EXECUTING...
```

The preamble before the numbered list shows the size of the compiled expression and the rarest characters found in the expression. This information is used by the internal regular expression tables during the actual execution. This information can also be invaluable if you want to see the advantage of using the **study** function (see Chapter 4).

The numbered lines display the individual nodes of the compiled regular expression that will be used during execution. The following summary statement gives the optimizer information for the compiled regular expression. The individual elements of the summary statement are made up of the fields shown in Table 18-3. The line after that shows whether the regular expression variable support has been enabled for this expression.

In our example, the regular expression compiles to starting with a value of "top" at the beginning of a line. The string "the world" can be matched between characters 5 and the end of the input line, remembering to check for the existence of "the world" before it checks for "top." The minimum length for a regular expression is 14 characters.

You may want to refer to the **perldebug** man page for details of the node types displayed during the expression compilation.

The Perl Profiler

Profiling is the process of reporting on the dynamic behavior of a program. Rather than identifying lexical errors in your script, profiling identifies performance issues in your script by monitoring the time taken to execute individual subroutines. The information for each subroutine call is recorded, and the information can then be collated to give a reasonable representation of how much overall execution time is made up of certain functions.

Armed with this information, you can identify which functions are soaking up the execution time of your script and, of those, which may require further optimization. You may need to make some modifications to your script, depending on the script's purpose. Scripts that wait for input from the user, or from an external pipe or network socket, may need to be modified. Any external source of information that causes the script to "wait" will skew the results and render the process useless unless you can identify which of the functions can be ignored. This is heavily dependent on the design

Field	Description
anchored **STRING** at **POS**	Shows that **STRING** has been identified as only appearing at the precise location specified by **POS**.
floating **STRING** at **POS1..POS2**	Shows that the **STRING** could be found within the character range **POS1** and **POS2**.
matching floating/anchored	Shows which substring should be checked first.
minlen	Shows the minimum length of the match.
stclass **TYPE**	The type of the first matching node.
noscan	Advises not to scan for the found substrings.
isall	Specifies that the optimizer info is in fact all that the regular expression contains. That is, the regular expression does not actually need to be executed in order for a match to be made. For example, the expression **/s/** doesn't require the expression engine to find a match; it's not a regular expression.
GPOS	Displayed if the pattern contains **\G**.
plus	Shown if the pattern starts with a repeated character, as in **/s+/**.
implicit	Shown if the pattern starts with **.***.
with eval	Shown if the patterns contains evaluated group expressions.
anchored(TYPE)	Shown if the pattern will only match at a number of places. **TYPE** is one of **BOL** (beginning of line), **MBOL** (beginning of multiline), **GPOS** (matches where the last **m//g** left off).

Table 18-3. *Summary Fields for Debugged Regular Expressions*

of your script, but my recommendation is to supply some "standard" information to the script that can be used to produce the profiling information.

The main profiling system for Perl is the Devel::Dprof module, available currently from CPAN, although it's expected to become part of the standard Perl distribution in the near future. It's composed of a single module that needs to be invoked via the debugging system. This produces a single file, called tmon.out, which contains the raw data of the profiling process. The Devel::DProf distribution comes with a Perl script, **dprofpp**, that analyzes this information and produces summarized reports detailing, to varying degrees, the execution profile of the subroutines defined in the script.

The options for the **dprofpp** script are shown in Table 18-4. If you regularly use a specific set of options, you can use the **DPROFPP_OPTS** environment variable to store the list of default options. The default value would be **–z –O 15 –E**.

For example, testing the script below:

```
package First;

$funca = { sin($_[0]) };
$funcb = { cos($_[0]) };

sub foo
{
    for ($i=0;$i<1000;$i++)
    {
        $funca;
        $funcb;
    }
}

package Second;

sub foo
{
    for ($i=0;$i<1000;$i++)
    {
        $i % 2;
      First::foo();
    }
}

package main;

sub bar
{
  Second::foo();
  First::foo();
}

bar();
```

Option	Description
-a	Sorts the list of subroutines alphabetically.
-A	Reports the time for functions loaded via the AutoLoad module as ***::AUTOLOAD**, showing the total time for all autoloaded modules. The default is for individual functions to have their own time calculated.
-E	This is the default option, displaying all subroutine times exclusive of child subroutine times.
-F	Generates fake exit time values. This gets around the problem introduced by subroutines calling **exit** or **exec**, which causes the normal execution process of the script to end prematurely.
-g subroutine	Shows only the results for **subroutine** and the subroutines it calls.
-I	Displays the execution times of child as well as parent execution times.
-l	Sorts the list of subroutines by the number of times each subroutine has been called.
-O cnt	Displays the first **cnt** subroutines, default is 15.
-p script	Executes **script** and then outputs report.
-Q	Quits after profiling the script with **–p** without producing a report.
-q	Displays report without headers.
-R	Counts anonymous subroutines within the same package scope individually. The normal operation is count each invocation separately.
-r	Displays only elapsed real times. Individual user and system times are not displayed.
-s	Displays only system times. User times are not displayed.

Table 18-4. *Options for the **dprofpp** Profiling System*

Option	Description
-S	Displays merged subroutine call tree, with statistical information for each branch, to **STDOUT**. Making multiple calls to the same function within the same branch creates a new branch at the next level. Repeat counts are displayed for each function within each branch. Sort order is by total time per branch.
-T	Displays subroutine call tree to **STDOUT**. Statistics are not printed.
-t	Displays subroutine call tree to **STDOUT**, and subroutines called multiple consecutive times are simply displayed with a repeat count. Statistics are not printed.
-U	Do not sort subroutine list.
-u	Displays only user times. System times are not displayed.
-V	Prints the version number of the **dprofpp** script, and prints the Devel::Dprof version number stored in the statistics file if found or specified.
-v	Sorts by the average time elapsed for child calls within each call.
-z	Sorts the subroutine list by the amount of user and system time used.

Table 18-4. *Options for the **dprofpp** Profiling System* (continued)

To create the raw data, you run the program through the interpreter and the profiling system:

```
$ perl -d:DProf t.pl
```

The default output of the **dprofpp** reporting system is shown here:

```
Total Elapsed Time = 40.28038 Seconds
  User+System Time = 40.18038 Seconds
Exclusive Times
```

```
%Time ExclSec CumulS #Calls sec/call Csec/c  Name
 100.    40.21 40.215   1001    0.0402 0.0402  First::foo
 0.31    0.125 40.291      1    0.1254 40.290  Second::foo
 0.00    0.000 40.340      1    0.0000 40.340  main::bar
```

The function called most often, and the one that soaks up the most amount of time, is the **foo** function in the **First** package. Let's just check where the function is called in the execution process by reporting the actual execution tree:

```
main::bar
   Second::foo
      First::foo (1000x)
   First::foo
```

Alternatively, you can combine the main report and the above tree to get an idea of how many times each group of calls to the function has been made, by using the **-S** option:

```
main::bar x 1    40.34s = (0.00 + 40.34)s
  Second::foo x 1        40.29s = (0.13 + 40.17)s
    First::foo x 1000    40.17s
  First::foo x 1         0.05s
```

If all you want is to produce a profile for a single hit of the script, you can use the **dprofpp** script directly:

```
$ dprofpp -S -p t.pl
```

However, if what you want is to continually probe the original results for different combinations and different reports, perhaps targeting a different selection of functions each time, then you should run the script through the profiler to create the tmon.out file. You can then compile reports based on the raw data without having to run the script again. Comparing the results of multiple executions of the script is often a waste of time, since the minor differences between each execution may introduce wildly different figures for certain functions.

Also be aware of the size of the raw data file created. For this small script, a 16K data file is generated. Larger scripts with more functions and, more importantly, more function calls will generate significantly more data.

For a simpler solution to the profiling problem, you may want to investigate the Benchmark module, which is part of the standard Perl distribution. It involves the inclusion of some code into your source code in order to report the time taken to execute certain blocks, but it may fill a requirement that the Devel::Dprof cannot. In particular, by using Benchmark, you can test the execution times of blocks of code instead of only reporting entire functions. On the other hand, it also requires more work to achieve the benchmark results, and the modifications will need to be removed before you distribute the script. With the Devel::Dprof module, the statistics are calculated for you automatically without requiring any code modifications.

Using the Compiler Interface

The Perl compiler modules B and O support many different backends that provide additional information about a Perl script. Two are relevant to the debugging process, Lint and Xref. The Lint backend checks a number of errors that are normally ignored by the standard Perl warnings. The possible bugs that it picks up include implicit use of arrays as scalars and implicit use of the **$_** variables. For aiding performance, it also identifies occurrences of the regular expression variables **$'**, **$&**, **$’**, which can slow down performance (see Chapter 4).

The Xref module produces a cross-reference report that lists the lines in which all subroutines and variables are called. Although not strictly a debugging tool, it does provide a useful list of references for tracing the use of specific functions and variables throughout a script. It also incorporates details for all of the imported modules, which makes it invaluable for tracing problems in all the components that make up the final executed script.

We'll look at the compiler and other backends in the next chapter.

Chapter 19

Perl Compiler

Chapter 16 details the internal processes involved in converting a Perl script into the internal opcodes that actually execute the Perl statements you have written. This process is conducted each time the Perl script is executed, and it has some major advantages. If you were writing the same program in C, C++, or Java, or another "compiled" language, the compilation process would convert the text-based source code into machine code. *Machine code* is the name for the actual binary instructions used by the computer's processor to perform different operations.

The compilation process is relatively long and complicated, as the code first has to be parsed into machine code, then linked with the standard operating system libraries to supply it with the base functions. The whole object file is then regurgitated into an executable—a compiled binary that can be executed without the need for any other external libraries (except those that can be dynamically loaded) or a separate program. Perl, however, is an interpreter. Perl is itself an executable, and it takes the source code and executes the code within the confines of the Perl interpreter.

The advantages and disadvantages between the two systems are simple. A compiled binary has some significant advantages. As a generalization, compiled binaries execute faster than most interpreted languages. They can also be supplied to users without the user requiring a separate application, and once received, the user cannot modify the application.

The disadvantage though is that different binaries must be compiled for different platforms, and the effects are felt both at a hardware and operating system level. Minor differences even between two different versions of the same operating system on the same hardware may require that a compiled binary be reproduced. Furthermore, any changes to the program require a recompilation and relinking process that even for relatively small programs requires a significant amount of time.

With Perl, because the script is written in plain text, you can send it to anybody with a Perl interpreter and expect him to be able to execute the program. Providing the Perl interpreter has been installed on the desired platform (barring minor differences), the script should run without error. Modifications to the script can be conducted very quickly, since all you need to do is edit the text file in any text editor. There is no recompilation process, either for the platform you are developing on or for any of the destination platforms.

The disadvantage is that this ease of modification also means users can unexpectedly modify the source and introduce errors. Furthermore, if you are trying to provide a commercial script, then any user to whom you supply the script will also have access to the source code, making it difficult for you to protect your own intellectual property and copyright.

Note *Actually, there are ways of getting around the problems of supplying Perl scripts in a textual, but encoded form that provides all the benefits without making the script readable to an end user. Check Appendix F for sample modules available from CPAN.*

Fortunately, the argument that Perl scripts run slower than their binary executable equivalents is normally a moot point. In most instances, Perl code often runs faster than programs written in native C or other languages. This is because of the highly optimized opcodes that execute the Perl script. The optimization on certain operations is so tight that without duplicating the optimization it would be impossible to achieve the same speed. There are of course some exceptions: repetitive loops and mathematical calculations take longer. In all instances, you need to consider the advantages of the Perl language. Handling large volumes of text in Perl is very easy, but in C it is very complex, for example. See the section "Speed Comparison" later in this chapter for some examples.

However, in some instances the conversion of a Perl script into an executable binary would be exceedingly useful. Perl actually provides two methods for achieving this, and we'll look in this chapter at the two methods and their relative merits. We'll also examine some of the differences in performance times between an "interpreted" Perl script and one converted to a binary executable.

Using dump

As you learned in Chapter 16, Perl effectively compiles a script into a series of highly optimized opcodes, all of which are basically links to the compiled C code that makes up the Perl interpreter. If you return to Figure 16-1 in Chapter 16, you will see the basic layout of the Perl interpreter. Once a script has reached the point of reduction to an optimized opcode tree, you effectively have an executable.

The combination of the script's opcode tree and Perl's opcode library with the Executor module of the Perl executable actually represents a complete executable program, or core image. You could make a complete stand-alone program by converting the running process consisting of all these elements into a stand-alone executable program.

Perl provides a method for dumping the core image of the current executable using the **dump** function. The idea is that this can then be turned into an executable using the system **undump** command. Unfortunately, the **undump** command is not supported on all systems.

```
dump LABEL
dump
```

If specified, execution will start from **LABEL** (by doing a **goto LABEL** when executed), or execution just starts from the beginning of the script.

What actually happens is that Perl calls the **abort** function, which causes a core dump. The contents of the core dump consist of all the current application data and code (core dumps are usually used when debugging an application). The state of the program, including any initialization in the original code, will be in place, so a script of the form

```
$message = "Hello World\n";
dump START;

START:
    print $message;
```

will already have the value of **$message** set when it is executed after being dumped. If you do not specify a label to the **dump** function, the program will just execute from the start.

Once dumped, you need to use the **undump** program to convert the dumped core into an executable. The **undump** program is not available on all platforms and, in fact, on some systems is not even possible. Most notably, any system that uses ELF (Executable and Linking Format) such as Solaris for its object format will not be able to use **undump**. ELF is incompatible with the principle of the **undump** process, although it does support the creation of an executable directly (see the discussion of **unexec** below).

In order to get the system working with Perl, you will need to have a version of **undump** installed on your system (it's available within the TeX distribution) and a copy of Perl compiled with static rather than dynamic libraries. You use the static version of Perl in combination with the dumped core file to produce an executable, for example:

```
$ dumpscript.pl
$ undump perl core
$ b.out
```

This example runs the dumpscript.pl script, which calls **dump**, then uses **undump** and the static Perl executable to create a new application, b.out, using the core file.

Although **dump** is very clumsy, it does provide the facility for creating a "saved state" of an executable program. Of course, without an easy way to return the execution to this state, the function is virtually useless.

In fact, **dump** can also be used in the debugging process since it causes a core dump that could be used by an external symbolic debugger such as **dbx** or **gdb**. You'll need to know the internals of Perl pretty well for it to be of any specific use since no C-level debugger will be able to understand the opcode format used internally by Perl scripts.

You can also use **dump** with the **unexec()** function (which is part of **emacs**) if you compile Perl with the **–DUNEXEC** flag. Unlike **dump**, **unexec** attempts to make an executable directly, instead of relying on an external program to produce the final executable. In theory, any platform that supports a "dumped" version of **emacs** should be able to use this method of producing executable Perl scripts.

Irrespective of which method you use to produce the executable, dumping an image of a running program is not very reliable. With the introduction of a Perl compiler, there seems little need for such convoluted methods.

Perl Compiler

The Perl compiler is a relatively new inclusion in the Perl distribution and is still considered largely experimental. When Perl 5 was introduced, it was a completely new version of Perl, which had been entirely rewritten to make some special changes to the way the internals worked. This change provided the ability to resolve a Perl script into a set of opcodes, as we saw in Chapters 16 and 17.

The Perl compiler uses the internal opcode tree and reproduces it with some wrapper code into the desired format. The wrapper code includes raw bytecode (a binary format), a simple textual opcode tree, and, of course, C source code. The C source code produced is not strictly a C version of the Perl script. In fact, it's a dump of the internal opcode tree in C format, which is then passed to a **PerlInterpreter()** object, identical to the system discussed in Chapter 17.

Although the code produced is not a recognizable C version of the Perl script, it is genuine C code. This can be compiled and linked with the Perl library in order to produce the final executable version of the original Perl script. The final executable is composed of the parsed opcode tree and a Perl interpreter that executes the opcode tree.

To make the process of compilation easier, the Perl distribution includes the **perlcc** Perl script, which can be used to compile a Perl script straight into an executable without any further intervention. The compiler can also be used to compile Perl modules into C libraries.

The actual internals of the Perl compiler are based on two modules, B and O, and a set of "backends" that translate Perl scripts into different target formats.

The perlcc Frontend

The main method for compiling a Perl script into a final executable is the **perlcc** script. This takes a number of command line options that control the generation process. It also automates the entire process from the generation of the C source code right through to the compilation and linking stages. Using it at its simplest level, the command

```
$ perlcc foo.pl
```

will compile the foo.pl script into the executable **foo**. It will also compile Perl modules into shared libraries that can then be accessed via the **AutoLoad** mechanism within Perl.

The process assumes you have installed Perl and have a C compiler on your system. The **perlcc** script (which is written in Perl) will try to account for the specific file locations of your Perl installation. Since all Perl distribution on both Windows and Unix platforms is done by source rather than executables, it can be assumed that both platforms should support the use of the Perl compiler. Support does not currently exist under MacOS. This is because MacOS does not support a command line interface, and there is no cheaply or widely available C compiler that could be used to produce the final executable. There are also other issues specifically related to the environment on a MacOS machine. Check Chapter 23 for the major differences between the MacOS platform and the "standard" Unix platform.

Command Line Options

The **perlcc** frontend supports a number of command line arguments. These control the compilation, code generation, and linking process for translating a Perl source script into an executable program. Most of the options are actually passed on to the underlying backend modules, which we'll be examining in greater detail later in this chapter.

The command line options also control the calls to the compiler and linker used to build the final executable. Certain options simplify both the process of compiling large programs that consist of many Perl scripts and modules, and the compilation of multiple scripts into multiple executables.

```
-L DIRS
```

Adds the directories specified in **DIRS** to the C/C++ compiler library path. Each directory should be separated by a colon.

```
-I DIRS
```

Adds the directories specified in **DIRS** to the C/C++ compiler include path. Each directory should be separated by a colon.

```
-C FILENAME
```

Gives the generated C code the file name specified by **FILENAME**. Only applicable when compiling a single source script.

```
-o FILENAME
```

Gives the generated executable the file name specified by **FILENAME**. Only applicable when compiling a single source script.

```
-e LINE
```

Identical to the Perl **–e** option. Compiles **LINE** as a single-line Perl script. The default operation is to compile and then execute the one-line script. If you want to save the executable generated, use the **–o** flag.

```
-regex NAME
```

NAME should specify a regular expression to be used when compiling multiple source files into multiple executables. For example, the command

```
$ perlcc -regex 's/\.pl/\.bin/' foo.pl bar.pl
```

would create two executables, foo.bin and bar.bin.

```
-verbose LEVEL
```

Sets the verbosity of the compilation process to the level specified by **LEVEL**. This should be in the form of either a number or a string of letters. Except where specified via the **–log** option, the information is sent to **STDERR**. The available levels are given in Table 19-1.

For example, to set the maximum verbosity level, you might use

```
$ perlcc -v 63 -log foo.out foo.pl
```

Note that some options require that the name of a suitable file be given via the **–log** option. See below for more details. If the **–log** tag has been given and no specific verbosity level has been specified, the script assumes a verbosity level of 63. If no verbosity or log file is specified, a level of 7 is implied.

```
-log NAME
```

Numeric	Letter	Description
1	g	Code generation errors to **STDERR**.
2	a	Compilation errors to **STDERR**.
4	t	Descriptive text to **STDERR**.
8	f	Code generation errors to file (**-log** flag needed).
16	c	Compilation errors to file (**-log** flag needed).
32	d	Descriptive text to file (**-log** flag needed).

Table 19-1. *Verbosity Levels for the **perlcc** Command*

Logs the progress of the compilation to the file **NAME**. Note that the information is appended to the file; the contents are not truncated before more information is added. The effect of this option is to make the entire process of compilation silent—all output is redirected to the specified file.

```
-argv ARGS
```

Must be used with the **–run** or **–e** options. Causes the value of **@ARGV** to be populated with the contents of **ARGS**. If you want to specify more than one argument, use single quotes and separate each argument with a space.

```
-sav
```

The intermediate C source code that is generated during the compilation is saved in a file with the same name as the source with ".c" appended.

```
-gen
```

Tells **perlcc** to generate only the C source code—the file will not be compiled into an executable.

```
-run
```

Immediately run the executable that was generated. Any remaining arguments to **perlcc** will be supplied to the executable as command line arguments.

```
-prog
```

Specifies that all files supplied are programs. This causes Perl to ignore the normal interpretation that .pm files are actually modules, not scripts.

```
-mod
```

Specifies that the files should be compiled as modules, not scripts. This overrides the normal interpretation that files ending in .p, .pl, and .bat are Perl scripts.

Environment

You can change some of the implied logic of the **perlcc** process using environment variables. These modifications will affect all compilation, unless you use the command line arguments to override the new defaults.

The **PERL_SCRIPT_EXT** variable contains a list of colon-separated regular expressions. These define the extensions that **perlcc** automatically recognizes as scripts. For example, the default value is

```
PERL_SCRIPT_EXT = '.p$:.pl$:.bat$';
```

Note the use of **$** to define that the extension should be at the end of the file name.

The **PERL_MODULE_EXT** operates in the same way, only for those files that should be recognized as modules. The default value is **.pm$**.

During the compilation process, the **perlcc** module creates a number of temporary files. All of these file's names are based on the value of the **$$** Perl variable, which refers to the current process ID. Thus the temporary file for the **–e** option is perlc$$.p, the file for temporary C code is perlc$$.p.c, and a temporary executable is stored in perlc$$.

The B and O Modules

The **B** and **O** modules provide the interface between the user and the actual compilation process. The core of the compilation process is actually handled by the **B** module. This supports the backends that translate the Perl source script into the various formats. In fact, the **B** module provides all the information you should need if you want to produce a different backend module. However, the **B** module is not the user interface to the internals of the compiler. For this you should use the **O** module, which provides a simpler interface to the compiler internals.

The internals of the **B** and **O** modules are really beyond this book; however, the different backends available are worth examining. They can provide some useful output, aside from the C source available with the normal **perlcc** frontend.

We will examine nine backends here: **C**, **CC**, **Bytecode**, **Terse**, **Debug**, **Xref**, **Lint**, **Deparse**, and **ShowLex**. All backends work in the same basic way. You call the **O** module as part of the command line to a normal Perl interpreter and then specify the backend and any options you want to define:

```
$ perl -MO=Backend[,OPTIONS] foo.pl
```

Most backends support three options. The **–v** option forces the backend to report all sorts of information about the compilation process. The **–D** option specifies debugging, using various option letters. The **–o** option enables the output of the compiler to be redirected to another file. Multiple options can be separated by commas.

You may also want to investigate the **assemble**, **disassemble**, and other scripts in the ext/B directory of the Perl distribution. These provide simple interfaces to some of the backends discussed in much the same way as the **perlcc** frontend we have already discussed.

Note that it's also possible (but probably not practical) to include the module within the source of the script. For example, to use the **C** backend without any options:

```
use O ('C','');
```

Whichever method is used, the process is the same. The **compile** function in the backend module is called, using the specified options. The function returns a subroutine reference, which will actually be called as part of the **B** module's **END** block, so it is the last thing executed after the internal compilation of the Perl script has been completed. The compile-only flag to Perl is switched on, and the compilation proceeds. Other than **BEGIN** blocks, the script does not actually execute. This allows for **use** and other initialization constructs to work normally.

Once the compilation has been completed, the subroutine from the backend module is called. The backend modules actually use a number of functions defined within the main **B** module, which allow the internal structures of the Perl interpreter environment to be accessed. Each backend module uses these functions to examine the opcode tree, data objects, and other information.

For example, the **Xref** backend actually just parses the opcode tree and symbol table in order to build up a picture of the script in terms of the objects and subroutines that are used, and where they are used. The compiled script and opcode itself is never used—no output, other than the cross-reference report, is produced.

At the other end of the scale, the **CC** backend reads the opcode tree and regurgitates the entire tree structure as C source code. It then adds the necessary wrapper code to enable the dumped opcode tree to execute once it has been compiled into an executable.

C Backend

The **C** backend is the fundamental part of the conversion of a Perl script into its **C** opcode equivalent. The backend produces code based on the state of the Perl script just before execution begins; that is, the compilation, parsing, and optimization processes normally conducted by the interpreter have already been completed. This allows a compiled program to execute more or less identically to the original interpreted version. Unfortunately, this also means that the speed of execution is identical.

The basic options, shared with the **CC** backend, are shown in Table 19-2. There are also a number of options specific to the **C** backend, shown in Table 19-3.

For example, to create the C source code of the **foo.pl** Perl script to the file **foo.c,** with optimization:

```
$ perl -MO=C,-O1,-ofoo.c foo.pl
```

You can then compile the **foo.c** program using any C compiler, remembering to link to the Perl library in order to produce a final executable.

Option	Description
-ofilename	Output the C source code to **filename** instead of **STDOUT**.
-v	Verbose mode; gives out compilation statistics.
--	End of options.
-uPackname	Include functions defined in **Packname** to be compiled if they have not otherwise been selected. Normally, only functions that are identified as being used are included in the opcode tree. Unused functions are ignored. Using this option allows for functions that are used via an **eval** to be compiled with the rest of the Perl script. Obviously, this also increases the size of the source code created, as well as the eventual size of the executable.

Table 19-2. *Basic **C** Backend Options*

CC Backend

The **CC** backend produces C code equivalent to the tree that would be executed at run time. This enables the code generated to be highly optimized, allowing for much better performance. The list of available optimizations is relatively small, but further optimizations are due to be added.

Option	Description
-Do	Debug opcodes; prints each opcode as it is processed.
-Dc	Debug construct opcodes (COPs); prints COPs as they are processed, including file and line number.
-DA	Debug; prints array value information.
-DC	Debug; prints code value information.
-DM	Debug; prints magic variable information.
-fcog	Copy-on-grow; string values are declared and initialized statically.
-fno-cog	No copy-on-grow; string values are initialized dynamically.
-On	Set optimization to the value of **n**. Values of one and higher set **–fcog**.

Table 19-3. *Options Specifically for the **C** Backend*

The **CC** backend supports the same basic options as the **C** backend that are shown in Table 19-2. The **CC**-specific options are shown in Table 19-4.

Option	Description
-mModulename	Generate source code for an XSUB, creating a hook function named **boot_Modulename** suitable for identification by the DynaLoader module.
-Dr	Debug: outputs debugging information to **STDERR**. If not specified, the debugging information is included as comments in the C source code produced.
-DO	Debug; prints with opcode as it's processed.
-Ds	Debug; prints the shadow stack of the opcode as it's processed.
-Dp	Debug; prints the contents of the shadow pad of lexials as loaded for each subroutine (including the main program).
-Dq	Debug; prints the name of each fake PP function just before it is processed.
-Dl	Debug; prints the source file name and line number of each line of Perl code as it is processed.
-Dt	Debug; prints the timing information for each compilation stage.
-ffreetmps-each-bblock	Forces the optimization of freeing temporaries to the end of each block until the end of each statement.
-ffreetmps-each-loop	Forces the optimization of freeing temporaries to the end of each enclosing loop, instead of the end of each statement. You can only set one of the **freetmps** optimizations at any one time.
-fomit-taint	Disables the generation of the tainting mechanism.
-On	Sets the optimization to level **n**. A level of **–O1** implies -ffreetmps-each-bblock, and -O2 implies -ffreetmps-each-loop.

Table 19-4. *Options Specifically for **CC** Backend*

For example, to create the C source code of the **foo.pl** Perl script to the file **foo.c**:

```
$ perl -MO=CC,-ofoo.c foo.pl
```

Bytecode Backend

The **Bytecode** backend produces a platform-independent version of the Perl script in a binary format. This is effectively the equivalent of the binary code generated when a normal C program is compiled. The difference is that it can be interpreted by a special version of the Perl interpreter and is therefore cross-platform compatible.

The bytecode produced is based on the state of the interpreter just before execution of the original script. The normal compilation process of the interpreter has already been completed, and so bytecode-compiled code executes significantly quicker than a raw script, albeit slower than a truly compiled version.

To use the **Bytecode** backend, you will need to have compiled the **byteperl** executable. Check the ext/B subdirectory of the Perl distribution for instructions. It's not compiled as part of the base distribution build process.

The **Bytecode** backend only supports the **–ofilename** and **--** options shown in Table 19-2, in combination with the specific options shown in Table 19-5.

To create a bytecode-compiled program from **foo.pl**:

```
$ perl -MO=Bytecode,-ofoo.bc foo.pl
```

To run the bytecode program, you supply the bytecode file to the **byteperl** executor:

```
$ byteperl foo.bc
```

Note that by default the bytecode file is sent to **STDOUT**, which will most likely upset your terminal. You should always use the **–ofilename** option to specify an alternative file in order to store the compiled program.

Terse Backend

The **Terse** backend is useful when you want to examine the exact execution path of a script in its opcode-compiled format. The information output is, as the name suggests, very terse, but it should provide you with a basic idea of the process that is taking

Option	Description
-Do	Debug; prints out each opcode as it is processed.
-Db	Debug; prints out the compilation progress.
-Da	Debug; includes source assembler lines in the bytecode as comments.
-DC	Debug; prints each code value as taken from the final symbol tree.
-S	Produces bytecode assembler source instead of the final bytecode binary.
-m	Compiles the script as a module.
-fcompress-nullops	Completes only the required fields of opcodes that have been optimized by the compiler. Other fields are ignored (saves space). Can be switched off with **-fno-compress-nullops**.
-fomit-sequence-numbers	Ignores the code normally produced that populates the **op_seq** field of each opcode (saves space). This is normally only used by Perl's internal compiler. Can be switched off with **-fno-omit-sequence-numbers**.
-fbypass-nullops	Ignores **null opcodes**; the code skips to the next **non-null opcode** in the execution tree (saves space and time). Can be switched off with **-fno-bypass-nullops**.
-fstrip-syntax-tree	Does not produce the internal pointers that compose the syntax tree. This does not affect execution, but the produced bytecode cannot be disassembled. This has the effect of rendering **goto LABEL** statements useless. It also works as a suitable security measure to stop bytecode-compiled scripts from being reverse engineered. Can be switched off with **-fno-strip-syntax-tree**.
-On	Sets optimization to level **n.** Currently, **-O1** implies -**fcompress-nullops** and **-fomit-sequence numbers. -O6** implies **-fstrip-syntax-tree**.

Table 19-5. *Options Specifically for* ***Bytecode*** *Backend*

place when a script executes. By default the information is formatted and printed in syntax order, for example:

```
$ perl -MO=Terse -e '$a = $b + 2;
-e syntax OK
LISTOP (0x13c530) pp_leave
    OP (0x1349a0) pp_enter
    COP (0x13c5f0) pp_nextstate
    BINOP (0x1435a0) pp_sassign
        BINOP (0x12eb40) pp_add [1]
            UNOP (0x12eb00) pp_null [15]
                GVOP (0x12eae0) pp_gvsv  GV (0xc9864) *b
            SVOP (0x1435c0) pp_const  IV (0xbc9d8) 2
        UNOP (0xbf6c0) pp_null [15]
            GVOP (0xbf660) pp_gvsv  GV (0xc6ba0) *a
```

You can compare this with the debugging output we saw when comparing the same statement in Chapter 16. You'll notice it looks remarkably similar, except that it's in much more compressed format.

The backend supports only one option, **exec**, which outputs the opcodes in execution order. Unfortunately, it removes much of the formatting available in the default mode:

```
$ perl -MO=Terse,exec -e '$a = $b + 2;'
-e syntax OK
OP (0x1349a0) pp_enter
COP (0x13c5f0) pp_nextstate
GVOP (0x12eae0) pp_gvsv  GV (0xc9864) *b
SVOP (0x1435c0) pp_const  IV (0xbc9d8) 2
BINOP (0x12eb40) pp_add [1]
GVOP (0xbf660) pp_gvsv  GV (0xc6ba0) *a
BINOP (0x1435a0) pp_sassign
LISTOP (0x13c530) pp_leave
```

Debug Backend

For a more detailed view of the execution of opcodes you can use the **Debug** backend. This works in a similar way to the **Terse** backend but provides more information. By default the information is output in syntax order:

```
$ perl -MO=Debug -e '$a = $b + 2;'
-e syntax OK
LISTOP (0x133530)
        op_next         0x0
        op_sibling      0x0
        op_ppaddr       pp_leave
        op_targ         0
        op_type         177
        op_seq          7065
        op_flags        13
        op_private      0
        op_first        0x151bf8
        op_last         0x141dc0
        op_children     3
OP (0x151bf8)
        op_next         0xcf1d0
        op_sibling      0xcf1d0
        op_ppaddr       pp_enter
        op_targ         0
        op_type         176
        op_seq          7058
        op_flags        0
        op_private      0
COP (0xcf1d0)
        op_next         0x12eae0
        op_sibling      0x141dc0
        op_ppaddr       pp_nextstate
        op_targ         0
        op_type         173
        op_seq          7059
        op_flags        1
        op_private      0
        cop_label
        cop_stash       0xbc87c
        cop_filegv      0xbca50
        cop_seq         7059
        cop_arybase     0
        cop_line        1
...
```

The output above has been trimmed for brevity. The full list from this simple statement is 173 lines long!

Like the **Terse** backend, **Debug** also supports the output in execution order, but once again the formatting is lost:

```
$ perl -MO=Debug,exec -e '$a = $b + 2;'|more
-e syntax OK
OP (0x151bf8)
        op_next         0xcf1d0
        op_sibling      0xcf1d0
        op_ppaddr       pp_enter
        op_targ         0
        op_type         176
        op_seq          7058
        op_flags        0
        op_private      0
COP (0xcf1d0)
        op_next         0x12eae0
        op_sibling      0x141dc0
        op_ppaddr       pp_nextstate
        op_targ         0
        op_type         173
        op_seq          7059
        op_flags        1
        op_private      0
        cop_label
        cop_stash       0xbc87c
        cop_filegv      0xbca50
        cop_seq         7059
        cop_arybase     0
        cop_line        1
```

The information provided here is probably only of real use to someone who is investigating the internal opcodes of a script. I've used this before to follow the information in a secure script when the **taint** option started doing what I thought was wrong. As it turned out, I'd merely forgotten one of the rules of the **taint** system, but the process was good background information!

Xref Backend

The **Xref** backend produces a report that details the use of all the variables, subroutines, and formats in a program. The information includes cross-references (including line numbers) for where the information is used and which subroutine uses which variable, along with other valuable cross-referencing detail. This provides information for a Perl script similar to that provided by the **cxref** program that does the same operation on C source code.

The level of detail includes not only the subroutines and variables from the original file but also all of the modules and files the original script relies upon. This means that even a relatively short script can produce a huge amount of information. The format of the report is as follows:

```
File filename1
      Subroutine subname1
        Package package1
          object1         line numbers
          object2         line numbers
          ...
        Package package2
        ...
```

Here's an example from a five-line script that prints the contents of a DBM file:

```
File /users/mc/etc/mcslp/books/perlaa/ch04/dbmdump.pl
  Subroutine (definitions)
    Package UNIVERSAL
      &VERSION          s0
      &can              s0
      &isa              s0
  Subroutine (main)
    Package main
      $!                11
      $0                3, 11
      $datafile         7
      $df               i5, 11, 11
      $key              15, 15
      %db               11, 13, 15, 17
      &O_RDONLY         &11
      *key              13
      @ARGV             3
```

The output has been trimmed for brevity; the full report runs to 246 lines.

The information can prove invaluable if you are trying to optimize the original source or find out which functions rely on certain variables. Normally this information should be obtainable through the use of the internal debugger, or by using one of the debugging methods outlined in Chapter 18. There are instances, however, when a cross-reference report is quicker, and it provides ancillary information that can help trace other bugs.

The function supports only two options, **-r** and **-D**. The **–r** option produces raw output. Rather than the formatted version shown above, a single line is printed for each definition or use of a function, package, or variable. Here's a fragment from the same script used to produce the above report:

```
dbmdump.pl (main)          3 main          @ ARGV        used
dbmdump.pl (main)          3 main          $ 0           used
dbmdump.pl (main)          5 main          $ df          intro
dbmdump.pl (main)          7 main          $ datafile    used
dbmdump.pl (main)         11 main          % db          used
dbmdump.pl (main)         11 main          $ df          used
dbmdump.pl (main)         11 main          & O_RDONLY    subused
dbmdump.pl (main)         11 main          $ 0           used
dbmdump.pl (main)         11 main          $ df          used
dbmdump.pl (main)         11 main          $ !           used
dbmdump.pl (main)         13 main          % db          used
dbmdump.pl (main)         13 main          * key         used
dbmdump.pl (main)         15 main          $ key         used
dbmdump.pl (main)         15 main          % db          used
dbmdump.pl (main)         15 main          $ key         used
dbmdump.pl (main)         17 main          % db          used
```

I've stripped the full pathname from the above example and, once again, trimmed it for size. Otherwise, this is identical to the output produced. The columns are, in order, file, full package name (includes references to functions included via **AutoLoad**), line number, short package name, object type, object name, and how it was used in the specified line. Once the information is produced, it is quite voluminous. Using a suitable Perl script, it should be possible to summarize the information in a more human-readable form, perhaps by selectively excluding those modules you are not interested in. I'll leave that particular exercise to the reader.

The **–D** option supports two sub-debugging flags, both of which are best used in combination with the **–r** option. Using **-Dt**, the object on top of the object stack is printed as it is tracked, allowing you to trace the object as it is being resolved in each of the packages. The **–DO** function prints each operator as it is processed during the cross-referencing process.

Remember that much of the information that can be gleaned from the data supplied is also available via more traditional debugging methods. By the same token, a similar proportion of the information is also only available via this backend.

Lint Backend

Under many C environments there is a program called **lint**, which checks C source code for any parsing errors, including those that may not normally have been picked up by the C compiler. The **Lint** backend is a similar module for Perl. It can pick up many errors that may not be identified by the Perl interpreter even with warnings switched on.

You can see from the options shown in Table 19-6 the errors that **Lint** attempts to identify.

Note that the use of this module is not intended as a replacement for either the **–w** command line option or the **use strict** pragma. It augments the options available for finding possible performance and/or parser problems.

Option	Description
context	Warns when an array is used in an implied scalar context such as **$foo = @bar.** Ordinarily the Perl interpreter ignores this and just sets the value of **$foo** to the scalar value of **@bar** (the number of elements in the array). You can prevent the error from being reported by explicitly using the **scalar** function.
implicit-read	Warns whenever a statement implicitly reads from one of Perl's special variables, such as **$_.**
implicit-write	Warns whenever a statement implicitly writes to a special variable.
dollar-underscore	Warns when the **$_** variable is used, either explicitly or implicitly, as part of a **print** statement.
private-names	Warns when a variable, subroutine, or method is used when the name is not within the current package, and when the name begins with an underscore.
undefined-subs	Warns when an undefined subroutine is called.
regexp-variables	Warns when one of the special regular expression variables, **$', $&,** or **$',** is used.
All	Turns on all warnings.
None	Turns off all warnings.

Table 19-6. *Options for the **Lint** Backend*

Deparse Backend

The **Deparse** backend produces a version of the supplied Perl script that represents the optimized version. That is, it regurgitates a textual representation of the original Perl script after the normal parsing and optimization process has taken place. See Chapter 16 for more information on the types of optimization that take place during the normal compilation of a script.

The specific options for the **Deparse** backend are shown in Table 19-7.

Option	Description
-p	Prints additional parentheses that would otherwise have been optimized away. Many parentheses can be ignored (or are implied) in the source code. For example, parentheses are not necessarily required around function arguments. This option ensures that all locations where parentheses are implied are actually printed. This can be useful when you want to discover how Perl has interpreted your implied parentheses in a statement. See the following examples for more information. Perl will reduce away any constant values, which will appear as **???** in the resulting output.
-uPACKAGE	Includes subroutines from **PACKAGE** that are not called directly (that is, by **AutoLoad,** and those that are not resolved to subroutines during run time). Normally these are ignored in the parsed output.
-l	Adds **#line** declarations to the output, based on the source code line and file locations.

-sC	**"Cuddle" elsif, else,** and **continue** blocks, for example,
	if () {
	}
	else {
	}
	will be printed as
	if () {
	} else {
	}

Table 19-7. *Options for the* ***Deparse*** *Backend*

The parentheses option is useful for demystifying the operator precedence that Perl uses. For example, here's a **Deparse**d calculation:

```
$ perl -MO=Deparse,-p -e '$a + $b * $c / $d % $e;'
-e syntax OK
($a + ((($b * $c) / $d) % $e));
```

See Chapter 2 for the list of operators and their precedence.

One school of thought says that all scripts could be processed and regurgitated by this process in order to produce "pretty" formatted Perl code. Unfortunately, because any constants will have been optimized away, this is not possible. But it's a nice thought.

Showlex Backend

The **Showlex** backend shows the lexical variables (those defined by **my** rather than **local**) used by a subroutine or file. Any options to the backend are assumed to be the names of the subroutines whose list of lexical variables you want to summarize.

For example, to summarize the lexical variables in the subroutine **bar**, which is part of the **foo.pl** script:

```
$ perl -MO=Showlex,bar foo.pl
```

Using the Compiler with XSUBS

Perl extensions that use XSUBS may not work. This is because an XSUB is loaded by the interpreter using the library file. The Perl compiler does introduce the necessary hooks into the source code to allow the XSUBS to be used, but you will need to manually incorporate them, or provide access to the libraries which the XSUB definitions provide.

Differences Between Interpreted and Compiled Code

Because of the methods used to produce an executable version of a Perl script, there are minor differences between interpreted and compiled code. For the most part, the bugs are related to the behavior of the compilation process, and in time they should be able to be modified such that the compiled and interpreted versions of the same script work identically. Unfortunately, other bugs are directly related to the way the compiler operates, and it's unlikely that these will be able to be changed.

The currently known list of differences are as follows:

- Compiled Perl scripts calculate the target of **next**, **last**, and **redo** loop control statements at compile time. Normally these values are determined at run time by the interpreter.

- The decision of Perl to interpret the .. operator as a range or flip-flop operator is normally decided at run time, based on the current context. In a compiled program the decision is made at compile time, which may produce unexpected results.
- Compiled Perl scripts use native C arithmetic instead of the normal opcode-based arithmetic used in interpreted scripts. This shouldn't cause too many problems (in fact, it makes things quicker), but it may affect calculations on large numbers, especially those at the boundaries of the number ranges.
- Many of the deprecated features of Perl are not implemented in the compiler. Check the Perl distribution for deprecated features, or use the short list in Chapter 16.

Speed Comparison

Many factors affect the speed of execution of a typical program. The platform on which you are running obviously has an effect, including the memory, hard disk, and other application requirements at the time the program is run. When considering a Perl script, there are additional overheads to the execution process.

With a C program, the time to execute a program can be split into three elements:

- The time to load the program, including any dynamic loading of libraries.
- The execution of any user-defined components.
- The execution of any system functions. These include any access to the operating system proper, such as files, network sockets, and any access to the memory system. Depending on the implementation, you can also add the library loading time to this figure.

With a Perl script that is interpreted, the list is longer, and as such the equivalent process should take longer, even for a very simple statement:

- The time to load the Perl interpreter.
- The time for Perl to load the Perl script.
- The time taken for the Perl interpreter to parse the script and translate it into the opcode tree.
- The execution of the Perl opcode tree.
- The execution of any system functions.

It should be obvious that Perl should, in theory, be a lot slower than a compiled version of the same program written in C. When a Perl script is compiled into a binary executable, two of the above elements can be removed. The script is already in the format of a binary executable; all you need to do is load the binary and execute it. This is where the speed advantage becomes apparent.

When comparing times, you need to compare the following operations:

- Time taken to compile the C program.
- Time taken to execute the C program.
- Time taken to execute the interpreted Perl script.
- Time taken to compile the Perl script into a binary.
- Time taken to execute the Perl binary.

It's also worth considering the overall time taken to

- Compile the C program and then execute it 100 times.
- Execute the Perl script 100 times with the interpreter.
- Compile the Perl script into a binary and then execute it 100 times.

These figures will show the difference in total execution time between the C program, interpreted Perl, and compiled Perl. Remember that when a Perl script is interpreted, it must be compiled before it is executed, which takes a finite amount of time.

Usually the reason for using a compiled binary is to increase the speed of execution. By checking the combined times for running the script 100 times, you should get a rough idea of how much of a speed increase you can expect. Obviously, it's likely that the script will be run significantly more than 100 times, but the same calculation can be applied to any number of executions.

Tests

We'll be comparing three basic programs. The first performs a repetitive calculation on an ascending number for a specific number of iterations. This tests the relative speed of calculations and loops, something we already know is slower in Perl than in a compiled C program. Below is the C version used in the tests:

```
#include <math.h>

int main()
{
  int i;

  for(i=0;i<10000;i++)
    {
      sqrt(abs(sin(i)+cos(i)));
    }
}
```

The code below shows the Perl version. Note that it's much slower; it shows the brevity with which programs can be written in Perl. You don't have to worry about any of the initialization that the C equivalent requires. Also notice that otherwise the two versions are very similar.

```
for(my $i=0;$i<10000;$i++)
{
    sqrt(abs(sin($i)+cos($i)));
}
```

The next test is a simple text-processing test. We'll count the number of lines in a document. The document in question is actually a list of all the words in a public domain dictionary that begin with "a," for reasons that will become apparent in the next script. This tests basic I/O in the two languages. Essentially, the performance of the two should be largely identical, since Perl will optimize the process down to an almost identical structure.

```
#include <stdio.h>

int main()
{
  char *line;
  FILE *data;
  long count=0;

  data = fopen("wordlist","rw");

  while(!feof(data))
    {
      fgets(line,255,data);
      count++;
    }
  printf("%d lines\n",count);
}
```

The Perl version of Test 2 can be seen below. Once again, note that the overall structure is largely identical, although Perl's **<FH>** operator makes reading in the information much easier.

```
open(DATA,"<wordlist")

while(<DATA>)
```

```
{
    $lines++;
}
close(DATA);

print "$lines lines\n";
```

The final test is an advanced version of Test 2. We'll read in the words from the file and then calculate the number of unique lines. Within C we'll use a simple keyword table stored in the **words** array. This will hold the list of words we have already recorded. To identify whether the word has already been seen, we just compare the new word against every entry in the array. This is slow, and inefficient, but the shortest (in lines) of the methods available. We could have used a binary tree or even a hashing system, but it would have added significantly more lines to an already long C program.

```
#include <stdio.h>

char words[32000][260];
long wordidx=0;

void addtolist(char word[255])
{
  int i=0;
  for(i=0;i<wordidx;i++)
    {
      if (strcmp(word,words[i]) == 0)
          return;
    }
  strcpy(words[++wordidx],word);
}

int main()
{
  char line[255];
  FILE *data;
  long count=0;

  data = fopen("wordlist","rw");

  while(!feof(data))
    {
```

```
        fgets(line,255,data);
        addtolist(line);
    }
  printf("%ld unique lines\n",wordidx);
}
```

The Perl script for Test 3 is significantly shorter, but only because we can directly use hashes, instead of having to use a separate function and loop to search an array.

```
open(DATA,"<wordlist") || die "Can't open file";

my %words;

while(<DATA>)
{
    $words{$_} = 1;
}
close(DATA);

print scalar keys %words," unique lines\n";
```

Summary Results

Each test was run three times, and the **times** command that is standard with the **bash** shell was used to test the execution of each item. This calculates the elapsed time and the user and system time for each command. The times shown are the elapsed amount of time for the program to load, execute, and quit.

The tests show a significant difference between execution times both between the C and Perl programs, and also between the interpreted and compiled versions of the Perl scripts. The times are shown in Table 19-8.

The figures show two things: first, the difference in execution time between a C program and a Perl script. Second, they show the performance gain between executing a Perl script in its interpreted form and then its compiled form. For additional cross-reference, the table also shows the time taken to perform 100 C, interpreted Perl, and compiled Perl executions.

Irrespective of the values, it should be noted that these are fairly immature benchmark tests, although they do show many of the advantages of compiling a Perl script into an executable. It's also worth remembering why the time taken to compile the Perl script into a binary is very high. Creating a Perl binary involves not only the compilation of the script into its native Perl format, but also a significant amount of translation to make that into a C source that can be compiled. It also needs to be linked to the Perl library that supplies all of the core Perl functions and the Perl interpreter.

Operation	Test 1	Test 2	Test 3
Compile C to binary	8.41	6.74	6.75
Execute C program	0.81	0.62	10.97
Compile C program once, execute 100 times	89.41	68.74	1103.75
Execute interpreted Perl script	2.48	1.04	1.97
Compile Perl script to binary	51.96	51.09	51.27
Execute Perl script binary	1.95	1.09	1.32
Execute interpreted Perl script 100 times	248.33	104.00	197.00
Compile Perl program once, execute 100 times	246.63	160.09	182.94

Table 19-8. *Summary Times for Comparison Tests*

The most obvious difference is the drop in speed from a raw C program to a Perl version. In the case of the interpreted version of the script, some of this can be attributed to the time taken to compile the script into opcodes, optimize it, and then execute the opcode tree. However, the difference in times is so great on the first test that it's obvious the problems are with the mathematical calculations in Perl, combined with the large loops.

The compiled version of the Perl script does at least narrow the gap. It is likely that a good deal of the overhead here is related to loading a binary that is about 686K, compared to the 23K for the C version. The Perl binary is large because we used a static, rather than a dynamic, Perl library. With a dynamic Perl library, the size is much smaller—about 11K—but many of the functions from the dynamic library will also need to be loaded.

For the second test, both the Perl and C versions are incredibly quick; the program is very simple, and probable differences between the core of both programs is likely to be very small. The biggest difference is of course in the last test, where the Perl version is significantly quicker than the C equivalent. The main difference is because we've cheated and used a hash to do the deduping operation. Within the C source we had to use a different method to achieve the same result. The C version is also much longer, source-lines-wise, and the algorithm used here is not ideal. Had I coded a binary tree or even a hash system in the C program, there might have been a smaller difference in the speed tests between the two. However, to add a C-based hashing system or binary tree system would have increased the length of the C program considerably.

The cross-reference figures between executing the interpreted Perl script 100 times and the compiled and then interpreted version are much more telling. You can see very clearly that executing the compiled Perl script is much faster than the interpreted version. This is significant if you are expecting to install a script in a live environment where it may be called a large number of times, for example, on a website.

The other benefit of a compiled executable is that you can continue to develop and test with the interpreted version while using a final compiled production version in the live environment. You can be guaranteed that the interpreted and compiled versions will work identically, and they will both retain the same compatibility. They can even use the same configuration and data files without requiring any modifications.

This is a much more efficient development environment than using C or some other language that requires separate compilation each time you want to test a feature or bug fix. As you saw in the last chapter when debugging a Perl program, you only need to change the source and run the interpreter again. With a C program it needs to be recompiled and relinked between each test of a bug fix.

As a further comparison, let's imagine the program in Test 2 is riddled with 100 bugs, and we recompile the program between each fix. Ignoring the time to edit the source, the C version would take 736 seconds for each compilation and execution. The Perl version would take 155.09 seconds, including a final compilation to an executable binary. That's an efficiency gain of 475 percent!

Chapter 20

Perl Makefiles

In Chapter 17, part of the process surrounding the development of extensions involved, in its easy form, the use of a Perl Makefile to produce, compile, and install the C library and associated extension. The Perl Makefile is, like many other parts of the Perl environment, just a Perl script. It uses a module that is part of the standard Perl distribution to create a Makefile that can be used with the **make** command.

The production of a customized Makefile is the last stage in the process of developing a customized extension. The **ExtUtils::MakeMaker** module uses the information gleaned during the installation and configuration process of the original Perl binary in order to provide the necessary information for the Makefile. As has also been stated before, the process of writing a Perl Makefile is made significantly easier through the use of the **h2xs** command, which will create a blank Makefile for you.

However, it is likely that you will want to modify the contents of the Makefile that has been produced. The module splits the task of the Makefile generation into several subroutines, and the overall configuration that is used with these subroutines is infinitely configurable. In each case, the subroutines provided by the module return the text that is required to be written to the Makefile.

The whole system is object oriented, and the production of individual files within the **MakeMaker** system is possible at all levels. Each file created is treated as a single object, and therefore a single **MakeMaker** configuration can generate a number of Makefiles both for the original target and for subdirectories and their targets.

The information in this chapter will be useful to you not only if you are creating your own Makefiles for the modules you are distributing, but also if you are installing modules on your system and want to customize the operation. In order to understand the process, you first need to appreciate the steps involved in compiling and installing an extension. Then you need to identify the process involved in creating the file that is used by **MakeMaker** and how to customize it to your own ends.

Extension Building and Installation Overview

Most of this process will be familiar; we've seen a lot of it already in Chapter 17. However, the build and installation process is slightly more complex than the examples we have already seen. You should already be aware that the extension uses the AutoLoader module to decide which function should be included. The AutoLoader module is actually capable of a number of different operations. Depending on the context and requirements, it can do one of the following:

- Perform the function itself; the caller will never know that the AutoLoader has been used.
- Create the function on the fly using an **eval** statement.
- Use the **system** function to launch an external program of the same name.
- Dynamically load a library using the **DynaLoader** module.

It is the last option that is used to load an external C library extension. The **AutoSplit** module is used to separate the original Perl module file into separate files, one per function, and a mapping within the split file then tells **DynaLoader** which library to load in order to implement the function. This loading mechanism requires a bootstrap file and an autoload file, which are both used to select the correct library location for the function, based on the library that was built and the split module. The whole system uses a specialized structure within the Perl module directory that accounts for both site and architecture differences.

The entire process for the **Makefile** produced by **MakeMaker** (under Solaris) is shown below. Entries taken from the **StatVFS** module we saw in Chapter 17 are used for reference:

1. Create a directory structure within the extensions directory that will hold the files produced during the build process before they are installed:

```
mkdir blib
mkdir blib/lib
mkdir blib/arch
mkdir blib/arch/auto
mkdir blib/arch/auto/StatVFS
mkdir blib/lib/auto
mkdir blib/lib/auto/StatVFS
mkdir blib/man3
cp StatVFS.pm blib/lib/StatVFS.pm
```

2. The module is split into individual functions. Each function is placed into the auto/StatVFS directory:

```
AutoSplitting blib/lib/StatVFS.pm (blib/lib/auto/StatVFS)
```

3. The XS file is parsed by **xsubpp**, producing the C file that contains the necessary functions:

```
/usr/bin/perl -I/usr/local/lib/perl5/5.00553/sun4-solaris
              -I/usr/local/lib/perl5/5.00553
              /usr/local/lib/perl5/5.00553/ExtUtils/xsubpp

              -typemap
              /usr/local/lib/perl5/5.00553/ExtUtils/typemap
              StatVFS.xs >xstmp.c && mv xstmp.c StatVFS.c
```

4. The source code is compiled into object format:

```
gcc -B/usr/ccs/bin/ -c  -I/usr/local/include
                    -DDEBUGGING -O -DVERSION=\"0.01\"
```

```
-DXS_VERSION=\"0.01\" -fPIC
-I/usr/local/lib/perl5/5.00553/sun4-solaris/CORE
StatVFS.c
```

5. The bootstrap code required for **DynaLoader** is produced. The StatVFS.bs file contains the necessary information to enable **DynaLoader** to relate the Perl call to the C function:

```
Running Mkbootstrap for StatVFS ()
chmod 644 StatVFS.bs
```

6. The library file is generated in its dynamic format:

```
LD_RUN_PATH="" gcc -B/usr/ccs/bin/ -o blib/arch/auto/StatVFS/StatVFS.so
                                   -G -L/usr/local/lib StatVFS.o
```

7. The library and the bootstrap code are copied into the correct location ready for installation, and the file modes are set to their correct values:

```
chmod 755 blib/arch/auto/StatVFS/StatVFS.so
cp StatVFS.bs blib/arch/auto/StatVFS/StatVFS.bs
chmod 644 blib/arch/auto/StatVFS/StatVFS.bs
```

8. The POD format documentation in the Perl module is extracted and converted into a man page, ready for installation:

```
Manifying blib/man3/StatVFS.3
```

The main process is now finished. The installation process just copies the structure below the blib directory into the site- or architecture-specific directories within the Perl library directory. At this point, if you want to test the module, you can use the **make test** command. The test files will need to include the just-built version of the library. See the **use blib** pragma in Chapter 16 for more information on this.

The actual installation process has its tricks too. The sample below is a continuation of the StatVFS module example.

1. Copy the files to the specified installation directory. This is defined as a whole by the **PREFIX** option and individually with the **INSTALL*** options.

```
Installing /usr/local/lib/perl5/site_perl/5.00553/sun4-
solaris/auto/StatVFS/StatVFS.so
Installing /usr/local/lib/perl5/site_perl/5.00553/sun4-
solaris/auto/StatVFS/StatVFS.bs
Files found in blib/arch --> Installing files in blib/lib into
architecture dependent library tree!
Installing /usr/local/lib/perl5/site_perl/5.00553/sun4-
solaris/auto/StatVFS/autosplit.ix
```

```
Installing /usr/local/lib/perl5/site_perl/5.00553/sun4-solaris/StatVFS.pm
Installing /usr/local/lib/perl5/5.00553/man/man3/StatVFS.3
```

2. A list of the files installed during the installation process is written in a special file, called .packlist in the module's AutoLoader directory. The actual location will depend on whether you have installed an architecture or site version. See the **INSTALLDIRS** option later in the chapter.

```
Writing /usr/local/lib/perl5/site_perl/5.00553/sun4-
solaris/auto/StatVFS/.packlist
```

3. The installation information, including the configuration details, is written to a general file that can later be consulted (preferably via a POD file viewer) to study which packages and extensions have been installed and when. This can also be a helpful starting point for tracing problems when a script or module suddenly stops working.

```
Appending installation info to /usr/local/lib/perl5/5.00553/sun4-
solaris/perllocal.pod
```

The rest of this chapter is devoted to describing the configurable parameters to the **MakeMaker** module. We'll also use the opportunity to look at some of the other modules that are used by the **MakeMaker** module to do its work.

MakeMaker Overview

The basic use of the MakeMaker module is very simple. The synopsis for the module is

```
use ExtUtils::MakeMaker;
WriteMakefile( ATTRIBUTE => VALUE [, ...] );
```

The basic method of operation is to create a simple file that imports the module and then calls the **WriteMakefile** function. You need to specify at least one attribute to the function, which is the name of the module. For example, to create the Makefile for building the **StatVFS** module we created in Chapter 17, you could get away with as little as the following in Makefile.PL:

```
use ExtUtils::MakeMaker;
WriteMakefile('NAME' -> 'StatVFS');
```

When run through a Perl interpreter, like this,

```
$ perl Makefile.PL
```

it automatically produces a Makefile capable of building and installing the extension. It accounts for the location of all the necessary libraries and include files, and it selects the correct C compiler and definitions in order to ensure that the extension is compiled properly. This information is selected from the information produced at build time and is specific to the platform on which you use the MakeMaker file. Thus the Perl Makefile is completely platform independent. Any platform on which you can build Perl should be able to produce a suitable Makefile for the platform for building an extension. The resulting Makefile produced is of course platform and build specific, even though the original Makefile.PL file is completely platform independent. It's the **MakeMaker** module that provides the platform independent information required to build the module.

The resulting Makefile is big—751 lines long. It is too long, and completely pointless, to reproduce here. The point about MakeMaker is that it hides all the complexity of the Makefile production from the user and just ensures that the file produced should work on whatever platform Perl is installed on.

MakeMaker Configurable Options

The bulk of the information that is produced by MakeMaker is gleaned from the configuration and environment of the machine on which the Makefile is extracted. MakeMaker uses a number of additional modules, including Config, which contains all of the information gained at the configuration of the Perl version.

All of the options can be modified to specify alternative install locations, installation procedures, and even the architecture and version of Perl that you want to install. The usual method is to specify the alternative values within Makefile.PL as part of the hash argument passed to **WriteMakefile**, for example:

```
use ExtUtils::MakeMaker;
WriteMakefile('NAME'    -> 'StatVFS',
              'PREFIX'  -> '/usr/lib',
              'VERSION' -> '1.01');
```

Alternatively, they can be specified as **NAME=VALUE** pairs on the command line, for example:

```
$ perl Makefile.PL PREFIX=/usr/lib
```

C This should be a reference to an array of C source file names. The information is not currently used by MakeMaker, but it can be a handy reference if you want to use some of the extensions available within the **MakeMaker** and other modules. See the section "Related Modules" at the end of this chapter.

CCFLAGS The string that will be passed to the compiler between the **INC** and **OPTIMIZE** options on the command line. You may want to include debugging options or special format handling (such as **–traditional** to **gcc**).

CONFIG An array reference to a list of configuration elements to be incorporated from the configuration information built at Perl's compile time. The following values are added to Config by MakeMaker: **ar**, **cc**, **cccdlflags**, **ccdlflags**, **dlext**, **dlsrc**, **ld**, **lddlflags**, **ldflags**, **libc**, **lib_ext**, **obj_ext**, **ranlib**, **sitelibexp**, **sitearchexp**, **so**.

CONFIGURE Should contain a reference to a section of code (anonymous or named function), which in turn should return a reference to a hash. The hash can contain the list of configurable elements for the MakeMaker module.

DEFINE A string containing the definitions required to compile the extension. For example, you may need to specify **–DHAVE_STRING_H**.

DIR A reference to an array containing a list of subdirectories that have their own Makefile.PL. The list will be used to determine the list of subdirectories and extensions that need to be included when each Makefile is written and also when the main Makefile is parsed by the **make** command.

DISTNAME The distribution name of the package that will be created when the directory is packaged by **tar** or **zip**. Defaults to the value of **NAME**.

DL_FUNCS A hash reference to a list of symbol names for functions that should be made available as universal symbols at compile time. This is currently only used under AIX and VMS.

DL_VARS An array reference to a list of symbol names for variables that should be made available as universal symbols at compile time. This is currently only used under AIX and VMS.

EXCLUDE_EXT An array reference to a list of extension names to be excluded when creating a new static Perl binary.

EXE_FILES An array reference to a list of executable files that will be installed into the **INST_SCRIPT** directory.

NO_VC If specified, then the normal check between the version of the Makefile that was created and the version of MakeMaker does not happen. Best used interactively, rather than as a hard option in the Makefile.PL.

FIRST_MAKEFILE A string defining the name of the Makefile to be produced for the **MAP_TARGET**. Defaults to the value of the **MAKEFILE** option.

FULLPERL A string defining the name of the Perl binary able to run this extension.

H A reference to an array of the header files within the extension distribution.

IMPORTS Valid only on the OS/2 version of Perl.

INC A string listing the names of the directories to be searched for header files during extension compilation, for example, **-I/usr/local/include**.

INCLUDE_EXT A reference to an array of extension names to be included in the Perl binary when creating a new statically linked Perl. Normally, **MakeMaker** automatically includes the list of currently installed extensions. This allows both the new extension and all the extensions already installed to be incorporated into the new static Perl binary. However, if you specify a list of specific options in **INCLUDE_EXT**, then only the extensions listed will be included in the final binary.

The DynaLoader extension (if supported) will always be included in the binary. If you specify an empty array, only the current extension (and DynaLoader) will be included.

INSTALLARCHLIB A string defining the name of the directory in which to install the files contained in **INST_ARCHLIB** if the value of **INSTALLDIRS** is **perl**.

INSTALLBIN A string defining the directory in which executable binaries should be installed.

INSTALLDIRS A string specifying which of the two directory sets in which to install the extension. The options are **perl**, which specifies that the extension should be installed into the architecture-specific **INSTALLPRIVLIB** and **INSTALLARCHLIB** directories, and **site**, which installs the extensions into the site-specific **INSTALLSITELIB** and **INSTALLSITEARCH** directories.

INSTALLMAN1DIR A string specifying the directory to be used for the section one (commands) man pages during installation. The value defaults to the value contained in **$Config{installman1dir}**.

INSTALLMAN3DIR A string specifying the directory to be used for the section three (functions/extensions) man pages during installation. The value defaults to the value contained in **$Config{installman3dir}**.

INSTALLPRIVLIB A string specifying the directory in which to install the built libraries. See **INSTALLDIRS**.

INSTALLSCRIPT A string specifying the directory in which to install any scripts. The contents of the directory specified by **INST_SCRIPT** is copied to this directory during installation.

INSTALLSITELIB A string specifying the directory in which to install the built libraries. See **INSTALLDIRS**.

INSTALLSITEARCH A string specifying the directory in which to install the contents of **INST_ARCH** during installation. See **INSTALLDIRS**.

INST_ARCHLIB A string specifying the local directory to be used for storing architecture-dependent libraries during build and before installation.

INST_BIN A string specifying the local directory to be used for storing binaries during build and before installation.

INST_EXE Deprecated; use the **INST_SCRIPT** option instead.

INST_LIB A string specifying the local directory to be used for storing libraries during build and before installation.

INST_MAN1DIR A string specifying the local directory to be used for storing section one man pages during build and before installation.

INST_MAN3DIR A string specifying the local directory to be used for storing section three man pages during build and before installation.

INST_SCRIPT A string specifying the local directory to be used for storing binaries and other executables during build and before installation. Defaults to blib/bin.

LDFROM A string specifying the list of files to be used to build the final library. Defaults to the value of **$OBJECTS**.

LIBPERL_A A string defining the name of the Perl library to be used with the extension. Defaults to libperl.a.

LIB A string specifying the directory into which the libraries will be installed. Has the effect of setting the values of **INSTALLPRIVLIB** and **INSTALLSITELIB**.

LIBS A reference to an anonymous array specifying the list of library specifications to be searched for, in order, until a suitable library is found. Each element should contain the full list of libraries to be searched. This can be used in situations where the functions required may be in any number of files. For example, DBM interfaces can exist in compatible forms in GDBM, NDBM, ODBM, and SDBM libraries. Other examples include compatibility libraries (such as BSD on an SVR4 platform) and extension libraries such as Tk and Tcl.

Note that because each element specifies the whole list, you will need to specify the same library a number of times if you are looking for other compatibility, for example:

```
'LIBS' => ["-ltk -lgdbm", "-ltk -lndbm", "-ltk -lodbm"]
```

If you only want to supply one list of libraries, you can supply a scalar, and **MakeMaker** will turn it into an array with only one element. Note that the specifications can also include a library path, as in **-L/usr/local/lib** in addition to the library list.

LINKTYPE A scalar specifying the type of linking to be used when creating the extension. This is usually **dynamic** unless your operating system does not support it. For a static build, use **static**.

MAKEAPERL A scalar; a value of 1 indicates that **MakeMaker** should incorporate the rules to make a new Perl binary.

MAKEFILE A scalar specifying the name of the Makefile to be produced.

MAN1PODS A reference to a hash of files containing documentation I POD format to be converted to man pages during installation. Defaults to **EXE_FILES**.

MAN3PODS A reference to a hash of files containing documentation in POD format to be converted to man pages during installation. Defaults to **EXE_FILES**.

MAP_TARGET A string containing the name of the new Perl binary to be produced if **static** linking is requested. Defaults to "perl".

MYEXTLIB A string containing the name of a custom library file built by the extension that should be included when linking the extension.

NAME A string specifying the name of the extension. If left unspecified, it will default to the name of the directory containing Makefile.PL.

NEEDS_LINKING If set, it indicates to **MakeMaker** that there is linkable code in one of the subdirectories. If not specified, **MakeMaker** will try to work it out and set this value as necessary.

NOECHO A string specifying the prefix to be placed in front of commands in the produced Makefile. By default it is set to @, which hides all the commands as they are executed. You can set this to an empty string to force the **make** process to output all of its commands, which can be useful for debugging.

NORECURS If set, **MakeMaker** will not recurse into subdirectories to create additional Makefiles. The default behavior is for **MakeMaker** both to create the Makefiles and ensure that the parent Makefile is capable of recursing into subdirectories to build additional targets.

OBJECT A string defining the list of object files to be created into a single library. Defaults to the single file specified by **$(BASEEXT)$(OBJ_EXT)**.

OPTIMIZE A string containing the flag to be passed to the compiler to make it optimize the code during compilation. Defaults to **-O**. Other options you may want to try are **-g**, to switch on debugging, and **-g -O**, to switch on debugging and optimization for the compilers that support it (GNU C does).

PERL A string containing the location of a Perl binary capable of doing the tasks normally executed by the **miniperl** binary created during a Perl build.

PERLMAINCC A string defining the program to use for compiling the perlmain.c file. The default is to use the value of **$(CC)**.

PERL_ARCHLIB A string defining the libraries to be used for building the Perl binary.

PERL_LIB A string specifying the directory containing the Perl library.

PERL_SRC A string specifying the location of the Perl source code. Normally unnecessary since the Perl source code is not required to build extensions or a new Perl binary.

PERM_RW A string defining the octal mode to be used for files that should be available for reading and writing. Defaults to **0644**, or read write for the owner and read-only for everybody else.

PERM_RWX A string defining the octal mode to be used for files that should be executable. Defaults to **0755**, or read, write and execute for the owner and read and execute for everybody else.

PL_FILES A reference to a hash that specifies the list of files to be processed as Perl scripts rather than native commands. The default is to use any files in the directory structure for the extension that end in .PL. The keys should be the full file name, and the corresponding value should be the base name of the file. This can be used to create custom installation routines.

PM A reference to a hash specifying the list of .pm and .pl files to be installed. The key should be the name of the file, and the corresponding value should equal the final installation location. By default this will be all the matching files found in **PMLIBDIRS**.

PMLIBDIRS A reference to an array of subdirectories containing library files to be installed. Defaults to **['lib', $(BASEEXT)]**. The entire contents of the directories is installed into the corresponding location according to their file type. The **libscan** method can be used to alter this behavior. See the section "Customizing Commands" for more details.

PREFIX A string defining the default prefix to be used in front of installation directories. The default is to use the value determined at configuration time.

PREREQ_PM A reference to a hash defining the list of modules that need to be available to run this extension. The key for the hash is the module/extension name, and the corresponding value is the minimum version number. If the value of the version number is zero, then **MakeMaker** only checks that the module or extension has been installed.

SKIP A reference to an array listing the parts of the Makefile that should be skipped during production. Should be avoided in nearly all cases.

TYPEMAPS A reference to an array of alternative typemap files to be used with **xsubpp**. This should only be used when you want to use a typemap file that is either not in the current directory or isn't called typemap. A typemap file in the current directory has the highest precedence, followed by the last element of **$(TYPEMAPS)**. The system typemap has the lowest precedence.

VERSION A string containing the version for this distribution of the package. This is gleaned from an alternative file if **VERSION_FROM** is defined.

VERSION_FROM A string specifying the name of a file to be searched to define the version number of the package distribution. The regular expression **/([\$*])(([\w\:\']*)\bVERSION)\b.*\=/** is used to find the version number in the file. This allows for unqualified definitions in the file, for example:

```
$VERSION = '1.00';
```

The result is parsed with **eval** to get the final value, which means you can also use arrays, hashes, and even functions if referenced by **$VERSION** or something similar. Variables qualified with **my** or **local**, or those specified with their full package name, will not be found. If you are using the **strict** pragma, then use the **use subs** pragma to predeclare the **VERSION** variable before assigning it a value.

XS A reference to a hash of XS files to be processed into C files. The key to the hash should contain the XS file name, and the value should contain the corresponding C source file name.

XSOPT A string specifying the options to be passed to **xsubpp**. Use the **TYPEMAP** option if you want to specify typemap files and the **XSPROTOARG** option for including prototypes.

XSPROTOARG A string that defines whether prototypes should be included (see Chapter 17). If blank (default), assumes prototypes should be included; a value of **-noprototypes** specifies that prototypes should not be created.

XS_VERSION A string defining the version number for the XS file in the current package. Defaults to **VERSION**.

Creating a Dummy Makefile

Not all Makefile.PL files are intended to create a Makefile suitable for creating an extension module. In these cases you can get **MakeMaker** to create a dummy Makefile that just does nothing. It will succeed for all the specified targets, but otherwise achieve nothing. To do this, you use a different function in the **MakeMaker** module:

```
ExtUtils::MakeMaker::WriteEmptyMakefile();
```

In most instances this is really only useful for creating a dummy Makefile that will be used by some automated process such as the **CPAN** module. The **CPAN** module tries to determine which packages and modules are required, automatically downloading and installing them as necessary. However, if the functionality of the module is supported by some other method on the current platform, you need some way to "trick" CPAN into believing that the installation was a success.

Default Makefile Targets

The Makefile created by **MakeMaker** produces a set of standard targets to be used during the build process. The default target always triggers the build process up to, but not including, the installation process. Other default targets are shown in Table 20-1.

Other targets deserving special mention are covered in the following sections.

Target	Description
test	Runs the defined test script(s).
testdb	Runs the defined test script(s) within the Perl debugger.
install	Installs the extension, modules, and support files, including documentation. The values of the **INSTALL*** options are used to define the final locations for the specified files.

Table 20-1. *Default **make** Targets*

Creating a New Perl Binary

The default operation for the produced Makefile is to create a library suitable for dynamic loading. A library file ending with .so on a Unix system and .dll on a Windows system signifies a dynamic library. However, not all systems support dynamic loading, and in these and other situations you may wish to create your own statically linked Perl executable that includes the new extension. If this is the case, you can use a special target, **perl**, to the Makefile produced by the **MakeMaker** module. The operation is then slightly different from the normal build process:

- The extension(s) is recompiled into a static rather than a dynamic library.
- A new Makefile is created—Makefile.aperl, although the exact name is system dependent. This contains the definitions for building a new Perl binary.
- The new Makefile is used to produce the new binary, first by creating a new file with a modified **main()** function, and then by linking the resulting object file with the main Perl library and the extension library to produce the final binary.

The new Perl binary is created within the current directory and can be installed over the existing binary using

```
$ make -f Makefile.aperl inst_perl
```

The final binary actually includes all the extensions specified in the **INST_ARCHLIB**, **SITELIBEXP**, and **PERL_ARCHLIB** options defined within the main **MakeMaker** definition.

You can create a Perl binary with a different file name by defining the value of **MAP_TARGET** in the Perl Makefile. The best way to do this is on the command line, since that overrides any options defined in the Makefile itself, which may well specify the default. For example, to change the name to **vfsperl**:

```
$ perl Makefile.PL MAP_TARGET=vfsperl
$ make vfsperl
```

As a final alternative, you may want to build a static Perl on a dynamically capable system. In this instance, you use the **LINKTYPE** value to specify the destination type:

```
$ perl Makefile.PL LINKTYPE=static
```

Targets for Package Builders

The built Makefile provides for some standard targets primarily aimed at developers. The targets are designed to test and package the final distribution file. Note that the tests are aimed at verifying that all of the required files are in the current directory structure. This is achieved by checking the contents of the MANIFEST file, which contains a list of all the files required before the package can be distributed.

The packaging process uses the defined archiving and compression programs to produce a final distributable package file. This is normally a combination of **tar** and **gzip**, but you can modify this if the file is aimed at Windows (which uses **zip**) or Linux (which occasionally uses **bzip2**). The list of "package" targets is summarized in Table 20-2.

Target	Description
distcheck	Provides a list of files that appear in the current directory structure, but not in MANIFEST, and vice versa. See the section on ExtUtils::Manifest at the end of this chapter for more details.
skipcheck	Provides a list of files that are skipped due to the list provided in MANIFEST.SKIP. See the section on ExtUtils::Manifest at the end of this chapter for more details.
distclean	Executes the **realclean** target and then the **distcheck** target. The result should be a set of files suitable for building a new distribution file or for returning the current directory to its distributed (supplied) state.
manifest	Recreates the MANIFEST file using the list of files found in the current directory.

Table 20-2. *Extension Developers' Targets*

distdir	Creates a new directory in the parent called **$(DISTNAME)-$(VERSION)** and copies the files listed in MANIFEST to the new directory. This does all of the steps necessary to create a new version-specific directory for the extension.
disttest	Does a **distdir** first and then runs **perl Makefile.PL**, **make**, and **make test** in the new directory. This should perform all of the steps necessary to create and test a new version of an extension.
tardist	Does a **distdir**, then runs **$(PREOP)** followed by **$(TOUNIX)**. Then it runs **$(TAR)** on the new directory (using **$(TARFLAGS)**) before deleting the directory and running **$(POSTOP)**. This target is intended to create, package, and delete a new version directory for the extension as a **tar** file, suitable for use by Unix machines. You can modify **$(TAR)** and the other options according to taste. See the section "Customizing Commands."
dist	Defaults to **$(DIST_DEFAULT)**, which in turn defaults to **tardist**.
uutardist	Runs a **tardist** first and then uuencodes the **tar** file (using **uuencode**).
shdist	Does a **distdir**, then runs **$(PREOP)** followed by **$(TOUNIX)**. Then it runs **$(SHAR)** on the new directory before deleting the directory and running **$(POSTOP)**. This target is intended to create, package, and delete a new version directory for the extension as a **shar** file, suitable for ASCII transmission. You can modify **$(SHAR)** and the other options according to taste. See the section "Customizing Commands."
zipdist	Does a **distdir**, then runs **$(PREOP)**. Then it runs **$(ZIP)** on the new directory (using **$(ZIPFLAGS)**) before deleting the directory and running **$(POSTOP)**. This target is intended to create, package, and delete a new version directory for the extension as a **zip** file, suitable for use by Windows machines. You can modify **$(ZIP)** and the other options according to taste. See the section "Customizing Commands."
ci	Checks in a version of each file in MANIFEST (using the value of **$CI**) and updates the RCS label (using **$RCS_LABEL**).

Table 20-2. *Extension Developers' Targets* (continued)

Customizing Commands

The developer targets default to use a number of commands that are expected to be on the host machine. The options can be configured where the destination or source requires a different format. For example, Linux often uses the **bzip2** command for compression, rather than **gzip** or **compress**.

The options in Table 20-3 should be passed as a hash reference to the special **dist** option to the **WriteMakefile** function.

Option	Default	Description
CI	ci -u	Program for "checking in" a revision.
COMPRESS	gzip--best	Program for compression.
POSTOP	@ :	Commands to be run after archive creation.
PREOP	@ :	Commands to be run before archive creation.
RCS_LABEL	rcs -q -Nv$(VERSION_SYM):	Extract the RCS label for a file.
SHAR	shar	Program to use for creating a **shar** file.
SUFFIX	.gz	Default suffix for compressed files.
TAR	tar	Program to use for creating a **tar** format archive.
TARFLAGS	cvf	Command line options to use for creating the **tar** file.
TO_UNIX	System dependent	Program used to convert the files into Unix format.
ZIP	zip	Command to use for **zip** files.
ZIPFLAGS	-r	Command line options to use for creating a **zip** file.

Table 20-3. *Options for Extension Developers' Targets*

Related Modules

A number of different modules are used and can help in the process of creating a Makefile using **MakeMaker**. It's unlikely that you will need to delve into the bowels of any of these modules, even when creating quite complex extensions. The information provided is merely background detail.

Config

The Config module exports a hash, **%Config**, that lists all of the configurable options that were calculated when Perl was built, with the values containing the necessary information. The **MakeMaker** module uses this information to select the correct C compiler and installation directories, among many other things.

ExtUtils::Command

This function is used under Win32 implementations. It defines a list of alternative functions to be used by the building and installation process in place of the usual Unix command line utilities.

ExtUtils::Embed

This module provides the necessary command line options and other information for use when you are embedding a Perl interpreter into an application. See Chapter 17 for more information.

ExtUtils::Install

This module defines two functions, **install** and **uninstall**, which are used during the installation and un-installation process.

ExtUtils::Installed

This module defines a suite of functions that can be used to query the contents of the .packlist files generated during module installation. If you call the **new** function, it constructs the internal lists by examining the .packlist files. The **modules** function returns a list of all the modules currently installed. The **files** and **directories** both accept a single argument—the name of a module. The result is a list of all the files installed by the package. The **directory_tree** function reports information for all the related directories. In all cases you can specify **Perl** to get information pertaining to the core Perl installation.

The **validate** function checks that the files listed in .packlist actually exist. The **packlist** function returns an object as defined by ExtUtils::Packlist for the specified module. Finally, **version** returns the version number of the specified module.

ExtUtils::Liblist

This module defines the libraries to be used when building extension libraries and other Perl-based binaries. The information provided here broaches much of the complexity involved in getting an extension to work across many platforms; the bulk of the code relates to the information required for individual platforms.

ExtUtils::Manifest

This module provides the functions that produce, test, and update the MANIFEST file. Five of the functions are the most useful, beginning with **mkmanifest**, which creates a file, based on the current directory contents. The **maincheck** function verifies the current directory contents against the MANIFEST file, while **filecheck** looks for files in the current directory that are not specified in the MANIFEST. Both **maincheck** and **filecheck** are executed by the **fullcheck** function, and **skipcheck** lists the files in the MAINFEST.SKIP file.

ExtUtils::Miniperl

This module provides the list of base libraries and extensions that should be included when building the **miniperl** binary.

ExtUtils::Mkbootstrap

This module makes a bootstrap file suitable for the **DynaLoader** module.

ExtUtils::Mksymlists

This module produces the list of options for creating a dynamically linked library.

ExtUtils::MM_OS2

MakeMaker specifics for the OS/2 operating system are produced by this module.

ExtUtils::MM_Unix

MakeMaker specifics for the Unix platform are produced by this module. It also includes many of the core functions used by the main **MakeMaker** module irrespective of the host platform.

ExtUtils::MM_VMS

This module produces **MakeMaker** specifics for VMS.

ExtUtils::MM_Win32

This module produces **MakeMaker** specifics for Windows 95/98/NT.

ExtUtils::Packlist

This module supplies the **Packlist** object used by the **ExtUtils::Installed** module.

The Complete Reference

Part VII

Cross-Platform Perl

Chapter 21

Perl Under Unix

Perl has its roots in the Unix operating system. Many of the built-in functions, and the built-in functionality, has been inherited from the features of Unix. Unix is therefore the common denominator across all of the different platforms on which Perl runs. The information provided in this chapter should be used as a reference point for the level of support provided in other platforms. The following two chapters detail the differences between Windows and MacOS implementations of Perl against the core Unix derived functionality detailed in this chapter.

The information in each of the three chapters is the same: we'll first look at the process of downloading and installing the application on the specified platform before looking at the methods available for running scripts. The installation of external modules, perhaps from the CPAN archives, is then covered in detail before we also examine the main details of the specification for Perl under each platform.

Installing and Running the Perl Application

Installation is a little more complex on Unix because for most implementations you will be compiling the actual Perl source code. Once you have downloaded the latest version of the Perl package (see Appendix A), check the documentation for the specific instructions for installing Perl. As a quick guide, you can try the following:

1. Extract the source code from the archive using **tar** and **gunzip**, for example:

   ```
   $ $ gunzip -c perl5.tar.gz | tar xvf -
   ```

2. Change to the newly created directory.

   It's worth checking the README and INSTALL files, which contain general Perl information and specific details on the installation process, respectively.

3. Run the configuration script:

   ```
   $ ./configure.gnu
   ```

   This is in fact a GNU-style execution of the real Configure script. The standard Perl Configure script is interactive, requiring input from you on a number of questions. The GNU-compatible execution answers the questions automatically for you, making a number of assumptions about your system, though it still shows the process going on behind the scenes.

4. Run **make** to build the application:

   ```
   $ make
   ```

   The application and support files have now been compiled. It's a good idea at this point to run **make test,** which will run a standard selection of tests to ensure that Perl has compiled properly. If there are any problems, you want to check the build process to see if anything failed. On the mainstream systems such as Linux and Solaris it's unlikely that you will notice any test failures.

5. Once the build has completed, install the application, scripts and modules using **make**:

   ```
   $ make install
   ```

   Providing you didn't specify different directories, the usual directory specification will install Perl into the /usr/local/bin and /usr/local/lib/perl5 directories. You will need to add /usr/local/bin, or the installation directory you chose (specified by the $installation_prefix/bin variable in the **Makefile**) to your **$PATH** environment variable, if it is not already in it.

If you don't want to compile the source yourself, the CPAN archives also now include prebuilt binaries ready to install onto your system. You can find the full list of ports that are available at ftp://ftp.funet.fi/pub/languages/perl/CPAN/ports/index.html.

Adding Extensions

If you want to include some of the options that have been discussed in this book, such as debugging with the **–DDEBUGGING**, or threads, you will need to modify the **config.sh** script before running **make**. You will need to add the options to the **ccflags** entry within the file and then do the following:

```
$ Configure -S
```

This re-creates the files required for the **make** process and scripts used to build the Perl application.

```
$ make depend
```

This resolves all of the required files for each stage of the build process. Then proceed, as from step 4 in the previous example.

Executing Scripts

There are two ways of executing a Perl script under Unix. You can run the Perl application, supplying the script's name on the command line, or you can place the following on the first line of the file,

```
#!/usr/local/bin/perl
```

where the path given is the path to the Perl application. You must then change the file mode of the script to be executable (usually 0755).

Note that it is common to have different versions of Perl on your system. In this case, the latest version will always have been installed as $prefix/bin/perl, which is linked to the version-specific file. This file includes the version number of the Perl being used, such as perl5.00553.

The Perl libraries and support files are installed in $prefix/lib/perl5. Since version 5.004, each version of Perl has installed its own subdirectory such that the actual location becomes $prefix/lib/perl5/5.00553/, or whatever the version number is. Platform-specific information is placed in a directory within that one specified as the platform name (see Chapter 24). User-installed scripts should be placed into $prefix/lib/perl5/5.00553/site-perl.

Whenever a script is run, unless it has been redirected, standard input, output, and errors are sent via the terminal or window, the same as the shell environment.

Installing Third-Party Modules

For most modules (particularly those from CPAN), the installation process is fairly straightforward:

1. Download the module, and extract it using **tar** and **gunzip**, for example:

   ```
   $ gunzip -c module.tar.gz | tar xf -
   ```

   This should create a new directory with the module contents.

2. Change to the module directory.
3. Type

   ```
   $ perl5 Makefile.PL
   ```

   This will check that the module contents are complete and that the necessary prerequisite modules are already installed. It will also create a **Makefile** that will compile (if necessary) and install the module.

As in the original installation process, a **make test** will verify that the compilation and configuration of the package works OK before you come to install it. You should report any problems to the package's author.

4. To install the module, type

   ```
   $ make install
   ```

   This will copy the modules and any required support files into the appropriate directories.

Most CPAN modules (except those specifically for another platform, such as the Win32 modules) are developed or supported under Unix. You should not have any compatibility problems. However, if you are using a Unix installation that does not have a bundled C compiler (such as Solaris 2.x), you may have trouble installing modules that use XS extensions.

Also note that you can use the CPAN module, which comes with the Perl distribution. This simplifies the process of downloading, configuring, and installing a module available on CPAN. See Appendix E for more details.

Platform-Specific Issues

The following sections include details on the platform-specific effects of the Unix platform.

Line Termination

The default line termination is **\n**, or ASCII **\012** (octal \x0A). Do not rely on this being compatible with other platforms directly. See Chapter 24 for specific details on all platforms.

Volumes, Pathnames, and Files

All files can be reached via the root directory, /. There are no separate volumes or drive identifiers. File names can be up to 256 characters in length, and there is theoretically no maximum length for a full pathname. In practice, most Unix flavors specify a maximum value of 2048 or 4096 characters.

Time

The time of the epoch is 00:00:00 on 1 January, 1970, UTC, and time values are calculated as the number of seconds since this date/time. The use of UTC or GMT specifies that the value is ignorant of the current time zone.

Running External Programs

You can use any of the methods we have discussed in this book to execute external programs, either directly or through the use of **open** statements. For example, the following line opens the file text.gz via the **gunzip** application to read uncompressed text from the file:

```
open(D,"gunzip -c text.gz|");
```

You can also run a program directly using the **system** function or using backticks. Note that unless you specify the location of the program absolutely, the program should be in the current **$ENV{PATH}** environment variable.

Networking

There are no specific issues regarding networking under Unix, since the original socket specification is a Unix feature. See Chapter 9 and the Socket module in Appendix E for further details on the standard Perl network implementation. Note as well that the file descriptors used for files are identical to those used for network sockets. Do not confuse the two values for two different ranges of values.

Memory and Performance

All varieties of Unix provide a virtual memory system that effectively provides an unlimited amount of memory to be available to a process. Allocation is done dynamically through the use of a single function, **malloc**, and some derivatives. It is therefore possible to use up all the memory within a script without realizing how much memory you are using. There are no standard ways to find out the amount of memory available, but if you are worried about using all of the available memory, you may want to make use of the **$^M** variable. This specifies the amount of memory for use in an emergency situation for closing files and exiting the script gracefully.

The only performance issue to keep in mind is that—although with Unix there are no limits for a typical program—there are physical and logical limits for all of the different resources available. Handling large volumes of memory, many simultaneously open files and network sockets all add extra weight to the interpretation process.

Web Servers and CGI

Because I/O is performed to the standard input and output devices, using Perl for CGI scripts is simply a case of installing the script into the CGI directory of your web server. If you are using Apache as your web server software, there is a Perl module, mod_perl, which effectively allows you to execute Perl code directly within the Apache server by providing a Perl interpreter as part of the Apache server. This increases performance dramatically by eliminating the need to run a separate external Perl interpreter. See Appendix F for more details.

Multiuser Issues

The default location for user and group information is the /etc/passwd and /etc/group files. However, different Unix flavors and different implementations may store the information elsewhere. This includes, but is not exclusive to, NIS (Network Information Service), NIS+, and Radius. Furthermore, even if the information is available in the /etc/passwd file, some of the secure information (especially the password) may be shadowed and only available to the superuser.

Usually, the system **getpwnam** and related functions will automatically refer to all of the available sources when accessing the information. If not, check the CPAN reference in Appendix F for some modules that will enable you to directly access NIS and other data sources.

The Complete Reference

Chapter 22

Perl Under Windows 95/98/NT/2000

The Windows port, otherwise known as Win32, is not vastly different from the Unix port. Win32 supports a very similar environment; indeed, large parts of the Windows NT environment are actually based on the same POSIX compliance as many Unix platforms. This means that many core features and functionality of the Perl interpreter are still available under the Windows platform, and you shouldn't have too many worries regarding the port from Unix to Win32.

Win32 Basics

The history of theWin32 port is slightly more complex than the traditional Perl history. The ActiveState port was originally a semicommercial effort to port Perl to the Windows platform. In time, the core Perl distribution was modified to include the differences and modifications required for the Win32 port. There are now two freely available distributions, the one from ActiveState and the core distribution from the main Perl source tree.

The ActiveState ports have been updated but are now slightly behind the core ports. The ActiveState version of Perl, downloadable from www.activestate.com will enable you to install a precompiled binary. The base version from ActiveState will work directly on Windows 95 and NT. There are also related extensions: PerlScript and ISAPI. PerlScript will run as an ActiveX scripting engine within Internet Explorer and Microsoft Internet Information Server. ISAPI is a dynamically loadable library (DLL) that will execute Perl scripts within the confines of an ISAPI-compliant web server. This is faster than the more generalized Perl binary, but otherwise provides no other benefits.

The core distributions are more up-to-date, and you can now compile a Perl interpreter for Win32 from the main Perl source tree providing you have the tools. Compilation requires a C compiler, which can be either one of the freely available Cygnus or GNU ports, or a commercial development system such as Microsoft's Visual C++. Because the core distribution is based on the latest core source code, it generally behaves more like the Unix equivalent, aside from the obvious differences between platforms. It is possible to use it with Microsoft's IIS and other web servers under Windows 95 and NT. If you want to use standard Perl under 95/NT, this is the best solution, and you should also think about installing Win32 Perl extensions, which provide a standard toolkit for using the features of the 32-bit Windows Perl port.

It was originally intended that the two versions of Perl available for Windows would eventually merge into a single distribution. Instead, ActiveState has rekindled its efforts and produced more regular updates to its own distribution. The Win32 modules supplied with the ActiveState distribution are now available separately from CPAN and can be installed with the core distribution. In essence there are few differences between the two versions, and it's unlikely that a script that runs under ActiveState Perl will not run under a core Perl distribution with the **libwin32** extensions installed.

Installing and Running the Perl Application

Once you have obtained the required version of the Perl distribution you want, you need to extract it with a Zip tool that supports long file names. I can recommend WinZip (http://www.winzip.com) and Aladdin's Expander for Windows (http://www.aladdinsys.com). Once extracted, it's a simple case of running install.bat and answering some simple questions. The result will be an installation in your selected directory of the entire Perl distribution and support modules.

The installation should update your PATH values so that you can type **perl** at the command line prompt and it will execute correctly. It will also associate the .pl extension to the Perl application so scripts can be double-clicked. If you have IIS installed, then an entry will be made against the script registry for IIS so that you can use Perl for CGI scripting.

Compiling Perl Under Win32

If you want to install a version of the Perl binary based on the latest source code, you will need to find a C compiler capable of compiling the application. It's then a case of following the instructions relevant to your C and development environment. The supported C compilers are described here. Other versions and C compilers may work, but it's not guaranteed.

- **Borland C++, version 5.02 or later**: With the Borland C++ compiler you will need to use a different **make** command, since the one supplied does not work very well and certainly doesn't support **MakeMaker** extensions. The documentation recommends the **dmake** application, available from http://www-personal.umich.edu/~gsar/dmake-4.1-win32.zip.
- **Microsoft Visual C++, version 4.2 or later**: You can use the **nmake** command that comes with Visual C++ to build the distribution correctly.
- **Mingw32 with EGCS, versions 1.0.2 and 1.1 or Mingw32 with GCC, version 2.8.1**: Both EGCS and GCC supply their own **make** command. You can download a copy of the EGCS version (preferred) from ftp://ftp.xraylith.wisc.edu/pub/khan/gnu-win32/mingw32/. The GCC version is available from http://agnes.dida.physik.uni-essen.de/~janjaap/mingw32/.

Windows 95 as a compilation platform is not supported, since the supported command shell does not work very well with the supplied scripts and **make** commands. The best platform to use is Windows NT, using the standard **cmd** shell. For all compilations, you can ignore the **Configure** utility, which probably won't run, and even if it did, it would probably configure the distribution incorrectly anyway.

Support for **MakeMaker** is included in the latest distributions, provided you have a compatible make, as specified in the compiler descriptions above.

Building

Once you have a suitable **make** utility, change to the win32 directory in the main distribution, and then just type

```
c:\perl\win32> dmake
```

Or type **nmake** if that's the version you are using. That should build and install everything for you.

Threads and Objects

You can build a version of Perl with native support for the threading mechanism. However, binaries built with threading enabled are not compatible with the standard C binary, and vice versa. This shouldn't affect scripts, but be aware of the incompatibilities if you expect to move the binary- and/or thread-enabled scripts.

From version 5.005, the core distribution also provides support for building a version with the object abstraction mechanism that was originally developed under the ActiveState version of Perl. Again, if built with this option, there is an incompatibility with the normal C Perl binary because the object version uses C++, but otherwise the two binaries are compatible.

Executing Scripts

Once installed correctly, there are two basic ways of executing a Perl script. You can either type

```
C:\> perl cat.pl
```

in a command window, or you can double-click on the script in Windows Explorer. The former method allows you to specify command line arguments; the latter method will require that you ask the user for any required information.

If you want a more Unix-like method of executing scripts, you can modify the **PATHEXT** environment variable (in the System control panel) to include .pl as a recognized extension. This allows you to call a script just like any other command line on the command line, but with limitations. The following will work:

```
C:\> cat readme.txt
```

But redirection and pipes do not work; so the following lines would do nothing:

```
C:\> cat <readme.txt

C:\> cat readme.txt|more
```

Note that this method only works under Windows NT, not Windows 95. It also does not support the "shebang" method of specifying Perl options, for example:

```
#!/usr/local/bin/perl5 -w
```

The "shebang" is the ***#!*** *string at the start of the file. This is used by Unix to identify an alternative program to the shell for executing the script.*

If you want to execute a script with warnings switched on, you must call Perl and the script from the command line. Input and output occurs in a command window (either the current window or a new one if the script was double-clicked), unless you have manually redirected within the script or you are using something like the Tk extension modules to create windows directly.

Third-Party Modules

How you install a third-party module is entirely dependent on the module in question. For the Win32 module, it is simply a case of extracting the zip file and then running install.bat. In contrast, for Dave Roth's **AdminMisc** module, you must install the module and support files manually. Once installed, you can call the modules as you normally would; no special handling is required.

When installing the Win32 module and Dave Roth's ***AdminMisc*** *module, you need to manually remove the* ***AdminMisc*** *module supplied with Win32. Otherwise, you will make calls to the Win32* ***AdminMisc*** *module that do not exist!*

If the module you are trying to install requires a C compiler, you will also have problems similar to the one described above. This is not an issue for Win32-specific modules that are supplied precompiled.

If you've managed to compile the Perl binary from source, then you can also use the traditional Unix method of

```
C:\> perl Makefile.PL
C:\> dmake
```

```
C:\> dmake test
C:\> dmake install
```

The **MakeMaker** module will make all the necessary decisions regarding file locations and install the module into a suitable directory. This is also the only way to genuinely install XS-reliant modules under Win32, since they all rely on an external C compiler.

Win32 Differences

Despite the similarities between the Win32 and Unix versions, there are still some minor differences between the two platforms.

Line Termination

Text files under Windows are terminated with "\r\n" (a carriage-return and a newline character, "\015\012"), and files are terminated by the SUB (^Z) character. However, within the C libraries that are used to build Perl, the end-of-line characters are converted to a single newline, "\n," on input, and a newline is converted to carriage-return newline on output. This means that Perl scripts using text files are interchangeable between Unix and Windows Perl implementations.

Incidentally, if you are using binary files directly within Perl, you must specify that the filehandle is to be treated as binary using the **binmode** function, as in:

```
open(D,"<file.bin");
binmode(D);
```

You need to do this before you read or write to the file. The change only occurs at the point the function is called.

Also be aware that if you are storing file locations as returned by **tell** externally when not in binary mode, the location is based on a "\n" terminated file, so a 100-line file will actually have 100 fewer characters in it. If you access the file with binary mode enabled and use the same values, you will end up in a different location.

Volumes, Pathnames, and Files

Volumes, or drives, under Windows are referenced by a drive letter, followed by a colon. The boot drive is generally C:, although it is possible to have further drives or multiple partitions of a physical disk. This means that if you use colons to separate drive information, you must account for the colon in any file specification. Directories and files are by default separated by the backslash "\." However, Perl for Windows uses the forward slash "/" as under Unix. This means that the code fragment

```
print "Exists\n" if (-f "C:/autoexec.bat");
```

works, but this one doesn't:

```
print "Exists\n" if (-f "C:\autoexec.bat");
```

Note *In the latter example, the lookup will actually fail because the double-quoted string causes Perl to interpret the "\a" at the start of the file name as a special character.*

It's also worth mentioning that files and directories can be specified irrespective of case. Windows does not distinguish between upper- and lowercase letters within the command prompt.

Time

The epoch is measured the same as in Unix—from 00:00:00 on 1 January 1970.

Running External Programs

Within the core Perl distribution it is possible to execute external programs in the same manner as you would under Unix. However, if you are using the ISAPI or Script versions of the ActiveState version of Perl, it is not a supported option. This is because scripts within these environments are executed within the confines of the host web server, and executing an external program would probably cause the host application to crash, if the attempt of the operation succeeded at all.

Networking

For most scripts, Unix-style networking will work. The standard **Socket** module is supplied. You can even run a simple TCP/IP server under Windows. However, it is not a good idea to use Windows as a server platform within Perl, because the Win32 implementation does not support **fork**, so you will only be able to support one connection at a time. The threaded version of the Perl interpreter may resolve this problem—check Chapters 9 and 11.

Web Servers and CGI

See the earlier sections on available versions and installing and executing Perl script.

Functional Differences

The functional differences are covered under the cross-platform compatibility guide in Chapter 24—see the section "Differences Between Functions."

Win32 Supplied/Specific Modules

The ActiveState version of Perl introduced a range of Win32-specific modules that provide a variety of additional functions for the Win32 port. These are now available separately within the CPAN archives, and information on their contents and use has been included here for reference. Also included here is information on the **Win32::AdminMisc** module from Dave Roth, which incorporates many additional functions to be used specifically for administration tasks.

Note that in all cases, except where otherwise noted, the functions return the normal zero (false) on failure and 1 (true) on success. You will also need to be aware with some modules of the Windows-specific programming requirements. I don't advise anybody without some Windows-specific programming experience to use these modules, especially those that provide access to the registry, ODBC, and administration features.

Also note that for nearly all modules the functions (not methods) are not included in the standard export list, and so will not automatically be imported into the caller's name space. You will therefore need to refer to them explicitly. For brevity, the module name has been stripped in the reference information below; remember to add the information back when you use the functions.

Win32

The base Win32 module provides a very simple set of functions that return information about the current Perl environment on which the Perl interpreter is running. In all cases the functions are not exported implicitly by the module, so you'll need to call them directly.

```
Win32::GetLastError
```

The **GetLastError** function is a vital part of the overall Win32 interface. It provides the extended error information returned by the Win32 subsystem when an error occurs. The value returned is a number, and it should be extracted as soon as an error occurs.

```
Win32::FormatMessage ERRORCODE
```

The error number returned by **GetLastError** can be converted into an error string by the **Win32::FormatMessage** function.

I generally use the **Win32::GetLastError** and **Win32::FormatMessage** functions as part of a custom subroutine that acts as an alternative to the normal **$!** handling supported by Perl:

```
sub win32die
{
```

```
    my $error=Win32::GetLastError();
    if ($error ne 0)
    {
        die $_[0] . Win32::FormatMessage($error);
    }
    return 1;
}
```

You can then call this directly within a function as a wrapper around the whole Win32 error-reporting process:

```
Win32::Spawn('dir') || win32die;
```

This is more practical than doing the testing manually, but be careful about using the functions without testing the return values from functions in the first place. And always make sure you call the **Win32::GetLastError** function immediately after an error occurs, otherwise you may get an unexpected return value.

```
Win32::LoginName
```

Returns the login name of the current user.

```
Win32::NodeName
```

Returns the node name (not necessarily the same as the Internet node name) of the current machine.

```
Win32::DomainName
```

Returns the domain name that the current user is logged into.

```
Win32::FsType
```

Returns a string defining the underlying file system type on which the script is being run.

```
Win32::GetCwd
```

Returns the current working directory. This should be more reliable than using the **Getcwd** module in the standard distribution.

```
Win32::GetOSVersion
```

Returns the current OS version.

```
Win32::Spawn COMMAND, ARGS, PID
```

Spawns a new process, running **COMMAND** with the specified **ARGS**. The **PID** should be a reference to a scalar, which will contain the process ID of the newly created process.

```
Win32::GetTickCount
```

Returns an integer, giving the number of milliseconds that the machine has currently been up—that is, the number of milliseconds since the last reboot.

```
Win32::IsWinNT
```

Returns true if the machine on which the interpreter is running is using Windows NT.

```
Win32::IsWin95
```

Returns true if the machine on which the interpreter is running is using Windows 95.

Win32API::Net

The **Win32API::Net** module provides a complete interface to the underlying C++ functions for managing accounts with the NT LanManager. The interface is more Perl specific, making use of references to pass the information between functions. You might also want to check out the **Win32::AdminMisc** module detailed later in this chapter. The module supports four main groups of functions for managing users, net groups, local groups, and finally, domain controller information.

The detail here should be enough to identify the individual functions you will require. Check the documentation pages for more details on specifics.

User Functions

The user functions make use of a "user-level" number. The user level is used to define the complexity of the hash supplied or returned by the function. The different levels are listed in Table 22-1.

The descriptions for each field can be found under the **GetMiscUserAttributes** function in the **Win32::AdminMisc** table. Table 22-2 lists the predefined constants for errors when updating user fields.

Level	Fields
0	name
1	name, password, passwordAge, priv, homeDir, comment, flags, scriptPath
2	name, password, passwordAge, priv, homeDir, comment, flags, scriptPath, authFlags, fullName, usrComment, parms, workstations, lastLogon, lastLogoff, acctExpires, maxStorage, unitsPerWeek, logonHours, badPwCount, numLogons, logonServer, countryCode, codePage
3	name, password, passwordAge, priv, homeDir, comment, flags, scriptPath, authFlags, fullName, usrComment, parms, workstations, lastLogon, lastLogoff, acctExpires, maxStorage, unitsPerWeek, logonHours, badPwCount, numLogons, logonServer, countryCode, codePage, userId, primaryGroupId, profile, homeDirDrive, passwordExpired
10	name, comment, usrComment, fullName
11	name, comment, usrComment, fullName, priv, authFlags, passwordAge, homeDir, parms, lastLogon, lastLogoff, badPwCount, numLogons, logonServer, countryCode, workstations, maxStorage, unitsPerWeek, logonHours, codePage
20	name, fullName, comment, flags, userId
21	Not supported
22	Not supported
1003	password
1005	priv
1006	homeDir
1007	comment
1008	flags
1009	scriptPath
1010	authFlags
1011	fullName

Table 22-1. *User Information Levels Supported*

Level	Fields
1012	usrComment
1013	parms
1014	workstations
1017	acctExpires
1018	maxStorage
1020	unitsPerWeek, logonHours
1023	logonServer
1024	countryCode
1025	codePage
1051	primaryGroupId
1052	profile
1053	homeDirDrive

Table 22-1. *User Information Levels Supported* (continued)

Constant	Description
USER_ACCT_EXPIRES_PARMNUM	The expiration value for the user's account is incorrectly specified.
USER_AUTH_FLAGS_PARMNUM	The authorization flags for the user are incorrect/invalid.
USER_BAD_PW_COUNT_PARMNUM	The user's password count was badly specified.
USER_CODE_PAGE_PARMNUM	The user's code page value was incorrectly specified or absent.
USER_COMMENT_PARMNUM	The user's comment was invalid.
USER_COUNTRY_CODE_PARMNUM	The user's country code was invalid.

Table 22-2. *Error Constants for the User Functions*

Constant	Description
USER_FLAGS_PARMNUM	The user's flags was invalid.
USER_FULL_NAME_PARMNUM	The user's full name was invalid.
USER_HOME_DIR_DRIVE_PARMNUM	The user's home directory drive was incorrectly specified or absent.
USER_HOME_DIR_PARMNUM	The home directory was incorrectly specified or absent.
USER_LAST_LOGOFF_PARMNUM	The last logoff value was incorrectly specified or absent.
USER_LAST_LOGON_PARMNUM	The last logon value was incorrectly specified or absent.
USER_LOGON_HOURS_PARMNUM	The logon hours field was incorrectly specified or absent.
USER_LOGON_SERVER_PARMNUM	The logon server for the user was incorrectly specified or absent.
USER_MAX_STORAGE_PARMNUM	The maximum storage value for the user was incorrectly specified or absent.
USER_NAME_PARMNUM	The user's name was incorrectly specified or absent.
USER_NUM_LOGONS_PARMNUM	The number of logons field was incorrectly specified or absent.
USER_PARMS_PARMNUM	The user parameters were incorrectly specified or absent.
USER_PASSWORD_AGE_PARMNUM	The password age was incorrectly specified or absent.
USER_PASSWORD_PARMNUM	The user's password was incorrectly specified or absent.
USER_PRIMARY_GROUP_PARMNUM	The user's primary group was incorrectly specified or absent.

Table 22-2. *Error Constants for the User Functions* (continued)

Constant	Description
USER_PRIV_PARMNUM	The user's privileges were incorrectly specified or absent.
USER_PROFILE_PARMNUM	The user's profile was incorrectly specified or absent.
USER_SCRIPT_PATH_PARMNUM	The user's script path was incorrectly specified or absent.
USER_UNITS_PER_WEEK_PARMNUM	The units per week was incorrectly specified or absent.
USER_USR_COMMENT_PARMNUM	The user's comment field was incorrectly specified or absent.
USER_WORKSTATIONS_PARMNUM	The user's workstations field was incorrectly specified or absent.

Table 22-2. *Error Constants for the User Functions* (continued)

```
UserAdd(SERVER, LEVEL, HASH, ERROR)
```

Adds a new user account to **SERVER**, to the **LEVEL**, using the information supplied in **HASH**. Any errors in the hash are reported into the **ERROR** scalar.

```
UserChangePassword(SERVER, USER, OLD, NEW)
```

Changes the password for **USER** on **SERVER** from **OLD** to **NEW**.

```
UserDel(SERVER, USER)
```

Deletes **USER** from **SERVER**.

```
UserEnum(SERVER, ARRAY [, FILTER])
```

Places the list of users on **SERVER**, starting with **FILTER** (if specified) into the array pointed to by **ARRAY**.

```
UserGetGroups(SERVER, USER, ARRAY)
```

Gets the list of valid groups for **USER** on **SERVER**, placing it into the array pointed to by **ARRAY**.

```
UserGetInfo(SERVER, USER, LEVEL, HASH)
```

Places the information for **USER** on **SERVER** into **HASH**, providing the list of fields specified by **LEVEL**.

```
UserGetLocalGroups(SERVER, USER, ARRAY [, FLAGS])
```

Gets the list of local groups of which **USER** on **SERVER** is a member. The list is placed in **ARRAY**. **FLAGS** can use the optional **LG_INCLUDE_DIRECT** constant, which includes the list of groups of which the user is indirectly a member.

```
UserSetGroups(SERVER, USER, ARRAY)
```

Sets the list of groups for **USER** on **SERVER** to that specified by the reference **ARRAY**.

```
UserSetInfo(SERVER, USER, LEVEL, HASH, ERROR)
```

Sets the information for **USER** on **SERVER**, using the information in the **HASH** reference. The **LEVEL** sets the fields that will be updated. Errors or missing fields are reported by setting the value of **ERROR**. See Table 22-2.

Also check the **Win32::AdminMisc** functions, which provide a less restrictive interface to the underlying C++ API.

Group Functions

Like the user functions, the group functions use a set of specific levels, as detailed in Table 22-3.

The fields of a group hash are **attributes** (unsupported), **comment**, **groupId**, and **name**.

The errors return when accessing and updating the groups can be matched against some predefined constants. **GROUP_ATTRIBUTES_PARMNUM** indicates that the **attributes** field was absent. **GROUP_COMMENT_PARMNUM** indicates that the **comment** field was absent or incorrectly specified. **GROUP_NAME_PARMNUM** indicates that the **name** field was absent.

```
GroupAdd(SERVER, LEVEL, HASH, ERROR)
```

Adds the group, specified by the **HASH** using the fields up to the **LEVEL**, on the **SERVER**. Errors are placed into **ERROR**.

Level	Fields
0	name
1	name, comment
2	name, comment, groupId, attributes
1002	comment
1005	attributes

Table 22-3. *Group Levels*

```
GroupAddUser(SERVER, GROUP, USER)
```

Adds **USER** to **GROUP** on **SERVER**.

```
GroupDel(SERVER, GROUP)
```

Deletes **GROUP** from **SERVER**.

```
GroupDelUser(SERVER, GROUP, USER)
```

Deletes **USER** from **GROUP** on **SERVER**.

```
GroupEnum(SERVER, ARRAY)
```

Places a list of groups into the array pointed to by **ARRAY** from **SERVER**.

```
GroupGetInfo(SERVER, GROUP, LEVEL, HASH)
```

Gets the group information to **LEVEL** for **GROUP** on **SERVER**, placing it into the hash pointed to by **HASH**.

```
GroupGetUsers(SERVER, GROUP, ARRAY)
```

Places the list of users for **GROUP** on **SERVER** into the array pointed to by **ARRAY**.

```
GroupSetInfo(SERVER, GROUP, LEVEL, HASH, ERROR)
```

Sets the fields of **GROUP** on **SERVER** from **HASH**. The list of specified fields is defined by **LEVEL**, and any errors are placed into **ERROR**.

```
GroupSetUsers(SERVER, GROUP, ARRAY)
```

Sets the membership of **GROUP** on **SERVER**, using the list of users in **ARRAY**.

Local Group Functions

This series of functions supports access and updating of the local groups. It uses the same group fields and other information supported by the group functions.


```
LocalGroupAdd(SERVER, LEVEL, HASH, ERROR)
```

Adds the group specified in **HASH**, using the fields **LEVEL** on **SERVER**. Errors are placed into **ERROR.**

```
LocalGroupAddMember()
```

Deprecated; use **LocalGroupAddMembers**.

```
LocalGroupAddMembers(SERVER, GROUP, ARRAY)
```

Adds the users in **ARRAY** to **GROUP** on **SERVER**.

```
LocalGroupDel(SERVER, GROUP)
```

Deletes the local **GROUP** on **SERVER**.

```
LocalGroupDelMember()
```

Deprecated; use **LocalGroupDelMembers** instead.

```
LocalGroupDelMembers(SERVER, GROUP, ARRAY)
```

Deletes the list of users in **ARRAY** from **GROUP** on **SERVER**.

```
LocalGroupEnum(SERVER, ARRAY)
```

Places the list of groups on **SERVER** into **ARRAY**.

```
LocalGroupGetInfo(SERVER, GROUP, LEVEL, HASH)
```

Gets the information for **GROUP** to **LEVEL** on **SERVER**, placing it into **HASH**.

```
LocalGroupGetMembers(SERVER, GROUP, ARRAY)
```

Puts the list of members of **GROUP** on **SERVER** into **ARRAY**.

```
LocalGroupSetInfo(server, level, hash, error)
```

Sets the information for the group defined in **HASH**, using the fields specified by **LEVEL** on **SERVER**. Errors are placed into **ERROR**.

```
LocalGroupSetMembers()
```

Not implemented.

Domain Functions

Only one function, **GetDCName** is supported:

```
GetDCName(MACHINE, DOMAIN, SERVER)
```

Places the domain controller for **MACHINE** within **DOMAIN** into **SERVER**.

Win32API::Registry

This module provides a low-level interface to the core API used for manipulating the registry. Since this is such a low-level interface, you may want to consider a more user-friendly interface such as **Win32::Registry** or, better still, **Win32::TieRegistry**.

The Windows registry is a complex informational source, and using it without knowledge of its layout and the dangers associated with making modifications is not advised.

Win32::ChangeNotify

The **ChangeNotify** module provides a simplified Perl interface to the Win32 change notification system. This enables you to monitor a directory and then be notified when the contents of the directory changes.

```
use Win32::ChangeNotify;

$notify = Win32::ChangeNotify->new(PATH, SUBTREE, EVENTS);
```

This creates a new object configured to monitor the **PATH** specified, which can either be a file or directory. If it is a directory, you can set **SUBTREE** to 1, which causes the new monitor object to include all of the subtree elements as well as the specific **PATH**.

The **EVENTS** argument is a string of the constants listed in Table 22-4. The constants should be separated either by white space or the | character.

Once created, two methods control the operation of the object. The **FindNext** method configures the system so that the object will be notified when a change occurs. The **Wait** takes a single argument, the time-out value, and blocks the process until the time-out expires, or when a change occurs on the specified object.

When you have finished monitoring an object, use the **Close** method.

Win32::Clipboard

This module provides simple access to the Windows clipboard.

```
use Win32::Clipboard;

$clipboard = Win32::Clipboard();
```

Constant	Description
ATTRIBUTES	Any changes to the file's/directory's attributes.
DIR_NAME	Any directory name change.
FILE_NAME	Any change to a file's name.
LAST_WRITE	Any change to the file, which implies an update of the file's last write time.
SECURITY	Changes to the security of the directory or file.
SIZE	Changes to the file's size.

Table 22-4. *Events to Monitor*

The newly created object then supports three methods, **Get**, **Set**, and **Empty**, which return the current clipboard contents, set the contents, and then empty the clipboard, respectively.

Win32::Console

This module provides simplified access to the Win32 console. It includes methods for controlling the input and output of the console that incorporate positions and colors, as well as other features. This is the equivalent of the Termcap interface covered in Chapter 13. There are two forms for creating new console objects.

```
use Win32::Console;

$console = new Win32::Console(HANDLE);
```

This creates a new object attached to the specified handle, which can be one of **STD_OUTPUT_HANDLE**, **STD_ERROR_HANDLE**, or **STD_INPUT_HANDLE**.

```
$console = new Win32::Console(ACCESSMODE, SHAREMORE);
```

This form creates a console in memory that can be modified and built "off screen." As soon as you've finished building the off-screen version, you can display it with the **Display** method. The **ACCESSMODE** is a combination of **GENERIC_READ** or **GENERIC_WRITE**, which defines the permissions you have on the created buffer. The **SHAREMODE** is a combination of **FILE_SHARE_READ** or **FILE_SHARE_WRITE**, which affects how the off-screen buffer can be shared. If you do not specify the options, then all four are automatically specified.

The supported methods are listed in Table 22-5.

The list of available constants for the flags is shown below. The relative result of each constant should be obvious.

```
BACKGROUND_BLUE            BACKGROUND_GREEN           BACKGROUND_INTENSITY
BACKGROUND_RED             CAPSLOCK_ON                CONSOLE_TEXTMODE_BUFFER
ENABLE_ECHO_INPUT          ENABLE_LINE_INPUT          ENABLE_MOUSE_INPUT
ENABLE_PROCESSED_INPUT     ENABLE_PROCESSED_OUTPUT ENABLE_WINDOW_INPUT
ENABLE_WRAP_AT_EOL_OUTPUT  ENHANCED_KEY               FILE_SHARE_READ
FILE_SHARE_WRITE           FOREGROUND_BLUE            FOREGROUND_GREEN
FOREGROUND_INTENSITY       FOREGROUND_RED             LEFT_ALT_PRESSED
LEFT_CTRL_PRESSED          NUMLOCK_ON                 GENERIC_READ
GENERIC_WRITE              RIGHT_ALT_PRESSED          RIGHT_CTRL_PRESSED
SCROLLLOCK_ON              SHIFT_PRESSED              STD_INPUT_HANDLE
STD_OUTPUT_HANDLE          STD_ERROR_HANDLE
```

Method	Description
Alloc	Allocates a new console for the current process. This creates a new console if the script is not currently within a console window. It returns **undef** if the script already has a console attached to it. There can only be one console per process.
Attr	Gets (or sets) the attributes for the console. See the list of flag constants at the end of this table.
Close	Explicitly closes a **Win32::Shortcut** object.
Cls	Clears the console (equivalent to the **cls** command). You can specify a list of attributes for the newly cleared screen.
Cursor	Gets (or sets) the cursor position and appearance. The fields to set or get are the X,Y coordinates of the cursor, the cursor size, and the visibility.
Display	Displays an off-screen console on screen.
FillAttr	Takes four arguments, **attribute**, **number**, **x**, **y**. This sets the specified attributes for **number** characters starting at location **x**, **y**.
FillChar	Takes four arguments, **char**, **number**, **x**, **y**. Fills the screen for **number** characters, starting at **x**, **y** with **char**.
Flush	Flushes the console's input buffer.
Free	Detaches the console from the process.
GenerateCtrlEvent	Accepts two arguments, **type** and **processgroup**. Sends the defined keyboard combination specified in **type** (one of **CTRL_BREAK_EVENT** or **CTRL_C_EVENT**) to the console. The **processgroup** argument should be the ID of a process sharing the same console.
GetEvents	Returns the number of events waiting in the input event buffer.

Table 22-5. *Methods for the **Console** Module*

Method	Description
Info	Returns an array defining the information about the console. The information returned is the number of columns; the number of rows; current X,Y location of the cursor; current attribute (used with the **Write** method); the X,Y position on screen of the top left corner of the window and the X,Y position of the bottom right corner of the window; and the maximum number of columns and rows for the current console window, taking into account the buffer size, font, and screen size.
Input	Reads an event from the input buffer. The first value returned is the type of event—1 for a keyboard event and 2 for a mouse event. The remainder of the list returned depends on the type: For a keyboard event: Keydown: true if a key is being pressed. Repeat count: the number of times the key was repeatedly pressed. Virtual keycode: the virtual code of the key. Virtual scancode: the virtual scan code of the key. Char: the ASCII code of the key (if it's an ASCII value, 0 otherwise) Control key state: the state of the modifier keys. For a mouse event: X,Y: the coordinates of the mouse. Button state: the mouse buttons being pressed. Control key state: the state of the modifier keys. Event flags: the type of mouse event.
InputChar	Returns the characters in the input buffer.
InputCP	Gets (or sets) the input code page of the console.

Table 22-5. *Methods for the* ***Console*** *Module* (continued)

Method	Description
MaxWindow	Returns the maximum size (in rows and columns) of a console window.
Mode	Gets (or sets) the current mode of the console. Flags can be one or more of the following (the results of each flag should be self-explanatory): **ENABLE_LINE_INPUT**, **ENABLE_ECHO_INPUT**, **ENABLE_PROCESSED_INPUT**, **ENABLE_WINDOW_INPUT**, **ENABLE_MOUSE_INPUT**, **ENABLE_PROCESSED_OUTPUT**, **ENABLE_WRAP_AT_EOL_OUTPUT**.
MouseButtons	Returns the number of buttons available on the mouse.
OutputCP	Gets (or sets) the output code page used by the console.
PeekInput	Examines the events in the input buffer without removing them.
ReadAttr	Takes three arguments, **number**, **x**, **y**. Returns the attributes for **number** characters starting at position **x**, **y**.
ReadChar	Reads **number** characters from the position **x**, **y** of the console.
ReadRect	Returns a string consisting of characters and attributes for the rectangle specified by the four arguments, which specify the X,Y position of the top left and bottom right corners of the rectangle.
Scroll	Takes these arguments: **left**, **top**, **right**, **bottom**, **col**, **row**, **char**, **attr**, [**cleft**, **ctop**, **cright**, **cbottom**]. Moves a rectangle, specified by the first four arguments, by the specified number of **col** columns or **row** rows. The characters remaining in the old rectangle are filled with **char** characters with **attr** attributes. The optional arguments specify a rectangle that should not be filled.
Select	Redirects the specified filehandle for the console object.

Table 22-5. *Methods for the **Console** Module* (continued)

Method	Description
Size	Gets (or sets) the console size by specifying the number of rows and columns in the buffer.
Title	Gets (or sets) the window title.
Window	When called with no arguments, returns the window size as a four-element list specifying the top left and bottom right corners of the window. To set the window size, you must supply a list of flags in the first argument in addition to the top left and bottom right coordinates.
Write	Writes the supplied string to the console using the current attribute.
WriteAttr	Writes the attributes in the first argument at the X,Y location specified in the next two arguments.
WriteChar	Writes the characters in the first argument starting at the X,Y location of the next two arguments without overwriting the existing attributes at that location.
WriteInput	Pushes the supplied event into the input buffer. The supplied event should be in the form of the corresponding event arguments.
WriteRect	Writes a rectangle of characters and attributes in the first argument into the rectangle specified by the top left and bottom right coordinates.

Table 22-5. *Methods for the **Console** Module* (continued)

For example, to set the size of the console buffer to 80x25 characters, set the window title, and clear the screen:

```
use Win32::Console;
$console = new Win32::Console();
$console->Size(80,25);
$console->Title('Perl Console');
$console->Cls();
```

Win32::Event

This module provides a simple interface to Win32 events, which are inherited from the **Win32::IPC** module. The state of a named event can be set and read and shared among threads and processes. The event is basically a flip-flop. The state of an event can be signaled or reset, and different threads can wait for a particular event to signal. The effect is similar to that of a semaphore with a maximum value of 1.

```
$event = Win32::Event->new([MANUAL [, INITIAL [, NAME]]])
```

Creates a new event object. If **MANUAL** is true, then the event must be manually reset after it has been signaled. If **INITIAL** is true, then the initial. The **NAME** is the string you want to use to identify the event. This will also create an object that refers to an existing event if **NAME** matches that of an existing entry.

```
$event = Win32::Event->open(NAME)
```

Opens the existing event **NAME**.

```
$event->pulse
```

Signals the event and immediately resets its status. If the corresponding event is set for manual reset, then it releases all threads currently waiting for the event. If the event is configured for autoreset, then this method releases just one thread.

```
$event->reset
```

Resets the event to a nonsignaled state.

```
$event->set
```

Sets the event to a signaled state

```
$event->wait([TIMEOUT])
```

Blocks the process until **$event** has been signaled for **TIMEOUT** seconds. If the time-out expires before the event is signaled, the function returns zero.

Win32::EventLog

You can read entries directly from the NT event log system using this module.

```
use Win32::EventLog;
Win32::EventLog::Open(EVENTOBJ, EVENTLOG, SERVER)
```

Creates a new object in **EVENTOBJ**, using the supplied **EVENTLOG** on **SERVER**. The default event logs on an NT machine are System, Application, Security. If **SERVER** is blank, it reads the log from the local machine.

The main method is **Read**, which gets an individual record from the specified event log:

```
Win32::EventLog($eventlog, 'Application', '');
$eventlog->Read(FLAG, RECORD, EVENT);
```

This reads a single record, populating the hash pointed to by **EVENT**. The **FLAG** should be a combination of the flags shown in Table 22-6. The **RECORD** is the record number to be retrieved. Records start at 1 (see the **GetNumber** and the **GetOldest** methods in this section).

Flag	Description
EVENTLOG_FORWARDS_READ	Reads the log in chronological order.
EVENTLOG_BACKWARDS_READ	Reads the log in reverse chronological order.
EVENTLOG_SEEK_READ	Reads from the record number specified in **RECORD**. This option must be used in conjunction with the **EVENTLOG_FORWARDS_READ** or **EVENTLOG_BACKWARDS_READ**.
EVENTLOG_SEQUENTIAL_READ	Reads the next record after a previous **Read** function, retaining the position and directional information.

Table 22-6. *Flags for the* ***EventLog*** *Module*

Note that these flags are mutually exclusive: **EVENTLOG_FORWARDS_READ** and **EVENTLOG_BACKWARDS_READ**. The keys of the hash are listed in Table 22-7.

The other methods supplied by the module are as follows:

```
$eventlog->Report(EVENT)
```


Key	Description
Category	An application-specific category number.
ClosingRecordNumber	The last record number in a multirecord entry.
Computer	The name of the computer from which the event was reported.
Data	The event data reported.
EventID	An application-specific ID number.
EventType	An integer equivalent to one of the following constants.
Length	The length of the application data.
Message	A short message string for the event.
RecordNumber	The record number within the event log.
Source	The name of the application or service that reported the entry.
Strings	Application-specific text strings.
TimeGenerated	The number of seconds since the epoch when the event was generated.
Timewritten	The number of seconds since the epoch when the event was added to the log.
User	The user name of the application that reported the event, if applicable.

Table 22-7. *Event Log Fields*

Adds the event specified in the hash **EVENT** to the log.

```
$eventlog->GetNumber(NUMBER)
```

Places the next record number for an event into the scalar pointed to by **NUMBER**.

```
$eventlog->GetOldest(NUMBER)
```

Places the oldest record number in the log into the scalar pointed to by **NUMBER**.

Win32::File

This module provides a simple interface to the attributes of the file, as shown in the File Properties dialog box. Two functions, **GetAttributes** and **SetAttributes**, return a number that can be matched with logical operators to the following constants:

```
ARCHIVE
COMPRESSED
DIRECTORY
HIDDEN
NORMAL
OFFLINE
READONLY
SYSTEM
TEMPORARY
```

The definitions for the two functions are

```
GetAttributes(FILE, ATTRIBUTES)
```

Places the attributes information for **FILE** into **ATTRIBUTES**. Returns false (zero) if the file does not exist or the attributes cannot be determined.

```
SetAttributes(FILE, ATTRIBUTES)
```

Sets the attributes for **FILE** to **ATTRIBUTES**.

Win32::FileSecurity

Aside from the simple attributes configurable via the **Win32::File** module, Windows NT also supports extended security via "Discretionary Access Control Lists." These allow more complex security options and therefore require a different module, **Win32::FileSecurity**.

The system works via a set of constants that define the different security options available. These constants, listed below, relate to the individual settings within the security properties dialog.

```
DELETE
READ_CONTROL
WRITE_DAC
WRITE_OWNER
SYNCHRONIZE
STANDARD_RIGHTS_REQUIRED
STANDARD_RIGHTS_READ
STANDARD_RIGHTS_WRITE
STANDARD_RIGHTS_EXECUTE
STANDARD_RIGHTS_ALL
SPECIFIC_RIGHTS_ALL
ACCESS_SYSTEM_SECURITY
MAXIMUM_ALLOWED
GENERIC_READ
GENERIC_WRITE
GENERIC_EXECUTE
GENERIC_ALL
FULL
READ
CHANGE
```

The main operations are supported by the **Get** and **Set** functions, which, respectively, get and set the access control lists for a file:

```
Get(FILE, PERMISSIONS)
Set(FILE, PERMISSIONS)
```

The access control information is placed into or taken from the hash pointed to by **PERMISSIONS**. The format of the permissions hash is as follows:

```
$permissions{USER} = ACL
```

The **USER** key is a recognized user name, and the **ACL** is a mask generated (or resolved) by the **MakeMask** and **EnumerateRights** functions:

```
MakeMask(LIST)
EnumerateRights(MASK, LIST)
```

The **MakeMask** function returns a mask based on the supplied list of constants, for example:

```
$mask = MakeMask(qw/READ_CONTROL GENERIC_READ/);
```

This can be converted back to the list of options using **EnumerateRights**:

```
EnumerateRights($mask, \@rights);
print join(' ', @rights),"\n";
```

Note that the information accepted and returned by these functions is in the form of strings, not strictly constants, although the overall effect is the same.

Win32::IPC

This module provides support for the IPC mechanism within Windows. You shouldn't need to use it directly, since it's automatically included by the modules that require IPC methods. Refer to the documentation if you need to use the module directly.

Win32::Internet

You can download web pages and connect to remote sites using FTP using the **Win32::Internet** module. This module uses the built-in Windows library directly for accessing this information. This is possibly more reliable, but it is also less platform specific than a module such as the **Net::FTP** and **LWP** modules (see Chapter 9). I prefer the **libnet** library because it provides both a cross-platform solution and a more useful set of additional utilities for controlling and accessing Internet information.

The module itself is huge and provides both low-level and high-level interfaces to the underlying Internet libraries supported under Win32. As with other modules in this group, access is via an object and corresponding method calls. The start of all operations is therefore:

```
use Win32::Internet;
$internet = new Win32::Internet();
```

This creates a generic Internet object, and you use the supported methods to define the connection protocol and to exchange information. The supported methods are detailed here.

```
CanonicalizeURL(URL, [flags])
```

Converts a URL into a normalized format, accounting for special characters (which are converted to the correct escape sequences), returning the new URL, or **undef** on error.

```
Close
```

Closes the Internet connection. This is implied when the object is destroyed; you do not need to explicitly close an open connection.

```
CombineURL(BASE, RELATIV [, FLAGS])
```

Combines a **BASE** URL (such as a home page) with a **RELATIVE** URL, returning the resolved URL, which refers directly to the **RELATIVE** URL.

```
ConnectBackoff([VALUE])
```

Reads the value of the connection time-out, defined in milliseconds, if no argument is supplied. If you specify a value, it sets the time-out to that value.

```
ConnectRetries([VALUE])
```

Reads (or sets) the number of times a connection is retried.

```
ConnectTimeout([VALUE])
```

Reads (or sets) the connection time-out value in milliseconds before a connection is defined as a failure.

```
ControlReceiveTimeout([VALUE])
```

Reads or sets the time-out value in milliseconds. Used for FTP control connections.

```
ControlSendTimeout([VALUE])
```

Reads or sets the time-out value in milliseconds. Used for FTP send requests.

```
CrackURL(URL [, FLAGS])
```

Returns an array containing the individual elements of a URL. The returned list contains the following fields: protocol, host, port, login, password, path, and any additional information (such as in-page anchor links).

```
CreateURL(PROTOCOL, HOST, PORT, LOGIN, PASSWORD, PATH, EXTRA [, FLAGS])
CreateURL(HASH [, FLAGS])
```

Returns a URL based on the individual arguments. With the hash version, you must supply a reference to a hash containing the information. The fields of the hash match the order of the argument-based function. They are as follows: **scheme**, **hostname**, **port**, **username**, **password**, **path**, **extrainfo**.

```
DataReceiveTimeout([VALUE])
```

Sets the time-out value, in milliseconds, for use when receiving data.

```
DataSendTimeout([VALUE])
```

Sets the time-out value, in milliseconds, for use when sending data.

```
Error
```

Returns the last error returned by the Win32 Internet subsystem. If the error contains additional information, this is returned as additional elements of the list. There are three levels of error: **1** indicates a trivial module-related error; numbers **1..11999** indicate a generic system error, which can be obtained using the **Win32::GetLastError** function; numbers above 12000 indicate an Internet subsystem error—additional information should have been returned.

Because there is no way of determining the error type until the call has been made, you will need to extract the error number and text when calling and determine later whether the second argument returned should be ignored.

```
FetchURL(URL)
```

Returns the content of **URL**, or **undef** on error.

```
FTP(FTPOBJECT, SERVER, USERNAME, PASSWORD, [PORT, PASV, CONTEXT])
FTP(FTPOBJECT, HASHREF)
```

This opens a connection to an FTP server, using the server and other information provided. Once the connection is complete, a new object is placed in **FTPOBJECT**. The new object can then be used to control the communication with the FTP server, and individual FTP commands are implemented as methods to the new object. If you use the hash method, the names of the hash keys are the lowercase equivalents of the arguments to the scalar version.

```
GetResponse
```

Returns the text received from the remote server in response to the last command transmitted.

```
GetStatusCallback(CONTEXT)
```

Returns information about the current status of an asynchronous operation. The list returned consists of two elements: a status code and an optional piece of information.

```
HTTP(HTTPOBJECT, SERVER, USERNAME, PASSWORD, [PORT, FLAGS, CONTEXT])
HTTP(HTTPOBJECT, HASHREF)
```

Opens an HTTP connection to a remote machine, using the information provided. Once again the hash version uses lowercase versions of the above arguments. The function creates an object in **HTTPOBJECT**, and you can then use the newly created object to access the remote server. The methods supported by the new object have the same names as the equivalent HTTP commands.

```
OpenURL(URLOBJECT, URL)
```

Creates a new object for accessing the information referred to by **URL**.

```
Password([PASSWORD])
```

Reads or sets the password used during an FTP or HTTP connection.

```
QueryDataAvailable
```

Returns the number of bytes in the buffer waiting to be received.

```
QueryOption(OPTION)
```

Queries an Internet option.

```
ReadEntireFile
```

Reads all the data available on an open URL request (via **OpenURL**).

```
ReadFile(EXPR)
```

Reads **EXPR** bytes of data from an open URL request (via **OpenURL**).

```
SetOption(OPTION, VALUE)
```

Sets the Internet option **OPTION** to **VALUE**.

```
SetStatusCallback
```

Initializes a callback routine to be used for accessing information on an asynchronous communications link. If you call this function before accessing a URL, you can use the return value of **GetStatusCallback** to determine whether there is information waiting to be read on a connection, without using a function such as **ReadFile**, which would otherwise block the process.

```
TimeConvert(TIME)
TimeConvert(SECONDS, MINUTE, HOURS, DAY, MONTH, YEAR, DAY_OF_WEEK, RFC)
```

Converts an HTTP date/time string, returning a list of date/time values as defined in the second form. The second form takes a list of the indicated arguments and produces an HTTP-formatted date/time string.

```
UserAgent([NAME])
```

Reads or sets the user agent used for HTTP requests.

```
Username([NAME])
```

Reads or sets the user name in use for the currrent HTTP or FTP connection.

```
Version
```

Returns the version numbers for the **Win32::Internet** module and the corresponding DLL version number for the Internet library.

Win32::Mutex

When accessing a resource on a Windows machine, it is necessary, as with any other shared resource, to control access via a system of resource locking. We looked at the default system in place for file locking in Chapter 6. Because you are dealing with resources, rather than files, which could potentially include printers, network connections, and other elements, you need a different system.

The **Win32::Mutex** module provides mechanisms for creating, working, and destroying with Mutexes. A Mutex is an object used to provide mutually exclusive access to a specific resource. The method is similar to file locks: A process creates a Mutex attached to a particular resource. Only one process can own a Mutex at any one time, and while the process owns it, it has exclusive access to the specified resource.

```
Use Win32::Mutex;
$mutex = new Win32::Mutex([INITIAL, [NAME]])
```

Creates a new Mutex. If **INITIAL** is true, assumes immediate ownership of the mutex. **NAME** is the name of the Mutex you want to create, or it opens an existing Mutex if one with the same name already exists. Alternatively, you can use the method below:

```
$mutex = Win32::Mutex->open(NAME)
```

In this instance you must specify the existing Mutex name.

```
$mutex->release
```

Releases ownership of the Mutex. Returns true if successful.

```
$mutex->wait([TIMEOUT])
```

Waits for the Mutex to be released by another process and immediately sets ownership of it. If **TIMEOUT** is specified, it waits for that number of seconds. If the time-out expires, the function returns false.

Win32::NetAdmin

This module provides control over the users and groups on a system. The functions provided are similar to those supported by both the **Win32API::Net** and **Win32::AdminMisc** modules. Although there is some crossover between this module and the others, there are functions in this module that are not available elsewhere.

```
GetDomainController(MACHINE, DOMAIN, RETURNEDNAME)
```

Returns the name of the primary domain controller for the specified **MACHINE** in **DOMAIN**, placing the name into **RETURNEDNAME**.

```
GetAnyDomainController(MACHINE, DOMAIN, RETURNEDNAME)
```

Returns the name of any domain controller (primary or backup) for the specified **MACHINE** in **DOMAIN**, placing the name into **RETURNEDNAME**.

```
UserCreate(SERVER, USERNAME, PASSWORD, PASSWORDAGE, PRIVILEGE,
           HOMEDIR, COMMENT, FLAGS, SCRIPTPATH)
```

Creates a user on **SERVER** with the properties of the specified arguments.

```
UserDelete(SERVER, USER)
```

Deletes **USER** from **SERVER**.

```
UserGetAttributes(SERVER, USERNAME, PASSWORD, PASSWORDAGE, PRIVILEGE,
                  HOMEDIR, COMMENT, FLAGS, SCRIPTPATH)
```

Gets the information for **USERNAME** from **SERVER**, placing the corresponding information into the supplied argument variables.

```
UserSetAttributes(SERVER, USERNAME, PASSWORD, PASSWORDAGE, PRIVILEGE,
                  HOMEDIR, COMMENT, FLAGS, SCRIPTPATH)
```

Updates the user on **SERVER** with the properties of the specified arguments.

```
UserChangePassword(DOMAINNAME, USERNAME, OLDPASSWORD, NEWPASSWORD)
```

Changes the password for **USERNAME** on **DOMAINNAME**. Because you are required to supply the old password as well as the new, this function can be used by any user.

```
UsersExist(SERVER, USERNAME)
```

Returns true if **USERNAME** exists on **SERVER**.

```
GetUsers(SERVER, FILTER, USERREF)
```

Fills the array pointed to by **USERREF** with the list of users from **SERVER**. If **USERREF** is a hash reference, then the hash contains user names and the corresponding full names. If **FILTER** is not blank, the list is restricted to those users starting with **FILTER**.

```
GroupCreate(SERVER, GROUP, COMMENT)
```

Creates **GROUP** on **SERVER**, with a suitable **COMMENT** if nonblank.

```
GroupDelete(SERVER, GROUP)
```

Deletes **GROUP** on **SERVER**.

```
GroupGetAttributes(SERVER, GROUP, COMMENT)
```

Places the comment for **GROUP** on **SERVER** into **COMMENT**.

```
GroupSetAttributes(SERVER, GROUP, COMMENT)
```

Sets the comment for **GROUP** on **SERVER** from **COMMENT**.

```
GroupAddUsers(SERVER, GROUP, USERS)
```

Adds the list of **USERS** to **GROUP** on **SERVER**.

```
GroupDeleteUsers(SERVER, GROUP, USERS)
```

Deletes the list of **USERS** from **GROUP** on **SERVER**.

```
GroupIsMember(SERVER, GROUP, USER)
```

Returns true if **USER** is a member of **GROUP** on **SERVER**.

```
GroupGetMembers(SERVER, GROUP, USERS)
```

Places the list of users that are members of **GROUP** into the array pointed to by **USERS**.

```
LocalGroupCreate(SERVER, GROUP, COMMENT)
```

Creates the local **GROUP**.

```
LocalGroupDelete(SERVER, GROUP)
```

Deletes the local **GROUP**.

```
LocalGroupGetAttributes(SERVER, GROUP, COMMENT)
```

Gets the comment for the local **GROUP**, putting it into **COMMENT**.

```
LocalGroupSetAttributes(SERVER, GROUP, COMMENT)
```

Sets the comment for the local **GROUP**, from the value in **COMMENT**.

```
LocalGroupIsMember(SERVER, GROUP, USER)
```

Returns true if **USER** is a member of the local **GROUP**.

```
LocalGroupGetMembers(SERVER, GROUP, USERS)
```

Places the list of members of **GROUP** into the array pointed to by **USERS**.

```
LocalGroupGetMembersWithDomain(SERVER, GROUPNAME, USERS)
```

Places a list of users that are members of **GROUP** into the array or hash pointed to by **USERS**. Unlike **LocalGroupGetMembers**, the user names include the domain name, in the form "DOMAIN\USERNAME."

```
LocalGroupAddUsers(SERVER, GROUP, USERS)
```

Adds the list of **USERS** to the local **GROUP**.

```
LocalGroupDeleteUsers(SERVER, GROUP, USERS)
```

Deletes the list of **USERS** from **GROUP**.

```
GetServers(SERVER, DOMAIN, FLAGS, SERVERS)
```

Places a list of server names in the array or hash pointed to by **SERVERS** for the specified **DOMAIN**. If you use a hash, then the values of the hash contain the contents of the comment field for the servers. The **FLAGS** argument specifies a suitable filter to be applied to the list of names returned. The list of valid values, which can be combined using a logical OR, are listed below:

SV_TYPE_WORKSTATION
SV_TYPE_SERVER
SV_TYPE_SQLSERVER
SV_TYPE_DOMAIN_CTRL
SV_TYPE_DOMAIN_BAKCTRL
SV_TYPE_TIMESOURCE

SV_TYPE_AFP
SV_TYPE_NOVELL
SV_TYPE_DOMAIN_MEMBER
SV_TYPE_PRINT
SV_TYPE_PRINTQ_SERVER
SV_TYPE_DIALIN
SV_TYPE_DIALIN_SERVER
SV_TYPE_XENIX_SERVER
SV_TYPE_NT
SV_TYPE_WFW
SV_TYPE_POTENTIAL_BROWSER
SV_TYPE_BACKUP_BROWSER
SV_TYPE_MASTER_BROWSER
SV_TYPE_DOMAIN_MASTER
SV_TYPE_DOMAIN_ENUM
SV_TYPE_SERVER_UNIX
SV_TYPE_SERVER_MFPN
SV_TYPE_SERVER_NT
SV_TYPE_SERVER_OSF
SV_TYPE_SERVER_VMS
SV_TYPE_WINDOWS
SV_TYPE_DFS
SV_TYPE_ALTERNATE_XPORT
SV_TYPE_LOCAL_LIST_ONLY
SV_TYPE_ALL


```
GetTransports(SERVER, TRANSPORTS)
```

Places a list of valid network transports into the array or hash pointed to by **TRANSPORTS**. If you specify a hash reference, then a hash of hashes is created and filled with all the data for the transports.

```
LoggedOnUsers(SERVER, USERS)
```

Places a list of users currently logged into **SERVER** into the array or hash pointed to by **USERS**. If **USERS** is a hash reference, the value is a semicolon-delimited list consisting of the user name, login domain, and server for each user.

```
GetAliasFromRID(SERVER, RID, RETURNEDNAME)
GetUserGroupFromRID(SERVER, RID, RETURNEDNAME)
```

Places the name of an alias or user group for the type specified in **RID** from **SERVER** into the **RETURNEDNAME** scalar. This provides you with the ability to obtain the real name of the specific general entity. Valid values for **RID** are listed below:

```
DOMAIN_ALIAS_RID_ACCOUNT_OPS
DOMAIN_ALIAS_RID_ADMINS
DOMAIN_ALIAS_RID_BACKUP_OPS
DOMAIN_ALIAS_RID_GUESTS
DOMAIN_ALIAS_RID_POWER_USERS
DOMAIN_ALIAS_RID_PRINT_OPS
DOMAIN_ALIAS_RID_REPLICATOR
DOMAIN_ALIAS_RID_SYSTEM_OPS
DOMAIN_ALIAS_RID_USERS
DOMAIN_GROUP_RID_ADMINS
DOMAIN_GROUP_RID_GUESTS
DOMAIN_GROUP_RID_USERS
DOMAIN_USER_RID_ADMIN
DOMAIN_USER_RID_GUEST
```

The individual constants should be self-explanatory.

```
GetServerDisks(SERVER, DRIVES)
```

Places a list of valid disk drives for **SERVER** into the array pointed to by **DRIVES**.

Win32::NetResource

Under Windows, individual resources (drives, printers) can be shared across the network. The **Win32::NetResource** module provides a suite of Perl functions for accessing and controlling the individual net resources.

The module relies on two hash structures, one is the "Net Resource" hash, which defines the format for returning information for an existing (and active) shared network resource. The second is the "Share Info" hash, which defines the information for creating a new shared resource. The formats of these hashes are shown in Tables 22-8 and 22-9, respectively.

The supported functions are as follows:

```
GetSharedResources(NETRESOURCES, TYPE)
```

Creates an array of Net Resource hashes in **NETRESOURCES**, using the specified **TYPE** (see Table 22-8).

Key	Value
Scope	The scope of the shared resource, which can be one of: **RESOURCE_CONNECTED** **RESOURCE_GLOBALNET** **RESOURCE_REMEMBERED**
Type	The type of resource to list: **RESOURCETYPE_ANY** **RESOURCETYPE_DISK** **RESOURCETYPE_PRINT**
DisplayType	The format of the returned resource information, which can be set using one of the following constants: **RESOURCEDISPLAYTYPE_DOMAIN** **RESOURCEDISPLAYTYPE_GENERIC** **RESOURCEDISPLAYTYPE_SERVER** **RESOURCEDISLPAYTYPE_SHARE**
Usage	Defines the resource's usage: **RESOURCEUSAGE_CONNECTABLE** **RESOURCEUSAGE_CONTAINER**
LocalName	The name of the local device the resource is connected to.
RemoteName	The network name/address of the resource.
Comment	The comment for the resource.
Provider	The name of the provider of the resource.

Table 22-8. *Net Resource Info*

Key	Description
netname	The share name.
type	The share type.
remark	Comment.
permissions	Share permissions.

Table 22-9. *Elements of the Share Info Hash*

Key	Description
maxusers	The maximum number of users able to connect to the shared resource.
current-users	The current number of users accessing the shared resource.
path	The absolute path to the shared resource.
passwd	The password required to use the shared resource.

Table 22-9. *Elements of the Share Info Hash* (continued)

```
AddConnection(NETRESOURCE, PASSWORD, USERNAME, CONNECTION)
```

Creates a connection to the network resource specified by the **NETRESOURCE** hash. The connection uses the **PASSWORD** and **USERNAME** if specified. The value of **CONNECTION** is either 1 for a persistent connection or zero for a temporary connection.

```
CancelConnection(NAME, CONNECTION, FORCE)
```

Cancels the connection **NAME**. If **FORCE** is 1, then the connection is canceled even if any errors that require intervention occur. **CONNECTION** was defined as persistent.

```
WNetGetLastError(ERRORCODE, DESCRIPTION, NAME)
```

Returns the error code, description, and name into the corresponding function arguments for the last network error.

```
GetError(ERRORCODE)
```

Gets the last error from a function call, placing the error code into **ERRORCODE**.

```
GetUNCName(UNCNAME, $LOCALPATH)
```

Returns the UNC (Universal Naming Convention) name for the specified **LOCALPATH**, placing the new name in **UNCNAME**.

```
NetShareAdd(SHARE, ERROR, SERVERNAME)
```

Adds a share using the information in the Share Info hash pointed to by **SHARE**. Errors are placed into **ERROR**. The value of **SERVERNAME** should be a valid machine in the local domain. This is generally zero.

```
NetShareCheck(DEVICE, TYPE, SERVER)
```

Checks if a share on **DEVICE** of the specified **TYPE** on **SERVER** is available to connect to.

```
NetShareDel(NETNAME, SERVER)
```

Removes the share **NETNAME** from **SERVER**.

```
NetShareGetInfo(NETNAME, SHARE, SERVER)
```

Inserts the information for the share called **NETNAME** on **SERVER** into the Share Info hash pointed to by **SHARE**.

```
NetShareSetInfo(NETNAME, SHARE, ERROR, SERVER)
```

Sets the information for the shared resource **NETNAME** to the values configured in **SHARE** on **SERVER**. Any errors are placed into **ERROR**.

Win32::ODBC

ODBC, short for Open Database Connectivity, is the database interface supported on Windows platforms. The **Win32::ODBC** module provides a direct method for accessing ODBC databases, which can be anything from traditional relational databases such as Microsoft Access or SQL Server to the more mundane sources such as Excel spreadsheets. If you want a cross-platform–capable system, you should look at the **DBI/DBD** toolkits, discussed in Chapter 8 and in the interface and drivers listed in Appendix F.

```
$database = new Win32::ODBC("DSN");
```

The DSN (Data Source Name) should be a recognized DSN, or it can be a DSN string. Check your documentation for more details. The new object will be undefined if the connection could not be made. Once opened, the object can be used to submit queries and retrieve information from the database. Unlike other objects in these modules, you must explicitly close the connection once you have finished using it:

```
$database->Close();
```

Other functions/methods are listed below. Refer to the documentation for your ODBC source for more information on how to use and access the data. Remember that accessing data from an ODBC source requires knowledge of SQL, the Structured Query Language.

```
Catalog(QUALIFIER, OWNER, NAME, TYPE)
```

Creates a new data set that contains the information for all the tables in the connection. You can restrict the search with **QUALIFIER**, **OWNER**, **NAME**, and **TYPE**. You need to use the **Fetch** and **Data** or **DataHash** functions to extract the data into a Perl structure.

```
ColAttributes(ATTRIBUTE, [FIELDNAMES])
```

Returns the attribute value for **ATTRIBUTE** on each of the fields **FIELDNAMES**, or all fields if they are not listed.

```
ConfigDSN(OPTION, DRIVER, (ATTRIBUTE1 [, ATTRIBUTE2, ATTRIBUTE3, ...]))
```

Configures the DSN. **OPTIONS** can be one of **ODBC_ADD_DSN**, which adds a new DSN; **ODBC_MODIFY_DSN**, which modifies an existing DSN; and **ODBC_REMOVE_DSN**, which removes an existing DSN. The **DRIVER** is the name of a valid driver. Use **DataSources** or **Drivers** to determine the available list. The attributes should be in the normal "ATTR=VALUE" format associated with DSN connections.

```
Connection()
```

Returns the connection number associated with the current ODBC connection.

```
Data([FIELDNAME])
```

Returns the data for **FIELDNAME** of the current data row.

```
DataHash([FIELD1, FIELD2, FIELD3, ...])
```

Returns a hash of all fields, or the fields specified for the current data row. The keys of the hash are the field names, and the values are the corresponding values.

```
DataSources()
```

Returns a hash of data sources and their descriptions.

```
Debug([1|0])
```

Switches debugging on and off.

```
Drivers()
```

Returns a hash of ODBC drivers and their attributes. Attributes are separated by commas.

```
DropCursor([CLOSETYPE])
```

Drops (deletes) the current cursor. The **CLOSETYPE** can be any valid close type supported by the ODBC driver.

```
DumpData()
```

Dumps the records for the current data set to the screen.

```
Error()
```

Returns the last error from the ODBC source. If you call the function in scalar context, it returns a string consisting of the error number, connection number, and associated error text. In a list context, it returns three values: the error number, error text, and connection number. Note the difference in order!

If debugging is enabled, then it also supplies the function in which the error occurred and additional error information returned by the function.

```
FetchRow([ROW [, TYPE]])
```

Retrieves the next row from the key set.

```
FieldNames()
```

Returns an array of field names from the current data set.

```
GetConnections()
```

Returns an array of currently open connection numbers.

```
GetConnectOption(OPTION)
```

Returns the value of the specified connection **OPTION**. Options are unique for different ODBC sources.

```
GetCursorName()
```

Returns the name of the current cursor.

```
GetData()
```

Retrieves the current row from the data set.

```
GetDSN([DSN])
```

Returns a hash containing the configuration information for the specified or current DSN.

```
GetFunctions([FUNCTION1, FUNCTION2, ...])
```

Returns a hash indicating the list of supported abilities/functions for the current ODBC connection. If you specify the individual functions, it only returns true for each valid function.

```
GetInfo(OPTION)
```

Returns the value of the specified option.

```
GetMaxBufSize()
```

Returns the maximum buffer size.

```
GetStmtCloseType([CONNECTION])
```

Returns the type of close that will be used each time the query statement is freed.

```
GetStmtOption($Option)
```

Returns the value of the statement option defined by **OPTION**.

```
MoreResults()
```

Returns true if there is more information to be returned from the query.

```
new(OBJECT | DSN [, (OPTION1, VALUE1), (OPTION2, VALUE2) ...])
```

Creates a new ODBC connection using the specified **OBJECT** or **DSN**. If you specify an existing object, then the connection will be duplicated.

```
RowCount(CONNECTION)
```

Returns the number of rows that are affected by the SQL **UPDATE**, **INSERT**, or **DELETE**.

```
Run(SQL)
```

Executes **SQL** statement, reporting data to the screen in the process. This is effectively a debugged version of the **Sql** function.

```
SetConnectOption(OPTION)
```

Sets the specified **OPTION** for the connection. Options are unique for the destination data source.

```
SetCursorName(NAME)
```

Sets the name of the current data cursor.

```
SetPos(ROW [, OPTION, LOCK])
```

Moves the data cursor to the specified **ROW** within the current keyset.

```
SetMaxBufSize(SIZE)
```

Configures the maximum size for the memory buffer used to hold data between the ODBC connection and Perl. The buffer size should increase automatically; you should only need this function to increase the maximum upper limit.

```
SetStmtCloseType(TYPE [, CONNECTION])
```

Sets the statement close type to **TYPE** for the current connection, or for the connection specified in **CONNECTION**. Valid types are **SQL_CLOSE**, **SQL_DROP**, **SQL_UNBIND**, **SQL_RESET_PARAMS**.

```
SetStmtOption(OPTION)
```

Configures options for a statement. This is unique for each ODBC source. Returns false if the change was unsuccessful.

```
ShutDown()
```

Closes the ODBC connection, dumping information about the connection during the process. This is effectively a debugging version of **Close**.

```
Sql(EXPR)
```

Executes the SQL expression **EXPR**.

```
TableList(QUALIFIER, OWNER, NAME, TYPE)
```

Returns a list of tables defined within the database connection. You can restrict the search using the **QUALIFIER**, **OWNER**, **NAME**, and **TYPE**. If they are blank, then it returns a list of all the available tables.

```
Transact(TYPE)
```

TYPE can be one of two types: **SQL_COMMIT**, which commits a transaction, and **SQL_ROLLBACK**, which rolls back a transaction. The ODBC connection must support the transaction. Returns false on error.

```
Version(LIST)
```

Returns a list of version numbers for the specified **LIST**.

Win32::OLE

The OLE (Object Linking and Embedding) system provides a mechanism within Perl for communicating with external OLE objects. The OLE system is used extensively within Windows for controlling and communicating between applications. The **Win32::OLE** module enables you to access and control an application directly from Perl. You will need to know the principles and basics of OLE automation to make use of this module. See Chapter 25 for an example involving Excel.


```
$ole = new Win32::OLE(PROGID [, DESTRUCTOR])
```

This creates a new OLE object for accessing an external application. The **PROGID** should be the name of a valid OLE object. This is typically an application, such as "Word.Application," but can be any valid OLE program. The **DESTRUCTOR** is an optional OLE function to call when the object is destroyed. Again, this should be an OLE function to be called on destruction—often the quit function to the application—so that it automatically closes when you have finished with it.

Once opened, you need to access the individual components of the OLE object using normal hash dereferences. Again, use the example in Chapter 25 as a guide.

```
Win32::OLE->GetActiveObject(CLASS)
```

This returns a reference to an OLE automation server and can be used to detect whether a particular application is installed on a machine. For example:

```
eval {$ex = Win32::OLE->GetActiveObject('Excel.Application')};
die "Excel not installed" if $@;
```

It returns **undef** if the OLE server is not running.

```
Win32::OLE->GetObject(OBJECT)
```

Returns an OLE reference to the object specified by **OBJECT**.

```
Win32::OLE->Initialize(COINIT)
```

Specifies an alternative apartment for the Perl interpreter. This method must be called before the first OLE object is created. The defined constants for **COINIT** are**Win32::OLE::COINIT_APARTMENTTHREADED** for single-threaded operation, **Win32::OLE::COINIT_MULTITHREADED**, for multithreaded operation (the default), and **Win32::OLE::COINIT_OLEINITIALIZE** for single-threaded operation with additional initialization abilities. This last option is sometimes needed when an external OLE object uses a nonstandard object model, which then requires additional OLE components in order to execute properly.

```
Invoke(METHOD, ARGS)
```

Invokes the specified OLE **METHOD** with the arguments specified in **ARGS**. This is equivalent to using **$oleobject->METHOD(ARGS)**.

```
LastError()
```

Returns the last error generated by the **OLE** object.

```
QueryObjectType(OBJECT)
```

Returns a list of the type libraries and object class for the specified **OBJECT**.

```
SetProperty(NAME, ARG, VALUE)
```

Modifies the property **NAME** using the additional arguments **ARGS**, setting the value of the property **VALUE**.

```
Win32::OLE->SpinMessageLoop
```

Retrieves all pending messages from the OLE message queue and sends them on to their corresponding window destinations.

```
Win32::OLE->Uninitialize
```

Uninitializes the OLE system and effectively disables the OLE system until a new initialization call is made or a new object is created.

Win32::PerfLib

Supports an interface to the Windows NT performance system. You can access the performance information on any Windows NT machine over the network (provided you have suitable access privileges).

```
$perflib = Win32::PerfLib->new (SERVER)
```

Creates a new performance object, connecting to **SERVER**. The data structures and contents are complex and may need further processing, which is beyond the scope of this book. Refer to the documentation for more information on these structures and calculations. The functions/methods are listed below, however.

```
Win32::PerfLib::GetCounterNames(SERVER, HASH)
```

Places the performance information for the counters and the related indices into the hash pointed to by **HASH**.

```
Win32::PerfLib::GetCounterHelp(SERVER, HASH)
```

Places the counter help strings into **HASH** from **SERVER**.

```
$perflib->GetObjectList(OBJECT,HASH)
```

Gets the object and counter information into **HASH** using the details in **OBJECT**.

```
$perflib->Close($hashref)
```

Closes the connection to the performance library.

```
Win32::PerfLib::GetCounterType(COUNTERTYPE)
```

Converts **COUNTERTYPE** to a readable string.

Win32::Pipe

Communicating between processes can be complex (just check Chapter 10), and not all the methods that have been described work under the different Windows platforms. A better solution is to use a Win32 named pipe, using the **Win32::Pipe** module. This gets around the limitation of the **pipe** function while providing a simple communication system that works across a network if you create the named pipe on a networked file system.

```
use Win32::Pipe;

$pipe = new Win32::Pipe(EXPR);
```

Creates a pipe with the name **EXPR**. If the pipe already exists, then **EXPR** should be the network path to the existing pipe file. Remaining methods are detailed below:

```
BufferSize()
```

Returns the current buffer size.

```
Connect()
```

Tells the named pipe object to create an instance of the named pipe and wait until a client connects.

```
Disconnect()
```

Disconnects the named pipe.

```
Error()
```

Returns the last error message.

```
Read()
```

Reads data from the named pipe.

```
ResizeBuffer(SIZE)
```

Sets the buffer size to **SIZE**.

```
Write(EXPR)
```

Writes **EXPR** to the named pipe.

Win32::Process

This module allows you to create manageable Win32 processes within Perl. The core of the module is the **Create** function:

```
use Win32;
use Win32::Process;

$process = Win32::Process::Create(APPL, CMDLINE, IHANDLES, OPTIONS, DIR)
```

The above line creates a new object in **$process**. **APPL** is the full pathname of the application you want to run. **CMDLINE** is how the command line would appear if you were to execute it within the **cmd** shell. **IHANDLES** defines whether the new process should inherit the filehandles of the caller. The **OPTIONS** is a list of flags that control the execution options of the process you are calling. **DIR** is the working directory of the new process.

For example:

```
$process = Win32::Process::Create("C:\\WinNT\\system32\\notepad.exe",
                                  "notepad source.txt",
                                  0,
                                  NORMAL_PRIORITY_CLASS,
                                  ".");
```

The flags to the process are defined in Table 22-10.

Flag	Description
CREATE_DEFAULT_ERROR_MODE	Gives the new process the default error mode.
CREATE_NEW_CONSOLE	The new process has a new console window created for it. This cannot be used with the **DETACHED_PROCESS** flag.
CREATE_NEW_PROCESS_GROUP	The new process is the root of a new process group.
CREATE_SEPARATE_WOW_VDM	The new process runs in its own 16-bit Virtual DOS Machine compartment.
CREATE_SUSPENDED	Starts the new process in a suspended (nonexecuting) state.
CREATE_UNICODE_ENVIRONMENT	The new process environment contains support for Unicode characters.
DEBUG_PROCESS	Sets up the called process to be debugged, using the calling Perl script as the debugger.
DEBUG_ONLY_THIS_PROCESS	The new process is not debugged, even if the current script is running in debug mode.

Table 22-10. *Option Flags When Creating a New Process*

Once created, the new process can be controlled via the created object and a number of methods:

```
$process->Suspend()
```

Suspends the process.

```
$process->Resume()
```

Resumes a process suspended either by the **Suspend** method or if the process was created with the **CREATE_SUSPENDED** flag.

```
$process->Kill($ExitCode)
```

Kills the process, causing it to die with the exit value specified by **$ExitCode**.

```
$process->GetPriorityClass($class)
```

Gets the priority class of the process.

```
$process->SetPriorityClass($class)
```

Sets the priority class of the process to the value of **$class**. The valid values are defined by a number of constants, listed in Table 22-11.

```
$process->GetProcessAffinitymask($processAffinityMask, $systemAffinitymask)
```

Gets a bitvector specifying the processors on which the process can run.

```
$process->SetProcessAffinitymask($processAffinityMask)
```

Sets the affinity mask that specifies the processors on which the process can run.

```
$process->GetExitCode($ExitCode)
```

Gets the exit code of the process.

```
$process->Wait($Timeout)
```

Waits for the specified process to die, waiting for a maximum of **$Timeout** seconds. The return value of **Wait** is false if the wait times out, setting the error code in **$!** to

Priority Class	Description
IDLE_PRIORITY_CLASS	The process will only run when the system is idle, soaking up all the available processor time that is left.
NORMAL_PRIORITY_CLASS	Standard process scheduling.
HIGH_PRIORITY_CLASS	Process runs at a higher than normal level, gaining more processor time.
REALTIME_PRIORITY_CLASS	Runs at the highest available priority. May cause a machine lockup if the process is not otherwise controlled properly, since it will suck up all available processor time.

Table 22-11. *Available Priority Classes for Processes*

WAIT_FAILED (see the **Win32::WinError** module). You can also use the predefined constant **INFINITE** to wait forever.

Win32::Registry

This module provides an interface to the Windows registry. See the **Win32::TieRegistry** module below for a more pragmatic interface. This module also defines many of the constants used in that module. There are too many to list here. Refer to the module for more information.

Win32::Semaphore

This module provides access to the Win32 semaphore system, which operates in a similar way to the equivalent System V IPC semaphores (see Chapter 10).

```
use Win32;
use Win32::Semaphore;

$sobj = Win32::Semaphore->new(INITIALCOUNT, MAXCOUNT, NAME);
```

The new object reference is placed into **$sobj**, the **INITIALCOUNT** argument specifies the initial semaphore value, and **MAXCOUNT** specifies the maximum value for the semaphore. The optional **NAME** is the name of an existing semaphore created by another process.

The **Wait** method waits for the semaphore to be released (see below):

```
$sobj->Wait($timeout);
```

The **$timeout** value is the number of seconds to wait for the semaphore to become free.

Once you have finished using a semaphore, you need to release it with the **Release** method:

```
$sobj->Release($ReleaseCount, $lastCount);
```

The value of the semaphore is increased by the value of **$ReleaseCount**, and the optional **$lastcount** is used to store the previous value. If **$ReleaseCount** plus **$lastcount** is greater than the **MAXCOUNT** value, then the value is not incremented.

Win32::Service

You can control Windows NT services directly within Perl using the **Win32::Service** module. This provides a functional interface to the service manager on a Windows NT machine. Because of NT's ability to manage machines remotely, the services for an individual machine can be controlled both locally and across the network, provided you have suitable privileges (administrator access) within the domain to which the machine belongs.

The module supports six functions, outlined below. As usual, you must use the **GetLastError** to determine whether the request to start, stop, pause, or resume the specified service properly. See the example at the end of the chapter for a sample service management script. The module does not import these functions into the calling package's name space, you must use the function names explicitly in your scripts.

```
StartService (HOST, SERVICE)
```

Starts **SERVICE** on **HOST**.

```
StopService(HOST, SERVICE)
```

Stops **SERVICE** on **HOST**.

```
GetStatus(HOST, SERVICE, STATUS)
```

Gets the status of **SERVICE** on **HOST**, placing the information into the hash pointed to by **STATUS**. The returned hash contains a number of keys, as shown in Table 22-12.

Key	Description
SeviceType	The type of service, as defined by one of the following constants: **SERVICE_WIN32_OWN_PROCESS** **SERVICE_WIN32_SHARE_PROCESS** **SERVICE_KERNEL_DRIVER** **SERVICE_FILE_SYSTEM_DRIVER**.
CurrentState	The status of the service. This is a combination of the "Status" and "Startup" information provided in the Services control panel. Valid constants for comparison are **SERVICE_START_PENDING** **SERVICE_STOP_PENDING** **SERVICE_RUNNING** **SERVICE_CONTINUE_RUNNING** **SERVICE_PAUSE_PENDING** **SERVICE_PAUSED**.
ControlsAccepted	The list of control codes accepted by the command.
Win32ExitCode	The generic error code returned when the service starts or stops.
ServiceSpecificExitCode	A service-specific error code.
CheckPoint	A simple increment that increases as the service runs; usually zero.
WaitHint	An estimate, in milliseconds, of the time left before the current state completes. A value of zero indicates that there is no pending change of state.

Table 22-12. *Status Information for a Running Service*


```
PauseService(HOST, SERVICE)
```

Pauses **SERVICE** on **HOST**, but doesn't actually stop it.

```
ResumeService(HOST, SERVICE)
```

Resumes a paused **SERVICE** on **HOST**.

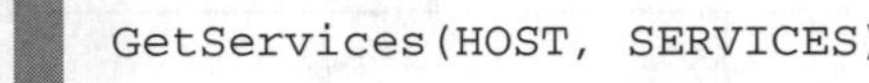

```
GetServices(HOST, SERVICES)
```

Gets a list of services from **HOST** and places the list into the hash referred to by **SERVICES**. The keys of the hash contain the full service name and the values of the shortened versions.

Win32::Shortcut

This module provides a simple hash-based interface to the shortcuts on Windows ("links" under Unix and "aliases" under MacOS):

```
use Win32::Shortcut;

$link = new Win32::Shortcut();
```

The above code creates a new **Win32::Shortcut** object, but does not automatically associate it with an existing file. For that you use the **Load** method:

```
$link->Load("C:\Everything.lnk");
```

Or you can combine the two by specifying the name of the link you want to load during object creation:

```
$link = new Win32::Shortcut("C:\Everything.lnk");
```

If you are creating a new link, just create the object, and then set the properties for it (see below) and use the **Save** method to create the shortcut file on disk:

```
$link->Save("C:\Nothing.lnk");
```

If you omit the file name in the method call, the method will take the name from the "File" property.

To resolve a shortcut without accessing the properties for the object, you can use the **Resolve** method:

```
$real=$link->Resolve();
```

If you supply a zero as the argument to the method, a dialog will be posted if the shortcut cannot be resolved to an existing file.

The **Set** method enables you to set the properties for a shortcut without using the hash method for accessing the properties:

```
$link->Set(PATH, ARGS, WORKINGDIR, DESC,
           SHOWCMD, HOTKEY, ICONFILE, ICONNUMBER);
```

A more pragmatic way of doing this is to use the object as a hash reference and access or update the information using the available list of properties, shown in Table 22-13. These are all equivalent to the individual boxes and options in a Properties dialog.

Property	Description
Arguments	The arguments to the file or command being linked to. This is the second half of the Target box in the Properties dialog.
Description	An optional description.
File	The name of the shortcut file. This is the location of the actual shortcut on disk, *not* the name of the file you are linking to.
Hotkey	The 2-byte shortcut key.
IconLocation	The path to the file that contains the icon you want to use for the shortcut.
IconNumber	The number of the icon within the **IconLocation** file.
Path	The path to the target file.
ShortPath	The DOS 8.3 character-compatible version of **Path**.
ShowCmd	The style of window in which the command will be executed. Can be one of **SW_SHOWNORMAL**, **SW_SHOWMAXIMIZED**, or **SW_SHOWMINNOACTIVE**, for normal, maximized, and minimized windows.
WorkingDirectory	The directory in which **Path** will be executed. Identical to the “Start in” field in the Properties dialog.

Table 22-13. *Shortcut Properties*

Once you have finished with the object, you can explicitly close it with the **Close** method, or just let it run out of scope.

Win32::Sound

This module provides a mechanism for playing external WAV files within Perl, or for playing one of the predefined sound names configured via the Sound control panel.

```
use Win32::Sound;

Win32::Sound::Play(SOUND, FLAG);
```

Plays the WAV file specified in **SOUND** or one the following predefined sound names:

```
SystemDefault
SystemAsterisk
SystemExclamation
SystemExit
SystemHand
SystemQuestion
SystemStart
```

The flags define the method used to play the sound, as shown in Table 22-14.

Flag	Description
SND_ASYNC	Sound is played asynchronously; the process does not block when the sound starts playing, and the function call returns immediately.
SND_LOOP	Sound loops repeatedly. You should specify **SND_ASYNC** as well, otherwise the process will block completely.
SND_NODEFAULT	Does not play the default sound if the sound you specify cannot be found.
SND_NOSTOP	Causes the function to fail if a sound is currently playing. Without this option, a sound already playing will stop in order to play the newly supplied sound.

Table 22-14. *Flags for Playing Sounds*

If you do not specify a sound, or if the sound you specify cannot be found, then the default Windows sound will be played instead. To switch this off, use the **SND_NODEFAULT** flag. To stop an asynchronous sound from playing, call the function again (with **SND_NOSTOP** if required), or use the **Win32::Sound::Stop** function.

Win32::TieRegistry

The **Win32API::Registry** and **Win32:Registry** support access to the Windows registry database. However, the method of access is less than clean, considering the systems available for accessing complex information within Perl. The **Win32::TieRegistry** supports a combination object/tied hash interface to the registry information that is more flexible and more Perl-like in its usage.

The Windows registry is a complex informational source, and using it without knowledge of its layout and the dangers associated with making modifications is not advised.

The method for using it is to import the **Win32::TieRegistry** module, which then provides immediate access to a **$Registry** object:

```
use Win32::TieRegistry(Delimiter => '/');
```

The delimiter arguments define the delimiter you want to use when accessing registry elements. To access a registry entry:

```
$swroot = $Registry->{"LMachine/Software/"};
```

The root of the registry is split into seven sections, which the **TieRegistry** module uses aliases for, as seen in Table 22-15.

The return value is a new object/hash reference that can be used to select further keys within a specific class. For example, to access the "Hewlett-Packard" key within the "Software" key:

```
$hpkeyroot = $swroot->{"Hewlett-Packard/"};
```

The trailing delimiter is required to indicate that you are accessing a root key and want an object returned, rather than the relevant key value, as in:

```
$installdir = $hpkeyroot->{"OfficeJet Series 600/Env/InstallRoot"};
```

Registry Root	TieRegistry Root
HKEY_CLASSES_ROOT	Classes
HKEY__CURRENT_USER	CUser
HKEY_LOCAL_MACHINE	LMachine
HKEY_USERS	Users
HKEY_PERFORMANCE_DATA	PerfData
HKEY_CURRENT_CONFIG	CConfig
HKEY_DYN_DATA	DynData

Table 22-15. ***TieRegistry*** *Root Keys*

If you want to obtain the data type for the specified value, then you must call the **ArrayValues** method:

```
$hpkeyroot->ArrayValues(1);
($installdir, $type) = $hpkeyroot->{"OfficeJet Series 600/Env/InstallRoot"};
```

The **$type** variable will now contain one of the registry types you have already seen in the **Win32::Registry** module above.

To update a value, you can simply assign the new value:

```
$hpkeyroot->{"OfficeJet Series 600/Env/InstallRoot"} = "E:\TEMP";
```

This assumes a data type of **REG_SZ**. If you want to assign a different data type, you can supply the data and type as an array reference:

```
$hpkeyroot->{"OfficeJet Series 600/Env/InstallRoot"}
                              = [ "E:\TEMP", "REG_MULTI_SZ" ];
```

Remember, though, if you want to assign a **BINARY** or **DWORD** value, you'll need to use **pack** to convert the value into a suitable format.

Other features work as you would expect. You can extract all the keys and values for a class, using **keys** and **values** and then use **grep** to extract the individual elements you're looking for. For example:

```
@swkeys = keys (%{$swroot->{"/"}});
```

Win32::WinError

This module provides the list of errors and error numbers used by the main **Win32::GetLastError** function. The list of supported error constants is far too long to list here.View the module source for a complete listing.

Win32::AdminMisc

The **Win32::AdminMisc** is a completely separate module, developed by Dave Roth (see Appendix A). It provides a number of administration functions that cross the boundaries of many of the functions in the main Win32 module set supplied with the ActiveState version.

CreateProcessAsUser

```
CreateProcessAsUser(CMD [, DIR]  [, CONFIG])
```

Creates a new process, using the command defined by **CMD**, in the directory **DIR** if defined. The **CONFIG** argument should be a hash defined using the values shown in Table 22-16.

Hash Element	Description
Title	The title of the processes window.
Desktop	A virtual desktop. Leave this blank if you are not familiar with it. The default is "winsta0\default".
X	The X coordinate of the upper left corner of the processes window.
Y	The Y corrdinate of the upper-left corner of the processes window.
XSize	The width of the processes window (in pixels).
YSize	The height of the processes window (in pixels).
XBuffer	Number of chars the X buffer should be. This applies only to console applications.
YBuffer	Number of chars the Y buffer should be. This applies only to console applications.

Table 22-16. *Options for the **CreateNewProcess** Function*

Hash Element	Description
Fill	The background color of the console window. Values can be logically **or**'d together: **BACKGROUND_RED** **BACKGROUND_BLUE** **BACKGROUND_GREEN** **BACKGROUND_INTENSITY** **FOREGROUND_RED** **FOREGROUND_GREEN** **FOREGROUND_BLUE** **FOREGROUND_INTENSITY**
Priority	The priority to use when running the process. See Table 22-2.
Flags	The process startup options. The values, as defined in Table 22-1, can be logically **or**'d together.
Show Window	The state of the process window during startup. The predefined constants are **SW_HIDE** **SW_MAXIMIZE** **SW_MINIMIZE** **SW_RESTORE** **SW_SHOW** **SW_SHOWDEFAULT** **SW_SHOWMAXIMIZED** **SW_SHOWMINIMIZED** **SW_SHOWMINNOACTIVE** **SW_SHOWNOACTIVATE** **SW_SHOWNORMAL**
StdInput StdOutput StdError	The filehandles to be used for the corresponding input, output, and error streams. You must define all these values explicitly if you want to define only one of the values. Use the **GetStdHandle** function to retrieve a reference to the current standard handle.
Inherit	Causes the subprocess to inherit the currently open filehandles in the calling script.
Directory	Specifies the directory in which the new process should run; equivalent to the **DIR** function argument.

Table 22-16. *Options for the **CreateNewProcess** Function* (continued)

The function returns the ID of the newly created process on success, or **undef** on error. Use the **Win32::GetLastError** function to check the reason for the error.

DelEnvVar

```
DelEnvVar(NAME [, TYPE] [, TIMEOUT])
```

The environment variables on a Windows machine can be modified locally with the **%ENV** hash, but to modify the environment variables used for all processes, you need to use the **DelEnvVar** function. This deletes both system- and user-defined environment variables directly.

The **NAME** is the name of the environment variable, and the type is **ENV_SYSTEM** by default, but you can also use **ENV_USER** to delete a user environmental variable. The optional **TIMEOUT** specifies the number of seconds that the change notification should be broadcast. If the time-out value is reached, the variable is still deleted, but the broadcast will be aborted.

The function returns 1 if successful, or zero on failure.

DNSCache

```
DNSCache([1|0])
```

Switches the local DNS cache on (1) or off (0), returning the new status. If nothing is supplied, no changes are made, but cache status is still returned.

DNSCacheCount

```
DNSCacheCount()
```

Returns the number of elements in the DNS cache.

DNSCacheSize

```
DNSCacheSize([SIZE])
```

Sets the size of the DNS cache to **SIZE**, returning the new current size. If the **SIZE** is not specified, it simply returns the current size.

ExitWindows

```
ExitWindows(FLAG)
```

Exits the current Windows session, using the method defined in the **FLAG**. Valid values are listed in Table 22-17.

The function returns zero if the operation was unsuccessful, or non-zero if the instruction to exit Windows was accepted successfully.

GetComputerName

```
GetComputerName()
```

Returns the Windows NT node name for the current machine. Equivalent to the **Win32::GetNodeName** function.

GetDC

```
GetDC(DOMAIN)
```

Returns the domain controller of **DOMAIN** if specified, or the domain controller of the current domain if none is specified. Returns the **undef** value if the name of the domain controller cannot be determined.

GetDrives

```
GetDrives([TYPE])
```

Flag	Description
EWX_LOGOFF	Log the user off, but don't shut down Windows. Applications will be asked to shut down gracefully.
EWX_POWEROFF	Shut down the machine, and switch off the power if power management is supported.
EWX_REBOOT	Shut down and reboot.
EWX_SHUTDOWN	Shut down the system, but don't power off or reboot.
EWX_FORCE	Log the user off, forcing applications to quit immediately.

Table 22-17. *Flags for Signifying the Method to Exit Windows*

Returns a list of valid drive letters for the current machine. If **TYPE** is specified, then it only returns the drive letters of the specified type. The list of valid type constants is shown in Table 22-18.

The function returns a list of letters, or an empty list if none of the specified types are found.

GetDriveType

```
GetDriveType(DRIVE)
```

Returns an integer relating to the drive type for **DRIVE** (such as "C:\"). Valid constants are listed in Table 22-18. On error it returns zero if the test was unsuccessful, and 1 if the type was unable to be determined.

GetDriveSpace

```
GetDriveSpace(DRIVE)
```

Returns an array consisting of the total drive capacity and free space on the specified **DRIVE**. In addition to the drive letter, you can also explicitly request the information from a remote mount such as "\\Atuin\MC\," but note that you must add the trailing slash. Returns nothing if the information could not be determined.

GetEnvVar

```
GetEnvVar(NAME [, TYPE])
```

Constant	Description
DRIVE_FIXED	Any fixed media (hard drive).
DRIVE_REMOVABLE	Any removable media.
DRIVE_REMOTE	Any drive remotely mounted from another machine.
DRIVE_CDROM	Any CD-ROM drive.
DRIVE_RAMDISK	Any drive emulated within memory.

Table 22-18. *Valid Drive Filters*

Returns the value of the environment variable **NAME**. If **TYPE** is specified, then it must be one of **ENV_SYSTEM** for a system variable or **ENV_USER** for a user variable. Returns **undef** if the variable could not be found.

GetFileInfo

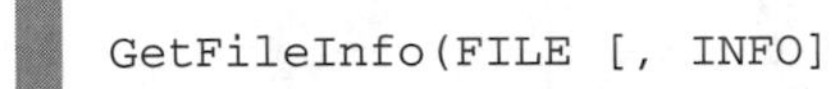

```
GetFileInfo(FILE [, INFO])
```

Places the attribute information for **FILE** into the hash pointed to by **INFO**. Returns 1 if successful, zero otherwise.

GetGroups

```
GetGroups([ MACHINE|DOMAIN ], TYPE, LIST [, PREFIX])
```

This will return a list of user groups that are of **TYPE**, placing the information into the array or hash reference pointed to by **LIST**. **TYPE** can be one of **GROUP_TYPE_LOCAL** (returns an array), which lists only groups defined only on the specified machine, or **GROUP_TYPE_GLOBAL** (array), which lists all groups defined in the current domain. You can also set **GROUP_TYPE_ALL** (hash) to get a list of all the groups, local and global.

The first parameter is either a server name, as in "\\Server," or a domain name such as "MCSLP." This value determines which machine will be used to determine the list of groups. If undefined, it uses the local machine. Returns a zero if the search was unsuccessful, 1 otherwise.

GetHostAddress

```
GetHostAddress(NAME)
```

Gets a host address using DNS, returning an IP address for the machine **NAME**.

GetHostName

```
GetHostName(ADDRESS)
```

Gets a host name from the supplied IP **ADDRESS**.

gethostbyname

```
gethostbyname(NAME)
```

Gets a host address using DNS, returning an IP address for the machine **NAME**.

gethostbyaddr

```
gethostbyaddr(ADDRESS)
```

Gets a host name from the supplied IP **ADDRESS**.

GetIdInfo

```
GetIdInfo()
```

Returns an array of information for the current thread/process:

```
($pid, $tid, $ppriority, $tpriority, $cmd) = GetIdInfo();
```

The elements are the process ID, the thread ID, the process priority, the thread priority, and the command line used to execute the script.

GetLogonName

```
GetLogonName
```

This returns the name of the user this account is logged on as. This is not necessarily the same as the user under which the script is running, since you can masquerade as another user under Windows the same way you can with setuid scripts under Unix. This correctly reflects the login account rather than the current user value returned by **Win32::GetLogonName**.

GetMachines

```
GetMachines(SERVER, TYPE, LIST [, PREFIX])
```

Populates **LIST**, which should be a reference to an array or hash, containing the names of computers matching **TYPE**. The **TYPE** should be one of **UF_SERVER_TRUST_ACCOUNTS**, which lists the domain server's machine accounts, **UF_INTERDOMAIN_TRUST_ACCOUNT**, which lists trusted accounts between machines, or **UF_WORKSTATION_TRUST_ACCOUNTS**, for workstation accounts.

If specified, **PREFIX** restricts the list of machines returned to only those starting with **PREFIX**. Returns 1 if successful, zero on failure.

GetMemoryInfo

```
GetMemoryInfo()
```

Returns a hash containing information about the current memory situation. The list of hash elements is shown in Table 22-19.

GetPDC

```
GetPDC([DOMAIN])
```

Returns the primary controller for the current domain, or the domain specified in **DOMAIN**. If **DOMAIN** is a machine, it returns the PDC for that machine.

Element	Description
Load	Percentage load on the available memory.
RAMTotal	Total amount, in bytes, of physical RAM.
RAMAvail	Total amount, in bytes, of available physical RAM.
PageTotal	Total amount, in bytes, of paged RAM.
PageAvail	Total amount, in bytes, of available paged RAM.
VirtTotal	Total amount, in bytes, of virtual memory.
VirtAvail	Total amount, in bytes, of available virtual memory.

Table 22-19. *Memory Information Returned by the **GetMemoryInfo** Function*

GetProcessorInfo

```
GetProcessorInfo()
```

Returns a hash of processor-related information, as shown in Table 22-20.

GetStdHandle

```
GetStdHandle(HANDLE)
```

Returns a Win32 handle for the filehandle specified by **HANDLE. HANDLE** should be one of **STD_INPUT_HANDLE**, **STD_OUTPUT_HANDLE**, or **STD_ERROR_HANDLE**. Returns **undef** on error.

GetTOD

```
GetTOD(MACHINE)
```

Returns the time of the specified **MACHINE**, in the number of seconds since the epoch.

Element	Description
OEMID	The OEM (Original Equipment Manufacturer) ID.
NumOfProcessors	The number of processors.
ProcessorType	Type of microprocessor.
ProcessorLevel	The level of processor (4=486, 5=586, etc.)
ProcessorRevision	The revision of the processor.
PageSize	The size of individual pages of memory (a page is the unit of information written swapped out to disk/virtual memory).

Table 22-20. *Information Gained from the **GetProcessorInfo** Function*

GetUsers

```
GetUsers(SERVER, PREFIX, LIST)
```

Populates the array or hash pointed to by **LIST** with the users on **SERVER**, starting with the specified **PREFIX**. If **PREFIX** is empty, then all users are returned.

GetVolumeInfo

```
GetVolumeInfo(DRIVE)
```

Returns a hash containing the current information for the specified drive (either "C:\" or "\\Atuin\MC." The elements of the hash are shown in Table 22-21.

Element	Description
Volume	The volume label.
Serial	The serial number for the drive, in decimal (rather than hexadecimal).
MaxFileNameLength	The maximum number of characters in a file name.
SystemFlag	A combination of the following predefined constants: **FS_CASE_IS_PRESERVED**—the character case is preserved on the drive. **FS_CASE_SENSITIVE**—the drive supports case-sensitive file names. **FS_UNICODE_STORED_ON_DISK**—supports Unicode formatted file names. **FS_PERSISTENT_ACLS**—stores and enforces access control lists. **FS_FILE_COMPRESSION**—the file system supports file-based compression (such as Windows NT file-based compression). **FS_VOL_IS_COMPRESSED**—signifies that the drive is a compressed device (as created by Stacker or Windows).

Table 22-21. *Hash Elements Returned by **GetVolumeInfo***

GetWinVersion

```
GetWinVersion()
```

Returns a hash defining the version information for the current Windows environment, as shown in Table 22-22.

LogoffAsUser

```
LogoffAsUser([1|0])
```

Logs the user off from an impersonated account (as initiated by **LogonAsUser**). If you supply a non-zero argument, the logoff is forced. Always returns 1.

LogonAsUser

```
LogonAsUser(DOMAIN, USER, PASSWORD [, LOGONTYPE])
```

This will log the current account on as an impersonated user. The login is valid for the specified **DOMAIN**, **USER**, and **PASSWORD**. If **DOMAIN** is blank, then **USER** is assumed to be in the current user's domain. The valid optional types for **LOGONTYPE** are shown in Table 22-23.

ReadINI

```
ReadINI(FILE, SECTION, KEY)
```

Element	Description
Major	The major release (for example, Windows NT 4).
Minor	The minor release.
Build	The build number.
Platform	One of **Win32s**, **Win32_95**, **Win32_NT**.
CSD	Currently installed service pack number.

Table 22-22. *Hash Elements Returned by* ***GetWinVersion***

Type	Description
LOGON32_LOGON_BATCH	Logs on as a noninteractive batch file.
LOGON32_LOGON_INTERACTIVE	Logs on as a normal interactive user.
LOGON32_LOGON_SERVICE	Logs on as a system service (under Windows NT).
LOGON32_LOGON_NETWORK	Logs on as a standard network user.

Table 22-23. *Logon Types for Impersonating Users*

Retrieves the specified value for the specified **KEY**, from the corresponding **SECTION** or the INI **FILE**. If **KEY** is empty, it returns a list of all the keys in the section, and if both **KEYS** and **SECTION** are blank, it returns a list of sections.

RenameUser

```
RenameUser(SERVER, USER, NEWUSER)
```

Changes the name of **USER** on the specified **SERVER** to **NEWUSER**. The update will change throughout the user database, updating the user and group information. If **SERVER** is the name of a domain, the PDC is found and the command sent to that machine. If **SERVER** is blank, it changes the name on the local machine.

ScheduleAdd

```
ScheduleAdd(MACHINE, TIME, DOM, DOW, FLAGS, COMMAND)
```

Schedules **COMMAND** to be run at a particular date and time. The **MACHINE** is the machine on which the command should be run. The **TIME** is the time at which the command should be run. The **DOM** and **DOW** arguments define the day of the month and the day of week on which the command should be run. The day of the month is a bitset, each bit, starting at zero, referring to subsequent days of the month. You can either use **vec** to create this or use the power of two to create the correct value. Values can be **or**'d together, such that **2****1 | 2**31** specifies the 1st and 31st of the month.

The **DOW** is also a bitset, but there are values predefined for **MONDAY**, **TUESDAY**, **WEDNESDAY**, **THURSDAY**, **FRIDAY**, **SATURDAY**, and **SUNDAY**. Values can be **or**'d together to specify multiple days.

The **FLAGS** is a list of options used for creating the scheduled entry. Valid values are listed in Table 22-24.

The function returns a unique job number for the scheduled command.

ScheduleDel

```
ScheduleDel(MACHINE, JOB [, MAXJOB])
```

Deletes the job number **JOB** from the schedule for **MACHINE**. If **MAXJOB** is specified, it removes all jobs with IDs from **JOB** to **MAXJOB**.

ScheduleGet

```
ScheduleGet(MACHINE, JOB, JOBINFO)
```

Places the information about **JOB** on **MACHINE** into the hash reference pointed to by **JOBINFO**. The elements of the hash are **Machine, Time, DOM, DOW, Flags, Command**. Refer to **ScheduleAdd** above for more information.

Flag	Description
JOB_RUN_PERIODICALLY	The job will be run every month on the specified days of the week and/or days of the week at the specified time.
JOB_ADD_CURRENT_DATE	The job will run today at the specified time, or tomorrow if the current time is greater than **TIME**.
JOB_EXEC_ERROR	Set if the last time the job was executed it failed.
JOB_RUN_TODAY	Set when the job's time has yet to pass for the current day. Set irrespective of the **DOM** or **DOW** settings.
JOB_NONINTERACTIVE	Set if the job is not allowed desktop interaction (a background job).

Table 22-24. *Flags for Creating Scheduled Jobs*

ScheduleList

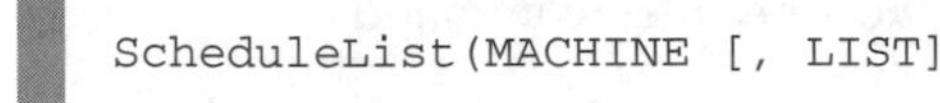

```
ScheduleList(MACHINE [, LIST])
```

Places a reference to a hash of hashes into the variable pointed to by **LIST**, defining the list of scheduled jobs for **MACHINE**. Returns the number of scheduled jobs on the machine, or **undef** if there was a problem.

SetComputerName

```
SetComputerName(NAME)
```

Sets the computer name to **NAME**. Using this on a machine within a domain will remove the machine from that domain.

SetEnvVar

```
SetEnvVar(NAME, VALUE [, TYPE [, TIMEOUT]])
```

Sets the value of the variable **NAME** to **VALUE**. If specified, creates the variable within the system variables (**ENV_SYSTEM**, the default) or user variables (**ENV_USER**). Changes are global and permanent, with the value change being broadcast to the other processes for a maximum of **TIMEOUT** seconds.

SetPassword

```
SetPassword(SERVER, USER, PASSWORD)
```

Changes the password for **USER** on the domain server **SERVER** to **PASSWORD**. **SERVER** can be the explicit name of a server, or the name of a domain, in which case the primary domain controller will be searched. You must have administration privileges for this to work. The function returns zero on failure. See the **UserChangePassword** function for a user-oriented version.

SetVolumeLabel

```
SetVolumeLabel(DRIVE, LABEL)
```

Sets the volume label for **DRIVE** to **LABEL**. Cannot be used on a network reference, only on a specific drive letter.

UserChangePassword

```
UserChangePassword(DOMAIN, USER, OLDPW, NEWPW)
```

Changes the password for **USER** in **DOMAIN** (or on the server **DOMAIN**) to **NEWPW**, providing that **OLDPW** matches the existing password. If **DOMAIN** is empty, assumes the current local domain. If **USER** is empty, then it assumes the current user. Returns zero if the password was not modified.

UserCheckPassword

```
UserCheckPassword(DOMAIN, USER, PASSWORD)
```

Verifies that the password for **USER** within **DOMAIN** matches **PASSWORD**. If **DOMAIN** is empty, assumes the current local domain. If **USER** is empty, then it assumes the current user. Returns zero if the password does not match.

UserGetAttributes

```
UserGetAttributes(SERVER, USER, NAME, PASSWORD, PASSWORDAGE, PRIVS,
                  HOMEDIR, COMMENT, FLAGS, SCRIPTPATH);
```

Gets the user information for the specified **USER**, placing the values into the remainder of the arguments supplied. If **DOMAIN** is empty, assumes the current local domain. If **USER** is empty, then it assumes the current user. You should use the **UserGetMiscAttributes**, which provides a more familiar hash-based interface to the information. Returns zero if the user could not be found.

UserGetMiscAttributes

```
UserGetMiscAttributes(DOMAIN, USER, INFO)
```

Places the attributes for **USER** in **DOMAIN** into the hash pointed to by **INFO**. The list of hash elements is shown in Table 22-25.

The valid user flags are listed in Table 22-26.

Element	Description
USER_ACCT_EXPIRES	When the user account is set to expire. Specified by the number of seconds since the epoch.
USER_AUTH_FLAGS	Defines the abilities of the user, existing constants are as follows: **AF_OP_PRINT**—user has print operator privileges. **AF_OP_COMM**—user has communications operator privileges. **AF_OP_SERVER**—user has server operator privilege. **AF_OP_ACCOUNTS**—user has accounts operator privilege.
USER_BAD_PW_COUNT	The number of times the user has supplied a bad password. Note that this value is recorded individually by each Backup Domain Controller; you will need to interrogate all BDCs and PDCs to get a complete value.
USER_CODE_PAGE	The code page of the user's language.
USER_COMMENT	The user's account comment.
USER_COUNTRY_CODE	The country code for the user's preferred language.
USER_FULL_NAME	User's full name.
USER_HOME_DIR	User's home directory.
USER_HOME_DIR_DRIVE	Drive letter assigned to the user's home directory during logon.
USER_FLAGS	A set of flags defining the current user account information. See Table 22-20.
USER_LAST_LOGOFF	The number of seconds since the epoch when the user last logged off. Note that this value is recorded individually by each Backup Domain Controller; you will need to interrogate all BDCs and PDCs to get a complete value.

Table 22-25. *User Information Fields*

Element	Description
USER_LAST_LOGON	The number of seconds since the epoch when the user last logged on. Note that this value is recorded individually by each Backup Domain Controller; you will need to interrogate all BDCs and PDCs to get a complete value.
USER_LOGON_HOURS	A string, 21 bytes in length, which specifies the times during which the user can log on. Each bit refers to a sequential hour in the week, with bit zero referring to Sunday, 0:00, to 0:59. You can extract the information using the **vec** function.
USER_LOGON_SERVER	The name of the server to which logon requests are sent.
USER_MAX_STORAGE	The maximum disk quote available to the user.
USER_NUM_LOGONS	The number of times the user has successfully logged on to the server. Note that this value is recorded individually by each Backup Domain Controller; you will need to interrogate all BDCs and PDCs to get a complete value.
USER_PARMS	A set of user-defined parameters. This information is used almost exclusively by Microsoft applications for some configuration information.
USER_PASSWORD	The encrypted version of the user's password.
USER_PASSWORD_AGE	The number of seconds since the password was last changed.
USER_PASSWORD_EXPIRED	Determines whether the user's password has expired.
USER_PRIMARY_GROUP_ID	The primary group to which the user belongs.

Table 22-25. *User Information Fields* (continued)

Element	Description
USER_PRIV	The privileges of the user: **USER_PRIV_GUEST**—guest privileges. **USER_PRIV_USER**—standard user privileges. **USER_PRIV_ADMIN**—administration privileges.
USER_PROFILE	The path to the user's profile information.
USER_SCRIPT_PATH	The path to the user's logon script.
USER_UNITS_PER_WEEK	Defines the number of equal units into which the week is divided.
USER_USER_ID	The relative ID of the user.
USER_NAME	The user's account name.
USER_WORKSTATIONS	The list of workstations, separated by commas, into which the user is allowed to log in.

Table 22-25. *User Information Fields* (continued)

Value	Description
UF_SCRIPT	The login script executed.
UF_ACCOUNTDISABLE	The user's account is disabled.
UF_HOMEDIR_REQUIRED	The user requires a home directory (ignored under Windows NT).
UF_PASSWD_NOTREQD	User does not require a password.
UF_PASSWD_CANT_CHANGE	User cannot change his password.
UF_LOCKOUT	The user account is currently locked out (disabled).
UF_DONT_EXPIRE_PASSWD	The user's password should never expire.

Table 22-26. *User Flags*

Value	Description
UF_NORMAL_ACCOUNT	The default account type.
UF_TEMP_DUPLICATE_ACCOUNT	The account is a duplicate temporary account.This is usually created when the user's primary account is in another domain.
UF_WORKSTATION_TRUST_ACCOUNT	This is a trusted workstation user account.
UF_SERVER_TRUST_ACCOUNT	This is a trusted server user account.
UF_INTERDOMAIN_TRUST_ACCOUNT	This is an interdomain account for allowing one domain to have trust to another domain.

Table 22-26. *User Flags* (continued)

To determine whether a user flag is set, you must logically **and** the value of **USER_FLAGS** with one of the constants in Table 22-20. To disable a flag, you must logically **and** the flag with the twos complement of the constant. To turn on a value, you need to logically **or** the user flags with the constant.

UserSetAttributes

```
UserSetAttributes(SERVER, USER, NAME, PASSWORD, PASSWORDAGE, PRIVS,
                  HOMEDIR, COMMENT, FLAGS, SCRIPTPATH)
```

Sets the attributes for **USER** on **SERVER** to the specified values. You should use the **UserSetMiscAttributes** function, which not only provides a more user-friendly interface but also allows you to set significantly more options.

UserSetMiscAttributes

```
UserSetMiscAttributes(DOMAIN, USER, USERINFO)
```

Sets the information in the hash **USERINFO** for **USER** in the domain **DOMAIN**. Use Tables 22-19 and 22-20 for details on the individual hash elements. Returns 1 if the update was successful.

WriteINI

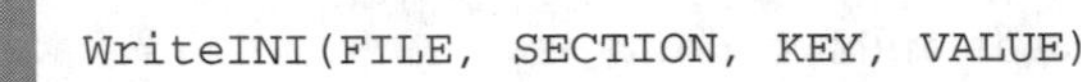

```
WriteINI(FILE, SECTION, KEY, VALUE)
```

Writes the **KEY/VALUE** pair into the INI file referred to by **FILE**, into the section defined by **SECTION**. If **VALUE** is empty, the **KEY** is removed. If **KEY** is empty, all keys in **SECTION** are removed, and if **SECTION** is empty, all sections in the entire file are removed. Returns one if successful, and **undef** on failure.

Examples

Aside from the obvious differences for error checking, there are a few tricks to making Perl scripts work under Win32. Provided you can follow the functions, methods, and structures above, you should be able to use the Win32 Perl environment very easily. To help you along, I've included two scripts below, which are mildly updated versions of scripts that first appeared in my book *Perl Annotated Archives* (see Appendix A).

Checking NT User Information

This script reads in the user data for a specific machine and/or domain and reports any inconsistencies or possible security traps in the information.

```
#!perl

use Win32::AdminMisc;
use Win32::NetAdmin;
use Getopt::Long;

my ($machine,$domain,@users,%attribs);

GetOptions("d=s" => \$domain);

$machine = Win32::NodeName();

$domain =Win32::DomainName()
    unless (defined($domain));

if (@ARGV)
{
    @users = @ARGV;
}
else
{
```

```
  Win32::NetAdmin::GetUsers(Win32::AdminMisc::GetDC($domain),
                            '',\@users);
}

if (@users)
{
    print "Domain: $domain\n";
}

for $user (sort @users)
{
    unless(Win32::AdminMisc::UserGetMiscAttributes($domain,
                                                    $user,
                                                    \%attribs))
    {
        opstatus();
    }
    else
    {
        if ($attribs{"USER_PASSWORD_EXPIRED"} == 1)
        {
            print "Error: $user : Password has expired\n";
        }
        if ($machine eq Win32::AdminMisc::GetDC($domain))
        {
            unless(-d $attribs{"USER_HOME_DIR"})
            {
                print("Error: $user : Home directory, ",
                      $attribs{"USER_HOME_DIR"},
                      " does not exist\n");
            }
        }
        if ($user !~ /Administrator/)
        {
            if ($attribs{"USER_PRIV"} == 2)
            {
                print("Warning: $user : User has ",
                      "administrator privileges\n");
            }
            else
            {
                if ($attribs{"USER_AUTH_FLAGS"} & 1)
```

```
                {
                    print("Warning: $user : User does not have ",
                          "administrator privileges but does ",
                          "have Print Admin privileges\n");
                }
                if ($attribs{"USER_AUTH_FLAGS"} & 4)
                {
                    print("Warning: $user : User does not have ",
                          "administrator privileges but does ",
                          "have Server Admin privileges\n");
                }
                if ($attribs{"USER_AUTH_FLAGS"} & 8)
                {
                    print("Warning: $user : User does not have ",
                          "administrator privileges but does ",
                          "have Accounts Admin privileges\n");
                }
            }
        }
        if ($attribs{"USER_PASSWORD_AGE"} > (31*24*60*60))
        {
            print("Error: $user : Password is more than ",
                  "one month (31 days) old\n");
        }
        if ($attribs{"USER_BAD_PW_COUNT"} > 0)
        {
            print("Warning: $user : User has had ",
                  $attribs{"USER_BAD_PW_COUNT"},
                  " bad password attempts\n");
        }
    }
}

sub opstatus
{
    my $error=Win32::GetLastError();
    if ($error ne 0)
    {
        print("\nERROR: ", Win32::FormatMessage($error),"\n");
    }
}
```

You should be able to follow the execution fairly easily. First of all you use the functions in the **Win32::NetAdmin** module to verify and/or resolve the supplied machine name, either for its validity or to determine the domain's primary controller. Then the **UserGetAdminMiscAttributes** function from Dave Roth's **Win32::AdminMisc** module is called to get the individual information for each user, before you go through and check individual components of the user's attributes.

Starting/Stopping NT Services

The second example script uses the **Win32::Service** module to selectively start and stop services on a local or remote machine, presuming you have suitable privileges to do so.

```
#!perl -w
use Win32::Service;
use Getopt::Long;

my ($upserv,$downserv,$server,%services);

GetOptions("u=s" => \$upserv,
           "d=s" => \$downserv
           );
if (@ARGV)
{
    $server = $ARGV[0];
}
else
{
    $server = Win32::NodeName();
}

Win32::Service::GetServices($server,\%services);

print "Server $server\n";

if ($upserv)
{
    startservices(split(/,/,$upserv));
}
elsif ($downserv)
{
    stopservices(split(/,/,$downserv));
}
else
```

```
{
    listservices();
}

sub startservices
{
    my (@servicelist) = @_;
    for my $service (@servicelist)
    {
        if (defined($services{$service}))
        {
            print "Starting the $service service...";
            Win32::Service::StartService($server,$service);
            opstatus("start $service");
            sleep 5;
            print "$service: ",chkstatus($service);
        }
        else
        {
            print "ERROR: Service $service does not exist\n";
        }
    }
}

sub stopservices
{
    my (@servicelist) = @_;
    for my $service (@servicelist)
    {
        if (defined($services{$service}))
        {
            print "Stopping the $service service...";
            Win32::Service::StopService($server,$service);
            opstatus("stop $service");
            sleep 5;
            print "$service: ",chkstatus($service);
        }
        else
        {
            print "ERROR: Service $service does not exist\n";
        }
    }
```

```
}

sub opstatus
{
    my ($opname) = @_;
    my $error=Win32::GetLastError();
    if ($error ne 0)
    {
        print("\n$opname: ", Win32::FormatMessage($error),"\n");
    }
}

sub chkstatus
{
    my ($service) = @_;
    my %status;
    Win32::Service::GetStatus($server,$service,\%status);
    if (defined($status{CurrentState})
        and $status{CurrentState} eq 4)
    {
        return "Started";
    }
    else
    {
        return "Stopped";
    }
}

sub listservices
{
    for my $service (sort keys %services)
    {
        print "$service: ",chkstatus($service),"\n";
    }
}
```

Again, the script is relatively straightforward. You check or ascertain the node name that you are managing and then start or stop the specified service using the **Win32::Service::StartService** and **Win32::Service::StopService** functions. Note that you check the result of each command using the same **opstatus** function as before, which resolves the error reported by the function if there was a problem.

Also note that you wait between stopping or starting the service and then reporting the new status. This is to give the service time to start or stop accordingly. If you don't supply any arguments to the script, then it just reports the status of all the currently configured services for the machine, as in:

```
Alerter: Started
ClipBook Server: Stopped
Computer Browser: Stopped
DHCP Client: Stopped
Directory Replicator: Stopped
EventLog: Started
MGACtrl: Started
McAfee Alert Manager: Started
McAfee VirusScan Task Manager: Started
Messenger: Started
NT LM Security Support Provider: Started
Net Logon: Stopped
Network DDE: Stopped
Network DDE DSDM: Stopped
Norton SpeedDisk: Started
Norton Unerase Protection: Started
Plug and Play: Stopped
Protected Storage: Started
Remote Access Autodial Manager: Stopped
Remote Access Connection Manager: Stopped
Remote Access Server: Stopped
Remote Procedure Call (RPC) Locator: Stopped
Remote Procedure Call (RPC) Service: Stopped
Retrospect Remote Client: Started
Schedule: Stopped
Server: Stopped
Spooler: Started
TCP/IP NetBIOS Helper: Started
Telephony Service: Stopped
UPS: Stopped
Workstation: Started
```

If you try to start a service, you get this result:

```
C:\> ntserv.pl -u
Server INSENTIENT
Starting the Server service...

Server: Started
```

Of course, this command could fail if you don't have the right permissions or authority to make any changes, and the script will report a suitable error via the **Win32::GetLastError** function.

More Information

The best place to go for more information is the Perl distribution directory on CPAN: http://www.cpan.org/ports/win32. There are ActiveState and core Perl executables here, along with FAQs and links to other sites.

The Complete Reference

Chapter 23

Perl Under MacOS

Compared to Unix and Windows, MacOS has one significant missing feature: it has no command line interface. MacOS is 100 percent a windowed GUI environment. This presents some potential problems when we consider the methods already suggested for running Perl programs.

The solution is a separate "development environment." The MacPerl application supports both the execution of Perl scripts and the creation of the scripts in the first place. In addition to direct access to the execution process (scripts can be started and stopped from menus and key combinations), you also have interactive use of the Perl debugger in a familiar environment and complete control of the environment in which the scripts are executed.

Quite aside from the simple interface problem, there are also underlying differences between text file formats, the value of the epoch used for dates and times, and even the supported commands and functions. There are ways of getting around these problems, both using your own Perl scripts and modifications and using a number of modules that are supplied as standard with the MacPerl application.

Looking to the future, there is a possible different path for MacPerl development. MacOS X is the new operating system from Apple. At the time of writing, MacOS X Server has just been released and shows a promising feature set. Unlike the main MacOS 8, and before that Systems 1 through 7, MacOS X is a completely new operating system. The core is based around a Mach BSD kernel (as used in the NeXT operating system), which effectively makes MacOS Unix based. This will eliminate many of the problems associated with running Perl on the MacOS X platform.

This won't, however, eliminate the need for MacPerl, since MacOS X still provides a Mac-like interface on top of the kernel. It also provides compatibility with the MacOS 8 environment. It's expected that with some minor modifications the MacPerl application should work in both these environments to provide compatibility with the older implementations, and to provide cross-platform support between traditional MacOS and MacOS X systems.

At the current time, only the Server version is available. This is not a suitable environment for desktop users, and there may be significant interface and implementation differences between the current MacOS X Server system and the client when it is released. The best advice is to check both the Apple website and the MacPerl website to keep abreast of the situation.

This chapter addresses these issues, with specific regard to the MacOS. For more general information on writing portable Perl code, see Chapter 24. MacPerl was originally ported, and is continually supported, by Matthias Neeracher.

Installing and Running the Perl Applications

Perl is available in a number of different guises, depending on what you want to do with it and how extensible and expandable you want the support modules to be. The basic distribution, "appl," includes the MacPerl binary, all the Perl and MacPerl libraries and modules, and the documentation. The "tool" distribution works with MPW (the Macintosh Programmers Workshop/Workbench), allowing you to develop and release Perl programs that are part of a larger overall application while presenting you with the same interface and development environment you use for C/C++ and Pascal Mac applications. Because MacPerl provides an almost transparent interface to the underlying Mac Toolbox, you can use Perl and C/C++/Pascal programs and code interchangeably. The source, in the "src" distribution, including all of the toolbox interfaces, is also available.

Installing the application is a case of downloading and decompressing the installer and then double-clicking on the installer application. This will install all the modules, application, and documentation you need to start programming in Perl. Starting MacPerl is a simple case of double-clicking on the application.

Executing Scripts

Perl scripts are identified using the MacOS Creator and Type codes. The MacPerl environment automatically sets this information when you save the script. In fact, MacPerl specifies three basic formats that are outlined in Table 23-1.

File Type	Description
Droplet	A droplet is a miniapplication that consists of the original Perl script and a small amount of glue code that uses AppleEvents to start MacPerl, if it is not already running, and then execute the script. Using droplets is the recommended method for distributing MacPerl scripts. To save a script as a droplet, go to Save As under the File menu, and choose Droplet in the file type pop-up at the bottom of the file dialog. Files dragged and dropped onto a droplet's icon in the finder have their names passed to the script as arguments (within @ARGV). If you plan on distributing your scripts to other people, droplets require that the destination users have MacPerl already installed. This might make initial distributions large (about 800K), although further updates should be smaller.

Table 23-1. *MacPerl Script Types*

File Type	Description
Stand-alone applications	A stand-alone application creates a file composed of the Perl application and the script and related modules. This creates a single, "double-clickable" application that runs and executes your script. This can be a great solution if you want to provide a single file solution for a client, or if you want to save clients the task of installing MacPerl on their machines. However, this is still an interpreted version. The script is not compiled into an executable, just bundled with the Perl interpreter into a single file.
Plain text file	A plain text file can be opened within the MacPerl environment and executed as a Perl script. Make sure that if the script has come from another platform, the script is in MacOS text format. These files will not automatically execute when you double-click them. They open either the built-in editor within MacPerl or the editor you usually use for editing text files (for example, SimpleText, BBEdit, or emacs).

Table 23-1. *MacPerl Script Types* (continued)

A fourth format, CGI Script, creates a script suitable for working with a Mac web server application. See "Web Servers and CGI" later in the chapter for more information.

When a script is executing, **STDIN**, **STDOUT**, and **STDERR** are supported directly within the MacPerl environment. If you want to introduce information on a "command line" (other than files if you are using a droplet), you will need to use the Mac-specific toolbox modules and functions to request the information from the user. See the section "MacOS Additional Functions," later in this chapter.

Installing Third-Party Modules

Modules that build on the modules supplied as part of a basic distribution should work without any problems. All of the modules in this book, for example, that do not rely on an external module set work OK.

Scripts that rely on external modules, such as those from CPAN (especially those that require C source code to be compiled), may cause difficulties, not all of which can be easily overcome. The process for installing a third-party module is as follows:

1. Download and then extract the module. Most modules are supplied as a Gzipped tar file. You can either use the individual tools MacGzip and suntar to extract the file, or use Aladdin System's Stuffit Expander with the Expander Extensions. Whichever application set you use, remember to switch line-feed conversion on. This will convert the Unix-style Perl scripts into Macintosh text files, which will be correctly parsed by the MacPerl processor.
2. Read the documentation to ensure the module or any modules on which it relies use XS or C source code. If they do, it's probably best to forget about using the module. If you have access to the MPW toolkit, you may be able to compile the extension, but success is not guaranteed. You can also ask another MacPerl user, via the MacPerl mailing list, to compile it for you.
3. Ignore the Makefile.PL file. Although it might run, it will probably report an error like this:

   ```
   # On MacOS, we need to build under the Perl source directory or
   have the MacPerl SDK installed in the MacPerl folder.
   ```

   Ignore it, because you need to install the Perl modules manually. Even if the Makefile.PL runs successfully, it will generate a Makefile that you can't use on the Mac without the addition of some special tools!
4. Create a new folder (if you don't already have one) to hold your site-specific and contributed modules. This is usually located in **$ENV{MACPERL}sitelib:**, although you can create it anywhere as long as you add the directory to the **@INC** variable via the MacPerl application preferences, or use the **use lib** pragma within a script.

   Remember to create a proper directory structure if you are installing a hierarchical module. For example, when installing Net::FTP, you need to install the FTP.pm module into a subdirectory called Net right below the site_perl or alternative installation location.
5. Copy across the individual Perl modules to the new directory. If the modules follow a structure, copy across all the directories and subdirectories.
6. Once copied across, try using the following script, which will automatically split the installed module, suitable for autoloading:

   ```
   use AutoSplit;
   my $instdir = "$ENV{MACPERL}site_perl";
   autosplit("$dir:Module.pm", "$dir:auto", 0, 1, 1);
   ```

   Change the **$instdir** and module names accordingly. See Appendix E for more details on the AutoSplit module.

7. Once installed, try running one of the test programs, or write a small script to use one of the modules you have installed. Check the MacPerl error window. If you get an error like this,

   ```
   # Illegal character \012 (carriage return).
   File 'Midkemia:MacPerl ƒ:site_perl:Net:DNS:Header.pm'; Line 1
   # (Maybe you didn't strip carriage returns after a network trans-
   fer?)
   ```

   then the file still has Unix-style line feeds in it. You can use BBEdit or a similar application to convert these to Macintosh text. Alternatively, you could write a Perl script to do it!

In my experience many of the modules on CPAN work OK, including libnet, Net-DNS, and libwww. One that doesn't is the DBD database module that relies on some C source code to interface between Perl and the outside world.

MacOS Differences

The main differences between the MacOS and Unix (our base platform) are detailed below. Some features rely on the availability of the MPW (a free development environment supported by Apple) or ToolServer (an application that supports the use of MPW tools from both the MPW environment and MacPerl). See the specific entries for details.

Line Termination

On the Mac, "\n" means ASCII 13, not ASCII 10 (under Unix). If you specifically want ASCII 10, you must specify the code, as in, "\012." All other conversions are done automatically. You should only have to change this if you are trying to read in a nontranslated Unix document, or if you're trying to do the translation.

Volumes, Pathnames, and Files

Directories are called "folders," and colons, rather than forward or backward slashes, separate files and folders. Individual disks or disk partitions are called "volumes." If you specify a file with

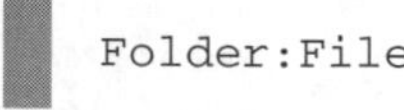

```
Folder:File
```

then the reference is considered relative. The reference will be relative to the current volume and folder. References of the form

```
:Folder:File
```

are relative to the current volume only. A reference like

```
File
```

refers to a file in the current directory. If you want to specify an absolute file name, just place the name of the volume in the path, for example:

```
Volume:Folder:File
```

Because you use colons to separate the path elements, care must be taken when storing the information in text-delimited databases. Using a colon to separate fields in a database, where one of the fields is a Mac pathname, will cause problems.

The individual elements of a pathname (volume, directory, file) have a limit of 31 characters each, although there is no theoretical limit on the size of a complete pathname.

Time

If you use the number of seconds since the epoch as a comparative measure, you need to be aware that the time within MacPerl is measured from an epoch of 1904, not 1970. This shouldn't be a problem under MacOS-only scripts because the comparisons will be using the same base reference, but if you are comparing or exchanging date information based on epoch references with other platforms, you will need to take account of the difference.

The best solution is to store the information in traditional date and time formats. You can then extract and/or format the information correctly. If you want to use the values for comparison, either write a special function for use with the **sort** function, or convert the date and time information into a numerical value. For example, the date "25 March, 1999, 10:15am" could be stored as a number with the value 199903251015. See Chapter 8 for more information.

Running External Programs

The MacOS does not have (currently) any notion of subprocesses. Therefore, entries like the following won't work:

```
open(d,"|command")
```

However, some backtick commands have been hard coded within MacPerl to support a certain level of cross-platform support. The entries supported are shown in Table 23-2.

Command	Description
'pwd' or 'Directory'	Returns the current working directory, followed by a newline. Case is significant.
'hostname'	Returns the name of the current machine if MacTCP or Open Transport are running.
'glob xxx'	Expands the glob pattern, returning a list of expanded file names. Only * and ? are supported. The internal **glob()** function also works.
'stty raw' and 'stty -raw'	Switches the console window between raw and sane modes, respectively.
'stty sane' and 'stty -sane'	Switches the console window between sane and raw modes.

Table 23-2. *MacPerl's "Built-in" External Programs*

If you have access to the ToolServer application, you can call a larger number of external command line programs both with **system** and through pipes with **open**.

Networking

MacPerl supports the standard Perl 5 Socket module, so basic TCP/IP networking works. I also have my MacPerl set up with the libnet and lwp modules without any problems (see Appendix F). If you want to use AppleTalk networking, MacPerl supports using and selecting certain AppleTalk devices and interfaces via the supplied Mac-specific toolboxes.

Web Servers and CGI

Any Mac-based web server that is MacHTTP and WebStar compliant should be able to use MacPerl and therefore Perl scripts for CGI operations. The MacPerl environment allows you to save a standard script as a CGI script. You can then install the "CGI" script into the CGI folder on the web server and reference it as you would a CGI script on a Unix platform.

The difference between a droplet and a CGI script is that the I/O is redirected to and from the web server interface. This allows you to obtain data using GET, PUT, and environment variables from the web server and HTML forms, just as you would with a Unix web server and script. Printing to **STDOUT** sends replies back as HTML to the client web browser.

MacOS Debugger

Because MacOS does not provide a command line as such, execution of the debugger is controlled slightly differently. To switch on debugging and invoke the debugger, make sure the Perl Debugger menu option in the Scripts menu is selected. You then execute the script as usual (double-clicking or choosing Run from the Scripts menu). This opens a new debugger window and restricts the execution process of MacPerl to the operations within the debugger. You cannot run a new script until the debugger has completed execution (or until you quit it).

Security

MacOS does not have a multiuser environment as supported by either Unix or Windows 95/NT, so security within MacOS requires some script-based implementation. If you are going to execute a script in a secure fashion, you may need to implement your own security entrance to the script, as well as your own password and validity checks.

If you want to enable taint checking, use the Taint Checking option within the Scripts menu. This is identical in every respect to the taint checking enabled under Unix and Windows.

DBM Compatibility

Currently the MacPerl implementation only supports two DBM implementations—NDBM and Berkeley DB. This should not provide too many compatibility problems, since NDBM is roughly compatible to the DBM/ODBM/SDBM implementations. The NDBM module is actually supported by the Berkeley DB system (which also supports the DB_File module), so it can be a bit misleading. See Chapter 8 for more information on DBM databases.

Environment Variables

You can set environment variables for all of your Perl scripts by adding new variables to the MacPerl applications environment through the Preferences option of the Edit menu. Variables set here are available as standard within the **%ENV** hash variable. If you do not want to be so globally specific, you can set the values of the **%ENV** variable at the start of the script (see Chapter 10 for more details).

Determining the MacPerl Environment

The **MacPerl** module (see "MacOS Additional Functions" below) provides a number of variables that supply information about the environment in which the MacPerl application is running. This information is particularly useful if you want to determine what type of MacPerl application is running, whether the ToolServer and MPW environments are available, and what platform (68K or PPC) you are currently running on. This is more specific than the information provided through the **$^O** variable.

The **$MacPerl::Version** variable contains the version number for the MacPerl application and includes the specification of the MacPerl application type, for example:

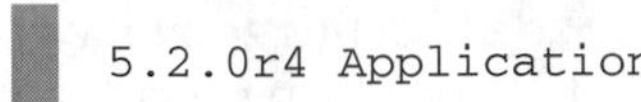

```
5.2.0r4 Application
```

Refer to "Installing and Running Perl Applications," at the beginning of the chapter, for more information on the available MacPerl types. Note as well that the Perl interpreter version number is still available via the **$]** variable.

The **$MacPerl::Architecture** variable returns the platform architecture that the script is currently running under, for example:

```
MacPPC
```

Alternatively, you can access a vast amount of information via the **Config** module, with the architecture name under which the MacPerl application was built available via the **$Config{'archname'}** variable.

Functional Differences

The functional differences are covered under the cross-platform portability issues in Chapter 24. See the section "Differences Between Functions."

Perl Documentation

The MacPerl distribution comes with an application called Shuck, which parses POD-based documentation into a formatted version suitable for viewing directly on screen. The quality and formatting is very good, and I find myself using the MacPerl distribution to view all POD documents when working because of the quality.

Although you can't print directly from this application, you can copy the formatted text into a word processor and print it from there. As with other MacOS elements, all the formatting is retained, and the result when printed is almost good enough to sell as a printed manual!

MacOS Additional Functions

As part of the compatibility process, the MacPerl distribution comes with a core MacPerl module that provides a number of MacPerl-specific functions used not only to bridge the gap between MacPerl and command line environments, but also to provide a simpler interface for Mac users when using Perl scripts.

I've included the most useful of the functions here. Refer to the **MacPerl** module for information on other functions.

Answer

The **Answer** function gives you a simple method for providing a dialog box, with a number of buttons, to the user. This is traditionally used for confirming a decision or for providing a simple notification dialog:

```
MacPerl::Answer(PROMPT)
MacPerl::Answer(PROMPT, BUTTON1)
MacPerl::Answer(PROMPT, BUTTON1, BUTTON2)
MacPerl::Answer(PROMPT, BUTTON1, BUTTON2, BUTTON3)
```

For example, the code snippet

```
MacPerl::Answer("Delete File","OK","Cancel");
```

would present a dialog with the message "Delete File" and two buttons, as seen in Figure 23-1.

The return value from the function would be 1 if OK was clicked, 0 if Cancel was clicked. As you add more options to the available list of buttons, the numbers increase, but remember that they work in opposite order to what you enter. You can only support three buttons with the **Answer** function; if you want to support more options, you will need to use the **Pick** function.

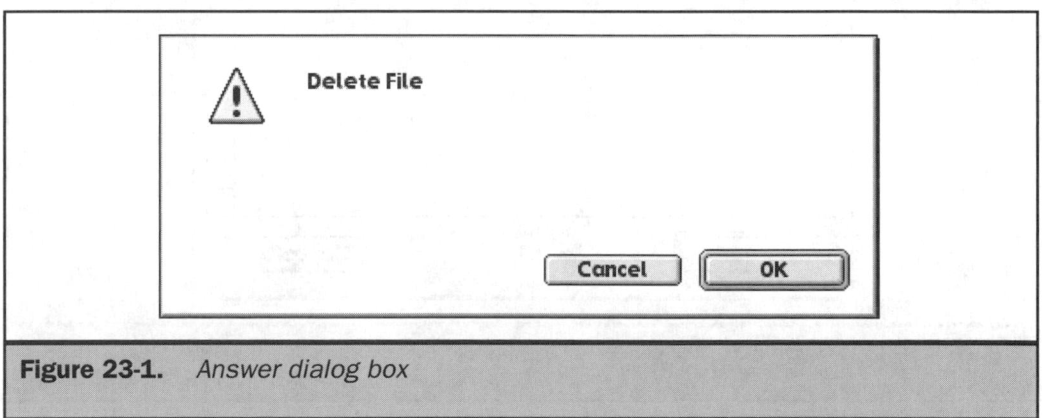

Figure 23-1. *Answer dialog box*

Ask

The most basic of the functions supported is the **Ask** function. This presents a dialog box to the user, either with buttons or a text field.

```
MacPerl::Ask(PROMPT, DEFAULT)
MacPerl::Ask(PROMPT)
```

For example:

```
$name = MacPerl::Ask('Enter your name');
```

You can supply a default value, which will be preentered into the field (and can obviously be overwritten) by specifying a second argument:

```
$name = MacPerl::Ask('Enter your name', 'Martin');
```

This presents a dialog like the one shown in Figure 23-2.

The value entered is returned by the function, or **undef** is returned if the Cancel button is clicked.

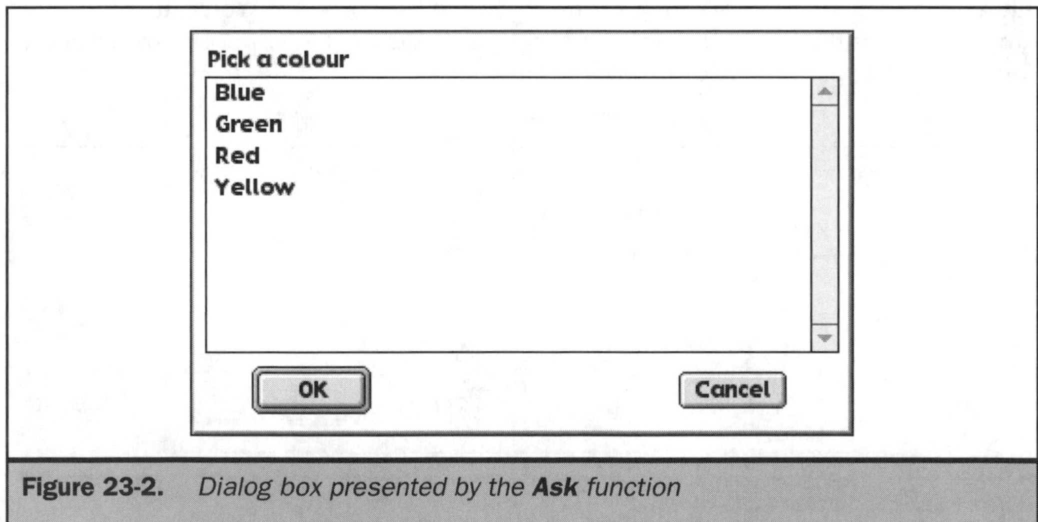

Figure 23-2. *Dialog box presented by the **Ask** function*

Pick

For multiple choice options in a dialog, you can use the **Pick** function. This provides a list of options and two buttons, OK and Cancel:

```
MacPerl::Pick(PROMPT, VALUES)
```

The prompt is the title of the window, and **VALUES** should be a list of strings that make up the list of available options. The value returned by the function is the string selected. For example, the function call

```
MacPerl::Pick("Pick a colour", "Blue", "Green", "Red", "Yellow");
```

produces a dialog box like the one shown in Figure 23-3.

Choose

The **Choose** function is a complex function that provides an interface to finding different types of information on the network through a unified functional interface. The interface is controlled through the use of a special **DOMAIN** argument, which is the first argument supplied to the function:

```
MacPerl::Choose(DOMAIN, TYPE, PROMPT, CONSTRAINT, FLAGS, DEFAULT)
MacPerl::Choose(DOMAIN, TYPE, PROMPT, CONSTRAINT, FLAGS)
MacPerl::Choose(DOMAIN, TYPE, PROMPT, CONSTRAINT)
MacPerl::Choose(DOMAIN, TYPE, PROMPT)
```

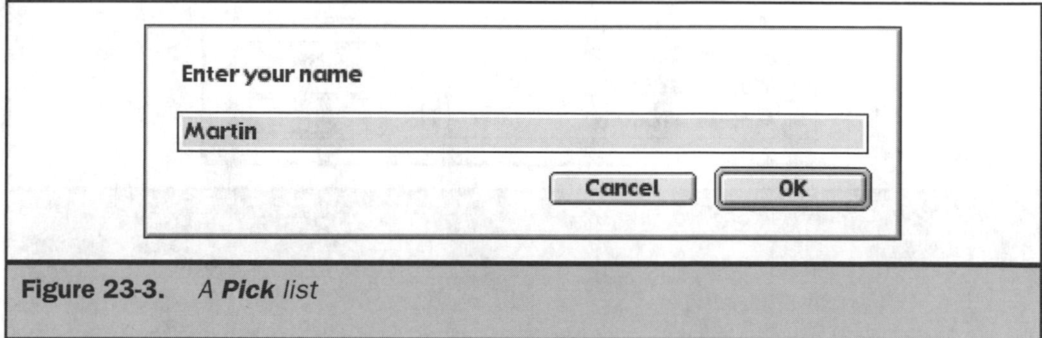

Figure 23-3. *A **Pick** list*

The function requires support from the **GUSI.ph** library which, among other things, supplies the packing and unpacking routines used for different arguments. The most useful of the domains specified is **AF_FILE**, which presents a modal dialog box, allowing the user to select a file (or directory) from a list.

For example, the code fragment below pops up a normal file selection dialog box, allowing you to select only text files:

```
require "GUSI.ph";

$file = MacPerl::Choose(&GUSI::AF_FILE, 0, "",
                        &GUSI::pack_sa_constr_file("TEXT", ""));
```

This presents you with a dialog box similar to the one shown in Figure 23-4.

For selecting a directory, rather than a file:

```
require "GUSI.ph";

$dir = MacPerl::Choose(&GUSI::AF_FILE, 0, "", "",
&GUSI::CHOOSE_DIR);
```

The dialog box displayed is shown in Figure 23-5.

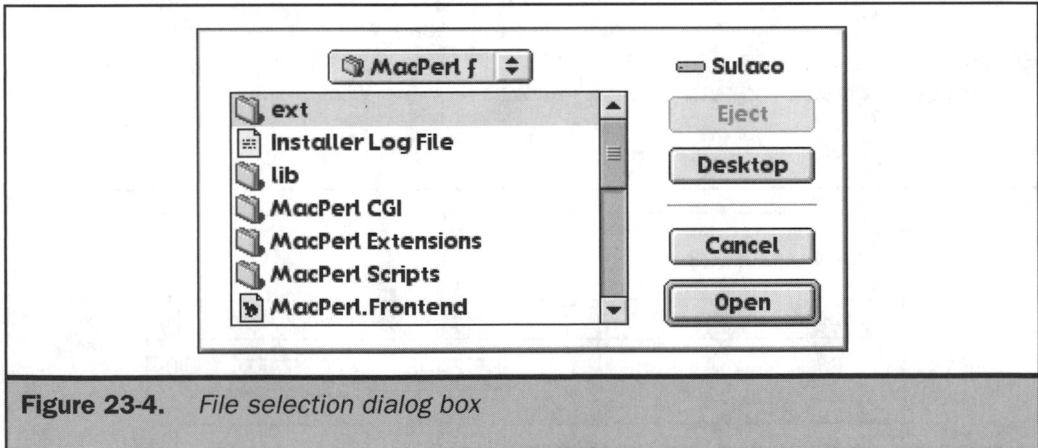

Figure 23-4. *File selection dialog box*

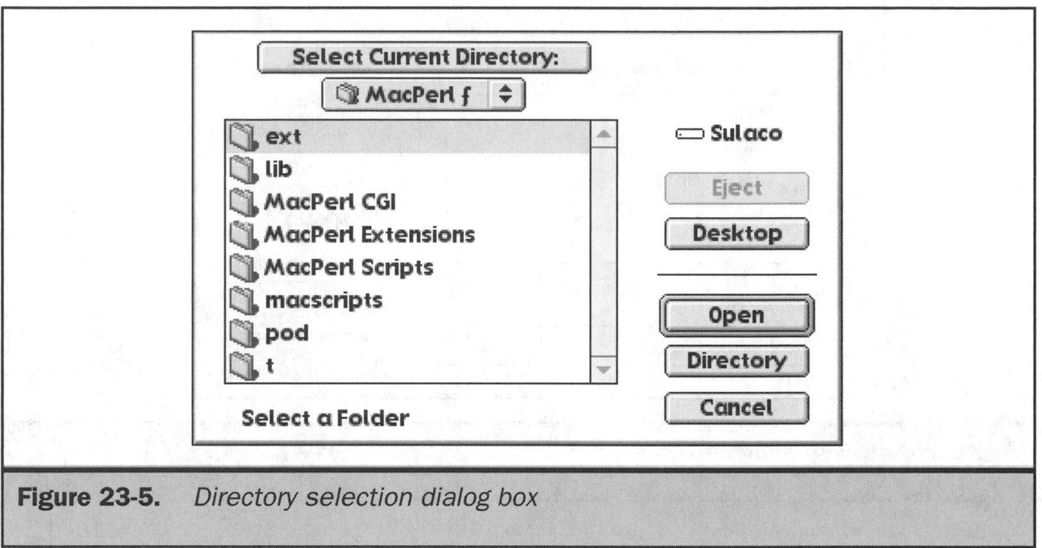

Figure 23-5. *Directory selection dialog box*

To present a dialog box that allows you to select a new file (and therefore enter a file name):

```
require "GUSI.ph";

$file = MacPerl::Choose(&GUSI::AF_FILE, 0, "", "",
                        &GUSI::CHOOSE_NEW + &GUSI::CHOOSE_DEFAULT,
                        "source.txt");
```

This displays a dialog box as shown in Figure 23-6, with the name of the file chosen by default highlighted.

GetFileInfo

The MacOS environment uses a completely different system for identifying the type of a particular file. Two 4-byte strings specify both the creating application (creator) and the type of document. The **GetFileInfo** function returns this information for a specified file:

```
MacPerl::GetFileInfo(FILE)
```

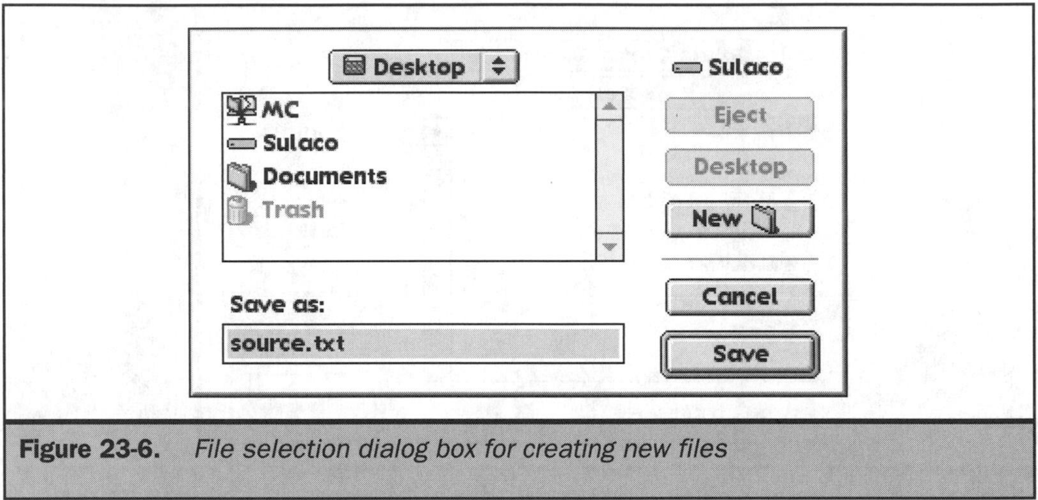

Figure 23-6. *File selection dialog box for creating new files*

In a scalar context it returns only the file type, but in a list context it returns both the creator and type. For example:

```
($type,$creator) = GetFileInfo("Sulaco::System Folder::System");
```

SetFileInfo

The **SetFileInfo** function—the logical opposite of the **GetFileInfo** function—allows you to set the type of a list of files:

```
SetFileInfo(CREATOR, TYPE, LIST)
```

This sets each of the files in **LIST** to the specified **CREATOR** and **TYPE**.

Quit

You can control how a script quits by using the **Quit** function:

```
MacPerl::Quit(LEVEL)
```

The easiest way to set the option is to use the predefined constants/functions defined within the MacPerl module. The list of those available is shown in Table 23-3.

Constant/Function	Description
kMacPerlNeverQuit	Don't quit after the script has finished executing. The MacPerl application will remain open.
kMacPerlQuitIfRuntime	Quit if you are running under a run-time-only version of the MacPerl interpreter.
kMacPerlAlwaysQuit	Always quit.
kMacPerlQuitIfFirstScript	Quit only if the script run was the first script to be executed when the MacPerl application ran. This forces MacPerl to quit if a standard Perl script is executed and MacPerl is automatically launched.

Table 23-3. *Options for Configuring How MacPerl Quits After a Script Invocation*

LoadExternals

The **LoadExternals** function allows you to import **XCMD** and **XFCN** extensions for a specified file:

```
MacPerl::LoadExternals(LIBFILE)
```

The imported functions are available directly within the scope of the current package.

AppleScript Interface

You can call AppleScript (under System 7.5 and higher) using a pair of functions, **DoAppleScript** and **Reply**. The AppleScript system is a MacOS-specific scripting environment that allows control of both the operating system and its configurable elements, as well as external applications that support the AppleScript system. Many applications support this option, including the heavyweights, such as Microsoft Word, and the lightweights, such as Apple's own MoviePlayer.

For more information on AppleScript programming, check the documentation that came with your MacOS computer or system software.

DoAppleScript

The **DoAppleScript** allows you to execute an AppleScript script directly within Perl. You pass a string to the **DoAppleScript** function, which then executes it via the AppleScript interface:

```
MacPerl::DoAppleScript(SCRIPT)
```

The best method for defining the AppleScript is to use a here document:

```
MacPerl::DoAppleScript(<<EOF);
tell application "Finder"
   activate
   empty trash
end tell
EOF
```

Using AppleScript is a more MacOS-friendly (and specific) way of controlling an external application, which may be more friendly than the traditional pipe methods used under Unix. However, be aware that to control the application, it must be AppleScript aware, and the MacPerl environment assumes you know how to program in AppleScript.

If you do not want to learn the complexities of AppleScript programming, consider using the Script Editor application, which comes with the AppleScript extensions. This provides a method for recording a sequence of steps as an AppleScript—recording the information in an interactive environment, much like the MacPerl application. You can then copy the script text directly into a MacPerl application.

Reply

The **Reply** function communicates information back to an AppleScript applet from the MacPerl environment. This enables you to call MacPerl from external applications that support AppleScript and control the MacPerl environment. Again, the best method if you do not already know how to program in AppleScript is to use the Script Editor application.

The function allows a value to be returned to the calling AppleScript:

```
MacPerl::Reply(ANSWER)
```

Here's an AppleScript recorded by the Script Editor application to generate and run the "Hello World!" application:

```
tell application "MacPerl"
   activate
   make new document
   set Spot 1 of document 1 to "print \"Hello World\n"
"
   Do Script "print \"Hello World\\n\";
" directory file "Sulaco:Applications:MacPerl ƒ:"
end tell
```


MacOS Support Modules

The MacPerl distribution comes with a standard set of Mac-specific modules that provide access to many of the MacOS features. The interface format for these follows the standard C/C++ functional interface very closely, and the module interfaces were designed with both Perl and C programmers in mind. The effect is that almost the full range of toolbox modules available to a C programmer are also available to a Perl programmer, albeit with all the facilities and advantages that an optimized scripting language provides.

The list of modules is shown in Table 23-4, but only the description of the contents is included. To make use of the Perl functions, you will need to know the data structures and functions in the C form. The best resource for this information is a suite of Inside Macintosh volumes, or the electronic forms of documentation supplied to you by Apple when you are a registered developer. I don't advise anybody to try these modules or toolkits without first having access to this information. You can easily corrupt information, and even the operating system, if you do not know how to use these functions correctly.

Module/Library	Description
Mac::AppleEvents	Apple Event Manager.
Mac::Components	Component Manager.
Mac::Controls	Control Manager.

Table 23-4. *Standard Mac-Specific Modules in the MacPerl Distribution*

Module/Library	Description
Mac::Dialogs	Dialog Manager.
Mac::Events	Event Manager.
Mac::Files	File Manager.
Mac::Fonts	Font Manager.
Mac::Gestalt	Gestalt Manager.
Mac::InternetConfig	Access and control of the InternetConfig System, which provides file extension mappings, email account details, and other information. This is now a standard part of MacOS 8.5.
Mac::Lists	Interface to the MacOS List Manager, which provides methods for controlling complex file selection and other lists.
Mac::Memory	Memory Manager.
Mac::Menus	Menu Manager.
Mac::MoreFiles	More File Manager–related routines.
Mac::Movies	Interface to the Movie Manager, which provides methods for using and controlling QuickTime movies.
Mac::OSA	Open Scripting Architecture.
Mac::Processes	Process Manager.
Mac::QDOffscreen	Offscreen QuickDraw.
Mac::QuickDraw	Functions and interface to the screen painting system provided by QuickDraw.
Mac::Resources	Resource Manager.
Mac::Speech	Functions and interface to the Speech Manager for selecting different MacInTalk voices and for speaking selected sequences of text direct from Perl.

Table 23-4. *Standard Mac-Specific Modules in the MacPerl Distribution* (continued)

Module/Library	Description
Mac::SpeechRecognition	Functions for controlling and accessing the Speech Recognition Manager.
Mac::StandardFile	Standard File dialogs (use the **Choose** function or the **StandardFile.pl** library for a more straightforward interface to this toolbox).
Mac::Types	Toolbox Types.
Mac::Windows	Window Manager.
StandardFile.pl	Calls for the standard file dialogs; makes for an alternative frontend interface to the underlying **MacPerl::Choose** function.
FindFolder.pl	Allows you to look for and return the pathnames for special folders (System, Preferences, Extensions).
CommConnect.pl	A simple serial interface toolbox.
GUSI.ph	Definitions for the socket-related calls (see the earlier section "Choose").
FAccess.ph	Definitions for the **MacPerl::FAccess** function.

Table 23-4. *Standard Mac-Specific Modules in the MacPerl Distribution* (continued)

Note that in all of the example modules in Table 23-4, you cannot always guarantee that a specific facility is available. For example, access to the Speech Recognition toolbox requires that the MacInTalk Speech Recognition extensions and control panels have been installed. All the modules provide functions for checking whether the system will be available, and even if you ignore this, all functions will return **undef** if they can't perform correctly.

Functions

All Perl functions take their arguments in the same order as the equivalent C functions (as you'd expect). Output values are returned as a list to the caller, rather than by references. In the event of an error, the toolbox functions return the normal **undef** or empty list, with error codes and/or strings being placed into the **$^E** variable.

Data Structures

Standard variable types are returned as the corresponding Perl variables, but complex data structures are returned as blessed object references. To access a single field within the data structure, you call a method with the same name as the field you are trying to access. The return value of the method call is the field data. You can also set field values this way by specifying the value as the first argument to the method call.

More Information

For more information, check out the extensive documentation supplied with the MacPerl application. I really can't praise the quality of this documentation enough. All of the standard Perl documents and man pages are supplied, in combination with Mac-specific information. The documentation interface is via a program called Shuck.

You can also visit the MacPerl website (see Appendix A), which has various links to other excellent MacPerl resources. And there is a MacPerl-specific book, which is available for download from the MacPerl website.

The Complete Reference

Chapter 24

Writing a Cross-Platform Script

Despite the complexities and differences we have seen in the last three chapters, the actual process of writing a cross-platform script is not as complex as it may seem. First of all, it should be apparent now that Perl is almost its own quasi-operating system. Providing one of the Perl functions can be supported by one or more of the underlying operating system functions, there is no reason why a script shouldn't work.

However, there is a difference between making the best use of Perl and making the best of the operating system on which you wish to run Perl. Perl can solve many problems of writing a program across many different platforms, but there is no reason why you should use it if it does not make sense. Most important of all, you should consider the implications of writing a cross-platform script. Using Perl across an array of Unix platforms is relatively easy, but writing a true cross-platform script does add overhead.

You also need to consider whether the project you are undertaking warrants the additional effort to make it compatible. If the script you are writing is a common script shared by many platforms, then it makes sense to make it cross-platform compatible. If it is simply a case of making a script work to get a specific task done, then writing individually on each platform may be quicker. Also, if you wish to take advantage of a particular operating system feature, then writing a platform-specific script will undoubtedly make more sense, even allowing for the wide range of external modules that support many of these external features.

Performance is also a critical consideration. Some of the methods we will examine in this chapter place an additional burden on the execution of a script, solely in the name of providing compatibility across platforms. By writing platform-specific code, particularly for those scripts that are executed many times (such as on a web server), you may save many processor cycles.

If you need to provide a core set of your functions or components to the different scripts on each platform, then the obvious solution is to use a custom module. Providing you don't use XS extensions or C code, there is no reason why your scripts and modules shouldn't be portable to any platform that supports Perl.

Let's assume, however, that you do need to support different platforms, whether within a single script or in multiple scripts. You need to know what the issues are and what the differences are for each platform, and these will both be covered in this chapter. Furthermore, we'll examine methods for identifying the different methods of determining what platform you are on, and what features the current Perl interpreter provides.

The common denominator across all platforms on which Perl is supported is, unsurprisingly, Perl. It hides many of the complexities and differences between the different platforms within the walls of its interpreter. If we look further, then it is more true to say that Perl is a Unix-derived scripting language. Therefore, Unix and related standards such as POSIX, Berkeley sockets, and System V interprocess communication systems are the real common denominators.

Taking this to its logical conclusion, it would make sense to assume that any operating system that is Unix related is therefore also pretty well covered by the core of the Perl interpreter. Such systems include, to a greater or lesser extent, QNX, RISC OS, BeOS, MacOS X, Linux (which could be classed as a true Unix, but that's a long debate), and even certain aspects of Windows NT. Those that are furthest removed from the Unix code base are the ones that present the most problems. These include VOS, VMS, MacOS, and other less well known operating systems.

This all makes for a much easier process than you may think. It's not actually that difficult to write a true cross-platform script if you keep a few basic ideas in mind. Most Perl scripts will run unhindered on all platforms without any modifications. It is only some very specific features that affect the process. When a function or feature is not supported, there is usually a workaround available in a module from CPAN.

The important thing to consider in all cases is what platforms you want to write for. If it is only for a few platforms, you will only need to consider the differences between them. Of course, it's likely that you will want to run the script on one of three platforms: Unix, Windows NT, and MacOS, and we have already seen the difference between those platforms in the previous three chapters.

Points to Consider

Irrespective of the specific platforms you are working on, and the functions or abilities they may have, there are some important core elements to consider. Minor differences between platforms, such as file formats, character sets, and even the characters used to separate file and path name elements will add complications to the missing functions.

Constant Compatibility

Wherever possible, you should avoid using your own static definitions for those constants that can be determined elsewhere. For example, the values that are passed to functions such as **fcntl**, **ioctl**, and **sysopen** can be obtained from one of the many Perl modules. The main **Fcntl** module is responsible for most of the constant definitions required for I/O. You may also want to use the **POSIX** module, which supplies the constants found in the fcntl.h header file.

Although it's true that other constants (such as those to **seek**) are less likely to change, if one is defined in the standard Perl distribution, then you should be using that value—it is far more likely to be correct than one of your selection.

Perl's Environment

Although Unix and Windows support environment variables, you shouldn't rely on their always being available. Without some effort on the user's part, MacOS does not support them, although you can set environment values with the MacPerl preferences panel. Other features of Perl that rely on the values of these external variables should also not be relied on. These include default paths, library paths, and module paths. For the latter, you can use the **use libs** pragma to define the locations of packages and modules without relying on any external influences, but remember to take account of the operating system on which you are running when you specify the values. See "Files and Pathnames" later in this chapter.

Note that all operating systems support the notion of different users. Again, the major odd one out is MacOS, but you should not always rely on the value of **$>** and variables to give you suitable ID numbers or reference points. Under MacOS, the **$>** and related variables all return zero, which to uninstructed script gives the user root access and priority to everything. This won't matter in the scope of a locally running Perl script, since users have access to do anything they want anyway, but imagine the limitations (or lack thereof) in a web server environment.

MacOS is also the odd one out when it comes to a command line interface. The operating system was never designed with one in mind. The effects, which are also felt on some other operating systems, affect seemingly unrelated operations such as opening a pipe to a command with **open**, as well as more obvious functions such as **system**. With the MacOS, if you have the MPW (Macintosh Programmers Workbench/Workshop) development environment, it provides a command line interface to many different commands, and it also solves the **open** and **system** problems.

Signals are supported on many systems, but not all. Even on those that support them, the list of supported signals may be very small. Unless they are vital to your application, avoid them where possible.

Interprocess communication is also an unsupported option on many platforms. Pipes, the **shm***, **msg***, and **sem*** functions, and pipes used with **open** are also sparse on non-Unix systems. Again, this affects a seemingly unusual set of abilities that some take for granted within Perl. The **sendmail**, **mail**, or **mailx** commands, often used to send email to other users, are good examples. If you cannot open a pipe to one of these commands, sending email may be difficult. The solution is to use something like Graham Barr's **Net::SMTP** module. See Chapter 9 for more details.

Character Sets

Different operating systems use different characters for line termination. In particular, Unix uses a newline (the **\n** or **\012** character) to terminate, whereas MacOS uses carriage return (the **\r** or **\015** character). To complicate matters, DOS/Windows uses the carriage-return, newline sequence (**\r\n** or **\015\012**). This is one of the most fundamental problems with Perl code. Simple constructs such as

```
while (<DATA>)
{
...
}
```

will not always work.

If you use the standard Perl system, then in fact it should work—Perl does the conversion for you automatically. Therefore, within Perl, **\n** will be interpreted as the corresponding character or character sequence for the current platform. Under MacOS, Perl simply interprets **\n** as **\015**, but under DOS/Windows, it is interpreted as **\015\012** when a file is accessed in text mode. To get the true value, you should use the **binmode** function.

This can cause a problem, seen below, when the **seek** and **tell** functions are being used, since Perl accounts for the two characters as a single one when in text mode, but identifies both characters literally when **binmode** has been used. However, you cannot expect Perl to convert locations returned by **tell** in text mode into their corresponding binary mode locations.

When used with network sockets, more direct specification is required. In all communication between sockets, you should use numerical values instead of their character versions to ensure that **\012** can be identified correctly. Otherwise the interpretation of **\n** on the two platforms may differ. See the discussion on character sets later in this section. To make the process easier, the **Socket** module, which is part of the standard Perl distribution, can supply the values for you.


```
use Socket qw(:DEFAULT :crlf);
print "Message$CRLF";
```

These provide three constant variables, **$CR**, **$LF**, and **$CRLF**, which map to **\015**, **\012**, and **\015\012**, respectively, which are identical irrespective of the platform on which you are running.

Another alternative is to use fixed-length records during network communication, if you are developing your own protocol. See Chapter 9 for more details on the different methods for networking.

Another popular misconception is that all platforms use the same character set. Although it's true most use the ASCII character set, you can only rely on the first 128 characters (values zero to 127, or **\00** to **\01727**) as being identical. Even with this consideration, you shouldn't necessarily rely on the values returned by **chr** or **ord** across different platforms. The actual values of the character set may include all manner of characters, including those that may have accents and may be in any order.

If you are worried about the character sets that you are using, you may want to consider the **UTF-8** character, which guarantees that the first 128 characters match the ASCII table, with each character being represented by a single byte. Further characters are represented by one or more bytes and include many of the accented and special characters. See Appendix E for more information.

For the support of international character sets, you should also consider Perl's locale system, demonstrated in Appendix E within the POSIX module.

Data Differences

Different physical and operating system combinations use different sequences for storing numbers. This affects the storage and transfer of numbers in binary format between systems, either within files or across network connections. The solution to the problem is either to use strings, which will of course be displayed in standard form, or use the **n** and **N** network orders with the **pack** and **unpack** functions. See Chapter 7.

All times are represented in Perl by the number of seconds since the epoch. On nearly all systems the epoch is 0:00:00, 1 January, 1970. However, other platforms define other values (MacOS, for example). If you want to store a date, use a format that is not reliant on the epoch value, such as a single string like **YYYYMMDDHHMMSS**.

Files and Pathnames

The main three platforms show the range of characters used to separate the directories and files that make up a file's path. Under Unix it is **/**, but under DOS/Windows it is ****, and on the Mac it's **:**. The Windows and DOS implementations also allow you to use the Unix **/** to separate the elements. To further complicate matters, only Unix and a small number of other operating systems use the concept of a single root directory.

On Windows and DOS, the individual drives, or partitions thereof, are identified by a single letter preceded by a colon. Under MacOS, each volume has a name that can precede a pathname, using the standard colon separator. The **File::Spec** module can create paths that use the appropriate character set and separator for you (see Appendix E).

Some consideration should also be given to file names. DOS supports only names with eight characters and three characters for an extension, and ignores case. Under Windows 95/NT the definition is slightly more complex: the full pathname has a maximum length of 256 characters and is case conscious. Under MacOS and older versions of Unix, any element can have up to 31 characters, while newer Unix versions have a limit of 256 characters. You should also try to restrict file names to use only standard alphanumeric characters. Although other scripts may support the use of other characters, support cannot be guaranteed.

Irrespective of the other features, do not rely on the location of a specific file, even within the realms of the same operating system group. Not all Unix flavors supply all the information about uses in /etc/passwd, for example. The password may be stored in a separate, hidden, or protected file, often called /etc/shadow. Use the **getpwuid** and similar functions to get the information.

Be aware that some operating systems do not allow you to open a file in more than one place at the same time. In some extreme cases you cannot set file permissions or options while the file is open elsewhere.

Modules

The modules provided as part of the standard Perl distribution are usually cross-platform compatible. There are some exceptions, including CPAN, which relies on external programs or contributed modules to work, and the DBM modules. There is no single DBM implementation that can be guaranteed across platforms. Although SDBM comes with Perl, there is no SDBM port for the MacOS platform. However, it does support the NDBM and DB_File implementations.

Also, modules that rely on external C code to operate may not be portable. Many platforms (DOS/Windows and MacOS included) do not include a C compiler, and even if they do, the C source for a Perl extension may rely on functions and header files not available on the desired platform. Writing modules that make use of the XS interface may therefore introduce many problems that cannot be easily solved.

Performance and Resources

Not all platforms have the seemingly unlimited resources of the Unix operating system available to them. Although Windows provides a similar memory interface, the available memory on a Windows machine may be significantly less in real terms (physical/virtual) than that available under a typical Unix implementation, although this is changing as RAM becomes cheaper. MacPerl must be allocated its own block of memory, and once exhausted, it cannot automatically gain new memory, even if there is some available. You should therefore take care with statements that arbitrarily create large internal structures; for example,

```
foreach (1..1000000)
```

creates a list with 1 million elements, which will take up a significant amount of memory. This has been fixed in Perl 5.005, but earlier versions, including MacPerl, which is currently based on 5.004, will generate the huge list.

Also remember that other operating systems do not provide the same protected memory spaces or the multitasking features of Unix. Use the tips in Chapter 16 for more information on optimizing memory and performance in your Perl scripts.

Differences Between Functions

Despite the efforts of the Perl porters, there are differences between platforms that cannot easily be hidden by the Perl language. This is usually because of major differences between how the operating system operates. As a classic example, MacOS does not have a command line interface like Windows, Unix, VMS, or even MS-DOS. Thus commands such as **system** or the backtick operators do not work, or certainly do not work as you expect. Furthermore, functions and operators that rely on pipes do not work under the MacOS either, so statements such as the following won't work:

```
open(DATA,"gunzip -c $file|") || die "Can't open $file";
```

Most of these differences, and possible workarounds, are covered in the previous chapters for Unix, Windows, and MacOS. You might want to keep the following points in mind though; they will help you to identify the most common of the missing elements on anything other than Unix.

- Functions that involve looking up details in one of the Unix files contained in **/etc**: generally these functions start with **set** or **get**. This includes everything from the network information routines and also those routines related to group and/or password information. There are usually equivalents in a platform-specific module. See the workarounds in Chapters 22 and 23 for more details.
- Functions that adjust elements of a file system: although all the basic file interfacing options will work, others, such as **–X**, **stat**, and more Unix-centric functions such as **chmod** and **chgrp**, are unsupported. You should also remember that although MacOS and Windows support the notion of links (via aliases and shortcuts, respectively), the **link** and **lstat** functions often do not work.
- Access to the internals of the operating system tables are also unsupported on many other platforms. In particular, those that return unique process and group IDs, or those that return parent group and parent owner information for a process ID. Most of the time, however, the **$$** variable should provide you with a reasonable amount of information.
- Unix-specific utility functions are also generally unimplemented: in particular the IPC systems such as **shm***, **msg***, and **sem***.

For a more specific list of functions supported under different operating systems, see Table 24-1 and the additional notes for platforms other than Unix, MacOS, and Win32. The letters in the table specify the following situations:

Y Supported
N Not supported/implemented
D Does nothing or returns useless information
S See one of the previous chapters
P Partial support/special action, see notes

The special notes (P) for individual functions and the operating systems listed in the table are given below. Note that more specific information on the Windows and MacOS platforms is available in Chapters 22 and 23.

Function	Unix	MacOS	Win32	VMS	AmigaOS	RISC OS	VOS
-X	Y	S	S	P	Y	Y, P	Y
binmode	Y	D	Y	Y,P	Y	Y,P	Y
chmod	Y	Y, S	Y, S	Y	Y	Y,P	Y
chown	Y	N	N,D	Y	Y	Y	N
chroot	Y	N	N	N	Y	Y	N
crypt	Y	Y	Y, S	Y	Y	Y	N
dbmclose	Y	Y	Y	N	Y	Y	N
dbmopen	Y	Y	Y	N	Y	Y	N
dump	Y	P, S	N	P	Y	D	Y
endgrent	Y	N	N	N	Y	N	Y
endhostent	Y	N	N	Y	Y	Y	Y
endnetent	Y	N	N	Y	Y	Y	Y
endprotoent	Y	N	N	Y	Y	Y	Y
endpwent	Y	N	N	Y	Y	Y	Y
endservent	Y	Y	N	Y	Y	Y	Y
exec	Y	N	Y	Y	Y	Y	Y
fcntl	Y	Y	N	N	Y	Y	Y
flock	Y	N	Y,P	N	Y	N	N
fork	Y	N	N	Y	N	N	N
getgrent	Y	N	N	N	Y	Y	Y
getgrgid	Y	N	N	N	Y	N	Y
getgrnam	Y	N	N	N	Y	N	Y
gethostent	Y	N	N	Y	Y	Y	Y
getlogin	Y	N	Y	Y	Y	N	Y
getnetbyaddr	Y	N	N	Y	Y	Y	Y

Table 24-1. *Function Support Summary*

Function	Unix	MacOS	Win32	VMS	AmigaOS	RISC OS	VOS
getnetbyname	Y	N	N	Y	Y	Y	Y
getnetent	Y	N	N	Y	Y	Y	Y
getpgrp	Y	N	N	N	Y	N	N
getppid	Y	N	N	N	Y	N	Y
getpriority	Y	N	N	N	Y	N	N
getprotobynumber	Y	N	Y	Y	Y	Y	Y
getprotoent	Y	N	N	Y	Y	Y	Y
getpwent	Y	N	N	Y	Y	Y	Y
getpwnam	Y	N	N	Y	Y	D	Y
getpwuid	Y	N	N	Y	Y	N	Y
getservbyport	Y	N	Y	Y	Y	Y	Y
getservent	Y	Y	N	Y	Y	Y	Y
getsockopt	Y	N	Y	Y	Y	Y	Y
glob	Y	S	S	Y	Y	Y, P	Y
ioctl	Y	Y	S	N	Y	Y, P	Y
kill	Y	N	S	Y	Y	N	Y
link	Y	N	N	N	Y	N	Y
lstat	Y	Y	D,S	N	Y	N	Y
msgctl	Y	N	N	N	Y	N	N
msgget	Y	N	N	N	Y	N	N
msgrcv	Y	N	N	N	Y	N	N
msgsnd	Y	N	N	N	Y	N	N
open	Y	N,S	Y,S	Y	Y	Y,P	Y
pipe	Y	N	Y	Y	Y	Y	Y
readlink	Y	Y	N	N	Y	N	Y
select	Y	Y	Y,S	Y	Y	N	Y
semctl	Y	N	N	N	Y	N	N

Table 24-1. *Function Support Summary* (continued)

Function	Unix	MacOS	Win32	VMS	AmigaOS	RISC OS	VOS
semget	Y	N	N	N	Y	N	N
semop	Y	N	N	N	Y	N	N
setgrent	Y	N	N	N	Y	N	Y
sethostent	Y	N	N	Y	Y	N	Y
setnetent	Y	N	N	Y	Y	N	Y
setpgrp	Y	N	N	N	Y	N	N
setpriority	Y	N	N	N	Y	N	N
setprotoent	Y	N	N	Y	Y	N	Y
setpwent	Y	N	N	Y	Y	N	Y
setservent	Y	Y	N	Y	Y	N	Y
setsockopt	Y	N	Y	Y	Y	N	N
shmctl	Y	N	N	N	Y	N	N
shmget	Y	N	N	N	Y	N	N
shmread	Y	N	N	N	Y	N	N
shmwrite	Y	N	N	N	Y	N	N
socketpair	Y	N	N	N	Y	N	N
stat	Y	Y,S	Y,S	Y,P	Y	Y,P	Y
symlink	Y	Y	N	N	Y	N	Y
syscall	Y	N	N	N	Y	N	N
sysopen	Y	Y,S	Y	Y	Y	Y	Y
system	Y	Y,S	Y,S	Y	Y	Y,P	Y
times	Y	Y, S	Y, D, S	Y	Y	Y, D	Y
truncate	Y	N	Y, S	N	Y	Y	Y, P
umask	Y	N, S	N, S	N, S	Y	N, P	Y
utime	Y	Y, S	Y	Y, S	Y	Y, P	Y, P
wait	Y	N	Y, S	Y	Y	D	N
waitpid	Y	N	Y, S	Y	Y	D	N

Table 24-1. *Function Support Summary* (continued)

-X

The **-X** tests are tailored for Unix information and are not supported across all platforms.

- **MacOS**: There is no difference between **-r** and **-R** and related tests; all directories and applications return true for **-x**; the **-s** test returns the size of the data fork, not the combined size of the file; tests **-b**, **-c**, **-k**, **-g**, **-p**, **-u**, **-A** are not implemented; the **-T** and **-B** tests may return bogus information.
- **Win32**: There is no difference between **-r** and **-R** and related tests; tests **-g**, **-k**, **-l**, **-p**, **-u**, **-A** are not implemented; the **-x**/**-X** tests return true if the file ends with one of the executable extensions (.bat, .exe, .com, etc.); **-S** is meaningless.
- **VMS**: The **-r**, **-w**, **-x**, and **-o** return true if the file is accessible, but may not reflect the true availability; tests **-g**, **-k**, **-l**, **-p**, **-u**, **-A** are not implemented; the **-d** test returns true if passed a device spec without an explicit directory.
- **RISC OS**: Tests **-g**, **-k**, **-l**, **-p**, **-u**, **-A** are not implemented; The **-x**/**-X** tests return true if the file has an executable file type.

binmode

The **binmode** function is often meaningless on most systems (Unix, RISC OS, and MacOS).

- **VMS**: The file is closed and reopened, resetting the pointer to the start of the file.
- **Win32**: The file pointer may be adjusted after changing the mode, due to the different interpretation.

chmod

The **chmod** function changes the file mode (read/write/execute permissions).

- **MacOS**: Does nothing; you cannot set such permissions on MacOS. The action of the disabling or enabling write permission is mapped to locking and unlocking the file.
- **Win32**: Changes only "owner" access.
- **RISC OS**: Changes only "owner" access.
- **VOS**: Changes are mapped to VOS access control lists.

dump

Under VMS, the **dump** function invokes the VMS debugger.

flock

The **flock** function is only supported under Windows NT, not under Windows 95/98.

glob

The **glob** function returns a list of matching characters.

- **MacOS**: Only the * and ? characters are supported.
- **Win32**: Support depends on the external perlglob.exe or perlglob.bat commands.
- **RISC OS**: Only the * and ? characters are supported.

ioctl

The **ioctl** function sets options on data handles.

- **Win32**: Only works on socket handles; uses the **ioctlsocket()** function.
- **RISC OS**: Only works on socket handles.

open

The **open** function associates an external data source with a filehandle.

- **MacOS**: The `|` variants, including the `|-` and `-|`, are only supported via the ToolServer application.
- **Win32**: The `|-` and `-|` variants are unsupported.
- **RISC OS**: The `|-` and `-|` variants are unsupported.

stat

The **stat** function returns status information for a file or filehandle.

- **MacOS**: The modification and access times return the same number, and the creation time is the creation time instead of inode modification time.
- **Win32**: The device and inode fields are meaningless.
- **VMS**: The device and inode fields are not reliable.
- **RISC OS**: The modification, access, and creation times all return the last modification time. The device and inode fields are not reliable.

system

The **system** function calls an external application.

- **MacOS**: Only implemented if ToolServer is installed.
- **Win32**: May not call the specified command shell. See Chapter 22 for more information.
- **RISC OS**: Since there is no external shell to process metacharacters, you may need to provide your own redirection and other operations. The exact

implementation of the call will vary according to the OS and Perl version, and whether the OS's Unix emulation library is available.

truncate

This function truncates the size of a file.

- **Win32**: There may be conflicts between open files and filehandles. If supplied a filehandle, it must have been opened with write access. If supplied a file name, it should not open by the same or other application.
- **VOS**: Truncates only to zero length.

umask

The **umask** function sets the permission mask for all of the files created. It returns **undef** if the function is not supported on the current operating system. If you need to use **umask**, use this test to decide how to proceed.

utime

The **utime** function updates a file's time stamps.

- **MacOS**: Updates only the modification time.
- **Win32**: Updates only the modification time.
- **VMS**: Updates only the modification time.
- **RISC OS**: Does not follow the true purpose of the function. The exact operation depends on the operating system version and the file system on which the file resides. See Chapter 22.

Signal Support

The list of supported signals under Perl depends entirely on the host OS, even down to individual version numbers. There is no guarantee that any platform supports a specific signal, you will need to test for the compatibility yourself. If you are writing for a platform that conforms to the POSIX you can afford to make at least some assumptions. Since you can test the existence of a signal with:

```
print "Have SIGALRM " if (exist $SIG{ALRM});
```

There's no excuse for you not to test for it. As a rough guide, see Table 24-2 for a list of supported signals on four of the main platforms, Solaris, MacOS, Windows NT and Linux.

Signal	Solaris 2.4 Perl 5.00502	MacOS 8.5.1 MacPerl 5.2.0r4 (Perl 5.004)	Windows NT 4 Perl 5.00502	RedHat Linux 5.2 Perl 5.00553
SIGABRT	X		X	X
SIGALRM	X	X	X	X
SIGBREAK			X	
SIGBUS	X			X
SIGCHLD	X		X	X
SIGCLD	X		X	X
SIGCONT	X		X	X
SIGEMT	X			
SIGFPE	X	X	X	X
SIGFREEZE	X			
SIGHUP	X			X
SIGILL	X	X	X	X
SIGINT	X	X	X	X
SIGIO	X			X
SIGIOT	X			X
SIGKILL	X		X	X
SIGLWP	X			
SIGPIPE	X		X	X
SIGPOLL	X			X
SIGPROF	X			X
SIGPWR	X			X
SIGQUIT	X		X	X
SIGRTMAX	X			
SIGRTMIN	X			

Table 24-2. *Signal Support Across Solaris, MacOS, Windows NT, and Linux*

Signal	Solaris 2.4 Perl 5.00502	MacOS 8.5.1 MacPerl 5.2.0r4 (Perl 5.004)	Windows NT 4 Perl 5.00502	RedHat Linux 5.2 Perl 5.00553
SIGSEGV	X	X	X	X
SIGSTKFLT				X
SIGSTOP	X		X	X
SIGSYS	X			
SIGTERM	X	X	X	X
SIGTHAW	X			
SIGTRAP	X			X
SIGTSTP	X			X
SIGTTIN	X			X
SIGTTOU	X			X
SIGURG	X			X
SIGUSR1	X			X
SIGUSR2	X			X
SIGVTALRM	X			X
SIGWAITING	X			
SIGWINCH	X			X
SIGXCPU	X			X
SIGXFSZ	X			X

Table 24-2. *Signal Support Across Solaris, MacOS, Windows NT, and Linux* (continued)

Tricks of the Trade

Beyond using Table 24-1 to identify any problems before they are incorporated within your script, there are tricks you can use within the scripts themselves to identify where the script is being executed. Most of the information is available as standard to the Perl interpreter; other pieces of information are available through the use of a supplied Perl module. In extreme cases you can use an external source to determine the system you are on, although for some systems, the act of calling external programs is not supported anyway.

Other information that is generally useful is the version of the Perl interpreter you are using. Although not an essential part of the cross-platform development process, it can provide helpful information about what may or may not be supported within your current environment. Using the information created during the configuration and build process of the Perl interpreter, you can determine the functions that are supported within your environment. Alternatively, you can use the **eval** function to trap and test for functions before you try to use them properly.

Finally, we'll look at the use of function overloading and module creation to provide an interface between the functions supported by the operating system and the functions you need to use.

Determining Your Platform

The **$^O** variable contains the name of the current platform. The information provided may not be very descriptive without knowing the significance of the name returned, but it should at the very least enable you to identify the main platform. Alternatively, you can use the value of the **$Config{'archname'}** variable (available via the **Config** module), which contains the name of the architecture on which the current Perl interpreter was compiled. The architecture string returned includes the platform name and the hardware architecture on which the binary was built.

Note the difference here: the build and current platform are not essentially identical, although it may be safe to assume they are compatible. For example, a Perl binary built on Solaris 2.4 will also run on Solaris 2.6, or even Solaris 7. However, a Perl binary for the Intel version of Solaris will not run on the SPARC version. The value of **$Config{'osname'}** will tell you the name of the operating system on which the binary was built.

Some sample operating system names, **$^O**, and **$Config{'archname'}** values are shown in Table 24-3.

On many platforms (particularly those derived from Unix), the value is extracted from that returned by **uname**. In all cases the value of **$^O** is probably of more use than the architecture name for writing cross-platform scripts.

Determining the Perl Version

The Perl version relates very little to the level of support on different platforms. However, it can sometimes be a useful indicator of whether an official release exists for a platform, as well as a useful reference point for a specific feature irrespective of the platform on which you are working.

If all you want to do is find out what version of Perl you are using, the obvious solution is to check the version of Perl using the **$]** variable. This is the version number of the Perl interpreter added to the patch level divided by a thousand. For example, v5.004 is

OS	$^O/$Config{'osname'}	$Config{'archname'}
MS-DOS	dos	
Windows 95	MSWin32	MSWin32-x86
Windows NT	MSWin32	MSWin32-x86
MacOS	MacOS	
Linux	linux	i686-linux
SunOS 4	sunos	sun4-sunos
Solaris	solaris	sun4-solaris

Table 24-3. *Operating Systems and Their Internal Equivalents*

Perl version 5, patch level 4. Subversion numbers to the patch level are included for the maintenance and development releases of Perl as the release number divided by 100,000, such that a value of 5.00553 is made up of Perl version 5, patch level 5, and development release 53. The maintenance release number increases from 1 to 49 and developmental releases from 50 to 99.

You can use the contents of the **perldelta** man page to determine what functions and abilities are available within each version of the Perl interpreter. Use the next section for specific ways of determining the supported functions without requiring prior knowledge.

If you want to restrict a script so it only runs on certain platforms, you should use the **require** keyword with a numerical, rather than alpha, value. The number specified is taken as the Perl version required to execute the script. For example, the statement

```
require 5;
```

places the simple restriction of requiring perl5 to continue. The value is taken literally, such that the comparison is made between the value passed to the **require** statement and the value of **$]**. If **$]** is numerically higher than the value passed to Perl, the script is allowed to continue. Thus, to ensure the script only runs on the very latest version of Perl, you might want to try,

```
require 5.00553;
```

although this will probably be out of date by the time you read this. If the value specified does not match the current Perl interpreter, a run-time error will be produced:

```
perl -e 'require 6;'
Perl 6 required--this is only version 5.00553, stopped at -e line 1.
```

Checking for Supported Functions

The Config module we used earlier to determine the architecture and operating system name used to build the current Perl interpreter actually contains all the information discovered during the configuration process. You can use this information to determine the functions and the extensions supported within the current Perl interpreter. The data is stored in the form of a hash, **%Config**; so to determine all of the values you might use

```
use Config;
foreach (sort keys %Config)
{
    print "$_ : $Config{$_}\n";
}
```

The values output are not cryptic, but also not obvious. The keys for underlying operating system functions start with **d_**, such that the existence of **chown** can be determined by

```
print "Have chown\n" if ($Config{'d_chown'} eq 'define');
```

Other features, such as extension modules to Perl (NDBM, Socket, for example), are in other keys within the same hash:

```
print "Extensions: $Config{extensions}\n";
```

To check for a specific function, use an **eval** block to execute the function within its own interpreter. If the call fails, the **eval** block will drop out, setting **$@** in the process. For example, to check once again for the **chown** function, you might use

```
eval { chown() };
warn "chown() $@" if $@;
```

Because **eval** blocks are executed within their own space at run time, this will report a suitable error.

Function Overloading

When you want to support a particular operation within a script that is not supported under multiple platforms, you may want to consider developing a special module that provides a personal interface to the built-in Perl functions. Another alternative is to provide your own set of "built-in" functions and then overload the real built-in functions with your own versions. You can do this through the use of a **BEGIN** block in your script and the **use subs** pragma.

The code fragment below shows the method required to determine which functions are supported:

```
BEGIN
{
    eval { chown() };
    push @functions,'chown' if $@;
}

use subs @functions;
use MyBuiltin @functions;

chown();
```

Note that the actual test must be done within the **BEGIN** block so that it is executed at compile rather than run time; then by the time compilation reaches the **use subs** pragma, the contents of **@functions** has already been populated with the required information.

The definition for **chown** is then placed into the **MyBuiltin** package, which is defined just like any other:

```
package MyBuiltin;
require Exporter;
@ISA = qw/Exporter/;
@EXPORT = ();
@EXPORT_OK = qw/chown/;

sub chown
{
```

```
    print "Changed mode!";
    return 1;
}
```

The contents of **@EXPORT** should be empty, since you don't want to import anything as standard. The value of **@EXPORT_OK** contains the list of built-in functions that you want to support and overload if necessary. Thus, when you call **use MyBuiltin** with a list of unsupported built-in functions, you import your own list of replacements. In this example a simple **print** statement is used to show that the overloading is working. In a real case you'll probably want to put some real functionality into the functions you want to overload.

If you are testing a lot of functions, you will need to use loops and references to test the functions you want to overload:

```
BEGIN
{
    @subtest = qw/chown exec/;
    foreach $function (@subtest)
    {
         eval { &$function };
         push @functions,$function if $@;
    }
}
```

It's not possible in this to optimize the loop by placing the **foreach** loop within the **eval** block, since you're using each **eval** invocation to test the existence of each function. This is a performance hit, but the overall process aids in compatibility, and it's one of the trade-offs examined at the beginning of the chapter.

The Complete Reference

Part VIII

Fun

Chapter 25

Things You Never Knew You Could Do with Perl

For years, rightly or wrongly, Perl has been labeled as a language used for developing CGI-based web applications. Although it's very good at this job, it's not really what the language was designed for. If we return to how I started this book, I explained that Perl is an acronym that stands for Practical Extraction and Report Language. Perl has its roots in the processing of text—particularly raw data—and manipulating, summarizing, and organizing that information into a simple report format that can be easily understood.

Perl has grown into a general-purpose programming language but still retains its text processing abilities. It's this that has enabled Perl to be a good choice as a CGI language, but it is not the reason it was invented. Aside from anything else, Perl's development precedes the development of HTML by a number of years.

Thus, in the same way that a pen is a tool for writing letters, so Perl is a good language for writing CGI programs. Also, like the pen, which can also be used to sign checks, draw pictures, and even act as a useful coffee stirrer, Perl can be used for many other things.

That's what this chapter is all about. There are things you can do with Perl that you might not expect. Some of these are straightforward, such as renaming files or updating a website with a new link. Others are more esoteric, such as the use of Perl for synchronizing files from one machine to another. Or how about downloading a website for viewing at your leisure rather than having to stay online as you click through each page?

Still more uses for Perl are just plain fun. IRC bots—so-called artificial intelligence agents—have been around for many years, and a large number of the systems use Perl as their background language. You can "talk" to a bot and have it supply you with information, perform tasks, and even act as a security guard to make sure you keep unwelcome people off your channel.

You probably are unaware that you can use Perl on a Windows machine to control another application. Using OLE you can tell other OLE-aware applications to perform all sorts of tasks without any interaction on your part—aside from calling the Perl script in the first place. You can do the same under MacOS by using AppleScript.

The last section of the chapter looks at Perl as a solution for writing games. Although you probably can't write a Perl program to produce the latest shoot-'em-up, there's no reason Perl can't be employed for the slower, more strategic games such as chess, adventures, or even a good game of tetris.

Renaming Files

One of my personal frustrations with Unix is that I can't do this

```
$ mv *.txt *.bak
```

and have it copy all files ending in .txt into files ending in .bak. As a DOS user for many years, this is the one thing I miss in the Unix environment. You can solve the problem, though, with the script below:

```
#!/usr/local/bin/perl

die "Usage: renspec.pl from_ext to_ext\n" unless (@ARGV);

$from=shift;
$to=shift;

@files = glob("*.$from");

foreach $file (@files)
{
     $old=$file;
     $file =~ s#\.$from#\.$to#g;
     rename($old,$file);
}
```

You grab a list of files using **glob** and then move the files with the old extension to files with the new extension, using **rename**.

This is a very specific script, and in the interests of making more generic Perl scripts for solving problems, it's a good idea to consider using a more configurable solution. You can do that by supplying a regular expression on the command line and then using **eval** to parse the regular expression on the file names:

```
#!/usr/local/bin/perl

($op = shift) || die "Usage: rename perlexpr [filenames]\n";

for (@ARGV)
{
    $old = $_;
    eval $op;
    die $@ if $@;
    rename($was,$_) unless $was eq $_;
}
```

You can now do this

```
$ rename.pl s/foo/bar/ foo*
```

and rename all the files starting with "foo" so they start with "bar." To process more complex renames, such as the extension one we started with:

```
$ rename.pl s/\.txt$/\.bak/
```

Replacing Text Across a Number of Files

You can use the **–i** and **–p** command line switches to replace text within files very easily. At its simplest, you can use it to translate DOS-formatted text files into Unix format:

```
perl -p -i.bak -e 's/[\012][\015]' file.in
```

However, it can also be used to perform more complex replacements across any number of files. This can be useful on websites where you want to update a link or other piece of text without editing every single file. For example:

```
perl -pi -e 's/help\.html/aid\.html/g'
```

Or you can embed it in a file if you want to do multiple replacements:

```
#!/usr/local/bin/perl -pi
next unless ($ARGV =~ /\.html/);
s/help\.html/aid\.html/g;
s#/cgi-bin/show\.pl#/cgi-bin/display\.pl#g/;
```

Essentially, anything you can do with Perl, you can do with an in-place edit and a set of files.

Synchronizing Files Across Servers

Here's a script from my personal collection, and one featured in my book *Perl Annotated Archives*. Despite my best efforts, the home network is missing a backup device for my Unix machines. To get around this, I wrote a very simple script, using Perl and Graham Barr's **libnet** bundle, which copies a directory tree from one machine to another using FTP. I use this to synchronize my vital files from my Unix machines to a directory on a server that is backed up. Furthermore, I actually use the same script for uploading websites from the Unix machine to my web hosting service.

Because it synchronizes from one machine to another, I know the contents will match, and I'll have easily retained the directory structure. Better still, if one of the Unix machines does go down, I can still access the files using a familiar directory layout without having to use a backup system to access them. Once a machine is back online, I can use the same script to copy the files back to the correct machine.

```
#!/usr/local/bin/perl5

use Net::FTP;
use Getopt::Long;
use File::Find;
use Cwd;

my $debug       = 1;
my $remserver   = undef;
my $remport     = '21';
my $user        = 'anonymous';
my $password    = 'me@foo.bar';
my $dir         = '.';
my $localdir    = './';
my $curxfermode = 'ASCII';

unless (GetOptions("d" => \$debug,
                   "s=s" => \$remserver,
                   "r=s" => \$dir,
                   "p=i" => \$remport,
                   "u=s" => \$user,
                   "w=s" => \$password,
                   "l=s" => \$localdir
                   ))
{
    usage();
}

usage() unless $remserver;

$localdir = './' unless ($localdir);
my $ftp = Net::FTP->new($remserver, 'Port' => $remport);
die "Could not connect to $remserver" unless $ftp;
$ftp->login($user, $password)
    or die "Couldn't login to $remserver";
$ftp->cwd($dir)
```

```
    or die "Invalid directory ($dir) on FTP Server";
$ftp->ascii()
    or warn "Couldn't change default xfer mode, continuing";

chdir($localdir);
my $currentdir = getcwd();
find(\&sendfile,'.');

$ftp->quit();

sub sendfile
{
    my $file      =  $File::Find::name;
    $file         =~ s#^\./##g;
    my $localfile =  "$currentdir/$file";
    $localfile    =~ s#//#/#g;
    my $remfile   =  $file;

    print "Processing $localfile rem($remfile)\n" if $debug;

    if (-d $localfile)
    {
        my $remcurdir = $ftp->pwd();
        unless($ftp->cwd($remfile))
        {
            unless ($localfile eq '..')
            {
                print "Attempting to make directory $remfile\n";
                $ftp->mkdir($remfile,1) or
                    die "Couldn't make directory $remfile";
            }
        }
        else
        {
            $ftp->cwd($remcurdir) or
                die "Couldn't change to directory $currentdir";
        }
    }
    else
    {
        my ($remtime,$localtime,$upload) = (undef,undef,0);
        unless($remtime = $ftp->mdtm($remfile))
```

```
{
    $remtime = 0;
}
$localtime = (stat($file))[9];
if (defined($localtime) and defined($remtime))
{
    if ($localtime > $remtime)
    {
        $upload=1;
    }
}
else
{
    $upload=1;
}
if ($upload)
{
    if (-B $localfile)
    {
        if ($curxfermode eq 'ASCII')
        {
            if ($ftp->binary())
            {
                $curxfermode = 'BIN';
                print "Changed mode to BINary\n"
                    if $debug;
            }
            else
            {
                warn "Couldn't change transfer mode";
            }
        }
    }
    else
    {
        if ($curxfermode eq 'BIN')
        {
            if ($ftp->ascii())
            {
                $curxfermode = 'ASCII';
                print "Changed mode to ASCII\n"
                    if $debug;
```

```
                    }
                    else
                    {
                        warn "Couldn't change transfer mode";
                    }
                }
            }
            print "Uploading $localfile to $remfile\n" if $debug;
            $ftp->put($localfile,$remfile)
                or warn "Couldn't upload $remfile";
        }
        else
        {
            print "File $remfile appears to be up to date\n"
                if $debug;
        }
    }
}

sub usage
{
    print <<EOF;
Usage:

    uplsite.pl [-d] [-r remdir] [-p remport] [-u user]
               [-w password] [-l localdir] -s server

Description:

Uploads a directory structure to the server using FTP.

Where:

-d  Switch on debugging output
-r  Remote directory to upload to (defaults to .)
-p  The remote port to use (defaults to 21)
-u  The user name to login as (defaults to anonymous)
-w  The password to use (defaults to me\@foo.bar)
-l  The local directory to upload from (defaults to .)
-s  The remote server address to upload to (required)

EOF
exit 1;
}
```

The script uses a combination of the **Net::FTP** modules and the **File::Find** modules to progress through a local directory tree, uploading files as it goes. It relies on the date and time stamp that may or may not be available on the destination host to check whether the local version of the file has been updated. For convenience, it also decides whether to upload each individual file as ASCII or binary, only switching when it needs to.

To use, supply the upload information on the command line:

```
$ uplsite.pl -d -r etc -s backup.mchome.com -u backup -w backup
```

The output looks something like this:

```
Processing /etc/. rem(.)
Processing /etc/.login rem(.login)
Uploading /etc/.login to .login
Processing /etc/cron.d rem(cron.d)
Attempting to make directory cron.d
Processing /etc/cron.d/.proto rem(cron.d/.proto)
Uploading /etc/cron.d/.proto to cron.d/.proto
Processing /etc/cron.d/logchecker rem(cron.d/logchecker)
Uploading /etc/cron.d/logchecker to cron.d/logchecker
Processing /etc/cron.d/queuedefs rem(cron.d/queuedefs)
Uploading /etc/cron.d/queuedefs to cron.d/queuedefs
Processing /etc/cron.d/at.deny rem(cron.d/at.deny)
Uploading /etc/cron.d/at.deny to cron.d/at.deny
Processing /etc/cron.d/cron.deny rem(cron.d/cron.deny)
Uploading /etc/cron.d/cron.deny to cron.d/cron.deny
Processing /etc/cron.d/FIFO rem(cron.d/FIFO)
```

Downloading Websites

As a web developer, and an avid Net user for almost ten years, I know how frustrating, time consuming, and, in the case of the UK at least, how expensive browsing websites can be. There have for many years been solutions to the problem, and most of them involve a custom-designed application for downloading HTML pages and the respective graphics to the local machine. You can then read the pages without being online.

The problem is that many of the programs are designed to download all the pages, links, and images, without taking the time to let you think or actively select the pages you want to download. Again, Perl comes to the rescue through the toolkit and modules provided by Gisle Aas. The **LWP** module provides a very simple way of downloading pages from the Internet without worrying about opening network sockets, using the HTTP protocol, or having to communicate with remote servers.

```
#!/usr/local/bin/perl

use LWP::Simple;
use LWP::UserAgent;
use HTML::LinkExtor;
use URI::URL;
use Getopt::Long;
use File::Basename;

my ($file,$host,$localdir,$curhost);
my ($url, $specdir, $quiet, $silent, $inchost, $unrestrict)
    = (undef, undef, undef, undef, undef);

usage() unless(GetOptions("d=s" => \$specdir,
                          "s"   => \$silent,
                          "q"   => \$quiet,
                          "h"   => \$inchost,
                          "u"   => \$unrestrict
                          ));

usage() unless($url=shift);
$specdir = '.' unless defined($specdir);
$specdir = "$specdir/" unless ($specdir =~ m#/$#);
$quiet = 1 if ($silent);

my %fullurl;
my @urlstack = ($url);
my @urls = ();
my $p = HTML::LinkExtor->new(\&callback);

my $ua = new LWP::UserAgent;
my $res = $ua->request(HTTP::Request->new(GET => $url));
my $base = $res->base;
$curhost = $host = url($url,'')->host;

print "Retrieving from $url to $specdir",
      ($inchost ? "$host\n" : "\n")
          unless ($silent);

while ($url = pop(@urlstack))
{
    $host = url($url,'')->host;
```

```
    if ($host ne $curhost)
    {
        my $ua = new LWP::UserAgent;
        my $res = $ua->request(HTTP::Request->new(GET => $url));
        my $base = $res->base;
        $host = url($url,'')->host;
        $curhost = $host;
        print "Changing host to $host\n" unless $quiet;
    }
    $localdir = ($inchost ? "$specdir$host/" : "$specdir/");

    $file = url($url,$base)->full_path;
    $file .='index.html' if ($file =~ m#/$#);
    $file =~ s#^/#$localdir#;

    print "Retrieving: $url to $file\n" unless ($quiet);
    my $dir = dirname($file);
    unless (-d $dir)
    {
        mkdirhier($dir);
    }
    getfile($url,$file);
    if (-e $file)
    {
        $p->parse_file($file);
        @urls = map { $_ = url($_, $base)->abs; } @urls;
        addtostack(@urls);
    }
}

sub addtostack
{
    my (@urllist) = @_;

    for my $url (@urllist)
    {
        next if ($url =~ /#/);
        next unless ($url =~ m#^http#);
        my $urlhost = url($url,$base)->host;
        unless (defined($unrestrict))
            { next unless ($urlhost eq $host); };
```

```
            push(@urlstack,$url) unless(defined($fullurl{$url}));
            $fullurl{$url} = 1;
        }
}

sub callback
{
    my($tag, %attr) = @_;
    push(@urls, values %attr);
}

sub getfile
{
    my ($url,$file) = @_;
    my $rc = mirror($url, $file);

    if ($rc == 304)
    {
        print "File is up to date\n" unless ($quiet);
    }
    elsif (!is_success($rc))
    {
        warn "sitemirr: $rc ", status_message($rc), " ($url)\n"
            unless ($silent);
        return(0);
    }
}

sub mkdirhier
{
    my ($fullpath) = @_;
    my $path;

    for my $dir (split(m#/#,$fullpath))
    {
        unless (-d "$path$dir")
        {
            mkdir("$path$dir",0777)
                or die "Couldn't make directory $path/$dir: $!";
        }
        $path .= "$dir/";
    }
```

```
}

sub usage
{
    die <<EOF;
Usage:
    sitemirr.pl [-d localdir] [-s] [-q] URL

Where:

localdir is the name of the local directory you want
         files copied to (default: .)
h        Include host in local directory path
q        Retrieve quietly (show errors only)
s        Retrieve silently (no output)
u        Unrestrict site match (will download ALL
         URL's, including those from other hosts)
EOF
}
```


For example, to download a copy of my MCwords site, www.mcwords.com:

```
$ sitemirr.pl -d . -s http://www.mcwords.com
```

This will copy the whole site into ./www.mcwords.com, including the structure and contents. It uses a simple loop to progress through the available pages that it downloads. The loop takes individual URLs off the stack, starting with the first. The bulk of the code centers around the divination of the URL from a local or relative location to a fully expanded URL so that you don't download the same URL multiple times.

The critical part of the code, though, is here:

```
$p->parse_file($file);
@urls = map { $_ = url($_, $base)->abs; } @urls;
addtostack(@urls);
```

This parses the file, using the **LWP** toolkit, before using **map** to translate partial URLs into full versions, and then adds them to the stack using the custom **addtostack** function. This checks a global hash to ensure the URL hasn't been downloaded or added to the list already before adding those needing to be downloaded onto the stack; and so the process continues and repeats until the whole site has been downloaded.

To prevent you from downloading the whole Internet (which may seem attractive at first!), you can use the **–u** option and compare the URL to be downloaded with the host of the original URL. If the two don't match, the URL is not added to the stack.

Controlling Windows Software

A fundamental problem with using a GUI application on a GUI operating system is that you lose much of the flexibility provided with command line tools. This is far from a criticism of the applications and operating systems involved, but it can sometimes be a frustration when you know how easy a particular operation would be if only you could write a small script to do the work for you.

This is the idea behind application-specific languages such as Visual Basic and the more generalized operating system scripting languages of OLE and AppleScript. In Chapter 22 we looked at the modules available when programming with Perl under Windows. One of these is the **Win32::OLE** module, which is part of the **libwin** bundle available from CPAN. This provides an interface between Perl and the OLE system. Using this you can communicate with Visual Basic and the other languages embedded in some applications.

As an example, let's look at how to control Microsoft Word. We'll use a common example—the need to convert a number of files simultaneously from one format to another. In our case, we'll convert Word documents to simple text files:

```
use strict;
use Win32::OLE;
my @files = @ARGV;
die "Usage:\n$0 files [...]\n" unless @files;
my $word = new Win32::OLE('Word.Application')
                || die "Can't open Word $!";

foreach $file (@files)
{
    next unless ($file =~ m/\.doc$/);
    $word->Documents->Open($file);
    (my $newfile = $file) =~ s/\.doc$/\.txt/ig;
    $word->ActiveDocument->SaveAs({FileName   => $newfile,
                                   FileFormat => 'wdFormatText'
                                  });
}
$word->Close();
```

It looks simple, and it is. You create a new OLE object, opening Word in the process; then you progress each of the files on the command line and call the **SaveAs** method on the active document to save the file to a new location. To use, just call it like this,

```
C:\> doc2txt.pl *.doc
```

and let Perl do the rest!

The same techniques can be employed with other OLE programs.

Controlling the MacOS

We looked at an example of controlling the MacOS in Chapter 23, but it's worth covering it again for those of you who skipped that chapter. The AppleScript language is much like OLE under Windows and provides a method for controlling an application, providing it supports AppleScript. The AppleScript system was originally released with System 7.5.2 and has since become a major component of the Mac operating system. The easiest way to do this is with the bundled Script Editor application. This creates an AppleScript script from your mouse movements, keyboard commands, and other information, just like other macro environments. You can then paste the generated script into a Perl program and use the **MacPerl::DoAppleScript** function. For example, to create a Mac version of the earlier OLE script for printing documents:

```
foreach $file (@ARGV)
{
    MacPerl::DoAppleScript(<<EOF)
    tell application "Finder"
        activate
        select file "$file"
        print selection
    end tell
EOF
}
```

If you created this in MacPerl, and saved it as a droplet, you could drag and drop files onto the newly created MacPerl script and have it print files.

This is not quite as elegant as the previous solution. You're actually relying on a feature of the MacOS that allows you to print a document directly from the finder, without having to interface with the application. However, you can also use AppleScript to interface to an underlying scripting language, again, if the application supports it. With Microsoft Word, it supports an interface between the AppleScript engine and the embedded Visual Basic engine, so you can also write AppleScript applications like this:

```
tell application "Microsoft Word"
   activate
   do Visual Basic "   Application.PrintOut FileName:=\"\",
Range:=wdPrintRangeOfPages, Item:= _
      wdPrintDocumentContent, Copies:=1, Pages:=\"1-1\", PageType:= _
      wdPrintAllPages, Collate:=True, Background:=False"
   close window 1
end tell
```

This sets the options for printing pages 1-1 in a document. You could combine it with the above to print only the first page of all the documents you dropped onto the droplet application:

```
foreach $file (@ARGV)
{
    MacPerl::DoAppleScript(<<EOF);
tell application "Finder"
   activate
   select file "$file"
   open selection
end tell
EOF

MacPerl::DoAppleScript(q/
tell application "Microsoft Word"
   activate
   do Visual Basic "   Application.PrintOut FileName:=\"\",
      Range:=wdPrintRangeOfPages, Item:= _
      wdPrintDocumentContent, Copies:=1, Pages:=\"1-1\", PageType:= _
      wdPrintAllPages, Collate:=True, Background:=False"
close window 1
end tell/);
}
```

This relies on dropping a Word document onto the newly created droplet, but you get the idea. Note that it uses the **q//** operator to quote the second AppleScript script. This is so that you retain the formatting, newlines, and especially the backslashes and double quotes.

IRC Bots

One of my "executive toys" is a channel bot called Spip, which, until very recently, resided in the IRCnet #beos channel. This particular bot is an information agent, and it uses the text processing abilities of Perl, in combination with its ability to easily store and recover information in multiple DBM databases, to provide an almost human interface for finding information.

The IRC channels use these bots to help answer the frequently asked questions that occur on the channel. For example:

```
Auth-MCB: Spip, status?
Spip: Since Tue May  4 22:18:46 1999, there have been 0 modifications and 0
questions.  I have been awake for 2 minutes, 29 seconds this session, and
currently reference 23 factoids.
Auth-MCB: rfc 21?
Spip: i guess rfc 21 is Network meeting. V.G. Cerf. Oct-17-1969. (Not
online) (Status: UNKNOWN)
```

The code for Spip is based on the Infobot code supported by Kevin Lenzo, at the Carnegie Mellon University. The core interface is large and provides and supports all sorts of features, using a combination of the text processing capabilities of Perl and the ability to embed simple Perl statements for actions such as simple mathematical calculations. The Infobot code even includes the ability to look up hosts and domains using **ping** and **whois**.

Perhaps best of all, you can customize the interface by using the **myRoutines.pl** script and by making modifications to the **myRoutines** function. The latest Spip version, before it was shut down, included the ability to "torture" other users, provide multiline replies to queries, and even to cook virtual meals. My favorite feature though was his temper—abuse him too many times, and he just stopped answering queries until you apologized.

Other Infobots are more practical and support routines that allow you to control the channel itself. Unfortunately, there are some irresponsible IRC users out there who abuse other genuine channel users, and so you need a way of protecting your channel and securing it from these users. You can do this with features built into any IRC server, but you must be connected and monitoring the traffic on the connection in order to kick these people, literally, into touch by blocking them out of the channel.

Although the Infobot code can do this quite effectively, you might want to develop a more pragmatic interface using the **Net::IRC** module available on CPAN. It was developed by Dennis Taylor, and the module supports an object-oriented interface to an IRC system. To create a connection to a machine is as easy as:

```
use strict;
use Net::IRC;

my $irc = new Net::IRC;

print "Connecting to IRC server\n";

my $conn = $irc->newconn(Server   => 'ircnet.demon.co.uk',
                         Port     => '6667',
                         Nick     => 'SonofSpip',
                         Ircname  => 'Son of Spip',
                         Username => 'sonofspip')
    or die "irctest: Can't connect to IRC server.\n";
```

Then to control a particular event, you install a handler. The one below shows what to do when a new user joins one of the monitored channels. In this case, you set the user to have administration ("ops") privileges on the channel if the name and host are matched by a particular expression. The bot obviously needs "ops" privilege itself for this handler to work. Once the function has been created, you then need to add it as a valid handler to the connection object.

```
sub on_join
{
    my ($self, $event) = @_;
    my ($channel) = ($event->to)[0];

    printf "*** %s (%s) has joined channel %s\n",
    $event->nick, $event->userhost, $channel;
    if ($event->userhost =~ /mc\@mcwords.com/)
    {
        $self->mode($channel, "+o", $event->nick);
    }
}
$conn->add_handler('join',   \&on_join);
```

Finally, you kick off the bot and let it do its thing:

```
$irc->start;
```

It's likely that if you use IRC at all, you'll spot these bots about on the different channels. There are a few on the #perl channels on different IRC networks, and all provide very similar features.

Games

Because Perl is a general-purpose language, you can use it to program all sorts of things, and almost since time began, computers have been used for programming games and other diversions. One of the oldest known games is shown below. It's the "guess what number I'm thinking of game," or Hi-Low (or any number of other names), which is probably centuries, if not millennia old, and can easily be emulated on a computer with some simple **if...elsif** statements.

```
#!/usr/local/bin/perl

srand(time);
$numbertoguess = int(rand(99))+1;

print "Guess a number between 1 and 100:\n";

for(;;)
{
    $guess = <STDIN>;
    if ($guess !~ /\d+/)
    {
        print "I was expecting a number\n";
        next;
    }
    if ($guess > $numbertoguess)
    {
        print "Too high, try again:\n";
        next;
    }
    elsif ($guess < $numbertoguess)
    {
        print "Too low, try again:\n";
        next;
    }
    elsif ($guess == $numbertoguess)
    {
        last;
    }
```

```
}

print "Correct! You win!\n";
```

Once run, it can provide endless hours of fun. Well, a good few minutes anyway:

```
Guess a number between 1 and 100:
50
Too low, try again:
80
Too high, try again:
60
Too high, try again:
55
Correct! You win!
```

Another alternative is sort of a personal version of the earlier IRC examples—the conversational application. The Turing test, in honor of Alan Turing, the "father" of the modern computer, attempts to identify whether an artificial intelligence program can effectively emulate a human and hold a "human" conversation. You've already seen how Perl can be used as a simple data repository for holding information and helping to control IRC channels. Spip, although seemingly intelligent, actually has just been given a lot of information about computer-related topics. In fact, at his core is a very simple program similar to the one shown below:

```
#!/usr/local/bin/perl -w

use GDBM_File;
use Fcntl;
use strict;

$| = 1;

my @unknowns = ('Eh?', 'What?', 'Pardon?', "Watcha talkin 'bout man?",
                'Er...?', "I'm not sure I understand you.");

tie my %respdb, 'GDBM_File', 'respdb', O_RDWR|O_CREAT, 0666
    or die "Can't open responsee: $!";

print ">> ";

while(<STDIN>)
{
    chomp;
```

```
    parse_query();
    print ">> ";
}

sub parse_query
{
    if (my ($key, $value) = m/(\S+)\s+is\s+(.*)/)
    {
        $respdb{lc($key)} = $value;
        print "Gotcha!\n";
    }
    else
    {
        if (exists($respdb{lc($_)}))
        {
            print "$respdb{lc($_)}\n";
        }
        else
        {
            print $unknowns[int(rand(@unknowns))],"\n";
        }
    }
}
```


Once you've taught him some information, he can almost seem human, but only because of his programmed responses:

```
>> hi
Hello. What do you want?
>> breakfast
Already cooking the eggs and bacon!
>> cancel
OK, I've stopped
>>
```

There are other uses for this sort of interface. Another of the age-old computer games is the adventure. Long before Quake or SimCity, there were Pawn, Lord of the Rings, Zork, and countless others. They all used a similar interface. You entered text queries and commands, and the computer would give you a programmed response based on the information you supplied. Although not "intelligent," the complexity of the interface and the information stored within the adventure database made for a very compelling game. Even now, similar immersing games exist, albeit with a different interface.

The logical extension of a single-player adventure game is the multiuser game (MUG) or multiuser dungeon (MUD). There is one available that has been written entirely in Perl, called PerlMUD, and available from http://www.boutell.com/perlmud/. It features a very advanced interface and a customizable world and environment.

If you are looking for a more graphical or interactive game, then a short search will provide you with some suitable links. You can find chess, card games (I've seen, but not played, blackjack and poker), and even checkers. Most of these are designed as CGI scripts that are two-way interfaces between users on a website, but they do help demonstrate the abilities of Perl as a general-purpose programming language.

Chapter 13 covered advanced user interfaces. One of the things covered was Tk. It provides a standard interface for developing Unix- and Windows-based GUI applications within Perl. Sriram Srinivasan has written a version of Tetris, another computer game favorite, using Perl/Tk. It is quite long—in fact, too long to include here comfortably—but you can find a copy on the O'Reilly FTP site at ftp.ora.com.

The Complete Reference

Part IX

Appendixes

Appendix A

Resources

From its humble beginnings many years ago, Perl has grown to be one of the "cult" languages on the Internet. Many websites, books, journals, mailing lists, and newsgroups supply a seemingly endless stream of information on the topic of Perl and Perl programming.

I've done my best to list a range of resources here that most people will find useful. Many of the entries are personal recommendations. Certainly, populating your shelf with the book list wouldn't be a bad idea!

However, this appendix is by no means an attempt to list all the possible entries and resources available. Perl is too popular, and the Internet is too fluid to make that sort of thoroughness possible.

Printed Material

While it's impossible to list all the books, journals, and other publications that promote Perl as a programming language, there are some standard books that all Perl programmers should probably keep on their bookshelf.

Books

Asbury, S., M. Glover, A. Humphreys, E. Weiss, J. Matthews, and S. Sol. 1997. *Perl 5 How-To*. 2d ed. Corte Madera, CA: Waite Group

By using a question-and-answer style, this book covers nearly the entire range of Perl's abilities. By solving specific problems and giving step-by-step examples of the solutions, the book manages to explain even the most complex areas of Perl development.

Brown, M. C. 1999. *Perl Annotated Archives*. Berkeley, CA: Osborne McGraw-Hill

This is a library of scripts and modules that are annotated, line by line, in order to demonstrate both the abilities of Perl and the logic behind the scripts' execution. The book should help both beginners and advanced users, and it is an excellent companion to *Perl: The Complete Reference.*

Brown, V., and C. Nandor. 1998. *MacPerl: Power and Ease*. Sunnyvale, CA: Prime Time Freeware

This book is a perfect guide to programming Mac-specific Perl scripts, as well as a general guide to Perl programming and making the best of the MacPerl development environment.

Johnson, E. F. 1996. *Cross-Platform Perl*. Foster City, CA: IDG Books Worldwide

This book concentrates on creating code that can be easily transported between Unix and NT hosts. Special attention is given to scripts that deal with systems administration and websites, although the book covers a wide range of other topics.

Orwant, J. 1997. *Perl 5 Interactive Course: Certified Edition*. Corte Madera, CA: Waite Group

This book is a thorough guide to Perl 5 programming, taking the reader through a series of different tasks and topics that range from building basic scripts to the proper use of variables, functions, and Perl-style regular expressions.

Srinivasan, S. 1997. *Advanced Perl Programming*. Sebastopol, CA: O'Reilly

This book is an excellent guide to data modeling, networking, and the Tk widget interface. It also covers the internal workings of Perl, which will help the advanced programmer write more efficient and smaller code, while providing all the information necessary for extending Perl with external C code.

Wall, L., T. Christiansen, and R. L. Schwartz. 1996. *Programming Perl*. 2d ed. Sebastopol, CA: O'Reilly

Written by the three modern Perl architects, this is the definitive guide to Perl programming. This is what most people refer to as the "Camel" book, since that is the picture used on the front.

Wall, L., T. Christiansen, and N. Torkington. 1998. *Perl Cookbook*. Sebastopol, CA: O'Reilly

This cookbook of recipes for programming in the Perl language is written by the same team as the classic Camel book and is based on two chapters from the original first edition.

Journals

The Perl Journal

A periodical devoted entirely to Perl, *The Perl Journal* covers a wide range of topics from basic principles for beginners to the advanced topics of Perl internals.

SunExpert Magazine

A magazine targeted at Sun and Unix users, *SunExpert* also covers the use of Perl in a systems administration and web serving role.

SunWorld Online (www.sunworldonline.com)

SunWorld Online is a monthly web magazine that covers a number of topics, including using Perl to help manage and monitor Sun workstations.

Web Resources

Although Perl's history is rooted in a simple reporting language, it became rapidly apparent that it could be used as a suitable language for CGI programming, and there are therefore a vast number of websites dedicated to Perl. The main site is the Perl Institute at www.perl.org. This is the home of Perl and is a good place to start looking for more information.

If you don't find what you are looking for under one of the sites in Table A-1, try visiting Yahoo (www.yahoo.com) or AltaVista (www.altavista.digital.com). The former lists hundreds of sites within its directory.

FTP Sites

If you are looking for a specific module, script, or idea, then it's best to visit the CPAN archives (see Table A-1), since the CPAN system will automatically take you to a local FTP

Site	Description
www.perl.org	The Perl Institute—the "official" home of Perl. You'll find general information on Perl, links to sources, ports, and a vast amount of background and support information on the Perl world.
www.perl.com	Tom Christiansen's Perl website. Tom is one of the major contributors to the modern Perl effort and Perl itself and author of a number of books on the topic. His site is primarily geared to providing general information and sample scripts and modules.
www.cpan.org	The Comprehensive Perl Archive Network (CPAN) is an online library of scripts, modules, and extensions to Perl. Originally produced with script-specific archives in mind, CPAN now concentrates on supporting and supplying perl5 modules. CPAN should be second port of call (after the CD-ROM) for the modules I've used throughout this book.
www.iis.ee.ethz.ch/~neeri/macintosh/perl.html	The MacPerl homepage contains links and information on using Perl on the Mac.
www.ActiveWare.com	ActiveWare offers a port of perl5 that is usable with Windows NT web servers (such as Microsoft's Internet Information Server (IIS)). If you want a more general version of Perl for NT, you need the "core" port available on CPAN.
www.roth.net/perl	This site is maintained by Dave Roth, the author of the Win32::AdminMisc Perl module for Windows 95 and NT. There is also some general information and other example scripts.
www.virtualschool.edu/mon/Perl/index.html	You'll find a wealth of information on both Mac- and Unix-based Perl scripts and modules here.
www.metronet.com/perlinfo/perl5.html	This brilliant independent source for perl5 scripts, modules, and examples is an excellent starting point for Perl programmers, beginner or advanced, to further their knowledge.

Table A-1. *Perl Websites*

site. However, if all you want to do is browse around the available files, or download the entire contents, then try some of the sites in Table A-2.

Server Name	Directory
coombs.anu.edu.au	/pub/perl/CPAN/src/5.0
ftp.cis.ufl.edu	/pub/perl/CPAN/src/5.0
ftp.cs.ruu.nl	/pub/PERL/perl5.0/src
ftp.funet.fi	/pub/languages/perl/CPAN/src/5.0
ftp.metronet.com	/pub/perl/source
ftp.netlabs.com	/pub/outgoing/perl5.0
sinsite.doc.ic.ac.uk	/pub/computing/programming/languages/perl/perl.5.0
sungear.mame.mu.oz.au	/pub/perl/src/5.0

Table A-2. *Perl FTP Sites*

Mailing Lists

Mailing lists fall into two distinct categories: announcements or discussions. If the list is for announcements, you are not allowed to post to the group. These tend to be low volume and are useful for keeping in touch with the direction of Perl. If it's a discussion list, you can post and reply to messages just as you would in a Usenet newsgroup. These are higher volume lists, and the number of messages can become unmanageable very quickly.

Saying that, a discussion list is likely to have the experts and users in it that are able to answer your questions and queries with authority.

General Mailing Lists

Perl Institute Announce

This list carries announcements from the Perl Institute on general Perl issues. To subscribe, send email to majordomo@perl.org with "subscribe tpi-announce" in the body of the message.

Perl-Unicode (from the Perl Institute)

This list is concerned with issues surrounding Unicode and Perl at both porting and using levels. To subscribe, send email to majordomo@perl.org with "subscribe perl-unicode" in the body of the message.

Perl5-Porters

If you are porting Perl or Perl modules or want to help in the development of the Perl language in general, you should be a member of this discussion list. Don't join if you are just interested. This is a high-volume, highly technical mailing list.

To subscribe, send email to majordomo@perl.org with "subscribe perl5-porters" in the body of the message.

Platform-Specific Mailing Lists

MacOS

This is a general discussion list of using Perl on the Mac. To subscribe, send email to mac-perl-request@iis.ee.ethz.ch with a body of "subscribe."

Windows Users

The Perl-Win32-Users mailing list is targeted for Perl installation and programming questions. There are two versions: standard and digest. To subscribe to the standard version, send email to ListManager@ActiveState.com with "SUBSCRIBE Perl-Win32-Users" in the body of the message. To subscribe to the digest version, send email to ListManager@ActiveState.com with "DIGEST Perl-Win32-Users" in the body of the message.

Windows Announce

This mailing list is for announcements of new builds, bugs, security problems, and other information. To subscribe to the standard version, send email to ListManager@ActiveState.com with "SUBSCRIBE Perl-Win32-Announce" in the body of the message. To subscribe to the digest version, send email to ListManager@ActiveState.com with "DIGEST Perl-Win32-Announce" in the body of the message.

Windows Web Programming

This focuses on using Perl as a CGI programming alternative on Windows NT servers. To subscribe to the standard version, send email to ListManager@ActiveState.com with "SUBSCRIBE Perl-Win32-Web" in the body of the message. To subscribe to the digest version, send email to ListManager@ActiveState.com with "DIGEST Perl-Win32-Web" in the body of the message.

Windows Admin

Here you will find information and discussion on using Perl for administering and managing Windows 95 and NT machines. To subscribe to the standard version, send email to ListManager@ActiveState.com with "SUBSCRIBE Perl-Win32-Admin" in the body of the message. To subscribe to the digest version, send email to ListManager@ActiveState.com with "DIGEST Perl-Win32-Admin" in the body of the message.

Newsgroups

To reach a more general Perl audience, you might want to post a question or announcement to one of the many Perl newsgroups. These are available on more ISP's Usenet news servers, and many will be happy to add them to their list if you ask nicely, the list is summarized in Table A-3.

You may also want to refer to "Joseph's Top Ten Tips for Answering Questions Posted to comp.lang.perl.misc," available at http://www.5sigma.com/perl/topten.html. This will provide you with some hints and tips on how best to make use of the question-and-answer nature of many of these groups.

Newsgroup	Description
comp.infosystems.www.authoring.cgi	Deals with using Perl as a tool for writing CGI programs. This is a general CGI discussion group; it is not specifically targeted at Perl users. However, it does provide a lot of useful information on extracting, receiving, and returning information from web servers and clients.
comp.lang.perl.announce	Used to announce news from the Perl world. This includes new book releases, new version releases, and occasionally major Perl module releases.
comp.lang.perl.misc	A general discussion forum for Perl. Everything from queries about how best to tackle a problem to the inside machinations of Perl are discussed here. Some of the discussion can get quite technical and be more biased to someone interested in the internal Perl workings, but it still represents the best port of call if you are having trouble with a problem or Perl script.
comp.lang.perl.modules	This was set up to specifically discuss the use and creation of Perl modules. Unlike comp.lang.perl.misc, you should only find problems related to modules in this group. If you are having trouble with something downloaded from CPAN, this is the best place to start asking questions.
comp.lang.perl.tk	Tk is a toolkit that provides a set of functions to support a graphical user interface (GUI) within Perl. Tk was originally developed in combination with Tcl (Tool command language) but has been massaged to work with other scripting systems, including Perl. Tk's strength, like Perl's, is that it is available for a number of platforms; and therefore building a GUI-style interface within X Windows (under Unix), Microsoft Windows (on the PC), and MacOS, among others, becomes very much easier.

Table A-3. *Perl-Friendly Newsgroups*

Appendix B

Function Reference

This appendix contains a complete functional reference for the built-in features of Perl. Additional functions and abilities may be provided by external packages and modules, both within the standard Perl distribution and from CPAN and other sources.

Note that this is intended as a quick reference for the arguments and values returned by each function. For a full discussion on how to use the function in a script, please refer to the corresponding chapter.

Note that in all cases, unless otherwise noted, the functions return either zero or **undef** on failure. Most functions will also set the value of **$!** to the corresponding system error number returned.

-X

```
-X FILEHANDLE
-X EXPR
-X
```

File test, where **X** is one or more of the letters listed in Table B-1. The function takes one operator, either a file name or a **FILEHANDLE**. The function tests the associated file to see if the selected option is true. If **EXPR** and **FILEHANDLE** are omitted, the function tests **$_**, except for **-t**, which tests **STDIN**.

Returns

1 if true
Special conditions exist for some operators; see Table B-1

REFERENCES Chapter 6; *see also* **stat**

abs

```
abs EXPR
abs
```

Returns the absolute value of **EXPR**, or **$_** if omitted.

Returns

Absolute value

REFERENCES Chapter 4

Test	Result
-r	File is readable by effective uid/gid.
-w	File is writable by effective uid/gid.
-x	File is executable by effective uid/gid.
-o	File is owned by effective uid.
-R	File is readable by real uid/gid.
-W	File is writable by real uid/gid.
-X	File is executable by real uid/gid.
-O	File is owned by real uid.
-e	File exists.
-z	File has zero size.
-s	File has non-zero size (returns size in bytes).
-f	File is a plain file.
-d	File is a directory.
-l	File is a symbolic link.
-p	File is a named pipe (**FIFO**), or **FILEHANDLE** is a pipe.
-S	File is a network socket.
-b	File is a block special file.
-c	File is a character special file.
-t	File is opened to a tty (terminal).
-u	File has setuid bit set.
-g	File has setgid bit set.
-k	File has sticky bit set.
-T	File is a text file.
-B	File is a binary file (opposite of -T).
-M	Age of file in days when script started.
-A	Time of last access in days when script started.
-C	Time of last inode change when script started.

Table B-1. *File Tests*

accept

```
accept NEWSOCKET, GENERICSOCKET
```

Accepts an incoming connection on **GENERICSOCKET**, assigning the new connection information to the **NEWSOCKET** filehandle.

Returns

0 on failure
Packed address of remote host on success

REFERENCES Chapter 9; *see also* **connect, listen**

alarm

```
alarm EXPR
alarm
```

Sets the "alarm," causing the current process to receive a **SIGALRM** signal in **EXPR** time. If **EXPR** is omitted, the value of **$_** is used instead. The actual time delay is not precise, since different systems implement the system differently. The actual time may be up to a second more or less than the requested value. You can only set one alarm timer at any one time. If a timer is already running and you make a new call to the alarm function, the alarm timer is reset to the new value. A running timer can be reset without setting a new timer by specifying a value of zero.

Returns

Integer, number of seconds remaining for previous timer

REFERENCES Chapter 10

atan2

```
atan2 Y,X
```

Returns the arctangent of Y/X in the range π to -π.

Returns

Floating point number

REFERENCES Chapter 4

bind

```
bind SOCKET, ADDRESS
```

Binds the network address **ADDRESS** to the **SOCKET** filehandle. The **ADDRESS** should be a packed address of the appropriate type for the socket being opened.

Returns

1 on success

REFERENCES Chapter 9; *see also* **connect**, **accept**, **socket**

binmode

```
binmode FILEHANDLE
```

Sets the format for **FILEHANDLE** to be read from and written to as binary on the operating systems that differentiate between the two. Files that are not in binary have **CR LF** sequences converted to **LF** on input and **LF** to **CR LF** on output. This is vital for operating systems that use two characters to separate lines within text files (MS-DOS), but has no effect on operating systems that use single characters (Unix, MacOS, QNX).

Returns

1 on success

REFERENCES Chapter 3

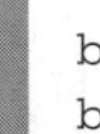

bless

```
bless REF, CLASSNAME
bless REF
```

Tells the entity referenced by **REF** that it is now an object in the **CLASSNAME** package, or the current package if **CLASSNAME** is omitted.

Returns

The reference **REF**

REFERENCES Chapter 7

caller

```
caller EXPR
caller
```

Returns the context of the current subroutine call; returns the caller's package name in a scalar context. Returns the package name, file name, and line within file in a list context, as in:

```
($package, $filename, $line) = caller;
```

If **EXPR** is specified, **caller** returns extended information, relative to the stack trace. That is, if you specify a value of 1, the parent subroutine information will be printed; a value of 2, the grandparent subroutine; and so forth. The information returned is

```
($package, $filename, $line, $subroutine,
 $hasargs, $wantarray, $evaltext, $is_require) = caller($i);
```

The **$evaltext** and **$is_require** values are only returned when the subroutine being examined is actually the result of an **eval()** statement.

Returns

undef on failure
Basic information (list) in a list context with no expression
Extended information (list) in a list context with an expression

REFERENCES Chapter 18

chdir

```
chdir EXPR
chdir
```

Changes the current working directory to **EXPR**, or user's home directory if none specified.

Returns

1 on success

REFERENCES Chapter 6

chmod

```
chmod MODE, LIST
```

Changes the mode of the files specified in **LIST** to the **MODE** specified. The value of **MODE** should be in octal.

Returns

0 on failure
Integer, number of files successfully changed

REFERENCES Chapter 6; *see also* **–X**, **stat**

chomp

```
chomp EXPR
chomp LIST
chomp
```

Removes the last character if it matches the value of **$/** from **EXPR**, each element of **LIST**, or **$_** if no value is specified. Note that this is a safer version of the **chop** function since it only removes the last character if it matches **$/**. Removes all trailing newlines from the string or strings if in paragraph mode (when **$/ = ""**).

Returns

Integer, number of bytes removed for all strings

REFERENCES Chapter 4; *see also* **chop**

chop

```
chop EXPR
chop LIST
chop
```

Removes the last character from **EXPR**, each element of **LIST**, or **$_** if no value is specified.

Returns

The character removed from **EXPR**, or from last element of **LIST**

REFERENCES Chapter 4; *see also* **chomp**

chown

```
chown USERID, GROUPID, LIST
```

Changes the user and group to the IDs specified by **USERID** and **GROUPID** on the files specified in **LIST**. Note that **USERID** and **GROUPID** must be the numeric IDs, not the names. If you specify a value of **–1** to either argument, then the user or group ID are not updated.

Returns

Number of files successfully changed

REFERENCES Chapter 6

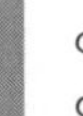

chr

```
chr EXPR
chr
```

Returns the character represented by the numeric value of **EXPR**, or **$_** if omitted, according to the current character set.

Returns

Character

REFERENCES Chapter 4

chroot

```
chroot EXPR
chroot
```

Changes the root directory for all pathnames beginning with "/" to the directory specified by **EXPR**, or **$_** if none is specified. For security reasons this function, which is identical to the system **chroot()** function, is restricted to the superuser and cannot be undone.

Returns

1 on success

REFERENCES Chapter 6

close

```
close FILEHANDLE
close
```

Closes **FILEHANDLE**, flushing the buffers, if appropriate, and disassociating the **FILEHANDLE** with the original file, pipe, or socket. Closes the currently selected filehandle if none is specified.

Returns

1 if buffers were flushed and the file was successfully closed

REFERENCES Chapter 3; *see also* **open**

closedir

```
closedir DIRHANDLE
```

Closes the directory handle **DIRHANDLE**.

Returns

1 on success

REFERENCES Chapter 6; *see also* **opendir**

connect

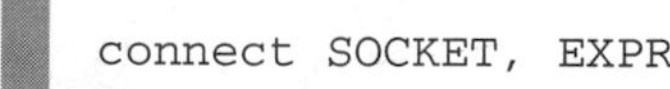

```
connect SOCKET, EXPR
```

Connects to the remote socket using the filehandle **SOCKET** and the address specified by **EXPR**. The **EXPR** should be a packed address of the appropriate type for the socket.

Returns

1 on success

REFERENCES Chapter 9

continue

```
continue BLOCK
```

Not a function. This is a flow control statement that executes **BLOCK** just before the conditional for the loop is evaluated.

Returns

Nothing

REFERENCES Chapter 2

cos

```
cos EXPR
cos
```

Returns the cosine of **EXPR**, or **$_** if **EXPR** is omitted. The value should be expressed in radians.

Returns

Floating point number

REFERENCES Chapter 4

crypt

```
crypt EXPR,SALT
```

Encrypts the string **EXPR** using the system **crypt()** function. The value of **SALT** is used to select an encrypted version from one of a number of variations.

Returns

Encrypted string

REFERENCES Chapter 6

dbmclose

```
dbmclose HASH
```

Closes the binding between a hash and a DBM file. Note that the use of this function has been deprecated, as it has been replaced with the more efficient facilities provided by **tie**.

Returns

1 on success

REFERENCES Chapter 8; *see also* **dbmopen**, **tie**

dbmopen

```
dbmopen HASH, EXPR, MODE
```

Binds the database file specified by **EXPR** to the hash **HASH**. If the database does not exist, then it is created using the mode specified by **MODE**. The file **EXPR** should be specified without the ".dir" and ".pag" extensions.

The use of **dbmopen** is now deprecated since the **tie** function provides a more advanced interface to DBM files and allows multiple types of DBM files to be used simultaneously.

Returns

1 on success

REFERENCES Chapter 8; *see also* **dbmclose**

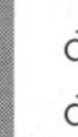

defined

```
defined EXPR
defined
```

Returns **TRUE** if **EXPR** has a value other than the **undef** value, or $_ if **EXPR** is not specified. This can be used with many functions to detect a failure in operation, since they return **undef** if there was a problem. A simple Boolean test does not differentiate between **FALSE**, zero, an empty string, or the string "0", which are all equally false.

If **EXPR** is a function or function reference, then it returns **TRUE** if the function has been defined. When used with entire arrays and hashes, it will not always produce intuitive results. If a hash element is specified, it returns **TRUE** if the corresponding value has been defined, but does not determine whether the specified key exists in the hash.

Returns
1 if **EXPR** has been defined

REFERENCES Chapter 4

delete

```
delete LIST
```

Deletes the specified keys and associated values from a hash. Deleting from the **$ENV** hash modifies the current environment, and deleting from a hash tied to a DBM database deletes the entry from the database file.

Returns
undef if the key does not exist
Each value associated with the corresponding key that was deleted

REFERENCES Chapter 7

die

```
die LIST
```

Prints the value of **LIST** to **STDERR** and calls **exit** with the error value contained in **$!**. If **$!** is zero, then it prints the value of (**$?** >> 8) (for use with backtick commands). If (**$?** >> 8) is zero, then the exit status value returned is 255.

Inside an **eval**, the value of **LIST** is inserted in the **$@** variable, and the **eval** block exits with an undefined value. You should therefore use **die** to raise an exception within a script.

If the value of **LIST** does not end in a newline, then Perl adds the current script and input line number to the message that is printed. If **LIST** is empty and **$@** already contains a value, then the string "\t...propagated" is appended, and if **LIST** is empty, the string "Died" is printed instead.

Returns
Nothing

REFERENCES Chapters 10 and 11; *see also* **exit**, **eval**, **warn**

do

```
do EXPR
```

If **EXPR** is a subroutine, executes the subroutine using the supplied arguments; otherwise, uses **EXPR** as a file name and executes the contents of the file as a Perl script.

Returns

undef if file is not accessible; on read error populates $!; compiler error populates $@
1 on success

REFERENCES Chapter 11

dump

```
dump LABEL
```

Dumps the currently executing Perl interpreter and script into a core dump. Using the **undump** program, you can then reconstitute the dumped core into an executable program. If so, execution in the dumped program starts at **LABEL**. The process is usually unsuccessful, since core dumps do not necessarily make good fodder for a new program. If you want to produce an executable version of a Perl script, use the Perl-to-C compiler.

Returns

Nothing

REFERENCES Chapters 11 and 19

each

```
each HASH
```

In a list context, returns a two-element list referring to the key and value for the next element of a hash, allowing you to iterate over it. In a scalar context, returns only the key for the next element in the hash. Information is returned in a random order, and a single iterator is shared among each—keys and values. The iterator can be reset by evaluating the entire hash or by calling the **keys** function in a scalar context.

Returns

In a list context, null array at end of hash
In a scalar context, **undef** at end of hash

In a list context, key and value for the next element of a hash
In a scalar context, key only for the next element of a hash

REFERENCES Chapter 7

endgrent

```
endgrent
```

Tells the system you no longer expect to read entries from the groups file using **getgrent**.

Returns

Nothing

REFERENCES Chapter 9; *see also* **getgrent**, **setgrent**

endhostent

```
endhostent
```

Tells the system you no longer expect to read entries from the hosts file using **gethostent**.

Returns

Nothing

REFERENCES Chapter 9; *see also* **gethostent**, **sethostent**

endnetent

```
endnetent
```

Tells the system you no longer expect to read entries from the networks list using **getnetent**.

Returns

Nothing

REFERENCES Chapter 9; *see also* **getnetent**, **setnetent**

endprotoent

```
endprotoent
```

Tells the system you no longer expect to read entries from the protocols list using **getprotoent**.

Returns

Nothing

REFERENCES Chapter 9; *see also* **getprotoent**, **setprotoent**

endpwent

```
endpwent
```

Tells the system you no longer expect to read entries from the password file using **getpwent**.

Returns

Nothing

REFERENCES Chapter 9; *see also* **getpwent**, **setpwent**

endservent

```
endservent
```

Tells the system you no longer expect to read entries from the services file using **getservent**.

Returns

Nothing

REFERENCES Chapter 9; *see also* **getservent**, **setservent**

eof

```
eof FILEHANDLE
eof()
eof
```

Returns true if the next read on the specified **FILEHANDLE** will return end of file, or if **FILEHANDLE** is not currently associated with an open file. If **FILEHANDLE** is not specified, it returns the condition for the last accessed file.

If the **eof()** format is used, it checks the input status of the list of files supplied on the command line and hence allows you to detect the end of the file list, instead of the end of the current file.

Normally, you should never need to use **eof** since all filehandle-compatible functions return false values when no data remains, or if there was an error.

Returns

1 if **FILEHANDLE** will report end of file on next read

REFERENCES Chapters 3 and 11; *see also* **while**, **open**, **close**

eval

```
eval EXPR
eval BLOCK
```

Evaluates **EXPR** at execution time as if **EXPR** was a separate Perl script. This allows you to use a separate, perhaps user-supplied, piece of Perl script within your program. An **eval EXPR** statement is evaluated separately each time the function is called.

The second form evaluates **BLOCK** when the rest of the script is parsed (before execution). Uses $_ if **BLOCK** or **EXPR** are not specified.

In both cases the evaluated **EXPR** or **BLOCK** have access to the variables, objects, and functions available within the host script.

Returns

Value of last evaluated statement in **EXPR** or **BLOCK**

REFERENCES Chapter 11

exec

```
exec LIST
```

Executes a system command (directly, not within a shell) and never returns to the calling script, except on error. The first element of **LIST** is taken as the program name; subsequent elements are passed as arguments to the command executed.

You should use **system** if you want to run a subcommand as part of a Perl script.

Returns

0 only if the command specified cannot be executed

REFERENCES Chapter 10

exists

```
exists EXPR
```

Returns **TRUE** if the specified hash key exists, regardless of the corresponding value.

Returns

1 if hash element does exist

REFERENCES Chapter 7

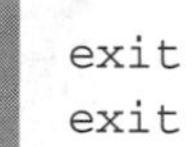

exit

```
exit EXPR
exit
```

Evaluates **EXPR**, exits the Perl interpreter, and returns the value as the exit value. Always runs all **END{}** blocks defined in the script (and imported packages) before exiting. If **EXPR** is omitted, then the interpreter exits with a value of zero. Should not be used to exit from a subroutine, either use **eval** and **die** or use **return**.

Returns

Nothing

REFERENCES Chapter 10

exp

```
exp EXPR
exp
```

Returns e (the natural logarithm base) raised to the power of **EXPR**, or **$_** if omitted.

Returns

e raised to the power

REFERENCES Chapter 4

fcntl

```
fcntl FILEHANDLE, FUNCTION, SCALAR
```

The Perl version of the system **fcntl()** function. Performs the function specified by **FUNCTION**, using **SCALAR** on **FILEHANDLE**. **SCALAR** either contains a value to be used by the function, or is the location of any returned information. The functions supported by **fcntl**() are entirely dependent on your system's implementation. If your system does not support **fcntl()**, then a fatal error will occur.

Returns

0 but true if the return value from the **fcntl()** is 0
Value returned by system

REFERENCES Chapter 6; *see also* **ioctl**

fileno

```
fileno FILEHANDLE
```

Returns the file descriptor number (as used by C and POSIX functions) of the specified **FILEHANDLE**. This is generally useful only for using the **select** function and any low-level tty functions.

Returns

undef if **FILEHANDLE** is not open
File descriptor (numeric) of **FILEHANDLE**

REFERENCES Chapter 3; *see also* **select**

flock

```
flock FILEHANDLE, OPERATION
```

Supports file locking on the specified **FILEHANDLE** using the system **flock()**, **fcntl()** locking, or **lockf()**. The exact implementation used is dependent on what your system supports. **OPERATION** is one of the static values defined in Table B-2.

In nearly all cases file locking is generally advisory, especially if the underlying implementation is through the **flock()** function.

Returns

1 on success to set/unset lock

REFERENCES Chapter 6; *see also* **fcntl**

fork

```
fork
```

Forks a new process using the **fork()** system call. Any shared sockets or filehandles are duplicated across processes. You must ensure that you wait on your children to prevent "zombie" processes from forming.

Returns

undef on failure to fork
Child process ID to parent on success
0 to child on success

REFERENCES Chapter 10

Operation	Result
LOCK_SH	Set shared lock.
LOCK_EX	Set exclusive lock.
LOCK_UN	Unlock specified file.
LONG_NB	Set lock without blocking.

Table B-2. *Locking Operations*

format

```
format NAME =
 picture line
 LIST
...
```

Declares a picture format for use by the **write** function.

Returns

Nothing

REFERENCES Chapter 12; *see also* **write**

formline

```
formline PICTURE, LIST
```

An internal function used by the **format** function and related operators. It formats **LIST** according to the contents of **PICTURE** into the output accumulator variable **$^**A. The value is written out to a filehandle when a write is done.

Returns

1 (always)

REFERENCES Chapter 12; *see also* **format**, **write**

getc

```
getc FILEHANDLE
getc
```

Reads the next character from **FILEHANDLE** (or **STDIN** if none specified), returning the value.

Returns

undef on error or end of file
Value of character read from **FILEHANDLE** empty string at end of file

REFERENCES Chapter 3

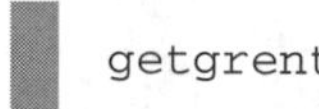

getgrent

```
getgrent
```

Iterates over the entries in the /etc/group file. Returns the following in a list context:

```
($name, $passwd, $gid, $members)
```

The **$members** scalar contains a space-separated list of the login names that are members of the group. Returns the group name in a scalar context.

Returns

Group name in a scalar context
Group information in list context

REFERENCES Chapter 6; *see also* **getgrgid**, **getgrnam**

getgrgid

```
getgrgid EXPR
```

Looks up the group file entry by group ID. Returns the following in a list context:

```
($name, $passwd, $gid, $members)
```

The **$members** scalar contains a space-separated list of the login names that are members of the group. Returns the group name in a scalar context. For a more efficient method of retrieving the entire groups file, see **getgrent**.

Returns

Group name in a scalar context
Group information in list context

REFERENCES Chapter 6; *see also* **getgrnam**, **getgrent**

getgrnam

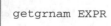

```
getgrnam EXPR
```

Looks up the group file entry by group name. Returns the following in a list context:

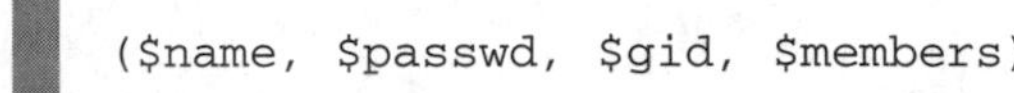

```
($name, $passwd, $gid, $members)
```

The **$members** scalar contains a space-separated list of the login names that are members of the group. Returns the group ID in a scalar context. For a more efficient method of retrieving the entire groups file, see **getgrent**.

Returns

Group ID in a scalar context
Group information in list context

REFERENCES Chapter 6; *see also* **getgrent**, **getgrgid**

gethostbyaddr

```
gethostbyaddr ADDR, ADDRTYPE
```

Contacts the system's name-resolving service, returning a list of information for the host **ADDR** of type **ADDRTYPE**, as follows:

```
($name, $aliases, $addrtype, $length, @addrs)
```

The **@addrs** array contains a list of packed binary addresses. In a scalar context, returns the host address.

Returns

undef on error in scalar context
Empty list on error in list context
Host name in scalar context
Host information array in list context

REFERENCES Chapter 9; *see also* **gethostbyname**

gethostbyname

```
gethostbyname NAME
```

Contacts the system's name-resolving service, returning a list of information for **NAME**, as follows:

```
($name, $aliases, $addrtype, $length, @addrs)
```

The **@addrs** array contains a list of packed binary addresses. In a scalar context, returns the host address.

Returns

undef on error in scalar context
Empty list on error in list context
Host address in scalar context
Host information array in list context

REFERENCES Chapter 9; *see also* **gethostbyaddr**

gethostent

```
gethostent
```

Returns the next entry from the hosts file as a list:

```
($name, $aliases, $addrtype, $length, @addrs)
```

Returns

undef on error in scalar context
Empty list on error in list context
Host name in scalar context
Host entry array in list context

REFERENCES Chapter 9; *see also* **sethostent, endhostent**

getlogin

```
getlogin
```

Returns the user's name, as discovered by the system function **getlogin()**.

Returns

undef on failure
User's login name

REFERENCES Chapter 6; *see also* **getpwuid**

getnetbyaddr

```
getnetbyaddr ADDR, ADDRTYPE
```

In a list context, returns the information for the network specified by **ADDR** and type **ADDRTYPE**:

```
($name, $aliases, $addrtype, $net)
```

In a scalar context, returns only the network address.

Returns

undef on error in scalar context
Empty list on error in list context
Network address in scalar context
Network address information in a list context

REFERENCES Chapter 9; *see also* **getnetbyname**

getnetbyname

```
getnetbyname NAME
```

In a list context, returns the information for the network specified by **NAME**:

```
($name, $aliases, $addrtype, $net)
```

In a scalar context, returns only the network address.

Returns

undef on error in scalar context
Empty list on error in list context
Network address in scalar context
Network address information in a list context

REFERENCES Chapter 9; *see also* **getnetbyaddr**

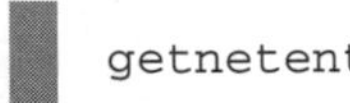

getnetent

```
getnetent
```

Gets the next entry from the /etc/networks file, returning:

```
($name, $aliases, $addrtype, $net)
```

Returns

undef on error in scalar context
Empty list on error in list context
Network name in a scalar context
Network entry in list context

REFERENCES Chapter 9; *see also* **setnetent**, **endnetent**

getpeername

```
getpeername SOCKET
```

Returns the packed socket address of the remote host attached via **SOCKET**.

Returns

undef on error
Packed socket address

REFERENCES Chapter 9; *see also* **accept**, **bind**, **socket**

getpgrp

```
getpgrp EXPR
getpgrp
```

Returns the process group for the process ID specified by **EXPR**, or the current process group if none specified.

Returns

Process group ID

REFERENCES Chapter 10; *see also* **setpgrp**

getppid

```
getppid
```

Returns the process ID of the parent process.

Returns

Process ID of the parent process

REFERENCES Chapter 10

getpriority

```
getpriority WHICH, WHO
```

Returns the current priority for a process (**PRIO_PROCESS**), process group (**PRIO_PGRP**), or user (**PRIO_USER**). The argument **WHICH** specifies what entity to set the priority for, and **WHO** is the process ID or user ID to set. A value of zero for **WHO** defines the current process, process group, or user. This produces a fatal error on systems that don't support the system **getpriority()** function.

Returns

undef on error
Current priority

REFERENCES Chapter 10; *see also* **setpriority**

getprotobyname

```
getprotobyname NAME
```

Translates the protocol **NAME** into its corresponding number in a scalar context, and its number and associated information in a list context:

```
($name, $aliases, $protocol_number)
```

Returns

undef on error in a scalar context
Empty list in a list context

Protocol number in a scalar context
Protocol information in a list context

REFERENCES Chapter 9; *see also* **getprotobynumber**

getprotobynumber

```
getprotobynumber NUMBER
```

Translates the protocol **NUMBER** into its corresponding name in a scalar context, and its name and associated information in a list context:

```
($name, $aliases, $protocol_number)
```

Returns

undef on error in a scalar context
Empty list in a list context
Protocol name in a scalar context
Protocol information in a list context

REFERENCES Chapter 9; *see also* **getprotobyname**

getprotoent

```
getprotoent
```

Returns the next entry from the list of valid protocols:

```
($name, $aliases, $protocol_number)
```

Returns

undef on error in scalar context
Empty list on error in list context
Protocol name in scalar context
Protocol entry in list context

REFERENCES Chapter 9; *see also* **setprotoent, endprotoent**

getpwent

```
getpwent
```

Returns the next password entry from the /etc/passwd file. This is used in combination with the **setpwent** and **endpwent** functions to iterate over the password file. In a list context, returns

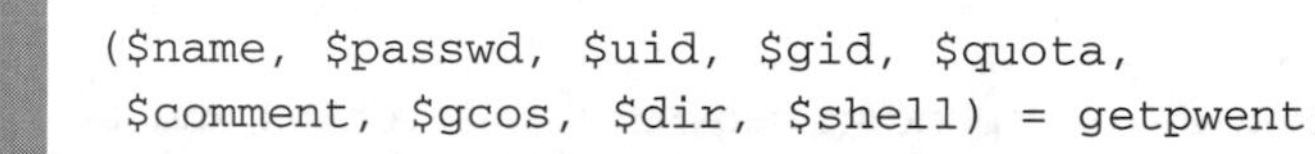

```
($name, $passwd, $uid, $gid, $quota,
 $comment, $gcos, $dir, $shell) = getpwent;
```

In a scalar context, just returns the user name.

Returns

User name in a scalar context
User information in a list context

REFERENCES Chapter 6; *see also* **getpwnam**, **getpwent**

getpwnam

```
getpwnam EXPR
```

In a list context, returns a list of fields, as extracted from the /etc/passwd file, based on the user name specified by **EXPR**. It's generally used like this:

```
($name, $passwd, $uid, $gid, $quota,
 $comment, $gcos, $dir, $shell) = getpwnam($user);
```

In a scalar context, returns the numeric user ID. If you are trying to access the whole /etc/passwd file, you should use the **getpwent** function. If you want to access the details by user ID, use **getpwuid**.

Returns

User ID in a scalar context
User information in a list context

REFERENCES Chapter 6; *see also* **getpwent**, **getpwuid**

getpwuid

```
getpwuid EXPR
```

In a list context, returns a list of fields, as extracted from the /etc/passwd file, based on the user name specified by **EXPR**. It's generally used like this:

```
($name, $passwd, $uid, $gid, $quota,
 $comment, $gcos, $dir, $shell) = getpwuid($uid);
```

In a scalar context, returns the user name. If you are trying to access the whole /etc/passwd file, you should use the **getpwent** function. If you want to access the details by user name, use **getpwnam**.

Returns

User name in a scalar context
User information in a list context

REFERENCES Chapter 6; *see also* **getpwent**, **getpwnam**

getservbyname

```
getservbyname NAME, PROTO
```

Translates the service **NAME** and for the protocol **PROTO**, returning the service number in a scalar context, and the number and associated information in a list context:

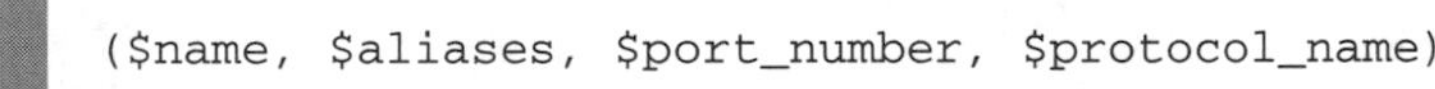

```
($name, $aliases, $port_number, $protocol_name)
```

Returns

undef on error in a scalar context
Empty list in a list context
Service number in a scalar context
Service information in a list context

REFERENCES Chapter 9; *see also* **getservbyport**

getservbyport

```
getservbyport PORT, PROTO
```

Translates the service number **PORT** and for the protocol **PROTO**, returning the service name in a scalar context, and the name and associated information in a list context:

```
($name, $aliases, $port_number, $protocol_name)
```

Returns

undef on error in a scalar context
Empty list in a list context
Service name in a scalar context
Service information in a list context

REFERENCES Chapter 9; *see also* **getservbyname**

getservent

```
getservent
```

Gets the next entry from the list of service entries, returning:

```
($name, $aliases, $port_number, $protocol_name)
```

Returns

undef on error in scalar context
Empty list on error in list context
Protocol name in scalar context
Protocol entry in list context

REFERENCES Chapter 9; *see also* **setservent**, **endservent**

getsockname

```
getsockname SOCKET
```

Returns a packed address of the local end of the network socket **SOCKET**.

Returns

undef on error
Packed address of local socket

REFERENCES Chapter 9; *see also* **getpeername, socket**

getsockopt

```
getsockopt SOCKET, LEVEL, OPTNAME
```

Gets the socket options set on **SOCKET**, at the socket implementation level **LEVEL** for the option **OPTNAME**. Some sample values for **OPTNAME** at a socket level are given in Table B-3. The values are defined in the Socket package.

Returns

undef on error
Option value

REFERENCES Chapter 9; *see also* **setsockopt**

OPTNAME	Result
SO_DEBUG	Get status of recording of debugging information.
SO_REUSEADDR	Get status of local address reuse.
SO_KEEPALIVE	Get status of keep connections alive.
SO_DONTROUTE	Get status of routing bypass for outgoing messages.
SO_LINGER	Get status of linger on close if data is present.
SO_BROADCAST	Get status of permission to transmit broadcast messages.
SO_OOBINLINE	Get status of out-of-band data in band.
SO_SNDBUF	Get buffer size for output.
SO_RCVBUF	Get buffer size for input.
SO_TYPE	Get the type of the socket.
SO_ERROR	Get and clear error on the socket.

Table B-3. *Options for* ***getsockopt***

glob

```
glob EXPR
glob
```

Returns a list of files matching **EXPR** as they would be expanded by the standard Bourne shell. If the **EXPR** does not specify a path, uses the current directory. If **EXPR** is omitted, the value of **$_** is used.

Returns

Empty list on error
List of expanded file names

REFERENCES Chapter 6; *see also* **chdir**

gmtime

```
gmtime EXPR
gmtime
```

Returns a list of values corresponding to the date and time as specified by **EXPR**, or date and time returned by the **time** function if **EXPR** is omitted, localized for the standard Greenwich mean time. The values returned are as follows:

```
#  0     1     2      3     4     5      6     7      8
($sec,$min,$hour,$mday,$mon,$year,$wday,$yday,$isdst)
    = gmtime(time);
```

The array elements are numeric, taken from the system **struct tm**. The value of **$mon** has a range of **0..11**, **$wday** has a range of **0..6** (Sunday–Saturday), and **$year** is returned as the number of years from 1900; so 2010 is 110.

Returns

In a scalar context, returns a formatted string
In a list context, returns a list of time values

REFERENCES Chapter 6; *see also* **localtime, time**

goto

```
goto LABEL
goto EXPR
goto &NAME
```

The first form causes the current execution point to jump to the point referred to as **LABEL**. A **goto** in this form cannot be used to jump into a loop or external function—you can only jump to a point within the same scope. The second form expects **EXPR** to evaluate to a recognizable **LABEL**. In general, you should be able to use a normal conditional statement or function to control the execution of a program, so its use is deprecated.

The third form substitutes a call to the named subroutine for the currently running subroutine. The new subroutine inherits the argument stack and other features of the original subroutine; it becomes impossible for the new subroutine even to know that it was called by another name.

Returns

Nothing

REFERENCES Chapters 2 and 17

grep

```
grep BLOCK LIST
grep EXPR, LIST
```

Similar to the standard Unix **grep** command. However, the selection process is more widespread and limited to regular expressions. Evaluates the **BLOCK** or **EXPR** for each element of **LIST**, returning the list of elements that the block or statement returns **TRUE**.

Returns

In a list context, list of matching elements

REFERENCES Chapter 7; *see also* **map**

hex

```
hex EXPR
hex
```

Interprets **EXPR** as a hexadecimal string and returns the value, or converts **$_** if **EXPR** is omitted.

Returns
Numeric value

REFERENCES Chapter 4; *see also* **oct**

index

```
index STR, SUBSTR, POSITION
index STR, SUBSTR
```

Returns the position of the first occurrence of **SUBSTR** in **STR**, starting at the beginning, or from **POSITION** if specified.

Returns
-1 on failure
Position of string

REFERENCES Chapter 4; *see also* **substr**

int

```
int EXPR
int
```

Returns the integer element of **EXPR**, or **$_** if omitted. The **int** function does not do rounding. If you need to round a value up to an integer, you should use **sprintf**.

Returns
Integer

REFERENCES Chapter 4; *see also* **abs**, **sprintf**

ioctl

```
ioctl FILEHANDLE, FUNCTION, SCALAR
```

Performs the function **FUNCTION** using the system function **ioctl()**, using **SCALAR** to set or receive information when appropriate. The available values for **FUNCTION** are completely system independent. You should refer to your ioctl.h C header file, if you have one available, for suitable values.

Returns

0 but true if the return value from the **ioctl()** is 0
Value returned by system

REFERENCES Chapter 6

join

```
join EXPR, LIST
```

Combines the elements of **LIST** into a single string using the value of **EXPR** to separate each element. Effectively the opposite of **split**.

Returns

Joined string

REFERENCES Chapter 7; *see also* **split**

keys

```
keys HASH
```

Returns all the keys of the **HASH** as a list. The keys are returned in random order but, in fact, share the same order as that used by **values** and **each**. You can therefore use the **keys** function to reset the shared iterator for a specific hash.

Returns

List of keys in list context, number of keys in scalar context

REFERENCES Chapter 7; *see also* **each**, **values**

kill

```
kill EXPR, LIST
```

Sends a signal of the value **EXPR** to the process IDs specified in **LIST**. If the value of **EXPR** is negative, it kills all processes that are members of the process groups specified. You can also use a signal name if specified in quotes. The precise list of signals supported is entirely dependent on the system implementation, but Table B-4 shows the main signals that should be supported by all POSIX-compatible operating systems.

Returns

Nothing

REFERENCES Chapter 10

last

```
last LABEL
last
```

Not a function. The **last** keyword is a loop control statement that immediately causes the current iteration of a loop to become the last. No further statements are executed, and the loop ends. If **LABEL** is specified, then it drops out of the loop identified by **LABEL** instead of the currently enclosing loop.

Name	Effect
SIGABRT	Aborts the process.
SIGARLM	Alarm signal.
SIGFPE	Arithmetic exception.
SIGHUP	Hang up.
SIGILL	Illegal instruction.
SIGINT	Interrupt.
SIGKILL	Termination signal.
SIGPIPE	Write to a pipe with no readers.
SIGQUIT	Quit signal.
SIGSEGV	Segmentation fault.
SIGTERM	Termination signal.
SIGUSER1	Application-defined signal 1.
SIGUSER2	Application-defined signal 2.

Table B-4. *POSIX-Compatible Signals*

Returns
Nothing

REFERENCES Chapter 2; *see also* **next, redo**

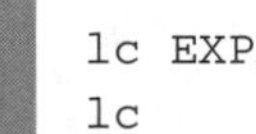

lc

```
lc EXPR
lc
```

Returns a lowercased version of **EXPR**, or **$_** if omitted.

Returns
String

REFERENCES Chapter 4; *see also* **lcfirst**

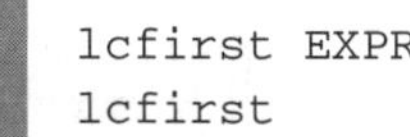

lcfirst

```
lcfirst EXPR
lcfirst
```

Returns the string **EXPR** or **$_** with the first character lowercased.

Returns
String

REFERENCES Chapter 4; *see also* **lc**

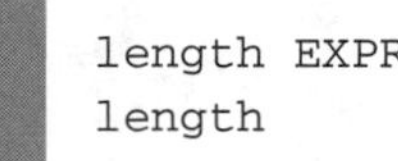

length

```
length EXPR
length
```

Returns the length, in bytes, of the value of **EXPR**, or **$_** if not specified.

Returns
Integer

REFERENCES Chapter 4

link

```
link OLDFILE,NEWFILE
```

Creates a new file name **NEWFILE** linked to the file **OLDFILE**. This is a hard link; if you want a symbolic link, use the **symlink** function.

Returns

1 on success

REFERENCES Chapter 6; *see also* **symlink**

listen

```
listen SOCKET, EXPR
```

Configures the network socket **SOCKET** for listening to incoming network connections. Sets the incoming connection queue length to **EXPR**.

Returns

1 on success

REFERENCES Chapter 9; *see also* **accept**, **connect**

local

```
local LIST
```

Sets the variables in **LIST** to be local to the current execution block. If more than one value is specified, you *must* use parentheses to define the list. You may wish to use **my** instead, as it's a more specific form of localization.

Returns

Nothing

REFERENCES Chapter 5; *see also* **my**

localtime

```
localtime EXPR
```

In a list context, converts the time specified by **EXPR**, returning a nine-element array with the time analyzed for the current local time zone. The elements of the array are

```
#  0    1     2     3     4    5     6     7     8
($sec,$min,$hour,$mday,$mon,$year,$wday,$yday,$isdst)
    = localtime(time);
```

If **EXPR** is omitted, uses the value returned by **time**.

In a scalar context, returns a string representation of the time specified by **EXPR**, roughly equivalent to the value returned by **ctime()**.

Returns

In a scalar context, returns a formatted string
In a list context, returns a list of time values

REFERENCES Chapter 6; *see also* **gmtime**, **time**

log

```
log EXPR
log
```

Returns the natural logarithm of **EXPR**, or **$_** if omitted.

Returns

Floating point number

REFERENCES Chapter 4

lstat

```
lstat FILEHANDLE
lstat EXPR
lstat
```

Performs the same tests as the **stat** function on **FILEHANDLE**, or the file referred to by **EXPR**, or **$_**. If the file is a symbolic link it returns the information for the link, rather than the file it points. Otherwise, it returns the information for the file.

Returns
1 on success

REFERENCES Chapter 6; *see also* **stat**

m//

```
m//
```

Match operator. Parentheses after initial **m** can be any character and will be used to delimit the regular expression statement.

Returns
1 on success
List of values in a grouped regular expression match

REFERENCES Chapter 4; *see also* **s///**, **tr///**

map

```
map EXPR, LIST
map BLOCK LIST
```

Evaluates **EXPR** or **BLOCK** for each element of **LIST**, locally setting **$_** to each element. Returns the evaluated list.

Returns
List of values

REFERENCES Chapter 7

mkdir

```
mkdir EXPR,MODE
```

Makes a directory with the name and path **EXPR** using the mode specified by **MODE** (specified as an octal number).

Returns

1 on success

REFERENCES Chapter 6

msgctl

```
msgctl ID, CMD, ARG
```

Calls the system function **msgctrl()** with the arguments **ID**, **CMD**, and **ARG**. You may need to include the **IPC::SysV** package to obtain the correct constants.

Returns

0 but true if the system function returns 0
1 on success

REFERENCES Chapter 10; *see also* **msgget**, **msgsnd**, **msgrcv**

msgget

```
msgget KEY, FLAGS
```

Returns the message queue ID, or **undef** on error.

Returns

undef on error
Message queue ID

REFERENCES Chapter 10; *see also* **msgctl**, **msgsnd**, **msgrcv**

msgrcv

```
msgrcv ID, VAR, SIZE, TYPE, FLAGS
```

Receives a message from the queue **ID**, placing the message into the variable **VAR** up to a maximum size of **SIZE**.

Returns
1 on success

msgsnd

```
msgsnd ID, MSG, FLAGS
```

Sends the message **MSG** to the message queue **ID**, using the optional **FLAGS**.

Returns
1 on success

REFERENCES Chapter 10; *see also* **msgctl**, **msgget**, **msgrcv**

my

```
my LIST
```

Declares the variables in **LIST** to be local within the enclosing block. If more than one variable is specified, all variables must be enclosed in parentheses.

Returns
Nothing

REFERENCES Chapter 5; *see also* **local**

next

```
next LABEL
next
```

Not a function. Causes the current loop iteration to skip to the next value or next evaluation of the control statement. No further statements in the current loop are executed. If **LABEL** is specified, then execution skips to the next iteration of the loop identified by **LABEL**.

Returns
Nothing

REFERENCES Chapter 2; *see also* **last**, **redo**

no

```
no MODULE LIST
no MODULE
```

If **MODULE** supports it, then **no** calls the **unimport** function defined in **MODULE** to unimport all symbols from the current package, or only the symbols referred to by **LIST**. Has some special meanings when used with pragmas.

Returns

Nothing

REFERENCES Chapters 5 and 16

oct

```
oct EXPR
oct
```

Returns **EXPR**, or **$_** if omitted, interpreted as an octal string. Most often used as a method for returning mode strings as octal values.

Returns

Octal value

REFERENCES Chapter 4; *see also* **hex**

open

```
open FILEHANDLE, EXPR
open FILEHANDLE
```

Opens the file specified by **EXPR**, associating it with **FILEHANDLE**. If **EXPR** is not specified, then the file name specified by the scalar variable of the same name as **FILEHANDLE** is used instead. The format of **EXPR** defines the mode in which the file is opened, as shown in Table B-5.

You should not ignore failures to the **open** command, so it is usually used in combination with **warn**, **die**, or a control statement.

If you are looking for the equivalent of the system function **open()**, see **sysopen**.

<table>
<tr><th>Expression</th><th>Result</th></tr>
<tr><td>"filename"</td><td>Opens the file for reading only.</td></tr>
<tr><td>"<filename"</td><td>Opens the file for reading only.</td></tr>
<tr><td>">filename"</td><td>Truncates and opens the file for writing.</td></tr>
<tr><td>">>filename"</td><td>Opens the file for appending (places pointer at end of file).</td></tr>
<tr><td>"+<filename"</td><td>Opens the file for reading and writing.</td></tr>
<tr><td>"+>filename"</td><td>Truncates and opens the file for reading and writing.</td></tr>
<tr><td>"| command"</td><td>Runs the command and pipes the output to the filehandle.</td></tr>
<tr><td>"command | "</td><td>Pipes the output from filehandle to the input of command.</td></tr>
<tr><td>"-"</td><td>Opens STDIN.</td></tr>
<tr><td>">-"</td><td>Opens STDOUT.</td></tr>
<tr><td>"<&FILEHANDLE"</td><td>Duplicates specified FILEHANDLE or file descriptor if numeric for reading.</td></tr>
<tr><td>">&FILEHANDLE"</td><td>Duplicates specified FILEHANDLE or file descriptor if numeric for writing.</td></tr>
<tr><td>"<&=N"</td><td>Opens the file descriptor N, similar to C's fdopen().</td></tr>
<tr><td>" |-" and "-| "</td><td>Opens a pipe to a forked command.</td></tr>
</table>

Table B-5. *Options for Opening Files*

Returns

undef on failure
non-zero on success (Process ID if open involved a pipe)

REFERENCES Chapter 3; *see also* **print**, **sysopen**, **close**

opendir

```
opendir DIRHANDLE, EXPR
```

Opens the directory **EXPR**, associating it with **DIRHANDLE** for processing, using the **readdir**, **telldir**, **seekdir**, and **closedir** functions.

Returns

1 on success

REFERENCES Chapter 6; *see also* **readdir**, **rewinddir**, **telldir**, **seekdir**, **closedir**

ord

```
ord EXPR
ord
```

Returns the ASCII numeric value of the character specified by **EXPR**, or **$_** if omitted.

Returns

Integer

REFERENCES Chapter 4; *see also* **chr**

pack

```
pack EXPR, LIST
```

Evaluates the expressions in **LIST** and packs it into a binary structure specified by **EXPR**. The format is specified using the characters shown in Table B-6.

Each character may be optionally followed by a number, which specifies a repeat count. A value of * repeats for as many values remaining in **LIST**. Values can be unpacked with the **unpack** function.

Returns

Formatted string

REFERENCES Chapter 7; *see also* **unpack**

package

```
package NAME
package
```

Changes the name of the current symbol table to **NAME**. The scope of the package name is until the end of the enclosing block. If **NAME** is omitted, there is no current package, and all function and variables names must be declared with their fully qualified names.

Returns

Nothing

REFERENCES Chapter 5

Character	Description
@	Null fill to absolute position.
a	An ASCII string, will be null padded.
A	An ASCII string, will be space padded.
b	A bitstring (ascending bit order).
B	A bitstring (descending bit order).
c	A signed char value.
C	An unsigned char value.
d	A double-precision float in the native format.
f	A single-precision float in the native format.
H	A hex string (high nibble first).
h	A hex string (low nibble first).
i	A signed integer value.
I	An unsigned integer value.
l	A signed long value.
L	An unsigned long value.
N	A long in "network" (big endian) order.
n	A short in "network" (big endian) order.
p	A pointer to a null-terminated string.
P	A pointer to a structure (fixed-length string).
s	A signed short value.
S	An unsigned short value.
u	A uuencoded string.
V	A long in "VAX" (little endian) order.
v	A short in "VAX" (little endian) order.
w	A BER compressed integer.
x	A null byte.
X	Back up a byte.

Table B-6. ***pack*** *Format Characters*

pipe

```
pipe READHANDLE, WRITEHANDLE
```

Opens a pair of connected communications pipes: **READHANDLE** for reading and **WRITEHANDLE** for writing.

Returns

1 on success

REFERENCES Chapter 10

pop

```
pop ARRAY
pop
```

Returns the last element of **ARRAY**, removing the value from the list. If **ARRAY** is omitted, it pops the last value from **@ARGV** in the main program and the @_ array within a subroutine. The opposite of **push**, which when used in combination, allows you to implement "stacks."

Returns

undef if list is empty
Last element from the array.

REFERENCES Chapter 7; *see also* **push**, **shift**, **unshift**

pos

```
pos EXPR
pos
```

Returns the position within **EXPR**, or **$_**, where the last **m//g** search left off.

Returns

Integer

REFERENCES Chapter 4

print

```
print FILEHANDLE LIST
print LIST
print
```

Prints the values of the expressions in **LIST** to the current default output filehandle, or to the one specified by **FILEHANDLE**. If **LIST** is empty, the value in **$_** is printed instead. Because **print** accepts a list of values, every element of the list will be interpreted as an expression. You should therefore ensure that if you are using print within a larger **LIST** context, you enclose the arguments to **print** in parentheses.

Returns

1 on success

REFERENCES Chapter 3; *see also* **printf**, **sprintf**

printf

```
printf FILEHANDLE FORMAT, LIST
printf FORMAT, LIST
```

Prints the value of **LIST** interpreted via the format specified by **FORMAT** to the current output filehandle, or to the one specified by **FILEHANDLE**. Effectively equivalent to

```
print FILEHANDLE sprintf(FORMAT, LIST)
```

Remember to use **print** in place of **printf** if you do not require a specific output format. The **print** function is more efficient. Table B-7 shows the list of accepted formatting conversions.

Perl also supports flags that optionally adjust the output format. These are specified between the % and conversion letter, as shown in Table B-8.

Returns

1 on success

REFERENCES Chapter 3; *see also* **print**, **sprintf**

Format	Result
%%	A percent sign.
%c	A character with the given ASCII code.
%s	A string.
%d	A signed integer (decimal).
%u	An unsigned integer (decimal).
%o	An unsigned integer (octal).
%x	An unsigned integer (hexadecimal).
%X	An unsigned integer (hexadecimal using uppercase characters).
%e	A floating point number (scientific notation).
%E	A floating point number (scientific notation using "E" in place of "e").
%f	A floating point number (fixed decimal notation).
%g	A floating point number (%e of %f notation according to value size).
%G	A floating point number (as %g, but using "E" in place of "e" when appropriate).
%p	A pointer (prints the memory address of the value in hexadecimal).
%n	Stores the number of characters output so far into the next variable in the parameter list.
%I	A synonym for %d.
%D	A synonym for C %ld.
%U	A synonym for C %lu.
%O	A synonym for C %lo.
%F	A synonym for C %f.

Table B-7. *Conversion Formats for* ***printf***

Flag	Result
space	Prefix positive number with a space.
+	Prefix positive number with a plus sign.
-	Left-justify within field.
0	Use zeros, not spaces, to right-justify.
#	Prefix non-zero octal with "0" and hexadecimal with "0x."
number	Minimum field width.
.number	Specify precision (number of digits after decimal point) for floating point numbers.
l	Interpret integer as C type "long" or "unsigned long."
h	Interpret integer as C type "short" or "unsigned short."
V	Interpret integer as Perl's standard integer type.

Table B-8. *Formatting Flags for* ***printf*** *Conversion Formats*

prototype

```
prototype EXPR
```

Returns a string containing the prototype of function or reference specified by **EXPR**, or **undef** if the function has no prototype.

Returns

undef if no function prototype
String

REFERENCES Chapter 5

push

```
push ARRAY, LIST
```

Pushes the values in **LIST** on to the end of the list **ARRAY**. Used with **pop** to implement stacks.

Returns

Number of elements in new array

REFERENCES Chapter 7; *see also* **pop**, **shift**, **unshift**

quotemeta

```
quotemeta EXPR
quotemeta
```

Returns the value of **EXPR** or **$_** with all nonalphanumeric characters backslashed.

Returns

String

REFERENCES Chapter 4

rand

```
rand EXPR
rand
```

Returns a random fractional number between zero and the positive number **EXPR**, or 1 if not specified. Automatically calls **srand** to seed the random number generator unless it has already been called.

Returns

Floating point number

REFERENCES Chapter 4; *see also* **srand**

read

```
read FILEHANDLE, SCALAR, LENGTH, OFFSET
read FILEHANDLE, SCALAR, LENGTH
```

Tries to read **LENGTH** bytes from **FILEHANDLE** into **SCALAR**. If **OFFSET** is specified, then reading starts from that point within the input string, up to **LENGTH** bytes. Uses the equivalent of the C **fread()** function. For the equivalent of the C **read()** function, see **sysread**.

Returns

0 at end of file
Number of bytes read

REFERENCES Chapter 3; *see also* **sysread**

readdir

```
readdir DIRHANDLE
```

In a scalar context, returns the next directory entry from the directory associated with **DIRHANDLE**. In a list context, returns all of the remaining directory entries in **DIRHANDLE**.

Returns

undef on failure in scalar context
Empty list on failure in list context

File name in scalar context
List of file names in list context

REFERENCES Chapter 6; *see also* **opendir, rewinddir**

readline

```
readline EXPR
```

Reads a line from the filehandle referred to by **EXPR**, returning the result. If you want to use a **FILEHANDLE** directly, it must be passed as a typeglob. In a scalar context, only one line is returned; in a list context, a list of lines up to end of file is returned. Ignores the setting of the **$/** or **$INPUT_RECORD_SEPARATOR** variable. You should use the <> operator in preference.

Returns

undef, or empty list, on error
One line in scalar context
List of lines in list context

REFERENCES Chapter 3

readlink

```
readlink EXPR
readlink
```

Returns the pathname of the file pointed to by the link **EXPR**, or **$_** if **EXPR** is not specified.

Returns

undef on error
String

REFERENCES Chapter 6; *see also* **link, symlink**

readpipe

```
readpipe EXPR
```

Executes **EXPR** as a command. The output is then returned, as a multiline string in scalar text, or with line returned as individual elements in a list context.

Returns
String in scalar context
List in list context

REFERENCES Chapter 10; *see also* **system**

recv

```
recv SOCKET, SCALAR, LEN, FLAGS
```

Receives a message on **SOCKET** attempting to read **LENGTH** bytes, placing the data read into variable **SCALAR**. The **FLAGS** argument takes the same values as the **recvfrom()** system function, on which the function is based. When communicating with sockets, this provides a more reliable method of reading fixed-length data than the **sysread** function or the line-based operator <>.

Returns
undef on error
Number of bytes read

REFERENCES Chapter 9

redo

```
redo LABEL
redo
```

Restarts the current loop without forcing the control statement to be evaluated. No further statements in the block are executed (execution restarts at the start of the block). A **continue** block, if present, will not be executed. If **LABEL** is specified, execution restarts at the start of the loop identified by **LABEL**.

Returns
Nothing

REFERENCES Chapter 2

ref

```
ref EXPR
ref
```

Returns a **TRUE** value if **EXPR**, or **$_**, is a reference. The actual value returned also defines the type of entity the reference refers to. The built-in types in:

```
REF
SCALAR
ARRAY
HASH
CODE
GLOB
```

Returns

1 if a reference

REFERENCES Chapter 7

rename

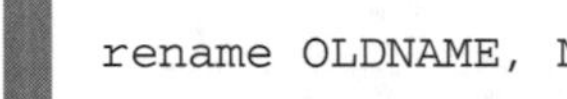

```
rename OLDNAME, NEWNAME
```

Renames the file with **OLDNAME** to **NEWNAME**. Uses the system function **rename()**, and so it will not rename files across file systems or volumes.

Returns

1 on success

REFERENCES Chapter 6

require

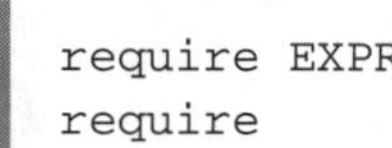

```
require EXPR
require
```

If **EXPR** (or **$_** if **EXPR** is omitted) is numeric, then it demands that the script requires the specified version of Perl in order to continue. If **EXPR** or **$_** are not numeric, it assumes that the name is the name of a library file to be included. You cannot include the same file with this function twice. The included file must return a true value as the last statement.

This differs from **use** in that included files effectively become additional text for the current script. Functions, variables, and other objects are not imported into the current name space, so if the specified file includes a package definition, then objects will require fully qualified names.

Returns

Nothing

REFERENCES Chapter 5; *see also* **use**

reset

```
reset EXPR
reset
```

Resets (clears) all package variables starting with the letter range specified by **EXPR**. Generally only used within a **continue** block or at the end of a loop. If omitted, resets **?PATTERN?** matches.

Returns

1 (always)

REFERENCES Chapter 4

return

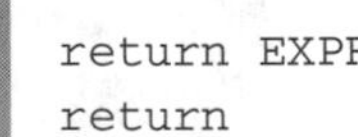

```
return EXPR
return
```

Returns **EXPR** at the end of a subroutine, block, or **do** function. **EXPR** may be a scalar, array, or hash value; context will be selected at execution time. If no **EXPR** is given, returns an empty list in list context, **undef** in scalar context, or nothing in a void context.

Returns

List, interpreted as scalar, array, or hash, depending on context

REFERENCES Chapter 5

reverse

```
reverse LIST
```

In a list context, returns the elements of **LIST** in reverse order. In a scalar context, returns a concatenated string of the values of **LIST**, with all bytes in opposite order.

Returns

String in scalar context
List in a list context

REFERENCES Chapter 7

rewinddir

```
rewinddir DIRHANDLE
```

Sets the current position within the directory specified by **DIRHANDLE** to the beginning of the directory.

Returns

Nothing

REFERENCES Chapter 6

rindex

```
rindex STR, SUBSTR, POSITION
rindex STR, SUBSTR
```

Operates similar to **index**, except it returns the position of the last occurrence of **SUBSTR** in **STR**. If **POSITION** is specified, returns the last occurrence at or before that position.

Returns

undef on failure
Integer

REFERENCES Chapter 4

rmdir

```
rmdir EXPR
rmdir
```

Deletes the directory specified by **EXPR**, or **$_** if omitted. Only deletes the directory if the directory is empty.

Returns

1 on success

REFERENCES Chapter 6; *see also* **mkdir**

s///

```
s/PATTERN/REPLACE/
```

This is the regular expression substitution operator. Based on the regular expression specified in **PATTERN**, data is replaced by **REPLACE**. Like **m//**, the delimiters are defined by the first character following **s**.

Returns

0 on failure
Number of substitutions made

REFERENCES Chapter 4

scalar

```
scalar EXPR
```

Forces the evaluation of **EXPR** to return a value in a scalar context.

Returns

Scalar

REFERENCES Chapters 5 and 7

seek

```
seek FILEHANDLE,POSITION,WHENCE
```

Positions the file pointer for the specified **FILEHANDLE**. **seek** is basically the same as the **fseek()** C function. The position within the file is specified by **POSITION**, using the value of **WHENCE** as a reference point, as follows:

0 sets the new position absolutely to **POSITION** bytes within the file.

1 sets the new position to the current position plus **POSITION** bytes within the file.

2 sets the new position to **POSITION** bytes, relative to the end of the file.

If you prefer, you can use the constants **SEEK_SET**, **SEEK_CUR**, and **SEEK_END**, providing you have imported the **IO::Seekable** or POSIX modules.

If you are accessing a file using **syswrite** and **sysread**, you should use **sysseek** due to the effects of buffering.

The **seek** function clears the **EOF** condition on a file when called.

Returns

1 on success

REFERENCES Chapter 3; *see also* **tell, sysseek**

seekdir

```
seekdir DIRHANDLE, POS
```

Sets the current position within **DIRHANDLE** to **POS**. The value of **POS** must be a value returned by **telldir**.

Returns

1 on success

REFERENCES Chapter 6; *see also* **rewinddir, telldir**

select

```
select FILEHANDLE
select
```

Sets the default filehandle for output to **FILEHANDLE**, setting the filehandle used by functions such as **print** and **write** if no filehandle is specified. If **FILEHANDLE** is not specified, then it returns the name of the current default filehandle.

Returns

Previous default filehandle if **FILEHANDLE** specified
Current default filehandle if **FILEHANDLE** was not specified

REFERENCES Chapter 3; *see also* **print**, **autoflush**, **write**

select

```
select RBITS, WBITS, EBITS, TIMEOUT
```

Calls the system function **select()** using the bits specified. The **select** function sets the controls for handling non-blocking I/O requests. Returns the number of filehandles awaiting I/O in scalar context, or the number of waiting filehandles and the time remaining in a list context.

TIMEOUT is specified in seconds, but accepts a floating point instead of an integer value. You can use this ability to pause execution for milliseconds instead of the normal seconds available with **sleep** and **alarm** by specifying **undef** for the first three arguments.

Returns

The number of filehandles awaiting I/O in a scalar context
The number of filehandles and time remaining in a list context

REFERENCES Chapter 6

semctl

```
semctl ID, SEMNUM, CMD, ARG
```

Controls a System V semaphore. You will need to import the **IPC::SysV** module to get the correct definitions for **CMD**. The function calls the system **semctl()** function.

Returns

0 but true if the return value from the **semctl()** is 0
Value returned by system

REFERENCES Chapter 10; *see also* **semget**, **semop**

semget

```
semget KEY, NSEMS, FLAGS
```

Returns the semaphore ID associated with **KEY**, using the system function **semget()**.

Returns

undef on error
Semaphore ID

REFERENCES *See also* **semctl**, **semop**

semop

```
semop KEY, OPSTRING
```

Performs the semaphore operations defined by **OPSTRING** on the semaphore ID associated with **KEY**. **OPSTRING** should be a packed array of **semop** structures, and each structure can be generated with

```
$semop = pack("sss", $semnum, $semop, $semflag);
```

Returns

1 on success

REFERENCES Chapter 10; *see also* **semctl**, **semget**

send

```
send SOCKET, MSG, FLAGS, TO
send SOCKET, MSG, FLAGS
```

Sends a message on **SOCKET** (the opposite of **recv**). If the socket is unconnected, you must supply a destination to communicate to with the **TO** parameter. In this case the **sendto** system function is used in place of the system **send** function.

The **FLAGS** parameter is formed from the bitwise **or** of zero and one or more of the **MSG_OOB** and **MSG_DONTROUTE** options. **MSG_OOB** allows you to send out-of-band data on sockets that support this notion. The underlying protocol must also support out-of-band data. Only **SOCK_STREAM** sockets created in the **AF_INET** address family support out-of-band data. The **MSG_DONTROUTE** option is turned on for the duration of the operation. Only diagnostic or routing programs use it.

Returns

undef on error
Integer, number of bytes sent

REFERENCES Chapter 9; *see also* **recv**

setgrent

```
setgrent
```

Sets (or resets) the enumeration to the beginning of the set of group entries. This function should be called before the first call to **getgrent**.

Returns

Nothing

REFERENCES Chapter 9; *see also* **getgrent**, **endgrent**

sethostent

```
sethostent STAYOPEN
```

Sets (or resets) the enumeration to the beginning of the set of host entries. This function should be called before the first call to **gethostent**. The **STAYOPEN** argument is optional and unused on most systems.

Returns

Nothing

REFERENCES Chapter 9; *see also* **gethostent**, **endhostent**

setnetent

```
setnetent STAYOPEN
```

Sets (or resets) the enumeration to the beginning of the set of network entries. This function should be called before the first call to **getnetent**. The **STAYOPEN** argument is optional and unused on most systems.

Returns

Nothing

REFERENCES Chapter 9; *see also* **getnetent, endnetent**

setpgrp

```
setpgrp PID, PGRP
```

Sets the current process group for the process **PID**. You can use a value of **0** for **PID** to change the process group of the current process. If both arguments are omitted, defaults to values of zero. Causes a fatal error if the system does not support the function.

Returns

undef on failure
New parent process ID

REFERENCES Chapter 10; *see also* **getpgrp**

setpriority

```
setpriority WHICH, WHO, PRIORITY
```

Sets the priority for a process (**PRIO_PROCESS**), process group (**PRIO_PGRP**), or user (**PRIO_USER**). The argument **WHICH** specifies what entity to set the priority for, and **WHO** is the process ID or user ID to set. A value of zero for **WHO** defines the current process, process group, or user. Produces a fatal error on systems that don't support the system **setpriority()** function.

Returns

1 on success

REFERENCES Chapter 10; *see also* **getpriority**

setprotoent

```
setprotoent STAYOPEN
```

Sets (or resets) the enumeration to the beginning of the set of protocol entries. This function should be called before the first call to **getprotoent**. The **STAYOPEN** argument is optional and unused on most systems.

Returns

Nothing

REFERENCES Chapter 9; *see also* **getprotoent**, **endprotoent**

setpwent

```
setpwent
```

Sets (or resets) the enumeration to the beginning of the set of password entries. This function should be called before the first call to **getpwent**.

Returns

Nothing

REFERENCES Chapter 9; *see also* **getpwent**, **endpwent**

setservent

```
setservent STAYOPEN
```

Sets (or resets) the enumeration to the beginning of the set of service entries. This function should be called before the first call to **getservent**. The **STAYOPEN** argument is optional and unused on most systems.

Returns

Nothing

REFERENCES Chapter 9; *see also* **getservent**, **endservent**

setsockopt

```
setsockopt SOCKET, LEVEL, OPTNAME, OPTVAL
```

Sets the socket option **OPTNAME** with a value of **OPTVAL** on **SOCKET** at the specified **LEVEL**. You will need to import the Socket module for the valid values for **OPTNAME** shown in Table B-9.

Returns

1 on success

REFERENCES Chapter 9; *see also* **getsockopt**, **socket**

shift

```
shift ARRAY
shift
```

Returns the first value in an array, deleting it and shifting the elements of the array list to the left by one. If **ARRAY** is not specified, shifts the @_ array within a subroutine, or

OPTNAME	Description
SO_DEBUG	Enable/disable recording of debugging information.
SO_REUSEADDR	Enable/disable local address reuse.
SO_KEEPALIVE	Enable/disable keep connections alive.
SO_DONTROUTE	Enable/disable routing bypass for outgoing messages.
SO_LINGER	Linger on close if data is present.
SO_BROADCAST	Enable/disable permission to transmit broadcast messages.
SO_OOBINLINE	Enable/disable reception of out-of-band data in band.
SO_SNDBUF	Set buffer size for output.
SO_RCVBUF	Set buffer size for input.
SO_TYPE	Get the type of the socket (get only).
SO_ERROR	Get and clear error on the socket (get only).

Table B-9. *Socket Options*

@ARGV otherwise. **shift** is essentially identical to **pop**, except values are taken from the start of the array instead of the end.

Returns

undef if the array is empty
First element in the array

REFERENCES Chapter 7; *see also* **pop**, **push**, **unshift**

shmctl

```
shmctl ID, CMD, ARG
```

Controls the shared memory segment referred to by **ID**, using **CMD** with **ARG**. You will need to import the **IPC::SysV** module to get the command tokens defined in Table B-10.

Returns

0 but true if the return value from the **shmctl()** is 0
Value returned by system

REFERENCES Chapter 10; *see also* **shmget**, **shmread**

Command	Description
IPC_STAT	Places the current value of each member of the data structure associated with **ID** into the scalar **ARG**.
IPC_SET	Sets the value of the following members of the data structure associated with **ID** to the corresponding values found in the packed scalar **ARG**.
IPC_RMID	Removes the shared memory identifier specified by **ID** from the system and destroys the shared memory segment and data structure associated with it.
SHM_LOCK	Locks the shared memory segment specified by **ID** in memory.
SHM_UNLOCK	Unlocks the shared memory segment specified by **ID**.

Table B-10. *Commands for Controlling Shared Memory Segments*

shmget

```
shmget KEY, SIZE, FLAGS
shmget KEY
```

Returns the shared memory segment ID for the segment matching **KEY**. A new shared memory segment is created of at least **SIZE** bytes, provided that either **KEY** does not already have a segment associated with it or that **KEY** is equal to the constant **IPC_PRIVATE**.

Returns

Shared memory ID

REFERENCES Chapter 10; *see also* **shmctl**, **shmread**, **shmwrite**

shmread

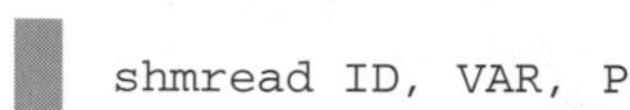

```
shmread ID, VAR, POS, SIZE
```

Reads the shared memory segment **ID** into the scalar **VAR** at position **POS** for up to **SIZE** bytes.

Returns

1 on success

REFERENCES Chapter 10; *see also* **shmctl**, **shmget**, **shmwrite**

shmwrite

```
shmwrite ID, STRING, POS, SIZE
```

Writes **STRING** from the position **POS** for **SIZE** bytes into the shared memory segment specified by **ID**. The **SIZE** is greater than the length of **STRING**. **shmwrite** appends null bytes to fill out to **SIZE** bytes.

Returns

1 on success

REFERENCES Chapter 10; *see also* **shmctl**, **shmget**, **shmread**

shutdown

```
shutdown SOCKET, HOW
```

Disables a socket connection according to the value of **HOW**. The valid values for **HOW** are identical to the system call of the same name. A value of **0** indicates that you have stopped reading information from the socket. A **1** indicates that you've stopped writing to the socket. A value of **2** indicates that you have stopped using the socket altogether.

Returns

1 on success

REFERENCES Chapter 9

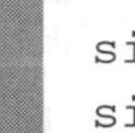

sin

```
sin EXPR
sin
```

Returns the sine of **EXPR**, or **$_** if not specified.

Returns

Floating point

REFERENCES Chapter 4

sleep

```
sleep EXPR
sleep
```

Pauses the script for **EXPR** seconds, or forever if **EXPR** is not specified. Returns the number of seconds actually slept. Can be interrupted by a signal handler, but you should avoid using **sleep** with **alarm** since many systems use **alarm** for the **sleep** implementation.

Returns

Integer, number of seconds actually slept

REFERENCES Chapter 6

socket

```
socket SOCKET, DOMAIN, TYPE, PROTOCOL
```

Opens a socket in **DOMAIN**, of **TYPE**, using **PROTOCOL** and attaches it to the filehandle **SOCKET**. You will need to import the Socket module to get the correct definitions. For most systems **DOMAIN** will be **PF_INET** for a TCP/IP-based socket. **TYPE** will generally be one of **SOCK_STREAM** for streams-based connections (TCP/IP) or **SOCK_DGRAM** for a datagram connection (UDP/IP). Values for **PROTOCOL** are system defined, but valid values include **TCP** for TCP/IP, **UDP** for UDP, and **RDP** for the "reliable" datagram protocol.

Returns

1 on success

REFERENCES Chapter 9

socketpair

```
socketpair SOCKET1, SOCKET2, DOMAIN, TYPE, PROTOCOL
```

Creates an unnamed pair of connected sockets in the specified **DOMAIN**, of the specified **TYPE**, using **PROTOCOL**. If the system **socketpair()** function is not implemented, then it causes a fatal error.

Returns

1 on success

REFERENCES Chapter 9; *see also* **pipe**, **socket**

sort

```
sort SUBNAME LIST
sort BLOCK LIST
sort LIST
```

Sorts **LIST** according to the subroutine **SUBNAME** or the anonymous subroutine specified by **BLOCK**. If no **SUBNAME** or **BLOCK** is specified, then sorts according to normal alphabetical sequence. If **BLOCK** or **SUBNAME** is specified, then the subroutine should return an integer less than, greater than, or equal to zero according to how the elements of the array are to be sorted.

Returns

List

REFERENCES Chapter 7

splice

```
splice ARRAY, OFFSET, LENGTH, LIST
splice ARRAY, OFFSET, LENGTH
splice ARRAY, OFFSET
```

Removes the elements of **ARRAY**, from the element **OFFSET** for **LENGTH** elements, replacing the elements removed with **LIST** if specified. If **LENGTH** is omitted, removes everything from **OFFSET** onwards.

Returns

undef if no elements removed in a scalar context
Last element removed in a scalar context
Empty list in a list context
List of elements removed in a list context

REFERENCES Chapter 7

split

```
split /PATTERN/, EXPR, LIMIT
split /PATTERN/, EXPR
split /PATTERN/
split
```

Splits a string into an array of strings, returning the resultant list. By default, empty leading fields are preserved, and empty trailing fields are deleted.

In a scalar context, returns the number of fields found and splits the values into the @_. In list context, you can force the split into @_ by array using **??** as the pattern delimiter. If **EXPR** is omitted, splits the value of **$_**. If **PATTERN** is also omitted, it splits on white space (multiple spaces, tabs). Anything matching **PATTERN** is taken to be a delimiter separating fields and can be a regular expression of one or more characters.

If **LIMIT** has been specified and is positive, splits into a maximum of that many fields (or fewer). If **LIMIT** is unspecified or zero, splitting continues until there are no more delimited fields. If negative, then **split** acts as if an arbitrarily large value has been specified, preserving trailing null fields.

A **PATTERN** of a null string splits **EXPR** into individual characters.

Returns

Integer, number of elements in scalar context
List of split elements

REFERENCES Chapter 7; *see also* **join**

sprintf

```
sprintf FORMAT, LIST
```

The **sprintf** function uses **FORMAT** to return a formatted string based on the values in **LIST**. Essentially identical to **printf**, but the formatted string is returned instead of being printed. The **sprintf** function is basically synonymous with the C **sprintf** function, but Perl does its own formatting; the C **sprintf** function is not used (except for basic floating point formatting).

The **sprintf** function accepts the same format conversions as **printf** (see Table B-7). Perl also supports flags that optionally adjust the output format. These are specified between the % and conversion letter and are the same as those for **printf** (see Table B-8).

Returns

undef on error
Preformatted string according to **FORMAT** and **LIST**.

REFERENCES Chapter 3; *see also* **print, printf**

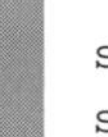

sqrt

```
sqrt EXPR
sqrt
```

Returns the square root of **EXPR**, or **$_** if omitted.

Returns

Floating point number

REFERENCES Chapter 4

srand

```
srand EXPR
srand
```

Sets the seed value for the random number generator to **EXPR**, or to a random value based on the time, process ID, and other values if **EXPR** is omitted.

Returns

Nothing

REFERENCES Chapter 4; *see also* **rand**

stat

```
stat FILEHANDLE
stat EXPR
stat
```

Returns a 13-element array giving the status info for a file, specified by either **FILEHANDLE**, **EXPR**, or **$_**. The list of values returned is shown in Table B-11. If used in a scalar context, returns **0** on failure, **1** on success.

Returns

1 on success in scalar context
Empty list on failure in list context
List of status on success values in list context

REFERENCES Chapter 6; *see also* **-X**

study

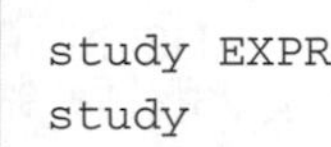

```
study EXPR
study
```

Takes extra time to study **EXPR** in order to improve the performance on regular expressions conducted on **EXPR**. If **EXPR** is omitted, uses **$_**. The actual speed gains may be very small, depending on the number of times you expect to search the string. You can only study one expression or scalar at any one time.

Element	Description
0	Device number of file system.
1	Inode number.
2	File mode (type and permissions).
3	Number of (hard) links to the file.
4	Numeric user ID of file's owner.
5	Numeric group ID of file's owner.
6	The device identifier (special files only).
7	File size, in bytes.
8	Last access time since the epoch.
9	Last modify time since the epoch.
10	Inode change time (*not* creation time!) since the epoch.
11	Preferred block size for file system I/O.
12	Actual number of blocks allocated.

Table B-11. *Values Returned by* ***stat***

Returns

Nothing

REFERENCES Chapter 4

sub

```
sub NAME BLOCK
sub NAME
sub BLOCK
```

Not a function. This is a keyword that signifies the start of a new subroutine definition. With **NAME** and **BLOCK**, it is a named function and definition. With only **NAME** (and optional prototypes), it is simply a declaration. With only **BLOCK**, it is an anonymous subroutine.

Returns

Nothing

REFERENCES Chapter 5

substr

```
substr EXPR, OFFSET, LEN, REPLACEMENT
substr EXPR, OFFSET, LEN
substr EXPR, OFFSET
```

Returns a substring of **EXPR**, starting at **OFFSET** within the string. If **OFFSET** is negative, starts that many characters from the end of the string. If **LEN** is specified, returns that number of bytes, or all bytes up until end of string if not specified. If **LEN** is negative, leaves that many characters off the end of the string. If **REPLACEMENT** is specified, replaces the substring with the **REPLACEMENT** string.

If you specify a substring that passes beyond the end of the string, then it returns only the valid element of the original string.

Returns
String

REFERENCES Chapter 4

symlink

```
symlink OLDFILE, NEWFILE
```

Creates a symbolic link between **OLDFILE** and **NEWFILE**. On systems that don't support symbolic links, causes a fatal error.

Returns
1 on success

REFERENCES Chapter 6

syscall

```
syscall EXPR, LIST
```

Calls the system function **EXPR** with the arguments **LIST**. Produces a fatal error if the specified function does not exist.

Returns

-1 on failure of system call
Value returned by system function

REFERENCES Chapter 10

sysopen

```
sysopen FILEHANDLE, FILENAME, MODE, PERMS
sysopen FILEHANDLE, FILENAME, MODE
```

Equivalent to the underlying C and operating system call **open()**. Opens the file specified by **FILENAME**, associating it with **FILEHANDLE**. The **MODE** argument specifies how the file should be opened. The values of **MODE** are system dependent, but some values are historically set. Values of zero, 1, and 2 mean read-only, write-only, and read/write. The supported values are available in the Fcntl module. Note that **FILENAME** is strictly a file name; no interpretation of the contents takes place, and the mode of opening is defined by the **MODE** argument.

If the file has to be created, and the **O_CREAT** flag has been specified in **MODE**, then the file is created with the permissions of **PERMS**. The value of **PERMS** must be specified in traditional Unix-style hexadecimal. If **PERMS** is not specified, then Perl uses a default mode of 0666.

Returns

1 on success

REFERENCES Chapter 3; *see also* **sysread**, **syswrite**, **sysseek**

sysread

```
sysread FILEHANDLE, SCALAR, LENGTH, OFFSET
sysread FILEHANDLE, SCALAR, LENGTH
```

Tries to read **LENGTH** bytes from **FILEHANDLE**, placing the result in **SCALAR**. If **OFFSET** is specified, then data is written to **SCALAR** from **OFFSET** bytes, effectively appending the information from a specific point. If **OFFSET** is negative, it starts from the number of bytes specified counted backwards from the end of the string. This is the equivalent of the C/operating system function **read()**. Because it bypasses the buffering system employed by functions like **print**, **read**, and **seek**, it should only be used with the corresponding **syswrite** and **sysseek** functions.

Returns

0 at end of file
Integer, number of bytes read

REFERENCES Chapter 3; *see also* **syswrite**, **sysseek**

sysseek

```
sysseek FILEHANDLE,POSITION,WHENCE
```

Sets the position within **FILEHANDLE** according to the values of **POSITION** and **WHENCE**. This function is the equivalent of the C function **lseek()**, so you should avoid using it with buffered forms of **FILEHANDLE**. This includes the **<FILEHANDLE>** notation and **print**, **write**, **seek**, and **tell**. Using it with **sysread** or **syswrite** is OK, since they too ignore buffering.

The position within the file is specified by **POSITION**, using the value of **WHENCE** as a reference point, as follows:

0 sets the new position to **POSITION**.

1 sets the new position to the current position plus **POSITION**.

2 sets the new position to **EOF** plus **POSITION**.

If you prefer, you can use the constants **SEEK_SET**, **SEEK_CUR**, and **SEEK_END**, respectively, providing you have imported the **IO::Seekable** or POSIX module.

Returns

undef on failure
A position of zero is returned as the string **0 but true**
Integer, new position (in bytes) on success

REFERENCES Chapter 3; *see also* **tell**, **seek**

system

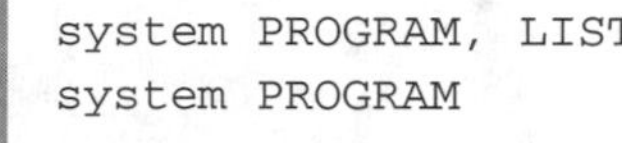

```
system PROGRAM, LIST
system PROGRAM
```

Executes the command specified by **PROGRAM**, passing **LIST** as arguments to the command. The script waits for execution of the child command to complete before continuing. If **PROGRAM** is the only argument specified, then Perl checks for any shell metacharacters and, if found, passes **PROGRAM** unchanged to the user's default command shell. If there are no metacharacters, then the value is split into words and passed as an entire command with arguments to the system **execvp** function.

The return value is the exit status of the program as returned by the **wait** function. To obtain the actual exit value, divide by 256. If you want to capture the output from a command, use the backticks operator.

Returns

Exit status of program as returned by **wait**

REFERENCES Chapter 10

syswrite

```
syswrite FILEHANDLE, SCALAR, LENGTH, OFFSET
syswrite FILEHANDLE, SCALAR, LENGTH
```

Attempts to write **LENGTH** bytes from **SCALAR** to the file associated with **FILEHANDLE**. If **OFFSET** is specified, then information is read from **OFFSET** bytes in the supplied **SCALAR**. This function uses the C/operating system **write()** function, which bypasses the normal buffering. You should therefore avoid using functions such as **print** and **read** in conjunction with this function.

Returns

undef on error
Integer, number of bytes written

REFERENCES Chapter 3; *see also* **sysread**, **sysseek**

tell

```
tell FILEHANDLE
tell
```

Returns the current position (in bytes) within the specified **FILEHANDLE**. If **FILEHANDLE** is omitted, then it returns the position within the last file accessed.

Returns

Integer, current file position (in bytes)

REFERENCES Chapter 3; *see also* **seek**, **sysseek**

telldir

```
telldir DIRHANDLE
```

Returns the current position within the directory listing referred to by **DIRHANDLE**.

Returns

Integer

REFERENCES Chapter 6

tie

```
tie VARIABLE, CLASSNAME, LIST
```

Ties the **VARIABLE** to the package class **CLASSNAME** that provides implementation for the variable type. Any additional arguments in **LIST** are passed to the constructor for the entire class. Typically used to bind hash variables to DBM databases.

Returns

Reference to tied object

REFERENCES Chapter 7; *see also* **tied**, **untie**

tied

```
tied VARIABLE
```

Returns a reference to the object underlying the tied entity **VARIABLE**.

Returns

undef if **VARIABLE** is not tied to a package

REFERENCES Chapter 7; *see also* **tie**, **untie**

time

```
time
```

Returns the number of seconds since the epoch (00:00:00 UTC, January 1, 1970, for most systems; 00:00:00, January 1, 1904, for MacOS). Suitable for feeding to **gmtime** and **localtime**.

Returns
Integer, seconds since epoch

REFERENCES Chapter 6; *see also* **gmtime**, **localtime**

times

```
times
```

Returns a four-element list giving the user, system, child, and child system times for the current process and its children.

Returns
User, system, child, child system times as integer

REFERENCES Chapter 6

tr///

```
tr/SEARCHLIST/REPLACEMENTLIST/
```

Not a function. This is the transliteration operator; it replaces all occurrences of the characters in **SEARCHLIST** with the characters in **REPLACEMENTLIST**.

Returns
Number of characters replaced or deleted

REFERENCES Chapter 4

truncate

```
truncate FILEHANDLE, LENGTH
```

Truncates (reduces) the size of the file specified by **FILEHANDLE** to the specified **LENGTH** (in bytes). Produces a fatal error if the function is not implemented on your system.

Returns
1 on success

REFERENCES Chapter 3

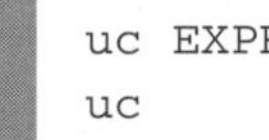

uc

```
uc EXPR
uc
```

Returns an uppercased version of **EXPR**, or **$_** if not specified.

Returns

String

REFERENCES Chapter 4; *see also* **lc**, **lcfirst**, **ucfirst**

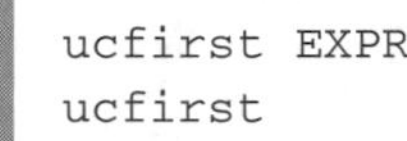

ucfirst

```
ucfirst EXPR
ucfirst
```

Returns the value of **EXPR** with only the first character uppercased. If **EXPR** is omitted, then uses **$_**.

Returns

String

REFERENCES Chapter 4; *see also* **lc**, **lcfirst**, **uc**

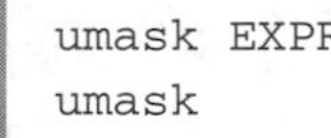

umask

```
umask EXPR
umask
```

Sets the umask (default mask applied when creating files and directories) for the current process. Value of **EXPR** must be an octal number. If **EXPR** is omitted, simply returns the previous value.

Returns

Previous umask value

REFERENCES *See also* **open**, **sysopen**, **mkdir**

undef

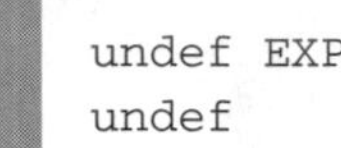

```
undef EXPR
undef
```

Undefines the value of **EXPR**. Use on a scalar, list, hash, function, or typeglob. Use on a hash with a statement such as **undef $hash{$key}**; actually sets the value of the specified key to an undefined value. If you want to delete the element from the hash, use the **delete** function.

Returns

undef

REFERENCES Chapter 4; *see also* **delete**

unlink

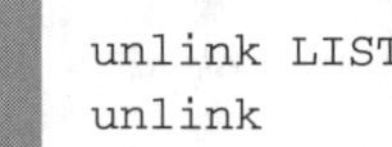

```
unlink LIST
unlink
```

Deletes the files specified by **LIST**, or the file specified by **$_** otherwise.

Returns

Number of files deleted

REFERENCES Chapter 6

unpack

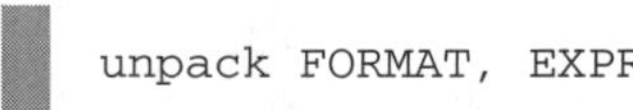

```
unpack FORMAT, EXPR
```

Unpacks the binary string **EXPR** using the format specified in **FORMAT**. Basically reverses the operation of **pack**, returning the list of packed values according to the supplied format.

You can also prefix any format field with a **%<number>** to indicate that you want a 16-bit checksum of the value of **EXPR**, instead of the value.

Returns

List of unpacked values

REFERENCES Chapter 7; *see also* **pack**

unshift

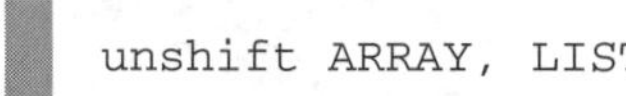

```
unshift ARRAY, LIST
```

Places the elements from **LIST**, in order, at the beginning of **ARRAY**.

Returns

Number of new elements in **ARRAY**

REFERENCES Chapter 7

untie

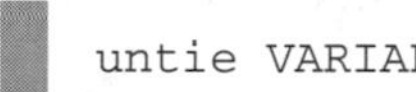

```
untie VARIABLE
```

Breaks the binding between a variable and a package, undoing the association created by the **tie** function.

Returns

1 on success

REFERENCES Chapter 7; *see also* **tie**

use

```
use MODULE LIST
use MODULE
use VERSION
use MODULE VERSION [LIST]
```

Imports all the functions exported by **MODULE**, or only those referred to by **LIST**, into the name space of the current package. If the VERSION formats are used then specifies either the minimum Perl version required, or the minimum version of the imported module required. Exits with a fatal error if the version condition is not met. Also used to impose compiler directives (pragmas) on the current script, although essentially these are just modules anyway.

Note that a **use** statement is evaluated at compile time. A **require** statement is evaluated at execution time.

Returns

Nothing

REFERENCES Chapter 5; *see also* **require**

utime

```
utime ATIME, MTIME, LIST
```

Sets the access and modification times specified by **ATIME** and **MTIME** for the list of files in **LIST**. The values of **ATIME** and **MTIME** must be numerical. The inode modification time is set to the current time.

Returns

Number of files updated

REFERENCES Chapter 6

values

```
values HASH
```

Returns the list of all the values contained in **HASH**. In a scalar context, returns the number of values that would be returned. Uses the same iterator, and therefore order, used by the **each** and **keys** functions.

Returns

Number of values in scalar context
List of values in list context

REFERENCES Chapter 7; *see also* **each**, **keys**

vec

```
vec EXPR, OFFSET, BITS
```

Treats the string in EXPR as a vector of unsigned integers and returns the value of the bit field specified by OFFSET. BITS specifies the number of bits reserved for each entry in the bit vector. This must be a power of two from 1 to 32.

Returns

Integer

REFERENCES Chapter 4

wait

```
wait
```

Waits for a child process to terminate, returning the process ID of the deceased process. The exit status of the process is contained in **$?**.

Returns

-1 if there are no child processes
Process ID of deceased process

REFERENCES Chapter 10; *see also* **waitfor**

waitpid

```
waitpid PID, FLAGS
```

Waits for the child process with ID **PID** to terminate, returning the process ID of the deceased process. If **PID** does not exist, then it returns **-1**. The exit status of the process is contained in **$?**.

If you import the POSIX module, you can specify flags by name, although all Perl implementations support a value of zero. Table B-12 lists the flags supported under Solaris. You will need to check your implementation for the flags your OS supports.

Returns

-1 if process does not exist
Process ID of deceased process

REFERENCES Chapter 10

Flag	Description
WIFEXITED	Wait for processes that have exited.
WIFSIGNALED	Wait for processes that received a signal.
WNOHANG	Nonblocking wait.
WSTOPSIG	Wait for processes that received STOP signal.
WTERMSIG	Wait for processes that received TERM signal.
WUNTRACED	Wait for processes stopped by signals.

Table B-12. *Flags for* ***waitpid***

wantarray

```
wantarray
```

Returns **TRUE** if the context of the currently executing function is looking for a list value. Returns **FALSE** in a scalar context.

Returns

0 in scalar context
1 in list context

REFERENCES Chapter 5

warn

```
warn LIST
```

Prints the value of **LIST** to **STDERR**. Basically the same as the **die** function except that no call is made to the exit and no exception is raised within an **eval** statement. This can be useful to raise an error without causing the script to terminate prematurely.

If the variable **$@** contains a value (from a previous **eval** call) and **LIST** is empty, then the value of **$@** is printed with "\t...caught" appended to the end. If both **$@** and **LIST** are empty, then "Warning: Something's wrong" is printed.

Returns

Nothing.

REFERENCES Chapter 10; *see also* **die**

write

```
write FILEHANDLE
write
```

Writes a formatted record, as specified by **format** to **FILEHANDLE**. If **FILEHANDLE** is omitted, then writes the output to the currently selected default output channel. Form processing is handled automatically, adding new pages, headers, footers, and so on, as specified by the format for the filehandle.

Returns

1 on success

REFERENCES Chapter 12; *see also* **format**

y///

```
y/SEARCHLIST/REPLACEMENTLIST/
```

Identical to the **tr///** operator; translates all characters in **SEARCHLIST** into the corresponding characters in **REPLACEMENTLIST**.

Returns

Number of characters modified

REFERENCES Chapter 4; *see also* **tr///**

Appendix C

Perl Entity Reference

This appendix contains a quick summary of the information provided in Chapters 2 and 3 that contain the basic statements and variables used throughout the rest of Perl.

Control Statements, Functions, Packages

Listed below are the Perl control statements and the definitions for creating new functions (subroutines) and packages. See Chapter 2 for more information on control statements. See Chapter 5 for more information on defining functions and packages.

```
if (EXPR)
if (EXPR) {BLOCK}
if (EXPR) {BLOCK} else {BLOCK}
if (EXPR) {BLOCK} elsif (EXPR) {BLOCK} ...
if (EXPR) {BLOCK} elsif (EXPR) {BLOCK} ... else {BLOCK}
```

The **if** statement tests **EXPR**; if it returns true, it executes the first block. If supplied, also tests additional **elsif** expressions. Once all **if** and **elsif** expressions have been resolved, executes the **else** block, if supplied.

```
while EXPR
LABEL while (EXPR) {BLOCK}
LABEL while (EXPR) {BLOCK} continue {BLOCK}
```

Executes **BLOCK** while **EXPR** returns true. Runs the **continue** block at the end of each loop.

```
until (EXPR) {BLOCK}
```

Executes **BLOCK** until **EXPR** returns true. Evaluates **EXPR** before executing the **BLOCK**.

```
do {BLOCK} until (EXPR)
```

Executes **BLOCK** until **EXPR** returns true. Executes **BLOCK** once before any evaluation.

```
LABEL for (EXPRA; EXPRB; EXPRC) {BLOCK}
```

Initializes the variables with **EXPRA** before loop, tests each iteration with **EXPRB**, and evaluates **EXPRC** at the end of each **BLOCK**.

```
LABEL foreach VAR (LIST) {BLOCK}
LABEL foreach VAR (LIST) {BLOCK} continue {BLOCK}
```

Iterates through each element of **LIST**, assigning the value of each element to **VAR** or to **$_** if not specified.

```
next LABEL
```

Skips execution to next iteration of the current loop, or the loop referred to by **LABEL**. Always runs **continue** block.

```
last
```

Ends iteration of the current loop, always skipping the rest of the statements in the main block and those that are defined by the **continue** block.

```
redo LABEL
```

Reexecutes the iteration of the current block without reevaluating the expression for the loop. Redoes the loop **LABEL** if specified.

```
sub NAME {BLOCK}
```

Defines the function (subroutine) **NAME** to execute the code contained in **BLOCK**. Can be used to define an anonymous function if **NAME** is skipped and result is assigned to a scalar reference.

```
package NAME;
```

Defines the current name space as **NAME**. When used within a script, defines a new package. See Appendix B for details on using **do**, **use**, and **require**.

Quoting

Perl supports two types of quoting: the customary (preferred) format and the alternative functional generic style. Different quote operators imply different evaluations, and only some interpolate values and variables. They are summarized in Table C-1. See Chapter 3 for more information on Perl quoting mechanisms.

Customary	Generic	Meaning	Interpolates
''	q//	Literal	No
""	qq//	Literal	Yes
``	qx//	Command	Yes
()	qw//	Word list	No
//	m//	Pattern match	Yes
s///	s///	Substitution	Yes
y///	tr///	Translation	No

Table C-1. *Perl Quotes*

Operators

Operators in Table C-2 are listed in precedence order. See Chapter 2 for more detailed information on the Perl operators available.

Order	Operator	Description
Left	List operators	Functions, variables, parentheses.
Left	->	Dereferencing operator.
NonA	++ --	Increment, decrement.
Right	**	Exponential.
Right	! ~ + - \	Not, bit negation, reference op, unary +/- (-4).
Left	=~. !~	Matching operators for regular expressions.
Left	* / % x	Multiplication, division, modulus, string multiplication.
Left	+ - .	Addition, subtraction, string concatenation.
Left	<< >>	Binary left and right shift.
NonA	Named unary operators	Functions that take one argument, file test operators.
NonA	< > <= >=	Numeric less than, greater than, less than or equal to, greater than or equal to.
NonA	lt gt le ge	Stringwise less than, greater than, less than or equal to, greater than or equal to.
NonA	== != <=>	Numeric equal to, not equal to, comparison operator.
NonA	eq ne cmp	String equal to, not equal to, comparison operator.

Table C-2. *Perl Operators*

<table>
<tr><th>Order</th><th>Operator</th><th>Description</th></tr>
<tr><td>Left</td><td>&</td><td>Bitwise AND.</td></tr>
<tr><td>Left</td><td>| ^</td><td>Bitwise OR and XOR.</td></tr>
<tr><td>Left</td><td>&&</td><td>AND.</td></tr>
<tr><td>Left</td><td>||</td><td>OR.</td></tr>
<tr><td>NonA</td><td>, ..</td><td>List generator.</td></tr>
<tr><td>Right</td><td>?:</td><td>Conditional.</td></tr>
<tr><td>Right</td><td>= += -= *= **=
&= <<= >>=
&&= ||=</td><td>Equals, plus equals, etc.</td></tr>
<tr><td>Left</td><td>=></td><td>List separators.</td></tr>
<tr><td>Left</td><td>NOT</td><td>Lower precedence !.</td></tr>
<tr><td>Left</td><td>AND</td><td>Lower precedence &&.</td></tr>
<tr><td>Left</td><td>OR</td><td>Lower precedence ||.</td></tr>
<tr><td>Left</td><td>xor</td><td>Lower precedence ^.</td></tr>
</table>

Table C-2. *Perl Operators* (continued)

Standard Variables

Table C-3 lists all of the standard variables available within any Perl script. Refer to Chapter 2 for in-depth information on the standard Perl variables. To use the long (named) variables, you must include the English module by placing

```
use English;
```

at the top of your program. By including this module, the longer names will be aliased to the shortened versions. Although there is no standard for using either format, because the shortened versions are the default, you will see them used more widely.

Variable	Description
$-	Number of lines available for printing for the current page.
$!	Returns the error number or error string, according to context.
$"	List separator.

Table C-3. *Standard Perl Variables*

Variable	Description
$#	Default number format when printing numbers.
$$	Process ID of the Perl interpreter.
$%	Current page number of the current output channel.
$&	String matched by the last successful pattern match.
$(	Real group ID of the current process.
$)	Effective group ID of the current process.
$*	Set to 1 to do multiline pattern matching. Use is deprecated by **/s** and **/m** modifiers.
$,	Current output field separator.
$.	Current input line number of the last file from which you read.
$/	Current input record separator.
$:	Set of characters after which a string may be broken to fill continuation fields.
$;	Separator used when emulating multidimensional arrays.
$?	The status returned by the last external command (via **system** or **qx//**).
$@	Error message returned by the Perl interpreter from an **eval** statement.
$[	Index of the first element in an array.
$	Current output record separator.
$]	Version + patch level/1000 of the Perl interpreter.
$^	Name of the current top-of-page output format for the current channel.
$^A	Variable used to hold formatted data before it is printed.
$^D	Value of the debugging flags.
$^E	Extended OS error information for OSs other than Unix.
$^F	Maximum file descriptor number.
$^H	Status of syntax checks enabled by the compiler.
$^I	Value of the in-place edit extension.
$^L	Character used to send a form feed to the output channel.
$^M	Size of the emergency memory pool.
$^O	Operating system name.
$^P	Internal variable that specifies the current debugging value.

Table C-3. *Standard Perl Variables* (continued)

Variable	Description
$^R	Value of the last evaluation in a block in a regular expression.
$^S	Current interpreter state.
$^T	Time the script started running in seconds since the epoch.
$^W	Current value of the warning switch.
$^X	Name of the Perl binary being executed.
$_	Default input/output and pattern matching space.
$|	Controls buffering on the currently selected output filehandle.
$~	Name of the current report format.
$`	String preceding the information matched by the last pattern match.
$'	String following the information matched by the last pattern match.
$+	Last bracket match by the last regular expression search pattern.
$<	Real ID of the user currently executing the interpreter.
$<digits>	Contains the result of the corresponding parentheses from the last regular expression match.
$=	Number of printable lines for the current page.
$>	Effective user ID of the current process.
$0	Name of the file containing the script currently being executed.
$ARGV	Name of the current file when reading from the default filehandle.
%ENV	List of environment variables.
%INC	List of files included via **do** or **require**.
%SIG	List of signals and how they are to be handled.
@_	List of parameters supplied to a subroutine.
@ARGV	List of command line arguments supplied to the script.
@INC	List of directories to be searched when importing modules.

Table C-3. *Standard Perl Variables* (continued)

Standard Filehandles

Table C-4 shows the standard filehandles available to all Perl scripts. See Chapter 3 for more information on using filehandles.

Filehandle	Description
ARGV	Special filehandle that iterates over command line file names in **@ARGV**. Usually written as the null filehandle <>.
STDERR	Used for printing error messages.
STDIN	Used for standard input.
STDOUT	Used for standard output.
DATA	Refers to the information contained after the **__END__** token in a script. Can also be used to read data after the **__DATA__** token.
_	Used to cache information from the last **stat**, **lstat**, or **file** test operator.

Table C-4. *Standard Perl Filehandles*

Appendix D

Errors and Warnings

The Perl parser and compiler produce error messages if they discover something that does not seem right. Because Perl parses the entire script before even attempting to execute, many problems, usually typographical errors, can be picked up before the program is actually executed. The executor picks up errors that are generated during the execution stage, and these usually relate to errors in inline statements, such as the **eval** function, or to other statements that are evaluated at execution rather than compilation time.

All errors and warning messages can be classified as shown in Table D-1.

Level	Perl Symbol	Display Status	Compilation/ Execution Process	Description
Warning	(W)	Optional	Continues	Simple warning. Either Perl will have made an educated decision on what to do, or it has ignored the error. In either case compilation and execution should continue.
Deprecation	(D)	Only	Continues	Method/function has been superseded.
Severe warning	(S)	Mandatory	Halts	An error in the syntax has occurred that will cause problems.
Fatal error	(F)	Trappable	Halts	A fatal error has occurred. It can be trapped with suitable constructs (signals, tests, or **eval** statement).
Internal error	(P)	Panic, trappable	Halts	An internal error within the parser, compiler or execution module of the Perl interpreter has occurred.
Very fatal error	(X)	Nontrappable	Halts	A nontrappable error has occurred. This usually only happens when an unforeseeable event occurs. Other instances include missing, or poorly supported, system functions.
Alien error	(A)	Not generated by Perl	Halts	An alien error message from an external program, function, or device has occurred that Perl could not identify.

Table D-1. *Perl Parser/Compiler/Interpreter Warning Types*

Most run-time errors (such as writing to a closed filehandle) can be trapped by correctly testing the original **open** statement. Some warnings will only appear if you've switched on warnings with the **-w** command line option. Fatal errors that are trappable can be evaluated with **eval** to prevent the main script from **die**ing.

All warnings can be captured by creating a signal handler for the special **$SIG{__WARN__}** signal. Trappable errors can be caught (but not prevented) using a handler on the **$SIG{__DIE__}** signal. See Chapter 10 for more details on capturing errors this way. The script will still exit if the faulty statement is outside of an **eval** block.

In the listings below, **%s** refers to a string (usually a variable, function, or operator name), while **%d** refers to a number in the error string.

Messages and Descriptions

```
"my" variable %s can't be in a package.
```

FATAL ERROR You've tried to declare a lexically scoped variable (via the **my** keyword) within a package. You cannot localize a variable in this way. Use the **local** keyword instead.

```
"my" variable %s masks earlier declaration in same scope
```

WARNING You've tried to redeclare a variable with the **my** keyword, for example:

```
my $var = "hello\n";
my $var = "world\n";
```

This is usually a typographical error. Perl will use the most recent declaration, although the previous declaration will not be deleted.

```
"no" not allowed in expression
```

FATAL ERROR You've tried to use the **no** keyword within an expression:

```
my $var = no diagnostics;
```

The **no** keyword is recognized at compile time, rather than during the execution stage. It returns no useful value, so the above statement is pointless anyway.

```
"use" not allowed in expression
```

FATAL ERROR The **use** keyword is recognized at compile time, not execution, so statements like

```
$debug = 1;
$debug && use diagnostics;
```

won't work.

```
% may only be used in unpack
```

FATAL ERROR You can't pack a string by supplying a checksum. This is because the check-summing process loses the information to be packed. Try doing it in two stages.

```
%s (...) interpreted as function
```

WARNING Any operator followed by parentheses is taken by Perl to be a function, with the original list elements being passed as arguments to the function. You may have inadvertently inserted an additional character into a statement where it doesn't need one.

```
%s argument is not a HASH element
```

FATAL ERROR You've tried to specify the element of a hash incorrectly. An element is always identified as **$hash{element}**.

```
%s argument is not a HASH element or slice
```

FATAL ERROR You've attempted to pass a list or scalar variable to a function or operator that expects a hash or hash slice.

```
%s did not return a true value
```

FATAL ERROR An imported module (by **use**, **require**, or **do**) must return a true value to indicate that the compilation and initialization process worked correctly.

```
%s found where operator expected
```

SEVERE WARNING You've inserted a function, variable, or static when Perl expected to see an operator. The most common reason for this message to appear is that you've forgotten to put a semicolon at the end of the previous line.

```
%s had compilation errors
```

FATAL ERROR This is the final summary message when a simple compilation test (via **perl -c**) fails.

```
%s has too many errors
```

FATAL ERROR The Perl parser only produces messages for the first ten errors. Most problems after the first ten errors are a result of an earlier problem anyway. This is the message produced when Perl gives up reporting errors.

```
%s matches null string many times
```

WARNING The regular expression pattern you've specified would be an infinite loop if the engine didn't specifically check for that.

```
%s never introduced
```

SEVERE WARNING The symbol disappeared from scope before it was required for use.

```
%s syntax OK
```

FATAL ERROR This is the final summary message when a compilation test (via **perl -c**) succeeds.

```
%s: Command not found
```

ALIEN ERROR This is actually produced by **csh**, not Perl, and signifies that you're trying to run your program with the wrong interpreter.

```
%s: Expression syntax
```

ALIEN ERROR This is actually produced by **csh**, not Perl, and signifies that you're trying to run your program with the wrong interpreter.

```
%s: Undefined variable
```

ALIEN ERROR This is actually produced by **csh**, not Perl, and signifies that you're trying to run your program with the wrong interpreter.

```
%s: not found
```

ALIEN ERROR This is actually produced by **sh** (the Bourne shell), not Perl, and signifies that you're trying to run your program with the wrong interpreter.

```
(Missing semicolon on previous line?)
```

SEVERE WARNING Usually produced in combination with the message "**%s found where operator expected**" to signify that you may have forgotten a semicolon. This doesn't always fix the problem, though.

```
-P not allowed for setuid/setgid script
```

FATAL ERROR You cannot use the C preprocessor and guarantee the security of your **setuid** or **setgid** Perl script.

```
-T and -B not implemented on filehandles
```

FATAL ERROR You can't expect Perl to access the stdio buffers if it's not allowed to use the stdio functions directly—which it isn't when taint checking is switched on.

```
-p destination: %s
```

FATAL ERROR Perl was unable to open the output file created during the "in-place" editing invoked by the **-p** command line switch.

```
?+* follows nothing in regexp
```

FATAL ERROR You've specified a regular expression with a quantifier, but supplied nothing to quantify. This usually indicates that you are trying to search for the literal equivalent. Use a backslash to ensure the character is interpreted correctly.

```
@ outside of string
```

FATAL ERROR You've specified an absolute position within a pack template that is outside the range of the string being unpacked.

```
accept() on closed fd
```

WARNING You've tried to **accept** a network connection on a closed socket.

```
Allocation too large: %lx
```

VERY FATAL ERROR You can't allocate more than 64K on an MS-DOS machine.

```
Applying %s to %s will act on scalar(%s)
```

WARNING When using pattern matching operators, you have specified an array or hash instead of a scalar. This has the effect of flattening the array or hash and performing the pattern matching on the flattened object. If you are trying to operate directly on an array or hash, see the **grep** or **map** function.

```
Arg too short for msgsnd
```

FATAL ERROR The **msgsnd** requires a string at least as long as **sizeof(long)**.

```
Ambiguous use of %s resolved as %s
```

WARNING, SEVERE WARNING Perl has made an assumption about the statement you have supplied. This can normally be resolved by inserting an operator, function, or parentheses.

```
Ambiguous call resolved as CORE::%s(), qualify as such or use &
```

WARNING You've declared a function with the same name as a Perl keyword, but haven't specified the call to the function with a prefix of **&**. Perl has therefore decided to use the built-in, not the declared, function. The alternative is to **use subs** the function to allow the core version to be redeclared. Alternatively, if you want to use the core function, then call it by its full name, **CORE::**.

```
Args must match #! line
```

FATAL ERROR The setuid emulator requires that the arguments Perl was invoked with match the arguments specified on the #! line.

```
Argument "%s" isn't numeric%s
```

WARNING A function expected a number when it actually detected a scalar or reference.

```
Array @%s missing the @ in argument %d of %s()
```

DEPRECATED FEATURE Very old versions of Perl let you omit the @ on array names in some spots. This is now heavily deprecated. You should always specify an array explicitly.

```
assertion botched: %s
```

INTERNAL ERROR The **malloc()** package that comes with Perl had an internal failure.

```
Assertion failed: file "%s"
```

INTERNAL ERROR A general assertion failed. The file in question must be examined.

```
Assignment to both a list and a scalar
```

FATAL ERROR An assignation to a conditional operator must have scalars or lists as the second and third arguments. You cannot mix scalars and lists in the assignment.

```
Attempt to free non-arena SV: 0x%lx
```

INTERNAL ERROR An internal scalar value had its storage space allocated from an arena that is not garbage collected.

```
Attempt to free nonexistent shared string
```

INTERNAL ERROR An attempt was made to decrement the reference count of a string in the internal tables, but the string did not exist.

```
Attempt to free temp prematurely
```

WARNING An internal function (**free_tmps()**) has tried to free a scalar value when the value has already been freed by another function.

```
Attempt to free unreferenced glob pointers
```

INTERNAL ERROR The reference counts got screwed up on symbol aliases.

```
Attempt to free unreferenced scalar
```

WARNING Perl tried to decrement the reference count of a scalar to see if it would go to zero, but found that the counter was already at zero and the scalar should have or had already been freed.

```
Attempt to pack pointer to temporary value
```

WARNING You tried to pass the **pack** function a temporary value (such as that returned by a function). The result in the packed string is a pointer to the location of the temporary value, which may or may not exist when the packed string is next accessed.

```
Attempt to use reference as lvalue in substr
```

WARNING You supplied a reference as the first argument to **substr** used as an lvalue, which is pretty strange.

```
Bad arg length for %s, is %d, should be %d
```

FATAL ERROR You passed a buffer of the wrong size to one of **msgctl()**, **semctl()**, or **shmctl()**.

```
Bad filehandle: %s
```

FATAL ERROR You passed a symbol as a filehandle when it wasn't, in fact, a filehandle.

```
Bad free() ignored
```

SEVERE WARNING An internal routine called **free()** on something that had never been **malloc()**ed in the first place. This message can be disabled by setting the environment variable **$PERL_BADFREE** to 1.

```
Bad hash
```

INTERNAL ERROR One of the internal hash routines was passed a null HV pointer.

```
Bad index while coercing array into hash
```

FATAL ERROR The index looked up in the hash found as the first element of a pseudo-hash is not legal. Index values must be at 1 or greater.

```
Bad name after %s::
```

FATAL ERROR A symbol was defined with a package prefix, but the symbol name within the package was never defined.

```
Bad symbol for array
```

INTERNAL ERROR An internal request asked to add an array entry to something that wasn't a symbol table entry.

```
Bad symbol for filehandle
```

INTERNAL ERROR An internal request asked to add a filehandle entry to something that wasn't a symbol table entry.

```
Bad symbol for hash
```

INTERNAL ERROR An internal request asked to add a hash entry to something that wasn't a symbol table entry.

```
Badly placed ()'s
```

ALIEN ERROR This is actually produced by **csh**, not Perl, and signifies that you're trying to run your program with the wrong interpreter.

```
Bareword "%s" not allowed while "strict subs" in use
```

FATAL ERROR When the **strict subs** pragma is in effect, you cannot specify bare words and expect them to be treated as strings.

```
Bareword "%s" refers to nonexistent package
```

WARNING You tried to reference a symbol by its full package name, but the package name space has not been defined or imported.

```
BEGIN failed--compilation aborted
```

FATAL ERROR One of the statements in a **BEGIN** subroutine raised an exception that wasn't otherwise trapped or handled. Compilation stops at this point, since **BEGIN** subroutines are executed at compile, not execution time.

```
BEGIN not safe after errors--compilation aborted
```

FATAL ERROR Perl found **BEGIN** statements after one or more earlier compilation errors. Since the stability of the program could not be guaranteed, Perl quits.

```
bind() on closed fd
```

WARNING You tried to do a bind on a closed socket.

```
Bizarre copy of %s in %s
```

INTERNAL ERROR Perl detected an attempt to copy an internal value that cannot be copied.

```
Callback called exit
```

FATAL ERROR A subroutine invoked from an external package via **perl_call_sv()** exited by calling **exit**.

```
Can't "goto" outside a block
```

FATAL ERROR A **goto** statement was executed to jump out of its enclosing block, which cannot be done. Usually this is a result of a subroutine calling an external block.

```
Can't "goto" into the middle of a foreach loop
```

FATAL ERROR You cannot jump to the inside of a **foreach** loop using **goto**. There shouldn't be any need to do so anyway.

```
Can't "last" outside a block
```

FATAL ERROR You tried to exit a block that wasn't a loop block. You cannot use **last** to extricate yourself from an **if** or **else** test. However, you can insert the **last** statement inside a new block, which Perl assumes is a loop that only executes once.

```
Can't "next" outside a block
```

FATAL ERROR You cannot reiterate over a block that isn't a loop block. However, you can insert the **next** statement inside a new block, which Perl assumes is a loop that only executes once.

```
Can't "redo" outside a block
```

FATAL ERROR You cannot **redo** a block that isn't a loop block. However, you can insert the **redo** statement inside a new block, which Perl assumes is a loop that only executes once.

```
Can't bless non-reference value
```

FATAL ERROR You cannot **bless** a soft or indirect reference, only a hard reference.

```
Can't break at that line
```

SEVERE WARNING A warning intended to be printed only while running within the debugger, indicating the line number specified wasn't the location of a statement where the debugger could stop.

```
Can't call method "%s" in empty package "%s"
```

FATAL ERROR You called a method correctly, and it correctly indicated a package functioning as a class, but that package doesn't have any definitions, functions, or other entities.

```
Can't call method "%s" on unblessed reference
```

FATAL ERROR You cannot call a method if the method does not know what object, and therefore what package, it is supposed to be working on. You haven't supplied an object to the method specified.

```
Can't call method "%s" without a package or object reference
```

FATAL ERROR You used the syntax of a method call, but the slot filled by the object reference or package name contains an expression that returns a defined value that is neither an object reference nor a package name.

```
Can't call method "%s" on an undefined value
```

FATAL ERROR You have specified a method call, but the object reference on which the method should act contains an undefined value, not an object.

```
Can't chdir to %s
```

FATAL ERROR You have tried to execute a script within another directory using the command line switch **-x**, but the directory does not exist.

```
Can't coerce %s to integer in %s
```

FATAL ERROR Not all internal scalars can be converted to an integer value.

```
Can't coerce %s to number in %s
```

FATAL ERROR Not all internal scalars can be converted to a numerical value.

```
Can't coerce %s to string in %s
```

FATAL ERROR Not all internal scalars can be converted to a string value.

```
Can't coerce array into hash
```

FATAL ERROR You used an array where a hash was expected, but the array has no information on how to map from keys to array indices. You can do that only with arrays that have a hash reference at index 0.

```
Can't create pipe mailbox
```

INTERNAL ERROR An error peculiar to VMS. The process is suffering from exhausted quotas or other plumbing problems.

```
Can't declare %s in my
```

FATAL ERROR Only scalar, array, and hash variables may be declared as lexical variables. They must have ordinary identifiers as names.

```
Can't do inplace edit on %s: %s
```

SEVERE WARNING The creation of the new file required for the in-place edit function failed for the indicated reason.

```
Can't do inplace edit without backup
```

FATAL ERROR You're on a system such as MS-DOS that gets confused if you try reading from a deleted (but still opened) file. If you want to continue using the in-place edit feature, use the **-i** command line option to specify an alternate backup file.

```
Can't do inplace edit: %s > 14 characters
```

SEVERE WARNING The file system you are working with does not support file names greater than 14 characters. Perl cannot generate a backup name for the file.

```
Can't do inplace edit: %s is not a regular file
```

SEVERE WARNING You tried to use a file that is not a regular file, with the **-i** command line option.

```
Can't do setegid!
```

INTERNAL ERROR The **setegid()** call failed for some reason in the **setuid()** emulator of **suidperl**.

```
Can't do seteuid!
```

INTERNAL ERROR The **setuid** emulator of **suidperl** failed for some reason.

```
Can't do setuid
```

FATAL ERROR The standard Perl interpreter tried to exec **suidperl** to allow the script to run with **setuid** emulation, but the required executable could not be found. It looks for a name of the form **sperl5.x** in the same directory that the Perl executable resides under the name perl5.x.

```
Can't do waitpid with flags
```

FATAL ERROR This machine doesn't have either **waitpid()** or **wait4()**, so only **waitpid()** without flags is emulated.

```
Can't do {n,m} with n > m
```

FATAL ERROR The value of **n** in the regular expression element must be smaller than the size of **m**.

```
Can't emulate -%s on #! line
```

FATAL ERROR The #! line specifies a switch that doesn't make sense at this point.

```
Can't exec "%s": %s
```

WARNING A **system**, **exec**, or piped **open** call could not execute the command specified. The problem is usually related to permissions or a bad file name, or the program cannot be found within the **$ENV{PATH}**. Other errors include bad executables or nonexistent programs that the called script or program relies on via the **#!** construct.

```
Can't exec %s
```

FATAL ERROR Perl was trying to execute the indicated program for you because that's what the #! line specified.

```
Can't execute %s
```

FATAL ERROR You've tried to execute a script using the value of **$PATH** via the **-S** switch, but the script cannot be found or does not have the right permissions.

```
Can't find %s on PATH, '.' not in PATH
```

FATAL ERROR You've tried to execute a script using the value of **$PATH** via the **-S** switch, but the script cannot be found or does not have the right permissions. However, the script does exist within the current directory, but **PATH** does not include "." (the current directory).

```
Can't find %s on PATH
```

FATAL ERROR You've tried to execute a script using the value of **$PATH** via the **-S** switch, but the script cannot be found.

```
Can't find label %s
```

FATAL ERROR You have attempted to jump to a label that does not exist.

```
Can't find string terminator %s anywhere before EOF
```

FATAL ERROR Perl cannot find the required terminator (closing quote) for a string and has now reached the end of the script looking for it. If the error is from a here document, check the definition for the end of the text marker. Perl includes any white space or other elements as part of the identifier.

```
Can't fork
```

FATAL ERROR A fatal error occurred while trying to fork when opening a pipeline.

```
Can't get filespec - stale stat buffer?
```

SEVERE WARNING This warning peculiar to VMS arises because of the difference between access checks under VMS and under the Unix model Perl assumes. Under VMS, access checks are done by file name rather than by bits in the **stat** buffer so that ACLs and other protections can be taken into account. Unfortunately, Perl assumes that the **stat** buffer contains all the necessary information and passes it, instead of the **filespec**, to the access checking routine. It will try to retrieve the **filespec** using the device name and FID present in the **stat** buffer, but this works only if you haven't made a subsequent call to the CRTL **stat()** routine, because the device name is overwritten with each call. If this warning appears, the name lookup failed, and the access checking routine gave up and returned FALSE, just to be conservative. (Note: The access checking routine knows about the Perl **stat** operator and file tests, so you shouldn't ever see this warning in response to a Perl command; it arises only if some internal code takes **stat** buffers lightly.)

```
Can't get pipe mailbox device name
```

INTERNAL ERROR An error peculiar to VMS. After creating a mailbox to act as a pipe, Perl can't retrieve its name for later use.

```
Can't get SYSGEN parameter value for MAXBUF
```

INTERNAL ERROR An error peculiar to VMS. Perl asked **$GETSYI** how big you want your mailbox buffers to be and didn't get an answer.

```
Can't goto subroutine outside a subroutine
```

FATAL ERROR The **goto subroutine** call can only replace one subroutine call for another.

```
Can't goto subroutine from an eval-string
```

FATAL ERROR The **goto subroutine** call can't be used to jump out of an **eval SCALAR**.

```
Can't localize through a reference
```

FATAL ERROR You've attempted to localize a dereferenced scalar with something like **local $$ref**. Perl cannot guarantee that the value of the reference scalar will still be a reference when the scope of the **local** definition ends.

```
Can't localize lexical variable %s
```

FATAL ERROR You cannot localize a variable with **local** that has previously been declared with **my**.

```
Can't localize pseudo-hash element
```

FATAL ERROR You cannot localize a reference to a pseudo-hash using a statement like

```
local $href->{'key'};
```

This isn't supported yet.

```
Can't locate auto/%s.al in @INC
```

FATAL ERROR You have tried to call a function within a package that supports autoloading, but the autoload system cannot find the necessary function to load.

```
Can't locate %s in @INC
```

FATAL ERROR You have tried to import a file that could not be found within the directories specified in the special **@INC** array.

```
Can't locate object method "%s" via package "%s"
```

FATAL ERROR You called a method correctly, and it correctly indicated a package functioning as a class, but that package doesn't define that particular method, nor does any of its base classes.

```
Can't locate package %s for @%s::ISA
```

WARNING The **@ISA** array, used by the **Exporter** module or one of its derived modules, contained the name of a package that doesn't seem to exist.

```
Can't make list assignment to \%ENV on this system
```

FATAL ERROR List assignment to **%ENV** is not supported on some systems, notably VMS.

```
Can't modify %s in %s
```

FATAL ERROR You aren't allowed to assign to the item indicated, or otherwise try to change its value.

```
Can't modify nonexistent substring
```

INTERNAL ERROR The internal routine that does assignment to a **substr** was handed a NULL.

```
Can't msgrcv to read-only var
```

FATAL ERROR The variable used as a receive buffer with the **msgrcv** function must be modifiable.

```
Can't open %s: %s
```

SEVERE WARNING The implicit opening of a file through use of the **<>** filehandle, or via the **-p** or **-n** command line switches, cannot be opened.

```
Can't open bidirectional pipe
```

WARNING The use of bidirectional pipes within the **open** command, as in

```
open (SHELL, "|sh|");
```

is not supported. Use the **IPC::Open2** or a similar module.

```
Can't open error file %s as stderr
```

FATAL ERROR An error peculiar to VMS. Perl does its own command line redirection and couldn't open the file specified after "2>" or "2>>" on the command line for writing.

```
Can't open input file %s as stdin
```

FATAL ERROR An error peculiar to VMS. Perl does its own command line redirection and couldn't open the file specified after "<" on the command line for reading.

```
Can't open output file %s as stdout
```

FATAL ERROR An error peculiar to VMS. Perl does its own command line redirection and couldn't open the file specified after ">" or ">>" on the command line for writing.

```
Can't open output pipe (name: %s)
```

INTERNAL ERROR An error peculiar to VMS. Perl does its own command line redirection and couldn't open the pipe into which to send data destined for stdout.

```
Can't open perl script "%s": %s
```

FATAL ERROR The script you specified can't be opened for the indicated reason.

```
Can't redefine active sort subroutine %s
```

FATAL ERROR Perl knows the location of the optimized subroutines supported by the sort function. If you want to specify your own sort subfunction, you must use **sort { func }** or another of the methods described in Chapter 7.

```
Can't rename %s to %s: %s, skipping file
```

SEVERE WARNING The creation of the backup file, implied by the rename operation as part of the **-i** command line switch, could not be completed.

```
Can't reopen input pipe (name: %s) in binary mode
```

INTERNAL ERROR An error peculiar to VMS. Perl thought **stdin** was a pipe and tried to reopen it to accept binary data. Alas, it failed.

```
Can't reswap uid and euid
```

INTERNAL ERROR The **setreuid()** call failed for some reason in the **setuid** emulator of **suidperl**.

```
Can't return outside a subroutine
```

FATAL ERROR You tried to return from somewhere other than a defined function.

```
Can't stat script "%s"
```

INTERNAL ERROR For some reason you can't **fstat()** the script even though you have it open already.

```
Can't swap uid and euid
```

INTERNAL ERROR The **setreuid()** call failed for some reason in the **setuid** emulator of **suidperl**.

```
Can't take log of %g
```

FATAL ERROR You cannot take the logarithm of a negative number of zero. If you need to do this, consider using the standard **Math::Complex** module.

```
Can't take sqrt of %g
```

FATAL ERROR You cannot take the square root of a negative number. If you need to do this, consider using the standard **Math::Complex** module.

```
Can't undef active subroutine
```

FATAL ERROR You can't undefine a routine that's currently running.

```
Can't unshift
```

FATAL ERROR You tried to unshift an "unreal" array that can't be unshifted, such as the main Perl stack.

```
Can't upgrade that kind of scalar
```

INTERNAL ERROR The internal sv_upgrade routine adds "members" to an SV, making it into a more specialized kind of SV. The top several SV types are so specialized, however, that they cannot be interconverted. This message indicates that such a conversion was attempted.

```
Can't upgrade to undef
```

INTERNAL ERROR The undefined SV is the bottom of the totem pole, in the scheme of upgradability. Upgrading to **undef** indicates an error in the code calling **sv_upgrade()**.

```
Can't use %%! because Errno.pm is not available
```

FATAL ERROR The first time the **%!** hash or its **$!** scalar equivalent is used, Perl automatically loads the **Errno** module. The **Errno** module is expected to tie the %**!** hash to provide symbolic names for the scalar errno values.

```
Can't use "my %s" in sort comparison
```

FATAL ERROR The global variables $a and $b are reserved for sort comparisons. You mentioned $a or $b in the same line as the **<=>** or **cmp** operator, and the variable had earlier been declared as a lexical variable. Either qualify the sort variable with the package name or rename the lexical variable.

```
Can't use %s for loop variable
```

FATAL ERROR Only a simple scalar variable may be used as a loop variable on a **foreach**.

```
Can't use %s ref as %s ref
```

FATAL ERROR You've mixed up your reference types. You have to dereference a reference of the type needed. You can use the **ref** function to test the type of the reference, if need be.

```
Can't use \1 to mean $1 in expression
```

WARNING You have tried to use the **\1** syntax (as used in **sed** and **emacs**) to reference a matched substring outside of a regular expression. Use the **$1** form instead.

```
Can't use bareword ("%s") as %s ref while \"strict refs\" in use
```

FATAL ERROR Only hard references are allowed by the **strict refs** pragma. Symbolic references are disallowed.

```
Can't use string ("%s") as %s ref while "strict refs" in use
```

FATAL ERROR Only hard references are allowed by the **strict refs** pragma. Symbolic references are disallowed.

```
Can't use an undefined value as %s reference
```

FATAL ERROR A value used as either a hard reference or a symbolic reference must be a defined value.

```
Can't use global %s in "my"
```

FATAL ERROR You tried to declare a magical variable as a lexical variable.

```
Can't use subscript on %s
```

FATAL ERROR You tried to access the subscript of an expression that didn't evaluate to a list. A common error is with functions that return different values based on context. The expression

```
my $hours = (localtime())[2];
```

will cause this error, because the assignation to a bare scalar forces **localtime** to return a scalar, not a list value. It should be written as

```
my ($hours) = (localtime())[2];
```

which will correctly indicate to **localtime** that a list should be returned.

Can't x= to read-only value

FATAL ERROR You tried to repeat a constant value (often the undefined value) with an assignment operator, which implies modifying the value itself.

```
Cannot find an opnumber for "%s"
```

FATAL ERROR You attempted to get the prototype information for a core function using

```
prototype(CORE::word);
```

But **word** does not exist as a built-in function or operator.

```
Cannot resolve method '%s' overloading '%s' in package '%s'
```

FATAL ERROR, INTERNAL ERROR An error occurred while resolving the overloading specified by a method name.

```
Character class syntax [. .] is reserved for future extensions
```

WARNING Within regular expression character classes ([]), the syntax beginning with "[." and ending with ".]" is reserved for future extensions.

```
Character class syntax [: :] is reserved for future extensions
```

WARNING Within regular expression character classes ([]), the syntax beginning with "[:" and ending with ":]" is reserved for future extensions.

```
Character class syntax [= =] is reserved for future extensions
```

WARNING Within regular expression character classes ([]), the syntax beginning with "[=" and ending with "=]" is reserved for future extensions.

```
chmod: mode argument is missing initial 0
```

WARNING The first argument to **chmod** must be an octal, not a decimal number. Octal constants are introduced with a leading 0 in Perl, as in C.

```
Close on unopened file <%s>
```

WARNING You tried to close a filehandle that was never opened.

```
Compilation failed in require
```

FATAL ERROR Perl could not compile a file specified in a **require** statement. Perl uses this generic message when none of the errors that it encountered were severe enough to halt compilation immediately.

```
Complex regular subexpression recursion limit (%d) exceeded
```

WARNING The regular expression engine uses recursion in complex situations where backtracking is required. Recursion depth is limited to 32,766, or perhaps less in architectures where the stack cannot grow arbitrarily. Try shortening the string under examination or looping within Perl code rather than in the regular expression engine. Alternatively, simply rewrite the regular expression so that it is simpler or backtracks less.

```
connect() on closed fd
```

WARNING You tried to do a **connect** on a closed socket.

```
Constant subroutine %s redefined
```

SEVERE WARNING You redefined a subroutine that had previously been eligible for inlining.

```
Constant subroutine %s undefined
```

SEVERE WARNING You undefined a subroutine that had previously been eligible for inlining.

```
Copy method did not return a reference
```

FATAL ERROR The method that overloads "=" is buggy.

```
Corrupt malloc ptr 0x%lx at 0x%lx
```

INTERNAL ERROR The **malloc** package that comes with Perl had an internal failure.

```
corrupted regexp pointers
```

INTERNAL ERROR The regular expression engine got confused by what the regular expression compiler gave it.

```
corrupted regexp program
```

INTERNAL ERROR The regular expression engine was passed a regular expression program without a valid magic number.

```
Deep recursion on subroutine "%s"
```

WARNING This subroutine has called itself (directly or indirectly) 100 times more than it has returned. This probably indicates an infinite recursion.

```
Delimiter for here document is too long
```

FATAL ERROR In a here document construct like **<<FOO**, the label **FOO** is too long for Perl to handle.

```
Did you mean &%s instead?
```

WARNING You referred to an imported subroutine **&FOO** as **$FOO**.

```
Did you mean $ or @ instead of %?
```

WARNING You specified a hash element as **%hash{$key}** when it should have been **$hash{$key}** or **@hash{@keys}**.

```
Died
```

FATAL ERROR You passed **die** an empty string, or you called **die** with no arguments, and both **$@** and **$_** were empty.

```
Do you need to predeclare %s?
```

SEVERE WARNING This is an educated guess made in conjunction with the message "%s found where operator expected." It often means a subroutine or module name is being referenced that hasn't been declared yet. This may be because of ordering problems in your file, or because of a missing **sub**, **package**, **require**, or **use** statement.

```
Don't know how to handle magic of type '%s'
```

INTERNAL ERROR The internal handling of magical variables has been cursed.

```
do_study: out of memory
```

INTERNAL ERROR An internal error with the memory allocation required for the **study** function has occurred.

```
Duplicate free() ignored
```

SEVERE WARNING The internal **free()** function attempted to free a block of memory that had already been freed.

```
elseif should be elsif
```

SEVERE WARNING You have used **elseif** when you meant **elsif**.

```
END failed--cleanup aborted
```

FATAL ERROR An untrapped exception was raised while executing an END subroutine. The interpreter is immediately exited.

```
Error converting file specification %s
```

FATAL ERROR An error peculiar to VMS. Because Perl may have to deal with file specifications in either VMS or Unix syntax, it converts them to a single form when it must operate on them directly. Either you've passed an invalid file specification to Perl or you've found a case the conversion routines don't handle.

```
%s: Eval-group in insecure regular expression
```

FATAL ERROR Perl detected tainted data when trying to compile a regular expression that contains the **(?{ ... })** zero-width assertion, which is unsafe.

```
%s: Eval-group not allowed, use re 'eval'
```

FATAL ERROR A regular expression contained the **(?{ ... })** zero-width assertion, but that construct is only allowed when the **use re 'eval'** pragma is used.

```
%s: Eval-group not allowed at run time
```

FATAL ERROR Perl tried to compile a regular expression containing the **(?{ ... })** zero-width assertion at run time, as it would when the pattern contains interpolated values. Since that is a security risk, it is not allowed.

```
Excessively long <> operator
```

FATAL ERROR The contents of a **<>** operator may not exceed the maximum size of a Perl identifier. If you're just trying to glob a long list of file names, use the **glob** operator, or put the file names into a variable and glob that.

```
Execution of %s aborted due to compilation errors
```

FATAL ERROR This is the final summary message when a Perl compilation fails.

```
Exiting eval via %s
```

WARNING You are exiting an **eval** by unconventional means, such as a **goto** or a loop control statement.

```
Exiting pseudo-block via %s
```

WARNING You are exiting a rather special block construct (such as a sort block or subroutine) by unconventional means, such as a **goto** or a loop control statement.

```
Exiting subroutine via %s
```

WARNING You are exiting a subroutine by unconventional means, such as a **goto** or a loop control statement.

```
Exiting substitution via %s
```

WARNING You are exiting a substitution by unconventional means, such as a return, a **goto**, or a loop control statement.

```
Explicit blessing to '' (assuming package main)
```

WARNING You are blessing a reference to a zero length string. This blesses the package main, which may not be what you want. Respecify the **bless** function with a full package name.

```
Fatal VMS error at %s, line %d
```

INTERNAL ERROR An error peculiar to VMS. Something untoward happened in a VMS system service or RTL routine; Perl's exit status should provide more details. The file name in "at %s" and the line number in "line %d" tell you which section of the Perl source code is distressed.

```
fcntl is not implemented
```

FATAL ERROR Your machine apparently doesn't implement **fcntl()**.

```
Filehandle %s never opened
```

WARNING An I/O operation was attempted on a filehandle that was never initialized. You need to do an **open** or a **socket** call, or call a constructor from the **FileHandle** package.

```
Filehandle %s opened for only input
```

WARNING You tried to write on a read-only filehandle. This means you probably forgot the + sign from the front of the file specification. Try using +< or +> or +>> rather than a single <.

```
Filehandle opened for only input
```

WARNING You tried to write on a read-only filehandle. This means you probably forgot the + sign from the front of the file specification. Try using +< or +> or +>> rather than a single <.

```
Final $ should be \$ or $name
```

FATAL ERROR You must now decide whether the final **$** in a string was meant to be a literal dollar sign or was meant to introduce a variable name that happens to be missing. So you have to put either the backslash or the variable name.

```
Final @ should be \@ or @name
```

FATAL ERROR You must now decide whether the final @ in a string was meant to be a literal "\@" sign or was meant to introduce a variable name that happens to be missing. So you have to put either the backslash or the variable name.

```
Format %s redefined
```

WARNING You redefined a format. To suppress this warning, write,

```
{
    local $^W = 0;
    eval "format NAME =...";
}
```

which has the effect of switching off warnings for the duration of the block by localizing the value of the special **$^W** warning variable to zero.

```
Format not terminated
```

FATAL ERROR A format must be terminated by a line with a solitary dot. Perl got to the end of your file without finding such a line.

```
Found = in conditional, should be ==
```

WARNING A common mistake by Pascal and BASIC programmers—you've tried to do a test like

```
    if ($foo = 123)
```

when you meant

```
    if ($foo == 123)
```

or some other form of test. Remember to use special characters for comparing numerical values and letters for string tests.

```
gdbm store returned %d, errno %d, key "%s"
```

SEVERE WARNING A warning from the GDBM_File extension that a store failed.

```
gethostent not implemented
```

FATAL ERROR Your C library apparently doesn't implement **gethostent()**.

```
get{sock,peer}name() on closed fd
```

WARNING You tried to get a socket or peer socket name on a closed socket.

```
getpwnam returned invalid UIC %#o for user "%s"
```

SEVERE WARNING A warning peculiar to VMS. The call to **sys$getuai** underlying the **getpwnam** operator returned an invalid UIC.

```
Glob not terminated
```

FATAL ERROR The Perl parser saw a left angle bracket in a place where it was expecting a term, so it's looking for the corresponding right angle bracket and cannot find it. This either points to a missing operator on the previous line or a typo when accessing a filehandle.

```
Global symbol "%s" requires explicit package name
```

FATAL ERROR You've written,

```
use strict vars
```

which indicates that all variables must either be lexically scoped (using **my**) or explicitly qualified to say which package the global variable is in (using ::).

```
goto must have label
```

FATAL ERROR The **goto** function must have a single argument for the LABEL to go to.

```
Had to create %s unexpectedly
```

SEVERE WARNING A routine asked for a symbol from a symbol table that ought to have existed already, but for some reason it didn't, and it had to be created on an emergency basis to prevent a core dump.

```
Hash %%s missing the % in argument %d of %s()
```

DEPRECATED FEATURE Very old versions of Perl let you omit the % on hash names in some spots. This is now heavily deprecated, and all hashes should be specified explicitly.

```
Identifier too long
```

FATAL ERROR Perl limits identifiers (names for variables, functions, and so on) to approximately 250 characters for simple names and somewhat more for compound names (such as **$A::B**).

```
Ill-formed logical name |%s| in prime_env_iter
```

WARNING A warning peculiar to VMS. A logical name was encountered when preparing to iterate over **%ENV**, which violates the syntactic rules governing logical names. Because it cannot be translated normally, it is skipped and will not appear in **%ENV**. This may be a benign occurrence, as some software packages might directly modify logical name tables and introduce nonstandard names, or it may indicate that a logical name table has been corrupted.

```
Illegal character %s (carriage return)
```

FATAL ERROR A carriage return character was found in the input. This is an error, and not a warning, because carriage return characters can break multiline strings, including here documents. The most common cause for this problem is a file imported from another platform without the necessary end-of-line conversion.

```
Illegal division by zero
```

FATAL ERROR You tried to divide a number by zero. Either something was wrong in your logic, or you need to put a conditional such as

```
if ($div == 0)
{
    return 0;
}
else
{
    return ($value/$div);
}
```

which will protect the interpreter from otherwise meaningless input.

```
Illegal modulus zero
```

FATAL ERROR You tried to divide a number by zero to get the remainder. See the example under the previous entry for a workaround.

```
Illegal octal digit
```

FATAL ERROR You used an 8 or 9 in an octal number.

```
Illegal octal digit ignored
```

WARNING You may have tried to use an 8 or 9 in an octal number. Interpretation of the octal number stopped before the 8 or 9.

```
Illegal hex digit ignored
```

WARNING You may have tried to use a character other than 0 through 9 or A through F in a hexadecimal number. Interpretation of the hexadecimal number stopped before the illegal character.

```
Illegal switch in PERL5OPT: %s
```

VERY FATAL ERROR The PERL5OPT environment variable may only be used to set the following switches: **-[DIMUdmw]**.

```
In string, @%s now must be written as \@%s
```

FATAL ERROR Perl interprets all @ signs in interpolated strings as identifiers for arrays. You have tried to use @ in an interpolated string without a matching array. You need to prefix a backslash to ensure it is identified as a literal. The most common cause for this error is introducing email addresses or other URL components.

```
Insecure dependency in %s
```

FATAL ERROR You tried to do something that the tainting mechanism didn't like. The tainting mechanism labels all data that's derived directly or indirectly from the user, who is considered to be unworthy of your trust. If any such data is used in a "dangerous" operation, you get this error. See Chapter 11.

```
Insecure directory in %s
```

FATAL ERROR You can't use **system**, **exec**, or a piped open in a **setuid** or **setgid** script if **$ENV{PATH}** contains a directory that is writable by the world.

```
Insecure $ENV{%s} while running %s
```

FATAL ERROR You can't use **system**, **exec**, or a piped open in a **setuid** or **setgid** script if any of **$ENV{PATH}**, **$ENV{IFS}**, **$ENV{CDPATH}**, **$ENV{ENV}**, or **$ENV{BASH_ENV}** are derived from data supplied (or potentially supplied) by the user.

```
Integer overflow in hex number
```

SEVERE WARNING The literal hex number you have specified is too big for your architecture. On a 32-bit architecture the largest hex literal is **0xFFFFFFFF**.

```
Integer overflow in octal number
```

SEVERE WARNING The literal octal number you have specified is too big for your architecture. On a 32-bit architecture the largest octal literal is **037777777777**.

```
Internal inconsistency in tracking vforks
```

SEVERE WARNING A warning peculiar to VMS. Perl keeps track of the number of times you've called **fork** and **exec**, to determine whether the current call to **exec** should affect the current script or a subprocess. Somehow, this count has become scrambled, so Perl is making a guess and treating this **exec** as a request to terminate the Perl script and execute the specified command.

```
internal disaster in regexp
```

INTERNAL ERROR Something went wrong in the regular expression parser.

```
internal error: glob failed
```

INTERNAL ERROR Something went wrong with the external program(s) used for the **glob** function and the **<>** globbing operator. This may mean that your **csh** (C shell) is broken. If so, you should change all of the **csh**-related variables in the **config.sh** script used to build Perl. If you make all **csh** references empty except **d_csh**, which should be **undef, Perl will assume that csh** is missing and instead emulate the code required internally. After editing config.sh, run **./Configure –S** and rebuild Perl.

```
internal urp in regexp at /%s/
```

INTERNAL ERROR Something went badly awry in the regular expression parser.

```
invalid [] range in regexp
```

FATAL ERROR The range specified in a character class had a minimum character greater than the maximum character.

```
Invalid conversion in %s: "%s"
```

WARNING Perl does not understand the given format conversion.

```
Invalid type in pack: '%s'
```

FATAL ERROR, WARNING The given character is not a valid pack type or the given character is not a valid pack type but used to be silently ignored.

```
Invalid type in unpack: '%s'
```

FATAL ERROR, WARNING The given character is not a valid unpack type or the given character is not a valid unpack type but used to be silently ignored.

```
ioctl is not implemented
```

FATAL ERROR Your machine does not support **ioctl**.

```
junk on end of regexp
```

INTERNAL ERROR The regular expression parser is confused.

```
Label not found for "last %s"
```

FATAL ERROR You named a loop to break out of, but you're not currently in a loop of that name, not even if you count where you were called from.

```
Label not found for "next %s"
```

FATAL ERROR You named a loop to continue, but you're not currently in a loop of that name, not even if you count where you were called from.

```
Label not found for "redo %s"
```

FATAL ERROR You named a loop to restart, but you're not currently in a loop of that name, not even if you count where you were called from.

```
listen() on closed fd
```

WARNING You tried to do a **listen** on a closed socket.

```
Method for operation %s not found in package %s during blessing
```

FATAL ERROR An attempt was made to specify an entry in an overloading table that doesn't resolve to a valid subroutine.

```
Might be a runaway multi-line %s string starting on line %d
```

SEVERE WARNING An advisory indicating that the previous error may have been caused by a missing delimiter on a string or pattern, because it eventually ended earlier on the current line.

```
Misplaced _ in number
```

WARNING An underline in a decimal constant wasn't on a three-digit boundary.

```
Missing $ on loop variable
```

FATAL ERROR You've tried to use a shell-like construct to specify the variable used in a loop. You must specify the scalar variable to be used in the loop with a leading **$** sign.

```
Missing comma after first argument to %s function
```

FATAL ERROR You have tried to specify a special variable (such as the **FILEHANDLE** argument on **print**) to a function that does not support it.

```
Missing operator before %s?
```

SEVERE WARNING This is an educated guess made in conjunction with the message "%s found where operator expected." Often the missing operator is a comma.

```
Missing right bracket
```

FATAL ERROR The Perl parser counted more opening curly brackets (braces) than closing ones.

```
Modification of a read-only value attempted
```

FATAL ERROR You tried, directly or indirectly, to change the value of a constant.

```
Modification of non-creatable array value attempted, subscript %d
```

FATAL ERROR You tried to make an array value spring into existence, and the subscript was negative, even when counting from end of the array backwards.

```
Modification of non-creatable hash value attempted, subscript "%s"
```

INTERNAL ERROR You tried to make a hash value spring into existence, and it couldn't be created.

```
Module name must be constant
```

FATAL ERROR Only a bare module name is allowed as the first argument to a **use**. If you want to import a package name derived from a variable, use the **require** function.

```
msg%s not implemented
```

FATAL ERROR You don't have System V message IPC on your system.

```
Multidimensional syntax %s not supported
```

WARNING Multidimensional arrays are specified using separate braces around each dimension, as in **$foo[1][2][3]**, not **$foo[1,2,3]**.

```
Name "%s::%s" used only once: possible typo
```

WARNING Typographical errors often show up as unique variable names. If you had a good reason for having a unique name, then either define or declare it earlier using **my** or the **use vars** pragma.

```
Negative length
```

FATAL ERROR You tried to do a **read/write/send/recv** operation with a buffer length that is less than zero.

```
nested *?+ in regexp
```

FATAL ERROR You can't quantify a quantifier without intervening parentheses.

```
No #! line
```

FATAL ERROR The **setuid** emulator requires that scripts have a well-formed **#!** line even on machines that don't support the **#!** construct.

```
No %s allowed while running setuid
```

FATAL ERROR Certain operations are deemed too insecure for a **setuid** or **setgid** script even to be allowed to attempt them.

```
No -e allowed in setuid scripts
```

FATAL ERROR A **setuid** script can't be specified by the user.

```
No comma allowed after %s
```

FATAL ERROR A list operator that has a filehandle or "indirect object" is not allowed to have a comma between that and the following arguments. Otherwise it would be just another one of the arguments.

```
No command into which to pipe on command line
```

FATAL ERROR An error peculiar to VMS. Perl handles its own command line redirection and found a "|" at the end of the command line, so it doesn't know where you want to pipe the output from this command.

```
No DB::DB routine defined
```

FATAL ERROR The currently executing code was compiled with the **–d** switch to drop you into the debugger, but for some reason the debugging module, defined in the perl5db.pl file, didn't define the required statement to trap each input line.

```
No dbm on this machine
```

INTERNAL ERROR This is counted as an internal error, because every machine should supply at least one version of **dbm**; Perl even comes with its own implementation.

```
No DBsub routine
```

FATAL ERROR The currently executing code was compiled with the **–d** switch to drop you into the debugger, but for some reason the debugging module, defined in the perl5db.pl file, didn't define the required **DB::sub** routine to be called at the beginning of each ordinary subroutine call.

```
No error file after 2> or 2>> on command line
```

FATAL ERROR An error peculiar to VMS. Perl handles its own command line redirection and found a "2>" or "2>>" on the command line, but can't find the name of the file to which to write data destined for **stderr**.

```
No input file after < on command line
```

FATAL ERROR An error peculiar to VMS. Perl handles its own command line redirection and found a "<" on the command line, but can't find the name of the file from which to read data for **stdin**.

```
No output file after > on command line
```

FATAL ERROR An error peculiar to VMS. Perl handles its own command line redirection and found a lone ">" at the end of the command line, so it doesn't know where you wanted to redirect **stdout**.

```
No output file after >> or >> on command line
```

FATAL ERROR An error peculiar to VMS. Perl handles its own command line redirection and found a ">" or a ">>" on the command line, but can't find the name of the file to which to write data destined for **stdout**.

```
No Perl script found in input
```

FATAL ERROR You called **perl -x**, but no line was found in the file beginning with **#!** and containing the word **perl**.

```
No setregid available
```

FATAL ERROR Configure didn't find anything resembling the **setregid()** call for your system.

```
No setreuid available
```

FATAL ERROR Configure didn't find anything resembling the **setreuid()** call for your system.

```
No space allowed after -I
```

FATAL ERROR The argument to **-I** must follow the **-I** immediately, with no intervening space.

```
No such array field
```

FATAL ERROR You tried to access an array as a hash, but the field name used is not defined. The hash at index 0 should map all valid field names to array indices for that to work.

```
No such field "%s" in variable %s of type %s
```

FATAL ERROR You tried to access a field of a typed variable where the type does not know about the field name. The field names are looked up in the **%FIELDS** hash in the type package at compile time. The **%FIELDS** hash is usually set up with the **fields** pragma.

```
No such pipe open
```

INTERNAL ERROR An error peculiar to VMS. The internal routine **my_pclose()** tried to close a pipe that hadn't been opened. This should have been caught earlier as an attempt to close an unopened filehandle.

```
No such signal: SIG%s
```

WARNING You specified a signal name as a subscript to **%SIG** that was not recognized.

```
Not a CODE reference
```

FATAL ERROR Perl was trying to evaluate a reference to a code value (that is, a subroutine) but found a reference to something else instead. You can use the **ref** function to find out what kind of reference it really was.

```
Not a format reference
```

FATAL ERROR You managed to generate a reference to an anonymous format, and it didn't exist.

```
Not a GLOB reference
```

FATAL ERROR Perl was trying to evaluate a reference to a **typeglob** but found a reference to something else instead. You can use the **ref** function to find out what kind of reference it really was.

```
Not a HASH reference
```

FATAL ERROR Perl was trying to evaluate a reference to a hash value but found a reference to something else instead. You can use the **ref** function to find out what kind of reference it really was.

```
Not a perl script
```

FATAL ERROR The **setuid** emulator requires that scripts have a well formed **#!** line even on machines that don't support the **#!** construct. The line must mention **perl**.

```
Not a SCALAR reference
```

FATAL ERROR Perl was trying to evaluate a reference to a scalar value but found a reference to something else instead. You can use the **ref** function to find out what kind of reference it really was.

```
Not a subroutine reference
```

FATAL ERROR Perl was trying to evaluate a reference to a subroutine but found a reference to something else instead. You can use the **ref** function to find out what kind of reference it really was.

```
Not a subroutine reference in overload table
```

FATAL ERROR An attempt was made to specify an entry in an overloading table that doesn't point to a valid subroutine.

```
Not an ARRAY reference
```

FATAL ERROR Perl was trying to evaluate a reference to an array value but found a reference to something else instead. You can use the **ref** function to find out what kind of reference it really was.

```
Not enough arguments for %s
```

FATAL ERROR The function requires more arguments than you specified.

```
Not enough format arguments
```

WARNING A format specified more picture fields than the next line supplied.

```
Null filename used
```

FATAL ERROR You can't require the null file name. On many machines the null file name refers to the current directory.

```
Null picture in formline
```

FATAL ERROR The first argument to **formline** must be a valid format picture specification.

```
NULL OP IN RUN
```

INTERNAL ERROR Some internal routine called **run()** with a null opcode pointer.

```
Null realloc
```

INTERNAL ERROR An attempt was made to **realloc**() NULL.

```
NULL regexp argument
```

INTERNAL ERROR The internal pattern matching routines failed to supply a suitable expression to the regular expression engine.

```
NULL regexp parameter
```

INTERNAL ERROR The internal pattern matching routines failed to supply a suitable expression to the regular expression engine.

```
Number too long
```

FATAL ERROR Perl limits the representation of decimal numbers in programs to about 250 characters. Try using scientific notation (for example, "1e6" instead of "1_000_000").

```
Odd number of elements in hash assignment
```

SEVERE WARNING You specified an odd number of elements to initialize a hash. Hashes should be initialized in key/value pairs.

```
Offset outside string
```

FATAL ERROR You tried to do a **read/write/send/recv** operation with an offset pointing outside the buffer.

```
oops: oopsAV
```

SEVERE WARNING An internal warning that the grammar is screwed up.

```
oops: oopsHV
```

SEVERE WARNING An internal warning that the grammar is screwed up.

```
Operation '%s': no method found, %s
```

FATAL ERROR An attempt was made to perform an overloaded operation for which no handler was defined. While some handlers can be autogenerated in terms of other handlers, there is no default handler for any operation, unless the **fallback** overloading key is specified to be true.

```
Operator or semicolon missing before %s
```

SEVERE WARNING You used a variable or subroutine call where the parser was expecting an operator.

```
Out of memory for yacc stack
```

FATAL ERROR The **yacc** parser wanted to grow its stack so it could continue parsing, but the system **realloc()** wouldn't give it more memory.

```
Out of memory during request for %s
```

VERY FATAL ERROR The **malloc()** function returned zero, indicating there was insufficient memory to satisfy the request.

FATAL ERROR The request was judged to be small, so the possibility to trap it depends on the way **perl** was compiled. By default it is not trappable. However, if compiled for this, Perl may use the contents of **$^M** as an emergency pool after **die**ing with this message. In this case the error is trappable.

```
Out of memory during "large" request for %s
```

FATAL ERROR The **malloc()** function returned zero, indicating there was insufficient memory to satisfy the request. However, the request was judged large enough (compile-time default is 64K), so a possibility to shut down by trapping this error is allowed.

```
Out of memory during ridiculously large request
```

FATAL ERROR You can't allocate more than 2^31+"small amount" bytes.

```
page overflow
```

WARNING A single call to **write** produced more lines than can fit on a page.

```
panic: ck_grep
```

INTERNAL ERROR Failed an internal consistency check trying to compile a **grep**.

```
panic: ck_split
```

INTERNAL ERROR Failed an internal consistency check trying to compile a **split**.

```
panic: corrupt saved stack index
```

INTERNAL ERROR The savestack was requested to restore more localized values than there are in the savestack.

```
panic: die %s
```

INTERNAL ERROR You popped the context stack to an **eval** context and then discovered it wasn't an **eval** context.

```
panic: do_match
```

INTERNAL ERROR The internal **pp_match()** routine was called with invalid operational data.

```
panic: do_split
```

INTERNAL ERROR The internal **split** function failed.

```
panic: do_subst
```

INTERNAL ERROR The internal **pp_subst()** routine was called with invalid operational data.

```
panic: do_trans
```

INTERNAL ERROR The internal **do_trans()** routine was called with invalid operational data.

```
panic: frexp
```

INTERNAL ERROR The library function **frexp()** failed, making **printf("%f")** impossible.

```
panic: goto
```

INTERNAL ERROR You popped the context stack to a context with the specified label and then discovered it wasn't a context we know how to do a **goto** in.

```
panic: INTERPCASEMOD
```

INTERNAL ERROR The Perl parser had problems with a case modification.

```
panic: INTERPCONCAT
```

INTERNAL ERROR The Perl parser had problems parsing a string with brackets.

```
panic: last
```

INTERNAL ERROR You popped the context stack to a block context and then discovered it wasn't a block context.

```
panic: leave_scope clearsv
```

INTERNAL ERROR A writable lexical variable became read-only somehow within the scope.

```
panic: leave_scope inconsistency
```

INTERNAL ERROR The savestack probably got out of sync.

```
panic: malloc
```

INTERNAL ERROR A internal function requested a negative number of bytes for allocation via the **malloc** function.

```
panic: mapstart
```

INTERNAL ERROR A problem occurred trying to execute a **map** function.

```
panic: null array
```

INTERNAL ERROR One of the internal array routines was passed a null AV (array value) pointer.

```
panic: pad_alloc
```

INTERNAL ERROR The compiler got confused about which scratch pad it was allocating and freeing temporary and lexical variables from.

```
panic: pad_free curpad
```

INTERNAL ERROR The compiler got confused about which scratch pad it was allocating and freeing temporary and lexical variables from.

```
panic: pad_free po
```

INTERNAL ERROR An invalid scratch pad offset was detected internally.

```
panic: pad_reset curpad
```

INTERNAL ERROR The compiler got confused about which scratch pad it was allocating and freeing temporary and lexical variables from.

```
panic: pad_sv po
```

INTERNAL ERROR An invalid scratch pad offset was detected internally.

```
panic: pad_swipe curpad
```

INTERNAL ERROR The compiler got confused about which scratch pad it was allocating and freeing temporary and lexical variables from.

```
panic: pad_swipe po
```

INTERNAL ERROR An invalid scratch pad offset was detected internally.

```
panic: pp_iter
```

INTERNAL ERROR The **foreach** iterator got called in a nonloop context frame.

```
panic: realloc
```

INTERNAL ERROR Something requested a negative number of bytes to the system **realloc()**.

```
panic: restartop
```

INTERNAL ERROR Some internal routine requested a **goto** or other jump statement and didn't supply the destination.

```
panic: return
```

INTERNAL ERROR You popped the context stack to a subroutine or **eval** context and then discovered it wasn't a subroutine or **eval** context.

```
panic: scan_num
```

INTERNAL ERROR The internal **scan_num()** function got called on something that wasn't a number.

```
panic: sv_insert
```

INTERNAL ERROR The internal **sv_insert()** routine was told to remove more string than there was string.

```
panic: top_env
```

INTERNAL ERROR The compiler attempted to do a **goto** and couldn't.

```
panic: yylex
```

INTERNAL ERROR The Perl parser had problems processing a case modifier.

```
Parentheses missing around "%s" list
```

WARNING You tried to specify a list without using parentheses, for example,

```
my $foo, $bar = @_;
```

instead of

```
my ($foo, $bar) = @_;
```

Remember that "my" and "local" bind closer than comma.

```
Perl %3.3f required--this is only version %s, stopped
```

FATAL ERROR The module in question uses features of a version of Perl more recent than the currently running version.

```
Permission denied
```

FATAL ERROR The **setuid** emulator in **suidperl** detected an unsafe operation and quit.

```
pid %d not a child
```

WARNING A warning peculiar to VMS. The **waitpid()** was asked to wait for a process that isn't a subprocess of the current process. While this is fine from VMS's perspective, it's probably not what you intended.

```
POSIX getpgrp can't take an argument
```

FATAL ERROR Your C compiler uses POSIX **getpgrp()**, which takes no argument, unlike the BSD version, which takes a pid.

```
Possible attempt to put comments in qw() list
```

WARNING **qw()** lists contain items separated by white space; as with literal strings, comment characters are not ignored, but are instead treated as literal data.

```
Possible attempt to separate words with commas
```

WARNING **qw()** lists contain items separated by white space; commas aren't needed to separate the items.

```
Possible memory corruption: %s overflowed 3rd argument
```

FATAL ERROR An **ioctl** or **fcntl** returned more information than Perl expected. Perl chooses a suitable buffer size and puts a sentinel byte at the end of the buffer to ensure that the buffer does not extend beyond the sentinel byte. In this instance the sentinel byte got clobbered, and Perl assumes that memory allocated to the buffer is now corrupted.

```
Precedence problem: open %s should be open(%s)
```

SEVERE WARNING Because of the precedence of operators, a statement like

```
open FOO || die;
```

is now misinterpreted as

```
open(FOO || die);
```

You must put parentheses around the filehandle, or use the **or** operator instead of `||`.

```
print on closed filehandle %s
```

WARNING You tried to print to a filehandle that was either closed before the **print** statement was reached or was never opened in the first place.

```
printf on closed filehandle %s
```

WARNING You tried to print to a filehandle that was either closed before the **printf** statement was reached or was never opened in the first place.

```
Probable precedence problem on %s
```

WARNING The compiler found a bare word where it expected a conditional operator.

```
Prototype mismatch: %s vs %s
```

SEVERE WARNING The subroutine being declared or defined had previously been declared or defined with a different function prototype.

```
Range iterator outside integer range
```

FATAL ERROR One (or both) of the numeric arguments to the range operator **..** are outside the range that can be represented by integers internally.

```
Read on closed filehandle E<lt>%sE<gt>
```

WARNING You tried to print to a filehandle that was either closed before the **print** statement was reached or was never opened in the first place.

```
Reallocation too large: %lx
```

FATAL ERROR You can't allocate more than 64K of memory on an MS-DOS machine.

```
Recompile perl with -D DEBUGGING to use -D switch
```

FATAL ERROR You can't use the **-D** option unless the code to produce the desired output is compiled into Perl.

```
Recursive inheritance detected in package '%s'
```

FATAL ERROR More than 100 levels of inheritance were used. This probably indicates an unintended loop in your inheritance hierarchy.

```
Recursive inheritance detected while looking for method '%s' in
package '%s'
```

FATAL ERROR More than 100 levels of inheritance were encountered while invoking a method. This probably indicates an unintended loop in your inheritance hierarchy.

```
Reference found where even-sized list expected
```

WARNING You gave a single reference where Perl was expecting a list with an even number of elements (for assignment to a hash).

```
Reference miscount in sv_replace()
```

WARNING The internal **sv_replace()** function was handed a new SV with a reference count of other than 1.

```
regexp *+ operand could be empty
```

FATAL ERROR The part of the regexp subject to either the * or + quantifier could match an empty string.

```
regexp memory corruption
```

INTERNAL ERROR The regular expression engine got confused by what the regular expression compiler gave it.

```
regexp out of space
```

INTERNAL ERROR The regular expression engine has run out of memory. This shouldn't happen because the internal **safemalloc()** function should have trapped the error.

```
regexp too big
```

FATAL ERROR The current implementation of regular expressions uses shorts as address offsets within a string. This means that if the regular expression compiles to longer than 32,767 bytes, the regular expression will fail.

```
Reversed %s= operator
```

WARNING You wrote your assignment operator backwards. The = must always come last, to avoid ambiguity with subsequent unary operators.

```
Runaway format
```

FATAL ERROR Your format contained the ~~ repeat-until-blank sequence, but it produced 200 lines at once, and the 200th line looked exactly like the 199th line.

```
Scalar value @%s[%s] better written as $%s[%s]
```

WARNING You've used an array slice (indicated by @) to select a single element of an array.

```
Scalar value @%s{%s} better written as $%s{%s}
```

WARNING You've used a hash slice (indicated by @) to select a single element of a hash.

```
Script is not setuid/setgid in suidperl
```

FATAL ERROR Oddly, the **suidperl** program was invoked on a script without the **setuid** or **setgid** bit set.

```
Search pattern not terminated
```

FATAL ERROR The Perl parser couldn't find the final delimiter of a // or **m{}** construct.

```
%sseek() on unopened file
```

WARNING You tried to use the **seek** or **sysseek** function on a filehandle that was either never opened or has since been closed.

```
select not implemented
```

FATAL ERROR This machine doesn't implement the **select** system call.

```
sem%s not implemented
```

FATAL ERROR You don't have System V semaphore IPC on your system.

```
semi-panic: attempt to dup freed string
```

SEVERE WARNING The internal **newSVsv()** routine was called to duplicate a scalar that had previously been marked as free.

```
Semicolon seems to be missing
```

WARNING A nearby syntax error was probably caused by a missing semicolon or possibly some other missing operator, such as a comma.

```
Send on closed socket
```

WARNING You tried to send data to a socket that was either closed before the **send** statement was reached or was never opened in the first place.

```
Sequence (? incomplete
```

FATAL ERROR A regular expression ended with an incomplete extension **(?**.

```
Sequence (?#... not terminated
```

FATAL ERROR A regular expression comment must be terminated by a closing parenthesis. Embedded parentheses aren't allowed.

```
Sequence (?%s...) not implemented
```

FATAL ERROR A proposed regular expression extension has the character reserved but has not yet been written.

```
Sequence (?%s...) not recognized
```

FATAL ERROR You used a regular expression extension that doesn't make sense.

```
setegid() not implemented
```

FATAL ERROR You tried to assign to the special **$)** variable, and your operating system doesn't support the **setegid()** system call.

```
seteuid() not implemented
```

FATAL ERROR You tried to assign to the special **$>** variable, and your operating system doesn't support the **seteuid()** system call.

```
setrgid() not implemented
```

FATAL ERROR You tried to assign to the special **$(** variable, and your operating system doesn't support the **setrgid()** system.

```
setruid() not implemented
```

FATAL ERROR You tried to assign to the special **$<** variable, and your operating system doesn't support the **setruid()** system call.

```
Setuid/gid script is writable by world
```

FATAL ERROR The **setuid** emulator won't run a script that is writable by the world, because it may have been modified by an non-secure user.

```
shm%s not implemented
```

FATAL ERROR You don't have System V shared memory IPC on your system.

```
shutdown() on closed fd
```

WARNING You tried to do a **shutdown** on a closed socket.

```
SIG%s handler "%s" not defined
```

WARNING The signal handler named in **%SIG** doesn't exist.

```
sort is now a reserved word
```

FATAL ERROR You cannot use the **sort** word as a keyword or function.

```
Sort subroutine didn't return a numeric value
```

FATAL ERROR A sort comparison routine must return a number.

```
Sort subroutine didn't return single value
```

FATAL ERROR A sort comparison subroutine may not return a list value with more or less than one element.

```
Split loop
```

INTERNAL ERROR The split was looping infinitely.

```
Stat on unopened file E<lt>%sE<gt>
```

WARNING You tried to use the **stat** function or **-X** file test on a filehandle that was either never opened or has since been closed.

```
Statement unlikely to be reached
```

WARNING You called **exec** with a statement containing something other than **die**.

```
Stub found while resolving method '%s' overloading '%s' in package '%s'
```

INTERNAL ERROR Overloading resolution over **@ISA** tree may be broken by importation stubs.

```
Subroutine %s redefined
```

WARNING You have tried to define a subroutine with the same name as one that already exists.

```
Substitution loop
```

INTERNAL ERROR The substitution was looping infinitely.

```
Substitution pattern not terminated
```

FATAL ERROR The Perl parser couldn't find the interior delimiter of a **s///** or **s{}{}** construct.

```
Substitution replacement not terminated
```

FATAL ERROR The Perl parser couldn't find the delimiter of a **s///** or **s{}{}** construct.

```
substr outside of string
```

SEVERE WARNING, WARNING You tried to reference a **substr** that pointed outside of a string. This usually indicates that the value of the offset was larger than the length of the string.

```
suidperl is no longer needed since %s
```

FATAL ERROR Your Perl was compiled with **-DSETUID_SCRIPTS_ARE_SECURE_NOW**, but a version of the **setuid** emulator was run.

```
syntax error
```

FATAL ERROR Probably means you had a syntax error. Common reasons include

- A keyword is misspelled.
- A semicolon is missing.
- A comma is missing.
- An opening or closing parenthesis is missing.
- An opening or closing brace is missing.
- A closing quote is missing.

Often there will be another error message associated with the syntax error giving more information. Your best solution is to switch on warnings with the **-w** switch to the Perl application. The error message itself often tells you where it was in the line when it decided to give up.

```
syntax error at line %d: '%s' unexpected
```

ALIEN ERROR You've accidentally run your script through the Bourne shell instead of Perl.

```
System V %s is not implemented on this machine
```

FATAL ERROR You tried to do something with a function beginning with **sem**, **shm**, or **msg**, but that System V IPC is not implemented in your machine.

```
Syswrite on closed filehandle
```

WARNING You tried to print to a filehandle that was either closed before the **print** statement was reached or was never opened in the first place.

```
Target of goto is too deeply nested
```

FATAL ERROR You tried to use **goto** to reach a label that was too deeply nested for Perl to reach.

```
tell() on unopened file
```

WARNING You tried to use the **tell** function on a filehandle that was either closed before the **tell** statement was reached or was never opened in the first place.

```
Test on unopened file E<lt>%sE<gt>
```

WARNING You tried to invoke a file test operator on a filehandle that isn't open.

```
That use of $[ is unsupported
```

FATAL ERROR Assignment to the special **$[** variable is now ignored and only interpreted as a compiler directive.

```
The %s function is unimplemented
```

FATAL ERROR The function indicated isn't implemented on this architecture, according to the tests of the **Configure** script used to build Perl.

```
The crypt() function is unimplemented due to excessive paranoia
```

FATAL ERROR Configure couldn't find the **crypt** function on your machine.

```
The stat preceding -l _ wasn't an lstat
```

FATAL ERROR It makes no sense to test the current **stat** buffer for a symbolic link if the last file tested resolved a symbolic link to a static file.

```
times not implemented
```

FATAL ERROR Your version of the C library apparently doesn't do **times**.

```
Too few args to syscall
```

FATAL ERROR There has to be at least one argument to **syscall** to specify the system call to call.

```
Too late for "-T" option
```

VERY FATAL ERROR The **#!** line (or local equivalent) in a Perl script contains the **–T** (taint) option, but Perl was not invoked with **-T** in its command line. This is flagged as an error because by the time Perl identifies the taint option in the script, the environment will already have been imported, thereby breaking the point of tainting external values in the first place.

```
Too late for "-%s" option
```

VERY FATAL ERROR The **#!** line (or local equivalent) in a Perl script contains the **–M** (module) or **–m** (module) option. Use the **use** pragma instead.

```
Too many ('s
Too many )'s
```

ALIEN ERROR This is actually produced by **csh**, not Perl, and signifies that you're trying to run your program with the wrong interpreter.

```
Too many args to syscall
```

FATAL ERROR Perl supports a maximum of only 14 arguments to **syscall**.

```
Too many arguments for %s
```

FATAL ERROR The function requires fewer arguments than you specified.

```
trailing \ in regexp
```

FATAL ERROR The regular expression ends with an unbackslashed backslash.

```
Transliteration pattern not terminated
```

FATAL ERROR The Perl parser couldn't find the interior delimiter of a **tr///** or **tr[][]** or **y///** or **y[][]** construct.

```
Transliteration replacement not terminated
```

FATAL ERROR The Perl parser couldn't find the final delimiter of a **tr///** or **tr[][]** construct.

```
truncate not implemented
```

FATAL ERROR Your machine doesn't implement a file truncation mechanism.

```
Type of arg %d to %s must be %s (not %s)
```

FATAL ERROR This function requires the argument in that position to be of a certain type.

```
umask: argument is missing initial 0
```

WARNING A function or operator is expecting an octal argument, and you have supplied a decimal constant.

```
umask not implemented
```

FATAL ERROR Your machine doesn't implement the **umask()** function.

```
Unable to create sub named "%s"
```

FATAL ERROR You attempted to create or access a subroutine with an illegal name.

```
Unbalanced context: %d more PUSHes than POPs
```

WARNING The exit code detected an internal inconsistency in how many execution contexts were entered and left.

```
Unbalanced saves: %d more saves than restores
```

WARNING The exit code detected an internal inconsistency in how many values were temporarily localized.

```
Unbalanced scopes: %d more ENTERs than LEAVEs
```

WARNING The exit code detected an internal inconsistency in how many blocks were entered and left.

```
Unbalanced tmps: %d more allocs than frees
```

WARNING The exit code detected an internal inconsistency in how many mortal scalars were allocated and freed.

```
Undefined format "%s" called
```

FATAL ERROR The format indicated doesn't seem to exist.

```
Undefined sort subroutine "%s" called
```

FATAL ERROR The sort comparison routine specified doesn't seem to exist.

```
Undefined subroutine &%s called
```

FATAL ERROR The subroutine indicated hasn't been defined, or if it was, it has since been undefined.

```
Undefined subroutine called
```

FATAL ERROR The anonymous subroutine you're trying to call hasn't been defined, or if it was, it has since been undefined.

```
Undefined subroutine in sort
```

FATAL ERROR The sort comparison routine specified is declared but doesn't seem to have been defined yet.

```
Undefined top format "%s" called
```

FATAL ERROR The format indicated doesn't seem to exist.

```
Undefined value assigned to typeglob
```

WARNING An undefined value was assigned to a typeglob.

```
unexec of %s into %s failed!
```

FATAL ERROR The **unexec()** routine failed for some reason.

```
Unknown BYTEORDER
```

FATAL ERROR There are no byte-swapping functions for a machine with this byte order.

```
unmatched () in regexp
```

FATAL ERROR Unbackslashed parentheses must always be balanced in regular expressions.

```
Unmatched right bracket
```

FATAL ERROR The Perl parser counted more closing curly brackets (braces) than opening ones, so you're probably missing an opening bracket.

```
unmatched [] in regexp
```

FATAL ERROR The brackets around a character class must match.

```
Unquoted string "%s" may clash with future reserved word
```

WARNING You used a bare word that might someday be claimed as a reserved word.

```
Unrecognized character %s
```

FATAL ERROR The Perl parser has no idea what to do with the specified character in your Perl script (or eval).

```
Unrecognized signal name "%s"
```

FATAL ERROR You specified a signal name to the **kill** function that was not recognized.

```
Unrecognized switch: -%s  (-h will show valid options)
```

FATAL ERROR You specified an illegal command line option to Perl.

```
Unsuccessful %s on filename containing newline
```

WARNING A file operation was attempted on a file name, and that operation failed.

```
Unsupported directory function "%s" called
```

FATAL ERROR Your machine doesn't support **opendir()** and **readdir()**.

```
Unsupported function fork
```

FATAL ERROR Your version of executable does not support forking.

```
Unsupported function %s
```

FATAL ERROR This machine doesn't implement the indicated function, apparently.

```
Unsupported socket function "%s" called
```

FATAL ERROR Your machine doesn't support the Berkeley socket mechanism.

```
Unterminated E<lt>E<gt> operator
```

FATAL ERROR The lexer saw a left angle bracket in a place where it was expecting a term, so it's looking for the corresponding right angle bracket and cannot find it.

```
Use of "$$<digit>" to mean "${$}<digit>" is deprecated
```

DEPRECATED FEATURE Perl versions before 5.004 misinterpreted any type marker followed by "$" and a digit. For example, "$$0" was incorrectly taken to mean "${$}0" instead of "${$0}." This bug is (mostly) fixed in Perl 5.004.

```
Use of $# is deprecated
```

DEPRECATED FEATURE This was an ill-advised attempt to emulate a poorly defined **awk** feature.

```
Use of $* is deprecated
```

DEPRECATED FEATURE The **$*** variable was used to switch on multiline pattern matching. You should now use the **/m** or **/s** modifiers.

```
Use of %s in printf format not supported
```

FATAL ERROR You attempted to use a feature of printf that is accessible only from C.

```
Use of bare << to mean <<"" is deprecated
```

DEPRECATED FEATURE You should use the explicitly quoted form if you wish to use an empty line as the terminator of the here document.

```
Use of implicit split to @_ is deprecated
```

DEPRECATED FEATURE You should split to a named array when using **split**, to prevent it from overwriting the arguments to a function.

```
Use of inherited AUTOLOAD for non-method %s() is deprecated
```

DEPRECATED FEATURE Autoloaded subroutines are looked up as methods via the modules and classes specified in **@ISA** even when the functions are referred to as functions, not methods. This has been fixed in v5.005.

```
Use of reserved word "%s" is deprecated
```

DEPRECATED FEATURE The indicated bare word is a reserved word.

```
Use of %s is deprecated
```

DEPRECATED FEATURE The construct indicated is no longer recommended for use, generally because there's a better way to do it, and also because the old way has bad side effects.

```
Use of uninitialized value
```

WARNING An undefined value was used as if it were already defined. It was interpreted as a "" (empty string) or a zero.

```
Useless use of "re" pragma
```

WARNING You inserted the **use re** pragma without any arguments.

```
Useless use of %s in void context
```

WARNING You did something without a side effect in a context that does nothing with the return value, such as a statement that doesn't return a value from a block, or the left side of a scalar comma operator.

```
untie attempted while %d inner references still exist
```

WARNING A copy of the object returned from **tie** was still valid when **untie** was called.

```
Value of %s can be "0"; test with defined()
```

WARNING In a conditional expression, you used **<HANDLE>**, **<*>** (glob), **each**, or **readdir** as a Boolean value.

```
Variable "%s" is not imported%s
```

FATAL ERROR While the **use strict** pragma is in effect, you referred to a global variable that you thought was imported from another module.

```
Variable "%s" may be unavailable
```

WARNING An inner (nested) anonymous subroutine is inside a named subroutine, and outside that is another subroutine; and the anonymous (innermost) subroutine is referencing a lexical variable defined in the outermost subroutine. For example:

```
sub outermost { my $a; sub middle { sub { $a } } }
```

If the anonymous subroutine is called or referenced (directly or indirectly) from the outermost subroutine, it will share the variable as you would expect. But if the anonymous subroutine is called or referenced when the outermost subroutine is not active, it will see the value of the shared variable as it was before and during the *first* call to the outermost subroutine.

```
Variable "%s" will not stay shared
```

WARNING An inner (nested) named subroutine is referencing a lexical variable defined in an outer subroutine.

```
Variable syntax
```

ALIEN ERROR This is actually produced by **csh**, not Perl, and signifies that you're trying to run your program with the wrong interpreter.

```
perl: warning: Setting locale failed.
```

SEVERE WARNING The whole warning message will look something like this:

```
perl: warning: Setting locale failed.
perl: warning: Please check that your locale settings:
        LC_ALL = "En_US",
        LANG = (unset)
    are supported and installed on your system.
perl: warning: Falling back to the standard locale ("C").
```

Exactly what were the failed locale settings varies. There is a default locale called "C" that Perl can use and the script will be run.

```
Warning: something's wrong
```

WARNING You passed **warn** an empty string, or you called it with no arguments and $_ was empty.

```
Warning: unable to close filehandle %s properly
```

SEVERE WARNING The implicit **close** done by an **open** got an error indication on the **close**. This usually indicates your file system ran out of disk space.

```
Warning: Use of "%s" without parentheses is ambiguous
```

SEVERE WARNING You wrote a unary operator followed by something that looks like a binary operator that could also have been interpreted as a term or unary operator.

```
Write on closed filehandle
```

WARNING The filehandle you are writing to was closed before you reached this point or was never opened in the first place.

```
X outside of string
```

FATAL ERROR You had a pack template that specified a relative position before the beginning of the string being unpacked.

```
x outside of string
```

FATAL ERROR You had a pack template that specified a relative position after the end of the string being unpacked.

```
Xsub "%s" called in sort
```

FATAL ERROR The use of an external subroutine as a sort comparison is not yet supported.

```
Xsub called in sort
```

FATAL ERROR The use of an external subroutine as a sort comparison is not yet supported.

```
You can't use -l on a filehandle
```

FATAL ERROR A filehandle represents an opened file, and when you opened the file, the symbolic link had already been resolved, so you cannot **stat** the original symbolic link.

```
You haven't disabled set-id scripts in the kernel yet!
```

FATAL ERROR This is an OS, not Perl, error. Your best bet is to use the **wrapsuid** script in the **eg** directory of the Perl distribution to put a **setuid** C wrapper around your script.

```
You need to quote "%s"
```

WARNING You assigned a bare word as a signal handler name.

```
[gs]etsockopt() on closed fd
```

WARNING You tried to get or set a socket option on a closed socket.

```
\1 better written as $1
```

WARNING Perl supports matching groups in a regular expression with **$1** rather than **\1** notation. Use the **$1** notation.

```
'|' and '<' may not both be specified on command line
```

FATAL ERROR An error peculiar to VMS. Perl does its own command line redirection and found that **STDIN** was a pipe, and that you also tried to redirect **STDIN** using **<**.

```
'|' and '>' may not both be specified on command line
```

FATAL ERROR An error peculiar to VMS. Perl does its own command line redirection and thinks you tried to redirect **stdout** both to a file and into a pipe to another command. You need to choose one or the other, though nothing is stopping you from piping into a program or Perl script, which "'splits'" output into two streams, such as,

```
open(OUT,">$ARGV[0]") or die "Can't write to $ARGV[0]: $!";
    while (<STDIN>) {
        print;

        print OUT;
    }
    close OUT;
```

which should achieve what you are trying to do.

```
Got an error from DosAllocMem
```

INTERNAL ERROR An error peculiar to OS/2. Most probably you're using an obsolete version of Perl.

```
Malformed PERLLIB_PREFIX
```

FATAL ERROR An error peculiar to OS/2. **PERLLIB_PREFIX** should be of the form

```
prefix1;prefix2
```

or

```
prefix1 prefix2
```

with nonempty **prefix1** and **prefix2**. If **prefix1** is indeed a prefix of a built-in library search path, **prefix2** is substituted. The error may appear if components are not found or are too long.

```
PERL_SH_DIR too long
```

FATAL ERROR An error peculiar to OS/2. **PERL_SH_DIR** is the directory to find the **sh** shell in.

```
Process terminated by SIG%s
```

WARNING This is a standard message issued by OS/2 applications, while Unix applications die in silence. It is considered a feature of the OS/2 port. You can easily disable this by installing appropriate signal handlers.

Appendix E

Standard Perl Library

The standard Perl library comes with a range of modules that have been deemed useful, if not essential, to developing Perl applications. Some of these modules, such as **AutoLoader**, **AutoSplit**, and much of the **ExtUtils** hierarchy, are an essential part of the development process. Others are utility modules, such as the **Text::Tabs** module that supports the expanding and compressing of tabs to and from spaces.

Please note the following:

- References to the **CORE** module refer to the core functions and operators supported natively by the Perl interpreter.
- The actual location of the files will vary according to platform and version. You may need to search the entire Perl 5 library directory to find a specific module. The titles given here will work inside any standard Perl script.
- The list of modules available on your system may be different from that listed here because of differences between the supported features of different operating systems.
- Only genuine modules have been included here. Older Perl libraries (with a .pl suffix) are not included.

AnyDBM_File

```
use AnyDBM_File;
```

This module imports a suitable DBM module to enable you to use a DBM database. Care should be taken, since you cannot normally mix DBM formats. By default, any program wanting to use a DBM file can use this module, which will try to inherit a DBM-handling class first from **NDBM_File** (which is also compatible with **ODBM_File**). Then the module tries to inherit its classes in turn from **DB_File**, **GDBM_File**, **SDBM_File** (which is part of the Perl distribution), and finally, **ODBM_File**.

To use, specify the DBM type as **AnyDBM_File** within the **tie** statement:

```
use Fcntl;
use AnyDBM_File;

tie %myhash, "AnyDBM_File", "mydbm", O_RDWR, 0644;
```

You can override the default list and sequence by redefining the contents of the **@ISA** array within the **AnyDBM_File** module:

```
@AnyDBM_File::ISA = qw(GDBM_File ODBM_File);
```

You can also specify your own preference by importing your DBM module directly. This is less portable, but if you are relying on the feature set of a DBM implementation, especially with the special abilities of **DB_File** and **GDBM_File** in mind, then you may want to use the module directly.

REFERENCES Chapter 8; *see also* **DB_File, GDBM_File, NDBM_File, ODBM_File, SDBM_File**

AutoLoader

This module provides a method for automatically loading Perl subroutines from external files that have been split by the **AutoSplit** module. Each subroutine is stored in an individual file within the ./auto directory with the rest of the Perl library modules. For example, the function **Auto::foo** would be in a file ./auto/Auto/foo.al.

```
package Auto;
use Exporter;
use AutoLoader;
@ISA = qw/Exporter AutoLoader/;
```

Any module using the **AutoLoader** should have the special marker **__END__** prior to any subroutine declarations. These will be used as the declarations for subroutines to be autoloaded from the corresponding .al files. Any code before the marker will be parsed and imported when the module is first used. Any subroutine declared that is not already in memory will then be loaded from the corresponding file by looking into the ./auto directory tree.

Since the **__END__** marker ends the current scope, you will need to use package globals rather than lexical variables declared with **my**. Remember to use the **vars** pragma to declare them if you are also using the **strict** pragma.

The easiest way to create a module supporting **AutoLoader** is to use the **AutoSplit** module. You may also want to see the **SelfLoader** module, which provides a similar mechanism for loading subroutines.

Also note that this is related to but does not provide the support for the **AUTOLOAD** special subroutine. See Chapter 5 for more information.

REFERENCES Chapters 5, 7, 16, 17; *see also* **AutoSplit, SelfLoader, strict, vars**

AutoSplit

This module provides a method for splitting modules into the individual files required by the **AutoLoader** module. This is generally used by the standard Perl library modules and by the XS and **MakeMaker** systems to split C extensions into individual loadable subroutines.

The main function is **autosplit**, and it supports the splitting process in a single hit. The typical use is

```
perl -MAutoSplit -e 'autosplit(FILE, DIR, KEEP, CHECK, MODTIME)'
```

where **FILE** is the module to split, and **DIR** is the base directory into which the file should be split. The **KEEP** argument defines whether existing .al files should be deleted as the module is split. This is the operation when false; if true, files are kept even if the functions do not appear in the new module.

The **CHECK** argument tells **AutoSplit** to check whether the specified module actually includes the **AutoLoader** module. If false, no checks are made. The **MODTIME** argument, if true, only splits the module if its modification time is later than that of the autosplit.ix index file.

Only those functions specified after the **__END__** marker are split; other functions are forced to load when the module is imported.

You will be warned if the functions to be split exceed the permitted length for file names on the desired file system. Because of the use of function names as file names, it presents possible naming conflicts that should be resolved. You will also be warned if the directory that you want to split the module into does not exist.

This module is normally only used as part of the **MakeMaker** process.

REFERENCES Chapters 5, 7, 16, 17; *see also* **AutoLoader**, **ExtUtils::MakeMaker**

autouse

```
use autouse 'Module' => qw(funca funcb);
```

The **autouse** pragma postpones the loading of the **Module** until one of **funca** or **funcb** is actually used. This is similar in principle but not identical to the **Autoloader** module. Note that you must specify the functions that will trigger the **autouse** process; otherwise there is no way for the Perl interpreter to identify the functions that should be imported. The line above is therefore equivalent to the standard method for importing selected functions:

```
use Module qw(funca funcb);
```

You can also supply a function prototype to the **autouse** pragma to trap errors during the compilation rather than execution stage:

```
use Module qw(funca($$) funcb($@));
```

REFERENCES Chapter 16

B

This module is part of the Perl compiler. The compiler uses many of the objects and methods defined within the **B** module and its hierarchy in order to provide the script with the necessary hooks into its own internals. The module does this by providing its own suite of classes, which allow a Perl script to examine its own objects and classes in detail.

```
use B;
```

Although this module provides the information required during the compilation process of a Perl script into a stand-alone executable, use of this module is not required to make a stand-alone program.

The bulk of the **B** module is the methods for accessing the fields of the objects that describe the internal structures. Note that all access is read-only: you cannot modify the internals by using this module.

The **B** module exports a variety of functions: some are simple utility functions; others provide a Perl program with a way to get an initial "handle" on an internal object. These are listed in Table E-1.

Function	Description
main_cv	Returns the (faked) **CV** corresponding to the main part of the Perl program.
main_root	Returns the root opcode of the main part of the Perl program.
main_start	Returns the starting op of the main part of the Perl program.
Comppadlist	Returns the **AV** object of the global comppadlist.
sv_undef	Returns the **SV** object corresponding to the C variable **sv_undef** (the undefined value).
sv_yes	Returns the **SV** object corresponding to the C variable **sv_yes** ("true").
sv_no	Returns the **SV** object corresponding to the C variable **sv_no** ("false").
walkoptree(OP, METHOD)	Does a tree-walk of the syntax tree starting at the opcode referenced by **OP**, calling **METHOD** on each opcode in the tree it visits. Each parent node is visited before its children.
walkoptree_debug(DEBUG)	Returns the current debugging flag for **walkoptree**. If the optional **DEBUG** argument is non-zero, it sets the debugging flag to that value.

Table E-1. *Functions in the **B** Module*

APPENDIXES

Function	Description
walksymtable(SYMREF, METHOD, RECURSE)	Walks the symbol table starting at **SYMREF** and calls **METHOD** on each symbol visited. When the walk reaches package symbols **Foo::**, it invokes **RECURSE** and only recurses into the package if that sub returns true.
svref_2object(SV)	Takes any Perl variable and turns it into an object in the appropriate **B::OP**-derived or **B::SV**-derived class.
ppname(OPNUM)	Returns the **PP** function name (for example, **pp_add**) of opcode number **OPNUM**.
hash(STRING)	Returns a string in the form "0x...", representing the hexadecimal value of the internal hash function used by Perl on string **STR**.
cast_I32(I)	Casts **I** to the internal **I32** type used by the current Perl interpreter.
minus_c	Does the equivalent of the **-c** command line option.
cstring(STR)	Returns a double-quote-surrounded escaped version of **STR**, which can be used as a string in C source code.
class(OBJECT)	Returns the class of an object without the part of the class name preceding the first **::**.
threadsv_names	In a Perl interpreter compiled for threads, this returns a list of the special per-thread **threadsv** variables.
byteload_fh(FILEHANDLE)	Loads the contents of **FILEHANDLE** as bytecode.

Table E-1. *Functions in the **B** Module* (continued)

A more in-depth discussion on the use of the Perl compiler, of which the **B** module is a critical part, can be found in Chapter 19.

REFERENCES *See* **O**; Chapters 16, 19

B::Asmdata

This module is used internally by the **B::Bytecode** and other modules to generate data about Perl opcodes.

REFERENCES *See* **B::Bytecode**, **O**; Chapters 16, 19

B::Assembler

The module used by the **O** Perl compiler interface to assemble Perl bytecode into executable opcodes.

REFERENCES *See* **B::Bytecode**, **O**; Chapters 16, 19

B::Bblock

The module used by the **O** Perl compiler interface to produce a report of the basic blocks that make up a Perl program.

REFERENCES *See* **O**; Chapters 16, 19

B::Bytecode

This module provides the necessary code for translating Perl scripts into Perl bytecode as used by the **O** module and the Perl compiler. For example, you can convert any Perl script into bytecode using

```
$ perl -MO=Bytecode foobar.pl
```

REFERENCES *See* **O**; Chapters 16, 19

B::C

The basic underlying module used by the Perl compiler that produces raw C code in a nonoptimized format, suitable for compiling into a stand-alone program. For an optimized version you should use the **B:CC** module. The default operation creates a C file that can be separately compiled:

```
$ perl -MO=C foobar.pl
```

If you want to compile a Perl script directly, then use the **perlcc** command:

```
$ perlcc foobar.pl
```

This will generate a stand-alone application called **foobar**.

REFERENCES *See* **O**; Chapters 16, 19

B::CC

This is the optimized interface for creating C code from Perl scripts for compilation into stand-alone applications. For example:

```
$ perl -MO=CC foobar.pl
```

Relatively simple optimizations are supported for the purposes of improving the performance of Perl code into C code.

REFERENCES *See* **O**; Chapters 16, 19

B::Debug

This module produces a Perl syntax tree, providing debug-level information about the opcodes being used. For example:

```
$ perl -M=Debug
```

For a simpler version you should try the **B::Terse** compiler interface module.

REFERENCES *See* **O**; Chapters 16, 19

B::Deparse

An interface used by the Perl compiler and the **O** module that regurgitates a Perl script based on the internal structure used by the Perl interpreter. The source output matches the format of the script after being parsed by the interpreter and may not match the original source script. It is normally used with the **O** module.

```
$ perl -MO=Deparse foobar.pl
```

REFERENCES *See* **O**; Chapters 16, 19

B::Disassembler

The backend used by the Perl compiler to translate compiled bytecode into raw source code.

REFERENCES *See* **B::Bytecode**, **O**; Chapters 16, 19

B::Lint

This module expands on the warnings provided by the **-w** switch with additional warnings for some specific statements and constructs in the Perl code. It is used as a backend to the Perl compiler.

```
$ perl -MO=Lint foobar.pl
```

REFERENCES *See* **O**; Chapters 16, 19

B::Showlex

A Perl compiler backend, used with the **O** module. The module produces a list of lexical values used within functions and files.

REFERENCES *See* **O**; Chapters 16, 19

B::Stackobj

A helper module for the Perl compiler.

REFERENCES *See* **O**; Chapters 16, 19

B::Terse

Used with the Perl compiler to provide the syntax tree for a Perl script. Unlike the **Debug** backend, information about individual opcodes within the tree is kept to a minimum.

```
$ perl -MO=Terse foobar.pl
```

REFERENCES *See* **O**; Chapters 16, 19

B::Xref

A Perl compiler backend that produces a report detailing and cross-referencing the variables, subroutines, and formats used in a Perl script on a line-by-line and file-by-file basis.

REFERENCES *See* **O**; Chapters 16, 19

base

The **base** pragma establishes a relationship with a base class at compile (rather than execution) time. In effect, this is equal to adding the specified classes to the **@ISA** array during the module initialization.

```
package Object;
use base qw(Foo Bar);
```

REFERENCES Chapters 5, 7, 16

Benchmark

```
use Benchmark;
```

This module provides a constant and consistent interface to aid in the production of benchmarking figures. You can use the **Benchmark** module to time the execution of any Perl statement, function, or even the entire script.

There are three main functions: **timeit**, **timethis**, and **timethese**:

```
timeit(COUNT, 'CODE');
```

Times the execution of a single piece of **CODE**, for **COUNT** iterations. Note that **CODE** is a string containing the code to benchmark. Use the object method shown below to benchmark an arbitrary piece of code.

For example, the code

```
$t = timeit(1000000,'cos(3.141)');
```

will place the timing information for a million iterations of the calculation into **$t**, which will be a reference to a **Benchmark** object. See below for more information on the object interface.

```
timethis(COUNT, 'CODE')
```

Uses **timeit** to run a piece of code, also printing a header to state that it is timing a piece of code and the resulting timing information.

```
timethese(COUNT, CODEHASH)
```

Runs **timethis** on multiple pieces of code. Each piece of code should be placed into the value of a hash element, and the corresponding key will be used as a label for the reported figures.

Note that in all the above cases, the code is embedded into a **for** loop and then **eval**'d in its entirety. As such, lexical values declared outside the **eval** block will not be available within it.

If you want to time arbitrary requests, you need to use the object interface to the module:

```
$ta = new Benchmark;
&render_object();
$tb = new Benchmark;
print "Calculation time: ", timestr(timediff($ta,$tb)), "\n";
```

The **timediff** function returns a new object detailing the time difference between two **Benchmark** objects, and you can then print a string of the time difference information with **timestr**.

In all cases, the times reported use the **times** function, so both CPU and user times are reported. The CPU time is the most important, since it should not be affected by other processes. Because it uses the **times** function, measurements are in milliseconds. You should aim to support enough iterations for a reasonable timing figure. Times of at least five seconds are advised; ten seconds or more may give a more precise figure.

REFERENCES Chapters 6, 19

blib

The **blib** pragma forces Perl to look in the local **blib** directory for modules. This directory structure is generated when an extension is being built via a Perl-produced Makefile. The normal way to use it is via the command line,

```
$ perl -Mblib script
```

although you can include it in the script if required. This is the usual method for tests conducted during the installation process.

REFERENCES Chapters 16, 17, 20

Carp

This module provides a simplified method for reporting errors within modules. A **die** call from a package will report an error with reference to the pacakge file in which it was called. This can cause problems if you are trying to trace errors in a calling script. The **Carp** module provides three functions: **carp**, **croak**, and **confess**. With each function the location of the error is specified relative to the package that called the function.

```
carp "Didn't work";
```

Equivalent of **warn**, reports an error to **stderr**.

```
croak "Definitely didn't work";
```

Equivalent of **die**.

```
confess "Failed around about there";
```

This is equivalent to **croak** except that a stack trace is printed.

For example, image that you have a package called **T**, used in a script called **tm.pl**. The package defines a single function, **only**, which calls **warn** and **carp**; the result is

```
Warning! at T.pm line 11.
Carp warning! at tm.pl line 3
```

You can see from this that the first message, using **warn**, reports the error with reference to the module. The second, using **carp**, reports an error with reference to the original script in which it was called.

The reference is obtained using **caller**, and goes up exactly one level, so if another package calls a **carp**-using function, the error will be reported with reference to the calling package.

REFERENCES Appendix B

CGI

This module provides a set of functions for drawing HTML pages and for both creating HTML forms and postprocessing them using the CGI interface.

```
use CGI;
```

The module's primary use is for producing web forms and parsing their contents once the information has been filled in and returned by a client. The module defines a simple CGI class that can be used to build the pages, although use of the class methods is not exclusive; they can be used as normal functions as well.

For example, to create a "Hello World!" page using the object method:

```
use CGI;
$page = new CGI;
print $page->header,
      $page->start_html('Hello World!'),
      $page->h1('Hello World!'),
      $page->end_html;
```

You can achieve the same result with the functional interface as follows:

```
use CGI qw/:standard/;

print header,
      start_html('Hello World!'),
      h1('Hello World!'),
      end_html;
```

The module provides three main elements: the HTTP header, HTML-formatted text, and a parsing engine for accepting input from browsers and forms using the various request methods available. In addition, it supports frames, cascading style sheets, cookies, and server-push technologies. Refer to Chapters 14 and 15 for more information on the use of the **CGI** module when writing HTML/CGI scripts.

Import Sets

The module supports the import sets shown in Table E-2.

REFERENCES Chapters 14, 15

CGI::Apache

This module supports the use of the **CGI** module when used within the confines of the Perl-Apache API, as supported by the **mod_perl** CPAN module.

```
require CGI::Apache;

my $query = new Apache::CGI;
$query->print($query->header);
```

The module provides a slightly modified interface in order to allow the **CGI** module to work when executing scripts with the Perl-Apache API environment. This imports, and also overrides, some of the methods defined by the **CGI** module.

REFERENCES *See* **CGI, CGI::Switch**

CGI::Switch

This module attempts to load **CGI** constructors from different modules until it successfully loads one.

```
use CGI::Switch;
```

Import Set	Exported Symbols/Symbol Sets
html2	h1 h2 h3 h4 h5 h6 p br hr ol ul li dl dt dd menu code var strong em tt u i b blockquote pre img a address cite samp dfn html head base body Link nextid title meta kbd start_html end_html input Select option comment
html3	div table caption th td TR Tr sup sub strike applet Param embed basefont style span layer ilayer font frameset frame script small big
netscape	blink fontsize center
form	textfield textarea filefield password_field hidden checkbox checkbox_group submit reset defaults radio_group popup_menu button autoEscape scrolling_list image_button start_form end_form startform endform start_multipart_form isindex tmpFileName uploadInfo URL_ENCODED MULTIPART
cgi	param path_info path_translated url self_url script_name cookie dump raw_cookie request_method query_string accept user_agent remote_host remote_addr referer server_name server_software server_port server_protocol virtual_host remote_ident auth_type http use_named_parameters save_parameters restore_parameters param_fetch remote_user user_name header redirect import_names put Delete Delete_all url_param
ssl	https
cgi-lib	ReadParse PrintHeader HtmlTop HtmlBot SplitParam
html	html2 html3 netscape
standard	html2 html3 form cgi
push	multipart_init multipart_start multipart_end
all	html2 html3 netscape form cgi internal

Table E-2. *Import Sets for the* ***CGI*** *module*

The default packages it attempts to load, in order, are **Apache::CGI**, **CGI::XA**, and **CGI**. You can define a different order or a different selection of modules by specifying them explicitly:

```
use CGI::Switch qw/CGI CGI::Apache/;
```

A call to the **new** method in **CGI::Switch** will return an object of the first found type:

```
$query = new CGI::Switch;
```

REFERENCES *See* **CGI**

Class::Struct

This module supports the construction of **struct**-like data types as Perl classes.

```
use Class::Struct;
```

It supports only one function, **struct**, which builds a new class based on the information you supply. The new class can be made up of multiple elements composed of scalars, arrays, hashes, and further class definitions. This is primarily used for designing or emulating C **struct** structures within Perl. The function has three forms:

```
struct(CLASS_NAME => [ ELEMENT_LIST ]);
struct(CLASS_NAME => { ELEMENT_LIST });
struct(ELEMENT_LIST);
```

The first two forms explicitly define the new class to be created, and the third form assumes the current package name as the new class. The first form creates an array-based class, which is fast; the second and third create a hash-based class, which is slower but more flexible and practical.

The newly created class must not be a subclass of anything other than **UNIVERSAL**. This is because it will inherit methods, including **new**, from its base class, which will override the methods generated by **struct**.

The **ELEMENT_LIST** argument has the format of a typical hash assignation:

```
NAME => TYPE
```

The **NAME** is the name of each element in the new class, and **TYPE** is one of **$**, **@**, or **%** to create a new scalar, array, or hash entry; or it can be the name of another class.

For example, to create a Perl version of the **hostent** structure:

```
struct('hostent' => {
                      'h_name' => '$',
                      'h_aliases' => '@',
                      'h_addrtype' => '$',
                      'h_length' => '$',
                      'h_addr_list' => '@',
                    });
```

The name of the new class is **hostent**, but you need to create a new object in order to make use of it; **struct** merely constructs the class definition. Thus,

```
$host = new hostent;
```

will create a new **hostent** structure.

Using Scalar Elements

The scalar is initialized with **undef**. To access the scalar:

```
$obj->scalar
```

To set the value of the scalar:

```
$obj->scalar(value)
```

When defined, if the element type is stated as **$**, then the element value is returned. If it is defined as ***$**, then a reference to the scalar element is returned.

Using Array Elements

The array is initialized as an empty list. To access the entire array:

```
$obj->array
```

Note that because there is no leading @ sign, you will need to use block notation to use the array in its entirety with many functions, for example:

```
sort @{$obj->array};
```

To access an element from the array,

```
$obj->array(index)
```

where **index** is the numerical index within the array.

To set a value in the array,

```
$obj->scalar(index, value)
```

where **index** is the numerical index within the array, and **value** is the value to be assigned.

When defined, if the element type is stated as @, then the element value is returned. If it is defined as *@, then a reference to the element is returned.

Using Hash Elements

The hash is initialized as an empty list. To access the entire hash:

```
$obj->array
```

Note that because there is no leading @ sign, you will need to use block notation to use the array in its entirety with many functions, for example:

```
sort @{$obj->array};
```

To access an element from the hash,

```
$obj->array(key)
```

where **key** is the string value.

To set a value in the hash,

```
$obj->scalar(key, value)
```

where **key** is the string index within the array, and **value** is the value to be assigned.

When defined, if the element type is stated as %, then the element value is returned. If it is defined as *%, then a reference to the element is returned.

Using Class Elements

The elements value must be a reference blessed to the named class or to one of its subclasses. The assigned class can have methods and structures and can be used like any other method, albeit within the confines of the class created by **struct**. The main use for this element is to support nested data structures within a **Class::Struct** created class.

Example

The code below builds on the **hostent** structure and populates it with the correct information based on the host given.

```
use Class::Struct;
use Socket;

struct('hostent' => {
    'h_name' => '$',
    'h_aliases' => '@',
    'h_addrtype' => '$',
    'h_length' => '$',
    'h_addr_list' => '@',
});

($name, $aliases, $addrtype, $length, @addresses) = gethostbyname($hostname);

my $host = new hostent;
```

```
host->h_name($name);

@aliases = split / /, $aliases;
foreach($i=0;$i<@aliases;$i++)
{
    $host->h_aliases($i, $aliases[$i]);
}
$host->h_addrtype($addrtype);
$host->h_length($length);

for($i=0;$i<@addresses;$i++)
{
    $host->h_addr_list($i,inet_ntoa($addresses[$i]));
}
```

REFERENCES Chapters 7, 17

Config

This module provides an interface to the configuration information determined during the build process.

```
use Config;
```

The module exports a single hash, **%Config**, which can be used to access individual configuration parameters by name, for example:

```
print "Built with: $Config{'cc'} $Config{'ccflags'}\n";
```

You can also optionally import the **myconfig**, **config_sh**, and **config_vars** functions:

```
myconfig
```

This returns a text summary of the main Perl configuration values. This is the method used by the **–V** command line option.

```
config_sh
```

This returns the entire set of Perl configuration information in the form of the config.sh file used during the building process.

```
config_vars(LIST)
```

Sends the configuration values for the names specified in **LIST** to **STDOUT**. The information is printed as you would output the values in a simple loop. Thus the code

```
use Config qw/config_vars/;

config_vars(qw/cc ccflags ldflags/);
```

outputs

```
cc='gcc -B/usr/ccs/bin/';
ccflags='-I/usr/local/include';
ldflags=' -L/usr/local/lib';
```

The information contained in the **Config** module is determined during the build process. Since this module could be modified and/or overwritten or copied, the actual configuration information may not match the binary you are currently using.

REFERENCES Chapters 11, 20; *see also* **ExtUtils::MakeMaker**

constant

The **constant** pragma enables you to create nonmodifiable constants. The advantages of a constant are obvious: if you use the same constant value throughout all of your calculations and programs, you can be guaranteed that the values calculated will also remain constant.

```
use constant PI => 3.141592654;
```

The value can be any normal Perl expression, including calculations and functions such that the following also work:

```
use constant PI   => 22/7;
use constant USER => scalar getpwuid($<);
```

REFERENCES Chapter 16

CPAN

This module provides a simple, and programmable, interface for downloading and installing modules from the CPAN archives. The module takes into account the requirements of the module you are downloading, automatically including the required modules during the installation process. The module makes use of the **Net::FTP** or **LWP** modules if they are available, or it uses the **lynx** web browser and even an external **ftp** client to download the information and modules it needs.

The **CPAN** module therefore takes out a lot of the manual work required when downloading and installing a **CPAN** module. It is in fact the best way to download **CPAN** modules, as it guarantees that you will get the latest version while also ensuring that any required modules will be downloaded and installed.

It works in one of two ways: either within an interactive shell, which is invoked like this:

```
$ perl -MCPAN -e shell;
```

or via a Perl script:

```
use CPAN;
```

Interactive Shell Interface

The shell interface, also known as interactive mode, puts Perl into a simple shell-style interface using the readline line input system. The first time the shell interface is run, you will go through a configuration process that sets up your environment for using the **CPAN** module. This includes configuration of the internal system used to access raw data from the Internet, your preferred download location, and proxy information.

The shell interface supports the commands listed in Table E-3. You can use the shell to query the CPAN archives and also to download and install modules.

To install a module with the interactive shell, the easiest method is to use the install command:

```
$ perl -MCPAN -e shell
cpan> install Nice
```

To install a CPAN bundle:

```
cpan> install Bundle::LWP
Fetching with Net::FTP:
  ftp://ftp.demon.co.uk/pub/mirrors/perl/CPAN/authors/id/GAAS/libwww-perl-5.42.tar.gz

  CPAN: MD5 security checks disabled because MD5 not installed.
  Please consider installing the MD5 module.

x libwww-perl-5.42/, 0 bytes, 0 tape blocks
x libwww-perl-5.42/t/, 0 bytes, 0 tape blocks
x libwww-perl-5.42/t/net/, 0 bytes, 0 tape blocks
x libwww-perl-5.42/t/net/cgi-bin/, 0 bytes, 0 tape blocks
x libwww-perl-5.42/t/net/cgi-bin/test, 526 bytes, 2 tape blocks
...
```

Command	Argument	Description
a	EXPR	Searches authors. **EXPR** should be a simple string, in which case a search will be made for an exact match with the author's ID. Alternatively, you can supply a regular expression that will search for matching author IDs and name details.
b		Displays a list of bundles.
d	EXPR	Performs a regular expression search for a package/module.
m	EXPR	Displays information about the expression matching **EXPR**.
I	EXPR	Displays information about a module, bundle, or user specified in **EXPR**.
r	EXPR	Displays a list of reinstallation recommendations, comparing the existing module list against installed modules and versions. If **EXPR** is not specified, lists all recommendations.
u	EXPR	Lists all modules not currently installed, but available on CPAN.
make	EXPR	Downloads the module specified in **EXPR**, builds it, and installs it. No check is performed to ensure that you need to install the module; it just does it. Use **install** if you want to update a module based on its version number.
test	EXPR	Runs **make test** on the module specified in **EXPR**.
install	EXPR	Downloads and installs the module specified in **EXPR**. Runs **make install**. If **EXPR** is a module, it checks to see if the currently installed version of the module specified in **EXPR** is lower than that available on CPAN. If it is, it downloads, builds, and installs it. If **EXPR** is a distribution file, then the file is processed without any version checking.
clean	EXPR	Runs a **make clean** on the specified module.
force	make | test | install EXPR	Forces a **make**, **test**, or **install** on a command within the current session. Normally, modules are not rebuilt or installed within the current session.
readme		Displays the README file.
reload	index | cpan	Loads the most recent CPAN index files, or the latest version of the **CPAN** module.
h | ?		Displays the help menu.
o		Gets and sets the various configuration options for the **CPAN** module.
!	EXPR	Evaluates the Perl expression **EXPR**.
q		Quits the interactive shell.

Table E-3. *Commands for the Interactive Shell*

In addition to the commands in Table E-3, the interactive shell supports two commands that should only be used by experienced users: **autobundle** and **recompile**.

The **autobundle** function writes a bundle file into the **$CPAN::Config->{cpan_home}/Bundle** directory. The new bundle contains all of the modules currently installed in the current Perl environment that are also available from CPAN. You can then use this file as the source for installing the same bundle of modules on a number of machines.

The **recompile** function forces the reinstallation of all the installed modules that make use of the XS extension system. This solves problems where an update to the operating system breaks binary compatibility. The function will re-download the necessary modules and rebuild them under the updated environment.

Programmable Interface

Depending on what you are trying to achieve, you might find the programmable interface to be more useful. All of the commands available in the interactive shell are also available as **CPAN::Shell** methods within any Perl script. The methods take the same arguments as their shell interface equivalents.

The **CPAN** module works with a series of subclasses for handling information about authors, bundles, modules, and distributions. The classes are **CPAN::Author**, **CPAN::Bundle**, **CPAN::Module**, **CPAN::Distribution**. Individual methods are identical to those outlined in the shell in Table E-3.

The core of the system is still the **CPAN::Shell** module. Individual methods are identical to their command equivalents, but instead of outputting a list to **STDOUT**, the methods return a list of suitable IDs for the corresponding entity type. This allows you to combine individual methods into entire statements—something not available in the shell. For example,

```
$ perl -MCPAN -e 'CPAN::Shell->install(CPAN::Shell->r)'
```

will reinstall all of the outdated modules currently installed.

The **CPAN::Shell** module also supports a further function, **expand**:

```
expand(TYPE, LIST)
```

This returns an array of **CPAN::Module** objects expanded according to their correct type. The **LIST** is the list of entries to expand. For example, you can expand and install a number of modules at once, using

```
for $module (qw/Bundle::libnet Bundle::LWP/)
{
    my $object = CPAN::Shell->expand('Module',$module);
    $object->install;
}
```

REFERENCES Appendix F

CPAN::FirstTime

This is a utility for configuring the **CPAN** module:

```
CPAN::FirstTime::init();
```

The **init** function asks some simple questions about the current environment and updates the **CPAN::Config** file that will be used by the **CPAN** module when downloading and building extensions.

REFERENCES *See* **CPAN**

CPAN::Nox

This module supports the normal **CPAN** functionality, but it avoids the use of XS extensions during execution.

```
$ perl -MCPAN::Nox -e shell
```

This is intended for use when the binary compatibility has been broken between the Perl binary and the extensions. The above command puts you into the familiar **CPAN** interactive state.

REFERENCES *See* **CPAN**

Cwd

This module provides a platform-independent interface for discovering the current working directory. The module provides three functions:

```
use Cwd;
$dir = cwd();
$dir = getcwd();
$dir = fastcwd();
```

The **cwd** function provides the safest method for discovering the current working directory. The **getcwd** function uses the **getcwd()** or **getwd()** C functions, if they are available on your platform.

The **fastcwd** function is a much faster version and can be used in situations where speed may be of great importance. However, it is not a reliable method and may mistakenly indicate that you can **chdir** out of a directory that you cannot change back into. As such, it shouldn't be relied on.

The **Cwd** module also optionally provides a replacement for the CORE **chdir** function that updates the value of the **PWD** environment variable:

```
use Cwd qw/chdir/;
chdir('/usr/local');
print $ENV{PWD};
```

REFERENCES Chapter 6; *see also* **File::Spec**

Data::Dumper

This module provides methods for resolving a data structure (including objects) into a string format that can be used both to "dump" the data for printing, and for evaluation so that a dumped structure can be reconstituted with **eval** into a valid internal structure.

```
use Data::Dumper;
```

The primary function is **Dumper**:

```
Dumper(LIST)
```

This function accepts a list of scalar references to data structures or objects. The return value is a string representation of the structure, produced in normal string syntax format.
For example:

```
use Data::Dumper;

my $ref = { "Name" => "Martin",
            "Size" => "Medium",
            "Dates" => { "Monday" => "170599",
                         "Tuesday" => "180599"
                       }
          };

print Dumper($ref);
```

generates the following:

```
$VAR1 = {
          'Dates' => {
                       'Monday' => 170599,
                       'Tuesday' => 180599
                     },
          'Name' => 'Martin',
          'Size' => 'Medium'
        };
```

Note that references to anonymous variables are labeled with **$VARn**, where **n** is a sequential number relating to the references as they were supplied.

REFERENCES See Chapters 7, 8

DB_File

This module provides access to the Berkeley DB system—probably the most flexible implementation of the DBM database system. Beyond the basic abilities of supporting a hash-style database, **DB_File** also provides the necessary functions and methods for accessing the database structures and for creating and managing B-Tree structures. The Berkeley DB system also supports a system based on fixed- and variable-length record numbers, which is supported within Perl as a hash using numerical rather than string references.

```
use DB_File ;

[$X =] tie %hash,  'DB_File', [FILENAME, FLAGS, MODE, $DB_HASH] ;
[$X =] tie %hash,  'DB_File', FILENAME, FLAGS, MODE, $DB_BTREE ;
[$X =] tie @array, 'DB_File', FILENAME, FLAGS, MODE, $DB_RECNO ;

# Methods for Hash databases
$status = $X->del(KEY [, FLAGS]);
$status = $X->put(KEY, VALUE [, FLAGS]);
$status = $X->get(KEY, VALUE [, FLAGS]);
$status = $X->seq(KEY, VALUE, FLAGS) ;
$status = $X->sync([FLAGS]);
$status = $X->fd;
```

```
 Methods for BTree databases
$count = $X->get_dup(KEY);
@list  = $X->get_dup(KEY);
%list  = $X->get_dup(KEY, 1);

# Methods for Record Number databases
$a = $X->length;
$a = $X->pop;
$X->push(LIST);
$a = $X->shift;
$X->unshift(LIST);

untie %hash;
untie @array;
```

The different database types are defined in the last argument to the **tie** function, using **DB_HASH** for hashes, **DB_BTREE** for binary trees, and **DB_RECNO** for the record number database.

A **DB_HASH** is identical in most respects to Perl's internal hash structure except that the key/data pairs are stored in data files, not memory. The functionality provided is basically identical to that provided by the other DBM-style database engines. **DB_File** uses its own hashing algorithm for storing and retrieving the key/data pairs, but you can supply your own system if you prefer.

The **DB_BTREE** format follows the same key/data pair structure, but the pairs are stored in a sorted, balanced binary tree. By default, the keys are sorted in lexical order, although you can supply your own comparison routine for use by the binary sorting subsystem.

DB_RECNO supports the storage of fixed- and variable-length records in a flat text using the same key/value hash interface. This may be more suitable to your requirements than using the DBI toolkit, covered later in this appendix. In order to make the record numbers more compatible with the array system employed by Perl, the offset starts at zero rather than 1 (as in the Berkeley DB).

You can also create an in-memory database (which is held entirely within memory, just like a standard hash) by specifying a NULL file name (use **undef**). You can use any of the database types for the in-memory database.

REFERENCES Chapter 8; *see also* **AnyDBM_File, GDBM_File, NDBM_File, ODBM_File, SDBM_File**

Devel::SelfStubber

This module generates subroutine stubs for use with modules that employ the **SelfLoader** module.

```
use Devel::SelfStubber;

Devel::SelfStubber->stub(MODULE, LIBDIR);
```

It analyzes the module specified in **MODULE** (which should be specified as if it were being imported). The **LIBDIR** argument specifies the directory to search for the module. If left as a blank string, the current directory is used.

The generated output displays the list of subroutine stubs you need to put before the **__DATA__** token in order to support autoloading via the **SelfLoader** module. The stub also ensures that if a method is called, it will get loaded according to the classes and normal inheritance rules, taking into account the effects of autoloading in the inherited modules and classes.

The basic method only produces a list of the correct stubs. To output a complete version of the whole module with the stubs inserted correctly, you need to set the value of the **$Devel::SelfStubber::JUST_STUBS** to zero. For example:

```
use Devel::SelfStubber;

$Devel::SelfStubber::JUST_STUBS = 0;
Devel::SelfStubber->stub(MODULE, LIBDIR);
```

The module uses the **SelfLoader** module to generate its list of stub subroutines and so can be useful if you want to verify what the **SelfLoader** thinks the list of stubs should be.

REFERENCES *See* **SelfLoader**

diagnostics

The **diagnostics** pragma prints out not only the terse one-line warnings but also the additional descriptive text that you find in the **perldiag** man page. It does not provide you with further information on the error, or the reason it has occurred, but it may help to serve as a reminder when a particular warning is produced.

The same module is also used to support the **splain** command, which takes ordinary warnings (from scripts without the **diagnostics** pragma) and regurgitates the errors produced with their full descriptions.

REFERENCES Chapter 16

DirHandle

This module supplies an object/method-based interface for directory handles.

```
use DirHandle;
```

It provides an object interface to the directory handle functions **opendir**, **readdir**, **closedir**, and **rewinddir**:

```
$dir = new DirHandle '.';
```

The only argument to the **new** method is the directory to be read, as specified in the **opendir** function. The supported methods then work in a manner identical to their functional equivalents, except that they are known as **open**, **read**, **close**, and **rewind**.

REFERENCES Chapter 6, Appendix B

DynaLoader

This module supports the dynamic loading of C libraries into Perl code.

```
package MyPackage;
require DynaLoader;
@ISA = qw/DynaLoader/;

bootstrap MyPackage;
```

It provides a generic interface to the various dynamic linking mechanisms available on the different platforms. This is primarily used with the XS extension system to load external C libraries and functions into the consciousness of the Perl interpreter. The **DynaLoader** module is designed to be easy to use from the user's point of view, in that using a module should be easy, even though the module itself may involve more complex processes to load the module.

In order to make use of the system within your own module, you only need to supply the information shown above, which will work whether your module is statically or dynamically linked. The Perl and C functions that need to be called in order to load the dynamic modules are automatically produced for you during the compilation of an XS interface.

The internal interface for communicating with the lower-level dynamic loading systems supported under SunOS/Solaris, HP-UX, Linux, VMS, Windows, and others is high level and generic enough to cover the requirements of nearly all platforms. However, the **DynaLoader** does not produce its own glue code between Perl and C—you must use the XS, SWIG, or other systems for that purpose.

Please refer to the **DynaLoader** man page for details on how to use the internal interface.

REFERENCES *See* **AutoLoader**, **SelfLoader**

English

This module produces a set of aliases that provide full text versions of the standard variables. These match those available in **awk**, and may also make more sense to most users. See Table E-4.

REFERENCES Chapter 2

<table>
<tr><th>Perl</th><th>English</th></tr>
<tr><td>@_</td><td>@ARG</td></tr>
<tr><td>$_</td><td>$ARG</td></tr>
<tr><td>$&</td><td>$MATCH</td></tr>
<tr><td>$’</td><td>$PREMATCH</td></tr>
<tr><td>$'</td><td>$POSTMATCH</td></tr>
<tr><td>$+</td><td>$LAST_PAREN_MATCH</td></tr>
<tr><td>$.</td><td>$INPUT_LINE_NUMBER
$NR</td></tr>
<tr><td>$/</td><td>$INPUT_RECORD_SEPARATOR
$RS</td></tr>
<tr><td>$|</td><td>$OUTPUT_AUTOFLUSH</td></tr>
<tr><td>$,</td><td>$OUTPUT_FIELD_SEPARATOR
$OFS</td></tr>
<tr><td>$\</td><td>$OUTPUT_RECORD_SEPARATOR
$ORS</td></tr>
<tr><td>$"</td><td>$LIST_SEPARATOR</td></tr>
<tr><td>$;</td><td>$SUBSCRIPT_SEPARATOR
$SUBSEP</td></tr>
<tr><td>$%</td><td>$FORMAT_PAGE_NUMBER</td></tr>
<tr><td>$=</td><td>$FORMAT_LINES_PER_PAGE</td></tr>
</table>

Table E-4. *Perl and English Variable Names*

Perl	English
$-	$FORMAT_LINES_LEFT
$~	$FORMAT_NAME
$^	$FORMAT_TOP_NAME
$:	$FORMAT_LINE_BREAK_CHARACTERS
$^L	$FORMAT_LINEFEED
$?	$CHILD_ERROR
$!	$OS_ERROR $ERRNO
$@	$EVAL_ERROR
$$	$PROCESS_ID $PID
$<	$REAL_USER_ID $UID
$>	$EFFECTIVE_USER_ID $EUID
$(	$REAL_GROUP_ID $GID
$)	$EFFECTIVE_GROUP_ID $EGID
$0	$PROGRAM_NAME
$]	$PERL_VERSION
$^A	$ACCUMULATOR
$^D	$DEBUGGING
$^F	$SYSTEM_FD_MAX
$^I	$INPLACE_EDIT
$^P	$PERLDB
$^T	$BASETIME
$^W	$WARNING
$^X	$EXECUTABLE_NAME
$^O	$OSNAME

Table E-4. *Perl and English Variable Names* (continued)

Env

This module imports environment variables into the current package as real scalars, rather than forcing you to use the **%ENV** hash. To import all the variables defined within the **%ENV** hash, just import the whole module:

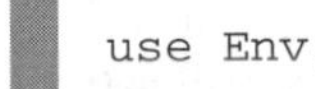

```
use Env;
```

To import specific environment variables, specify them during the import:

```
use Env qw/PATH/;
```

You can now use and update **$PATH** as if it was **$ENV{PATH}**.

The internal method for supporting this is actually to tie scalar values to the **%ENV** hash. The tie remains in place until the script exits, or until you remove a tied variable with **undef**:

```
undef $PATH;
```

REFERENCES Chapters 2, 6, 7

Errno

This module defines and exports the constants defined in errno.h for error numbers on your system.

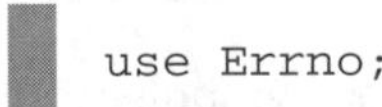

```
use Errno;
```

Importing this module has the added effect of exporting %!. This allows you to access **$!{}** as a hash element, retaining the look and feel of the special **$!** variable. Each key of the hash is one of the exported error numbers. When an error occurs, the corresponding error(s) that occurred have a non-zero value. Thus you can do more complex error trapping and management by identifying and handling individual error types.

Exporter

This module implements the default import method for modules.

```
package MyModule;
use Exporter;
@ISA = qw/Exporter/;
```

It implements a default **import** method that is called during the **use** statement. Although it is possible for any module to define its own **import** method, this module supplies a sample **import** method that can be inherited by your module to enable you to export symbols to the calling script.

The **Exporter** module and the supplied **import** method use the **@EXPORT**, **@EXPORT_OK**, and **%EXPORT_TAGS** variables to select which symbols to import. The symbols in **@EXPORT** are exported by default, and the symbols in **@EXPORT_OK** only when specifically requested. The **%EXPORT_TAGS** hash defines a number of import sets that can be used to import a named set of symbols at one time.

For example, if the module defines the following variables:

```
@EXPORT      = qw/A B C D E F/;
@EXPORT_OK   = qw/G H I J K L/;
%EXPORT_TAGS = (FIRST => [qw/D E F/],
                SECOND => [qw/J K L/]
                );
```

then you can use the following constructs in a calling script:

```
use MyModule;                      # Imports all of @EXPORT
use MyModule qw/G H/               # Only symbols G and H
use MyModule qw/:DEFAULT/;         # All the symbols in @EXPORT
use MyModule qw/:FIRST A B C/;     # The symbols in group FIRST and A B C
use MyModule qw(/^[ACGH]/);        # Only the symbols matching the regex
use MyModule qw/!:FIRST/;          # Only A B C
```

A leading colon indicates that you want to load the symbols defined in the specified group, as defined by **%EXPORT_TAGS**. Note that the symbols exported here must appear either in **@EXPORT** or **@EXPORT_OK**.

A leading exclamation mark indicates that you want to delete the specified symbols from the import list. If such a definition is the first in the import list, then it assumes you want to import the **:DEFAULT** set.

A *//* regular expression imports the symbols defined in **@EXPORT** and **@EXPORT_OK** according to the regular expression.

You can display the list of symbols to be imported as they are determined by setting the value of **$Exporter::Verbose** to true. You'll need to do this in a **BEGIN** block:

```
BEGIN { $Exporter::Verbose = 1 }
```

Unknown Symbols

You can prevent certain symbols from being exported. You should place the names of symbols that should not be listed into the **@EXPORT_FAIL** array. Any attempt to import any of these symbols will call the **export_fail** method (in the host module) with a list of failed symbols.

If **export_fail** returns an empty list, no error is recorded and the requested symbols are exported. If the list is not empty, an error is generated for each return symbol and the export fails. The default **export_fail** method supported by **Exporter** just returns the list of symbols supplied to it.

Tag Handling Functions

You can modify the contents of the **@EXPORT_OK** and **@EXPORT** arrays using the tag sets defined by the **%EXPORT_TAGS** hash and the **Exporter::export_tags** and **Exporter::export_ok_tags** methods.

For example, consider our original example, in which you could have built the contents of **@EXPORT** and **@EXPORT_OK** using:

```
@EXPORT      = qw/A B C/;
@EXPORT_OK   = qw/G H I/;
%EXPORT_TAGS = (FIRST => [qw/D E F/],
                SECOND => [qw/J K L/]
                );
Exporter::export_tags('FIRST');
Exporter::export_ok_tags('SECOND');
```

This would populate the arrays with your original values, without requiring you to specify the symbols explicitly. Any names not matching a tag defined in **%EXPORT_TAGS** will raise a warning when the **–w** command line switch is enabled.

Version Checking

The **require_version** method validates that the module being loaded is of a value equal to or greater than the supplied value. The **Exporter** module supplies this method for you, or you can define your own. In the case of the **Exporter** version, it uses the value of the **$VERSION** variable in the exporting module.

Note that the comparison made is numeric, so the version 1.10 will be treated as a lower version than 1.9. You should therefore use an explicit two-digit (or more) format for the version number, for example, 1.09.

REFERENCES Chapter 5

ExtUtils::Command

This function is used under Win32 implementations to provide suitable replacements for core Unix commands used by the extension development process. You should not need to use this module directly, but it defines the following functions/commands:

```
cat
eqtime src dst
rm_f files....
touch files ...
mv source... destination
cp source... destination
chmod mode files...
mkpath directory...
test_f file
```

ExtUtils::Embed

This module provides the necessary command line options and other information for use when you are embedding a Perl interpreter into an application. It supports the following functions:

```
xsinit
```

Generates code for the XS initializer function.

```
ldopts
```

Generates command line options for linking Perl to an application.

```
ccopts
```

Generates command line options for compiling embedded Perl programs.

```
perl_inc
```

Generates the command line options for including Perl headers.

```
ccflags
```

Outputs the contents of the **$Config{ccflags}** hash element.

```
ccdlflags
```

Outputs the contents of the **$Config{ccdlflags}** hash element.

```
xsi_header
```

Outputs the string defining the **EXTERN_C** macro used by perlmain.c and includes statements to include perl.h and EXTERN.h.

```
xsi_protos(LIST)
```

Outputs the corresponding **boot_MODULE** prototypes for the modules specified in **LIST**.

```
xsi_body(LIST)
```

Returns a list of the calls to **newXS** that glue each module **bootstrap** function to the **boot_MODULE** function for each module specified in **LIST**.

REFERENCES Chapter 17; *see also* **Config**, **ExtUtils::MakeMaker**

ExtUtils::Install

This module defines two functions: **install** and **uninstall**. These are used during the installation process by the **MakeMaker** system to install files into the destination directory.

ExtUtils::Installed

This module defines a suite of functions that can be used to query the contents of the .packlist files generated during module installation. If you call the **new** function, it constructs the internal lists by examining the .packlist files. The **modules** function returns a list of all the modules currently installed. The **files** and **directories** both accept a single argument—the name of a module. The result is a list of all the files installed by the package. The **directory_tree** function reports information for all the related directories. In all cases you can specify **Perl** to get information pertaining to the core Perl installation.

The **validate** function checks that the files listed in .packlist actually exist. The **packlist** function returns an object as defined by **ExtUtils::Packlist** for the specified module. Finally, **version** returns the version number of the specified module.

ExtUtils::Liblist

This module defines the libraries to be used when building extension libraries and other Perl-based binaries. The information provided here broaches much of the complexity involved in getting an extension to work across many platforms; the bulk of the code relates to the information required for individual platforms.

ExtUtils::MakeMaker

The **MakeMaker** package provides a Perl-based system for producing standard **make** files suitable for installing Perl applications and, more specifically, Perl extensions.

REFERENCES Chapter 20

ExtUtils::Manifest

This module provides the functions that produce, test, and update the MANIFEST file. Five of the functions are the most useful, beginning with **mkmanifest**, which creates a file, based on the current directory contents. The **maincheck** function verifies the current directory contents against the MANIFEST file, while **filecheck** looks for files in the current directory that are not specified in the MANIFEST. Both **maincheck** and **filecheck** are executed by the **fullcheck** function, and **skipcheck** lists the files in the MAINFEST.SKIP file.

ExtUtils::Miniperl

This module provides the list of base libraries and extensions that should be included when building the **miniperl** binary.

ExtUtils::Mkbootstrap

This module makes a bootstrap file suitable for the **DynaLoader** module.

ExtUtils::Mksymlists

This module produces the list of options for creating a dynamically linked library.

ExtUtils::MM_OS2

MakeMaker specifics for the OS/2 operating system are produced by this module.

ExtUtils::MM_Unix

MakeMaker specifics for the Unix platform are produced by this module. It also includes many of the core functions used by the main **MakeMaker** module irrespective of the host platform.

ExtUtils::MM_VMS

This module produces **MakeMaker** specifics for VMS.

ExtUtils::MM_Win32

This module produces **MakeMaker** specifics for Windows 95/98/NT.

ExtUtils::Packlist

This module supplies the **Packlist** object used by the **ExtUtils::Installed** module.

REFERENCES *See* **ExtUtils::Installed**

Fatal

This module provides a system for overriding functions that normally provide a true or false return value so that they instead fail (using **die**) when they would normally return false. For example,

```
use Fatal qw/open/;
```

overrides **open** so that a failure will call **die** and raise an exception that can be caught with a suitable **$SIG{__DIE__}** handler. This allows you to bypass the normal checking that you would conduct on each call to **open** and instead install a global handler for all **open** calls.

To trap your own calls:

```
sub mightfail {};
import Fatal 'mightfail';
```

Note that you cannot override the **exec** and **system** calls.

REFERENCES Chapters 3, 11

Fcntl

This module supplies the constants that are available as standard within the fcntl.h file within C. This supplies all the constants directly as functions—the same as other modules. This information is gleaned during the installation and build process of Perl and should be correct for your operating system, supporting a compatible set of constants.

The module exports the following constants by default. The exact list will vary from system to system; this list comes from MacPerl 5.2.0r4:

```
F_DUPFD F_GETFD F_GETLK F_SETFD F_GETFL F_SETFL F_SETLK F_SETLKW
FD_CLOEXEC F_RDLCK F_UNLCK F_WRLCK
O_CREAT O_EXCL O_NOCTTY O_TRUNC
O_APPEND O_NONBLOCK
O_NDELAY O_DEFER
O_RDONLY O_RDWR O_WRONLY
O_EXLOCK O_SHLOCK O_ASYNC O_DSYNC O_RSYNC O_SYNC
F_SETOWN F_GETOWN
O_ALIAS O_RSRC
```

The following symbols are available, either individually or via the **flock** group:

```
LOCK_SH LOCK_EX LOCK_NB LOCK_UN
```

To import this group:

```
use Fcntl qw/:flock/;
```

REFERENCES Chapter 6

fields

The **fields** pragma affects the compile time error checking of objects. Using the **fields** pragma enables you to predefine class fields, such that a call to a specific class method will fail at compile time if the field has not been specified. This is achieved by populating a hash called **%FIELDS**. When you access a hash with a typed variable holding an object reference, the type is looked up in the **%FIELDS** hash, and if the variable type exists, the entire operation is turned into an array access during the compilation stage. For example:

```
{
    package Foo;
    use fields qw(foo bar _private);
}
...
my Foo $var = new Foo;
$var->{foo} = 42;
```

If the specified field does not exist, then a compile time error is produced.

For this to work, the **%FIELDS** hash is consulted at compile time, and it's the **fields** and **base** pragmas that facilitate this. The **base** pragma copies fields from the base class definitions, and the **fields** pragma adds new fields to the existing definitions. Field names that start with an underscore character are private to a class; they are not even accessible to subclasses.

The result is that objects can be created with named fields that are as convenient and quick to access as a corresponding hash. You must access the objects through correctly typed variables, or you can use untyped variables, provided that a reference to the **%FIELDS** hash is assigned to the 0th element of the array object. You can achieve this initialization with

```
sub new
{
    my $class = shift;
    no strict 'refs';
    my $self = bless [\%{"$class\::FIELDS"], $class;
    $self;
}
```

REFERENCES Chapter 16

FileCache

This module enables you to keep more files open than the system permits.

```
use FileCache;
```

It remembers a list of valid pathnames that you know you will want to write to, and opens and closes the files as necessary to stay within the maximum number of open files supported on your machine. To add a path to the list, you call the **cacheout** function:

```
cacheout $path;
```

FileHandle

This module supports an object-based interface for using filehandles.

```
use FileHandle;
```

The **new** method creates a new **FileHandle** object, returning it to the caller. Any supplied arguments are passed on directly to the **open** method. If the **open** fails, the object is destroyed and **undef** is returned. The newly created object is a reference to a newly created symbol as supported by the **Symbol** module.

```
$fh = new FileHandle;
```

Alternatively, you can use the **new_from_fd** method to create a new **FileHandle** object. It requires two parameters that are passed to **FileHandle::fdopen**.

The **open** method attaches a file to the new filehandle:

```
$fh->method(FILE [, MODE [, PERMS]])
```

The **open** method supports the options as the built-in **open** function. The first parameter is the file name. If supplied on its own, you can use the normal **open** formats such as > or >>, and then it uses the normal **open** function.

If you supply a **MODE** in the format of the **POSIX fopen()** function—for example, "w" or "w+"—then the built-in **open** function is also used. If given a numeric **MODE**, then the built-in **sysopen** function is used instead. The module automatically imports the **O_*** constants from **Fcntl** if they are available.

The **fdopen** method is like **open** except that its first argument should be a filehandle name, **FileHandle** object, or a file descriptor number.

If supported on your system, the **fgetpos()** and **fsetpos()** functions are available as the **getpos** and **setpos** methods, respectively. The **getpos** works like **tell** and returns the current location. You can then revisit the location within the file using **setpos**.

The **setvbuf** method is available to you if your system supports the **setvbuf()** function, and it sets the buffering policy for the filehandle:

```
$fh->setvbuf(VAR, TYPE, SIZE)
```

The **VAR** parameter should be a suitable scalar variable to hold the buffer data, and **SIZE** defines the maximum size of the buffer. The **TYPE** is specified using a constant, and these are exported by default by the module. The constants are described in Table E-5.

Constant	Description
_IOFBF	Causes the input and output to be fully buffered.
_IOLBF	Causes the output to be line buffered. The buffer will be flushed when a newline character is written to the filehandle, when the buffer is full, or when input is requested on the handle.
_IONBF	Causes the input and output to be completely unbuffered.

Table E-5. *Options for the **FileHandle->setvbuf** Method*

You should not modify the contents of the scalar variable you use for the buffer while it is in use.

The **FileHandle** module also supports the following methods, which are simply aliases for the corresponding functions. See Chapters 3, 6, and/or Appendix B for more information on the following functions:

clearerr	**close**	**eof**	**fileno**	**getc**
gets	**print**	**printf**	**seek**	**tell**

The module also supports methods for setting the individual variables that affect the use of the filehandle directly:

autoflush	**format_formfeed**
format_line_break_characters	**format_lines_left**
format_lines_per_page	**format_name**
format_page_number	**format_top_name**
input_line_number	**input_record_separator**
output_field_separator	**output_record_separator**

Finally, the module also supports two further methods for reading lines from the file:

```
$fh->getline
$fh->getlines
```

The **getline** method returns a single line from the filehandle, just like the **<$fh>** operator when used in a scalar context. The **getlines** method returns a list of lines in a manner identical to the **<$fh>** operator in a list context. The **getlines** method will **croak** if called in a scalar context.

REFERENCES Chapters 2, 3, 6; *see also* **Symbol**, **POSIX**

File::Basename

This module supports the **basename** and **dirname** functions for extracting file and directory names for complete paths. It also supports more complex file path parsing functions.

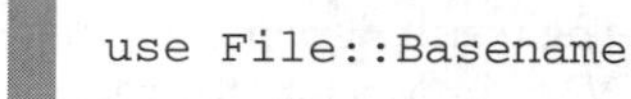

```
use File::Basename;
```

The **File::Basename** module supplies functions for parsing pathnames and extracting the directory, file name, and optionally, the extension. The extraction can be made to account for different operating systems and can therefore be used as a cross-platform tool for parsing paths.

The main function is **fileparse**:

```
fileparse PATH, EXTENSION
```

The **fileparse** function separates **PATH** into its components: a directory name, a file name, and a suffix. The directory name should contain everything up to and including the last directory separator in **PATH**. The remainder is then separated into the file name and suffix based on the **EXTENSION** definitions you supply.

This argument should be a reference to an array, where each element is a regular expression used to match against the end of the file name. If the match succeeds, the file is split into its file name and extension. If it does not match, the whole file name is returned and the suffix remains empty.

For example:

```
($name, $path, $suffix) = fileparse('/usr/local/bin/script.pl', '\.pl');
```

This will return "script," "/usr/local/bin/," and ".pl," in that order. Note that this is not the same as the order you might expect. The function guarantees that if you combine the three elements returned, you will end up with the original file path.

The syntax used to separate the path depends on the setting of the module. You can change the specification syntax using the **fileparse_set_fstype** function:

```
fileparse_set_fstype EXPR
```

The supplied expression defines the operating system syntax to be used. If **EXPR** contains one of the substrings "VMS," "MSDOS," or "MacOS," then the corresponding syntax is used in all future calls to the **fileparse** function. If **EXPR** does not contain one of these strings, the Unix syntax is used instead. Note that the default operation depends on the value of **$Config{osname}** as determined during the build process.

Two functions, **basename** and **dirname**, are supplied for Unix compatibility:

```
basename EXPR
```

The **basename** function returns the file name of a path. The function uses **fileparse** for its result.

```
dirname EXPR
```

The **dirname** function returns the directory portion of a file path. The result depends on the current syntax being used to extract the information. When using VMS or MacOS, the result is the same as the second argument returned by **fileparse**. If Unix or MSDOS syntax is used, the value matches what would be returned by the **dirname** Unix command. The function uses **fileparse** for its result.

REFERENCES Chapter 6

File::CheckTree

This module provides a mechanism for validating a series of files using the standard built-in tests for files. The method is to call the **validate** function with a textual list of files and tests, for example:

```
use File::CheckTree;
$errors += validate(q{
/test/test.c                    -e  || die "Can't find test.c"
/test/test.o                    -e  || warn "Object file not found"
/test/test                      -ex || warn
});
```

The above tests that the **test.c** file exists; a failure will cause a call to **die**. Warnings are produced if the object and executable do not exist, and also if the executable is not actually executable. The default method is to produce a warning (effectively || **warn**) if a file is not specified. Note that the files must be specified exactly. See the **File::Find** module for another alternative.

You can also use a method of **cd**, which indicates the following entries are within the specified directory. Thus the above example could be rewritten:

```
use File::CheckTree;
$errors += validate(q{
/test                       cd
   test.c                   -e  || die "Can't find test.c"
   test.o                   -e  || warn "Object file not found"
   test                     -ex || warn
});
```

In all cases, providing a fatal error has not occurred, the return value is the number of files that failed the test.

REFERENCES *See* **File::Find**

File::Compare

This module compares files or filehandles.

```
use File::Compare;
```

To compare files, you use the **compare** function:

```
print "Equal\n" if (compare('f1','f2) == 0);
```

Either argument to the function can be a file name or filehandle. The function returns zero if the files are equal, 1 otherwise, or –1 if an error was encountered.

File::Copy

This module copies or moves files or filehandles.

```
use File::Copy;
```

It supports two functions: **copy** and **move**. The **copy** function accepts two arguments and copies from the first to the second file. Either argument can be a file name or filehandle. The following examples are valid:

```
copy('f1', 'f2');
copy(\*STDIN, 'console');
copy('f1', \*STDOUT);
```

The **move** function will move a file from one location to another:

```
move('f1', 'f2');
```

If possible it will rename the file; but if this does not work, the contents will be copied to the new file, and the old file will be deleted when the copy is complete.

Both functions are platform independent and return 1 on success, zero on failure.

REFERENCES *See* **Shell**

File::DosGlob

This module provides a DOS-like globbing functionality, with the addition that wildcards are supported in directory and file names.

```
require 5.004;
use File::DosGlob qw/glob/;
```

Note that this function overrides the **CORE** function within the scope of the current package. To override the function in all pacakges:

```
use File::DosGlob qw/GLOBAL_glob/;
```

You can use spaces to separate individual patterns within the file specification given, for example:

```
$executables = glob('*.exe *.com');
```

Note that in all cases you may have to double the backslashes in file specifications to override the normal parsing that Perl does on quoted strings. Alternatively, use the **q//** operator.

REFERENCES Chapter 6

File::Find

This module supports the traversal of a directory tree.

```
use File::Find;
```

It supports two functions: **find** and **finddepth**. The **find** function accepts at least two arguments:

```
find(\&wanted, '/foo', '/bar');
```

The first argument is a reference to a subroutine called each time a file is found. This is called the "wanted" function and is used to process each file as it is found. Further arguments specify the individual directories to traverse.

Because the wanted function is called each time a file is found, the function can perform whatever functions or verifications on each file it needs to. The **$File::Find::dir** variable contains the name of the current directory. Note that the function calls **chdir** to change into each found directory. The special **$_** variable contains the current file name. You can also access **$File::Find::name** to get the full pathname of the current file. Setting the value of **$File::Find::prune** prunes the directory tree.

For example, the script below would print files and directories in the /usr/local tree that are executable by the real and effective uid/gid:

```
use File::Find;

find(\&wanted, '/usr/local');

sub wanted
{
    next unless (-x $_ and -X _);
    print "$File::Find::name\n";
}
```

If you are creating complex wanted functions and know how to use the Unix **find** command, you can use the **find2perl** script, which generates the necessary stand-alone code for you. For example,

```
$ find2perl /usr/local -name "*.html" -mtime -7
```

produces the following stand-alone script:

```
#!/usr/local/bin/perl
    eval 'exec /usr/local/bin/perl -S $0 ${1+"$@"}'
        if $running_under_some_shell;

require "find.pl";

# Traverse desired filesystems


&find('/usr/local');

exit;
sub wanted {
    /^.*\.html$/ &&
    (($dev,$ino,$mode,$nlink,$uid,$gid) = lstat($_)) &&
    (int(-M _) < 7);
}
```

The **finddepth** function is identical to **find** except that it does a depth first search, rather than working from the lowest to the highest depth.

REFERENCES Chapters 6, 25

File::Path

This module creates or removes a directory tree.

```
use File::Path;
```

It supplies two functions, **mkpath** and **rmtree**, which make and remove directory trees.

```
mkpath(ARRAYREF, PRINT, MODE)
```

The **ARRAYREF** should either be the name of the directory to create or a reference to a list of directories to be created. All intermediate directories in the specification will also be created as required. If **PRINT** is true (default is false), the name of each directory created will be printed to **STDOUT**. The **MODE** is octal mode to be used for the newly created directories. The function returns a list of all the directories created. For example, to create a typical /usr/local structure:

```
mkpath(['/usr/local/bin',
        '/usr/local/etc',
        '/usr/local/lib'], 0, 0777);
```

The **rmtree** function deletes a directory subtree. All of the directories specified will be deleted, in addition to the subdirectories and files contained within them.

```
rmtime(ARRAYREF, PRINT, SKIP)
```

The **ARRAYREF** should either be the name of a directory to delete or a reference to an array of directories to be deleted. The directory specified and all its subdirectories and files will be deleted.

The **PRINT** argument, if set to true, prints each file or directory and the method used to remove the file or directory. The default value is false. The **SKIP** argument, if set to true, causes the function to skip files and directories that it is unable to remove due to access privileges. The default value for **SKIP** is false.

The function returns the number of files successfully deleted.

Note that you will need to use a **$SIG{__WARN__}** handler to identify files or directories that could not be deleted.

REFERENCES Chapters 6, 10

File::Spec

This module is a cross-platform-compatible library for performing operations on file names and paths.

```
use File::Spec;
```

The module is supported by a number of platform-specific modules that are imported as required, depending on the platform on which the script is running. You shouldn't need to import the support modules individually; use the **File::Spec** module and let it decide which module is required. See the **File::Spec::Unix** module for a list of the supported methods. Other modules override the necessary methods that are specific to that platform.

Since the interface is object oriented, you must call the functions as class methods:

```
$path = File::Spec->('usr','local');
```

REFERENCES Chapters 21, 22, 23, 24; *see also* **File::Spec::Mac**, **File::Spec::OS2**, **File::Spec::Unix**, **File::Spec::VMS**, **File::Spec::Win32**

File::Spec::Mac

This module supports the MacOS-specific methods for manipulating file specifications.

```
use File::Spec::Mac;
```

It overrides the default methods supported by **File::Spec**. Note that you should not normally need to use this module directory. The methods overridden by this module are given here.

```
canonpath
```

Returns the path it's given; no process is required under MacOS.

```
catdir
```

Concatenates directory names to form a complete path ending with a directory. Under MacOS, the following rules are followed:

- Each argument has any trailing : removed.
- Each argument except the first has any leading : character removed.
- All arguments are then joined by a single : character.

To create a relative rather than absolute path, precede the first argument with a : character, or use a blank argument.

```
catfile
```

Concatenates directory names and a file into a path that defines an individual file. Uses **catdir** for the directory names. Any leading or trailing colons are removed from the file name.

```
curdir
```

Returns a string defining the current directory.

```
rootdir
```

Returns a string defining the root directory. Under MacPerl this returns the name of this startup volume; under any other Perl, returns an empty string.

```
updir
```

Returns the string representing the parent directory.

```
file_name_is_absolute
```

Returns true if the supplied path is absolute.

```
path
```

Returns the null list under MacPerl, since there is no execution path under MacOS. When used within the MPW environment, returns the contents of **$ENV{Commands}** as a list.

REFERENCES *See* **File::Spec**

File::Spec::OS2

This module supports methods for manipulating file specifications under the OS/2 platform.

```
use File::Spec::OS2;
```

It overrides the default methods supported by **File::Spec**. Note that you should not normally need to use this module directory. The supported methods are detailed in the **File::Spec:Unix** module.

REFERENCES *See* **File::Spec**

File::Spec::Unix

This module supports Unix-specific methods for file specifications.

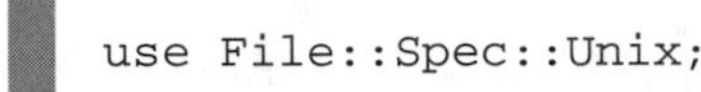

```
use File::Spec::Unix;
```

It imports and overrides the methods supported by **File::Spec**. It is normally imported by **File::Spec** as needed, although you can import it directly if required. The following methods are supplied:

```
canonpath
```

Cleans up a given path, removing successive slashes and /.. Note that the physical existence of the file or directory is not verified.

```
catdir
```

Concatenates one or more directories into a valid path. This strips the trailing slash off the path for all but the root directory.

```
catfile
```

Concatenates one or more directories and a file name into a valid path to a file.

```
curdir
```

Returns a string representing the current directory (.).

```
rootdir
```

Returns a string representing the root directory (/).

```
updir
```

Returns a string representing the parent directory (..).

```
no_upwards
```

Removes references to parent directories from a given list of file paths.

```
file_name_if_absolute
```

Returns true if the given path is absolute.

```
path
```

Returns the **$ENV{PATH}** variable as a list.

```
join
```

Identical to **catfile**.

REFERENCES *See* **File::Spec**

File::Spec::VMS

This module supports VMS-specific methods for file specifications.

```
use File::Spec::VMS;
```

It is imported and overrides the methods supplied by **File::Spec** under the VMS platform. The following methods are supported:

```
catdir LIST
```

Concatenates a list of specifications and returns a VMS syntax directory specification.

```
catfile LIST
```

Concatenates a list of specifications and returns a VMS syntax file specification.

```
curdir
```

Returns the current directory as a string.

```
rootdir
```

Returns the root directory as a string.

```
updir
```

Returns the parent directory as a string.

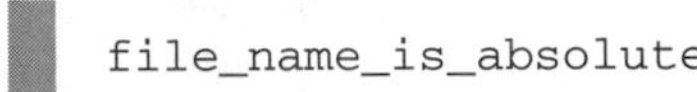

```
path
```

Translates the logical VMS path defined in **DCL$PATH** rather than splitting the value of **$ENV{PATH}**.

```
file_name_is_absolute
```

Checks that a VMS directory specification is valid. Note that this does not check the physical existence of a file or directory, only that the specification is correct.

REFERENCES *See* **File::Spec**

File::Spec::Win32

This module provides Win32-specific methods for file specifications.

```
use File::Spec::Win32;
```

This is the module imported internally by **File::Spec** under Win32 platforms. The package overrides the following methods supported by the **File::Spec** module.

```
Catfile LIST
```

Concatenates one or more directory names and a file name to form a complete path to a file.

```
canonpath EXPR
```

Cleans up a supplied pathname for use on Win32 platforms.

REFERENCES *See* **File::Spec**

FindBin

This module exports variables that define the directory of the original Perl script.

```
use FindBin;
```

It locates the full path to the script's parent directory, as well as the name of the script. This can be useful if you want to install a script in its own directory hierarchy but do not want to hard code the directory location into the script.

The variables available are shown in Table E-6. The variables are not exported by default; you must explicitly request them or use the fully qualified values.

Variable	Description
$Bin	Path to the directory where the script was located.
$Script	The name of the script that was invoked.
$RealBin	The value of **$Bin** with all the links resolved.
$RealScript	The value of **$Script** with all the links resolved.

Table E-6. *Variables Available via* ***FindBin***

Note that if the script was invoked from **STDIN** or via the **–e** command line option, the value of **$Bin** is set to the current directory.

GDBM_File

This module provides an interface to the GDBM database system. The main benefit of GDBM over other systems (except Berkeley DB) is that it provides rudimentary database locking and does not have a restricted bucket size, allowing you to store any size object within a GDBM database.

```
use GDBM_File;
tie %db, 'GDBM_File', 'db', &GDBM_WRCREAT, 0640;
untie %db;
```

Instead of using the modes for opening the database that are ordinarily supplied by the **Fcntl** module, the **GDBM_File** module provides its own constants, listed in Table E-7.

REFERENCES Chapter 8; *see also* **AnyDBM_File, DB_File, NDBM_File, ODBM_File, SDBM_File**

Constant	Description
GDBM_READER	Open for read only.
GDBM_WRITER	Open for read/write.
GDBM_WRCREAT	Open for read/write, creating a new database if it does not already exist, using the mode specified.
GDBM_NEWDB	Open for read/write, creating a new database even if one already exists, using the mode specified.

Table E-7. *Modes for Opening GDBM Tied Databases*

Getopt::Long

This module is suitable for simple scripts and argument passing. However, it falls over if you try to do more complex processing or want to place the extracted information into specific variables and structures. The **Getopt::Long** module implements a more advanced system. It is **POSIX** compliant and therefore suitable for use in scripts that require **POSIX** compliance.

POSIX compliance allows not only the standard single-character matching supported by the **Getopt::Std** module, but also string arguments. For example:

```
$ script.pl --inputfile=source.txt
```

The command line option in this case is **--inputfile**. Note that long names as arguments are supported by both the single and double hyphen, although the double hyphen is the **POSIX** default.

Note *The* **+** *sign is also supported, but the use of this is deprecated and not part of the* ***POSIX*** *specification.*

The selection of additional arguments to command line options is supported by appending a specific character sequence to the end of the option name. The list of available modifiers is defined in Table E-8.

Any elements in the argument list not identified as options remain in the **@ARGV** array.

Linkage

When using a hash reference as the first argument to the **GetOptions** function, additional facilities are available to you for processing more complex command lines. By default, the operation is identical to the **getopts** function. You can also use a trailing @ or % sign to signify that an array or hash reference should be returned. In the case of an array reference, this allows you to supply multiple values for a single named option.

For a hash, it supports "-option name=value" command line constructs, where **name** and **value** are the key and value of the returned hash.

If you do not specify a hash reference as the first argument, the function will instead create a new variable of the corresponding type, using the argument name prefixed by **opt_**. So a function call

```
GetOptions("file=s","files=s@","users=s%");
```

may result in a similar assignment to the following:

```
$opt_file = "source.txt";
@opt_files = ('source.txt', 'sauce.txt');
%opt_users = ( 'Bob'  => 'Manager',
               'Fred' => 'Salesman' );
```

Option Specified	Description
!	The option does not accept an optional piece of information and may be negated by prefixing **no**. For example, **opt!**, will set the value of an option **--opt** to one, and **--noopt** to zero.
+	The option does not accept an additional piece of information. Each appearance in the command line options will increment the corresponding value by 1, such that **--opt --opt --opt** will set a value of 3, providing it doesn't already have a value.
=s	The option requires an additional string argument. The value of the string will be placed into the corresponding variable.
:s	The option accepts an optional string argument. The value of the string will be placed into the corresponding variable.
=i	The option requires an integer argument. The value will be placed into the corresponding variable.
:i	The option accepts an optional integer argument. The value will be placed into the corresponding variable.
=f	The option requires a real number argument. The value will be placed into the corresponding variable.
:f	The option accepts an optional real number argument. The value will be placed into the corresponding variable.

Table E-8. *Definitions for Use with the **Getopt::Long** Module*

You can also use the hash argument feature to update your own variables directly:

```
GetOptions("file=s"   => \$file,
           "files=s@" => \@files,
           "users=s%" => \%users);
```

This last specification method also supports a function that will handle the specified option. The function will receive two arguments—the true option name (see below) and the value supplied.

Aliases

You can support alternative argument names by using | characters to separate individual names. For example:

```
GetOptions("file|input|source=s");
```

The "true" name would be "file" in this instance, placing the value into **$opt_file**. This true name is also passed to a function if specified (see above).

Callback Function

If **GetOptions** cannot identify an individual element of the **@ARGV** array as a true argument, you can specify a function that will handle the option. You do this by using a value of <> as the argument name, as in

```
GetOptions("<>" => \&nonoption);
```

Remember that the **GetOptions** function removes identifiable arguments from **@ARGV** and leaves the remainder of the elements intact if you don't use this facility. You can then process the arguments as you wish after **GetOptions** has completed successfully.

Return Values

The **GetOptions** function returns true (1) if the command line arguments could be identified correctly. If an error occurs (because the user has supplied a command line argument the function wasn't expecting), the function returns false and uses **warn** to report the bad options. If the definitions supplied to the function are invalid, the function calls **die**, reporting the error.

Customizing GetOptions

You can control the operation of the **GetOptions** function by passing arguments to **Getopt::Long::Configure**. The list of options is shown in Table E-9. The values shown in the table *set* the option; to unset, prefix the option with **no_**.

For example, to set auto abbreviation and allow differentiation between upper- and lowercase arguments:

```
Getopt::Long::Configure('auto_abbrev','no_ignore_case');
```

Variables

You can monitor the version number of the **Getopt::Long** module with the **$Getopt::Long::VERSION** variable. You can also identify the major and minor versions using the **$Getopt::Long::major_version** and **$Getopt::Long::minor_version** variables. If you want to identify the version number during import, use the usual:

```
use Getopt::Long 3.00;
```

<table>
<tr><th>Option</th><th>Description</th></tr>
<tr><td>default</td><td>Sets all configuration options to their default values.</td></tr>
<tr><td>auto_abbrev</td><td>Supports abbreviated option names, providing the arguments supplied can be identified uniquely. This is the default operation, unless the POSIXLY_CORRECT environment variable is set.</td></tr>
<tr><td>getopt_compat</td><td>Supports the use of + as the prefix to arguments. This is the default operation, unless the POSIXLY_CORRECT environment variable is set.</td></tr>
<tr><td>require_order</td><td>This specifies that your options must be supplied first on the command line. This is the default operation, unless the POSIXLY_CORRECT environment variable is set. This is the opposite of permute. If require_order is set, processing terminates on the first nonorder item found in the argument list.</td></tr>
<tr><td>permute</td><td>Specifies that nonoptions are allowed to be mixed with real options. This is the default operation, unless the POSIXLY_CORRECT environment variable is set. This the opposite of require_order.</td></tr>
<tr><td>bundling</td><td>Setting this allows single-character options to be bundled into single strings. For example, if set, the string "-vax" will be equivalent to "-v -a -x." This option also allows for integer values to be inserted into the bundled options, such that "-d256aq" is equivalent to "-d 256 -a -q."</td></tr>
<tr><td>bundling_override</td><td>If set, the bundling option is implied. However, if an option has been defined with the same full name as a bundle, it will be interpreted as the name, not the individual options. For example, if "vax" was specified, then "-vax" would be interpreted as "-vax", but "-avx" would be interpreted as "-a -v -x."</td></tr>
<tr><td>ignore_case</td><td>Default; string command line options are interpreted ignoring case.</td></tr>
<tr><td>ignore_case_always</td><td>When bundling is set, case is also ignored on single-character options.</td></tr>
<tr><td>pass_through</td><td>Unrecognized options remain in the @ARGV array, instead of producing and being flagged as errors.</td></tr>
<tr><td>prefix</td><td>Takes the next argument to the function as a string defining the list of strings that identify an option. The default value is (—|-|\+), or (—|-) if the POSIXLY_CORRECT environment variable is set.</td></tr>
<tr><td>debug</td><td>Enables debugging output.</td></tr>
</table>

Table E-9. *Configurable Variables for the **Getopt::Long** Module*

When using the callback function (with <>) you may want to report an error back to the main **GetOptions** function. You can do this by incrementing the **$Getopt::Long::error** variable.

REFERENCES Chapter 12

Getopt::Std

This module provides two functions: **getopt** and **getopts**.

```
use Getopt::Std;

getopt('ol');
getopts('ol:');
```

Both functions require a single argument that specifies the list of single-letter arguments you would like to identify on the command line.

In the case of the **getopt** function, it assumes that all arguments expect an additional piece of information. With the **getopts** function, each character is taken to be a Boolean value. If you want to accept arguments with additional information, append a colon.

Variables are created by the function with a prefix of **$opt_**. The value of each variable is one in the case of a Boolean value, or the supplied additional argument. If the command argument is not found, the variable is still created, but the value is **undef**.

In addition, for either function, you can supply a second argument that should be a reference to a hash:

```
getopts('i:',\%opts);
```

Each supplied argument will be used as the key of the hash, and any additional information supplied will be placed into the corresponding values. Thus a script with the above line when called,

```
$ getopts -i Hello
```

will place the string "Hello" into the **$opts{'i'}** hash element.

If you have the **use strict 'vars'** pragma in effect (see Chapter 16), you will need to predefine the **$opt_** and hash variables before they are called. Either use a **my** definition before calling the function, or, better still, predeclare them with **use vars**.

REFERENCES Chapter 12

I18N::Collate

The functionality of the **I18N::Collate** module has been integrated into Perl from version 5.003_06. See the **perllocale** man page for details.

integer

Forces integer-based math.The **use integer** pragma only lasts as long as the current block, so it can safely be used within individual functions without affecting the rest of the script. In addition, you can switch off the **integer** pragma with the **no** keyword:

```
use integer;
print 67/3,"\n";
no integer;
print 67/3,"\n";
```

You can also use **no** within an enclosed block to temporarily turn off integer math.

REFERENCES Chapter 16

IO

This module automatically imports a number of base IO modules.

```
use IO;
```

It doesn't provide any modules or functionality on its own, but does attempt to import the following modules for you:

```
IO::File
IO::Handle
IO::Pipe
IO::Seekable
IO::Socket
```

REFERENCES *See* **IO::File, IO::Handle, IO::Pipe, IO::Seekable, IO::Socket**

IO::File

This module supports the methods for accessing and using filehandles.

```
use IO::File;
```

The **new** method creates a new filehandle, and any arguments are passed to the **open** method. If the **open** fails, the object is destroyed; otherwise it is returned to the caller.

```
new_tmpfile
```

Creates a new filehandle opened for read/write on the newly created temporary file.
Once created, the object supports the following methods:

```
open(FILENAME [, MODE [, PERMS]])
```

The **open** method supports the options as the built-in **open** function. The first parameter is the file name. If supplied on its own, you can use the normal **open** formats, such as > or >>, and then it uses the normal **open** function.

If you supply a **MODE** in the format of the **POSIX fopen()** function—for example, "w" or "w+"—the built-in **open** function is also used. If given a numeric **MODE**, the built-in **sysopen** function is used instead. The module automatically imports the **O_*** constants from **Fcntl** if they are available.

The **fdopen** method is like **open** except that its first argument should be a filehandle name, **FileHandle** object, or a file descriptor number.

Additional methods are inherited from **IO::Handle** and **IO::Seekable**.

REFERENCES *See* **IO**, **IO::Handle**, **IO::Seekable**

IO::Handle

This module supports the object methods available for use with other IO handles.

```
use IO::Handle;
```

It provides the base class from which all other IO handle classes inherit.

```
new
```

The **new** method creates a new **IO::Handle** object.

```
new_from_fd(FD, MODE)
```

Creates a new **IO::Handle** object. The **FD** and **MODE** are passed on to the **fdopen** method.

Additional methods match the functionality supported by the following functions. See Chapters 3, 6, and Appendix B for more details.

close **fileno** **getc** **eof** **read**
truncate **stat** **print** **printf** **sysread**
syswrite

The following methods are handle-specific versions of the corresponding Perl variables. See Chapter 2 for more information.

autoflush **format_formfeed**
format_line_break_characters **format_lines_left**
format_lines_per_page **format_name**
format_page_number **format_top_name**
format_write **input_line_number**
input_record_separator **output_field_separator**
output_record_separator

Additional module-specific methods are described here.

```
$fh->fdopen(FD, MODE)
```

This opens the file like the built-in **open**. The **FD** parameter takes a filehandle name, **IO::Handle** object, or a file descriptor number. The **MODE** is a valid **Fcntl** mode, and the module attempts to import the **O_*** series of constants from **Fcntl**, but doesn't **croak** if the modules cannot be imported.

```
$fh->opened
```

Returns true if the object is currently a valid file descriptor.

```
$fh->getline
$fh->getlines
```

The **getline** method returns a single line from the filehandle, just like the **<$fh>** operator when used in a scalar context. The **getlines** method returns a list of lines in a manner identical to the **<$fh>** operator in a list context. The **getlines** method will **croak** if called in a scalar context.

```
$fh->ungetc(ORD)
```

Pushes the character that is the ordinal value **ORD** onto the input stream.

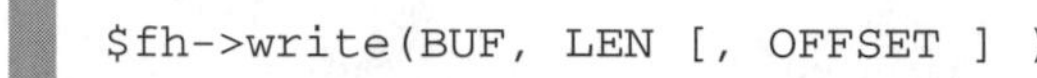

```
$fh->write(BUF, LEN [, OFFSET ] )
```

Writes **BUF** of size **LEN** to the filehandle. This is the implementation of the **write()** C function. If given, then **OFFSET** specifies the location within the file to write the data, without requiring you to move to that spot, and without modifying the current file pointer. Note that this is identical to the **pwrite()** C function.

```
$fh->flush
```

Flushes the filehandle's buffer.

```
$fh->error
```

Returns true if the filehandle has experienced any errors.

```
$fh->clearerr
```

Clears the error indicator.

```
$fh->untaint
```

Marks the data received on the handle as taint safe.

The **setvbuf** method is available if your system supports the **setvbuf()** function, and it sets the buffering policy for the filehandle:

```
$fh->setvbuf(VAR, TYPE, SIZE)
```

The **VAR** parameter should be a suitable scalar variable to hold the buffer data, and **SIZE** defines the maximum size of the buffer. The **TYPE** is specified using a constant, and these are exported by default by the module. The constants are described in Table E-10.

Warning *You should not modify the contents of the scalar variable you use for the buffer while it is in use.*

REFERENCES *See* **IO, IO::File, Symbol**

IO::Pipe

This module supports methods for pipes.

```
use IO::Pipe;
```

It provides an object interface for creating pipes between processes.

Constant	Description
_IOFBF	Causes the input and output to be fully buffered.
_IOLBF	Causes the output to be line buffered. The buffer will be flushed when a newline character is written to the filehandle, when the buffer is full, or when input is requested on the handle.
_IONBF	Causes the input and output to be completely unbuffered.

Table E-10. *Options for the **FileHandle->setvbuf** Method*

```
new([READER, WRITER])
```

This creates a new object (as supplied by the **Symbol** package). It takes two optional arguments, which should be **IO::Handle** objects, or an object that is a subclass of **IO::Handle**. These arguments will be used during the **pipe()** system call. If no arguments are supplied, the **handles** method is called.

Supported methods are described here.

```
reader([ARGS])
```

The object is reblessed into a subclass of **IO::Handle** and is the handle at the reading end of the pipe. Any supplied **ARGS** are used when calling **exec** after a **fork**.

```
writer([ARGS])
```

The object is reblessed into a subclass of **IO::Handle** and is the handle at the writing end of the pipe. Any supplied **ARGS** are used when calling **exec** after a **fork**.

```
handles
```

This method returns two objects blessed into **IO::Pipe::End** or a subclass thereof.

REFERENCES *See* **IO**, **IO::Handle**, **Symbol**

IO::Seekable

This module supplies base seek methods for IO objects.

```
use IO::Seekable;
package IO::Package;
@ISA = qw/IO::Seekable/;
```

APPENDIXES

It provides base methods for other **IO::*** modules to implement the positional functionality normally handled by the **seek** and **tell** built-in functions. Note that the module does not support any constructor methods of its own. The methods support the seek and location within file descriptors, using the **fgetpos()** and **fsetpos()** C functions. The methods are supported within **IO::File** as **IO::File::getpos** and **IO::File::setpos** methods, respectively. See the **seek** and **tell** functions in Appendix B for more information.

REFERENCES Chapters 3, 6, Appendix B; *see also* **IO**, **IO::File**

IO::Select

This module supports an object-oriented interface to the **select()** system call.

```
use IO::Select;
```

The module allows you to monitor which **IO::Handle** objects are ready for reading or writing or have an error pending, just like the **select** built-in function.

You can create a new **IO::Select** object with the **new** method:

```
new([HANDLES])
```

The optional **HANDLES** argument is a list of **IO::Handle** objects to initialize into the **IO::Select** object.

Once created, the new object supports the following, more pragmatic, interface to the **select** function.

```
add(HANDLES)
```

Adds the list of **IO::Handle** objects, integer file descriptor, or array reference, where the first element is an **IO::Handle** object or integer. It is these objects that will be returned when an event occurs. This works by the file descriptor number (as returned by **fileno**), so duplicated handles are not added.

```
remove(HANDLES)
```

Removes the given handles from the object.

```
exists(HANDLE)
```

Returns true if **HANDLE** is a part of the set.

```
handles
```

Returns an array of all the handles within the set.

```
can_read([TIMEOUT])
```

Returns an array of handles that are ready for reading. The method blocks for a maximum of **TIMEOUT** seconds. If **TIMEOUT** is not specified, the call blocks indefinitely.

```
can_write([TIMEOUT])
```

Returns an array of handles that are ready for writing. The method blocks for a maximum of **TIMEOUT** seconds. If **TIMEOUT** is not specified, the call blocks indefinitely.

```
has_error([TIMEOUT])
```

Returns an array of handles that have a pending error condition. The method blocks for a maximum of **TIMEOUT** seconds. If **TIMEOUT** is not specified, the call blocks indefinitely.

```
count
```

Returns the number of handles that will be returned when a **can_*** method is called.

```
bits
```

Returns a bitstring suitable for passing to the built-in **select** function.

```
IO::Select::select(READ, WRITE, ERROR, [, TIMEOUT])
```

The **select** method is a static method that must be called with the package name, as shown above. The function returns an array of three elements. Each is a reference to an array holding the reference to the handles that are ready for reading, writing, and have error conditions waiting, respectively.

The **READ**, **WRITE**, and **ERROR** arguments are **IO::Select** objects, or **undef**. The optional **TIMEOUT** value is the number of seconds to wait for a handle to become ready.

REFERENCES *See* **IO, IO::File, IO::Handle**

IO::Socket

This module supports an object interface for socket communications.

```
use IO::Socket;
```

This class supports socket-based communication. It exports the functions and constants supported by **Socket** and also inherits methods from **IO::Handle** in addition to defining a number of common methods suitable for all sockets. The **IO::Socket::INET** and **IO::Socket::UNIX** classes define additional methods for specific socket types.

The **new** method creates a new **IO::Socket** object using a symbol generated by the **Symbol** package.

```
$socket = IO::Socket->new(Domain => 'UNIX');
```

The constructor only identifies one option, **Domain**, which specifies the domain in which to create the socket. Any other options are supplied to the **IO::Socket::INET** or **IO::Socket::UNIX** constructor accordingly.

Note *The newly created handle will be in autoflush mode. This is the default operation from versions above 1.1603 (Perl 5.004_04). You will need to specify this explicitly if you want to remain compatible with earlier versions.*

The class supports the following methods:

```
accept([PKG])
```

This accepts a new socket connection like the built-in **accept** function, returning a new **IO::Socket** handle of the appropriate type. If you specify **PKG**, the new object will be of the specified class, rather than that of the parent handle. In a scalar context, only the new object is returned; in a list context, both the object and the peer address are returned. The method will return **undef** or an empty list on failure.

```
timeout([VALUE])
```

If supplied without any arguments, the current time-out setting is returned. If called with an argument, it sets the time-out value. The time-out value is used by various other methods.

```
sockopt(OPT [, VALUE])
```

Gets/sets the socket option **OPT**. If the method is only supplied **OPT**, it gets the current value of the option. To set a value, use the two-argument form.

```
sockdomain
```

Returns the numerical value of the socket domain type.

```
socktype
```

Returns the numerical value of the socket type.

```
protocol
```

Returns the numerical value of the protocol being used on the socket. If the protocol is unknown, zero is returned.

```
peername
```

This is identical to the built-in **getpeername** function.

```
sockname
```

This is identical to the built-in **getsockname** function.

The class also supplies frontend methods for the following built-in functions:

```
socket
socketpair
bind
listen
send
recv
```

Please refer to Chapter 9 and Appendix B for more information on these functions/methods.

IO::Socket::INET

The **IO::Socket::INET** class provides a constructor to create a socket within the **AF_INET** family/domain. The constructor accepts a hash that takes the options shown in Table E-11.

If passed a single argument, the constructor assumes that it's a **PeerAddr** specification. For example, to create a connection to a web server on port 80:

```
$socket = IO::Socket::INET->new(
                    PeerAddr => 'www.mcwords.com:http(80)');
```

Or to create a local socket for listening:

```
$socket = IO::Socket::INET->new(LocalAddr => 'localhost',
                                LocalPort  => '7000',
                                Listen     => '5',
                                Proto      => 'tcp');
```

Option	Format	Description
PeerAddr	hostname[:port]	Remote host address (and port). The **address** can be specified as a name (which will be resolved) or as an IP address. The **port** (if specified) should be a valid service name and/or port number as defined in **PeerPort**.
PeerPort	service(port) | port	The service port name and number, or number only.
LocalAddr	hostname[:port]	Local host address to bind to.
LocalPort	service(no) | no	The local service port name and number, or number only.
Proto	"tcp" | "udp" | ...	The protocol name or number. If this is not specified and you give a service name in the **PeerPort** option, then the constructor will attempt to derive **Proto** from the given service name. If it cannot be resolved, then "tcp" is used.
Type	SOCK_STREAM | SOCK_DGRAM | ...	The socket type, specified using a constant as exported by **Socket**. This will be deduced from **Proto** if not otherwise specified.
Listen		The queue size for listening to requests.
Reuse		If true, then it sets the **SO_REUSEADDR** option before binding to the local socket.

Table E-11. *Options for Creating an **IO::Socket::INET** Object*

Note that by specifying **LocalAddr** and **Listen**, the constructor builds a local socket suitable for acting as a server-side socket. You can use the **accept** method (inherited from **IO::Socket**), which works just like the built-in function.

Beyond the methods inherited from **IO::Socket** and **IO::Handle**, the **IO::Socket::INET** class also supports the following methods:

```
sockaddr
```

Returns the 4-byte packed address of the local socket.

```
sockport
```

Returns the port number used for the local socket.

```
sockhost
```

Returns the IP address in the form xxx.xxx.xxx.xxx for the local socket.

```
peeraddr
```

Returns the 4-byte packed address of the remote socket.

```
peerport
```

Returns the port number used for the remote socket.

```
peerhost
```

Returns the IP address in the form xxx.xxx.xxx.xxx for the remote socket.

IO::Socket::UNIX

The **IO::Socket::UNIX** class provides a constructor to create a socket within the **AF_UNIX** family/domain. The constructor accepts a hash that takes the options shown in Table E-12.

Like the **IO::Socket::INET** class, this class supports the methods inherited from **IO::Socket** and **IO::Handle**, in addition to the following methods:

```
hostpath
```

Returns the pathname to the FIFO file at the local end.

Option	Description
Type	The socket type, **SOCK_STREAM**, **SOCK_DGRAM**, or one of the other constants supported in **Socket**.
Local	Path to the local FIFO file.
Peer	Path to the peer FIFO file.
Listen	If set to true, it creates a socket that can be used to accept new client connections.

Table E-12. *Options for Creating a New **IO::Socket::Unix** Object*

```
peerpath
```

Returns the pathname to the FIFO file at the peer end.

REFERENCES Chapter 9; *see also* **IO::Handle, IO::Socket, Socket**

IPC::Msg

This module is an object-oriented interface to the System V message system.

```
use IPC::Msg;
```

It provides an alternative interface to the **msg*** range of IPC message queue functions. The **new** method creates a new message queue.

```
new KEY, FLAGS
```

Creates a new message queue associated with **KEY** using **FLAGS** as the permissions for accessing the queue. You will need to import suitable constants from **IPC::SysV**. A new object is created only under the following conditions:

- **KEY** is equal to **IPC_PRIVATE**.
- **KEY** does not already have a message queue associated with it.
- **FLAGS** contains the **IPC_CREAT** constant.

Once created, the following methods are supported:

```
id
```

Returns the system message queue identifier.

```
rcv BUF, LEN [, TYPE [, FLAGS]])
```

Receives a message from the queue into the variable **BUF**, up to a maximum length **LEN**.

```
remove
```

Removes (destroys) the message queue from the system.

```
set STAT
set(NAME => VALUE [, NAME => VALUE...])
```

Sets the values using either an **IPC::Msg::stat** object or the specified hash. Supported elements are **uid**, **gid**, **mode**, and **qbytes**.

```
snd
```

Sends a message to the queue of **TYPE**.

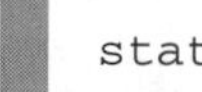

```
stat
```

Returns an **IPC::Msg::stat** object that is a subclass of the **Class::Struct** class. The object consists of the following fields:

uid	**gid**	**cuid**	**cgid**	**mode**	**qnum**	**qbytes**
lspid	**lrpid**	**stime**	**rtime**	**ctime**		

REFERENCES Chapter 10; *see also* **Class::Struct**, **IPC::SysV**

IPC::Open2

This module allows you to open a piped process for both reading and writing.

```
use IPC::Open2;

$pid = open2(READER, WRITER, LIST);
```

The **open2** function supports the functionality not provided in the built-in **open** function to allow you to open a command for both reading and writing. The **READER** and **WRITER** arguments should be references to existing filehandles to be used for reading from and writing to the piped command. The function does not create the filehandles for you. The **LIST** is one or more arguments defining the command to be run. For example:

```
$pid = open2(\*READ, \*WRITE, '|bc|');
```

The returned value is the process ID of the child process executed. Errors are raised by an exception matching **/^open2:/**. You should probably use this within an **eval** block.

If **READER** is a string and it begins with ">&", then the child will send output directly to that filehandle. If **WRITER** is a string that begins with "<&", then **WRITER** will be closed in the parent, and the child process will read from the filehandle directly. In both cases the filehandle is duplicated with **dup()** instead of **pipe()**.

The function assumes you know how to read from and write to the child process while preventing deadlocking. Commands that use a fixed input or output length (specified in a number of characters or lines) should prevent the problem.

REFERENCES Chapters 3, 6, 10; *see also* **IPC::Open3**

IPC::Open3

This module is similar to **IPC::Open2**, but it opens a command for reading, writing, and error handling.

```
use IPC::Open3;

$pid = open3(WRITER, READER, ERROR, LIST);
```

The **WRITER**, **READER**, and **ERROR** should be references to existing filehandles to be used for standard input, standard output, and standard error from the command and arguments supplied in **LIST**. Note that the order of the **READER** and **WRITER** arguments is different from that in **open2**. If '' is given as the argument for **ERROR**, then **ERROR** and **READER** use the same filehandle.

All other details are identical to the **open2** call, including the warning on deadlocking.

REFERENCES Chapters 3, 6, 10; *see also* **IPC::Open2**

IPC::Semaphore

This module is an object class definition for System V semaphore–based IPC.

```
use IPC::Semaphore;
```

It provides an object interface to the System V semaphore system used for interprocess communication. The **new** method creates a new **IPC::Semaphore** object:

```
$sem = new IPC::Semaphore(KEY, NSEMS, FLAGS);
```

Creates a new semaphore set associated with **KEY**, with **NSEMS** semaphores in the set. The value of **FLAGS** is a list of permissions for the new semaphore set. You will need to import suitable constants from the **IPC::SysV** module.

A new semaphore is created only under the following conditions:

- **KEY** is equal to **IPC_PRIVATE**.
- **KEY** does not already have a semaphore identifier associated with it.
- **FLAGS** contains the **IPC_CREAT** constant.

Once created, the new object supports the following methods:

```
getall
```

Returns the values contained in the semaphore set as a list.

```
getnccnt SEM
```

Returns the number of processes waiting for **SEM** to become greater than the current value.

```
getpid SEM
```

Returns the process ID of the last process that used **SEM**.

```
getval SEM
```

Returns the current value of **SEM**.

```
getzcnt SEM
```

Returns the number of processes waiting for **SEM** to become zero.

```
id
```

Returns the system identifier for the semaphore set.

```
op OPLIST
```

Performs a specific operation on the semaphore set. **OPLIST** is a multiple of a three-value list that defines the operation to perform. The first argument is the semaphore number, the second is the operator, and the last is the **FLAGS** value.

```
remove
```

Removes (destroys) the semaphore set.

```
set STAT
set(NAME => VALUE [, NAME => VALUE...])
```

Sets the **uid**, **gid**, and **mode** of the semaphore set. Accepts either an **IPC::Semaphore::stat** object, as returned by the **stat** method (see below), or a hash.

```
setall LIST
```

Sets all the values in the set to those given in **LIST**. The **LIST** must be of the correct length.

```
setval N, VALUE
```

Sets the value of the semaphore at index **N** to **VALUE**.

```
stat
```

Returns an **IP::Semaphore::stat** object that is a subclass of the **Class::Struct** class. The object consists of the following fields:

uid	**gid**	**cuid**	**cgid**	**mode**	**ctime**	**otime**	**nsems**

REFERENCES Chapter 10; *see also* **Class::Struct**, **IPC::SysV**

IPC::SysV

This module supplies the System V IPC constants used by the built-in IPC calls.

```
use SysV::IPC;
```

Note that the module does not import any symbols implicitly. You need to specify the symbols you want to use. The list of available symbols is shown below:

GETALL	**GETNCNT**	**GETPID**	**GETVAL**
GETZCNT			
IPC_ALLOC	**IPC_CREAT**	**IPC_EXCL**	**IPC_GETACL**
IPC_LOCKED	**IPC_M**	**IPC_NOERROR**	**IPC_NOWAIT**
IPC_PRIVATE	**IPC_R**	**IPC_RMID**	**IPC_SET**
IPC_SETACL	**IPC_SETLABEL**	**IPC_STAT**	**IPC_W**

IPC_WANTED			
MSG_FWAIT	**MSG_LOCKED**	**MSG_MWAIT**	**MSG_NOERROR**
MSG_QWAIT			
MSG_R	**MSG_RWAIT**	**MSG_STAT**	**MSG_W**
MSG_WWAIT			
SEM_A	**SEM_ALLOC**	**SEM_DEST**	**SEM_ERR**
SEM_ORDER	**SEM_R**	**SEM_UNDO**	
SETALL	**SETVAL**		
SHMLBA			
SHM_A	**SHM_CLEAR**	**SHM_COPY**	**SHM_DCACHE**
SHM_DEST	**SHM_ECACHE**	**SHM_FMAP**	**SHM_ICACHE**
SHM_INIT	**SHM_LOCK**	**SHM_LOCKED**	**SHM_MAP**
SHM_NOSWAP	**SHM_R**	**SHM_RDONLY**	**SHM_REMOVED**
SHM_RND	**SHM_SHARE_MMU**	**SHM_SHATTR**	**SHM_SIZE**
SHM_UNLOCK	**SHM_W**		
S_IRUSR	**S_IWUSR**	**S_IRWXU**	
S_IRGRP	**S_IWGRP**	**S_IRWXG**	
S_IROTH	**S_IWOTH**	**S_IRWXO**	

You can also optionally import the **ftok** function:

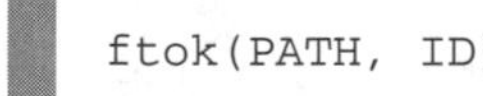

```
ftok(PATH, ID)
```

This creates a unique key suitable for use with the **msgget**, **semget**, and **shmget** functions.

REFERENCES *See* **IPC::Msg, IPC::Semaphore**

less

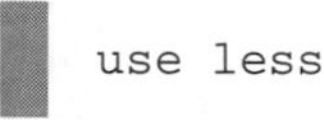

```
use less;
```

The intention is to allow you to specify reductions for certain resources such as memory or processor space.

REFERENCES Chapter 16

lib

The **lib** pragma specifies additional libraries to be added to the search path for modules imported by **use** and **require**, adding them to the **@INC** array. This is a neater solution for solving the problem of updating the list of library directories that need to be populated at compilation rather than run time.

```
use lib LIST;
```

Note that the directories are added before (using **unshift**) the standard directories to ensure that you use the local modules in preference to the standard ones. For all directories added in this way, the **lib** module also checks that a $dir/$archname/auto exists, where $archname is the name of the architecture of the current platform. If it does exist, then it is assumed to be an architecture-specific directory and is actually added to **@INC** before the original directory specification.

REFERENCES Chapter 16

locale

The **locale** pragma specifies that the current locale should be used for internal operations such as regular expression, string comparisons, and sorts. To use the current locale:

```
use locale;
```

The default operation for Perl is to ignore locales, meaning that most operations are actually in a quasi-C locale, which sorts and does comparisons based on the ASCII table. If you have switched locales on, you can switch them off with

```
no locale;
```

REFERENCES Chapter 16

Math::BigFloat

This module supports the use of floating point numbers of arbitrary length.

```
use Math::BigFloat;
$bigfloat = Math::BigFloat->new($string);
```

The **new** method creates a new floating point object based on the supplied string.

Most operators are overloaded to support the new floating point objects, provided you create the number with

```
$bigfloat = new Math::BigFloat '1.23456789012345678901234567890';
```

In addition, you can use the following methods.

```
fadd(STRING)
```

Adds the number **STRING** to the object, returning a number string.

```
fsub(STRING)
```

Subtracts the number **STRING** from the object, returning a number string.

```
fmul(STRING)
```

Multiplies the object by the number **STRING**, returning a number string.

```
fdiv(STRING [,SCALE])
```

Divides the object by the number **STRING**, to the specified **SCALE** places.

```
fneg()
```

Negates the number.

```
fabs()
```

Returns the absolute number.

```
fcmp(STRING)
```

Compares the object to the number **STRING**, returning a value less than, equal to, or greater than zero according to whether the number is less than, equal to, or greater than the given number.

```
fround(SCALE)
```

Rounds the number object to **SCALE** digits, returning the number strings.

```
ffround(SCALE)
```

Rounds the number at the **SCALE**th place within the number.

```
fnorm()
```

Normalizes the floating point, returning a number string.

```
fsqrt([SCALE])
```

Returns the square root of the number object, rounded to the specified **SCALE** if supplied.

REFERENCES *See also* **Math::BigInt**

Math::BigInt

Supports math with integer values of arbitrary sizes.

```
use Math::BigInt;
$int = Math::BigInt->new($string);
```

Basic operators are overloaded, providing you create the new integer with

```
$int = new Math::BigInt '1234567890123456789012345678901234567890';
```

The following methods are supported by the new object.

```
bneg return BINT                    negation
```

Negates the integer, and returns an integer string.

```
babs
```

Returns the absolute value as an integer string.

```
bcmp(STRING)
```

Compares the object with the supplied integer **STRING**, returning a value smaller, equal to, or greater than zero depending on the relationship between the object and the supplied **STRING**.

```
badd(STRING)
```

Adds **STRING** to the object.

```
bsub(STRING)
```

Subtracts **STRING** from the object.

```
bmul(STRING)
```

Multiplies the object by **STRING**.

```
bdiv(STRING)
```

Divides the object by **STRING**, returning the quotient and remainder as strings.

```
bmod(STRING)
```

Returns the modulus of the object and **STRING**.

```
bgcd(STRING)
```

Returns the largest common divisor.

```
bnorm
```

Normalizes the object.

REFERENCES *See also* **Math::BigFloat**

Math::Complex

This module supports the use of complex numbers in mathematical computations.

```
use Math::Complex;
```

You create a new complex number with the **make** method:

```
$z = Math::Complex->make(1,2);
```

the **cplx** function:

```
$z = cplx(1, 2);
```

or directly, using complex notation:

```
$z = 3 + 4*i;
```

In addition, you can specify them in the polar form:

```
$z = Math::Complex->emake(5, pi/3);
$x = cplxe(5, pi/3);
```

The first argument is the modulus, and the second is the angle in radians.

The module also overloads the following operations to allow complex math directly within Perl, where **z** is an imaginary variable.

```
z1 + z2 = (a + c) + i(b + d)
z1 - z2 = (a - c) + i(b - d)
z1 * z2 = (r1 * r2) * exp(i * (t1 + t2))
z1 / z2 = (r1 / r2) * exp(i * (t1 - t2))
z1 ** z2 = exp(z2 * log z1)
~z = a - bi
abs(z) = r1 = sqrt(a*a + b*b)
sqrt(z) = sqrt(r1) * exp(i * t/2)
exp(z) = exp(a) * exp(i * b)
log(z) = log(r1) + i*t
sin(z) = 1/2i (exp(i * z1) - exp(-i * z))
cos(z) = 1/2 (exp(i * z1) + exp(-i * z))
atan2(z1, z2) = atan(z1/z2)
```

You can also use the following methods:

Im(z)	**Re(z)**	**abs(z)**	**acos(z)**
acosh(z)	**acot(z)**	**acoth(z)**	**acsc(z)**
acsch(z)	**arg(z)**	**asec(z)**	**asech(z)**
asin(z)	**asinh(z)**	**atan(z)**	**atanh(z)**
cbrt(z)	**cosh(z)**	**cot(z)**	**coth(z)**
csc(z)	**csch(z)**	**log10(z)**	**logn(z,n)**
sec(z)	**sech(z)**	**sinh(z)**	**tan(z)**
tanh(z)			

Math::Trig

This module defines the full set of trigonometric functions.

```
use Math::Trig;
```

The supplied functions are as follows.

```
tan
```

Returns the tangent.

```
csc, cosec, sec, cot, cotan
```

The cofunctions of sine, cosine, and tangent. The **csc** and **cosec** are aliases for each other, as are **cot** and **cotan**.

```
asin, acos, atan
```

The arcus (inverse) of sin, cos, and tan.

```
atan2(y, x)
```

The principle value of the arctangent of **y/x**.

```
acsc, acosec, asec, acot, acotan
```

The arcus cofunctions.

```
sinh, cosh, tanh
```

The hyperbolic functions.

```
csch, cosech, sech, coth, cotanh
```

The cofunctions of the hyperbolics.

```
asinh, acosh, atanh
```

The arcus of the hyperbolics.

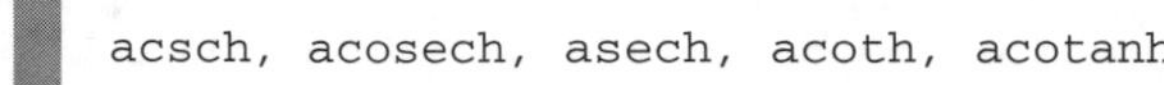

```
acsch, acosech, asech, acoth, acotanh
```

The arcus cofunctions of the hyperbolics.

The module also defines the constant **pi**.

Net::Ping

This module supports a simplified interface to the process of determining a remote host's accessibility.

```
use Net::Ping;
```

The module uses an object-oriented interface and makes use of the **alarm** function and associated signal to test for a suitable time-out value. To create a new **Ping** object:

```
Net::Ping->new([PROTO [, TIMEOUT [, BYTES]]]);
```

The **PROTO**, if specified, should be one of "tcp," "udp," or "icmp." You should use "udp" or "icmp" in preference to "tcp" due to network bandwidth. The default is "udp."

The default **TIMEOUT** should be specified in seconds and be greater than zero. The default value is five seconds. The **BYTES** parameter specifies the number of bytes to be sent to the remote host. The minimum value should be 1 if the protocol is "udp", zero otherwise. The maximum size is 1,024 bytes.

The following methods are supported by the new object.

```
ping(HOST [, TIMEOUT]);
```

Pings the remote **HOST** and waits for a response. The method waits the number of seconds defined when the object was created, or **TIMEOUT** seconds if specified. The method returns 1 if the lookup was successful, zero otherwise. The **undef** value is returned if the host cannot be resolved.

```
close();
```

Closes the network connection. The connection is automatically closed if the object goes out of scope.

The module also supports a single function, **pingecho**, for backward compatibility:

```
pingecho(HOST [, TIMEOUT])
```

This pings **HOST** using the **tcp** protocol, returning 1 if the host can be reached, zero otherwise. If the **HOST** cannot be resolved, the function returns **undef**.

REFERENCES Chapter 9

NDBM_File

```
use NDBM_File;
use Fcntl;

tie(%db, 'NDBM_File', 'db', O_RDWR|O_CREAT, 0640);
untie %db;
```

This module is an interface supporting, via **tie**, the new (standard) DBM data storage format.

REFERENCES Chapter 8; *see also* **AnyDBM_File, DB_File, GDBM_File, ODBM_File, SDBM_File**

O

This module supports the generic interface to the Perl compiler backends.

```
perl -MO=Backend[OPTIONS] foo.pl
```

Most backends support the following **OPTIONS**. These should be supplied a comma-separated list of words without white space.

- -V Puts the backend into verbose mode
- -oFILE Specifies the name of the output **FILE**
- -D Switches on backend debugging flags

REFERENCES Chapters 16, 19; *see also* **B, B::Asmdata, B::Bblock, B::Bytecode, B::C, B::CC, B::Debug, B::Deparse, B::Disassembler, B::Lint, B::Showlex, B::Stackobj, B::Terse, B::Xref**

ODBM_File

```
use ODBM_File;
use Fcntl;
tie(%db, 'ODBM_File', 'db', O_RDWR|O_CREAT, 0640);
untie %db;
```

This is an interface supporting, via **tie**, the old DBM data storage format.

REFERENCES Chapter 8; *see also* **AnyDBM_File**, **DB_File**, **GDBM_File**, **NDBM_File**, **SDBM_File**

Opcode

This module is used by the **Safe** module and **ops** pragma to disable named opcodes when compiling Perl scripts.

```
use Opcode;
```

An opcode is the smallest executable element of a Perl program, and it is the internal format of a Perl script once it has been compiled. You shouldn't normally need to use this module; the **Safe** and **ops** interfaces are more practical. However, the information provided here is useful background and reference for both modules.

The module works by creating an opcode mask using the supported functions and defined opcode names and sets. Once the opcode mask has been created, you can execute your program. The execution will croak if an attempt is made to use an opcode defined in the current mask. Note that the created opcode mask only affects the *next* compilation, that is, one executed by **eval**. It does not affect the current script.

Functions

Most functions accept a number of arguments, and these are defined as **OPNAME**, which is the individual name of an opcode, **OPTAG**, for a group of opcodes, or an **OPSET**, which is a binary string that holds a set or zero or more operators. Functions are provided for building **OPSET** strings. Both **OPNAME** and **OPTAG** can be negated by prefixing the name or set with an exclamation mark. **OPTAG** names start with a colon.

```
opcodes
```

In a scalar context, returns the number of opcodes in the current Perl binary. In a list context, returns a list of all the opcodes This is not yet implemented, so use

```
@names = opset_to_opts(full_opset);
```

to get the full list.

```
opset(OPNAME, ...)
```

Returns an **OPSET** containing the listed operators.

```
opset_to_ops(OPSET)
```

Returns a list of operator names corresponding to those operators in the **OPSET**.

```
opset_to_hex(OPSET)
```

Returns a string representation of an **OPSET**.

```
full_opset
```

Returns an **OPSET** that includes all operators.

```
empty_opset
```

Returns an **OPSET** that contains no operators.

```
invert_opset(OPSET)
```

Returns an **OPSET** that is the inverse set of the one supplied.

```
verify_opset(OPSET, ...)
```

Returns true if **OPSET** is valid; returns false otherwise. If you supply a second argument and it is true, the function calls **croak** if the **OPSET** is invalid.

```
define_optag(OPTAG, OPSET)
```

Creates **OPTAG** as a symbolic name for **OPSET**.

```
opmask_add(OPSET)
```

Adds **OPSET** to the current opcode mask. You cannot unmask opcodes once added.

```
opmask
```

Returns the **OPSET** corresponding to the current opcode mask.

```
opdesc(OPNAME, ...)
```

Returns a list of descriptions for the supplied **OPNAME**s.

```
opdump(PAT)
```

Prints to **STDOUT** a list of opcode names and corresponding descriptions. If **PAT** is supplied, only lines that match the pattern will be listed.

Opcode Sets

A number of predefined **OPSET** values are supplied as standard. They are logically divided into both function and security-conscious sets.

:base_core

aassign	**abs**	**add**	**aelem**
aelemfast	**and**	**andassign**	**anoncode**
aslice	**av2arylen**	**bit_and**	**bit_or**
bit_xor	**chomp**	**chop**	**chr**
complement	**cond_expr**	**const**	**defined**
delete	**die**	**divide**	**each**
enter	**entersub**	**eq**	**exists**
flip	**flop**	**ge**	**gt**
helem	**hex**	**hslice**	**i_add**
i_divide	**i_eq**	**i_ge**	**i_gt**
i_le	**i_lt**	**i_modulo**	**i_multiply**
i_ncmp	**i_ne**	**i_negate**	**i_postdec**
i_postinc	**i_predec**	**i_preinc**	**i_subtract**
index	**int**	**keys**	**lc**
lcfirst	**le**	**leave**	**leaveeval**
leavesub	**left_shift**	**length**	**lineseq**
list	**lslice**	**lt**	**match**
method	**modulo**	**multiply**	**ncmp**
ne	**negate**	**nextstate**	**not**
null	**oct**	**or**	**orassign**
ord	**pop**	**pos**	**postdec**
postinc	**pow**	**predec**	**preinc**
prototype	**push**	**pushmark**	**qr**
quotemeta	**return**	**reverse**	**right_shift**
rindex	**rv2av**	**rv2cv**	**rv2hv**
rv2sv	**sassign**	**scalar**	**schomp**
schop	**scmp**	**scope**	**seq**

sge sgt shift sle
slt sne splice split
stringify stub study substr
subtract trans uc ucfirst
undef unshift unstack values
vec wantarray warn xor

:base_mem

concat repeat join range
anonlist anonhash

:base_loop

enteriter enterloop goto grepstart
grepwhile iter last leaveloop
mapstart mapwhile next redo

:base_io

enterwrite eof formline getc
leavewrite print rcatline read
readdir readline recv rewinddir
seek seekdir send sysread
sysseek syswrite tell telldir

:base_orig

bless crypt dbmclose dbmopen
entertry gelem getpgrp getppid
getpriority gmtime gv gvsv
leavetry localtime padany padav
padhv padsv pipe_op prtf
pushre ref refgen regcmaybe
regcomp regcreset rv2gv select
setpgrp setpriority sockpair sprintf
srefgen sselect subst substcont
tie untie

:base_math

atan2	cos	exp	log
rand	sin	sqrt	srand

:base_thread

lock	threadsv

:default

This set is made up of the following other sets.

:base_core	:base_mem	:base_loop	:base_io
:base_orig	:base_thread		

:filesys_read

fileno	ftatime	ftbinary	ftblk
ftchr	ftctime	ftdir	fteexec
fteowned	fteread	ftewrite	ftfile
ftis	ftlink	ftmtime	ftpipe
ftrexec	ftrowned	ftrread	ftrwrite
ftsgid	ftsize	ftsock	ftsuid
ftsvtx	fttext	fttty	ftzero
lstat	readlink	stat	

:sys_db

egrent	ehostent	enetent	eprotoent
epwent	eservent	getlogin	ggrent
ggrgid	ggrnam	ghbyaddr	ghbyname
ghostent	gnbyaddr	gnbyname	gnetent
gpbyname	gpbynumber	gprotoent	gpwent
gpwnam	gpwuid	gsbyname	gsbyport
gservent	sgrent	shostent	snetent
sprotoent	spwent	sservent	

:browser

This collection of opcodes is more practical than the **:default** set.

:default	:filesys_read	:sys_db

:filesys_open

binmode	close	closedir	open
open_dir	sysopen	umask	

:filesys_write

chmod	chown	fcntl	link
mkdir	rename	rmdir	symlink
truncate	unlink	utime	

:subprocess

backtick	fork	glob	system
wait	waitpid		

:ownprocess

exec	exit	kill	time	tms

:others

This set holds a list of other opcodes that are not otherwise handled and don't deserve their own tags.

msgctl	msgget	msgrcv	msgsnd
semctl	semget	semop	shmctl
shmget	shmread	shmwrite	

:still_to_be_decided

accept	alarm	bind	caller
chdir	connect	dbstate	dofile
entereval	flock	getpeername	getsockname
gsockopt	ioctl	listen	pack

require **reset** **shutdown** **sleep**
socket **sort** **ssockopt** **tied**
unpack

:dangerous

These are possibly dangerous tags not mentioned elsewhere.

syscall **dump** **chroot**

ops

The **ops** pragma switches off specific opcodes during the compilation process. The synopsis is as follows:

```
perl -Mops=:default
```

which enables only reasonably safe operations. Or you can specify opcodes to be removed from those available using

```
perl -M-ops=system
```

Note that the best way to use this option is via the command line incorporation; otherwise you open yourself up to abuse before the compilation process starts through the use of **BEGIN {}** statements. This pragma makes use of the **Opcode** module.

REFERENCES Chapter 16; *see also* **Opcode**

overload

The **overload** pragma enables you to install alternative functions for the core operators defined in Perl. The main syntax is

```
use overload
    '+' => \&myadd,
    '-' => \&mysubtract;
```

The arguments are specified here as a hash, and each key/value pair assigns the operator defined in the key to use the function in the value, instead of using one of the built-in opcodes. The module operates on objects and classes, so the **myadd** function will be called to execute the statement **$a + $b** operator if **$a** is a reference to an object blessed into the current package, or if **$b** is a reference to an object in the current package.

You can overload the following operators and functions:

```
+ += - -= * *= / /= % %= ** **= << <<= >> >>= x x= . .=
<  <= >  >= == != <=>
lt le gt ge eq ne cmp
& ^ | neg ! ~
++ --
atan2 cos sin exp abs log sqrt
bool "" 0+
```

The pragma also supports three special operators: **nomethod**, **fallback**, and **=**.

REFERENCES Chapter 16

Pod::Functions

Used by the internal **Pod** libraries. You shouldn't need to use this function on its own, unless you are developing your own Pod interface.

REFERENCES Chapter 12; *see also* **Pod::Html**, **Pod::Text**

Pod::Html

Supports a single function, **pod2html**, for translating POD formatted documents into HTML documents.

```
use Pod::Html;
pod2html("pod2html",
             "--podpath=lib",
             "--podroot=/usr/local/lib/perl5/5.00502/",
             "--htmlroot=/usr/local/http/docs",
             "--recurse",
             "--infile=foo.pod",
             "--outfile=/perl/foo.html");
```

For a full list of supported options see Table E-13.

REFERENCES Chapter 12; *see also* **Pod::Text**

Option	Description
--flush	Flushes the contents of the item and directory caches created during the parsing of a POD document.
--help	Prints a help message.
--htmlroot	The base directory from which you reference documents relatively. This is required if you expect to install the generated HTML files onto a web server. The default is /.
--index	Generates an index of =head1 elements at the top of the HTML file that is generated (default).
--infile	The file name to convert. You don't have to use this element; the first nonhyphenated argument is taken as a file name. If you don't specify a file by either method, it will accept input from standard input.
--libpods	A colon-separated list of pages searched when referencing =item entries. These are not the file names, just the page names, as they would appear in L<> link elements.
--netscape	Uses Netscape-specific browser directives when necessary.
--nonetscape	Prevents the use of Netscape-specific browser directives (default).
--outfile	The destination file name for the generated HTML. Uses standard output if none is specified.
--podpath	A colon-separated list of directories containing pod files and libraries.
--podroot	The base directory prepended to each entry in the **podpath** command line argument. The default is ".", the current directory.
--noindex	Don't generate an index at the top of the HTML file that is generated.
--norecurse	Don't recurse into the subdirectories specified in the **podpath** option.
--recurse	Recurse into the subdirectories specified in the **podpath** option (this is the default behavior).
--title	The contents of the <**TITLE**> tag in the created HTML document.
--verbose	Produces status and progress messages during production.

Table E-13. *Options for Translating POD to HTML*

Pod::Text

Supports the **pod2text** script for translating documents from POD format to normal text.

```
use Pod::Text;
pod2text(LIST);
```

If **LIST** is only one argument, it is taken as the name of a file to translate. The translated output is automatically sent to **STDOUT**. If a second argument is specified, it is taken as a reference to a filehandle to which the output should be sent.

You can optionally insert two arguments before the input file. The **–a** option instructs the function to use an alternative format that does not make assumptions about the abilities of the destination output stream. Without this option, termcap may be used to format the document (you can force this by setting **$Pod::Text::termcap** to a value of 1), or if termcap is not available, backspaces will be used to simulate boldfaced and underlined text.

The **–width** argument should be the width of the output device, where **width** is the number of characters to use (the default value is 72 characters), or the value of your terminal if this can be determined with termcap.

REFERENCES Chapter 12; *see also* **Pod::Html**

POSIX

```
use POSIX;
```

The **POSIX** module provides an interface to the POSIX standard—a set of standards designed to provide a common set of features across operating systems, primarily Unix. The **POSIX** module also supports many of the constants and static definitions required when using **fcntl**, **ioctl**, and other I/O-related functions.

The full range of the POSIX functions has been the subject of many books. The best of these is *The POSIX Programmers Guide* by Donald Lewine (O'Reilly & Associates, Sebastopol, CA, 1991).

Where possible, the interface to the underlying POSIX library is made as Perl compatible as possible. This means that some of the interface is handled by functions and some is handled by objects and classes. As a general rule, when a structure would normally be returned by a function, the Perl equivalent returns a list.

The list of functions supported by the module is shown in Table E-14. Note that some functions are C specific and therefore not supported within the interface.

Constant	Description
_exit	Exits the current process.
abort	Aborts the current script, sending the **ABRT** signal to the Perl interpreter.
abs	Identical to the Perl function; returns the absolute value.
access	Returns true if the file can be accessed to the specified level.
acos	Returns the arc cosine of a number.

Table E-14. *Functions in the **POSIX** Module*

APPENDIXES

Constant	Description
alarm	Identical to the Perl **alarm** function.
asctime	Converts a time structure to its string equivalent.
asin	Returns the arcsine of a number.
assert	Currently unimplemented. Aborts the current program if the assertion fails.
atan	Returns the arctan of a number.
atan2	Identical to the Perl function.
atexit	Not supported. Use an **END{}** block instead.
atof	C specific.
atoi	C specific.
atol	C specific.
bsearch	Not supported. The functionality can normally be supported by using a hash.
calloc	C specific.
ceil	Identical to the C function; returns the smallest integer value greater than or equal to the supplied value.
cfgetispeed	Method for obtaining the input baud rate. See the section on the **POSIX::Termios** import set.
cfgetospeed	Method for obtaining the output baud rate. See the section on the **POSIX::Termios** import set.
cfsetispeed	Method for setting the input baud rate. See the section on the **POSIX::Termios** import set.
cfsetospeed	Method for setting the output baud rate. See the section on the **POSIX::Termios** import set.
chdir	Identical to the Perl function.
chmod	Identical to the Perl function.
chown	Identical to the Perl function.
clearerr	Not supported. Use the **FileHandle::clearerr** function.
clock	Returns an approximation of the amount of CPU time used by the program.
close	Closes the file descriptor created by the **POSIX::open** function.
closedir	Identical to the Perl function.
cos	Returns the cosine of a value.
cosh	Returns the hyperbolic cosine of a value.

Table E-14. *Functions in the **POSIX** Module* (continued)

Constant	Description
creat	Creates a new file, returning the file descriptor.
ctermid	Returns the pathname to the device for controlling terminal for the current program.
ctime	Returns a formatted string for the supplied time. Similar to the scalar value returned by **localtime**.
cuserid	Returns the current user name.
difftime	Returns the difference between two times.
div	C specific.
dup	Duplicates an open file descriptor.
dup2	Duplicates an open file descriptor.
errno	Returns the value of **errno**.
execl	C specific. Use the built-in **exec** function instead.
execle	C specific. Use the built-in **exec** function instead.
execlp	C specific. Use the built-in **exec** function instead.
execv	C specific. Use the built-in **exec** function instead.
execve	C specific. Use the built-in **exec** function instead.
execvp	C specific. Use the built-in **exec** function instead.
exit	Identical to the Perl function.
exp	Identical to the Perl function.
fabs	Identical to the built-in **abs** function.
fclose	Use the **FileHandle::close** method instead.
fcntl	Identical to the Perl function.
fdopen	Use the **FileHandle::new_from_fd** method instead.
feof	Use the **FileHandle::eof** method instead.
ferror	Use the **FileHandle::error** method instead.
fflush	Use the **FileHandle::flush** method instead.
fgetc	Use the **FileHandle::getc** method instead.
fgetpos	Use the **FileHandle::getpos** method instead.
fgets	Use the **FileHandle::gets** method instead.
fileno	Use the **FileHandle::fileno** method instead.
floor	Returns the largest integer not greater than the number supplied.
fmod	Returns the floating point remainder after dividing two numbers using integer math.

Table E-14. *Functions in the **POSIX** Module* (continued)

Constant	Description
fopen	Use the **FileHandle::open** method instead.
fork	Identical to the Perl function.
fpathconf	Returns the configural limit for a file or directory using the specified file descriptor.
fprintf	C specific. Use the built-in **printf** function instead.
fputc	C specific. Use the built-in **print** function instead.
fputs	C specific. Use the built-in **print** function instead.
fread	C specific. Use the built-in **read** function instead.
free	C specific.
freopen	C specific. Use the built-in **open** function instead.
frexp	Returns the mantissa and exponent of a floating point number.
fscanf	C specific. Use **<>** and regular expression instead.
fseek	Use the **FileHandle::seek** method instead.
fsetpos	Use the **FileHandle::setpos** method instead.
fstat	Gets the file status information for a given file descriptor.
ftell	Use **FileHandle::tell** method instead.
fwrite	C specific. Use the built-in **print** function instead.
getc	Identical to the Perl function.
getchar	Returns one character read from **STDIN**.
getcwd	Returns the path to the current working directory.
getegid	Returns the effect group ID for the current process. Use **$)**.
getenv	Returns the value of the specified environment variable. Use **%ENV**.
geteuid	Identical to the Perl function.
getgid	Returns the current process's real group ID. Use **$(**.
getgrgid	Identical to the Perl function.
getgrnam	Identical to the Perl function.
getgroups	Identical to the Perl function.
getlogin	Identical to the Perl function.
getpgrp	Identical to the Perl function.
getpid	Gets the current process ID. Use the **$$** value.
getppid	Identical to the Perl function.
getpwnam	Identical to the Perl function.
getpwuid	Identical to the Perl function.

Table E-14. *Functions in the **POSIX** Module* (continued)

Constant	Description
gets	Returns a line from **STDIN**.
getuid	Gets the current user ID. Use the value of $<.
gmtime	Identical to the Perl function.
isalnum	Returns true if the string is composed only of letters (irrespective of case) or numbers.
isalpha	Returns true if the string is composed only of letters (irrespective of case).
isatty	Returns true if the specified filehandle is connected to a TTY device.
iscntrl	Returns true if the string is composed only of control characters.
isdigit	Returns true if the string is composed only of digits.
isgraph	Returns true if the string is composed only of printable characters, except space.
islower	Returns true if the string is composed only of lowercase characters.
isprint	Returns true if the string is composed only of printable characters, including space.
ispunct	Returns true if the string is composed only of punctuation characters.
isspace	Returns true if the string is composed only of white space characters. Within the default C and POSIX locales are space, form feed, newline, carriage return, horizontal tab, and vertical tab.
isupper	Returns true if the string is composed only of uppercase characters.
isxdigit	Returns true if the string is composed only of hexadecimal characters, "a-z", "A-Z", "0-9".
kill	Identical to the Perl function.
labs	C specific. Use the built-in **abs** function.
ldexp	Multiplies a floating point number by a power of 2 (**ldexp(num,pow)**).
ldiv	C specific. Use **int($a/$b)** instead.
localeconv	Gets numeric formatting information. See the **locale_h** import set below.
localtime	Identical to the Perl function.
log	Identical to the Perl function.
log10	Computes the logarithmic value in base 10.
longjmp	C specific. Use **die** instead.
lseek	Moves the read/write pointer within an open file descriptor.
malloc	C specific.

Table E-14. *Functions in the* ***POSIX*** *Module* (continued)

Constant	Description
mblen	Returns the length of a multibyte string.
mbstowcs	Converts a multibyte string to a wide character string.
mbtowc	Converts a multibyte character to a wide character.
memchr	C specific. Use the built-in **index** function.
memcmp	C specific. Use **eq** instead.
memcpy	C specific. Use = instead.
memmove	C specific. Use = instead.
memset	C specific. Use **x** instead.
mkdir	Identical to the Perl function.
mkfifo	Creates a fifo (named pipe).
mktime	Converts date and time information to a calendar time.
modf	Returns the integral and fractional parts of a floating point number.
nice	Changes the execution priority of a process.
offsetof	C specific.
open	Opens a file, returning a file descriptor. Accepts three arguments: the file name, mode, and permissions (in octal).
opendir	Identical to the Perl function.
pathconf	Gets configuration values for a specified file or directory.
pause	Suspends the execution of a process until it receives a signal with an associated handler.
perror	Prints the error message associated with the error in **errno**.
pipe	Creates an interprocess communication channel returning file descriptors for use with **open** and related functions.
pow	Raises a number to the specified power (**pow(num,power)**.
printf	Identical to the Perl function.
putc	C specific. Use the built-in **print** instead.
putchar	C specific. Use the built-in **print** instead.
puts	C specific. Use the built-in **print** instead.
qsort	C specific. Use the built-in **sort** instead.
raise	Sends the specified signal to the current process.
rand	Not supported. Use the built-in **rand** function.
readdir	Identical to the Perl version.
realloc	C specific.

Table E-14. *Functions in the **POSIX** Module* (continued)

Constant	Description
remove	Identical to the Perl **unlink** function.
rewind	Seeks to the beginning of the specified filehandle.
rewinddir	Identical to the Perl version.
scanf	C specific. Use the **<>** operator and regular expressions.
setbuf	Sets how a filehandle will be buffered.
setgid	Sets the group ID for the process. Equivalent to setting the value of **$(**.
setjmp	C specific. Use **eval** instead.
setlocale	Sets the current locale. See the **local_h** import set section below.
setpgid	Sets the process group ID.
setsid	Creates a new session and sets the process group ID of the current process.
setuid	Sets the user ID. Equivalent to setting the value of **$<**.
setvbuf	Sets and defines how the buffer for a filehandle works.
sigaction	Defines a signal handler. See the **POSIX::SigAction** section below.
siglongjmp	C specific. Use the **die** function instead.
signal	C specific. Use the **%SIG** hash instead.
sigpending	Returns information about signals that are blocked and pending. See the **POSIX::SigSet** section below.
sigprocmask	Changes or examines the current process's signal mask. See the **POSIX::SigSet** section below.
sigsetjmp	C specific. Use **eval** instead.
sigsuspend	Installs a signal mask and suspends the process until a signal arrives. See the **POSIX::SigSet** import set section below.
sin	Returns the sine for a given value.
sinh	Returns the hyperbolic sine for a given value.
sleep	Identical to the Perl function.
sprintf	Identical to the Perl function.
sqrt	Identical to the Perl function.
srand	Identical to the Perl function.
sscanf	C specific. Use regular expressions.
stat	Identical to the Perl function.
strcat	C specific. Use **.=** instead.
strchr	C specific. Use the built-in **index** function instead.

Table E-14. *Functions in the **POSIX** Module* (continued)

Constant	Description
strcmp	C specific. Use **eq** instead.
strcoll	Compares two strings using the current locale.
strcpy	C specific. Use = instead.
strcspn	C specific. Use regular expressions instead.
strerror	Returns the error string for a specific error number.
strftime	Returns a formatted string based on the supplied date and time information.
strlen	C specific. Use the built-in **length** function instead.
strncat	C specific. Use **.=** or **substr** instead.
strncmp	C specific. Use **eq** or **substr** instead.
strncpy	C specific. Use **eq** or **substr** instead.
strpbrk	C specific.
strrchr	C specific. Use **eq** or **substr** instead.
strspn	C specific.
strstr	Identical to the Perl **index** function.
strtod	C specific.
strtok	C specific.
strtol	C specific.
strtoul	C specific.
strxfrm	Transforms the supplied string.
sysconf	Retrieves values from the system configuration tables.
tan	Returns the tangent of a value.
tanh	Returns the hyperbolic tangent of a value.
tcdrain	See the section on the **POSIX::Termios**.
tcflow	See the section on the **POSIX::Termios**.
tcflush	See the section on the **POSIX::Termios**.
tcgetattr	See the section on the **POSIX::Termios**.
tcgetpgrp	See the section on the **POSIX::Termios**.
tcsendbreak	See the section on the **POSIX::Termios**.
tcsetattr	See the section on the **POSIX::Termios**.
tcsetpgrp	See the section on the **POSIX::Termios**.
time	Identical to the Perl function.

Table E-14. *Functions in the* ***POSIX*** *Module* (continued)

Constant	Description
times	Similar to the Perl function, but returns five values (realtime, user, system, childuser, and childsystem) counted in clock ticks rather than seconds.
tmpfile	Use the **FileHandle::new_tmpfile** method instead.
tmpnam	Returns the name for a temporary file.
tolower	Identical to the Perl **lc** function.
toupper	Identical to the Perl **uc** function.
ttyname	Returns the path to the terminal associated with the supplied filehandle.
tzname	Returns the offset and daylight savings time settings for the current time zone.
tzset	Sets the current time zone using the **$ENV{TZ}** variable.
umask	Identical to the Perl function.
uname	Returns the system name, node name, release, version, and machine for the current operating system.
ungetc	Use the **FileHandle::ungetc** method instead.
unlink	Identical to the Perl function.
utime	Identical to the Perl function.
vfprintf	C specific.
vprintf	C specific.
vsprintf	C specific.
wait	Identical to the Perl function.
waitpid	Identical to the Perl function.
wcstombs	Converts a wide character string to a multibyte character string.
wctomb	Converts a wide character to a multibyte character.
write	Writes to a file descriptor opened with **POSIX::open**.

Table E-14. *Functions in the **POSIX** Module* (continued)

Supported Classes

The **POSIX** module provides three new classes: **POSIX::SigSet**, **POSIX::SigAction**, and **POSIX::Termios**.

POSIX::SigSet

This provides an interface to the **sigset** function for creating signal sets. For installing handlers for these sets use the **SigAction** class. See the **signal_h** import set for information about the available signal constants to use with the methods.

```
$sigset = POSIX::SigSet->new;
```

Creates a new **SigSet** object. Additional methods are described here.

```
addset SIGNAL
```

Adds a **SIGNAL** to an existing set.

```
delset SIGNAL
```

Deletes a **SIGNAL** from a set.

```
emptyset
```

Empties a signal set.

```
fillset
```

Populates a signal set with all the available signals.

```
ismember SIGNAL
```

Returns true if the signal set contains the specified signal.

POSIX::SigAction

This installs a signal handler against a specific **SigSet** object.

```
$sigaction = POSIX::SigAction->new('main::handler', $sigset, $flags);
```

The first parameter must be the fully qualified name of the signal handler routine. The second argument is the previously created **SigSet** object. The value of flags is a list of signal actions.

POSIX::Termios

This supports an interface to the termios interface driving system.

```
$termios = POSIX::Termios->new;
```

Creates a new **Termios** object. The following additional methods are supported.

```
getattr FD
```

Gets the attributes for the file descriptor specified. Uses zero (**STDIN**) by default.

```
getcc EXPR
```

Gets the value from the **c_cc** field. The information is an array, so you must use an index value.

```
getcflag
```

Returns the value of the **c_cflag**.

```
getiflag
```

Returns the value of the **c_iflag**.

```
getispeed
```

Returns the input baud rate.

```
getlflag
```

Returns the value of the **c_lflag**.

```
getoflag
```

Returns the value of the **c_oflag**.

```
getospeed
```

Returns the output baud rate.

```
setattr FD, EXPR
```

Sets the attributes for the file descriptor **FD**.

```
setcc EXPR, INDEX
```

Sets the value of the **c_cc** field. The information is an array, so you must specify an index value.

```
getcflag EXPR
```

Sets the value of the **c_cflag**.

```
getiflag EXPR
```

Sets the value of the **c_iflag**.

```
getispeed EXPR
```

Sets the input baud rate.

```
getlflag EXPR
```

Sets the value of the **c_lflag**.

```
getoflag EXPR
```

Sets the value of the **c_oflag**.

```
getospeed EXPR
```

Sets the output baud rate.

See the **termios_h** import set for the lists of supported constants.

Symbol Sets

For convenience and compatibility, the functions and constants defined within the **POSIX** module are also grouped into symbol sets to import the required elements. The sets are grouped by the name of the header file that would be required if you were programming directly in C. To use, specify the header name, substituting underscores for periods, and prefixing the name with a colon. For example, to include the elements of the fcntl.h file:

```
use POSIX qw/:fcntl_h/;
```

For reference, the sets and functions they import, along with the constant they define, are listed below.

assert_h

This symbol set imports the following function: **assert**.

The following constant function is also imported: **NDEBUG**.

ctype_h

This symbol set imports the following functions:

isalnum	**Isalpha**	**iscntrl**	**isdigit**
isgraph	**Islower**	**isprint**	**ispunct**
isspace	**Isupper**	**isxdigit**	**tolower**
toupper			

dirent_h

There are no imported elements for this symbol set, since the functions of dirent.h are supported as built-in functions within Perl.

errno_h

The constants defined within errno.h are those that specify the numerical error number normally contained within **$!**. The list of imported constants is as follows:

E2BIG	EACCES	EADDRINUSE
EADDRNOTAVAIL	EAFNOSUPPORT	EAGAIN
EALREADY	EBADF	EBUSY
ECHILD	ECONNABORTED	ECONNREFUSED
ECONNRESET	EDEADLK	EDESTADDRREQ
EDOM	EDQUOT	EEXIST
EFAULT	EFBIG	EHOSTDOWN
EHOSTUNREACH	EINPROGRESS	EINTR
EINVAL	EIO	EISCONN
EISDIR	ELOOP	EMFILE
EMLINK	EMSGSIZE	ENAMETOOLONG
ENETDOWN	ENETRESET	ENETUNREACH

ENFILE	ENOBUFS	ENODEV
ENOENT	ENOEXEC	ENOLCK
ENOMEM	ENOPROTOOPT	ENOSPC
ENOSYS	ENOTBLK	ENOTCONN
ENOTDIR	ENOTEMPTY	ENOTSOCK
ENOTTY	ENXIO	EOPNOTSUPP
EPERM	EPFNOSUPPORT	EPIPE
EPROCLIM	EPROTONOSUPPORT	EPROTOTYPE
ERANGE	EREMOTE	ERESTART
EROFS	ESHUTDOWN	ESOCKTNOSUPPORT
ESPIPE	ESRCH	ESTALE
ETIMEDOUT	ETOOMANYREFS	ETXTBSY
EUSERS	EWOULDBLOCK	EXDEV

fcntl_h

This symbol set imports the following function: **creat**.

This symbol set imports the following constants:

FD_CLOEXEC	F_DUPFD	F_GETFD	F_GETFL
F_GETLK	F_RDLCK	F_SETFD	F_SETFL
F_SETLK	F_SETLKW	F_UNLCK	F_WRLCK
O_ACCMODE	O_APPEND	O_CREAT	O_EXCL
O_NOCTTY	O_NONBLOCK	O_RDONLY	O_RDWR
O_TRUNC	O_WRONLY	SEEK_CUR	SEEK_END
SEEK_SET	S_IRGRP	S_IROTH	S_IRUSR
S_IRWXG	S_IRWXO	S_IRWXU	S_ISBLK
S_ISCHR	S_ISDIR	S_ISFIFO	S_ISGID
S_ISREG	S_ISUID	S_IWGRP	S_IWOTH
S_IWUSR			

float_h

This symbol set imports the following constants:

DBL_DIG	DBL_EPSILON	DBL_MANT_DIG
DBL_MAX	DBL_MAX_10_EXP	DBL_MAX_EXP
DBL_MIN	DBL_MIN_10_EXP	DBL_MIN_EXP
FLT_DIG	FLT_EPSILON	FLT_MANT_DIG

FLT_MAX	FLT_MAX_10_EXP	FLT_MAX_EXP
FLT_MIN	FLT_MIN_10_EXP	FLT_MIN_EXP
FLT_RADIX	FLT_ROUNDS	LDBL_DIG
LDBL_EPSILON	LDBL_MANT_DIG	LDBL_MAX
LDBL_MAX_10_EXP	LDBL_MAX_EXP	LDBL_MIN
LDBL_MIN_10_EXP	LDBL_MIN_EXP	

limits_h

This symbol set imports the following constants:

ARG_MAX	CHAR_BIT	CHAR_MAX
CHAR_MIN	CHILD_MAX	INT_MAX
INT_MIN	LINK_MAX	LONG_MAX
LONG_MIN	MAX_CANON	MAX_INPUT
MB_LEN_MAX	NAME_MAX	NGROUPS_MAX
OPEN_MAX	PATH_MAX	PIPE_BUF
SCHAR_MAX	SCHAR_MIN	SHRT_MAX
SHRT_MIN	SSIZE_MAX	STREAM_MAX
TZNAME_MAX	UCHAR_MAX	UINT_MAX
ULONG_MAX	USHRT_MAX	_POSIX_ARG_MAX
_POSIX_CHILD_MAX	_POSIX_LINK_MAX	_POSIX_MAX_CANON
_POSIX_MAX_INPUT	_POSIX_NAME_MAX	_POSIX_NGROUPS_MAX
_POSIX_OPEN_MAX	_POSIX_PATH_MAX	_POSIX_PIPE_BUF
_POSIX_SSIZE_MAX	_POSIX_STREAM_MAX	_POSIX_TZNAME_MAX

locale_h

This symbol set imports the following functions:

localeconv **setlocale**

The **localeconv** function returns a reference to a hash with the following, self-explanatory, elements:

currency_symbol	decimal_point	frac_digits
grouping	int_curr_symbol	int_frac_digits
mon_decimal_point	mon_grouping	mon_thousands_sep
n_cs_precedes	n_sep_by_space	n_sign_posn
negative_sign	p_cs_precedes	p_sep_by_space
p_sign_posn	positive_sign	thousands_sep

This symbol set imports the following constants:

LC_ALL	LC_COLLATE	LC_CTYPE
LC_MONETARY	LC_NUMERIC	LC_TIME
NULL		

math_h

This symbol set imports the following functions:

acos	**asin**	**atan**	**ceil**
cosh	**fabs**	**floor**	**fmod**
frexp	**ldexp**	**log10**	**modf**
pow	**sinh**	**tan**	**tanh**

This symbol set imports the following constant: **HUGE_VAL**.

setjmp_h

This symbol set imports the following functions:

longjmp	**setjmp**	**siglongjmp**	**sigsetjmp**

signal_h

This symbol set imports the following functions:

raise	**sigaction**	**signal**	**sigpending**
sigprocmask	**sigsuspend**		

This symbol set imports the following constants:

SA_NOCLDSTOP	SA_NOCLDWAIT	SA_NODEFER
SA_ONSTACK	SA_RESETHAND	SA_RESTART
SA_SIGINFO	SIGABRT	SIGALRM
SIGCHLD	SIGCONT	SIGFPE
SIGHUP	SIGILL	SIGINT
SIGKILL	SIGPIPE	SIGQUIT
SIGSEGV	SIGSTOP	SIGTERM
SIGTSTP	SIGTTIN	SIGTTOU
SIGUSR1	SIGUSR2	SIG_BLOCK
SIG_DFL	SIG_ERR	SIG_IGN
SIG_SETMASK	SIG_UNBLOCK	

stddef_h

This symbol set imports the following function: **offsetof**.

This symbol set imports the following constant: **NULL**.

stdio_h

This symbol set imports the following functions:

clearerr	**fclose**	**fdopen**	**feof**	**ferror**
fflush	**fgetc**	**fgetpos**	**fgets**	**fopen**
fprintf	**fputc**	**fputs**	**fread**	**freopen**
fscanf	**fseek**	**fsetpos**	**ftell**	**fwrite**
getchar	**gets**	**perror**	**putc**	**putchar**
puts	**remove**	**rewind**	**scanf**	**setbuf**
setvbuf	**sscanf**	**stderr**	**stdin**	**stdout**
tmpfile	**tmpnam**	**ungetc**	**vfprintf**	**vprintf**
vsprintf				

This symbol set imports the following constants:

BUFSIZ	EOF	FILENAME_MAX	L_ctermid
L_cuserid	L_tmpname	NULL	SEEK_CUR
SEEK_END	SEEK_SET	STREAM_MAX	TMP_MAX

stdlib_h

This symbol set imports the following functions:

abort	**atexit**	**atof**	**atoi**	**atol**
bsearch	**calloc**	**div**	**free**	**getenv**
labs	**ldiv**	**malloc**	**mblen**	**mbstowcs**
mbtowc	**qsort**	**realloc**	**strtod**	**strtol**
strtoul	**wcstombs**	**wctomb**		

This symbol set imports the following constants:

EXIT_FAILURE	EXIT_SUCCESS	MB_CUR_MAX	NULL
RAND_MAX			

string_h

This symbol set imports the following functions:

memchr	**memcmp**	**memcpy**	**memmove**	**memset**
strcat	**strchr**	**strcmp**	**strcoll**	**strcpy**

strcspn	**strerror**	**strlen**	**strncat**	**strncmp**
strncpy	**strpbrk**	**strrchr**	**strspn**	**strstr**
strtok	**strxfrm**			

This symbol set imports the following constant: **NULL**.

sys_stat_h

This symbol set imports the following functions:

fstat **mkfifo**

This symbol set imports the following constants:

S_IRGRP	S_IROTH	S_IRUSR	S_IRWXG	S_IRWXO
S_IRWXU	S_ISBLK	S_ISCHR	S_ISDIR	S_ISFIFO
S_ISGID	S_ISREG	S_ISUID	S_IWGRP	S_IWOTH
S_IWUSR	S_IXGRP	S_IXOTH	S_IXUSR	

sys_utsname_h

This symbol set imports the following function: **uname**.

sys_wait_h

This symbol set imports the following constants:

WEXITSTATUS	WIFEXITED	WIFSIGNALED	WIFSTOPPED
WNOHANG	WSTOPSIG	WTERMSIG	WUNTRACED

termios_h

This symbol set imports the following functions:

cfgetispeed	**cfgetospeed**	**cfsetispeed**	**cfsetospeed**
tcdrain	**tcflow**	**tcflush**	**tcgetattr**
tcsendbreak	**tcsetattr**		

This symbol set imports the following constants:

B0	B110	B1200	B134
B150	B1800	B19200	B200
B2400	B300	B38400	B4800
B50	B600	B75	B9600

BRKINT	CLOCAL	CREAD	CS5
CS6	CS7	CS8	CSIZE
CSTOPB	ECHO	ECHOE	ECHOK
ECHONL	HUPCL	ICANON	ICRNL
IEXTEN	IGNBRK	IGNCR	IGNPAR
INLCR	INPCK	ISIG	ISTRIP
IXOFF	IXON	NCCS	NOFLSH
OPOST	PARENB	PARMRK	PARODD
TCIFLUSH	TCIOFF	TCIOFLUSH	TCION
TCOFLUSH	TCOOFF	TCOON	TCSADRAIN
TCSAFLUSH	TCSANOW	TOSTOP	VEOF
VEOL	VERASE	VINTR	VKILL
VMIN	VQUIT	VSTART	VSTOP
VSUSP	VTIME		

time_h

This symbol set imports the following functions:

asctime	**clock**	**ctime**	**difftime**
mktime	**strftime**	**tzset**	**tzname**

This symbol set imports the following constants:

CLK_TCK	CLOCKS_PER_SEC	NULL

unistd_h

This symbol set imports the following functions:

_exit	**access**	**ctermid**	**cuserid**
dup	**dup2**	**execl**	**execle**
execlp	**execv**	**execve**	**execvp**
fpathconf	**getcwd**	**getegid**	**geteuid**
getgid	**getgroups**	**getpid**	**getuid**
isatty	**lseek**	**pathconf**	**pause**
setgid	**setpgid**	**setsid**	**setuid**
sysconf	**tcgetpgrp**	**tcsetpgrp**	**ttyname**

This symbol set imports the following constants:

F_OK	NULL
R_OK	SEEK_CUR
SEEK_END	SEEK_SET
STDIN_FILENO	STDOUT_FILENO
STRERR_FILENO	W_OK
X_OK	_PC_CHOWN_RESTRICTED
_PC_LINK_MAX	_PC_MAX_CANON
_PC_MAX_INPUT	_PC_NAME_MAX
_PC_NO_TRUNC	_PC_PATH_MAX
_PC_PIPE_BUF	_PC_VDISABLE
_POSIX_CHOWN_RESTRICTED	_POSIX_JOB_CONTROL
_POSIX_NO_TRUNC	_POSIX_SAVED_IDS
_POSIX_VDISABLE	_POSIX_VERSION
_SC_ARG_MAX	_SC_CHILD_MAX
_SC_CLK_TCK	_SC_JOB_CONTROL
_SC_NGROUPS_MAX	_SC_OPEN_MAX
_SC_SAVED_IDS	_SC_STREAM_MAX
_SC_TZNAME_MAX	_SC_VERSION

REFERENCES Chapters 3, 4, 6, 7, 10, 11, 13, Appendix B

re

The **re** pragma alters regular expression behavior. The pragma has three options: **taint**, **debug**, and **eval**. One additional pragma is really just a modification of an earlier one, called **debugcolor**. The only difference is in the color of the output.

The **taint** option ensures that variables modified with a regular expression are tainted in situations where they would be considered clean:

```
use re 'taint';
```

That is, in situations where matches or substitutions on tainted variables would ordinarily produce an untainted result, the results are in fact marked as tainted. See Chapter 11 for more information on tainted execution.

The **debug** and **debugcolor** options force Perl to produce debugging messages during the execution of a regular expression:

```
use re 'debug';
use re 'debugcolor';
```

This is equivalent to using the **–Dr** switch during execution if the **–DDEBUGGING** option was specified during the build process. The information provided can be very large, even on a relatively small regular expression. The **debugcolor** option prints out a color version if your terminal supports it.

The **eval** option enables regular expressions to contain the **(?{...})** assertions, even if the regular expression contains variable interpolation:

```
use re 'eval';
```

Ordinarily, this is disabled because it's seen as a security risk, and the pragma is ignored if the **use re 'taint'** pragma is in effect.

REFERENCES Chapter 16

Safe

This module creates a safe compartment for executing a Perl script.

```
use Safe;

$compartment = new Safe;
```

The created compartment has the following attributes:

- A new name space. The new package has a new root name space, and code within the compartment cannot access the variables outside of this root name space. The parent script can optionally insert new variables into the name space, but the reverse is not true. Only the "underscore" variables (**$_**, **@_**, and **%_**) are shared between the parent and safe compartment.
- An operator mask. This is generated using the opcode names and tags as defined in the **Opcode** module. Executing code within the new compartment that contains a masked operator will cause the compilation of the code to fail. By default, the operator mask uses the **:default** opcode set.

To create a new compartment:

```
$compartment = new Safe;
```

An optional argument specifies the name of the new root name space. The module then supports the following methods.

```
permit(OP, ...)
```

Adds the specified opcodes or sets to the mask when compiling code in the compartment.

```
permit_only(OP, ...)
```

Exclusively sets the specified opcodes or sets in the mask when compiling code in the compartment.

```
deny(OP, ...)
```

Deletes the specified opcodes or sets from the current mask.

```
deny_only(OP, ...)
```

Denies only the listed opcodes or sets.

```
trap(OP, ...)
```

Synonymous with **deny**.

```
untrap(OP, ...)
```

Synonymous with **permit**.

```
share(NAME, ...)
```

Shares the specified variables with the compartment.

```
share_from(PACKAGE, ARRAY)
```

Shares the list of symbols defined in the array of references **ARRAY** from the specified **PACKAGE** with the compartment.

```
varglob(VARNAME)
```

Returns a glob reference for the symbol table entry of **VARNAME** with the package of the compartment.

```
reval(STRING)
```

Evaluates **STRING** within the compartment.

```
rdo(FILENAME)
```

Executes the script **FILENAME** in the compartment.

```
root(NAMESPACE)
```

Returns the name of the package that is the root of the compartment's name space.

```
mask(MASK)
```

When **MASK** is not specified, returns the entire operator mask for the compartment. If **MASK** is specified, then it sets the compartment's operator mask.

REFERENCES Chapter 11, 16, 17; *see also* **Opcode**, **ops**

SDBM_File

```
use SDBM_File;
use Fcntl;

tie(%db, 'SDBM_File', 'db', O_RDWR|O_CREAT, 0640);
untie %db;
```

This is an interface supporting access to the Perl-supplied **SDBM** database using **tie**.

REFERENCES Chapter 8; *see also* **AnyDBM_File**, **DB_File**, **GDBM_File**, **NDBM_File**, **ODBM_File**

Search::Dict

```
use Search::Dict;
look *FILEHANDLE, $key, $dict, $fold;
```

The **look** function sets the current location within the **FILEHANDLE** to the first occurrence of **$key**, or the closest match that is greater than or equal to it. This can be used, as the name suggests, to locate a word within a dictionary that lists words, one per line. If **$dict** is true, the search is conducted in strict dictionary (alphabetical) order, ignoring everything that is not a word character. The dictionary file should have been sorted with the Unix **sort** command and the **-d** option. If **$fold** is true, the case is ignored.

REFERENCES Chapter 8; *see also* **Text::Abbrev**, **Text::Soundex**

SelectSaver

This module provides an alternative to the **select** function for selecting the default output filehandle.

```
use SelectSaver;
```

You use it within a block:

```
use SelectSaver;

#STDOUT is selected
{
    my $saver = new SelectSaver(MYOUT);
    #MYOUT is selected
}
#STDOUT is selected again
```

Once the block exits, the selected filehandle returns to the value selected before the block.

REFERENCES Chapters 3, 6

SelfLoader

This module provides a system similar to **AutoLoader** except that functions are self-loaded from the script rather than from separate files.

```
package MyPackage;
use SelfLoader;
```

Like **AutoLoader**, the module delays the loading of functions until they are called. Unlike **AutoLoader**, the functions themselves are defined after the **__DATA__** token. This token signifies to Perl that the code to be compiled has ended, and the functions defined in **__DATA__** are available via the **MyPackage::DATA** filehandle.

The **__DATA__** definitions for a single package can span multiple files, but the last **__DATA__** token in a given package is the one accessible via the **MyPackage::DATA** filehandle. Reading from the **DATA** filehandle ends when it sees the **__END__** token. But it will restart if the **__END__** token is immediately followed by a **DATA** token (not to be confused with the **__DATA__** token).

The method used by the **SelfLoader** package is to read in the contents of the filehandle to identify the defined functions. When the function is first called, it uses **eval** to parse the requested subroutine. The **SelfLoader** exports an **AUTOLOAD** subroutine to be used for loading the packages from the **DATA** filehandle.

Unlike **AutoLoader**, there is a small overhead for having the definitions parsed once at compile time. Other than that, execution will seem faster because functions are only compiled when used, thus negating the need to compile unused functions. There is no advantage to defining often used functions with **SelfLoader**.

Note that lexically defined values (via **my**) are visible to functions only up to the **__DATA__** token. Functions that rely on lexicals cannot be autoloaded, either by **AutoLoader** or **SelfLoader**. Remember to use the **vars** pragma if you are also using the **strict** pragma.

REFERENCES Chapters 5, 13, 16, 17; *see also* **AutoLoader**, **Devel::SelfStubber**

Shell

This module allows you to use shell commands directly without the need to use backticks or the **system** function.

```
use Shell;
```

If you do not specify explicitly any commands, then all are assumed.

Once loaded, you can use the shell commands just like a normal Perl function:

```
use Shell;

print ps('-ef');
```

If you want to use them without parentheses, either import explicitly or declare the shell command as a function before you use it:

```
use Shell;
sub ps;
print ps -ef;
```

The actual method of supporting this operation is to use the **AUTOLOAD** system to call the supported command.

REFERENCES Chapters 10, 11

sigtrap

The **sigtrap** pragma enables simple signal handling without the complexity of the normal signal handling routines.

```
use sigtrap;
```

The pragma supports three handlers: two are supplied by the module itself (one provides a stack trace, and the other just calls **die**), and the third is one that you supply yourself. Each option supplied to the module is processed in order, so the moment a signal name is identified, the signal handler is installed.

Without any options specified, the module defaults to the **stack-trace** and **old-interface-signals** options. The individual options are listed below.

```
use sigtrap qw/stack-trace HUP INT KILL/;
```

Generates a Perl stack trace to **STDERR** when the specified signals are received by the script. Once the trace has been generated, the module calls **dump** to dump the core.

```
use sigtrap qw/die HUP INT KILL/;
```

Calls **croak**, reporting the name of the message that was caught.

```
use sigtrap 'handler' => \&my_handler, HUP, INT, KILL;
```

Installs the handler **my_handler** for the specified signals.

The pragma defines some standard signal lists. If your system does not support one of the specified signals, the signal is ignored rather than producing an error.

```
normal-signals
```

These are signals that might ordinarily be trapped by any program: **HUP**, **INT**, **PIPE**, **TERM**.

```
error-signals
```

These are the signals that indicate a serious error: **ABRT**, **BUS**, **EMT**, **FPE**, **ILL**, **QUIT**, **SEGV**, **SYS**, **TRAP**.

```
old-interface-signals
```

The list of signals that were trapped by default by the old **sigtrap** pragma. This is the list of signals that are used if you do not specify others and include **ABRT**, **BUS**, **EMT**, **FPE**, **ILL**, **PIPE**, **QUIT**, **SEGV**, **SYS**, **TERM**, **TRAP**.

```
untrapped
```

This special option selects from the following signal list or specification all the signals that are not otherwise trapped or ignored.

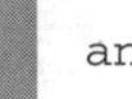

```
any
```

Applies handlers to all subsequently listed signals; this is the default.

REFERENCES Chapter 16

Socket

This module defines the core functions and utility routines for supporting socket-based communication.

```
use Socket;
```

The module defines a core set of functions, as shown in Table E-15.

REFERENCES Chapter 9; *see also* **IO::Socket**

strict

The **strict** pragma restricts those constructs and statements that would normally be considered as unsafe.

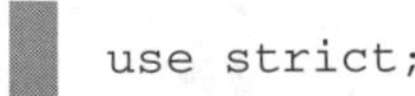

```
use strict;
```

In particular, it reduces the effects of assumptions Perl makes about what you are trying to achieve and, instead, imposes limits on the definition and use of variables, references, and bare words that would otherwise be interpreted as functions. These can be individually turned on or off using **vars**, **refs**, and **subs**.

Although it imposes these limits, the pragma generally encourages (and enforces) good programming practice. However, for casual scripts it imposes more restrictions than are really necessary. In all cases the pragmas are lexically scoped, which means you must specify **use strict** separately within all the packages, modules, and individual scripts you create.

REFERENCES Chapter 16

subs

The **subs** pragma predeclares **func** so that the function can be called without parentheses even before Perl has seen the full definition.

```
use subs qw(func);
```

Function	Description
inet_aton HOSTNAME	Returns a 4-byte packed IP address for **HOSTNAME**, or **undef** if it cannot be resolved.
inet_ntoa IP_ADDRESS	Returns a string in the form **x.x.x.x** based on the supplied 4-byte packed IP address.
INADDR_ANY	Returns a 4-byte packed string defining the wildcard address for accepting connections.
INADDR_BROADCAST	Returns a 4-byte packed string defining the broadcast address
INADDR_LOOPBACK	Returns a 4-byte packed string defining the loopback address for the current host.
INADDR_NONE	Returns a 4-byte packed string defining the invalid IP address.
sockaddr_in PORT, ADDRESS	Packs **PORT** and **ADDRESS** into a **sockaddr_in** structure.
sockaddr_in SOCKADDR_IN	Unpacks and returns the **SOCKADDR_IN** structure into port and IP address.
pack_sockaddr_in PORT, ADDRESS	Packs **PORT** and **ADDRESS** into a **sockaddr_in** structure.
unpack_sockaddr_in SOCKADDR_IN	Unpacks and returns the **SOCKADDR_IN** structure into port and IP address.
sockaddr_un PATHNAME	Packs **PATHNAME** into a **sockaddr_un** structure.
sockaddr_un SOCKADDR_UN	Unpacks **SOCKADDR_UN** structure into a pathname.
pack_sockaddr_un PATHNAME	Packs **PATHNAME** into a **sockaddr_un** structure.
unpack_sockaddr_un SOCKADDR_UN	Unpacks **SOCKADDR_UN** structure into a pathname.

Table E-15. *Functions Defined in the* ***Socket*** *Module*

This can also be used to override internal functions by predefining subroutines:

```
use subs qw(chdir);
chdir $message;
sub chdir
{
...
}
```

REFERENCES Chapter 16

Symbol

This module provides a set of functions for manipulating Perl symbols and their names.

```
use Symbol;

$glob = gensym;
print qualify($symbol, $pkg);
print qualify_to_ref($symbol, $pkg);
```

The **gensym** function returns a reference to an anonymous glob. The resulting reference is suitable for use as a file or directory handle. This is useful when you want to use a filehandle but do not want to name it directly.

The **qualify** function returns a string containing the qualified variable name for the supplied **$symbol** (which should be a string). If you supply **$pkg**, it will be used as the default package for variables not defined within a separate package in place of the normal **main::**. In all cases, the returned string contains the true qualification, such that function **foo** in package **Bar** will always resolve to **Bar::foo**. The two lines below would print the same value:

```
print qualify('foo','Bar'),"\n";
print qualify('foo','foo'),"\n";
```

References are assumed to be glob references and therefore return their true, qualified name by their very nature.

The **qualify_to_ref** function is identical to **qualify** except that it returns a glob reference rather than a string.

The optional **delete_package** function deletes all of the symbol table entries and therefore the related variables, functions, and other structures:

```
use Symbol qw/delete_package/;

delete_package('Foo');
```

REFERENCES Chapter 5

Sys::Hostname

This module provides a semireliable method of determining a host's name by trying every conceivable method until the hostname is found.

```
use Sys::Hostname;
print "Hostname is ", hostname, "\n";
```

It tries **syscall(SYS_gethostname), 'hostname'**, **'uname -n'**, and the file /com/host, stripping any white space, line termination, or null characters as necessary. If it is still unable to find the hostname, it calls **croak**.

Note that this method may fail on non-Unix operating systems.

REFERENCES Chapter 9; *see also* **Carp**

Sys::Syslog

This module supports an interface to the Unix **syslog** logging system.

```
use Sys::Syslog;
```

There are four main functions imported by default: **openlog**, **syslog**, **setlogmask**, and **closelog**:

```
openlog IDENT, LOGOPT, FACILITY
```

Opens the system log. The string **IDENT** will prepend every message. The **LOGOPT** is a comma-separated list of options that equate to the standard **openlog** constants. See Table E-16 for a list.

The **FACILITY** argument is a string that defines the part of the system for which to record the log entries. Valid values are **user** for user-level entries, **kern** for kernel problems, and **daemon** for system daemons. These equate to the **LOG_USER**, **LOG_KERN**, and **LOG_DAEMON** constants used in the C interface. The exact list of supported values is system dependent.

String	C Constant	Description
pid	LOG_PID	Logs the process ID with each message.
ndelay	LOG_NDELAY	Opens the connection to the **syslogd** daemon immediately. Normally the interface waits until the first message is posted to open the log.
cons	LOG_CONS	Writes messages to the system console if the **syslogd** daemon cannot be contacted.
nowait	LOG_NOWAIT	Don't wait for child processes (from **fork**) to log messages to the console.

Table E-16. *Syslog Options in Perl*

```
syslog PRIORITY, FORMAT, LIST
```

This records an entry in the system log, of the level specified by **PRIORITY**. Note that the priority definition is the same as for the **LOGOPT** parameter to the **openlog** function and should be expressed as a string. See Table E-17. Individual priorities can be combined using the | symbol. The **FORMAT** and **LIST** are passed to **sprintf** to format and output the supplied arguments in a formatted format. The resulting string is then used as the log entry.

The **FORMAT** string supports one additional option not supported by **printf**. The **%m** format inserts the value of the latest error message found in **$!**.

```
setlogmask MASK
```

Sets the mask priority for further **syslog** calls. Returns the old mask value.

```
closelog
```

Closes the connection to the **syslogd** daemon.

You can optionally import the **setlogsock** function, which allows you to change the type of socket used to communicate with the **syslogd** daemon.

```
setlogsock SOCKTYPE
```

Valid values for **SOCKTYPE** are "unix," for Unix domain sockets, and "inet" for INET domain sockets. The function returns true on success and **undef** on failure.

REFERENCES Chapters 3, 6, 9, Appendix B

String	C Constant	Description
emerg	LOG_EMERG	A panic condition, normally broadcast to all users.
alert	LOG_ALERT	An urgent problem that needs immediate attention.
crit	LOG_CRIT	Critical error such as a hardware error/failure.
err	LOG_ERR	Simple errors.
warning	LOG_WARNING	Warning messages.
notice	LOG_NOTICE	Notification of particular events. Not considered critical, but may still require immediate attention.
info	LOG_INFO	Informational messages.
debug	LOG_DEBUG	Debugging information, normally of no use outside a debugging procedure.

Table E-17. *Syslog Priorities*

Term::Cap

This module provides a simplified interface to the termcap terminal driver system.

```
use Term::Cap;
```

The module supports an object interface to **Tgetent**:

```
Tgetent(TERM)
```

The **Tgetent** function extracts the entry of the specified terminal type **TERM**, returning a reference to a **Term::Cap** object. For example:

```
$terminal = Tgetent Term::Cap { TERM => 'vt220', OSPEED => $ospeed };
```

The **OSPEED** is the output bitrate for the terminal, specified either in POSIX format (absolute bitrates such as 9600), or as BSD-style relative values, where 13 equals 9600.

```
$terminal->Trequire(LIST)
```

The **Trequire** method enables you to specify the list of required capabilities for the terminal driver.

```
$terminal->Tgoto(EXPR, COL, ROW, HANDLE)
```

This decodes a cursor addressing string **EXPR**, passing it **COL** and **ROW**. The value of the string is returned, or printed directly to the **HANDLE** if specified.

```
$terminal->Tputs(EXPR, COUNT, HANDLE)
```

Caches the control string **EXPR** for **COUNT** times, returning the string. Alternatively, you can have it sent directly to **HANDLE** if specified.

You can access the extracted termcap entry by accessing the **TERMCAP** hash key element.

REFERENCES Chapter 13

Term::Complete

This module provides an interface for completing words on a command line interface, similar to that provided by the Bourne Again SHell (**bash**).

```
use Term::Complete;
```

It supports a single function, **Complete**:

```
Complete(PROMPT, LIST)
```

This provides **PROMPT** to the screen and supports completion on the words in **LIST**. The return value is the completed word:

```
$input = Complete('$ ', qw/echo ls/);
```

You can type any character into the prompt. Pressing TAB completes the word (if possible). The default **^D** prints a list of completion words. The **^U** combination deletes the current line, and the DEL and BACKSPACE keys work as you would expect. You can modify the keys used for the last four options using the **$Term::Complete::complete**, **$Term::Complete::kill**, **$Term::Complete::erase1**, and **$Term::Complete::erase2** variables.

Specification should be done using the normal **stty** values, and the **stty** command is required for the module to function correctly. Note that you can continue to edit the line using the above keyboard sequences. The completion value is not returned until ENTER is pressed.

REFERENCES Chapter 13; *see also* **Text::Abbrev**

Term::ReadLine

This module supports an interface to the available readline packages.

```
use Term::ReadLine;
```

Readline is a function library that supports the input of text in a line-by-line editable format. The interface is object based:

```
use Term::ReadLine;

$line = new Term::ReadLine 'Line Interface';
$input = $line->readline('Name? ');

print "Got $input\n";
```

The supported methods are described here.

```
readline(EXPR)
```

Returns the string entered, using the value of **EXPR** as a prompt. The trailing newline character is removed from the returned value.

```
ReadLine
```

Returns the name of the actual package being used to support the readline operation.

```
new
```

Creates a new **Term::ReadLine** object. You can optionally supply two arguments that specify the input and output filehandles to use for the readline operation.

```
addhistory(EXPR)
```

Adds **EXPR** to the history of input lines.

```
IN
OUT
```

Returns the filehandles for input or output.

```
MinLine(EXPR)
```

If specified, defines the minimal size of a line to be included in the history list.

```
findConsole
```

Returns an array of two strings containing the names for files for input and output, specified in the normal **shell** style of **<file** and **>file**.

```
Attribs
```

Returns a hash reference describing the internal configuration parameters of the package.

```
Features
```

Returns a hash reference describing the features of the current readline package being used.

REFERENCES Chapter 13

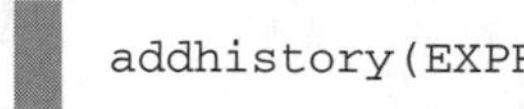

Test

This module provides a simple framework for writing Perl test scripts, using a format similar to Perl's own testing systems.

```
use Test;
```

You use the framework by importing the module and then using a **BEGIN** block to specify the parameters for the tests you are about to conduct. For example:

```
use Test;
BEGIN { plan tests => 2}

ok(1);
ok(0);
```

Each call to **ok** should indicate a successful test or failure. The resulting report and output matches the format used by Perl's own testing system available when Perl has been built from a raw distribution. For example, the above script would output

```
1..2
ok 1
not ok 2
# Failed test 2 in test.pl at line 5
```

Note that each call to **ok** iterates through the available test numbers, and failures are recorded and reported.

You can embed expressions into the **ok** call:

```
ok(mytest());
```

The return value or resolved expression must be expected to return true or false according to the success or otherwise of the test. You can also use a two-argument version that compares the values of the two arguments:

```
ok(mytest(),mytest());
```

If you want to trap additional information with the error, you can append additional arguments to the **ok** function:

```
ok(0,1,'Math Error');
```

The resulting error and mismatch information is reported when the script exits:

```
1..2
ok 1
not ok 2
# Test 2 got: '0' (test.pl at line 5)
#   Expected: '1' (Didnt work)
```

You can mark tests as "to do" tests by specifying which test numbers are to be fixed directly within the test suite. These tests are expected to fail. You specify the information to the **plan** function during the **BEGIN** block:

```
use Test;
BEGIN { plan tests => 2, todo = [2]}

ok(1);
ok(0);
```

The resulting failure message notes the existence of an expected failure,

```
1..2 todo 2;
ok 1
not ok 2 # (failure expected in test.pl at line 5)
```

and also warns you when it sees a success in a test it was expecting to fail:

```
1..2 todo 2;
ok 1
ok 2 # Wow! (test.pl at line 5)
```

You can skip tests based on the availability of platform-specific facilities, using the **skip** function:

```
skip(TEST, LIST)
```

TEST is a test that evaluates to true only if the required feature is *not* available. Subsequent values in **LIST** work identically to the **ok** function.

You can supply a subroutine to handle additional diagnostics after the tests have completed. The function is passed an array reference of hash references that describe each test failure. The keys of each hash are **package**, **repetition**, and **result**. To configure the function, specify its reference in the call to **plan** in the **BEGIN** block:

```
BEGIN { plan tests => 2, onfail => \&errdiags }
```

The resulting function is executed within an **END** block and is therefore subject to the normal limitations of such a block.

REFERENCES Chapters 5, 16, 17, 18, 20

Test::Harness

This module processes the output of multiple Perl test scripts and reports the success or failure of the scripts accordingly.

```
use Test::Harness;
runtests(LIST)
```

LIST should be a list of valid test scripts to be executed. It parses the output produced by a typical Perl test script and analyzes the output. The output produced by the **Test** module is suitable for correct parsing.

For example, a nine-test script with three failures would output the following:

```
t.p.................# Failed test 2 in t.pl at line 5
# Failed test 5 in t.pl at line 8
# Failed test 9 in t.pl at line 12
FAILED tests 2, 5, 9
        Failed 3/9 tests, 66.67% okay
Failed Test  Status Wstat Total Fail  Failed  List of failed
----------------------------------------------------------------------
t.pl                         9    3  33.33%  2, 5, 9
Failed 1/1 test scripts, 0.00% okay. 3/9 subtests failed, 66.67% okay.
```

REFERENCES Chapter 17, 18, 20; *see also* **Test**

Text::Abbrev

Given a list of words, this module generates an abbreviation table in a hash. The generated list accounts for possible duplications of abbreviations within the supplied list.

```
use Text::Abbrev;
%abbrev = ();
abbrev(\%abbrev, LIST);
```

For example, the call

```
abbrev(\%abbrev, 'better');
```

will produce a hash like this:

```
b      => better,
be     => better,
bet    => better,
bett   => better,
bette  => better,
better => better,
```

APPENDIXES

While the call

```
abbrev(\%abbrev, qw/be bet better/);
```

will populate the **%abbrev** hash with

```
b      => be,
be     => be,
bet    => bet,
bett   => better,
bette  => better,
better => better,
```

REFERENCES *See also* **Term::Complete**

Text::ParseWords

This module parses an array of lines into a list of words using a specified delimiter. Any words or strings contained within quotes are treated as single words, effectively ignoring the supplied delimiter.

```
use Text::ParseWords;
@words = quotewords($delim, $keep, LIST);
```

The **$delim** element is the delimiter to use. This can be a raw string or a regular expression. The **$keep** element affects the way text within the lines is treated. If set to true, quotes are retained in the list of words returned; otherwise they are removed. Also, if **$keep** is true, then the backslashes are preserved in the returned list. If false, then a double backslash is converted to a single backslash, and a single backslash disappears entirely.

REFERENCES Chapter 7, Appendix B

Text::Soundex

The **Text::Soundex** module generates a four-character soundex string using the algorithm designed by Donald Knuth. The algorithm translates individual words into the string, which can then be used for comparison and hashing of the supplied words as they sound when they are spoken, rather than how they are spelled.

```
use Text::Soundex;

soundex LIST
```

The **soundex** function hashes the words supplied in **LIST**, returning a list of soundex codes. Each code is made up a single character, matching the first character of the supplied word, and three digits. For example,

```
print join(' ',soundex('Martin', 'Brown'),"\n");
```

prints

```
M635 B650
```

On the other hand,

```
print join(' ',soundex('Martin', 'Martian'),"\n");
```

produces

```
M635 M635
```

Note that the soundex string produced cannot be mapped back to the original string. The above example should demonstrate the fact, since M635 refers both to "Martin" and "Martian." Note however that the algorithm is not completely fail-safe:

```
print join(' ',soundex('Wood', 'Would'),"\n");
```

This produces the following, perhaps incorrect, sequence:

```
W300 W430
```

If a suitable soundex string cannot be produced, then the function returns **$soundex_nocode**, which is initially set to the undefined value. You can, however, set the value of this variable for your own purposes.

Text::Tabs

This module expands tabs into spaces and "unexpands" spaces into tabs.

```
use Text::Tabs;

$tabstop = 8;
expand LIST
unexpand LIST
```

The **$tabstops** scalar specifies the number of spaces to replace a single tab with **expand**, or the number of spaces to convert into a single tab with **unexpand**. Both functions accept a list of scalars, and each scalar should contain a string to be expanded or unexpanded as appropriate. Each element of **LIST** should not contain any newlines; they should be **split** first into a suitable list. The return value is a list of converted elements.

For example, here is a script for expanding the tabs of files supplied on the command line into four spaces:

```
#!/usr/local/bin/perl -pi.bak

BEGIN
{
        use Text::Tabs;
        $tabstop = 4;
}

$_ = expand $_;
```

You can now do

```
$ expand file.txt
```

To convert it back, create a new script with **unexpand** instead of **expand**:

```
#!/usr/local/bin/perl -pi.bak

BEGIN
{
        use Text::Tabs;
        $tabstop = 4;
}

$_ = unexpand $_;
```

Text::Wrap

This module intelligently wraps text into paragraphs.

```
use Text::Wrap;

$Text::Wrap::columns = 70;
wrap PREFIRST, PREOTHER, EXPR
```

The width of the resulting paragraph is specified directly in the **$Text::Wrap::columns** scalar. The **wrap** function then wraps **EXPR** indenting the first line of the paragraph with **PREFIRST** and subsequent lines in the paragraph with **PREOTHER**.

Tie::Array

This module provides some simple base class definitions for tying arrays. You normally use this module to inherit base methods from, for example:

```
package MyArray;
use Tie::Array;
@ISA = qw/Tie::Array/;
```

It provides stub **DELETE** and **EXTEND** methods, and also **PUSH**, **POP**, **SHIFT**, **UNSHIFT**, **SPLICE**, and **CLEAR** in terms of basic **FETCH**, **STORE**, **FETCHSIZE**, **STORESIZE**, in addition to the mandatory **new** method for creating the new object.

When developing your own tied-array classes, you will need to define the following methods:

```
TIEARRAY classname, LIST
STORE this, index, value
FETCH this, index
FETCHSIZE this
STORESIZE this, count
EXTEND this, count
CLEAR this
DESTROY this
PUSH this, LIST
POP this
SHIFT this
UNSHIFT this, LIST
SPLICE this, offset, length, LIST
```

REFERENCES Chapter 7

Tie::Handle

This module provides core methods for tying handles.

```
package MyHandle;
use Tie::Handle;
@ISA = qw/Tie::Handle/;
```

It supports the basic **new** method in addition to **TIESCALAR**, **FETCH**, and **STORE**.

For developing your own tied-handle classes, you will need to define the following methods:

```
TIEHANDLE classname, LIST
WRITE this, scalar, length, offset
PRINT this, LIST
PRINTF this, format, LIST
READ this, scalar, length, offset
READLINE this
GETC this
DESTROY this
```

REFERENCES Chapter 7

Tie::Hash

This module provides base class definitions for tied hashes. It provides the **new**, **TIEHASH**, **EXISTS**, and **CLEAR** methods.

```
package MyHash;
use Tie::Hash;
@ISA = qw/Tie::Hash/;
```

When developing your own class for tying hashes, you will need to implement the following methods:

```
TIEHASH classname, LIST
STORE this, key, value
FETCH this, key
FIRSTKEY this
NEXTKEY this, lastkey
EXISTS this, key
DELETE this, key
CLEAR this
```

REFERENCES Chapter 7

Tie::RefHash

This module supports the facility to use references as hash keys through a tied hash. This is normally not allowed, and if **strict refs** is switched on, Perl will fail on compilation.

```
use Tie::RefHash;
tie %hash, 'Tie::RefHash', LIST;
```

REFERENCES Chapter 7

Tie::Scalar

This module provides base class definitions for tying scalars. The basic **Tie::Scalar** package provides the **new**, **TIESCALAR**, **FETCH**, and **STORE** methods.

```
package myScalar;
use Tie::Scalar;
@ISA = qw/Tie::Scalar/;
```

If you are developing your own tied scalars, you will need to define the following methods:

```
TIESCALAR classname, LIST
FETCH this
STORE this, value
DESTROY this
```

REFERENCES Chapter 7

Tie::SubstrHash

This module provides a class for supporting a hash with fixed key and value sizes. The resulting hash algorithm is a factor of the key and value sizes specified, and the hash is optimized for the specified size. This improves performance, but also limits the size of the hash you create. Any attempt to add keys into the hash beyond the specified size results in a fatal error.

```
require Tie::SubstrHash;
tie %hash, 'Tie::SubstrHash', KEYLEN, VALUELEN,  TABLE_SIZE;
```

The above creates a hash in **%hash**. Each key within the hash will be **KEYLEN** long (in bytes), and values will be **VALUELEN** long. Note that **KEYLEN** and **VALUELEN** are not maximum sizes; they are fixed. Attempts to insert data with a key size greater or less than **KEYLEN** will cause a fatal error, as will storing values that are greater or less than **VALUELEN**. The maximum size for the hash is specified as the number of key/value pairs, as specified in **TABLE_SIZE**.

There are two main benefits to this system: speed and memory. With a fixed-size hash the memory footprint is much smaller, and the resulting internal tables used to look up individual key/value pairs are therefore much smaller, resulting in faster and more efficient searches for information.

REFERENCES Chapter 7

Time::Local

This module provides the reverse functionality of the **localtime** and **gmtime** functions; that is, it converts a date and time specified in individual variables into the number of seconds that have elapsed since the epoch:

```
use Time::Local;

$time = timelocal(SEC, MIN, HOURS, MDAY, MON, YEAR);
$time = timegm(SEC, MIN, HOURS, MDAY, MON, YEAR);
```

The functions accept the arguments in the same range as the corresponding **localtime** and **gmtime** function, such that the code

```
use Time::Local;

$time = time;

print "Time!" if ($time = (timelocal((localtime)[0..5])));
```

should always print "Time!"

Both **timelocal** and **timegm** return –1 if the upper limit is reached for the integer that stores the time value. On most systems this will be Jan 1 2038.

REFERENCES Chapter 6

Time::gmtime

Overrides the built-in **gmtime** function with one that returns an object based on the **Time::tm** module. The individual methods within the returned object are the individual fields of the new time structure. For example:

```
use Time::gmtime;

$time = gmtime;

print "Date is: ",
      join('/',$time->mday,($time->mon+1),($time->year+1900)), "\n";
```

The individual methods (fields) match the names of the **struct tm** structure, that is, **sec**, **min**, **hour**, **mday**, **mon**, **year**, **wday**, **yday**, and **isdst**.

It's also possible to obtain the time from the last **gmtime** call via predefined variables. These variables have the same name as the structure fields and object methods with a **tm_** prefix. For example:

```
use Time::gmtime qw/:FIELDS/;

gmtime;

print "Date is: ",join('/',$tm_mday,($tm_mon+1),($tm_year+1900)),"\n";
```

The time variables will not be updated until **gmtime** is called again.

You can access the original **CORE::gmtime** function in a scalar context using the new **gmctime** function:

```
print gmctime(time);
```

To use the object-oriented interface without overriding the **CORE::localtime** function, import the module with an empty import list, and then call the functions explicitly:

```
use Time::gmtime qw//;

$time = Time::gmtime::gmtime;

print "Date is: ",
      join('/',$time->mday,($time->mon+1),($time->year+1900)), "\n";
```

REFERENCES *See* **Time::tm**; Chapter 6

Time::localtime

This module overrides the built-in **localtime** function with one that returns an object based on the **Time::tm** module. The individual methods within the returned object are the individual fields of the new time structure. For example:

```
use Time::localtime;

$time = localtime;

print "Time is: ",join(':',$time->hour,$time->min,$time->sec),"\n";
```

The individual methods (fields) match the names of the **struct tm** structure, that is, **sec**, **min**, **hour**, **mday**, **mon**, **year**, **wday**, **yday**, and **isdst**.

It's also possible to obtain the time from the last **localtime** call via predefined variables. These variables have the same name as the structure fields and object methods with a **tm_** prefix. For example:

```
use Time::localtime qw(:FIELDS);

localtime;

print "Time is: ",join(':',$tm_hour,$tm_min,$tm_sec),"\n";
```

The time variables will not be updated until **localtime** is called again.

You can access the original **CORE::localtime** function in a scalar context using the new **ctime** function:

```
print ctime(time);
```

To use the object-oriented interface without overriding the **CORE::localtime** function, import the module with an empty import list, and then call the functions explicitly:

```
use Time::localtime qw//;

$time = Time::localtime::localtime;

print "Time is: ",join(':',$time->hour,$time->min,$time->sec),"\n";
```

REFERENCES *See* **Time::tm**; Chapter 6

Time::tm

This module supports the internal functionality of the **Time::localtime** and **Time::gmtime** modules.

REFERENCES *See* **Time::localtime, Time::gmtime**

UNIVERSAL

The **UNIVERSAL** module provides the base class from which all other classes are based. This module provides the essential grounding for all blessed references within. Because all new objects inherit from the base class, the **UNIVERSAL** module also provides same base methods that are automatically inherited by all classes and objects. Two of the methods, **can** and **isa**, are supported both as methods and functions:

```
isa(TYPE)
UNIVERSAL::isa(REF, TYPE)
```

Returns true if the object or **REF** is blessed into the package **TYPE**, or has inherited from the package **TYPE**.

```
can(METHOD)
UNIVERSAL::can(REF, METHOD)
```

Returns a reference to the subroutine supporting **METHOD** if **METHOD** is supported within the class of the object or **REF**. If the specified method does not exist, then it returns **undef**.

```
VERSION ([REQUIRE])
```

Returns the contents of the **$VERSION** variable within the object's class. If the **REQUIRE** value is specified, the script will die if **REQUIRE** is less than or equal to the **$VERSION** variable.

REFERENCES Chapter 7

User::grent

This module supports an object-oriented interface to the built-in **getgr*** functions:

```
use User::grent;
$grent = getgrnam('staff');
```

Individual fields are then available as methods to the **$grent** object. The supported methods are **name**, **passwd**, **gid**, and **members**. This last item returns a reference to a list; the first three simply return scalars.

REFERENCES Chapter 6; *see also* **User::pwent**

User::pwent

This module provides an object-based interface to the built-in **getpw*** functions.

```
use User::pwent;
$pwent = getpwnam('root');
```

Once retrieved, individual fields of the password entry are available as methods to the newly created object. For example,

```
print "User ID: ",$pwent->uid,"\n";
```

prints the uid of the **root** user. The list of methods supported is **name**, **passwd**, **uid**, **gid**, **quota**, **comment**, **gecos**, **dir**, and **shell**.

REFERENCES Chapter 6; *see also* **User::grent**

utf8

The **utf8** pragma tells Perl to use the UTF-8 (Unicode) character set for internal string representation. The pragma is block scoped. For most installations there are no differences between Unicode and normal ASCII representation, since the first 128 characters of the ASCII code are stored within a single byte. For patterns that are greater than this value, or for multibyte characters, the differences are significant.

```
use utf8;
```

Once switched on, you can switch off Unicode operation with **no**:

```
no utf8;
```

The main effects of the module are as follows:

- Strings and patterns may contain characters that have an ordinal value greater than 255. You can explicitly specify a Unicode character by specifying the hexadecimal prefix with braces and the Unicode character in a 2-byte hexadecimal string, for example **\x{263A}**.

- Symbol table entries within Perl may be specified in Unicode format.
- Regular expressions match characters (including multibyte characters) instead of individual bytes.
- Character classes in regexps match characters instead of bytes.
- You can match Unicode properties using the **\p{}** (which matches a property) and **\P{}** (which does not match a property).
- The **\X** pattern match matches any extended Unicode string.
- The **tr///** operator translates characters instead of bytes.
- Case translation with the **uc**, **lc**, **ucfirst**, and **lcfirst** functions uses internal Unicode tables for conversion.
- Functions that use or return character positions, return positions correctly in characters, not bytes.
- The **pack** and **unpack** functions are unaffected (the "c" and "C" letters still pack single-byte characters). The "U" specifier can instead be used to pack Unicode characters.
- The **chr** and **ord** functions work on Unicode characters.
- Use of **reverse** in a scalar context works correctly on characters, not bytes.

REFERENCES *See also* **File::Find**, **File::CheckTree**

vmsish

This module is a pragma for imposing VMS-specific and/or style features. This allows for the differences between the VMS platform and Perl's normal behavior.

```
use vmsish;
```

The options for the **vmsish** pragma are listed in Table E-18.

REFERENCES Chapter 16

Option	Description
status	Implies VMS-style treatment of the values returned by backticks and **system**.
exit	Causes the **SS$NORMAL** variable to contain the correct exit status.
time	Forces time values to be localized rather than referenced to GMT.

Table E-18. *Options for the **vmsish** Pragma*

APPENDIXES

vars

The **vars** pragma predeclares the variables specified. This solves problems when the **use strict** is in force and also provides the best mechanism for exporting variables from modules and packages.

```
use vars qw/$foo @bar %poo/;
```

REFERENCES Chapter 16; *see also* **subs**

warnings

This module is a pragma that can help to control the level of warnings that are produced. There are three options to the pragma: **all**, **deprecated**, and **unsafe**.

```
use warnings 'all';
```

Switches on all warnings for the script.

```
use warnings 'deprecated';
```

Only lists warnings for features that are deprecated in the current version of Perl.

```
use warnings 'unsafe';
```

Only lists warnings that are considered unsafe.

You can switch off specific sets with **no**:

```
no warnings 'deprecated';
```

REFERENCES Chapter 16

The Complete Reference

Appendix F

CPAN Module Reference

This appendix contains a list of CPAN modules. CPAN is a huge archive of contributed modules for use with Perl. At the beginning of May 1999, it consisted of almost 900 module distributions, which provide almost 3,000 individual modules that can be imported for use in your scripts. Some of them are well known and have been included in this book—for example, the **libnet** bundle by Graham Barr, which includes the **Net::FTP** and **Net::SMTP** modules, among many others.

For brevity's sake, the list provided here is a shortened version of the full CPAN list because only "release-quality" modules are provided; alpha, beta, initial, and placeholder modules are not listed. The only exceptions are for modules that have been mentioned in this book. Note, however, that this is not a reflection on the quality of the modules that are at either alpha or beta stages. Many of these "prerelease" modules are used in live production systems, including some that I've used and developed myself.

The first column is the name of the module, and the second column is the description. Due to the dynamic nature of the CPAN system, I have not included the file names for the individual modules, since they change weekly, and sometimes even daily. Visit CPAN or your local mirror to download one of these modules. The status of the module is given in the third column of all tables. For a full list, visit www.cpan.org, or your local mirror (see Appendix A). The fourth column denotes the requirements for using the module; the possible values are shown in Table F-1.

For modules that appear in CPAN, but are actually supplied as part of the standard Perl distribution, please see Appendix E.

You may also want to investigate the **CPAN** module, which will automatically download and install modules from CPAN for you, including all the required modules. See **CPAN** in Appendix E for more details.

Requirement	Description
P	Only requires Perl and should therefore be cross-platform compatible. However, be aware that some modules make use of functions that are not supported across all platforms.
C	Needs a C compiler.
C++	Needs a C++ compiler.
Opt. C	May optionally need a C compiler for some elements of the module.
O	Requires another language or nonstandard extension.

Table F-1. *Requirements for CPAN Modules*

Module Support

Module::Reload	Enables you to reload modules that have already been imported (according to the **%INC** hash), based on the time stamp of the module. Thus you can reload a module within a script without invoking the Perl interpreter afresh each time.	Release	P

Development Support

ExtUtils::F77	Supports the use of the FORTRAN language from both Perl and XS code.	Release	P
Devel::CallerItem	Supports an object-based wrapper around the **caller** function, and additional methods not supported within the base environment.	Release	P
Devel::DProf	Perl equivalent of the C profiler for monitoring the execution speed of individual functions and blocks within a Perl program. See Chapter 18.	Release	C
Devel::DumpStack	Creates a dump of the current function execution stack.	Release	C
Devel::Leak	Finds "loose" Perl objects that are not reclaimed.	Release	C
Devel::Symdump	Functional interface to the Perl symbol table, which can be both modified and dumped using this module.	Release	C
VCS::CVS	Functional interface to the GNU CVS version control system.	Release	C

Operating System Interfaces, Hardware Drivers

BSD::Resource	Implements an interface to the **getrusage()**, **s/getrlimit()**, and **s/getpriority()** system functions.	Release	C
Proc::Forkfunc	Simple wrapper to the **fork()** function.	Release	C
Schedule::At	Operating-system–independent interface to the **at** command and **cron** scheduling system.	Release	C

Quota	Interface to file system quotas. You can get and set quotas on an individual file system and user basis. Also supports remote quota calculations.	Release	C
Sys::AlarmCall	Supports a simple time-out on any subroutine. You can nest multiple time-outs for different subroutines.	Release	P

Platform-Specific Modules

Mac::AppleEvents	Access to the MacOS AppleEvent manager used to share information and execution control between processes.	Beta	P
Mac::AppleEvents::Simple	A simple interface to the **Mac::AppleEvents** module.	Release	P
Mac::Apps::Anarchie	Control of the Anarchie application. Anarchie supports FTP access on a Mac, and also Archie web searching.	Release	P
Mac::Apps::Launch	Module for launching and quitting individual Mac applications.	Release	P
Mac::Apps::MacPGP	Controls the MacPGP security application.	Release	P
Mac::Apps::PBar	Controls the Progress Bar system.	Release	P
Mac::Comm::OT_PPP	Controls the Open Transport PPP/Remote Access systems.	Release	P
Mac::OSA::Simple	Simple access to **Mac::OSA**.	Release	P
OS2::ExtAttr	A tied interface to the extended attributes on an OS/2 file system.	Release	C
OS2::PrfDB	A tied interface to the .INI initialization and configuration tables used for applications.	Release	C
OS2::REXX	Interface to the REXX scripting language, both the run-time and dynamic libraries.	Release	C
Unix::UserAdmin	Platform-independent interface to the Unix user account databases.	Release	P
VMS::Persona	Interface to the VMS Persona services.	Release	C
VMS::Priv	Accesses VMS Privileges for processes.	Release	C
VMS::Process	Supports a process management interface under VMS.	Release	C
VMS::System	VMS-specific system calls.	Release	C

Note that the **Win32::** modules come with their own DLLs in a prepackaged format, suitable for immediate use. Although some of them may be marked as requiring either C or C++, you shouldn't need a compiler to use them unless you expect to make modifications to your code.

Win32::AbsPath	Converts relative paths to absolute paths, taking into account both local directory specifications and network mounted devices (UNCs). See Chapter 22.	Release	C
Win32::AdminMisc	Miscellaneous administration functions for both local and remote machines. Also supports a number of network-specific functions for determining the local networking environment. See Chapter 22.	Release	C
Win32::ASP	Easier interface to PerlScript ASP development.	Release	C
Win32::ChangeNotify	Interface to the NT Change/Notify system for monitoring the status of files and directories transparently. See Chapter 22.	Beta	C
Win32::Clipboard	Access to the global system clipboard. You can add/remove objects from the clipboard directory. See Chapter 22.	Beta	C
Win32::Console	Terminal control of an MSDOS or Windows NT command console. See Chapter 22.	Beta	C
Win32::Event	Interface to the Win32 event system for IPC. See Chapter 22.	Beta	C
Win32::EventLog	Interface to reading from and writing to the Windows NT event log system. See Chapter 22.	Beta	C
Win32::File	Allows you to access and set the attributes of a file. See Chapter 22.	Beta	C
Win32::FileOp	Win32-specific file operations and dialogs. Also supports the use and modification of .INI files.	Mature	C
Win32::FileSecurity	Interface to the extended file security options under Windows NT. See Chapter 22.	Beta	C
Win32::FileType	Modifies Win32 file typemapping.	Release	C
Win32::GD	A Win32 port of the GD gif creation module.	Release	C
Win32::Internet	Interface to Win32's built-in Internet access system for downloading files. For a cross-platform solution see **Net::FTP**, **Net:HTTP**, or the **LWP** modules elsewhere in this appendix. See also Chapter 22.	Beta	C

Win32::IPC	Base methods for the different IPC techniques supported under Win32. See Chapter 22.	Beta	C
Win32::Mutex	Interface to the Mutex (Mutual/Exclusive) locking and access mechanism. See Chapter 22.	Beta	C
Win32::NetAdmin	Network administration functions for individual machines and entire domains. See Chapter 22.	Alpha	C
Win32::NetResource	Provides a suite of Perl functions for accessing and controlling the individual Net resources. See Chapter 22.	Alpha	C
Win32::ODBC	ODBC interface for accessing databases. See also the **DBI** and **DBD** toolkits elsewhere in this appendix. See Chapter 22.	Release	C++
Win32::OLE	Interface to OLE automation. See Chapters 22, 25.	Release	C++
Win32::PerfLib	Supports an interface to the Windows NT performance system. See Chapter 22.		C
Win32::Pipe	Named pipes and assorted functions.	Release	C++
Win32::Process	Allows you to create manageable Win32 processes within Perl. See Chapter 22.	Alpha	C
Win32::Registry	Provides an interface to the Windows registry. See the **Win32API::Registry** module and the **Win32::TieRegistry** module for a tied interface. See also Chapter 22.	Alpha	C
Win32::Semaphore	Interface to the Win32 semaphores. See Chapter 22.	Beta	P
Win32::Service	Allows the control and access of Windows NT services. See Chapter 22.	Beta	C
Win32::Shortcut	Access (and modification) of Win32 shortcuts. See Chapter 22.	Beta	C
Win32::Sound	Allows you to play .WAV and other file formats within a Perl script. See Chapter 22.	Beta	C
Win32::TieRegistry	A tied interface to the Win32 registry system. See Chapter 22.	Beta	C
Win32::WinError	Access to the Win32 error system. See Chapter 22.	Alpha	C
Win32API::Net	Provides a complete interface to the underlying C++ functions for managing accounts with the NT LanManager. See Chapter 22.	Alpha	C++

Win32API::Registry	Provides a low-level interface to the core API used for manipulating the registry. See Chapter 22.	Alpha	C

Networking, Device Control, and Interprocess Communication

Net::DNS	Functional interface to the NetDNS system. See Chapter 25.	Beta	C
Net::DummyInetd	A Perl-based, dummy Inetd Internet network daemon manager.	Release	P
Net::FTP	Functional interface to the FTP protocol. See Chapters 9, 25.	Alpha	P
Net::Hotline	Interface to the Hotline protocol.	Release	P
Net::Ident	Enables you to perform Ident identification/authentication system.	Release	P
Net::IRC	Module for creating IRC clients. See Chapter 25.	Pre-Alpha	P
Net::LDAPapi	Interface to both the UMICH LDAP server and to Netscape's LDAP server (which is based on the UMICH code).	Release	C
Net::PH	Enables Ph lookups and resolving.	Release	P
Net::SMTP	Interface to the SMTP protocol. See Chapter 25.	Alpha	P
IPC::ChildSafe	Controls child process without risk of deadlock.	Release	C
RPC::pServer	Interface for building Perl servers using RPCs (Remote Procedure Calls).	Release	P
RPC::pClient	Interface for building RPC clients (to the **pServer** module).	Release	P

Data Types and Data Type Utilities

Math::Amoeba	Multidimensional Function Minimization.	Release	P
Math::Brent	One-Dimensional Function Minimization.	Release	P
Math::Derivative	1st and 2nd order differentiation of data.	Release	P
Math::Fortran	Implements FORTRAN math functions.	Release	P
Math::Interpolate	Polynomial interpolation of data.	Release	P

Math::MatrixBool	Supports matrices of Booleans for doing Boolean algebra.	Release	C
Math::MatrixReal	Matrix math.	Release	P
Math::Polynomial	Object-based polynomials.	Release	P
Math::Spline	Cubic Spline Interpolation of data.	Release	P
Math::VecStat	Statistics for vector data.	Release	P
Statistics::ChiSquare	Chi Square test. Used for checking the randomness of your data.	Release	P
Statistics::Descriptive	Descriptive statistical methods.	Release	P
Statistics::LTU	Implements Linear Threshold Units.	Release	P
Statistics::MaxEntropy	Maximum entropy modeling.	Release	P
Algorithm::Shuffle	Donald Knuth's shuffle algorithm.	Release	P
Algorithm::Sample	Donald Knuth's sample algorithm.	Release	P
PDL::Options	Provides hash options handling for the Perl Data Language.	Release	P
Bit::Vector	Efficient bit vector and set base class.	Release	C
Set::IntRange	Supports "sets" of integers.	Release	C
Graph::Element	Base class for the element of directed graph.	Release	P
Graph::Node	A node in a directed graph.	Release	P
Graph::Edge	An edge in a directed graph.	Release	P
Graph::Kruskal	Kruskal Algorithm for Minimal Spanning Trees.	Release	P
Date::Calc	Gregorian calendar date calculations.	Release	C
Date::Format	Date formatter, similar to the **strftime()** function.	Release	P
Date::Manip	Parsing module for international dates/times.	Release	P
Date::Parse	ASCII date parser for translating string dates into the internal structures used by Perl.	Release	P
Time::CTime	Formats times similar to the **ctime()** function. Supports many different formats.	Release	P
Time::DaysInMonth	Returns the number of days in a month.	Release	P
Time::HiRes	High-resolution **time**, **sleep**, and **alarm**.	Release	C
Time::JulianDay	Converts a date (y/m/d) into seconds.	Release	P
Time::ParseDate	Parses dates and times into numerical values.	Release	P

Time::Period	Calculations of time periods.	Release	P
Time::Timezone	Calculates time zone offsets.	Release	P
Time::Zone	Time zone information and translation routines.	Release	P
Tie::DBI	Ties a hash to a DBI handle. See **DBI** elsewhere in this appendix.	Release	P
Tie::Handle	Base class for implementing tied filehandles.	Release	P
Tie::IxHash	Indexed hash supports ordered array/hash structures. See also the **DB_File** module in Chapter 8 and Appendix E.	Release	P
Class::Eroot	Eternal Root—object persistence system for storing object data.	Release	P
Class::Template	Struct/member template builder.	Release	P
Class::Tree	C++ class hierarchies and disk directories.	Mature	P
Class::TOM	Transportable Object Model.	Release	P
Object::Info	General information about objects (is-a, ...).	Release	P
Ref	Print, compare, and copy Perl structures.	Release	P
Sort::ArbBiLex	Enables the sorting of data in an arbitrary sort order.	Release	P
Sort::Versions	Sorts revision and version numbers.	Release	P

Data Type Conversion and Persistent Storage

Data::Dumper	Converts a data structure into Perl code.	Release	P
Data::Flow	Acquires data based on format "recipes." This allows the parsing of complex data streams into Perl structures.	Release	P
Data::Locations	Handles nested insertion points in your data.	Release	P
Data::Reporter	ASCII report generator.	Release	P

Database Interfaces

DBI	Generic database interface to different database systems. Uses a **DBD** module to provide access to a specific DB system. See Chapter 8	Alpha	C

DBD::CSV	SQL engine and DBI driver for using CSV (comma-separated values) files for databases. See Chapter 8 for some examples.	Alpha	C
DBD::DB2	DB2 **DBI** interface.	Alpha	C
DBD::Informix	Informix **DBI** interface.	Alpha	C
DBD::ODBC	ODBC **DBI** interface.	Alpha	C
DBD::Oracle	Oracle **DBI** interface.	Alpha	C
DBD::mSQL	Msql **DBI** interface.	Release	C
DBD::mysql	Mysql **DBI** interface.	Release	C
Oraperl	Oraperl emulation interface for **DBD::Oracle**.	Release	P
Sybase::BCP	Sybase BCP interface.	Release	C
Sybase::DBlib	Sybase DBlibrary interface.	Release	C
Sybase::Sybperl	A sybperl 1.0xx compatibility module.	Release	P
Sybase::CTlib	Sybase CTlibrary interface.	Release	C
Datascope	Interface to Datascope RDBMS.	Release	C
Msql	Mini-SQL database interface.	Release	C
Mysql	Mysql database interface.	Release	C
ObjStore	ObjectStore OODBMS interface.	Release	C++
Pg	PostgreSQL SQL database interface.	Release	C
Postgres	PostgreSQL SQL database interface employing objects/methods.	Release	C
Sprite	Limited SQL interface to flat file databases.	Release	P

Tied Hash File Interfaces

MLDBM	Transparently stores multilevel data in DBM. See the discussion on DBM techniques in Chapter 8.	Release	P

User Interfaces (Character and Graphical)

Term::ANSIColor	Supports color output to a terminal using ANSI escape sequences.	Release	P
Term::Query	Intelligent user prompt/response driver.	Release	P

Term::ReadKey	Reads keystrokes and changes terminal modes.	Release	P
Term::Screen	Basic screen and input classes using the **Term::Cap** module. See Appendix E.	Release	P
Term::ReadLine::Perl	GNU Readline history and completion in Perl. See also the **Term::Complete** module in Appendix E.	Release	P
Term::ReadLine::Gnu	GNU Readline XS library wrapper.	Release	C

Major Character-based User Interface Modules

PerlMenu	Curses-based menu and template system.	Mature	P
Cdk	Collection of Curses widgets.	Release	C

Tk Interfaces

Tk	Object-oriented interface to the Tk windowing system	Beta	C

Other Major X Windows User Interface Modules

Gimp	Perl-based plug-in builder for the Gimp image processor.	Beta	C
Gnome	Interface to the Gnome Desktop Toolkit.	Beta	C
Gtk	Interface to Gimp's Gtk library.	Beta	C
Sx	Simple Athena widget interface.	Release	C
X11::Fvwm	Simple interface to the FVWM window manager API.	Release	C

Interfaces/Emulations of Other Programming Languages

C::Scan	Heuristic parse of C files.	Release	P
Tcl	Complete access to Tcl (Tool Command Language).	Release	C

Tcl::Tk	Complete access to the Tk interface builder using the Tcl language (instead of a direct interface).	Release	C

File Names, File Systems, and File Locking

File::CounterFile	Persistent counter class.	Release	P
File::Sort	Emulates some functionality of the **sort** command for sorting files.	Release	P
Filesys::AFS	AFS Distributed File System interface.	Release	C
Filesys::Df	Functions for performing **df**-style reports, based on the **Filesys::Statvfs**.	Release	P
Filesys::Statvfs	Interface to the **statvfs()** system call.	Release	C
LockFile::Simple	Locking facilities within Perl based at an application rather than system level.	Alpha	P
Stat::lsMode	Translates octal modes into their "ls" format. For example, converts the mode 0644 to the string -rw-r—r—.	Release	P

String/Language Text Processing, Parsing, and Searching

String::Approx	Approximate string matching and substitution functions.	Release	P
String::CRC	Cyclic redundancy check generation.	Release	C
String::Scanf	Implementation of C **sscanf()** function.	Release	P

Language and Text-Related Modules

Text::DelimMatch	Matches (possibly nested) delimited strings.	Release	P
Text::Format	Advanced paragraph formatting. See also **Text::Wrap** in Appendix E.	Release	P
Text::Graphics	Graphics-rendering toolkit with text output.	Release	P
Text::Refer	Parses bibliography files written using the **refer** command.	Release	P
Text::Vpp	Versatile text preprocessor.	Release	P

Text::Balanced	Extracts balanced-delimiter substrings.	Release	P

Natural Languages

Lingua::EN::Infinitive	Finds the infinitive of a conjugated word.	Mature	P
Lingua::EN::Inflect	English singular and plural/ "a" and "an" formatter for sentences.	Release	P
ERG	An extensible report generator framework.	Release	P
PostScript::Font	Analyzes PostScript font files.	Release	P
PostScript::FontMetrics	Analyzes Adobe Font Metric files.	Release	P
PostScript::FontInfo	Analyzes Windows font info files.	Release	P
Font::AFM	Parses Adobe Font Metric files.	Release	P
Parse::ePerl	Embedded Perl (ePerl) parser.	Release	C
Parse::RecDescent	Recursive descent parser generator.	Release	P
SGMLS	A postprocessor for SGMLS and NSGMLS parsed files.	Release	P
XML	Large collection of XML-related modules.	Release	Opt. C

Option, Argument, Parameter, and Configuration File Processing

Getopt::Declare	An easy-to-use WYSIWYG command line parser.	Release	P
Getopt::EvaP	Supports both the long and short options supported by **Getopt::Std** and **Getopt::Long**. Also supports a multilevel help interface.	Mature	P
Getopt::Mixed	Supports both the long and short options supported by **Getopt::Std** and **Getopt::Long**.	Release	P
Getopt::Simple	A simple-to-use interface to the **Getopt::Long** module. See Appendix E.	Mature	P

Internationalization and Locale

I18N::Charset	Character set names and aliases. This was part of the **I18N** module, which has now been wrapped into the core of Perl. See the **perllocale** man page.	Release	P
I18N::LangTags	Extracts Language tags.	Release	P
Locale::Country	ISO 3166 two-letter country codes.	Release	P
Locale::Language	ISO 639 two-letter language codes.	Release	P
Locale::Msgcat	Access to XPG4 message catalog functions.	Release	C
Locale::gettext	Gets multilanguage messages.	Release	C

Authentication, Security, and Encryption

MD5	MD5 message digest algorithm.	Release	C
Crypt::OpenCA	Tools for running a Certification Authority.	Release	P

World Wide Web, HTML, HTTP, CGI, MIME

URI::Escape	Escapes/unescapes URL strings.	Alpha	P
URI::URL	Uniform Resource Locator objects.	Release	P
CGI::Authent	Requests the HTTP authentication information. Extension to the base **CGI** module. See Chapters 14 and 15 and Appendix E.	Mature	P
CGI::Base	Complete CGI interface class.	Release	P
CGI::BasePlus	Additional **CGI::Base** methods.	Release	P
CGI::Deurl	Decodes the URLs.	Mature	P
CGI::Enurl	Encodes URLs.	Mature	P
CGI::Formalware	Converts an XML file to a suite of CGI forms.	Mature	P
CGI::MiniSvr	Forks CGI app as a per-session mini server.	Release	P
CGI::Request	Parses CGI request and handle form fields.	Release	P
HTML::Embperl	Embeds Perl in HTML documents.	Release	C
HTML::Stream	HTML output stream.	Release	P
HTTP::Request::Form	Generates **HTTP::Request** objects out of forms.	Release	P

LWP::MediaTypes	Media types and mailcap processing.	Release	P
LWP::Parallel	Allows parallel HTTP and FTP access with the LWP toolkit.	Release	P
LWP::Protocol	LWP support for different protocol families.	Release	P
LWP::RobotUA	A UserAgent for robot applications.	Release	P
LWP::Simple	Simple procedural interface to the **LWP** toolkit for downloading and parsing web pages.	Release	P
LWP::UserAgent	Simple UserAgent class for downloading pages from the Internet.	Release	P
MIME::Base64	Encodes/decodes Base 64 (RFC 1521) email messages and attachments.	Release	P
MIME::QuotedPrint	Encodes/decodes Quoted-Printable email messages and attachments.	Release	P
MIME::Lite	Simple module for composing MIME-compliant email messages.	Release	P
Apache	Interface to the Apache server API. See **CGI::Apache** in the standard distribution.	Release	C
CGI_Lite	Lightweight interface for fast apps.	Mature	P
FCGI	Fast CGI for use with Open Market's Fast CGI system. See also the **CGI::Fast** module in the standard distribution.	Release	C
WING	Apache-based IMAP/NNTP gateway.	Release	Opt. C

Server and Daemon Utilities

EventServer	Simple event server. Triggers objects on input/output, timers, and interrupts.	Release	P
EventServer::Functions	Utility functions for initializing event servers.	Release	P
EventServer::*Wrapper	Wrappers for different server types.	Release	P
EventServer::Gettimeofday	Wrapper around the **gettimeofday()** system call on different platforms.	Release	P
EventServer::Signal	Signal handler interface for the **EventServer** module.	Release	P
EventServer::EventDriven	Compatibility module for **EventServer**.	Release	P

Archiving, Compression, and Conversion

Compress::Bzip2	Interface to the Bzip2 compression library.	Release	C
Compress::LZO	Interface to the LZO compression library.	Release	C
Compress::Zlib	Interface to the Info-Zip zlib library.	Release	C
Convert::Translit	String conversion among many character sets.	Mature	C

Images, Pixmap and Bitmap Manipulation, Drawing and Graphing

PGPLOT	PGPLOT plotting library. Used for plotting scientific graphs.	Release	Other
GIFgraph	Package to generate GIF graphs, uses GD.pm.	Release	Other
VRML	VRML methods independent of specification. Requires VRML libraries.	Release	Other
VRML::VRML1	VRML interface to the VRML 1.0 standard. Requires VRML libraries.	Release	Other
VRML::VRML2	VRML interface to the VRML 2.0 standard. Requires VRML libraries.	Release	Other
VRML::Color	Color functions and manipulations for VRML files. Also supports translation of VRML colors to/from their X Windows equivalents. Requires VRML libraries.	Release	Other
VRML::Base	Common base methods for the **VRML** modules. Requires VRML libraries.	Release	Other
Graphics::Libplot	Bindings for the C libplotter plotting library.	Release	C
Graphics::Plotter	Bindings for the C++ libplotter plotting library.	Release	C++
Image::Grab	Tool for grabbing images off the Internet.	Release	P
Image::Magick	Reads, queries, transforms, and writes images.	Release	C
Image::Size	Measures size of images in common formats.	Release	P
Chart::Base	Business chart widget collection.	Release	P
Chart::GnuPlot	Access to the gnuplot library.	Release	P
Chart::XMGR	Interface to XMGR plotting package.	Release	P

Gimp	Rich interface to write plug-ins for the Gimp image processor.	Mature	C

Mail and Usenet News

Mail::Field	Base class for handling mail header fields.	Release	P
Mail::Header	Manipulates mail headers (RFC822 compliant).	Release	P
Mail::POP3Client	Support for clients of POP3 servers.	Release	P
Mail::Sender	Supports the sending of email using SMTP and the built-in **socket** functions.	Mature	P
Mail::Sendmail	Simple platform-independent mailer.	Release	P
IMAP::Admin	IMAP administration.	Release	P

Control Flow Utilities

AtExit	Supports the facility to register callback functions to be executed when a script exits, similar to the C **atexit()** function.	Release	P
Callback	Defines easy-to-use function callback objects.	Release	P

Filehandle, Directory Handle, and Input/Output Stream Utilities

IO::Scalar	I/O handle to read/write to a string.	Release	P
IO::ScalarArray	I/O handle to read/write to array of scalars.	Release	P
IO::Tee	Multiplex output to multiple handles.	Release	P
IO::Wrap	Wrap old-style filehandles in standard OO interface.	Release	P
Log::Topics	Controls the flow of topic-based logging messages.	Release	P
Expect	Supports a similar set of functionality to Don Libes' Expect.	Release	P

Miscellaneous Modules

Module	Description	Status	Language
Archie	Runs Archie queries via the Prospero ARDP protocol.	Release	C++
BnP	Build'n'Play, an all-purpose batch installation tool.	Release	Opt. C
Roman	Converts Roman numbers to and from Arabic.	Release	P
Wais	Interface to the free WAIS-sf libraries.	Release	C
Business::CreditCard	Credit card number check digit test.	Release	P
Business::ISBN	Works with ISBN numbers as objects.	Release	P
ARS	Interface to Remedy's Action Request API.	Release	P
Penguin	Remote Perl in Secure Environment. See also **Safe** and **Opcode** in Appendix E.	Release	P
Penguin::Easy	Provides quick, easy access to the Penguin API.	Release	P
MIDI	Object interface to MIDI files.	Release	P
Logfile	Generic methods to analyze log files.	Release	P
Chemistry::Elements	Interface for working with chemical elements.	Release	P
FAQ::Omatic	A CGI-based FAQ/help database maintainer.	Release	P
Geo::METAR	Processes Aviation Weather (METAR) data.	Release	P
Geo::WeatherNOAA	Current/forecast weather from NOAA.	Release	P

Index

A

B

C

D

E

F

M

N

O

P

Q

R

T

W

X

Y

Z